EQUITY AND TRUSTS IN SANSKRIT JURISPRUDENCE

A British Academy Monograph

The British Academy has a scheme for the selective publication of monographs arising from its British Academy Postdoctoral Fellowships, British Academy Newton International Fellowships and British Academy / Wolfson Fellowships. Its purpose is to assist individual scholars by providing a prestigious publishing opportunity to showcase works of excellence.

Christopher T. Fleming studied Sanskrit at Balliol College, Oxford (DPhil 2018) and taught at the University of Southern California before returning to the University of Oxford as a British Academy Postdoctoral Fellow and as the Bowra Junior Research Fellow at Wadham College. His publications include a monograph, *Ownership and Inheritance in Sanskrit Jurisprudence* (OUP 2020) and a co-edited volume, *Science in Society in the Sanskrit World* (Brill 2023). Currently, Fleming is a student at the Faculty of Law and an associate member of the Faculty of Asian and Middle Eastern Studies at the University of Oxford.

EQUITY AND TRUSTS IN SANSKRIT JURISPRUDENCE

Christopher T. Fleming

Published for THE BRITISH ACADEMY
by OXFORD UNIVERSITY PRESS

Oxford University Press, Great Clarendon Street, Oxford OX2 6DP

First edition published in 2025

British Library Cataloguing in Publication Data
Data available

Library of Congress Cataloguing in Publication Data
Data available

Typeset by Newgen Publishing UK
Printed in Great Britain by CMP, Poole, Dorset

ISBN 978-0-19-726787-5 (hardback)
ISBN 978-0-19-897154-2 (UPDF)
ISBN 978-0-19-897155-9 (ebook)
ISBN 978-0-19-897156-6 (online)

vāgarthāviva saṃpṛktau vāgarthapratipattaye / jagataḥ pitarau vande pārvatīparameśvarau //1//

ākāśātpatitaṃ toyaṃ yathā gacchati sāgaram / sarvadevanamaskāraḥ keśavaṃ pratigacchati //2//

Contents

List of Illustrations

Maps

Figures

Tables

Table of Cases

Glossaries

Chapter 1: Glossary of Sanskrit terms

Abhiṣeka:	Coronation
Ādhi:	Pledge
Adhikāra:	Entitlement/duty/authority
Akṣapaṭala:	Bureau of Official Records
Āmātya:	Minister
Anātha:	Person without a protector
Apogaṇḍa:	Person under the age of sixteen
Apratibandhasvatva:	Unobstructed ownership
Āropajñāna:	Suppositious knowledge
Arthaśāstra:	Sanskrit political science
Āśrayadāna:	Gift of shelter
Aupacārika:	Conventional/figurative
Āvāhana:	Invocation
Bāla:	Child
Bhāṣya:	Commentary
Bhogyādhi:	Usufructuary pledge
Bhṛti:	Wages
Bhukti:	Possession/enjoyment
Brāhmacārin:	Student
Brāhmadeya/Brāhmāgrahāra:	Brāhmaṇical estate
Buddhi:	Cognition
Caritra:	Customary rules (in the context of jurisprudence)
Dāna:	Gift
Deśadharma:	Local law
Deva/Devatā:	Deity
Devālaya/Devagṛha/Devagṛha:	Temple
Devalaka:	Temple servant
Devapaśu:	Deities' animal
Devasva:	Deities' property

***Devatādhyakṣa*:**	Deity-supervisor
***Dharmaśāstra*:**	Sanskrit jurisprudential literature
***Dharmaśāstrin*:**	Sanskrit jurist
***Dīkṣā*:**	Initiation
***Dravya*:**	Assets
***Gauṇa*:**	Secondary
***Gopyādhi*:**	Custodial pledge
***Iṣṭāpūrta/Yogakṣema*:**	Charities
***Jaḍa*:**	Mentally incapacitated
***Jalāśaya*:**	Reservoirs
***Janmasvatva*:**	Ownership-by-birth
***Kalpita*:**	Artificial
***Klība*:**	Impotent
***Kuladharma*:**	Congenital law
***Laukika*:**	Local/private (as opposed to royal)
***Maṭha*:**	Monastery
***Mīmāṃsā*:**	Sanskrit ritual hermeneutical literature
***Mukhya*:**	Primary
***Mūrti*:**	Image
***Naigama*:**	Corporate body
***Nibandha*:**	Corrody/mortgage/lien/ also – legal digest
***Nikṣepa*:**	Deposit
***Nyāya*:**	Logic
***Pālana/Paripālana*:**	Protection
***Paribhāṣa*:**	Meta-rule
***Pāribhāṣikadharma*:**	Supplemental law
***Paricāra*:**	Conventional usage
***Parigraha*:**	Acceptance (of a gift, etc.)
***Pariṣad*:**	Assembly
***Pāṣaṇḍa*:**	'Heretical' – non-Vedic – religious community
***Pratimā*:**	Image (of a deity)
***Pratiṣṭhā*:**	Consecration
***Purāṇa*:**	Mythological literature
***Pūrvapakṣin*:**	Prima facie opinion
***Rāja*:**	King
***Rājadharma*:**	Laws governing the king
***Rājaśāsana*:**	Royal edict
***Rakṣaṇa*:**	Protection

Śabdamātradevatā:	Theory that deities are merely liturgical phonemes
Samayadharma/Sāmayikadharma:	Conventional law
Samayasyānapakarman:	Breach of convention
Saṃkalpa:	Intention
Sampradāna:	Primary recipient (of a gift)
Samvid:	Contract/compact
Sapratibandhasvatva:	Obstructed ownership
Śāsana:	Edict
Sattra:	Alms house
Sevaka:	Servant
Snātaka:	Vedic graduate
Śrāddha:	Funerary ritual
Śreṇidharmu:	Guild law
Sthiti:	Usage (of a particular group)
Strī:	Woman
Śuddhavadha:	'Clean death' – capital punishment
Sūtrādhyakṣa:	Superintendent of yarns
Svam:	Property
Svasvāmisambandha:	Relationship between owner and property
Svatva:	Ownership
Unmatta:	Mentally unhealthy person
Upacāra:	Convention/practice
Utsarga:	Relinquishment (of ownership)
Uttamadaṇḍa:	Highest fine/punishment
Vivādapada:	Title of law
Vyavahāra:	Legal procedure
Yāga:	Sacrifice

Chapter 2: Glossary of Sanskrit and Prakrit terms

Akṣapaṭala:	Bureau of Official Records
Akṣayanīvī:	Perpetual endowment
Bali:	Tax (in Aśokan inscriptions), a form of ritual offering (in Brāhmaṇical inscriptions)
Bhikkuhala:	Monks' land (i.e., land assigned to Buddhist monks)
Caru/Charu:	Oblation offered to deity

Devabhoga:	For the benefit of the deity
Devabhogasamaya:	Rule for divine enjoyment
Devadāya:	Divine endowment
Devāgrahāra:	Divine estate
Devālaya/Devagṛha/Devagṛha:	Temple
Devaparicārikas:	Servants of a deity
Devasva:	Deities' property
Deyadharma:	Religious gift
Dharmaśāstra:	Sanskrit jurisprudential literature
Dharmasthāna:	Dharma-site
Dhaṁmamahāmātras:	Dharma agents
Gandhakuṭi:	Perfume chamber of Buddhist monastery
Jayastambha:	Pillar of victory
Mahāmātras:	Officers of the Crown (in Aśokan inscirptions)
Maṭha:	Monastery/College
Mūlya:	Endowment (the principal of a financial endowment)
Niyama:	Legal instrument
Pāṣaṇḍas:	Religious communities (in Arthaśāstra and in Mauryan epigraphy), but 'heretical' non-Vedic religious communities in Dharmaśāstra
Pratiṣṭhā:	Consecration (of image of deity or of relic)
Praśasti:	Eulogy
Pratimā/Mūrti:	Image (of Buddha or of deity)
Pratyaya:	Suffix indicating that the prefixed person holds an asset in trust for a beneficiary (expressed in the dative case)
Rājasāsana:	Royal edict
Rajūkas:	Provincial governors
Samayadharma:	Conventional dharma
Sattra:	Alms house
Śrotaka:	Debt
Sthiti:	Legal convention
Vārika:	Servant/fiduciary
Vihohālakas:	Judicial officers
Vyavasthā:	Legal settlement
Yogakṣema:	Custody

Chapter 3: Glossary of Sanskrit, Arabic, and Persian terms

ahl aḏ-ḏimmah:	Protected subjects
'ajam:	Non-Arab peoples
al-Andalus:	Arabic name for Iberian peninsula
al-Hind:	Arabic name for India
al-Ka 'ba:	Axis mundi of the Islamic world in Mecca
al-Sind:	Arabic name for Sindh
Amīr:	Islamic term for king – technically 'commander'
Dharmasabhā:	Brāhmaṇical judicial assembly
Budh:	Islamic name for indigenous religions of Sind
Caliph:	The chief Muslim civil and religious ruler, regarded as the successor of Muhammad
Daftar-i divān-i sa'adat:	Department of pious foundations and religious affairs
Ḏhimmī:	Protected individuals under Islamic law
Dīwānī:	Right to revenue collection held by a Dīwān
Farmān:	Royal decree
Fiqh:	Islamic jurisprudence
Ijārah:	Lease used in revenue farming
'inām:	Grant of a share of income from a taxable jurisdiction
Iqṭā':	Islamic feudal tenure
Jāgīrdar:	Holder of a revenue assignment
Jiziya:	Islamic poll tax
Kanīsa:	Temple
Kharāj:	Islamic land tax
Kūladharma:	Congenital law
Madrassa:	Islamic pedagogical institution
Manāt:	Pre-Islamic Arab Goddess
Mleccha:	Foreigner, barbarian
Mušrikūn:	Idolaters/polytheists
Nayamkara:	Vijayanagara analogue to Iqṭā' system
Qāḍī:	Magistrate of a Sharī'a court

Qaṣīdas:	Panegyric poetry
Razmiyas:	Persian war epics
Saadni/Sādin:	Custody of pre-Islamic deities and of the Ka'ba
Sanam:	Idol
Širk:	Idolatry/polytheism
Sūbedār:	Governor of a subah, a province of the Mughal Empire
Surati:	Temple image
Tājika:	'Turk' in Sanskrit
Turuṣka:	'Turk' in Sanskrit
Ulamā:	Islamic scholarly community
Wakfs (plural awqāf):	Islamic charitable trust
Yavana:	Foreigner, Greek, barbarian

Chapter 4

Collector:	Chief Revenue Administrator for the British East India Company
Daftar-i divān-i sa'adat:	Department of religious and public works under the Mughal Empire
Dāya:	Inheritance
Debutter:	Property belonging to a deity
Dharmakarta:	Manager of a Hindu temple (fiduciary)
Diwān:	Holder of a Diwānī
Diwānī:	Right of revenue collection under the Mughal Empire
Res extra commercium:	Non-circulating property
Imperium et Libertas:	Empire and liberty
Inām:	Land grant under Mughal and sulṭānate regimes
Lehkiraj:	Lands assigned rent-free for a charitable or religious purpose
Mofussil:	Areas of company control outside of the Presidency Towns (of Calcutta, Madras, and Bombay)
Nawāb:	A native governor under the Mughal Empire
Parens Patriae:	Parent of the nation
Prochein Amis:	Next friend in law

Ṣadr Dīwānī 'Adālat: Super civil court in the Mofussil
Ṣadr Nizāmat 'Adālat: Super criminal court in the Mofussil
Shebait: Fiduciary guardian of deity (a 'trustee')
Subāh: An administrative province of the Mughal Empire
Svatva: Ownership (or property)
Vyavasthā: Brāhmaṇical responsa
Zamīndār: Local gentry/landowner/revenue farmer

Acknowledgements

My British Academy mentor

Christopher Z. Minkowski

Sanskrit friends and colleagues

Diwakar Acharya, Patrick Olivelle, John Lowe, Sir James Mallinson, Alex Watson, James McHugh, James Benson, Tim Lubin, Vishal Sharma, Richard Salomon, Tara Fabienne Hathaway, Pranav Prakash, Barbora Sojkova, Jonathan Walters, Tim Lorndale, Caley Smith

Law friends and colleagues

Charles Foster, Jeffery Hackney, Kristin van Zwieten, Haley Hooper, Edward Lui, Sandy Steel, Christos Mentis, Nathan Oliver, Kenneth Poh, Scott Altman, Susan Bright

Ecclesiastic friends and colleagues

Father Dr Nicholas Austin, S.J; Fathers Dr. Richard Robert Marsh, Francis Turner, Patrick Riordan, Brian Mac Cuarta, Gigigimon Joseph, Phillip Moller, Jayme Stayer, Joseph Simmons, S.J; Professors, Jane Stevenson, Peter Davidson, and Gavin Flood; Mr. Rodrigo de la Flor; Mrs. Rebecca White and Ms. Trudi Preston; Principal Revd Canon Dr Robin Ward, Revds Andreas Wenzel and Lucy Gardner

Equestrian friends and colleagues

Dianna Pritchard, Sally Webb, Arebella Whelan, Betsy Irwin, Sarah Hill, Elise Clements, Nicole Wieclaw, Mustafa Bakr, Yvonne Storrs, Joanna Remzi, Boldi Paladi-Kovacs, Kento Ohara, Daniel O. Cluanaigh, Beverly Adrian, Melody, Langford

My family

Tim, Brenda, Michael, Anna, Margot, and Lucie Fleming; Katherine Spencer; Joy Barkey; JGAD; Ashley M. Eden

Fide et fiducia

Special thanks to Portia Taylor at the British Academy. I completed this monograph as a member of the Society of Fellows in the Humanities at the University of Southern California, as a British Academy Postdoctoral Fellow at the University of Oxford, as a Bowra Junior Research Fellow at Wadham College, Oxford, and as a student of English jurisprudence at Harris Manchester College, Oxford.

Map 0 Contemporary India, showing locations of the High Courts

Introduction: Equity and Trusts in Sanskrit Jurisprudence

A king rescues his people from fear, and protects them. Therefore, being their protector, a king is to his subjects a father. Of this there is no doubt.'

Brahmavaivartapurāṇa[1]

the King is to be considered as the parens patriae... the protector of every part of his subjects, and... therefore, it is the duty of his officer, the Attorney-General, to see that justice is done to every part of those subjects.

Lord Eldon in ***Corporation of Ludlow v Greenhouse*** *(1817) 1 Bli. N.S. 17*[2]

This monograph outlines theories of Equity and Trusts in Sanskrit jurisprudence (Dharmaśāstra) and traces their variegated connections to the practical administration of religious endowments from classical to contemporary India. Dharmaśāstra describes phenomena that, in Anglo-American jurisprudence, are associated with courts of equity: the management of religious and charitable trusts; and the guardianship of minors, women, the infirm, and other categories of non *sui iuris* persons (those who lack legal capacity). Furthermore, Dharmaśāstra recognises deities as juridical persons and owners of temple property, who, like minors, require fiduciaries (guardians who hold a relationship of *trust* toward other parties) to protect their interests.

Equity and Trusts in Sanskrit Jurisprudence focuses on 'deities' property' (*devadhana/devadravya*), a quintessentially Indian form of trust in which the tutelary deities of temples and monasteries are treated as the legal owners and beneficiaries of temple and monastic property (if only in an 'ideal' or 'figurative' sense). The management of Hindu temples and monasteries and their often-substantial

[1] Quoted in Rajah Tagore, *Hindu Loyalty* (Calcutta: I.C. Bose & Co., 1883): bhayatrātā ca rājā syāt sarveṣāṃ pālakaḥ sadā / yo rājā sa pitā pātā prājānām eva niścaya //49// For the history and date (possibly 16th century) of the *Brahmavaivartapurāṇa*, see Greg Bailey (trans), *Brahmavaivarta Purāṇa* (New Delhi: Motilal Banarsidass, 2022).

[2] Cited in Gareth Jones, *History of the Law of Charity, 1532–1827* (Cambridge: Cambridge University Press 1969), 160.

endowments vests in various servants (*sevakas/dharmakartṛs*), who owe fiduciary duties to their tutelary deities. These deities are analogised to perpetual minors and the Crown (or the State), as *parens patriae*, serves as a bulwark against breach of trust and as a protector of 'orphaned' deities.

Furthermore, Dharmaśāstra articulates a theory of Equity, as conventional (*sāmayikadharma*) or supplemental (*pāribhāṣika*) law (*dharma*), in which guilds, corporations, monasteries, and temples, among other organisational groupings, enjoy *sui iuris* powers to set their own by-laws and adjudicate internal disputes among members provided that said by-laws do not conflict with the core principles of Dharmaśāstric jurisprudence. In this account of Equity, Dharmaśāstra delimits the boundaries of its own positive law and accepts the necessity of supplementing it with meta-law in the pursuit of justice.

The Crown, for its part, has a right of supervision over these conventional laws and a duty to protect these corporations and institutions from internal or external interference. In short, Dharmaśāstric Equity involves the recognition of the legality of extra-Dharmaśāstric conventions and the subordination of those conventions to the administrative apparatus of the Crown.

Since the early centuries of the Common Era, Dharmaśāstric theories of Equity and Trusts have served, and continue to serve, as a touchstone for the practical administration of Hindu religious endowments under numerous political regimes. During the classical and early medieval eras (3rd century BCE–6th century CE and 6th century CE–12th century CE), Buddhist, Jain, and Hindu sovereigns, as well as private individuals, deployed Dharmaśāstric concepts and principles, often directly, in thousands of charters (inscribed on copper plates or on stone) for temples, monasteries, rest-houses, granaries, reservoirs, Brāhmaṇical settlements (*brahmadeyas*) and other religious and charitable institutions. Dharmaśāstric Equity enabled a diverse array of religious communities to participate in a shared, secular, Sanskrit cosmopolitan legal and political order which lasted around a thousand years.[3]

During the late medieval and early modern periods (12th–16th centuries CE and 16th–18th centuries CE), the arrival of Islamic rulers into the Indian subcontinent dramatically altered the indigenous religious, legal, and political order. Many Islamic rulers, such as Maḥmūd of Ghazni (r. 998–1030 CE) and Alā' al-Dīn Khaljī (r. 1290–96 CE), looted and pillaged Hindu, Buddhist, and Jain religious institutions in India such as the famous Somanātha temple in Veraval, Gujarat. Other Islamic rulers, however, including as Jalal-ud-Dīn Muhammad Akbar (r. 1556–1605 CE)

[3] For the Sanskrit cosmopolis, see Donald Davis, 'A Historical Overview of Hindu Law', in Timothy Lubin, Donald Davis, and Jayanth Krishnan (eds), *Hinduism and Law: An Introduction* (Cambridge: Cambridge University Press, 2010): 17–27, 18. Davis is summarising Sheldon Pollock's, *The Language of the Gods in the World of Men* (Berkeley: University of California Press, 2006). See also Chapter 2, §2.1.1, 'Theory'.

and Tipu Sulṭān (r. 1782–99 CE), actively patronised Hindu religious institutions. They also incorporated, to a limited extent, Dharmaśāstric theories of Equity and Trusts in their administration of non-Islamic religious endowments.

Hindu rulers, such as the Vijayanagara emperors (1336–1646 CE), the semi-independent Rajpūt kingdoms, and the Marāṭhā Confederacy (1674–1818 CE), synthesised Dharmaśāstric jurisprudence and Islamicate (or Persianate) bureaucratic techniques in order to create a legal system that exercised considerably greater supervision over religious endowments than during pre-Islamic times. Notably, as Hindu polities adopted the increasingly centralised administrative paradigms of the Indian sulṭānates (often wrapping these paradigms in Dharmaśāstric terminology), Hindu deities were sometimes viewed as the sovereign proprietor of the realm, with human kings serving as trustees on behalf of their tutelary deities.

The ascension of the British East India Company as a puissant territorial power following the Battle of Buxar in 1764 and the Treaty of Allahabad in 1765 led to the gradual creation of a new political and legal order for India and its religious trusts. Beginning with Governor-General Warren Hastings' Judicial Plan of 1772, Company and Crown courts adjudicated civil disputes among the native population concerning inheritance, contracts, trusts, adoptions, etc. according to the laws and customs of Islamic and Hindu law. The relative paucity of Dharmaśāstric discussions of trusts, in comparison to inheritance and adoption meant that colonial efforts to legally regulate Hindu religious and charitable endowments relied heavily on English concepts of Equity and Trusts from the Court of Chancery. In practice, colonial jurists drew on a mixture of Sanskrit and English theories of Equity and Trusts and created a hybrid, Anglo-Hindu law of Hindu religious and charitable trusts.

After Indian independence in 1947 and the introduction of the Constitution of the Republic of India in 1950, the newly formed Supreme Court reformed the Anglo-Hindu law of religious and charitable trusts by bringing it into alignment with the fundamental rights to religious freedom and protections from discrimination enshrined in the Constitution. As with previous shifts in political sovereignty, the advent of a constitutional republic entailed a *transformation* rather than an *abrogation* of the previous jurisprudence of Equity and Trusts. In shifting from a focus on private property rights towards an emphasis on public freedoms and interests, the Supreme Court expanded the idea of *what* could be recognised as a Hindu deity under the law while simultaneously constraining the exclusionary practices (against women or low caste individuals) that constituted the ancient customary practices (or conventional dharmas) of religious institutions. Nevertheless, theories of Equity and Trusts, however hybrid, lie at the heart of the modern jurisprudence of Hindu endowments.

This ancient, hybrid jurisprudence of Equity and Trusts, fashioned over more than two thousand years of Indian history, lies at the heart of some of the most contentious legal disputes in contemporary India, such as the communal disputes over sacred sites in Ayodhyā, Mathurā, and Vārāṇasī.[4] Understanding and addressing current controversies concerning the ownership and administration of (sometimes former) Hindu temples and monasteries require us to uncover their legal and cultural histories.

0.1 Equity and Trusts in England and in India

It is vital to have an appreciation for the technical meaning of *Equity* and *Trusts* in Western legal parlance before querying the extent to which classical Sanskrit jurisprudential literature describes analogous phenomena. From the English legal perspective, *etic* to India, Equity and Trusts forms a distinctive and highly specialised body of law and jurisprudence.[5] Unfortunately for comparative purposes, Equity and Trusts is probably the least understood body of English law from a jurisprudential perspective.[6] Certainly, we know a great deal about the law of different remedies available from courts of Equity – trusts, injunctions, specific performance, equitable estoppel, and the appointment of fiduciaries (such as guardians for wards) – and the doctrine of unjust enrichment, but devising a comprehensive jurisprudential description of what principles, if any, actually unite these disparate phenomena has proven elusive.[7]

Attending to the complex historical and jurisprudential debates concerning Equity and Trusts in the British context can, however, enable us to make more nuanced comparisons between English and Sanskritic legal theories and practices, especially with reference to Hindu religious and charitable trusts. I agree with the late Chief Justice of the Supreme Court of India, B.K. Mukherjea, who noted that, 'religious and charitable trusts are found to exist, in some shape or other, in almost all civilized countries'.[8] The question for this monograph, is: what are the principles of jurisprudence which govern English and Sanskritic trusts? The answer, I argue, is Equity.

[4] For socio-legal studies of these conflicts, see the special edition of *Contemporary South Asia*, edited by Vera Lazzaretti and Knut Jacobsen in *Contemporary South Asia* 32.1 (2024).

[5] See, for example, the innumerable textbooks for practitioners on the subject: Alastair Hudson, *Equity and Trusts*, 10th edn. (London: Routledge, 2021); Graham Virgo, *The Principles of Equity and Trusts*, 4th edn. (Oxford: Oxford University Press, 2020); Mohamed Ramjohn, *Unlocking Equity and Trusts*, 7th edn. (London: Routledge, 2019); and Gary Watt, *Trusts and Equity*, 9th edn. (Oxford: Oxford University Press, 2020).

[6] For an account of Equity as a jurisprudence of conscience, see Mike MacNair, 'Equity and Conscience', *Oxford Journal of Legal Studies* 27.4 (2007): 659–81.

[7] See Lord Neuberger's comments: 'Far from being a seamless collection of clear principles, equity sometimes appears to be a hot-bed of uncertainty where the judicial foot not merely comes in all shapes and sizes, but seems to set off in opposite directions.' In 'Equity: the Soul and Spirit of all Law or a Roguish Thing? Lehane Lecture 2014', *Australian Law Journal* 88.11 (2014): 802–11.

[8] B.K. Mukherjea, *The Hindu Law of Religious and Charitable Trusts*, 5th edn. (Calcutta: Eastern Law House, 2016), 1.

0.1.1 Equity

In its simplest, Aristotelian sense, Equity (επιείκεια) denotes fairness, or decency. 'The function of Equity is the correction of the (civil or common) law where it is deficient by reason of its universality (i.e.: its tendency to establish rules without exceptions). In this broad, general sense, Equity is the body of principles which provide and govern exceptions to the law.'[9] As Mike McNair explains, this well-known meaning of Equity has its origins in 'Aristotle's *Nicomachean Ethics*, where the idea is explained in terms of the difficulty of making general definite rules cover the indefinite range of possible factual situations'.[10] In the *Nicomachean Ethics*, Equity is: 'like the lead ruler allegedly invented in ancient Lesbos, which adapts the fixed measurements (the terms of the law) to the irregular stone (the particular situation)'.[11]

This relatively straightforward theory of Equity was adopted by St Thomas Aquinas in his *Summa Theologiæ*, from where it became 'a commonplace of medieval legal thought'.[12] In its medieval legal incarnation, in works such as John Fortescue's *De Natura Legibus Naturae*, Equity became closely associated with 'the idea that a king ruling "politically", i.e. under law, must or may at some times rule "regally", i.e. by absolute power'.[13] In the 16th century, Christopher St German's seminal *Doctor and Student* (*Dialogus de Fundamentis Legum Anglie et de Conscientia*), published in Latin and in English in 1528 and 1530–31, respectively, 'partially (and rather imperfectly or inconsistently) explained' the workings of the English Court of Chancery as 'as an application of επιείκεια'.[14] Whatever be the veracity of the historical connection between Aristotelian επιείκεια and the jurisprudence of the English Court of Chancery, this theory of Equity as a corrective supplement to the universality of the Common Law has remained deeply

[9] Howard Oleck, 'Historical Nature of Equity Jurisprudence', *Fordham Law Review* 20.23 (1951): 23–44.

[10] MacNair, 'Equity and Conscience', 660. For Aristotle and Equity, see Allan Beever, 'Aristotle on Equity, Law, and Justice', *Legal Theory* 10.1 (2004): 33–50.

[11] MacNair, 'Equity and Conscience', 660. Citing Terence Irwin (trans.), *Nicomachean Ethics*, 2nd edn. (Indianapolis: Hackett, 1999), 1137a–38a

[12] MacNair, 'Equity and Conscience', 660. Citing ST 1a2æ. 96, 6, in Thomas Gilby (ed.), *St Thomas Aquinas Summa Theologiæ* Vol. 28 (Cambridge: Blackfriars 1966), at 138–41; and N. Doe, *Fundamental Authority in Late Medieval English Law* (Cambridge: Cambridge University Press, 1990) at 101–3, 'and literature cited therein'.

[13] MacNair, 'Equity and Conscience', 660. Citing Ch. 24, in Thomas Fortescue, Lord Clermont (ed.), *The Works of Sir John Fortescue* (London: Privately Printed, 1869), 85–86 and trans. at 214–15.

[14] MacNair, 'Equity and Conscience', 661. Citing, *inter alia*, Lord Nottingham, 'Prolegomena of Chancery and Equity', Ch. 7 ss 1 and 3, in D.E.C. Yale (ed.), *Lord Nottingham's 'Manual of Chancery Practice' and 'Prolegomena of Chancery and Equity'* (Cambridge: Cambridge University Press, 1965). For an excellent account of Christopher St Germain and Equity, see Timothy Endicott, 'The Conscience of the King: Christopher St. German and Thomas More and the Development of English Equity', *University of Toronto Faculty of Law Review* 47.2 (1989): 549–70.

imbedded in contemporary accounts of the discipline – so much so, that it has become the 'general modern usage for the jurisdiction'.[15]

Of course, Christopher St Germain's association of *επιείκεια* with the Court of Chancery was an *ex post facto* jurisprudential explanation of procedures and remedies that had been in operation since at least the reign of Henry V (r. 1413–22).[16] In his lectures on Equity, the legendary English legal historian Frederic William Maitland provided an accurate, and circular definition of Equity as 'that body of rules administered by our English Courts of justice which, were it not for the operation of the Judicature Acts [of 1873 and 1875], would be administered only by those courts which would be known as Courts of Equity'.[17] The early Court of Chancery, according to Oliver Wendell Holmes: 'Had the "examination and oath of the parties according to the form of the civil law and the law of Holy Church in subversion of the common law"... it had the subpoena, which also it did not invent, and it had a form of decree requiring personal obedience.'[18] As Holmes notes, with the exception of uses, 'the parent of our modern trusts' and 'a peculiar view of contract, [that] has left no traces in modern law', the early Court of Chancery simply applied the principles of Common Law in cases where, 'for some reason [a suit] without the jurisdiction of the King's ordinary courts' was brought before the Lord Chancellor.[19] In time, however, the jurisdiction and jurisprudence of the Court of Chancery expanded greatly, and by the 17th century, it held an equitable jurisdiction over, *inter alia*, guardians and wards, trusts, and charities.[20]

By whatever quirk of history, we find remarkably similar accounts of Equity in Sanskrit jurisprudential literature. Obviously, Dharmaśāstra does not describe Equity as a philosophical principle, or Equity as a juridical practice in precisely the same terms as those found in English law. Nevertheless, a theory of

[15] MacNair, 'Equity and Conscience', 660. Debates about the relevance of *επιείκεια* started as soon as St Germain published *Doctor and Student*. See Georg Behrens, 'An Early Tudor debate on the Relation between Law and Equity', *The Journal of Legal History* 19.2 (1998): 143–61, 143.

[16] Oliver Wendell Holmes, 'Early English Equity', *Law Quarterly Review* 1.2 (1885): 162–74.

[17] F.W. Maitland, *Equity: Also the Forms of Action at Common Law* (Cambridge: Cambridge University Press, 1910), 1.

[18] Holmes, 'Early English Equity', 162. Citing 4 Rot. Parl. 84 (3 Hen-V-, Pt 2, 46, no. xxiii). For the early Court, see William Lindsay Carne, 'A Sketch of the History of the High Court of Chancery from its Origin to the Chancellorship of Wolsey', *Virginia Law Register* 13.7 (1927): 391–421.

[19] Holmes, 'Early English Equity', 163.

[20] For general histories of the early modern Court of Chancery, see Alfred Marsh, *History of the Court of Chancery and of the Rise and Development of the Doctrines of Equity* (Toronto: Carswell & Co, 1890). Also see W. J. Jones, *The Elizabethan Court of Chancery* (Oxford: Oxford University Press, 1967). For the Chancery Court's jurisdiction over uses and trusts, see James Ames, 'The Origin of Uses and Trusts', *Harvard Law Review* 21.4 (1908): 261–74; and Austin Scott, 'The Nature and Rights of *Cestui Que Trust*', *Columbia Law Review* 17.4 (1917): 269–90. For the fusion of Common Law and Equity, see Michael Lobban, 'Preparing for Fusion: Reforming the Nineteenth-Century Court of Chancery (Parts 1 and 2)', *Law and History Review* 22.2–3 (2004). For a critical appraisal of the 'fusion' theory, see John Goldberg, Henry E. Smith, and P.G. Turner (eds), *Equity and Law: Fusion and Fission* (Cambridge: Cambridge University Press, 2019).

supplemental, or corrective meta-law lies at the very heart of Sanskrit jurisprudence. In Dharmaśāstra and in Sanskrit political science (*Arthaśāstra*), the king is duty-bound to investigate (*parīkṣaṇa*) and to protect (*paripālana*), a wide array of supplemental laws (*pāribhāṣikadharmas*) that includes congenital laws (*kuladharmas*), regional customs (*deśadharmas*), the conventions (*samayas*) of commercial guilds (*śreṇidharmas*), religious institutions of 'heretics' (*pāṣaṇḍas*), charities (*iṣṭāpūrta/yogakṣema*) and, of course, the established terms of trust of temples (*devagṛha/devālaya/devakula/*etc.). These terms are not merely theoretical: we find references to supplemental law in many of the thousands of classical and medieval Indian inscriptions that established and regulated temples, charities, and other foundations.

Donald Davis compares Dharmaśāstric accounts of supplemental laws with similar meta-rules (*paribhāṣas*) in Sanskrit grammatical literature (*Vyākaraṇa*), where they 'provide the correct interpretation of rules, remove conflicts between rules, or establish supplementary rules'.[21] In Sanskrit jurisprudence, *pāribhāṣikadharmas* 'elaborated and specified certain additional or supplementary rules, both adjective and substantive in nature, that shaped and filled in the law propounded in the textual tradition itself'.[22] While English Equity – in the Aristotelian sense of corrective law – focused on the power of the Crown, through the chancellor, to issue equitable remedies, Sanskrit Equity focused on the equitable duty of the Crown to protect legal remedies and institutions that had been fashioned by semi-*sui iuris* communities.

While the connection between Equity as a philosophical concept and the practices of the Court of Chancery were debatable and far from absolute, the connection between Dharmaśāstric accounts of Equity and the practical administration of law in India was more or less total. To the extent that epigraphic records from medieval India attest to real legal practice – a matter of contention explored in the second chapter of this monograph – they are almost invariably in conversation with the principles of Dharmaśāstric Equity. We might say, then, that Dharmaśāstric Equity was more equitable in an Aristotelian sense than English Equity.

Furthermore, Dharmaśāstra and Arthaśāstra articulate a theory of kingship in which the Crown or its agents are responsible for adjudicating many of the same disputes that were delegated to the Court of Chancery in England: trusts, charities, guardianship, etc. As in English jurisprudence, Dharmaśāstra contains a sophisticated theory of *parens patriae* jurisdiction in which the king, as father of the country has a feudal duty to secure the interests of women, children, the mentally

[21] Donald Davis, 'Intermediate Realms of Law: Corporate Groups and Rulers in Medieval India', *Journal of the Economic and Social History of the Orient* 48.1 (2005): 92–117, 97.

[22] Ibid., 97. Davis compares this theory to Hart's 'rules of recognition' but I argue that a comparison to Equity is equally valid.

unfit and other categories of non-legally competent individuals.[23] Intriguingly, as in English law, this royal *parens patriae* jurisdiction is extended to charities and churches.[24] Deities in particular became *the* definitive analogue to minors, especially with regard to the operation of civil law. Take, for example, a 1307 case from the reign of Edward I:

> A church is always under age and is to be treated as an infant, and it is not according to law that infants should be disinherited by the negligence of their guardians or be barred of an action in case they would complain of things wrongfully done by their guardians while they were under age.[25]

In time, the Crown delegated its role as *parens patriae* to the Court of Chancery and guardianship became a core facet of its equitable jurisdiction. As Lord Donaldson notes in ***Re R***:

> [T]he practical jurisdiction [of a court exercising *parens patriae* powers] is wider than that of parents … [T]his jurisdiction is not derivative from the parents' rights and responsibilities, but derives from, or is, the delegated performance of the duties of the Crown to protect its subjects and particularly children…[26]

My broader point is that Sanskrit jurisprudence and classical Indian legal practice have theoretical and practical analogues to the jurisprudence and practice of Equity in the English context. While scholarship on English Equity tends to highlight the uniqueness of this branch of legal history on the basis of the highly circumscribed social and administrative contexts from which it emerged, nevertheless, it bears

[23] For the Crown and the Chancery Court's right of supervision of guardians/wards in its role as *parens patriae*, see John Seymour, 'Parens Patriae and Wardship Powers: Their Nature and Origins', *Oxford Journal of Legal Studies* 14.2 (1994): 159–88; Jennifer Alkire, 'Incompetency from an Equitable Perspective: Chancery and the Guardianship Doctrine', *The Journal of Legal Medicine* 1.1 (1979): 80–109; John Chambers, *A Practical Treatise on the Jurisdiction of the High Court of Chancery Over the Persons and Property of Infants* (London: Saunders and Bennin, 1842); and Deborah Wilson, *Women and Legal Guardianship* (Manchester: Manchester University Press, 2013).

[24] For the Court of Chancery's right of supervision over charities, see David Patton, 'The Queen, the Attorney General, and the Modern Charitable Fiduciary: A Historical Perspective on Charitable Enforcement Reform', *University of Florida Journal of Law and Public Policy* 11.2 (2000): 131–78, 131–45; Theodore Dwight, 'The Jurisdiction of the Court of Chancery to Enforce Charitable Uses', *University of Pennsylvania Law Review* 10.3 (1862): 129–147; and Gareth Jones, *History of the Law of Charity, 1532–1827*, 2nd edn. (Cambridge: Cambridge University Press, 2011).

[25] Frederick Pollock and Frederic William Maitland, *The History of English Law Before the Time of Edward I*, 2nd edn., Vol. 1 (Cambridge: Cambridge University Press, 1898), 503–4 citing Placit. Abbrev. 304 (Noff). Y.B. 21–2 Edw I. p. 33: 'le eglise est dedeinz age'. Compare with Bract., *De legibus et Consuetudinibus Angliæ* f. 226b: 'Et cum ecclesia fungatur vice minoris, acquiritur per rectorem et retinet per eundem, sicut minor per tutorem. Et quamvis moriatur rector, non tamen cadit ecclesia a seisina sua, de aliquo de quo rector seisitus moritur nomine ecclesiae suae, non magis quam minor si custos suus moriatur.' 'And when the church functions like a minor, it is acquired by the ruler and retained by the same, like a minor by a guardian. And although the rector dies, the church does not lose its property, since the dead rector possesses (that property) in the name of his church. No more than a minor if its guardian dies.'

[26] ***Re R* (a minor) (wardship: medical treatment)** (1991) 4 All ER 177 at 186. Cited in Seymour, 'Parens Patriae', 159.

more than a passing resemblance to what we see in the Indian context. English Equity may be *etic* to India, but it accords, nevertheless, with *emic* Indian theories of supplemental law.

0.1.2 Trusts

Like Equity, the term Trust in its peculiar English legal sense is also difficult to define. As B.K. Mukherjea notes: 'The conception of "trust" in its technical sense was devised by the Chancery Courts in England, which as Courts of Conscience attempted to supply the deficiencies of the English Common Law, by administering what were known as principles of equity and natural justice.'[27] Trusts and their practical, if not conceptual forebear, Uses, solved a deficiency in the Common Law wherein a legal conveyance of property to one party for the explicit benefit of a third party was unenforceable by contract. In its most basic form, a Trust is a legal mechanism to compel someone who has received legal ownership of some property to utilise said property for a particular purpose imposed by the settlor.[28]

Chancery procedure, however, 'being entirely one *in personam*' (against the person) rather than *in rem* (against a thing), frames a Trust as imposing duties on the *individual* holding the asset rather than as governing the asset itself.[29] These unique procedural doctrines of the Court of Chancery gave rise to several technically accurate, but ideologically hollow definitions of Trusts. In his seminal treatise on the law of Trusts, Thomas Lewin offers the following definition of a Trust as: 'A confidence reposed in some other, not issuing out of the land, but as a thing collateral, annexed in privity to the estate of the land, for which cestui que [the person for whose benefit] trust has no remedy but by Subpoena in the Chancery.'[30]

Despite its general accuracy (before the fusion of the Common Law and Chancery Court in 1875), this procedural definition of Trusts hardly helps us to understand the jurisprudence behind it. Moreover, it suffers from the defect of applying 'to real estates only, whereas there can be trust in favor of personal property as well'.[31] Alternatively, one could define a Trust from the perspective of the beneficiary, as Justice Story does in his *Equity Jurisprudence*: 'an equitable title or interest in property real or personal distinct from the legal ownership thereof'.[32]

Mukherjea notes that modern writers tend to focus on a person's status – and corresponding duties – as a trustee who has a duty 'to hold the [Trust] property or

[27] Mukherjea, *Hindu Law*, 4.
[28] For definitions of Trust, see Joseph Long, 'The Definition of a Trust', *Virginia Law Review* 8.6 (1922): 426–33.
[29] Mukherjea, *Hindu Law*, 4.
[30] Ibid., 4. Citing Thomas Lewin, *A Practical Treatise on the Law of Trusts and Trustees*, 10th edn. (London: Maxell, 1837), 11.
[31] Mukherjea, *Hindu Law*, 5.
[32] Ibid., 5, citing Joseph Story, *Equity Jurisprudence*, 2nd edn. (England: Stevens and Haynes, 1892), 960.

exercise his powers for the benefit of others persons or for the accomplishment of some particular purpose'.[33] This focus on the trustee as a fiduciary, who is bound by a legal and ethical relationship of trust with other parties in respect to property, is a far happier definition and it enables a more constructive comparison to classical Indian phenomena.

As B.K. Mukherjea observes, given that the '"Trust" in its origin was a highly artificial concept which had its foundation upon a dual system of law... in England under peculiar political and historical conditions' one could 'not naturally expect to find a trust in this form in the Hindu system', or, I might add, in *any* non-English legal system.[34] What we find, however, in virtually every sophisticated legal system in the history of global jurisprudence are *fiduciaries*. Focusing on fiduciary relations in the general sense helps us to avoid the technical intellectual baggage of the English ancient dual system of law and to see commonalities between different systems of trusts (again, in the general sense) in global legal history.

Mike MacNair's model of Equity Jurisdiction as being tethered to the core principle of *confidence* is apposite here:

> Confidence is a synonym for trust, but this was wider than technical trusts, extending beyond fiduciary relations in the narrow sense (agency and partnership) to all cases where one party placed reliance on another's good faith, as, for example, by going surety on another's debt, or giving a security for a loan which on its face gave more than merely security rights, and to legal co-owners. As the equity jurisdictions expanded and developed (and in some areas contracted) after Egerton's reinstatement of these ideas, they never completely lost their conceptual links to this core.[35]

Classical Sanskrit jurisprudence developed a sophisticated theory of fiduciary law which, like its English analogue in Chancery, described trusts in terms of the duty of care owed by a holder of property in which another party enjoyed an interest – either legal or ethical.[36] *Pace* Justice Ali's observation in ***Vidya Varuthi Thirtha v Balusami Ayyar***, that 'the conception of a trust apart from a gift was introduced in India with the establishment of Moslem rule', I demonstrate, particularly in the

[33] Mukherjea, *Hindu Law*, 5.

[34] Ibid., 6.

[35] MacNair, 'Equity and Conscience', 677.

[36] For discussions of fiduciary relations more broadly, see David Seipp, 'Trust and Fiduciary Duty in the Early Common Law', *Boston University Law Review* 91.3 (2011): 1011–38; Leonard Rotman, 'Fiduciary Law's Holy Grail: Reconciling Theory and Practice in Fiduciary Jurisprudence', *Boston University Law Review* 91.3 (2011): 921–72; and Tamar Frankel, 'Fiduciary Law', *California Law Review* 71.3 (1983): 795–836. For guardians as fiduciaries, see Len Sealy, 'Fiduciary Relationships', *Cambridge Law Journal* 20.1 (1962): 119–40, 70 & 74–5; and Alkire, 'Incompetency from an Equitable Perspective'. For the Roman origins of guardianship, see Charles Sherman, 'Debt of the Modern Law of Guardianship to Roman Law', *Michigan Law Review* 12.2 (1913–14): 124–31.

first two chapters of this monograph, that trusts were an integral part of Indian law and religion long before the arrival of Islam on the subcontinent in 711 CE.[37]

Sanskrit jurisprudence describes a variety of legal situations involving fiduciaries and complex ownership. For example, the settlement of Brāhmaṇas on estates (*Brahmadeyas/Brāhmāgrahāras*), or the establishment of alms houses (*sattras*) are relatively straightforward purpose trusts: liquid cash or the income from certain lands are given to trustees for specific purposes and those trustees are answerable to the Crown if they fail to use the trust properties for the stated purpose. The property vests in the donee, but the donee is bound by obligation to use the donated assets for the donor's stipulated purposes.

Other fiduciary circumstances involve the overlapping ownership of the parties involved. Deposits (*nikṣepas*), pledges (*ādhis*), mortgages (*nibandhas*) or the heritable assets of a Joint Hindu Family (*dāya*), involve the blocking (*bandhana*) of simultaneous co-inherence of the ownership (*svatva*) of multiple parties. The co-inherence of multiple ownerships – partial or full – compelled individuals who held possession of an asset to utilise it for the collective interest of all parties.[38] In these circumstances, a fiduciary's obligations derive as much from a relationship of trust as they do from the operation of property law. In the course of time, competing juridical models of inheritance – in which families held property in trusts or in tenancies-in-common – developed in conjunction with the emergence of different philosophical understandings of ownership in the Sanskrit text-traditions of hermeneutics (*Mīmāṃsā*) and logic (*Nyāya*), respectively.[39]

Finally, and most importantly, divine trusts, i.e., individuals taking possession of assets in the name of a deity – with or without stated purposes – present a much more complicated picture. The *Kautilīyārthaśāstra* (1st century BCE to 2nd century CE), an influential treatise on statecraft, articulates an extensive jurisprudence of divine trusts: deities are recognised as legal persons – analogised to minors – that may hold assets which are, in turn managed by trustees. These trustees are answerable to the Crown for breaches of trust. The *Arthaśāstra* describes deity-supervisors (*devatādhyakṣas*), who like the agents of India's modern Devaswom Boards (temple trust boards), are duty-bound to monitor divine endowments and bring suit in the name of the deity.[40]

[37] (1922) 24 Bom LR 629 ¶11 [Ali, J]. Of course, there is stronger evidence that *English* Trusts have their origin in the Islamic *waqf*. See Monica Gaudiosi, 'The Influence of the Islamic Law of *Waqf* on the Development of the Trust in England: The Case of Merton College', *University of Pennsylvania Law Review* 136 (1987): 1231–61.

[38] See Christopher T. Fleming, *Ownership and Inheritance in Sanskrit Jurisprudence* (Oxford: Oxford University Press, 2020), Chapter 2.

[39] Ibid.

[40] For the *Arthaśāstra* see Patrick Olivelle, *King, Governance, and Law in Ancient India: Kauṭilya's Arthaśāstra* (Oxford: Oxford University Press, 2013).

Authors of Dharmaśāstra texts took a different route to explaining divine trusts than the Arthaśāstric tradition, but they also arrived at a theory of deities' agents as fiduciaries. Medieval authors of Dharmaśāstra commentaries (*bhāṣyas*), including Bhāruci (6th–7th centuries CE) and Medhātithi (9th–11th centuries CE), redeployed arguments drawn from Sanskrit ritual hermeneutical philosophy (*Mīmāṃsā*) to argue that deities' ownership is a secondary (*gauṇa*) form of ownership that imposes certain fiduciary duties on temple servants (*sevakas*) who appropriate these assets.[41] These fiduciaries were answerable to the Crown in both the Arthaśāstric tradition and as in English Equity jurisprudence. The Crown enjoys a general *parens patriae* jurisdiction which entails the supervision of charities and other trusts.

Sanskrit jurists analysed various legal phenomena associated with divine endowments such as the gift of cows to temples, prohibitions on the misuse of 'divine property' (*devasva*), and a wide array of mythological dicta concerning charities (*iṣṭāpūrta/yogakṣema*). As in the case of deposits and other fiduciary phenomena, Sanskrit jurists employed the concept of ownership (*svatva*) to construct a jurisprudential account of legal phenomena in which someone holds property for the benefit of another.

Over the centuries, this ownership-oriented logic inspired the development of a jurisprudence of divine endowments in which: 1) deities are legal persons who may own assets according to custom and tradition; 2) on account of the deities' *alieni juris* (under the legal control of another) status this 'ownership' is secondary (*gauṇa*) or artificial (*kalpita*); 3) the deities' hypothetical ownership imposes fiduciary duties on the deities' guardians; 4) the rules governing divine trusts fall under the category of supplemental law (*pāribhāṣikadharma*), or Equity in the Sanskritic sense. If a deity's fiduciaries expropriate divine assets, then they will be answerable to the Crown for breach of trust.

In short, Sanskrit jurists articulated jurisprudential principles of Equity and Trusts that bear a great deal of similarity to their English counterparts, especially when we take a broad view of the English phenomena. Over the centuries, Sanskrit jurisprudential treatises developed a sophisticated theory of Trusts using property theory and these treatises linked the theory of trusts with a theory of Equity in which the Crown was duty-bound to recognise and protect the conventional laws of religious communities. The two key differences between English and Sanskrit theories of Equity and Trusts were: 1) English Equity entailed the Crown (or its delegated agent, the chancellor) dispensing remedies not otherwise known in the Common Law, while Sanskrit Equity entailed the Crown (or its agent) recognising

[41] For Medhātithi and other commentators' theories of deities' 'secondary' ownership, see Chapter 1, §1.6.2.iii, 'Divine endowments in medieval Dharmaśāstra'. For the dates of these authors, see P.V. Kāṇe, *History of Dharmaśāstra*, Vol. 1 (Pune: Bhandarkar Oriental Research Institute, 1930): 264–6 & 266–75, respectively.

and enforcing remedies that existed outside of the purview of Dharmaśāstric positive law; and 2) while English Trusts recognised the legal ownership of trustees, Sanskrit Trusts recognised the legal ownership of the beneficiary, but typically only in a 'secondary' (*gauṇa*) or 'figurative' (*aupacārika*) way. Nevertheless, both jurisprudential systems describe similar phenomena and it is readily understandable why English jurists during the colonial period assimilated Hindu endowments to trusts in Company and Crown courts.

0.2 World history as the history of endowments

Systems of endowments governed by trustees appear in virtually every ancient legal system. Michael Borgolte notes in his account of world history as the history of foundations: 'it is a fascinating insight that human ingenuity, apparently independent of prototypes, begets similar or even identical solutions for the same problems or tasks'.[42] For millennia, people have dedicated properties to pious, charitable, or other aims and developed systems of control for these endowments. Understanding what makes India's iterations unique requires us to delve into a general history of the theory and practice of endowments in the ancient world.

Borgolte describes a foundation as an instance in which 'a sum of capital is allocated, with whose revenues a certain goal can be followed over the long term'.[43] For Borgolte, this sense of financial and legal permanency is the essential feature of a foundation (as opposed to a gift). To an extent, Borgolte takes the financial and legal elements of a foundation for granted and uses the concept of a permanent endowment as a hermeneutical tool to analyse shifting theological and social paradigms over four and a half millennia, from ancient Mesopotamia to Oxford in the 16th century.

In what follows, I use Borgolte's historical account as a springboard to examine religious trusts (or foundations) involving deities in a series of classical and medieval civilisations: 1) ancient Mesopotamia; 2) classical Greece and Rome (Republic and Empire); and 3) early Christendom. Taken collectively, I argue that the data from these civilisations demonstrates that the Indian model of divine trusts, in which deities own property and make use of it commercially, was the *norm* rather than the *exception* in the ancient and medieval world. Far from being an exotic anomaly, the juristic personality of Hindu deities is representative of a widespread, almost universal phenomenon.

[42] Michael Borgolte, *World History as the History of Foundation, 3000 BCE to 1500 CE*, translated by Zachary Chitwood (Leiden: Brill, 2020), 1.
[43] Ibid., 2.

0.2.1 Deities as owners in Ancient Mesopotamia

During the Akkadian Empire (2334–2154 BCE), 'the first large territorial empire of Mesopotamia', temple deities emerged as the nexus of large economic, religious, and political formations.[44] Notably, kings as the 'favorites of the gods', had an obligation, according to Mesopotamian myths, 'to provide for… [deities'] lasting nourishment, care and preservation'.[45] Here, as in India, royal sovereignty was thoroughly interconnected with the capacity of the Crown to serve as a protector and endower of a tutelary deity, which in the Akkadian context was Anunītu.[46]

Conversely, in Mesopotamian ideology, 'the gods themselves were seen as the owners of the land or the world, so that kings were only returning to the gods what always belonged to them'.[47] Divine ownership was an integral feature of this exceptionally early economy, and the theory of the Crown as the guardian of deities and their assets expanded into a wider *parens patriae* jurisdiction over 'care for orphans, widows' and other categories of unprotected people.[48] Deities held significant assets in the ancient Mesopotamian world, such as flocks and fields. Deities also engaged in money-lending at interest.[49] As Johannes Renger notes:

> The human ruler of the state was considered the god's deputy (*vicarius*) on earth. In this capacity he headed the household of the god, i.e., the temple household. The arable land in a given state was part of the divine *patrimonium* and as such was administered by the god's deputy. The spouse of the main god, as well as the children of the divine couple, had their own temples, including agricultural do- mains of substantial size. Still other gods within the state were hierarchically and genealogically linked with the main god…. Accordingly, all individual divine or temple households were subordinated to his household. Consequently, the ruler… governed all divine households and their agricultural domains.[50]

[44] Ibid., 139. Citing Hans Neumann, 'Mesopotamien', in Albrecht Jockenhovel (ed.), *Grundlagen der Globalen Welt vom Beginn bis 1200 v. Chr* (Darmstadt: Wissenschaftliches Buchgesellschaft), 2009): 184–215, & 476–7.

[45] Borgolte, *World History*, 139.

[46] For Akkadian religion, see Beate Pongratz-Leisten, *Religion and Ideology in Assyria* (Berlin: De Gruyte, 2015).

[47] Borgolte, *World History*, 139. Compare with fn. 660, where Aššur was considered the absolute owner of land in Assyria.

[48] Ibid., 139–40. For early Mesopotamian temple economies and political theory see Johannes Renger, 'Economy of Ancient Mesopotamia: A General Outline', in Gwendolyn Leick (ed.), *The Babylonian World* (London: Routledge, 2007): 187–97; Johannes Renger, 'Interaction of Temple, Palace, and "Private Enterprise" in the Old Babylonian Economy', in Edward Lipinski (ed.), *State and Temple Economy*, Vol. 1 (Leuven: Departement Oriëntalistiek 1979): 249–56; and Johannes Renger, 'Institutional, Communal, and Individual Ownership or Possession of Arable Land in Ancient Mesopotamia from the end of the Fourth to the end of the First Millennium BC', *Chicago-Kent Law Review* 71.1 (1995): 269–319.

[49] For examples of divine assets being loaned at interest, see Claude Johns, *Assyrian Deeds and Documents Recording the Transfer of Property, Volume 3* (Cambridge: Cambridge University Press, 1901), 9, 254, & 340.

[50] Renger, 'Ownership', 279.

Alongside these temple assets, Mesopotamian kings granted substantial endowments to deities and their temples, in no small part to legitimate their rule. For example, from the time of the great law-maker, Hammurabi (1793–1750 BCE), the deity 'Marduk rose from being a civic deity to the premiere god of the land, and his temple became a depot for meals and other foodstuffs from the entire realm'.[51] Similarly, a 'clay nail' from a ruined temple of the deity Enil at Lagash records that 'King Enmetena (around 2400 BCE) had made a pious gift of land to the god Enlil'.[52]

This theory of kings as protectors of sovereign deities suffused the jurisprudence of ancient Mesopotamia. In an excellent article on Mesopotamian jurisprudence and the Laws of Hammurabi, Martha Roth opens with the acknowledgement that: 'The "law" and the "law collections" throughout Mesopotamia, considering the variety of social, linguistic, political, economic, and ethnic changes over three millennia, contain a rich multitude of layers of meaning. Although there are shared traditions, there is no single "common law" throughout the ancient Near East.'[53] Turning away from the Code of Hammurabi and other ancient legal texts as sources of positive law, Roth examines their wider ideological significance in Babylonian society jurisprudence.

Hammurabi's code, whatever its practical application, had as its premise a jurisprudential theory of the king as the representative of the sovereign deity – in this case, Marduk. As Roth relates:

> First and foremost, we must never forget that the composition was intended for the gods. The gods, and especially Marduk, Hammurabi's patron deity of Babylon, and Shamash, the god of justice, entrusted the king with the administration and equitable application of the principles of 'truth and justice' (*kittum u migarum*). It was in order to 'provide just ways and appropriate behavior for the people of the land', as the prologue expresses it (v 16–19), that the gods gave into Hammurabi's hands more than a score of powerful and wealthy cities (as enumerated in the prologue).[54]

[51] Borgolte, *World History*, 5.

[52] Ibid., 6, citing Edward Chiera, *They Wrote on Clay: The Babylonian Tablets Speak Today* (Cambridge: Cambridge University Press, 1939), 93–101. For Enlil's assets and economic activities, see J.F. Robertson, *Redistributive Economies in Ancient Mesopotamian Society: A Case Study from Isin-Larsa Period Nippur* (Unpublished PhD Dissertation: University of Michigan, 1981); J.F. Robertson, 'The Internal Political and Economic Structure of Old Babylonian Nippur: The *Guennakkum* and His "House"', *Journal of Cuneiform Studies* 36 (1984): 145–90; and J.F. Robertson, 'The Temple Economy of Old Babylonian Nippur: The Evidence for Centralized Management', in J. Ellis (ed.), *Nippur at the Centennial: Papers Read at the 35 Rencontre Assyriologique Internationale, Philadelphia* (Philadelphia: University Museum Press, 1988): 177–88.

[53] Martha Roth, 'Mesopotamian Legal Traditions and the Laws of Hammurabi', *Chicago-Kent Law Review* 71.1 (1995): 13–40, 13.

[54] Ibid., 17. For an account of Marduk's shifting fortunes (metaphorically and literally) in ancient Mesopotamia, see Jennifer Finn, *Much Ado About Marduk: Questioning Discourses of Royalty in First Millennium Mesopotamian Literature* (Berlin: De Gruyter, 2017).

This close association between a deity, a king, and the administration of civil and criminal law also accounts for Cyrus the Great's (r. 559–530 BCE) proclamation in his Cylinder Inscription, that his conquest of Babylon 539 BCE was the result of Nabonid's breach of trust with the Babylonian pantheon.[55] In Cyrus' account, his maintenance, protection, and endowment of the Babylon pantheon was the basis of his claim to rule these conquered territories.

My intention in adumbrating these phenomena is not to craft a phenomenological study of divine ownership – although one is a desideratum in our field – but, rather to demonstrate that Sanskrit jurisprudence was far from the first ancient system of legal thought to consider the relationship between divine legal persons and material assets within the wider rubric of rulership and economics. The Crown as *parens patriae*, protecting both gods and humans is an ancient and fundamental jurisprudential principle.

0.2.2 Temples and deities in Greco-Roman legal history

Classical Greco-Roman theories and practices of divine endowments present a more ambiguous and legally complex picture. On the one hand, temples, along with their deities, endowments, and administrative functionaries played an active, dynamic economic role. Temples served as repositories for sealed deposits, offered lines of credit to city-states, the Roman State, and private individuals, financed commercial ventures, and owned substantial productive and liquid assets.

On the other hand, the jurisprudence of these divine endowments is less clear than their Babylonian or Sanskritic analogues. Greek and Roman jurists discuss temples and other religious and charitable institutions typically from the political rather than the contractual point of view: the Greeks examined temples from the standpoint of the administration of the *polis* and the Romans examined temples and religious institutions from the standpoint of centrally governed religious law. Nevertheless, as in Babylon and India, deities were very much a part of the legal and commercial landscape.

0.2.2.i Grecian deities and the law

Véronique Chankowski's 'Divine Financiers', together with her wider scholarly corpus, are some of the most important studies of the economic role and

[55] Borgolte, *World History*, 146. For the Cylinder text, see H. C. Rawlinson, 'Notes on a Newly-Discovered Clay Cylinder of Cyrus the Great', *Journal of the Royal Asiatic Society of Great Britain and Ireland* New Series 12.1 (1880): 70–97.

regulation of religious temples in ancient Greece.[56] Chankowski observes that the ancient Greeks, 'always drew a clear-cut distinction between sacred and public finances, [and] recognized sacred property'.[57] While much past scholarship frames Greek temples as recipients of donations whose 'accumulation immobilizes wealth in an unproductive fashion… offer[ing] the (perhaps reassuring) image of sacred domains that stay purely sacred, far from the temptations of money, and originate in a sort of economic irrationality', the truth is far more complicated.[58] The recent shift, towards a 'completely different perspective' that focuses on temple economies has largely been the product of the influence of Near Eastern (especially Babylonian) studies on the Classics.[59]

In the ancient Greek world, 'the gods got on well with money' and their sanctuaries accumulated vast quantities of assets, 'as much in the form of precious metals as in coin and real estate', but crucially, these temples 'also created channels of distribution[:] auctioning contracts for construction work, hiring craftsmen, farming taxes, and leasing properties, as well as by banking activities'.[60] In his study of classical temple banking, Raymond Bogaert describes the various financial practices of over thirty sanctuaries. While many 'establishments accepted funds on deposit (*παρακαταθήκη*) without such activity involving circulation or profit' others 'practised lending' to 'private individuals on the one hand, [and] the city that managed the sanctuary on the other'.[61]

The financial practices at temples, however, were often intimately linked with the civil administration of the city-states. For example, at Amorgos:

> The regulations for the foundation of Kritolaos (*IG* XII 7, 515, lines 17–19) at the end of the second century refer to clauses which govern loans from sacred funds (*καθάπερ τὰ ἱερὰ χρήματα*): interest of 10 per cent was payable each year to the

[56] Véronique Chankowski, 'Divine Financiers: Cults as Consumers and Generators of Value', in Zosia Archibald, John Davies, and Vincent Gabrielsen (eds), *The Economies of Hellenistic Societies, Third to First Centuries BC* (Oxford: Oxford University Press, 2011): 142–65; Véronique Chankowski, 'Techniques Financières, Influences, Performances dans les Activités Bancaires des Sanctuaires Grecs', *Topoi Orient-Occident* 12.1 (2005): 69–93; Véronique Chankowski, 'Les Places Financières dans le monde Grec Classique et hellénistique des Cités', *Pallas* (2007): 93–112; Véronique Chankowski, *Athenes et Delos a l'epoque Classique: Recherches sur l'administration du Sanctuaire d'apollon Delien* (Unpublished PhD Dissertation: EPHE, 1999); and Véronique Chankowski, *Parasites du Dieu: Comptables, Financiers et Commerçants dans la Délos Hellénistique* (Athens: École Française d''Athènes, 2020).

[57] Chankowski, 'Divine Financiers', 142, citing Léopold Migeottee, 'La Gestion des Biens Sacrés dans les Cités Grecques', in H. Rupprecht (ed.), *Symposion 2003, Vorträge zur griechischen und Hellenistischen Rechtsgeschichte* (Vienna: Austrian Academy of Sciences 2006): 233–46.

[58] Chankowski, 'Divine Financiers', 142.

[59] Ibid., 142–3.

[60] Ibid., 143.

[61] Ibid., 149. Citing Raymond Bogaert, *Banques et Banquiers dans les Cités Grecques* (Leiden: Sijthoff, 1968), 281–8.

> Council in the month of *Apatourion* under penalty of reclamation by the *logistai* and a fine amounting to as much as half the principal borrowed.[62]

In some instances, 'the city entrusted with the administration of the sanctuary' used the deity's funds as a line of public credit.[63]

The Athenian democracy was particularly adept at exploiting divine endowments at home and within its realm of influence. For example, the city made significant use of 'the treasury of Athena and that of "the Other Gods" in the fifth century' and, of course, took control of the treasury of Apollo at Delos when Pericles moved it to Athens in 454 BCE.[64] The Delian League was as much a financial system as it was a political alliance. As Chankowski notes: 'after the departure of the Athenians in 314, the opportunities for borrowing were shut off and lending became almost exclusively the province of the Delians and their city; the sacred funds thus functioned as a spare account for the city of Delos and the Delians'.[65]

The legal regulation of these temple funds lay in the individual city-states that held responsibility for the temple itself. In (pre and post-Athenian) Delos, for example, 'it was the same administrators of Apollo's sacred wealth, the *hieropoioi*, an annually selected college of magistrates, who concurrently managed the sacred funds and the public funds'.[66] Likewise, in the Athenian Constitution (*Ἀθηναίων πολιτεία*), Aristotle discusses the management and importance of deities and their temples within the wider remit of civic virtue.[67] Aristotle describes the executive council and its relationship with 'other magistrates' such as:

> the treasurers of Athena, ten in number, elected by lot, one from each tribe. According to the law of Solon – which is still in force – they must be *Pentacosiomedimni*, but in point of fact the person on whom the lot falls holds the office even though he be quite a poor man. These officers take over charge of the statue of Athena, the figures of Victory and all the other ornaments of the temple, together with the money, in the presence of the Council.[68]

In his comments on this passage, the translator, Frederic Kenyon, observes that: 'Every temple in Athens had its own treasurers, those of the temple of Athena being by far the most important; but in 435 B.C. the various treasurers, with the

[62] Chankowski, 'Divine Financiers', 150. See pages 150–2 for several additional examples of local financial regulations governing temple credit, including: the sanctuaries of Apollo at Delos and Delphi; the sanctuary at Dystos near Eretria; and the sanctuary of Pythian Apollo.
[63] Ibid., 151.
[64] Ibid. For Athenian finance, see Loren Samons, *Empire of the Owl: Athenian Imperial Finance* (Stuttgart: Franz Steiner, 2000).
[65] Chankowski, 'Divine Financiers', 151, see fn. 43: 'Around 280, the Delians received help from Philokles, king of Sidon, supported by Ptolemy I, to recover funds that were in circulation and oblige debtor cities to repay their debts. This external support is undoubtedly what terminated the lending circuit which the Athenians had initiated with island cities.'
[66] Ibid., 152.
[67] Frederic Kenyon, *Aristotle on the Athenian Constitution* (London: George Bell and Sons, 1901).
[68] Ibid., 86, §47.

exception of those of Athena, were united in a single board under the title of *ταμίαι των ἀλλων θεών*.'[69] Furthermore, the supervision of the temples themselves was handled by the 'Commissioners for Repairs of Temples, elected by lot, who receive a sum of thirty minas from the Receivers-General, and therewith carry out the most necessary repairs in the temples'.[70]

In short, the administration of temples and their finances reflected the wider political theology of Hellenic political theology in which power was distributed municipally. The law of temple regulation by municipal authorities follows the wider, decentralised jurisprudence of classical Greece in which diverse local legal conventions at individual city-states shared broad, cultural conventions concerning law and justice.[71] Conversely, sanctuaries were the foremost location for engraving or otherwise displaying municipal legal conventions when they were fixed. As Karl Hölkeskamp observes:

> The overwhelming majority of early laws, however, were either kept in sanctuaries, like the *Elean rhetrai*, which were written on bronze plaques and deposited at Olympia – one of them even requires explicitly that this 'tablet'... be 'sacred at Olympia'; or they were inscribed on the walls of the major temple of the city, such as, for example, the early laws of Gortyn at the local sanctuary of Apollo Pythios and the sixth-century *lex sacra* at the temple of Athena Polias in Argos.[72]

Ancient Greece lacked the central authority of the Crown, and as such, it was likely impossible to develop the sort of divine royal authority that coalesced in ancient Babylon. Nevertheless, the jurisprudence and political theology of the decentralised Greek city-states led to a different, if analogically comparable model of divine ownership, and municipal management of endowments. Sovereignty lay in the polis, which in turn managed temple endowments. As Aristotle states in his *Politics*:

> Another kind of supervision, however, is that concerned with the gods – for example, priests, supervisors of matters relating to the temples (such as the preservation of existing buildings, the restoration of decaying ones), and all other things that are ordered in relation to the gods. In some places it happens that a single office supervises all this – for example, in small cities. But in other places there are many

[69] Frederic Kenyon, *Aristotle on the Constitution of Athens* (London: British Museum, 1892), 104–5 fn. 10.

[70] Kenyon, *Aristotle* (1901 edition), 92, §50.

[71] For classical Greek jurisprudence, George Calhoun, 'The Jurisprudence of the Greek City', *Columbia Law Review* 24.2 (1924): 154–71; and Paul Vinogradoff, *Outlines of Historical Jurisprudence, Volume 2: The Jurisprudence of the Greek City* (Oxford: Oxford University Press, 1922). For Athens in particular, see Christopher Carey, 'Legal Space in Classical Athens', *Greece & Rome*, 41.2 (2009): 172–86; Victoria Wohl, *Law's Cosmos: Juridical Discourse in Athenian Forensic Oratory* (Cambridge: Cambridge University Press, 2010); and Christopher Carey, Ifigeneia Giannadaki, and Brenda Griffith-Williams (eds), *Use and Abuse of Law in the Athenian Courts* (Leiden: Brill, 2018).

[72] Karl Hölkeskamp, 'Written Law in Archaic Greece', *Proceedings of the Cambridge Philological Society (Second Series)*, 38 (1993): 87–117, 100.

> officials who are separate from the priesthood – for example, supervisors of sacrifices, temple-guardians, and treasurers of sacred funds. Next after this is the office set aside for all the public sacrifices that the law does not assign to the priests but which have the honor [of being celebrated].[73]

0.2.2.ii The Roman State and the law of religious endowments

The status of deities and other charitable and religious foundations under Roman law presents a more complicated picture than that in ancient Greece. On the one hand, the Roman State was highly centralised, legally sophisticated, and geographically expansive. One would thus imagine that Roman jurisprudence would contain extensive discussions about the regulation of temple trusts and so forth. On the other hand, *res sacrae* (sacred things) existed largely outside the operation of Roman private law as *res extra commercium*.[74]

As Rudolph Sohm notes, 'in regard to *res sacrae* the idea was not that they were the private property of a Juristic person, e.g., the gods or some religious institution, but rather they were excluded from all private ownership'.[75] Furthermore, the general assumption has been that dedications made to the 'certain and specific deities' authorised by a *Senatus Consultum* or an Imperial constitution, were the property of the State 'as the administration was carried on by Magistrates and not by the temple priests'.[76] The inscribed law (*lex*) of the *Colonia Genetiva Iulia* from Urso, dating to 44 BCE, 'stipulates that sacred offerings of money (*pecunia stipis*) given to the temple, as well as monetary surpluses from sacrifices, should be expended within the temple and not reused for other purposes… [and] refer[s] to the control of the incomes of sacred places by public authorities'.[77]

[73] Aristotle, *Politics*, 1322b 18–29, cited in Franciszek Bryk, *What Role Do Religious Institutions Play in Aristotle's Ideal Polis?* (Unpublished MSt Thesis: University of Oxford, 2023), 15–16.

[74] Mukherjea, *Hindu Law*, 7.

[75] Rudolph Sohm, *Institutes of Roman Law* (Oxford: Oxford University Press, 1892), cited in Mukherjea, *Hindu Law*, 7.

[76] Mukherjea, *Hindu Law*, 8, citing William Buckland, *A Text-Book of Roman Law: From Augustus to Justinian* (Cambridge: Cambridge University Press, 1921), 177. For authorized deities, see Andrew Wilson, 'Introduction', in Andrew Wilson, Nick Ray, and Angela Trentacoste (eds), *The Economy of Roman Religion* (Oxford: Oxford University Press, 2023): 1–29, 11 fn. 51 (citing Ulpian): 'deos heredes instituere non possumus praeter eos, quos senatus consulto constitutionibusve principum instituere concessum est, sicuti Iovem Tarpeium, Apollinem Didymaeum Mileti, Martem in Gallia, Minervam Iliensem, Herculem Gaditanum, Dianam Ephesiam, Materem Deorum Sipylenen, Nemesim, quae Smyrnae colitur, et Caelestem Salinensem Carthagini.' ('We cannot designate the gods as heirs, except for those whom it has been allowed so to designate by a decree of the senate or constitutions of the emperor, such as Tarpeian Jove, Apollo Didymaeus of Miletus, Mars in Gaul, Trojan Minerva, Hercules of Cadiz, Diana of Ephesos, the Mother of the Gods of Mt Sipylos, Nemesis who is worshipped at Smyrna, and Caelestis Salinensis at Carthage.')

[77] Marta García Morcillo, 'Sacred Gifts, Profane Uses? Transfers and the Roman Religious Sphere', in Andrew Wilson, Nick Ray, and Angela Trentacoste (eds), *The Economy of Roman Religion* (Oxford: Oxford University Press, 2023): 245–66, 254–5.

While past scholarship tended to take this characterisation of Roman law at face value, the recent groundbreaking edited volume *The Economy of Roman Religion* challenges that assumption considerably.[78] The work of Beate Dignas, for example, demonstrates that: 'Temple economies were not simply subsumed into civic funds but were separate and sometimes at odds with civic aims and funding, finding themselves in conflict with city councils over revenues and resources.'[79]

Roman temples, like Greek temples, functioned as locations for safe deposits. For example, 'the Temple of Vesta we know that in addition to its being a place for the deposit of wills and treaties it was also a convenient sanctuary for funds'.[80] Furthermore: 'There is some evidence that in early days the temple of Jupiter Capitolinus had been used as a state treasury (there being a secret hiding-place in the throne of the god) and during the later republic the state treasury was housed in the temple of Saturn, as the phrase aerarium Saturni shows.'[81] Benjamin Bromberg argues that Roman temples 'did not lend any money at all', but recent work suggests the opposite. David Wigg-Wolf observes that, 'there was a clear differentiation between offerings made to the gods, which were temple property, and private deposits, which could later be withdrawn and recovered'.[82] Nevertheless, while 'evidence for temples lending money during the Roman Empire is scarcer' than for Greece, Wigg-Wolf notes two instances in the wider Roman Empire where temple deities lent funds at interest.[83] Additionally:

> Temples were also economic actors in their own right… [and] they might on occasion even act as civic benefactors: at Aphrodisias, 'Aphrodite' dedicated the marble entablature of the eastern forecourt of the Hadrianic baths from her own resources and from the bequest given to her by Epigonos, son of Dioscourides – in other words, the goddess, or rather her temple, was acting on a par with other civic donors drawn largely from the ranks of the town council.[84]

Greco-Roman deities might make poor financial decisions. The temple of Artemis at Ephesos, discussed above, which 'had a widespread reputation as a safe repository' was a noted money lender in the 1st century BCE, and in 37 CE, 'poor administration of lending by the temple led to intervention by the Proconsul

[78] Ibid.

[79] Beate Dignas, *Economy of the Sacred in Hellenistic and Roman Asia Minor* (Oxford: Oxford University Press, 2002), paraphrased in Wilson, 'Introduction', 2. Also see Padilla Peralta, *Divine Institutions: Religions and Community in the Middle Roman Republic* (Princeton: Princeton University Press, 2020).

[80] Benjamin Bromberg, 'Temple Banking in Ancient Rome', *The Economic History Review* 10.2 (1940): 128–31, 129.

[81] Ibid., 130.

[82] David Wigg-Wolf, 'Moneychangers in the Temple? Coins and Religion in the Roman World', in Andrew Wilson, Nick Ray, and Angela Trentacoste (eds), *The Economy of Roman Religion* (Oxford: Oxford University Press, 2023): 130–54, 145.

[83] Ibid., 146.

[84] Wilson, 'Introduction', 15.

of Asia, Paullus Fabius Persicus'.[85] Furthermore, we have several fragmentary papyri from the temple of Jupiter at Arsinoe, 'evidently run on Roman rather than Egyptian lines', that record the various lines of credit extended by the temple to private creditors.[86] The historical archive, however, suggests that such temples were the exception, rather than the rule. Marta Morcillo, however, observes, 'the consecration of things given to a temple depended ultimately on the Roman public authorities under which the temple or sanctuary was administrated, usually a local magistrate' and, consequently, the 'expropriation' of sacred assets and their resumption for secular uses, 'was not considered a sacrilege *per se*, as long as this was authorized by the relevant authority'.[87]

Finally, Roman economy and religion were closely aligned in the context of *collegia* (societies), the quintessential legal persons of Roman jurisprudence.[88] *Collegia*, which had the capacity to hold property as legal persons (corporations), often combined religious, social, economic, and legal aspects and they likely served as the basis for the rise of the modern corporation – albeit through the intermediary of Roman Catholic Canon Law.[89] *Collegia*, which set their own bylaws and received recognition by the State, in many ways typify a Sanskritic model of Equity: an association forms according to its local conventions, is granted protection (subject to revocation) by the State (or Crown), and operates for a particular purpose.

The Senate, and later Princeps, acted as guarantor, protector, and rescinder of *collegia* during the Roman period. The central Roman Government regulated

[85] Wigg-Wolf, 'Moneychangers', 145–6.

[86] Ibid., 146–7. The more widespread practice of temple loans in Roman Egypt is attested by 'the code of regulations of the *idiologus*, the chief financial official in Roman Egypt, issued in AD 150–61.... [which contains a] section dealing with priests and temples [that] states: "It is forbidden to lend temple revenues on second mortgages"'.

[87] Morcillo, 'Sacred Gifts', 255–6. See Thomas Harrington, 'Stewardship and Ownership of Material Goods: Discipline and Order in the Pre-Constantinian Church', *Catholic Lawyer* 33.2 (1990): 109–30, 122–3, for a 58 BCE record in which the priests of the Temple of Jove in Rome 'were permitted to sell certain items which had been dedicated to the god... [following] a formal procedure involving a declaration on the part of the responsible sacral stewards conducted in the presence of the aediles'.

[88] Koenraad Verboven, 'Guilds and Gods Religious Profiles of Occupational *Collegia* and the Problem of the *Dendrophori*', in Andrew Wilson, Nick Ray, and Angela Trentacoste (eds), *The Economy of Roman Religion* (Oxford: Oxford University Press, 2023): 267–309.

[89] For Roman *collegia* as economic institutions, see N. Tran, *Les membres des associations Romaines: Le rang social des collegiati en Italie et en Gaules sous le haut-empire* (Rome: Collection de l'École française de Rome 367, 2006); Nicholas Rauh, *The Sacred Bonds of Commerce: Religion, Economy, and Trade Society at Hellenistic Roman Delos, 166–87 BC.* (Leiden: Brill, 1993); and Inge Kroppenberg, 'Law, Religion, and Constitution of the Vestal Virgins', *Law & Literature* 22.3 (2010): 418–39. For the evolution of Roman *collegia* into modern corporations, see Samuel Williston, 'History of the Law of Business Corporations before 1800. I', *Harvard Law Review* 2.3 (1888): 105–24; John Dewey, 'The Historic Background of Corporate Legal Personality', *Yale Law Journal* 35.6 (1926): 655–73; Patrick Duff, *Personality in Roman Private Law* (Cambridge: Cambridge University Press, 1938); and Geoffrey Poitras, 'The *Societas Publicanorum* and Corporate Personality in Roman Private Law', *Business History* 63.7 (2021): 1055–78.

these institutions, sometimes abolishing or reforming them.[90] For example, the Roman Senate dissolved 'those associations deemed to be against the Roman constitution'.[91] Some *collegia* were reintroduced in the following decades; however, according to Suetonius, Julius Caesar, '"dissolved all the associations, except the ancient ones" and those that the Senate chose to allow on the ground of *utilitas civitatis*'.[92] According to the two documents which governed *collegia* in the early Empire – the *Lex Iulia de Collegiis* and the *Senatus Consultum Distraxit* – it was required that *collegia*, like public temples, be formally approved by the Senate (or emperor).[93] While these restrictions would wax and wane over time, the core feature of the Roman law of *collegia* was *control*: the State always exercised the right to regulate, supervise, and, if necessary, dissolve these associations.

In concert with the centralisation of State authority over religious and civic institutions, the Romans developed the theory of the Princeps as *parens patriae*. The term, in various forms – *parens urbis Romanae* (parent of the Roman city), or *pater patriae* (father of the fatherland) – had been bestowed by the Senate on notable Romans for their contributions: including Romulus, Marcus Furius Camillus, Cicero, and Julius Caesar.[94] Augustus' eventual acceptance of the title for himself in 2 BCE represents, in some ways, the culmination of his gradual establishment of the imperial identity of the Julian Caesars' royal identity. As Tom Stevenson notes:

> Valerius Messala… was once a civil war opponent of the emperor… [and] Suetonius says explicitly that he is reproducing the exact words used by Messala… 'May it be good and auspicious for you and your house, Caesar Augustus! For in this way we think to be praying for the lasting good fortune of the *res publica* and happiness for it: the Senate, in agreement with the Roman people, hails you as Father of the Fatherland.'[95]

Augustus' imperial role as the father of the nation, guarding its public institutions, bears as close a resemblance to classical Indian theories of *parens patriae* as it does to the system of feudal supervision that developed during the reign

[90] Ilias N Arnaoutoglou, 'Roman Law and Collegia in Asia Minor', *Revue Internationale des droits de l'Antiquité* 49 (2002): 27–44.

[91] Ibid., 30. Note that the 'first ban on associations, SC de Bacchanalibus (ILS 18 = FIRA I2 30), was issued in 186 BC. The decree banned the gatherings for the worship of Bacchus'.

[92] Ibid., 31.

[93] Luuk de Ligt, 'D. 47,22, 1, pr.-1 and the Formation of Semi-Public "Collegia"', *Latomus* 60.2 (2001): 345–58, 346.

[94] For the history of *pater patriae* and *parens patriae* in Rome, see Tom Stevenson, 'Acceptance of the Title *Pater Patriae* in 2 BC', *Antichthon* 43 (2009): 97–108.

[95] Ibid., 103, citing Suetonius (*Aug.* 58.2): 'quod bonum faustumque sit tibi domuique tuae, Caesar Auguste! sic enim nos perpetuam felicitatem rei p. et laeta huic precari existimamus: senatus te consentiens cum populo R. consalutat patriae patrem'.

of Edward I (r. 1272–1307), in which 'the English crown had claimed a particular type of wardship over all natural fools and idiots, a claim that was formally recognised by the passage of the Statute *Prerogativa Regis* in 1324'.[96] As in India and England, Augustus' claim to *parens patriae* status went hand-in-glove with his efforts to rebuild eighty-two temples and to promote the 'public cults' as '*sacra publica*'.[97] The relationship between emperor and deities was also circular: a statue of Augustus from a ruined temple to the imperial cult at Pompeii, for example, is inscribed 'Augustus Caesar, parent of the fatherland, *parens patriae*'.[98] Temple protection and the regulation of corporate bodies (religious or civic) thus played a central role in the theory of the concept (if not the jurisprudence) of *parens patriae* in classical Rome.

In short, while the ancient Greeks had a robust theory of deities as legal owners who could own property, lease assets, and offer lines of credit, their jurisprudence behind such activities was largely limited to the recognition that the divine activities – ritual or financial – should be overseen by the polis that is tasked with the responsibility of protecting the temple in question. The Romans, in contrast, had a significantly more centralised state and a more comprehensive jurisprudence than the Greeks, but generally, divine assets were separated from the operation of private law and existed outside of commercial circulation.[99]

Ultimately, these two phenomena – strong legal personality for religious institutions and a sophisticated jurisprudential account of the legal relations involved in endowments – would coalesce in medieval Christian Canon Law. Likewise, the *fideicommissum*, a testamentary bequest in which the beneficiary must use parts of the estate for someone else, influenced the subsequent development of charity and trusts law in medieval Europe.[100]

0.2.3 Christian theories and practices of endowments

One simple truism of the historical development of Chancery jurisprudence in England is the relationship between the Crown and the Church before the

[96] Lawrence Custer, 'The Origins of the Doctrine of *Parens Patriae*', *Emory Law Journal* 27.2 (1978): 195–208, 195.
[97] Borgolte, *World History*, 206.
[98] J. Bert Lott, 'The Earliest Augustan Gods Outside of Rome', *The Classical Journal* 110.2 (2014–15): 129–58, 139.
[99] For the Roman jurisprudence of sacred things (*res sacrae*) see Olga Tellegen-Couperu, 'Sacred Law and Civil Law', in Olga Tellegen-Couperu (ed.), *Law and Religion in the Roman Republic* (Leiden: Brill, 2012): 145–64; Yan Thomas, '*Res Religiosae*: On the Categories of Religion and Commerce Under Roman Law', in Alain Pottage and Martha Mundy (eds), *Law, Anthropology, and the Constitution of the Social: Making Persons and Things* (Cambridge: Cambridge University Press, 2009): 40–72; and Duncan MacRae, 'The Laws of the Rites of the Priests: Varro and Late Republican Roman Sacral Jurisprudence', *Bulletin of the Institute of Classical Studies* 60.2 (2017): 34–48.
[100] For Roman *fideicommissums* and trusts and charities law, see David Johnston, *The Roman Law of Trusts* (Oxford: Oxford University Press, 1988); and C. Rickett, 'Charitable Giving in English and Roman Law: A Comparison of Method', *The Cambridge Law Journal* 38.1 (1979): 118–47.

Reformation in the 16th century. W.T. Barbour argued that 'the ecclesiastical chancellors of the fifteenth century had established the groundwork of principle and practice upon which the structure of modern equity would be built'.[101] Additionally, R.A. Marchant, posited that: 'It was from canon law that the developing court of equity, the Chancery Court, received some of its basic principles and also its method of procedure – not unnaturally, as many of the medieval lord chancellors were clerics.'[102] Helmut Coings' argument, as summarised by Haskett provides the standard account of Equity's post-reformation history in England:

> They [the clerical Chancellors] found in the canon law basic principles but no specific rules they could take, for as the *denunciatio evangelica* and English equity supplemented different legal systems there needed to be adaptation along different lines. Because the common law prevailed in England, English equity became something much different than equity on the Continent, with its civil and canon law context.[103]

The broader point is that English Chancellors drew on Canon Law jurisprudence as a source of basic principles in their efforts to develop an equitable jurisprudence that was adapted to the unique historical and legal circumstances of the Court of Chancery as a parallel institution to the King's Bench.[104] This process bears a close similarity to the approach taken by colonial jurists of the British East India Company and Crown Courts, who drew on Sanskrit jurisprudence for basic principles of jurisprudence, rather than written rules of positive law when they crafted an Anglo-Hindu jurisprudence of Hindu religious and charitable trusts that combined elements of indigenous Indian practice and English Equity law.

The history of English Equity entails elements of Canon Law jurisprudence, and the Roman Catholic Church's Canon Law's origins lie in no small part in the old Roman Law. Therefore, it is vital to examine the emergence of the Church as a legal entity under Roman Law as we explore the historical development of the law of religious and charitable institutions in European (and by colonial extension, India).[105]

In contrast to its later institutional and legal unity under the Bishop of Rome, the early Christian Church was divided 'into separate communities, largely

[101] Quoted in Timothy Haskett, 'The Medieval English Court of Chancery', *Law and History Review* 14.2 (1996): 245–314, 259.

[102] Ibid., 259. Citing Ronald Marchant, *The Church under the Law. Justice, Administration and Discipline in the Diocese of York, 1560–1640* (Cambridge: Cambridge University Press, 1969), 2.

[103] Haskett, 'The Medieval English Court', 264. Referring to Helmut Coing, 'English Equity and the Denunciatio Evangelica of the Canon Law', *Law Quarterly Review* 71 (1955): 223–41.

[104] For the wider influence of Canon Law in medieval England, see David Seipp, 'The Reception of Canon Law and Civil Law in the Common Law Courts before 1600', *Oxford Journal of Legal Studies* 13.3 (1993): 388–420.

[105] For Roman Law and Canon Law, see Albert Gauthier, *Roman Law and its Contribution to the Development of Canon Law* (Ottawa: Faculty of Canon Law, Saint Paul University, 1996). Also see R.H. Helmholz, 'Canon Law and Roman Law', in David Johnston (ed.), *The Cambridge Companion to Roman Law* (Cambridge: Cambridge University Press, 2015): 396–422.

withdrawn from official Roman society'.[106] Until the Emperor Constantine's (r. 306–337 CE) issuance of the Edict of Milan in 312, 'at civil law, the Christian collectivities remained *collegia illicita*, devoid of legal standing, deprived of any caput. The Christian communities did not enjoy and could not attain the *ius coeundi*'.[107] From a legal perspective, the Edict of Milan brought about a landmark shift in the legal constitution of the Roman Catholic Church: it restored confiscated Church property, authorised bequests to the Church (like the authorised state deities of earlier centuries), and granted the Church legal status analogous to a collegium.[108]

As the Canon Law developed, it did so in conversation with the Roman civil law, with the effect that 'this new convergence of Roman and Christian beliefs allowed the Christian church to imbue the Roman law with a number of its basic teachings'.[109] As R.H. Helmholz notes, 'the early church's dependence on the civil law was pithily stated in an oft-repeated maxim, as found, for example, in the *Lex Ribuaria*: "The church lives according to the Roman law" (*Ecclesia vivit iure Romano*)'.[110] Not only did this maxim set the Roman Church, its possessions, and its clergy, outside of the jurisdiction of local (often Germanic) courts after the fall of Rome, but it also established intimate links between the Emperor and the Church. It comes as no surprise, therefore, that 'the first book of Justinian's Code, for example, begins with titles on churches and their possessions, bishops and clerics, episcopal jurisdiction, heresy, baptism, and apostasy'.[111]

In the medieval ages, of course, the Roman Church gained immense influence and property across a multitude of kingdoms. The totality of these holdings and the complex and contested relationships between the Church and Crowns is beyond the scope of this introduction, but I reflect on one key legal phenomenon that emerged from medieval Canon Law: the corporation.[112] As Luka Ribaravić evocatively describes: 'The character of communal life in Europe was profoundly transformed by the appearance of an immense variety of associations in the twelfth and

[106] John Witte, 'Introduction', in John Witte and Frank Alexander (eds) *Christianity and Law: An Introduction* (Cambridge: Cambridge University Press, 2008): 1–32, 7.

[107] Harrington, 'Stewardship', 129.

[108] There is much debate about whether the Edict of Milan ever existed, or if it refers to a series of edicts issued by Constantine that gradually extended legal rights to the Church. See Gregory Armstrong, 'Church and State Relations: The Changes Wrought by Constantine' *Journal of the American Academy of Religion* 32.1 (1964): 1–7.

[109] Witte, 'Introduction' 7.

[110] Helmholz, 'Canon Law', 404–5.

[111] Ibid., 405–6.

[112] Studies of the Church and economy are legion. The standard work of reference is Robert Ekelund *et al.*, *Sacred Trust: The Medieval Church as an Economic Firm* (Oxford: Oxford University Press, 1996). Also see Susan Wood, *The Proprietary Church in the Medieval West* (Oxford: Oxford University Press, 2006). For English examples, see Alisdair Dobie, 'The Development of Financial Management and Control in Monastic Houses and Estates in England c. 1200–1540', *Accounting, Business & Financial History* 18.2 (1980): 141–59; and Nancy Warren, *Spiritual Economies: Female Monasticism in Later Medieval England* (Philadelphia: University of Pennsylvania Press, 2001).

thirteenth centuries… both ecclesiastical and lay… [and] a generic term for these different types of medieval corporations, taken over from the earlier Roman law of corporations, is universitas.'[113] At the very heart of the matter is Ribaravić's observation that: 'Rapidly developing after Gratian finished compiling the *Decretum* in the middle of the twelfth century, canonistic legal thought successfully effected the fusion of Roman law legacy with centuries long experience of living in ecclesiastical corporate communities.'[114] This wellspring of jurisprudential thought concerning legal personality in Canon Law would give rise to the sorts of civic, religious, and charitable institutions of the medieval and modern world: charitable trusts, schools, colleges, and universities, professional guilds, chartered companies, and, eventually, the limited liability company.[115]

It was in the Canon Law, primarily, that the precursor to the modern law of Equity and Trusts emerged, but the origins of Equity and Trusts jurisprudence have Greco-Roman antecedents. Furthermore, even before the development of Greco-Roman law, the ancient Babylonians developed a sophisticated system of Equity and Trusts – even if it seems to have had little known influence on European developments. The general point is twofold: 1) English Equity jurisprudence has a long, complicated history which, when we examine its manifold historical influences, reveals a model of divine ownership (and the Crown as *parens patriae*) that looks remarkably similar in many ways to parallel developments in classical India; and 2) classical Sanskrit theories of Equity and Trusts are not exotic outliers to European analogues when viewed within the wider, global history of foundations.

Equity and Trusts as global phenomenon has always involved an idiosyncratic admixture of multiple strands of legal thought combined with a healthy dose of mercurial sovereign power. Seeing the larger picture can thus help us to appreciate the various strands that, threaded together, make up the ancient and modern jurisprudence of Hindu religious and charitable trusts.

[113] Luka Ribaravić, 'Leviathan and Medieval "Universitas": Hobbes' Debt to Canon Law', *History of Political Thought*, 38.1 (2017): 92–109, 100.

[114] Ibid., 100

[115] Of note, George Makdisi, 'The Guilds of Law in Medieval Legal History: An Inquiry into the Origins of the Inns of Court', *Cleveland State Law Review* 34.1 (1985–86): 3–18, argues for an Islamic influence for English corporations based on contact between the crusaders in the near east and the Inns of Court at the Temple in London. This idea is very similar to Monica Gaudiosi's argument concerning the creation of *trusts* at the same point in English history (see Note 37). For Makdisi's argument, see page 15: 'It was only after the Merton model of 1274 that *hospitia* became colleges in the sense of *collegia*. But associations, such as unincorporated guilds, have a development that goes further back into history to at least the tenth century in Baghdad and other parts of Eastern Islam. The scholastic guild development may be divided, legally speaking, into two main categories: (1) the guild as an unchartered institution or an eleemosynary institution based on the waqf or charitable trust; and (2) a charitable-trust guild capped with the protective cover of incorporation.'

0.3 Précis of chapters

This monograph is divided into five chapters, which introduce the core principles of the Sanskrit jurisprudence of Equity and Trusts and then examine how those principles influenced the practical administration of Hindu religious and charitable trusts over several epochs in Indian history. One broad argument of this monograph is that Sanskrit jurisprudential concepts have influenced and continue to influence the decision-making processes of government administrators with reference to Hindu religious institutions.

This influence has sometimes been direct, with medieval kings and private donors invoking Sanskrit jurisprudential texts verbatim when creating deeds of endowments for monasteries and temples. At other times, this influence was indirect: Islamic rulers of India, such as the Mughals, seem to have been aware of the principles of Hindu law even if they administered Hindu religious institutions according to Persianate administrative paradigms. The administrators of the British East India Company, and later the Crown, tried with mixed success to supervise Hindu religious endowments according to the 'laws and usages' of Dharmaśāstra, but in practice, they incorporated many elements of English Equity and Trusts jurisprudence in the process.

Finally, the Supreme Court of India has endeavoured to use Dharmaśāstric treatises as a source of juridical knowledge about core Hindu beliefs and practices about deities and their endowments. During different epochs, ruling governments adapted Sanskrit jurisprudential ideas to the unique legal and political circumstances of their day, but in each instance, we can detect the clear presence of the core principles that I shall outline in the next chapter.

Jurisprudential theory is very different from actual historical legal practice. This invites a brief reflection on *what* exactly Sanskrit jurisprudence *is*. Dharmaśāstra is the science of Dharma.[116] Dharma, as Patrick Olivelle notes:

> Constitute[s] the most central feature of Indian civilization... , irrespective of linguistic, sectarian, or regional differences... One has only to pick up any introduction to Hinduism or Buddhism to note the prominence given to this term by the authors... One is also left with the impression that, following the orientalist image of the 'unchanging' India, dharma has always been the central concept of Indian religion and culture.[117]

[116] For justifying the translation of *śāstra* as 'science', see Christopher T. Fleming, 'Introduction', in Christopher T. Fleming *et al.* (eds), *Science and Society in the Sanskrit World* (Leiden: Brill, 2023): 1–46, 9–19.

[117] Patrick Olivelle, 'Introduction', *Journal of Indian Philosophy* 32.5–6 (2004): 421–2. Citied in Fleming, *Ownership and Inheritance*, 7.

While Dharma was relatively obscure in the Vedic period (1500–600 BCE), it became *the* central pillar of the moral universe of the *śramaṇic* traditions (Buddhism and Jainism) in the 5th century BCE and the core principle of the Mauryan Empires (321–185 BCE) pan-Indian political theology.[118]

The revival of Brāhmaṇical hegemony and the introduction of image-oriented temple cults following the collapse of Mauryan power in the 'Age Between the Empires' (c. 100 BCE–300 CE) led to the creation of a new concept of Dharma: as 'the privileges, duties and obligations of a man [sic], his standard of conduct as a member of the *Āryan* community, as a member of one of the castes, as a person, in a particular stage of life [*Varṇāśramadharma*]'.[119] This version of Dharma was not limited to morality. Rather, it: 'Encompasses the prescriptions for, the acts of, and the effects of ritual, purification, diet, statecraft, and penance in addition to rules for legal procedure, contracts, property, corporations and partnerships, inheritance, marriage, and crimes of various sorts.'[120]

Over the centuries, Brāhmaṇa scholars compiled a vast corpus of Dharmaśāstric literature that discussed these facets of an ordered, Dharmic life in great detail. Dharmaśāstrins (scholars of Dharmaśāstra) developed sophisticated accounts of contract, marriage, crime, royal sovereignty, and personal piety, but it is vital to recognise that Dharmaśāstra is *not* positive law. Instead, as has been noted elsewhere:

> Dharmaśāstra is a technical, scholastic science (*śāstra*) that portrays itself as a comprehensive guide to Dharma, the various duties incumbent on individuals (whose archetype is an able-bodied Brāhmaṇa male). In this system, seemingly distinct activities ranging from making one's toilet to dividing one's estate among one's children are facets of a larger, transcendent model of how society ought to be organized according to caste and class.[121]

However theoretical Dharmaśāstra may have been, *internally* as a discipline, its principles have clearly been deployed by human agents for a diverse array of purposes at various points in history. The theoretical, jurisprudential nature of Dharmaśāstra by no means elides its practical applications in different contexts, but it is important to remember that, whatever its rhetorical pretences, Dharmaśāstra is an *intellectual* discipline that aims to equip the reader with an understanding of the themes and concepts to which practical legal discourse appeals.

[118] Fleming, *Ownership and Inheritance*, 7.
[119] Ibid., 7, citing P.V. Kāṇe, *A History of Dharmaśāstra*, Vol. 1. Part 2, 2nd edn. (Pune: Bhandarkar Oriental Research Institute, 1968), 3.
[120] Fleming, *Ownership and Inheritance*, 7, citing Donald Davis, 'Hinduism as a Legal Tradition', *Journal of the American Academy of Religion* 75.2 (2007): 241–67, 243.
[121] Fleming, *Ownership and Inheritance*, 12.

0.3.1 Chapter 1: The Sanskrit Jurisprudence of Equity and Trusts

Contemporary scholarship has long accepted that, in contrast to its intricate, if highly scholastic, discussions of inheritance, adoption, legal procedure, gift, etc., Dharmaśāstra is remarkably taciturn concerning the management of Hindu religious endowments.[122] One ostensible reason for this is that the Sanskrit text tradition of ritual hermeneutics (*Mīmāṃsā*) provided the interpretive frame for Dharmaśāstra. Scholars of Mīmāṃsā (*Mīmāṃsakas*) argued for a theory of deities as being, merely, liturgical phonemes (*śabdamātra*) and were deeply opposed to temple worship. Consequently, scholars of Dharmaśāstra (*Dharmaśāstrins*) could not countenance divine ownership of temple and monastic property.[123]

Another reason, coloured, in part, by an orientalist stereotype of Brāhmaṇical rapacity, is that the authors of Dharmaśāstra did not want to create any obstacles to *their* ownership or temples and other religious endowments (such as monasteries).[124] This argument, however, ignores the fact that political scientific (*Arthaśāstric*) and legendary (*Purāṇic*) sources, both authored by Brāhmaṇas, attest to the ownership of deities.

Chapter 1 qualifies the standard narrative in two ways. First, Mīmāṃsā and Dharmaśāstra authors describe a theory of a figurative (*aupacārika*), or artificial (*kalpita*) ownership (*svatva*) on the part of temple deities that, while not constituting ownership in a strict sense, nevertheless imposes legal duties on temple managers. Oftentimes, especially in classical Dharmaśāstra (Bhāruci and Medhātithi's commentaries on the *Mānavadharmaśāstra*, for example), and Mīmāṃsā (the *Śābarabhāṣya*, and *Mīmāṃsānayaviveka*, for example), this form of figurative ownership is portrayed as a legally recognised form of popular practice rather than as an injunction originating directly from canonical scriptural interpretation. Nevertheless, it is vital to note that classical Dharmaśāstra and Mīmāṃsā authorities *explicitly recognise* the social reality and legal validity of divine ownership. Furthermore, in late-medieval and early-modern works (Anantadeva's *Rājadharmakaustubha*, Kamalākarabhaṭṭa's *Dānakamalākara*, Nīlakaṇṭhabhaṭṭa's *Pratiṣṭhāmayūkha*, and Raghunandana's *Devapratiṣṭhātattva*, for example) Brāhmaṇical authors interpreted some canonical textual passages in accordance with popular practices.

Second, drawing on the work of Donald Davis and Timothy Lubin, Chapter 1 demonstrates that Dharmaśāstra advances a model of supplementary

[122] See, for example, Justice B.K. Mukherjea's observation in *Hindu Law*, 1–2.

[123] The argument appears, most influentially, in Günther-Dietz Sontheimer, 'Religious Endowments in India: The Juristic Personality of Hindu Deities', in Heidrun Brückner *et al.* (eds), *Essays on Religion, Literature and Law* (New Delhi: Manohar, 2004): 15–68.

[124] See J. Duncan Derrett 'Religious Endowments, Public and Private', in J. Duncan Derrett (ed.), *Religion, Law and the State in India* (Delhi: Oxford University Press, 1999): 482–512, for a vociferous, if largely unwarranted defense of Brāhmaṇical ownership of temple assets.

law, or meta-law (*pāribhāṣikadharma*), wherein the responsibility of generating rules governing religious endowments (including the ownership of deities) is delegated to the founders of these institutions – including kings, princes, merchants, and, sometimes, even deities themselves.[125] Colonial jurists and Indological scholars have long noted that Dharmaśāstra enjoins the Crown, as *parens patriae*, to protect temples and to ensure the observance of conventions. Eventually, colonial jurists linked Sanskrit jurisprudential principles regarding the Crown and *pāribhāṣikadharma* to Dharmaśāstric (and Mīmāṃsā) descriptions of deities' figurative ownership. Consequently, Chapter 1 shows that there is a Dharmaśāstric theory of Equity (meta-legal rules enforced by the Crown) and Trusts (wherein fiduciaries exercise possession of property on behalf of another). To uncover the specific rules of these endowments, however, we must turn to the epigraphic tradition.

0.3.2 Chapter 2: Equity and Trusts in Classical Indian Legal History

Chapter 2 provides a phenomenological and chronological account of the dedication and regulation of classical and medieval religious endowments – Jain, Buddhist, Vaiṣṇava, and Śaiva – through a close examination of India's epigraphic records. The model for the juridical personality of classical and medieval Hindu deities (and the language of establishing trusts for their benefit) lay, I argue, in the ownership of Buddhist and Jain monasteries.

There is an extraordinarily large corpus of Indian inscriptions and copperplates which describe deities as the owners of temples and monasteries (and which outline the fiduciary duties of their legal guardians). Chapter 2 distils the core phenomena of classical Indian trusts from these epigraphic records and produces a history of their evolution. I follow Timothy Lubin and Gerard Colas' recent exploration of cosmopolitan norms and regional idioms in the use of documents in classical and medieval India.[126] Scholastic Dharmaśāstric theory provided a discursive language for the practical law of temple management and that the foundation and preservation of temples (owned by their tutelary deities) in accordance with Dharmaśāstric and Purāṇic principles. Such practices were the most important method for royal dynasties to articulate their place within India-wide 'imperial formations' (to borrow Ronald Inden's historiographic model of the political constitution of India from the Gupta period to the rise of the Delhi Sulṭānate).

[125] See, for example, Davis, 'Intermediate Realms of Law'.

[126] Gerard Colas, 'Images and Territory of Gods: From Precepts to Epigraphs', in Daniela Berti and Gilles Tarabout (eds), *Territory, Soil and Society in South Asia* (New Delhi: Manohar, 2009): 99–142; and Timothy Lubin, 'Towards a South Asian Diplomatics: Cosmopolitan Norms and Regional Idioms in the Use of Documents', in Simon Cubelic, Axel Michaels, and Astrid Zotter (eds), *Studies in Historical Documents from Nepal and India* (Heidelberg: Heidelberg University Publishing, 2018): 37–84.

Chapter 2 opens with a survey of some of the oldest strata of Indian epigraphy: deeds of dedication to Buddhist and Jain monasteries by the rulers of, among others, the Mahāmēghavāhana (2nd century BCE–4th century CE) and Sātavāhana (2nd century BCE–3rd century CE) dynasties. These deeds of endowment gift properties to the Jain and Buddhist *Saṃghas* (often to a Jina or to the Buddha), with various stipulations. Unlike contemporaneous gifts to Brāhmaṇas (usually for the stipulated purpose of performing sacrifices), disciplinary restrictions on Jain and Buddhist ascetics (not to own property, among other things) led to the introduction of various conceits in the epigraphic, legal record: the Buddha as owner, a *stūpa* as owner, the lineage as owner, or the Sangha as owner (similar to the proposed origin of English trusts law in the vexed problem of the ownership of Christian monastic property). This aspect of the chapter builds on Gregory Schopen's influential work on the economic and legal history of Buddhist monasteries.[127]

The emergence of Purāṇic, temple-based Hinduism associated with Vaiṣṇava and Śaiva political theology (as well as Hindu monastic institutions) in early centuries of the Common Era led to the appropriation and transformation of Jaina and Buddhist models of religious endowments – wherein Hindu *deities* rather than the Buddha, Jina, or monastic Sanghas were framed as legal owners. The rulers of the Gupta (275–897 CE), Cola (3rd century BCE–1279 CE), Pallava (275–897 CE), Puṣyabhūti (6th–7th century CE), Cālukya (543–753 CE), and Rāṣṭrakūṭa (753–982 CE) dynasties endowed temple complexes and monasteries (with the deity as owner and with elaborate systems of fiduciaries and royal supervision) as part of their claims to the paramountcy in India's medieval imperial formation.

Lower-level regional rulers and corporate guilds also endowed temples and monasteries as part of an interconnected, hierarchical religio-political system. Invariably, these endowments followed the theoretical models set out in Dharmaśāstra.[128] Furthermore, the chapter explores epigraphic records of legal disputes (fiduciaries in breach of trust with their deity, boundaries between temples, the plundering/non-plundering of a temple by a neighbouring king) where kings followed their Dharmaśāstric duty to ensure the proper administration of religious endowments within their realms.

[127] Gregory Schopen, 'The Buddha as an Owner of Property and Permanent Resident in Medieval Indian Monasteries', *Journal of Indian Philosophy* 18.3 (1990): 181–217.

[128] See, for example, Donald Davis' analysis of documents 'lekhya' in the *Smṛticandrikā*: 'Toward a History of Documents in Medieval India: The Encounter of Scholasticism and Regional Law in the *Smṛticandrikā*', *The Medieval Globe* 2.2 (2016): 167–97.

0.3.3 Chapter 3: Hindu Temple Trusts in Islamic India

Chapter 3 attends to one of the most controversial epochs and issues in Indian history: the arrival of Muslim rulers in the Indian subcontinent and the relationship between these rulers and Hindu temples within their realms. Examples of eristical interactions are legion: the Somanātha temple in Gujarat, the Kṛṣṇajanmastha temple in Mathurā, and the Kāśīviśvanātha temple in Vārāṇasī, for example, were destroyed repeatedly (being rebuilt in the intervals) – most notably by Mahmud of Ghazni in 1024 and 1017 (Kāśīviśvanātha was destroyed first in 1194) and by Aurangzeb in 1665, 1670, and 1669, respectively. In many instances, Muslim rulers raised mosques on the sites of temples from spoliated materials, and control over these locations is the subject of considerable conflict in contemporary India. Furthermore, the legacy of these events lies at the heart of communalist narratives of Indian history.

Pace these narratives of religious *prejudice* being the *primary* cause of temple destruction, and in line with the work of Richard Eaton, Richard Davis, and Audrey Truschke, I explore temple destruction within the rubrics of *political* domination and *legal* regulation.[129] Chapter 2 showed that temple endowment and protection were the cornerstone of medieval Hindu political sovereignty, and, consequently, the destruction of these same temples should be viewed as politically strategic acts *primarily* and as reflections of religious prejudice *secondarily*. The chapter focuses on Hindu temples under two influential regimes: under the Delhi Sulṭānate (1206–1526 CE) and the Mughal Empire (1526–1857 CE).

Although the Delhi Sulṭānate is often viewed as a period of extensive temple destruction, there are several instances in which the sultans and their regional governors protected temples, permitted repairs to damaged temples, and even made donations to some temples. Some Mughal emperors, most notably Akbar, but even Aurangzeb, issued decrees (*farmāns*) that set aside funds for the creation of new temples and the management of their endowments as part of a wider political strategy for securing the loyalty of various Hindu princes – assuming, strategically, the role of a Dharmaśāstric ruler. Furthermore, Mughal legal records detail instances wherein Hindus petitioned the state, successfully, to intervene in the management of temple endowments. These efforts entailed assimilating Hindu endowments to the Islamic/Islamicate legal models of the Mughal bureaucracy (*waqfs*, most notably).

This chapter also examines the flip-side of the coin: the ways in which Hindu sovereigns and subjects of Muslim rulers built, endowed, and protected

[129] Richard Eaton, *India in the Persianate Age* (Berkeley: University of California Press, 2019); Richard Davis, *Lives of Indian Images* (Princeton: Princeton University Press, 1997); and Audrey Truschke, *The Language of History: Sanskrit Narratives of Indo-Muslim Rule* (New York: Columbia University Press, 2021).

temples and monasteries. Rāja Ṭoḍar Mal, who patronised the compilation of a Dharmaśāstra digest, the *Ṭoḍarānanda*, rebuilt and endowed the Kāśīviśvanātha temple at Vārāṇasī, which supported a series of illustrious scholars of Dharmaśāstra. One family of these scholars, the Bhaṭṭas, formed a close relationship with Śivājī Bhonsle, and Śivājī's rebellion against the Mughal Empire in 1657 explains, partially, Aurangzeb's destruction of the Kāśīviśvanātha temple in 1669. Later, the Dharmaśāstric writings of the Bhaṭṭas (which include discussions of Equity and Trusts) became a core component of the Marāṭhā Empire's legal system (in the management of temples, among other issues) and the Maratha Chatrapatis, who framed themselves as Dharmaśāstric sovereigns, emphasised their guardianship of temples from Mughal desecration as part of their strategy of political legitimation.

Finally, in southern India, much of which remained independent of Muslim rulers, the medieval model of kings as donors reached a zenith in the Vijayanagara Empire, where the deity Virūpākṣa was enshrined as the sovereign owner of the realm, with the 'king' ruling in his name. After the fall of Vijayanagara in 1565, many smaller kingdoms, including Travancore, continued to follow this model. Although Hindu rulers adapted to or resisted the suzerainty of Muslim rulers in different ways, the Sanskrit jurisprudence of Equity and Trusts formed a key facet of their varied political strategies.

0.3.4 Chapter 4: Equity and Trusts in Anglo-Hindu Jurisprudence

Chapter 4 recounts the creation of the Anglo-Hindu law of Equity and Trusts. In 1765, the Mughal Emperor Shāh 'Ālam II (r. 1760–1806 CE) granted the British East India Company the *Dīwānī* (the right to collect revenue on behalf of the Emperor) to the provinces of Bihar, Bengal, and Orissa. As the *Dīwān*, the East India Company was also responsible for the administration of justice (including the supervision of religious endowments) in these territories. After a period of chaotic rule, in 1772, Governor-General Warren Hastings introduced a *Judicial Plan*, which established a series of civil courts (*Dīwānī 'Adālats*) in its Indian territories, where Hindu and Muslims could have their cases adjudicated according to their indigenous legal systems – by British judges. To aid the courts, philologists worked with native scholars of Sanskrit jurisprudence to codify and to translate Dharmaśāstra as a source of laws for Hindu subjects. Donald Davis and Ludo Rocher have written convincingly that in doing so, colonial philologists and jurists mistook Dharmaśāstric legal *theory* as positive *law*.

Unlike Dharmaśāstric discussions of, say, inheritance or adoption (for example), Dharmaśāstric theories of equity and trusts were very much part of the practical legal systems of pre-colonial India. Inscriptions quote Dharmaśāstric verses on the protection of temple property; deeds of endowment follow Dharmaśāstric descriptions of documents; temples employ the conceit of the deity as an 'owner'; and sovereigns often utilised their Dharmaśāstric right of supervision over temple and monastery endowments. In the late 18th and early 19th centuries, as the *Ṣadr Dīwānī 'Adālats* (and later, the Supreme Courts) of the Bengal, Bombay, and Madras presidencies developed a body of Anglo-Hindu Equity and Trusts, they repeatedly invoked Dharmaśāstric injunctions – the same injunctions that court-appointed *paṇḍitas* (traditional scholars of Sanskrit) cite in their letters of judgment (*vyavasthās*). We find a similar phenomenon in the Company's Courts of Wards, where the Company invoked Dharmaśāstric injunctions concerning a king's duty to guard the property of minors in order to authorise their 'management' of native princes.

The chapter traces the development of the Anglo-Hindu jurisprudence of equity and trusts (through case law and statutory reform) alongside the expansion of British dominion over the subcontinent. Although colonial jurists concluded correctly, I argue, that Hindu sovereigns enjoyed a right of visitation over religious trusts and that deities are 'owners' in a figurative, but legally efficacious manner, they erred in not looking – as Dharmaśāstra enjoins – for the *pāribhāṣikadharmas* (inscriptions, copper-plate charters, etc.) that outline the fiduciary duties of the trustees of specific deities. Had they done so, these jurists might not have needed to introduce the paradigm of 'Justice, Equity, and Good Conscience' in 1781, in which the ostensible paucity of Dharmaśāstric discussions of divine endowments was supplemented with English principles of equity and trust. The introduction of 'Justice, Equity, and Good Conscience' led to a gradual assimilation of Sanskritic legal theories to the terminology of the English Court of Chancery – beneficiary, next friend, equitable right, etc.

The key innovation was to frame temple deities as the personification of the 'pious, benevolent purpose' of the temple's founder. Although this theory of a deity as pious, religious purpose was part of a hybrid synthesis of Dharmaśāstric theories and English trusts law it was *not* as radical a departure from pre-colonial systems as J. Duncan Derrett and others have claimed. Nor was it the result of relying on '*Mīmāṃsā*' theories (as contemporary legal historians often claim).[130]

[130] This chapter also corrects the reading of this body of case law by Ritua Birla, *Stages of Capital: Law, Culture, and Market Governance in Late Colonial India* (Durham: Duke University Press, 2009). It engages more positively with Nandini Chatterjee, *The Making of Indian Secularism: Empire, Law and Christianity, 1830–1960* (Cambridge: Cambridge University Press, 2011).

0.3.5 Chapter 5: The Supreme Court of India and Hindu Religious Trusts

Chapter 5 examines the evolution of Hindu religious trusts in the wake of Indian independence (1947) and the introduction of the Indian Constitution (1950). The Indian Constitution established the Supreme Court (instead of the Judicial Committee of the Privy Council) and outlined specific freedoms of religion (in Articles 25–8). Notably, Article 26 ensures that 'every religious denomination… shall have the right… to establish and maintain institutions for religious and charitable purposes'.[131]

This chapter details the ongoing process whereby India's independent courts have attempted to bring the principles and precedents of the colonial-era Anglo-Hindu jurisprudence of Equity and Trusts into alignment with a constitutional, rights-based regime. In most areas of Anglo-Hindu law, such as inheritance and adoption, the passage of the Hindu Code Bill (1955–56) supplanted Dharmaśāstra with statutory law in virtually its entirety. While individual Indian states assumed control over Hindu religious endowments, the Hindu law of equity and trusts was never supplanted by extensive legislation. Consequently, the courts have and continue to engage with Dharmaśāstra (along with judicial precedent) when adjudicating disputes involving temple and monastery management.

Article 26 rights are not absolute and the courts have laboured (with mixed success) to balance a series of competing interests: 1) constitutional and legislative prohibitions on caste, gender, and religious discrimination; 2) the ability of individual states to manage temples for the 'public good'; and 3) the applicability of civil procedure (such as the bar of limitation) and of income tax to deities and their fiduciaries. In doing so, the Supreme Court developed an 'essential practices' doctrine (originating in 1954 in ***Commissioner, Hindu Religious Endowments, Madras v Sri Lakshmindra Thirtha Swamiar of Sri Shirur Mutt***), where the courts assumed the ability to separate the core, *essential*, constitutionally protected features of a religious institution or community from non-essential, non-protected aspects. Drawing the line between 'essential' and 'non-essential' practices requires the court to take an active role in understanding and managing religious institutions (often on the basis of Dharmaśāstric sources).[132]

As Deepa Das Acevedo has argued convincingly, the courts have recognised the sovereignty of temple deities and their private property rights (as well as the rights of deities' fiduciaries) while simultaneously acknowledging the public's

[131] For freedom of religion and deities, see Deepa Das Acevedo, 'Temples, Courts, and Dynamic Equilibrium in the Indian Constitution', *The American Journal of Comparative Law* 64.3 (2016): 555–82.
[132] 1954 AIR 282, 1954 SCR 1005. Also see Deepa Das Acevedo, 'Celibate Gods and "Essential Practices" Jurisprudence at Sabarimala, 1991–2011', in Daniela Berti *et al.* (eds), *Filing Religion: State, Hinduism, and Courts of Law* (Oxford: Oxford University Press, 2016): 101–23.

beneficial interest in the worship of these deities. The result was that, in virtually all instances, temple deities were re-cast as the legal personification of the pious benevolent purpose of the *public's right to worship the deity*. This merged Indian constitutional thinking with British notions of the legal personification of religious/charitable trusts and corporations (as pious and profit-oriented institutions, respectively).

The chapter attends to a variety of influential cases between 1950 and 2020, but two warrant particularly detailed attention: 1) the conflict over the admission of women to the Sabarimala temple; and 2) litigation concerning the ownership of the vast fortune housed in the Padmanābhasvāmi temple. In the first case, the managers of the Sabarimala temple (whose tutelary deity is celibate) refused, on the basis of longstanding tradition and Article 26, to admit women between the ages of ten and fifty (out of concern for menstrual pollution). A group of women filed suit, alleging that this violated Article 25 (the freedom to worship). In 2018, the Supreme Court ruled, on the basis of gender equality and the right to religious freedom, that women must be allowed entry into the temple. In the second case, the State of Kerala attempted to replace the titular Mahārāja of Travancore as the manager of Padmanābhasvāmi temple's vast wealth (the Mahārāja had donated the entire kingdom to the deity 'Padmanābhasvāmi' in 1750) on the basis that the public had a right to the temple treasure.

The Supreme Court ruled, however, that although the public had a right to worship at the temple (according to Article 25), the Mahārāja's right to serve as the deity's fiduciary was protected by Article 26. To arrive at this conclusion, the Supreme Court navigated Sanskrit deeds of dedication, Dharmaśāstric sources on Equity and Trusts, colonial-era judicial precedent, the Instrument of Accession (through which Travancore joined the Union of India) and their applicability of all of these sources to Constitutional rights concerning the freedom of religion.

This chapter also attends to one of the most controversial and influential Supreme Court Cases in recent Indian history, ***M. Siddiq v Suresh Das***.[133] The case concerned the disputed ownership of a parcel of land in Ayodhyā, a city in the State of Uttar Pradesh where, according to popular Hindu belief, the deity Rāma was born and where, until its destruction by a violent mob of Hindu extremists in 1992, a Mughal-era mosque stood. Until 1949, Hindus and Muslims shared access to the site (although not without significant tensions), with Hindus worshipping an image of Rāma in the outer courtyard of the mosque and Muslims worshipping in the mosque itself. In December of 1949, Hindu parties installed the idol of Rāma under the central dome of the mosque – where it remained, despite riots, under the custody of court-appointed priests, until the Supreme Court's verdict.

[133] 1 SCC 1 (2020).

In 2019, the Supreme Court awarded the area in its entirety to the juridical person, Rām Virajman, the tutelary deity of the site, with the specific instruction that a trust be formed to build and maintain a temple to Rāma. In doing so, the Supreme Court overturned a ten-thousand page, 2010 Allahabad High Court judgment that had divided the land. The Supreme Court's landmark thousand-page judgment, provided the most influential and comprehensive account of the current status of the Hindu law of equity and trusts in Indian legal history. After outlining the facts of the Ayodhyā dispute, the chapter compares the Supreme Court and Allahabad High Court's rulings vis-à-vis two seminal jurisprudential issues: 1) the legal *personality* of the Hindu deities at Ayodhyā; and 2) the *representation* of these deities in civil proceedings by various parties who portrayed themselves as Rāma's legal guardians (fiduciaries).

In the first debate, the courts were called upon to determine *what* a Hindu deity *is*, while in the second debate, the courts were tasked with determining *who* is obligated to secure a deity's best interests. Both courts navigated the tension between the Hindu community's rights of religious freedom under Articles 25 and 26 of the Indian Constitution and the applicability of civil law. Civil legal issues included evidence of title, the bar of limitation (time-limits within which an aggrieved party can file suit), and adverse possession (whereby a party can acquire legal ownership based on continuous possession).

Two justices of the Allahabad High Court argued, on the basis of Articles 25 and 26 of the Indian Constitution, and a strident application of Dharmaśāstric reasoning, for a capacious theory of Hindu equity and trusts in which deities such as Rām Virajman should be wholly immune to dispossession. The Supreme Court rejected much of the Allahabad High Court's more assertive Sanskrit-derived reasoning and defended established judicial precedent concerning the application of civil procedure to Hindu deities. The Supreme Court did, however, recognise Rām Virajman, characterised as 'the underlying purpose of continued worship' by Hindus at the disputed site, as a juridical person. Once it had recognised Rām Virajman – and afforded him the legal vestments of a religious endowment under Article 26 – the Supreme Court produced an historical narrative in which the State, since the British annexation of Oudh in 1856, protected the Hindu community's *idealised religious purpose of worship at Ayodhyā* – even when the Muslim community was dispossessed illegally. Although the Supreme Court largely ignored Sanskrit sources in its reasoning (and claimed to rely on precedent exclusively), it nevertheless engaged significantly with the Dharmaśāstra-derived arguments of the Allahabad High Court. The Sanskrit jurisprudence of Hindu equity and trusts lingers, I argue, as a spectral figure in the margins of the Supreme Court's verdict: unseen, but influential.

The broad arc of this book is to show the reader that, contrary to many previous scholars' opinions, India boasts a long and distinguished heritage of *theories* and *practices* of Equity and Trusts. While not as ancient as the grand temple economies of ancient Mesopotamia, India nevertheless developed one of the earliest and most sophisticated theories of trusts law. The assumption that India did not lies mostly in the East India Company's administrators' misguided quest to find *positive law* rather than *jurisprudential principles* in Dharmaśāstra treatises. Ironically, however, the system that developed in colonial India was, largely because of paucity of positive legal statements in India, more closely in alignment with pre-colonial theories and practices than other areas of Anglo-Hindu law such as inheritance. Despite the best efforts of many to ignore or overturn Dharmaśāstric jurisprudence in modern India, it has and will likely continue to serve as a jurisprudential wellspring for the administration of Hindu religious and charitable trusts.

1

The Sanskrit Jurisprudence of Equity and Trusts

> *It strikes one as... anomalous that notwithstanding the existence of richly endowed Hindu... religious institutions all over India, the subject of endowment should receive a most niggardly treatment in the hands of the Smriti writers... There is no statement of law, directly on the subject, in any of the Smriti works. Stray passages having only an incidental bearing on the matter occur here and there in the midst of dissertations on other topics, and no workable law could be constructed on the basis of scanty materials like these. Some of the later commentators... have paid a little more attention to the subject than what their predecessors did and they have drawn largely on the Pouranic literature; but what they talk of is not law but religion and rituals and it is often difficult to extricate any legal rule from a mass of religious rites and ceremonies.*
>
> Justice B.K. Mukherjea[1]

No scholar of the jurisprudence of Hindu endowments carries the same gravitas as Bijan Kumar Mukherjea, the fourth Chief Justice of the Supreme Court of India. *The Hindu Law of Religious and Charitable Trusts* is a ubiquitous presence in legal pleadings, judicial judgments, and scholarly work on the equally ubiquitous cultural institution of Hindu temples and other forms of religious endowment.[2] Mukherjea's provocative observation highlights a fundamental problem that has vexed centuries' worth of prominent juridical minds as they strive to distil a functional body of practical trusts law from India's vast ocean of Sanskrit jurisprudential literature. It is astonishing that, given the central importance of Hindu temple (and monastery) endowments to Indian culture, politics,

[1] Mukherjea, *Hindu Law*, 1–2.

[2] For Mukherjea's importance, see Rajeev Dhawan, 'The Supreme Court and Hindu Religious Endowments 1950–1975', *Journal of the Indian Law Institute* 20.1 (1978): 52–102, 54–5: 'From about 1950 to 1954, the law was shaped under the guiding hand of B.K. Mukherjea, J., who wrote the judgments in eight of the ten cases that were reported during this period. He was a distinguished authority on the subject and had delivered the Tagore Law lectures on this very subject in 1951.'

economy, and faith over the last two millennia, and given the infamous prolixity of Sanskrit jurists' (Dharmaśāstrins') efforts to prescribe *every* facet of human life, that India's greatest Sanskrit jurists – Manu, Yājñavalkya, Vijñāneśvara, Raghunandana, and Kamalākarabhaṭṭa – had so little to say about the financial arrangement of the religious institutions which often brought them substantial pecuniary advantages.[3]

Lamentations about the paucity of positive law concerning temple endowments have been *de rigueur* for scholars of the Hindu law of Equity and Trusts for some two-hundred years, beginning with Thomas Strange's observation that: 'Of the property of religious institutions, and of that partaking of Jura Regalia something will be incidentally said in parts of this work in which a reference to them connects with other subjects of discussion; materials covering them, that are accessible, being too scanty to admit of any extended investigation.'[4] Perhaps this truism is more dogmatic than axiomatic. Sanskrit studies have advanced remarkably since Strange and Mukherjea's remarks from the 19th and 20th centuries, respectively. This chapter is the product of my extended investigation into an archive of Sanskrit resources that are much less scanty than those of Strange, Mukherjea, or even Günther-Dietz Sontheimer, whose 1965 'Religious Endowments in India: The Juristic Personality of Hindu Deities' remains the standard work of reference for the Sanskritic side of this subject.[5]

Much Sanskrit jurisprudential literature (Dharmaśāstra) has been edited, published, and even made searchable through the efforts of Patrick Olivelle and Donald Davis at the University of Texas.[6] Similarly, our knowledge of

[3] For the universality of Dharmaśāstra, see Davis, 'Hinduism as a Legal Tradition', 243: '[Dharmaśāstra] encompasses the prescriptions for, the acts of, and the effects of ritual, purification, diet, statecraft, and penance in addition to rules for legal procedure, contracts, property, corporations and partnerships, inheritance, marriage, and crimes of various sorts.'

[4] Thomas Strange, *Hindu Law*, Vol. 1 (London: Parbury Allen & Co., 1830), 32. Also see P.V. Kāṇe *History of Dharmaśāstra*, Vol. 2.2 (Pune: Bhandarkar Oriental Research Institute, 1941), 910: 'Throughout India for many centuries there have been well-endowed temples and *maṭhas*. But how the rulers or the ancient and medieval courts of justice regulated the administration of these institutions or their funds or how they prevented or stopped maladministration or misappropriation is not dealt with exhaustively anywhere.... In the following some of the meagre material that can be gathered from Dharmaśāstra works and analogous writings is set out'; Richard H. Davis, 'Images and Temples', in Patrick Olivelle and Donald R. Davis (eds), *The Oxford History of Hinduism: Hindu Law* (Oxford: Oxford University Press, 2018): 347–67, 347: 'Considering the importance of these religious practices in classical and medieval India... it is surprising that discussion of them in Dharmaśāstra literature is quite sparse'; and Patrick Olivelle, 'The Temple in Sanskrit Legal Literature', in H. P. Ray (ed.), *Archaeology and Text: Temple in South Asia* (Delhi: Oxford University Press, 2010): 191–204, 177–88, 193: 'Ironically... the temple is conspicuous by its absence or insignificance in the legal literature of ancient India.'

[5] Sontheimer, 'Religious Endowments'.

[6] The Dharmaśāstra Resource Library at the University of Texas, Austin has benefitted tremendously from Patrick Olivelle's transcription and annotation of dozens of influential Dharmaśāstra treatises: https://sites.utexas.edu/sanskrit/resources/dharmasastra/

Sanskrit ritual hermeneutical literature (*Mīmāṃsā*), a core interpretive philosophy for Sanskrit jurisprudence, and a notoriously abstruse scholarly idiom has expanded considerably.[7] And, of great aid to this chapter of Hindu religious trusts, I recently published a comprehensive account of ownership (*svatva*) in pre-colonial, colonial, and post-colonial Indian history.[8]

1.1 Introduction

With the aid of these advancements in Sanskrit studies, I was able to cast a wider net into the seas of Sanskrit jurisprudence and to snare a few more legal fish to add to our catch. In the aggregate, we have many additional 'stray passages' from Dharmaśāstra and aligned intellectual disciplines with which to attempt to construct a more 'workable law', or at least a less skeletal Sanskrit jurisprudence of Equity and Trusts. I do not argue that these additional gleanings can or should viewed as being as comparatively detailed and comprehensive as Dharmaśāstric discussions of property, ownership, etc. We can, however, flesh out the bones of earlier accounts of the Sanskrit jurisprudence of Equity and Trusts with an eye to providing, in the aggregate, more nuance and detail to contemporary jurists, to legal historians, and to Indologists. Here, then, are the fundamental principles of this jurisprudence.

1.1.1 Equity

The broad theme of this monograph is that we find phenomena in Sanskrit jurisprudence that are broadly equivalent to legal phenomena that, in Anglo-American jurisprudence, were once associated with 'courts of equity': trusts, charitable endowments, and the administration of the estates of minors, women, etc., by the Lord Chancellor as the Keeper of the King's Conscience.[9] I focus on three aspects of this system of equitable jurisprudence: guardianship; supplementary law; and trusts.

[7] For the relationship between Dharmaśāstra and Mīmāṃsā, see Lawrence McCrea, 'Hindu Jurisprudence and Scriptural Hermeneutics', in Timothy Lubin *et al.* (eds), *Hinduism and Law: An Introduction* (Cambridge: Cambridge University Press, 2010): 123–36.

[8] Fleming, *Ownership and Inheritance*.

[9] For shifting understandings of this role – from ecclesiastic to secular – see Endicott, 'The Conscience of the King'.

1.1.1.i Guardianship

Guardianship is a fiduciary duty of care owed by guardians to their wards (in a broad sense) that is, in the last instance, enforceable by the Crown.[10] The dissolution of the Court of Chancery, the 'fusion' of Equity and the Common Law, and the creation of a specialised Family Division of the High Court – all the result of the 'Judicature Acts' of 1873 and 1875 – (36 & 37 Victoria. c. 66 and 38 & 39 Victoria. c. 77), and a further series of amending acts (twelve in all by 1899) – most people tend to think of 'Equity' as referring exclusively to the specialised property-focused jurisprudence of the Chancery Bar.[11] It is salutary to remember that the Court of Chancery once had a much wider equitable jurisdiction that covered, *inter alia*, guardianship and that these principles also shaped the laws of Equity and Trusts in colonial India.[12]

In Sanskrit jurisprudence, the Crown (*rāja*), as *parens patriae*, is duty-bound, according to his personal (*sva*) royal Dharma (*rājadharma*), to protect (*rakṣaṇa*/*pālana*) women (*strīs*), children (*bālas*), students (*brāhmacārins*), the mentally unhealthy (*unmatta*), Brāhmaṇas, and people without protection (*anātha*), through his ministers (*āmātyas*) and courts. To this list we sometimes see – although not often – deities (*devas*). Nevertheless, the analogous relationship between deities and minors appears sporadically in several chronological layers of Sanskrit jurisprudence. An analogous relationship between Church and infant runs long and deep in English jurisprudence. As Pollock and Maitland note, citing a 1307 case from the reign of Edward I: 'A church is always under age and is to be treated as an infant, and it is not according to law that infants should be disinherited by the negligence of their guardians or be barred of an action in case they would complain of things wrongfully done by their guardians while they were under age.'[13]

[10] For the emergence of the Crown's (and, later, chancellors') right of supervision of guardians/wards in its role as *parens patriae*, see Seymour, 'Parens Patriae'. For Chancery and legal incompetents, see Alkire, 'Incompetency from an Equitable Perspective'. For Chancery and children, see Chambers, *A Practical Treatise*. For Chancery and women as both guardians and wards, see Wilson, *Women and Legal Guardianship*.

[11] For the fusion of common law and equity, see Lobban, 'Preparing for Fusion'. For a critical appraisal of the 'fusion' theory, see Goldberg *et al.*, *Equity and Law*.

[12] I discuss the fusion of English and Sanskritic theories of Equity and Trusts during the colonial period in Chapter 4. For an overview of the colonial law of guardianship, see Ernest Trevelyan, *The Law Relating to Minors: As Administered in the Provinces Subject to the High Courts of British India. Together with the Practice of the Courts of Wards in Bengal, Madras, Bombay, and the United Provinces of Agra and Oudh*, 4th Ed. (London: Thacker & Co., 1912).

[13] Pollock and Maitland, *The History of English Law*, 503–4, citing Placit. Abbrev. 304 (Noff). Y.B. 21–2 Edward I. p. 33: 'le eglise est dedeinz age'. Compare with Bract., *De legibus et Consuetudinibus Angliæ* f. 226b: 'Et cum ecclesia fungatur vice minoris, acquiritur per rectorem et retinet per eundem, sicut minor per tutorem. Et quamvis moriatur rector, non tamen cadit ecclesia a seisina sua, de aliquo de quo rector seisitus moritur nomine ecclesiae suae, non magis quam minor si custos suus moriatur.' 'And when the church functions like minor, it is acquired by the ruler and retained by the same, like a minor by a guardian. And although the rector dies, the church does not lose its property, since the dead rector possess (that property) in the name of his church. No more than a minor if its guardian dies.'

1.1.1.ii Supplemental law

The origins of contemporary Equity as what Maitland defines as 'the rules which were applied in the Court of Chancery in 1875, as developed by the modern court system since' lay in the broader, Greco-Romanic formulation of a distinction between justice (*iustitia*) and equity (*aequitas*).[14] As Howard Oleck notes, 'in this broad, general sense, Equity is the body of principles which provide and govern exceptions to the law'.[15] In fact, post-fusion scholars, such as Henry Smith, among others, have argued, persuasively, for a similar view of modern Equity as a form of supplemental, meta-law that acts as a 'safety valve' for structural inequities in the Common Law.[16] Derrett argues that Equity has the dual functions, '(i) to correct, modify and if necessary, amend statute law… and (ii) to supplement, make good, and otherwise remove the deficiencies of the written… source of law'.[17]

The specific jurisprudence of Equity once applicable to the Court of Chancery and now more widely applicable in Common Law is but one iteration of Equity as corrective meta-law.[18] This aspect of Equity has a long and notorious presence in Anglo-Indian and contemporary Indian law – beginning with the introduction of 'Justice, Equity and Good Conscience' as a legal mechanism (from Regulation 60 of Warren Hastings' 1781 *Regulations for the Administration of Justice* to Article 142(1) of the Constitution of the Republic of India) for English judges to supplement or override indigenous Indian laws.

In Sanskrit jurisprudence, the king has a similar Dharmic duty to investigate (*parīkṣaṇa*) and protect (*paripālana*) a wide series of supplemental laws (*pāribhāṣikadharmas*), provided that they do not violate Dharmaśāstric precepts. These supplemental laws include congenital laws (*kuladharmas*) and regional customs (*deśadharmas*), as well as the conventions (*samayas*) of commercial guilds (*śreṇis*), religious institutions of 'heretics' (*pāṣaṇḍas*), charities (*iṣṭāpūrta*/*yogakṣema*) and, of course, temples (*devagṛha*/*devālaya*/*devakula*/etc). Classical Sanskrit jurisprudence's theory of supplemental laws are similar enough to the aforementioned, second aspect of Equity to justify a productive comparison.[19]

[14] For a comparison of Roman and English views of Equity, see W.J. Zwalve and E. Koops, 'Introduction: The Equity Phenomenon', in W.J. Zwalve and E. Koops (eds), *Law & Equity Approaches in Roman Law and Common Law* (Leiden: Brill, 2013): 1–13. For the Aristotelian origins of the Roman concept of Equity, see MacNair, 'Equity and Conscience', 660–1.

[15] Oleck, 'Historical Nature', 23.

[16] Henry E. Smith, 'Equity as Meta-Law', *Yale Law Journal* 130 (2021): 1050–134; Henry E. Smith, 'Equity as Second-Order Law: The Problem of Opportunism', *Harvard Public Law Working Paper No. 15-13* (2015).

[17] J. Duncan Derrett, 'Justice, Equity, and Good Conscience', in J.D. Anderson (ed.), *Changing Law In Developing Countries* (New York Frederick Praeger, 1963): 114–54, 118–19.

[18] Maitland, *Equity*, 1, cited in MacNair, 'Equity and Conscience', 659.

[19] Donald Davis has written extensively on this topic, although he does not use the term 'Equity' to refer to this second-order, supplementary aspect of *pāribhāṣikadharma*. See Davis, 'Toward a History of Documents'; Davis, 'Intermediate Realms of Law'; and Donald Davis, 'Centres of Law: Duties, Rights, and Jurisdictional Pluralism in Medieval India', in Paul Dresch and Hannah Skoda (eds), *Legalism: Anthropology and History* (Oxford: Oxford University Press, 2012): 85–113.

As Donald Davis notes, in ritual and grammatical texts, meta-rules (*paribhāṣas*) function to 'provide the correct interpretation of rules, remove conflicts between rules, or establish supplementary rules'.[20] In Sanskrit jurisprudence, *pāribhāṣikadharmas* 'elaborated and specified certain additional or supplementary rules, both adjective and substantive in nature, that shaped and filled in the law propounded in the textual tradition itself'.[21] It is essential to note that the Dharmaśāstric jurisprudential principal of *parens patriae* is what obliges the Crown to protect supplemental laws *like it protects the well-being of minors, women, and legal incompetents, etc.* Even if the *contents* of *pāribhāṣikadharmas* are not prescribed by Dharmaśāstric sources (they are certainly described though) the *enforcement* and *stewardship* of them are explicitly prescribed as one of the core features of Dharmaśāstric jurisprudence. This element of Dharmaśāstric Equity was probably the most important jurisprudential principle for the practical administration of religious and charitable trusts in pre-modern Indian legal history.

1.1.2 Trusts

The legal historian, F.W. Maitland (1850–1906) wrote that 'it is a big affair our Trust... [and] anyone who wishes to know England... should know a little of our Trust'.[22] The Trust, although thoroughly English, is also thoroughly perplexing. As Mukherjea notes, Thomas Lewin's well-known definition of a Trust as 'a confidence reposed in some other, not issue out of the land, but as a thing collateral, annexed in privity to the estate of the land, for which *cestui que* trust has no remedy but by *Subpoena* in the Chancery' is, although accurate from an historical perspective, 'not a happy one' from the standpoint of perspicuity.[23] Hardinge Halsbury's (1823–1901) more general definition of a trust as 'a confidence reposed in a person with respect to property of which he has possession or over which he can exercise a power, to the intent that he may hold the property or exercise the power for the benefit of some other person or object' is a much happier one, because, as Mukherjea notes, 'there may be trusts in a form other than the English form'.[24] Mukherjea defines a Trust as, 'the conception... of a fiduciary relation under which a person in possession of or having control over any property is bound to use that property for the benefit of certain named persons, or specified objects' and notes that, 'obviously, there are trusts in Hindu law in that sense'.[25]

[20] Davis, 'Intermediate Realms of Law', 97.

[21] Ibid., 97. Davis compares this theory to H.L.A. Hart's 'rules of recognition' but I argue that a comparison to Equity is equally valid.

[22] F.W. Maitland, *State, Trust and Corporation*, eds. David Runciman and Magnus Ryan (Cambridge: Cambridge University Press, 2003): 76, cited in Birla, *Stages of Capital*, 67.

[23] Mukherjea, *Hindu Law*, 4–5. Citing Lewin, *A Practical Treatise*, 11.

[24] Mukherjea, *Hindu Law*, 5–6.

[25] Ibid., 6.

There are a wide variety of trusts in Sanskrit jurisprudence. Some, like the settling of Brāhmaṇas on estates (*brahmadeyas/brāhmāgrahāras*), or the establishment of alms houses (*sattras*) are relatively straightforward purpose trusts: liquid cash or the income from certain lands are given to trustees for specific purposes and those trustees are answerable to the Crown if they fail to use the trust properties for the stated purpose. Other trusts, such as deposits (*nikṣepas*), pledges (*ādhis*), mortgages (*nibandhas*), or the heritable assets of a Joint Hindu Family (*dāya*), involve the blocking (*bandhana*) of the simultaneous co-inherence of the ownership (*svatva*) of multiple parties. The co-inherence of multiple ownerships – partial or full – compelled individuals who held possession of asset to utilise it for the collective interest of all parties.[26] In the course of time, competing juridical models of inheritance – in which families held property in Trusts or in tenancies-in-common – developed in conjunction with the emergence of different philosophical understanding of ownership in the Sanskrit text-traditions of hermeneutics (*Mīmāṃsā*) and logic (*Nyāya*) respectively.

Divine trusts, i.e., individuals taking possession of assets in the name of a deity – with or without stated purposes – present a much more complicated picture. The *Kautilīyārthaśāstra* (1st century BCE–2nd century CE), an influential treatise on statecraft, articulates an extensive jurisprudence of divine trusts: deities are recognised as legal persons – analogised to minors – that may hold assets which are, in turn managed by trustees. In case of breach of trust, the Crown, through its deity-supervisors (*devatādhyakṣas*) are duty-bound to initiate suits in the name of the deity.[27] I will discuss the *Kautilīyārthaśāstra* in more detail, but, for whatever reason, the Brāhmaṇa authors of early Dharmaśāstric literature did not adopt the Arthaśāstric jurisprudence of divine endowments. Instead, medieval authors of Dharmaśāstra commentaries (*bhāṣyas*), including Bhāruci (6th–7th century) and Medhātithi (9th–11th century) redeployed arguments drawn from Sanskrit ritual hermeneutical philosophy (*Mīmāṃsā*) to argue that deities' ownership is a secondary (*gauṇa*) form of ownership that may (or may

[26] See Fleming, *Ownership and Inheritance*, Chapter 2.

[27] For the *Arthaśāstra* see Olivelle, *King, Governance, and Law*; Mark McClish, *The History of the Arthaśāstra: Sovereignty and Sacred Law in Ancient India* (Cambridge: Cambridge University Press, 2019). For the appropriation of the Vivādapadas (titles of law), see Mark McClish, 'Titles of Law: *Vyavahārapada*', in Patrick Olivelle and Donald Davis (eds), *Hindu Law: A New History of Dharmaśāstra* (New York: Oxford University Press, 2018): 299–312. The dating of the *Arthaśāstra* is complicated, because, as Olivelle notes, 'several books [5, 8, 11, 12, 14, and 15]… were added by the śāstric [2nd century CE] redactor'. Nevertheless, the majority of the material I examine here belongs to the earlier, 'Kauṭilya' recension whose sources Olivelle assigns 'to a period between the middle of the first century BCE and the middle of the first century CE'. For the potentially Mauryan (300 BCE) origin of the earliest bits of the Arthaśāstra, potentially shared with the Dharmasūtra tradition, see Mark McClish, 'Is the Arthaśāstra a Mauryan Document?', in Patrick Olivelle *et al.* (eds), *Reimagining Asoka* (Oxford: Oxford University Press, 2012): 280–309.

not) impose certain fiduciary duties on temple servants (*sevakas*) who appropriate these assets.[28]

Over the subsequent centuries, Sanskrit jurists analysed – in a largely piecemeal fashion – various legal phenomena associated with divine endowments such as the gift of cows to temples, prohibitions on the misuse of 'divine property' (*devasva*), and a wide array of Purāṇic dicta concerning charities (*iṣṭāpūrta/yogakṣema*). The jurists did so, just as they did with deposits and other fiduciary phenomena, through the lens of ownership (*svatva*). These discussions of divine property do not usually rise to the level of providing a comprehensive jurisprudence – being diffusely spread and often somewhat critical of deities' capacious legal personality – but, nevertheless, they describe five *essential* principles of the Sanskrit jurisprudence of divine trusts.

These core principles are: 1) it is a legally recognised fact that social custom recognises deities as legal persons who may own property; 2) nevertheless, because deities cannot utilise this property, they are 'owners' only in a secondary (*gauṇa*), or in figurative or conventional (*aupacārika/sāmayika*) sense; 3) that 'secondary' ownership of the deity imposes fiduciary duties on the real persons who receive or manage that property on the deity's behalf because; 4) the rules governing divine endowments are a form of supplemental law (*pāribhāṣikadharma*); and 5) the deity's fiduciaries and the wider public are legally accountable if they expropriate the deity's assets. This jurisprudence of divine trusts is, of course, more or less identical to that of the *Kauṭilīyārthaśāstra* and to that of the modern law of Hindu religious and charitable trusts. To reiterate, even though the Dharmaśāstric tradition does *not* offer a series of positive precepts that outline the *content* of divine ownership (viewing that as a matter of popular, rather than śāstric behaviour) it *does*, emphatically, describe divine endowments as a form of Trust whose regulations *must*, on the basis of Dharmaśāstric principles of Equity, be protected by the Crown – just like minors, women, etc.

1.2 The problem

In outlining the core principles of the Sanskrit jurisprudence of Equity and Trusts, this chapter tackles a major conceptual problem in Günther-Dietz Sontheimer's 'Religious Endowments in India: The Juristic Personality of Hindu Deities': the presumption – an unwarranted one in my estimation – of a fundamental distinction between Sanskrit jurisprudence (and its *Mīmāṃsā*-derived metaphysical theory of deities as mere phonemes) on the one hand and 'popular' practice on the other hand. According to Sontheimer, although 'the negation of the deity

[28] For the dates of these authors, see Kāṇe, *History of Dharmaśāstra*, Vol. 1, 264–6 & 266–75, respectively.

as personified and symbolized by an idol is supported by *pūrvamīmāṃsaka* authors, this theory is not endorsed by popular opinion or practice'.[29]

Sontheimer's thesis, that Dharmaśāstric authors' invocation of *Pūrvamīmāṃsā* denials of the ownership of deities (in a primary sense) was an effective method of combating 'the popular form of worship… [temple Hinduism, wherein] spiritual merit could be gained by donating property to a deity and by pleasing it thereby' seems plausible.[30] Sontheimer presents compelling evidence for what Richard Davis describes as an 'iconophobic orientation… in texts such as the Dharmaśāstra of Manu'. The works of Stietencron, Granoff, Colas, and Inden have outlined the history of the 'bitter feuds between traditionalists [i.e., Vedic Brāhmaṇas] and innovators [the proponents of image worshipping temple Hinduism]'.[31]

Manu and Śabara's 'iconophobia' notwithstanding, however, the intellectual arc among Mīmāṃsakas and Dharmaśāstrins in the following centuries was *towards* rather than *away* from accommodation of image worship within their ritual and legal frameworks. Mīmāṃsakas' and Dharmaśāstrins' iconophobia can then be viewed as primarily *metaphysical* rather than *legal*. As Gerard Colas notes, since Kumārila, like Śabara, 'implicitly recognized… the principle of donation of lands to a deity… as an acceptable current socio-religious convention' then 'the thesis of a conflict between ancient Mīmāṃsā… and an image worship that would have been "popular"… needs to be seriously reconsidered'.[32] In fact, as Colas and others have observed, even a cursory inspection of India's medieval epigraphic temple records reveal that the elite, Sanskrit-proficient authors of royal copper-plate records and stone engravings – the paradigmatic 'popular' people of Sontheimer's analysis – explicitly invoked Dharmaśāstric jurisprudential principles when endowing deities with substantial assets.[33]

[29] Sontheimer, 'Religious Endowments', 16.

[30] Ibid., 26. For 'Temple Hinduism' see Richard Davis, *Ritual in an Oscillating Universe* (Princeton: Princeton University Press, 1991), 6ff. where he attributes the term to Ronald Inden. Also see Elisabeth Raddock, *Listen How the Wise One Begins Construction of a House for Visnu: Chapters 1–14 of the Hayasirsa Pancaratra* (Unpublished PhD Dissertation: UC Berkeley, 2011), 5–19.

[31] Davis, 'Images and Temples', 348. Heinrich von Stietencron, 'Orthodox Attitudes Towards Temple Service and Image Worship in Ancient India', *Central Asiatic Journal* 21.2 (1977): 126–38; Phyllis Granoff, 'Images and Their Ritual Use in Medieval India: Hesitations and Contradictions', in Phyllis Granoff *et al.* (eds), *Images in Asian Religions* (Vancouver: UBC Press, 2004): 19–55; Gerard Colas, 'The Competing Hermeneutics of Image Worship in Hinduism (Fifth to Eleventh Century AD)', in *Images in Asian Religions*, 149–79; and Ronald Inden, 'Changes in the Vedic Priesthood', in A.W. Van den Hoek *et al.* (eds), *Ritual, State and History in South Asia: Essays in Honour of J.C. Heesterman* (Leiden: Brill, 1992), 556–78. Manu's inclusion of temple priests (*devalakas*) in a list of individuals banned from Śrāddhas (3.150–66) is one notable example.

[32] Colas, 'Images and Territory of Gods', 109 & 115. Michael Willis, *The Archaeology of Hindu Ritual: Temples and the Establishment of the Gods* (Cambridge: Cambridge University Press, 2009), 214–15 reads the same inscriptions and Mīmāṃsā materials from the implicit perspective of Sontheimer's elite/popular divide.

[33] See Lubin, 'South Asian Diplomatics'; Timothy Lubin, 'The Theory and Practice of Property in Premodern South Asia: Disparities and Convergences', *Journal of the Economic and Social History of the Orient* 61.5/6 (2018): 803–50; and Timothy Lubin, 'Religious Endowments in Ancient India and the Institutionalization of Brahmin Caste Status', *American Journal of Legal History*, 63.2 (2023): 97–114.

While it is important to acknowledge that an initial iconophobic reaction to the advent of Temple Hinduism from traditional Brāhmaṇical authors left its imprint on Sanskrit jurisprudential discussions of Equity and Trusts, it is equally important to acknowledge that Sanskrit jurists' discussion of Equity and Trusts served as an authoritative jurisprudential lynchpin for the practical legal administration of thousands of religious and charitable endowments in India over the centuries. Whatever the metaphysical apprehensions of some Sanskrit jurists, Dharmaśāstric theories of Equity very clearly had an influential bearing upon the actual historical practice of law regarding Hindu temples in various periods of Indian history.

A further consequence of Sontheimer's postulation of an intellectual rupture between Sanskrit jurisprudence and popular practice lies in its uncritical application to post-colonial studies of Anglo-Hindu and contemporary Hindu law. The core issue is a presupposition that the development of the doctrine of legal personhood for Hindu deities was a novel development borne out of the (*Mīmāṃsā*-inflected) imaginations of colonial jurists. As Richard Davis notes, 'however, the discrepancy between Dharmaśāstra principle and public practice did pose a problem for legal theory in the colonial period. This led to the new concept of the deity as "juristic person".'[34]

Arguably, the most important case in Indian legal history in terms of the courts exploring the relationship between classical Sanskrit jurisprudence and modern Hindu temple trusts was ***Bhupati Nath Smrititirtha v Ram Lal Maitra*** (1909).[35] This case overturned 'the proposition that a gift to a Hindu deity, whose image is to be established and consecrated in future, is void'.[36] Justice Mookerjee cited a mélange of Mīmāṃsā and Dharmaśāstra texts, to advance the argument that:

> The Hindu law recognises dedications for the establishment of the image of a deity and for the maintenance and worship thereof. The property so dedicated to a pious purpose is placed extra-commercium and is entitled to special protection at the hands of the Sovereign whose duty it is to intervene to prevent fraud and waste in dealing with religious endowments.[37]

With reference to the deity itself, Justice Jenkins observed, on the basis of Mīmāṃsā and Dharmaśāstric sources, that 'the dedication to a deity is a compendious expression of the pious purposes for which the dedication is designed'.[38] This is, to reiterate, more or less synchronous with pre-colonial Sanskrit jurisprudence and epigraphic practice. It is patently untrue that the juridical personality of Hindu deities was a product of colonial courts' efforts to reconcile 'public practice' and 'Dharmaśāstra principles'.

[34] Richard Davis, 'Temples, Deities, and the Law', in Timothy Lubin, Donald Davis, and Jayanth Krishnan (eds), *Hinduism and Law: An Introduction* (Cambridge: Cambridge University Press, 2010): 195–206, 204.

[35] ***Bhupati Nath Smrititirtha v Ram Lal Maitra*** (1909) ILR 37 Cal 128.

[36] Ibid., Jenkins, ¶1.ii.

[37] Ibid., Mookerjee, ¶66.ii.

[38] Ibid., Jenkins at ¶15.

Sontheimer draws on S.C. Bagchi's 1931 Asutosh Mookerjee Lectures to defend a conclusion that 'neither the ancient discussions of the *Mīmāṃsakas* nor the modern doctrines based in part on Western models are apt for the situations we have been discussing.'[39] For Bagchi, the Mīmāṃsā and Dharmaśāstric view of deities' ownership as a 'secondary' (*gauṇa*) or 'figurative' (*aupacārika*) ownership meant, in his estimation, that because, 'there is no acceptance [of a gift] on the part of the deity... [the] material benefit accrues to the person in charge of the worship.'[40] Consequently, according to Bagchi, 'the attempt at making an idol a plaintiff or defendant in a lawsuit is based on a wrong notion of juristic personality.'[41] Bagchi's excellent translations of Sanskrit sources notwithstanding, his recommendation, that 'religious endowments can be assimilated to purpose trusts' is, however, entirely at odds with the epigraphic record, with pre-colonial early modern practices and, as we shall see, with the very Dharmaśāstric sources that he analyses.[42]

In *Stages of Capital*, Ritu Birla takes the position that: 'In the 1870s... the deity's ability to hold property was by no means an accepted legal concept or, indeed, an accurate reflection of the meanings of ritual convention.'[43] Birla argues that 'the translation of customary Hindu endowments into modern legal trust contracts... was encapsulated in a masterful turn of legal idolatry... the deity, to which Hindu endowments were consecrated was rendered a legal subject and thus the beneficiary.'[44]

Birla supports this argument on the basis of Jonathan Duncan Derrett's invective against the newly independent state of India's statutory regulation of religious endowments in the 1950s and 1960s.[45] Derrett's position, articulated at greater length elsewhere – and based on the Sanskrit sources of Bagchi and Sontheimer – is, broadly, that 'there is no doubt that but that orthodox śāstric learning denies that idols have any property.'[46] Derrett asks: 'Where did the money [offered to a deity] go previously? Nobody bothered much, until this century saw a dramatic and continuous pressure to place the finances of such temples and mutts under secular control.'[47] This statement is simply untrue and relies on a superficial reading of the Sanskritic sources that Sontheimer

[39] Sontheimer, 'Religious Endowments,' 57.

[40] S.C. Bagchi, *Juristic Personality of Hindu Deities* (Calcutta: University of Calcutta, 1933), 78.

[41] Ibid., 78.

[42] Ibid.

[43] Birla, *Stages of Capital*, 83–4.

[44] Ibid., 71–2. Birla defines 'market governance' (22–3) as: 'the production of "the economy" as an object of governance, but also the utopic production of "the market" as an ethico-political sovereign: that is, as a model for social relations.'

[45] J. Duncan Derrett, 'The Reform of Hindu Religious Endowments,' in D.E. Smith (ed.), *South Asian Politics and Religion* (Princeton: Princeton University Press, 1966): 311–36.

[46] Derrett, 'Religious Endowments, Public and Private,' 484.

[47] Ibid., 488.

and Bagchi cite in their respective works.[48] Dharmaśāstric authorities are very clear that there *are* rules governing the property of deities, that these rules are conventional rather than śāstric, and that, whatever their origins, they must be protected by the Crown exercising an equitable jurisdiction (that is imposed by Dharmaśāstra).

Furthermore, this errant reading leads Birla to argue against centuries of pre-colonial legal usage and jurisprudence. Birla examines ***Mahrani Shibessouree v Mothooranath Acharjo***, an 1869 Privy Council appeal that, *inter alia*, affirmed the status of deity-as-owner and attendant-as-fiduciary.[49] According to Birla, the case 'overrode the predominant view of orthodox Hindu jurisprudence… [in which]… the widespread perception… that the temple priest often lived on the offerings to the deity had been legitimated by the *mimamsa* system of Hindu philosophy'.[50] Birla lets the tail (*Mīmāṃsā*) wag the dog (Dharmaśāstric principles of Equity and Trusts, and centuries of legal historical practice) here. The situation becomes even more sadly ironic when Birla inveighs against the Bombay High Court's 1887 judgment in ***Manohar Ganesh Tambekar v Lakhmiram Govindram***, the infamous and influential 'Dakor Temple Case'.[51] In this case, the fiduciaries (*sevakas*) of a Kṛṣṇa temple in Dakor, near Baroda argued, as a defence to the claim that they had flagrantly misappropriated properties dedicated to the deity whom they served, that they 'are the owners, for all secular purposes, of the idol… [and] the offerings made at the shrine, the cattle, and even the land presented by devotees are, they assert, their property free from any secular obligation'.[52] Justice West of the Bombay High Court ruled, on the basis of a body of precedent and Sanskrit jurisprudential literature, that the deity of the temple could not be 'conceived as a mere slave or property of the shevaks whose very title implies not ownership, but service of the god'.[53]

Again, West's judgment is more or less completely in line with pre-colonial theories and practices of divine endowments, but Birla reads this case as evidence that proves her thesis that 'the making of deities into legal persons with the power to be sued, and hold property reflected the slow transformation of the Hindu endowment into a form of contractual private property'.[54]

[48] Even Derrett acknowledges, ibid., 485–6, that 'there are many inscriptions extant which show the idol actually making decisions and announcing them… the legal personality of the idol was therefore a popular concept long before it became part of the Anglo-Indian law'.
[49] Birla, *Stages of Capital*, 83. ***Mahrani Shibessouree v Mothooranath Acharjo*** (1869) 13 Moore's Indian Appeals 270.
[50] Birla, *Stages of Capital*, 3–4.
[51] Ibid., 83–7.
[52] ***Manohar Ganesh Tambekar v Lakhmiram Govindram*** (1888) ILR 12 Bom 247 ¶3 [West, J].
[53] Ibid., ¶11.
[54] Birla, *Stages of Capital*, 87.

Finally, Deepa Das Acevedo's recent analysis of prominent temple-related disputes in contemporary India recapitulates these same series of errors. Drawing on Birla, Sontheimer, and Richard Davis, Das Acevedo argues that:

> Davis and Sontheimer explicitly connect the case law's conceptualization of deities as legal persons, as well as its insistence that such personhood is figurative rather than literal, to the Purva Mimamsa exegetical school… [which] contrasted and continues to contrast with popular belief, according to which deities do literally receive gifts, and in which gifts to temples… become part of a deity's personal wealth. Ethnographic studies of temples have thus argued that they combine spatial, processual, and symbolic attributes centred on a sovereign deity who receives and redistributes gifts, and who in the process leads worshippers to cooperate with one another while affirming their individuality.[55]

Unlike Appadurai or Das Acevedo, Sanskrit jurists were not anthropologists and Medhātithi was uninterested in the 'ethnographic attributes' of image worship. Dharmaśāstrins were interested in providing a jurisprudential description of very real legal practices in premodern South Asia. Birla and Das Acevedo are, however, probably correct in acknowledging that Anglo-Hindu law limited the redistributive capacities of Hindu deities' fiduciaries.

We shall see in Chapter 2 that Dharmaśāstra recognised (and enforced) supplemental laws that chartered religious and charitable trusts in classical and early modern India. The supplemental laws often permitted deities' fiduciaries to redistribute wealth in accordance with the terms of the endowment.[56] Birla and Das Acevedo, however, are certainly incorrect in asserting that colonial judicial restrictions on the redistribution of religious endowments were the result of a *correct* interpretation of Sanskrit jurisprudence. Rather, Dharmaśāstric theories of Equity and Trusts *support* the legal recognition of the unique redistributive practices of many of India's religious endowments.

If, as Gerard Colas concludes, 'the thesis of a conflict between ancient Mīmāṃsā… and an image worship that would have been "popular"… needs to be seriously reconsidered' then, similarly, Birla, Das Acevedo, and other contemporary legal scholars' arguments that a 'colonial fixation with the purity of the Vedas melded with the desire of some jurists to view Hindus as having their own law' led colonial jurists to privilege '*Mīmāṃsā* theories of Equity and Trusts over an alternative, popular, view' needs to be reconsidered as well.[57] Arguing persuasively about how the judicial precedents of the colonial period may or may not have distorted

[55] Deepa Das Acevedo, 'Divine Sovereignty, Indian Property Law, and the Dispute over the Padmanabhaswamy Temple', *Modern Asian Studies* 50.3 (2016): 841–65, 861. Das Acevedo's examples of sovereign deities are drawn from the work of Arjun Appadurai, *Worship and Conflict Under Colonial Rule: A South Indian Case* (Cambridge: Cambridge University Press, 1981) and C.J. Fuller, *Servants of the Goddess: The Priests of a South Indian Temple* (Cambridge: Cambridge University Press, 2008).
[56] See Chapter 2, §2.6.3, 'Deities' complex assets'.
[57] Colas, 'Images and Territory of Gods', 109 & 115. Das Acevedo, 'Divine Sovereignty', 862.

the pre-colonial jurisprudence and practical legal practice of Equity and Trusts requires, *a priori*, an accurate understanding of those pre-colonial phenomena.

1.3 The solution

1.3.1 The solution, part 1 – Arthaśāstra

The solution I propose is simple: outlining – as far as is possible – a synchronic jurisprudence of Equity and Trusts using Sanskritic textual sources. Thinking synchronically does not always entail thinking diachronically (or historically). Rather, a synchronic approach mines various epochal layers of textual accretion to distil what are the core, recurrent themes of the jurisprudential record. Certainly, this chapter attends to the historical chronology of developments in the law (diachronically), but it does so with an eye to providing a *comprehensive* summary of the data in their aggregate.

One obstacle to this project is that the earliest Dharmaśāstric texts – the *Dharmasūtras* ('the beginning of the third to the middle of the second centuries BCE, and somewhat later for Vasiṣṭha') and the *Dharmasmṛtis* (1st–8th centuries CE) – say very little about temples or their endowments.[58] This paucity of evidence is particularly suspicious in consideration of the many detailed statements concerning divine endowments in Kauṭilya's *Arthaśāstra* (1st century BCE–2nd century CE). Perhaps Kauṭilya's legal model of divine endowments fell victim to the early Dharmaśāstrins' wider elision of aspects of secular royal authority from their Brāhmaṇa-normative jurisprudence that Mark McClish and Patrick Olivelle discuss in the context of the 'four feet' (*catuṣpād*) of legal procedure (*vyavahāra*).[59] Unfortunately, the *Kauṭilīyārthaśāstra* was not re-discovered until 1905; furthermore, a high-quality edition of it was not accessible until 2013. Consequently, it has never factored in colonial-era jurisprudence, or in most of the secondary scholarship on Hindu religious endowments. Had Justice Mookerjee buttressed his ruling in ***Bhupati*** with some Arthaśāstric dicta concerning the legal personality of deities and the State's responsibility for safeguarding their final interests, he

[58] For the date and compositional history of the Dharmasūtras, see Patrick Olivelle, *Dharmasūtras: The Law Codes of Āpastamba, Gautama, Baudhāyana, and Vasiṣṭha* (Oxford: Oxford University Press, 1999): xxviii–xxxv. Text and translations cited here are from Olivelle's edition. For dating the Dharmasmṛtis, see Kāṇe, *History of Dharmaśāstra*, Vol. 1, 131–5.

[59] Patrick Olivelle and Mark McClish, 'The Four Feet of Legal Procedure and the Origins of Jurisprudence in Ancient India', *Journal of the American Oriental Society* 135.1 (2015): 33–47, 46: 'in terms of the early development of South Asian jurisprudence, particularly its initial systematization in the Arthaśāstra, it is vyavahāra – not as legal procedure or lawsuit, but in an earlier and more elementary meaning as rules governing public transactions – that is the central term and that it leads us to identify the origin of systematic jurisprudence in the manner through which the state created a public space by systematizing and enforcing rules of public commerce'.

may well have staved off Bagchi, Sontheimer, Birla, and others' indictment of the Anglo-Hindu law of religious and charitable trusts.

The discovery of 'a complete manuscript… written in Grantha script' of the *Kauṭilīyārthaśāstra*, in what Olivelle describes as 'an Indiana Jones-like moment in the rather drab history of ancient Indian scholarship' permits us to employ the treatise as a form of independent verification for the veracity of the courts' interpretation of the pre-colonial jurisprudence of Equity and Trusts (based on Dharmaśāstric sources).[60] Kauṭilya offers a remarkably comprehensive account of divine trusts wherein an agent of the Crown, the 'overseer of temples' (*devatādhyakṣa*), is tasked with ensuring the proper administration of temples. In fact, this function is remarkably similar to contemporary State-level *devasvom* (temple property) boards. This is part of the *Arthaśāstra*'s wider theory of Equity as supplemental laws – such as those involving guilds, communities, and religious institutions. According to Kauṭilya, the king should establish a 'Bureau of Official Records' (*Akṣapaṭala*) and the superintendent of that bureau must:

> Have the following entered in the registry books: concerning departments the totality of their number, procedures, and income;
>
> concerning factories – the extent of the following: gain and loss of material in the manufacturing process, expenses, additional weight, surcharge, admixture, location, wages, and labor;
>
> concerning precious stones, articles of high value, articles of low value, and forest produce – price, sample, size, weight, height, depth, and container;
>
> concerning regions, villages, castes, families, and associations – *dharma*, *vyavahāra*, *caritra*, and *saṃsthāna* (*deśagrāmajātikulasaṃghānāṃ dharmavyavahāracaritrasaṃ sthānam*);
>
> concerning those in the king's service – the receipt by them of favors, land, benefits, exemptions, rations, and wages; concerning the king's wives and sons – the receipt by them of precious stones and land, and of special allowances and remedial measures during disasters;
>
> concerning allies and enemies – payments and receipts in connection with peace pacts and declarations of war (KaŚ 2.7.2).[61]

In case of a breach of these conventions (*samayasyānapakarman*) 'within regions, castes, families, and associations' (*deśajātikulasaṃghānāṃ*), the contracting individuals will be held liable (3.10.35–46).

Furthermore, as Olivelle notes, in the *Arthaśāstra*, 'we see the temple or the temple god emerging as a legal entity with legal rights that can be defended in a court of law'.[62] The *Arthaśāstra* generally employs the term deity (*deva/devatā*)

[60] Olivelle, *King, Governance, and Law*, 1.

[61] Olivelle and McClish, 'Four Feet', 40: KaŚ, 2.7.1–2: akṣapaṭalam adhyakṣaḥ prāṅmukham udaṅmukhaṃ vā vibhaktopasthānaṃ nibandhapustakasthānaṃ kārayet… deśagrāmajātikulasaṃghānāṃ dharmavya vahāracaritrasaṃsthānam rājopajīvināṃ pragrahapradeśabhogaparihārabhaktavetanalābham.

[62] Olivelle, 'The Temple', 200

synecdochally when describing temples (*devālaya/devagṛha*). This may reflect a recognition of the juridical personality of temple deities. The legal rights of deities as legal persons and the concomitant duties of their legal guardians are remarkably similar to those delineated by colonial and contemporary courts. Deities are compared analogously to women, minors, and other legally incompetent individuals whose interests must be protected by the king in his role of *parens patriae*.

The temples of the *Arthaśāstra* were likely 'roadside shrines, [that were] probably small structures' rather than the large, politically central, imperial complexes of Purāṇic Temple Hinduism.[63] Nevertheless, these temples and their deities possessed large enough endowments for Kauṭilya to advise a prince, who is out of favour with his father, to 'secretly steal the property of 'heretical' religious orders (*pāṣaṇḍasaṃgha*) of temples (*deva*) – except what is meant for use by Vedic scholars'.[64] In a similar way, Kauṭilya suggests that, in times of adversity, the king should expropriate deities' assets:

> Executive officers should bring over the property of religious orders or the property of temples, except what is meant for use by Vedic scholars, stating that it was deposited with a person who has died or whose house has been burnt down. The Temple Superintendent should gather individually the treasures belonging to the temples of the city and the provinces in one place, and bring them over in the same manner. [as other expropriated assets].[65]

What kinds of assets (*dravya*) did these deities possess? The *Arthaśāstra* mentions 'female slaves of gods whose divine service has ended' (*vyuparatopasthānadevadāsī*) as amongst those who should be employed by the 'Superintendent of Yarns' (*Sūtrādhyakṣa*),[66] 'chariots for the gods' (*devaratha*) amongst a list of construction projects for the 'superintendent of chariots' (*Rathādhyakṣa*)[67] and 'bulls belonging to a god or a village' as among those animals exempt from fines'.[68] Kauṭilya neatly indexes species of divine assets when he prescribes 'the highest fine' (*uttamadaṇḍa*) or 'a clean death' (*śuddhavadha*) 'for someone stealing an animal, an icon, a man, a field, a house, money, gold, gems, or crops belonging to a deity'.[69] Furthermore, deities could be the object of royal largesse: Kauṭilya

[63] Ibid., 202.

[64] All translations are Olivelle's and all Sanskrit text is from R.P. Kangle (ed.), *The Kauṭilīya Arthaśāstra: A Critical Edition with a Glossary*, 2nd edn. (Bombay: University of Bombay, 1969), 1.18.09: pāṣaṇḍasaṃghadravyam aśrotriyopabhogyaṃ vā devadravyam… gūḍham anupraviśya.

[65] Ibid., 5.2.37–8: pāṣaṇḍasaṃghadravyam aśrotriyopabhogyaṃ devadravyaṃ vā kṛtyakarāḥ pretasya dagdhagṛhasya vā haste nyastam ity upahareyuḥ. devatvādhyakṣo durgarāṣṭradevānāṃ yathā svam ekasthaṃ kośaṃ kuryāt, tathaiva copaharet.

[66] Ibid., 2.23.2: vyuparatopasthānadevadāsībhiś ca kartayet [sūtrādhyakṣaḥ].

[67] Ibid., 2.33.5: devarathapuṣyarathasāṃgrāmikapāriyāṇikaparapurābhiyānikavainayikāṃś ca rathān kārayet.

[68] Ibid., 3.10.24 (21 in Olivelle's translation): grāmadevavṛṣā vā… adaṇḍyāḥ.

[69] Ibid., 4.10.16: devapaśupratimāmanuṣyakṣetragṛhahiraṇyasuvarṇaratnasasyāpahāriṇa uttamo daṇḍaḥ, śuddhavadho vā. Also see 4.10.13 for a similar formulation of punishment for the appropriation of devadravya.

describes the 'allocations for the worship of gods and ancestors and for gifts' (*deva pitṛpūjādānārtham*) as a component of 'the corpus of expenditure'.[70]

Deities owned significant assets and it is unsurprising that, in recognising this, the *Arthaśāstra* articulates complex methods of remedy in the event that people would fail to protect the deity. Crucially, however, the method of doing so was twofold: 1) to analogise deities legally to women, animals, children, and others who lack legal capacity; and 2) to hold these individuals' fiduciaries (husbands, guardians, fathers, and servants) accountable for breach of trust. The Crown, we are told:

> Should try the cases – those relating to gods, hermitages, members of religious orders, Vedic scholars, farm animals, and holy places; those relating to children, the elderly, the sick, those in distress, and the helpless; and those relating to women – in that order, or according to the gravity of the case or its urgency.[71]

This is probably the earliest Sanskrit formulation of the longstanding juridical position that Hindu deities are legally analogous to women, animals, and others who cannot act on their own behalf. Of crucial importance here is the fact that the Crown's duty to protect these sundry individuals and communities is a constituent part of its *parens patriae* jurisdiction.

Also note, that the formulation is 'deities' and not 'deities' servants'. As in Anglo-Indian law, these individuals require someone to initiate legal proceedings for them and their lack of legal capacity ensures that they are protected from the bar of limitation or adverse possession.[72] Kauṭilya argues that:

> In the case of gods, Brāhmaṇas, recluses, women, children, the aged, the sick, and the helpless, who may not come (to the court) themselves, the Justices should initiate lawsuits on their behalf, and they should not dismiss their cases under the pretext of place, time, or enjoyment.[73]

[70] Ibid., 2.6.11: devapitṛpūjādānārtham.... iti vyayaśarīram. For punishment for voiding faeces near temples, see 2.36.28: paṇyasthānodakasthānadevagṛharājaparigraheṣu paṇottarā viṣṭādaṇḍāḥ, mūtreṣv ardhadaṇḍāḥ'. For punishment for slander against deities, see 3.18.12: 'svadeśagrāmayoḥ pūrvaṃ madhyamaṃ jātisaṃghayoḥ / ākrośād devacaityānām uttamaṃ daṇḍam arhati.

[71] Ibid., 1.19.29: devatāśramapāṣaṇḍaśrotriyapaśupuṇyasthānānāṃ bālavṛddhavyādhitavyasanyanāth ānāṃ strīṇāṃ ca krameṇa kāryāṇi paśyet, kāryagauravād ātyayikavaśena vā. Also see 1.19.31.

[72] The analogous relationship between deities and minors is a vexed question in Anglo-Hindu and contemporary Indian law and served as a fault-line in the Ayodhyā dispute. See Chapter 5, §5.3.2.i, 'Deities and adverse possession'.

[73] *Arthaśāstra*, 3.20.22: devabrāhmaṇatapasvistrībālavṛddhavyādhitānām anāthānām anabhisaratāṃ dharmasthāḥ kāryāṇi kuryuḥ, na ca deśakālabhogacchalenātihareyuḥ. Also see the discussion of minors, etc. (but not deities) in 3.16.30: jñātayaḥ śrotriyāḥ pāṣaṇḍā vā rājñām asaṃnidhau paravāstuṣu vivasanto na bhogena hareyuḥ, upanidhim ādhiṃ nidhiṃ nikṣepaṃ striyaṃ sīmānaṃ rājaśrotriyadravyāṇi ca... 'When someone pays no heed while his property is being enjoyed by others for ten years, he forfeits it, except in the case of children, old people, the sick, those who have fallen on hard times, those who have gone abroad, and those who have migrated, and when there is a tumult in the country'; and in 3.16.32: jñātayaḥ śrotriyāḥ pāṣaṇḍā vā rājñām asaṃnidhau paravāstuṣu vivasanto na bhogena hareyuḥ, upanidhim ādhiṃ nidhiṃ nikṣepaṃ striyaṃ sīmānaṃ rājaśrotriyadravyāṇi ca. 'Relatives, Vedic scholars, or members of religious orders residing – outside the presence of kings – in immovable properties belonging to others do not obtain ownership over them through enjoyment; nor over a deposit, a pledge, a treasure trove, a consignment, a woman, a boundary, and the property of the king or a Vedic scholar.'

So, deities who own complex properties, are, like women, minors, and animals, entitled to legal protection by the Crown (in the case of deities, seemingly as legal persons) and shielded from some of the constraints which might render other lawsuits invalid. But what about the duties of the deities' legal guardians? Kauṭilya offers the most comprehensive account of the duties of guardianship – at least as they apply to deities – in Sanskrit jurisprudence. On the one hand, the king, as *parens patriae*, 'should enforce discipline on slaves, persons given as pledges, and relatives, when they fail to obey. The king should, moreover, provide for children, old people, those fallen into misfortune, and the helpless, as also for women who have not borne children and the sons of women who have borne children.'[74] The deity is likened, explicitly, to a minor and Kauṭilya notes that:

> The elders of a village should make the property of minors increase in value until they reach the legal age, as also the property of a temple. When a person who has the capacity does not provide for his children, wives, mother, father, brothers who are minors, or unmarried and widowed sisters, he should be fined 12 Paṇas, unless they have fallen from their caste, except the mother.[75]

Here we have a two-layered approach to guardianship: on the first level, a deity's attendants, like the heads of families, are responsible for looking after the interests of their ward. On the second level, when these individuals breach their relationship of trust with the guardians, then the king must act to secure the welfare of the helpless. In his modern, *Śrīmūlā* commentary, T. Gaṇapati Śāstrī explains that, unlike a minor (whose property should be managed by elders until he reaches the age of legal majority), 'the village elders should manage temple property in perpetuity because of the impossibility of an end (to the inability to conduct legal transactions)'.[76]

Taken collectively, the data indicates the existence of a substantial jurisprudence of Equity and Trusts in Sanskrit sources far before the emergence of Purāṇic Temple Hinduism in the second half of the first millennium. It also indicates that, *pace* Sontheimer, Derrett, Birla, and Das Acevedo, the juridical personality of Hindu deities was not *originally* an invention of colonial courts. Certainly, the elision of Kauṭilya's model of divine temple trusts from the subsequent strata of Sanskrit jurisprudence (the *Dharmasūtras* and the *Dharmasmṛtis*) suggests an element of iconophobia on their authors' part. However, I will demonstrate that, in the long arc of time, Sanskrit jurists articulated, if somewhat diffusely and chronologically unevenly, jurisprudential

[74] Ibid., 2.1.25–6: dāsāhitakabandhūn aśṛṇvato rājā vinayaṃ grāhayet. bālavṛddhavyasanyanāthāṃś ca rājā bibhṛyāt, striyam aprajātāṃ prajātāyaś ca putrān.

[75] Ibid., 2.1.27–8: bāladravyaṃ grāmavṛddhā vardhayeyur ā vyavahāraprāpaṇāt, devadravyaṃ ca. apatyadāraṃ mātāpitarau bhrātṝn aprāptavyavahārān bhaginīḥ kanyā vidhavāś cābibhrataḥ śaktimato dvādaśapaṇo daṇḍaḥ, anyatra patitebhyaḥ, anyatra mātuḥ.

[76] *Kauṭalīyamarthaśāstram of Ācārya Viṣṇugupta: with Four Commentaries*, Vol. 2.1., Śrī Viśvanātha Śāstrī Dātāra (ed.) (Varanasi: Sarasvatībhāvana-Granthamālā No. 130, 1991), 15 (2.1.27): 'devālayadravyaṃ ca grāmavṛddhā varjayeyuḥ avadhir ayogān nityam'.

themes about Equity and Trusts that were very similar to those discussed by Kauṭilya in the *Arthaśāstra*.

1.3.2 The solution, part 2 – a synchronic account of equity and trusts

The outlier of Kauṭilya's *Arthaśāstra* notwithstanding, the jurisprudence of Equity and Trusts is spread so diffusely within Sanskrit literature that the most efficient means of outlining these disparate fragments is to arrange them thematically in a synchronic, rather than a diachronic format. In what follows, I discuss guardianship and supplemental law as Sanskritic theories of Equity. Second, I discuss various kinds of complex property relations that can be characterised as Trusts: secular and divine. For each theme, I start with the earliest strata of Dharmaśāstric literature, introduce non-Dharmaśāstric (Purāṇic and Tantric) sources from the corpus of Temple Hinduism and record Mīmāṃsā responses to those developments. I then explore the reception of Purāṇic, Tantric, and Mīmāṃsā ideas in early medieval commentaries on Dharmaśāstra treatises. Finally, I turn to the final, 'mature' phase of Sanskrit jurisprudence with the writings of several famous Dharmaśāstrins who wrote in Bengal and Vārāṇasī during the early modern period (1400–1700 CE).

This approach builds a synchronic account of core jurisprudential themes in Sanskrit jurisprudential literature from the ground up: moving from the earliest layers to more recent layers. Although I make several observations about the broad developmental arc of jurisprudence over the centuries, the diffuse spread of discussions of some themes of Equity and Trusts (particularly divine endowments) in the literature requires a greater emphasis on synthesis. Thinking historically about the diachronic shifts in jurisprudential literature helps us to appreciate the context of particular authors' arguments and make some broad observations about long-term developments. Nevertheless, this is done in the service of the wider project of distilling and explicating as broad and comprehensive an account of the Sanskrit jurisprudence of Equity and Trusts as the materials permit. I do so with an eye towards two goals: 1) tracing the *application* of these core themes throughout Indian legal history in Chapters 2–5; and 2) assisting contemporary jurists in India and abroad with an accessible account of Equity and Trusts in Sanskrit jurisprudence.

Before outlining this synchronic account of the Sanskrit jurisprudence of Equity and Trusts, I want to present a brief, four-part diachronic account of the data from which I gleaned the various components of that account. First, by the early centuries of the Common Era (before the development of what Richard Davis describes as 'Temple Hinduism'), Kauṭilya's *Arthaśāstra* articulated a substantial jurisprudence which viewed deities as analogous to legal minors (and other legally protected categories of people), outlined the fiduciary duties owed to them by their guardians, and enjoined the Crown to enforce the customary arrangements relating to them. While the *Dharmasūtras* and *Dharmasmṛtis* incorporated Kauṭilya's theories of guardianship, supplemental law, and trusts, they were largely silent on the issue of deities' rights within that system. As Patrick Olivelle notes, temples receive no mention in the *Āpastambadharmasūtra*, but are mentioned once by Gautama and by Baudhāyana, and thrice by Vasiṣṭha – only 'in passing in the context of other discussions'.[77]

Second, the compilers of the Purāṇas, along with Mīmāṃsakas, Vedāntins, and logicians, attempted, in the first half of the first millennium CE, to accommodate – or compartmentalise – the emergent ritual and legal phenomenon of elaborate temple-based worship of images with their metaphysical and epistemological systems associated with Temple Hinduism.[78] The early centuries of the Common Era saw the rise of devotional, theistic traditions, including Pāñcarātras, Pāśupātas, and Śaivasiddhāntas. These devotional traditions' Āgamic (received) textual sources were sometimes at a variance with normative, Brāhmaṇical textual categories and their tantric practices varied (broadly speaking), with traditional Vedic sacrifices.[79] These Āgamic traditions endorsed the consecration (*pratiṣṭhā*) of images, the initiation (*dīkṣā*) of their followers, and the construction and patronage of large-scale, public temple structures (along with a bevy of other devotional practices).

In many respects, the Purāṇas served a mediating function, compiling the ritual practices of Āgamic traditions along with cosmology, dynastic genealogy, sacred geography, and, *inter alia*, Dharmaśāstra in manifold attempts, to shape and transform, what Ronald Inden describes as, the 'polities and the disciplinary orders that

[77] Olivelle, 'The Temple', 193. See Gautama, 9.66: praśastamaṅgalyadevatāyatanacatuṣpadam pradakṣiṇam āvarteta, 'when he passes people or things that are distinguished as auspicious, as also temples, intersections of two roads, and the like, he should keep to the right side towards them'; Baudhāyana, 2.5.8.1: śmaśānam āpo devagṛhaṃ goṣṭhaṃ yatra ca brāhmaṇā aprakṣālya pādau tan na praveṣṭavyam, 'A cemetery, water, a temple, a cowpen, and a place where there are Brahmins – one should not enter them without washing the feet'; and Vasiṣṭha, 6.17: antarjale devagṛhe valmīke mūṣakasthale, 'earth from under water, a temple, anthill, or a mound over a rathole, and earth left behind by someone after his purification – he should not take these five types of earth'; 10.3: grāmānte devagṛhe śūnyāgāre vā vṛkṣamūle vā, 'staying in the outskirts of a village, in a temple or an abandoned house, or at the foot of a tree'; and 11.31: devatāyatane kṛtvā tataḥ śrāddhaṃ pravartayet, 'he should place it in a temple and then continue with the ancestral offering'.

[78] See Note 30.

[79] For the Pañcarātras, see Diwakar Acharya, *Early Tantric Vaiṣṇavism: Three Newly Discovered Works of the Pañcarātra: Devāmṛtapañcarātra and Aṣṭādaśavidhāna: Critically Edited from their 11th and 12th-Century Nepalese Palm Leaf Manuscripts with an Introduction and Texts* (Paris: EFEO, 2015). For the Pāśupātas, see Gavin Flood, 'The Śaiva Traditions', in Gavin Flood (ed.), *The Blackwelll Companion to Hinduism* (Oxford: Blackwell, 2003): 200–28. For the Śaiva Siddhānta tradition, see Davis, *Ritual in an Oscillating Universe*.

sought their recognition and adherence'.[80] The success of the Purāṇic compilers (whom Inden characterises as 'complex authors') in manifesting their treatises' prescriptive visions of imperial temple polities is attested by the wide array of richly endowed temple complexes that sprang up in India during the early medieval period (roughly 700–1200 CE).[81] The economic arrangements for these temples – recorded on stone or on copper plates – are the subject of sustained analysis in the following chapter, but in this chapter, I attend to reception of Temple Hinduism in Sanskrit jurisprudence. This is no small matter, because, as Richard Davis notes:

> During this period [of medieval Temple Hinduism] the worship of animated icons of the gods, who resided in monumental temples teeming with divine imagery, was the primary form of public religiosity in the subcontinent. Temple priests elaborated liturgical procedures of great intricacy for the proper consecration and respectful treatment of these iconic deities, and rulers of the time vied with one another in sponsoring ever more ostentatious sacred structures in their own dominions. By the beginning of the eleventh century the Indian landscape was covered with myriad temples small and large, each filled with hosts of divine figures. When the Ghaznavid ruler Mahmud arrived in the holy city of Mathura on his military campaign of 1006, he was astonished by the extravagant structures that confronted him there.[82]

Third, medieval authors of legal compendia, commentaries, and monographs sought to canonise the vast array of Purāṇic dicta and to harmonise these passages within the legal parameters of the *Dharmasmṛtis* and the philosophical parameters of Mīmāṃsā.[83] The Purāṇas say little about the legal governance of temples or of the juridical personality of Hindu deities: consecratory or dedicatory acts typically end without any of the acts of proprietary abandonment (*utsarga*) or exhortatory warnings not to misuse the deities' properties that occupied the legal imaginations of later Dharmaśāstra authors. There are, however, many statements that enjoin gifts of specific assets, including land, that are clearly meant for temple deities.[84] The Purāṇas presented later Dharmaśāstrins with a juridical dilemma: how to

[80] Ronald Inden, 'Imperial Purāṇas: Kashmir as the Center of the World', in Ronald Inden, Jonathan Walters, and Daud Ali (eds), *Querying the Medieval: Texts and the History of Practices in South Asia* (Oxford: Oxford University Press, 2000): 29–98, 55.

[81] For complex agents, see ibid., 29–41. Inden also provides an account of how the *Viṣṇudharmottarapurāṇa* (in conjunction with the *Viṣṇusmṛti*) functioned, in medieval Kashmir, to 'persuade an imperial king, a "king of kings," of the truth of its particular wish for and account of the world, that of the Pāñcarātra Vaiṣṇavas' in opposition to 'that of their rivals, the Pāśupata Śavias'.

[82] Richard H. Davis, 'Indian Image-Worship and its Discontents', in Jan Assmann and Albert I. Baumgartner (eds), *Representation in Religion* (Leiden: Brill, 2001): 107–32.

[83] For Dharmaśāstra in Purāṇic materials and Dharmaśāstric citations of Purāṇic materials, see Kāṇe, *History of Dharmaśāstra*, Vol. 1, 160–7. The best work on the relationship between Purāṇas and devotional practices is R.C. Hazra, *Studies in the Purāṇic Records on Hindu Rites and Customs* (Dacca: University of Dacca, 1940). Also see Ludo Rocher, *The Purāṇas*: (Wiesbaden: Otto Harrassowitz, 1986).

[84] Prannath Sarasvati, *The Hindu Law of Endowments* (Calcutta: Thacker, Spink, & Co., 1897), 136, ¶6 lists several verses from Purāṇas that support the gift of land to various deities.

weave the vast array of Purāṇic statements endorsing temple dedication and gifts to deities within the parameters of Dharmaśāstric jurisprudence?

Some Sanskrit jurists, such as Lakṣmīdhara (12th century), wrote legal digests (*nibandhas*) that incorporated and domesticated Purāṇic discussions on topics such as gifting (*dāna*) and the consecration (*pratiṣṭhā*) of temples (*devagṛhas*), images (*mūrtis*), reservoirs (*jalāśayas*), and monasteries (*maṭhas*).[85] As David Brick notes, 'Brahmanical authors had trouble determining the total contents of their accepted Smṛtis and, thus, many of them would have likely welcomed an authoritative… and topically arranged collection of this literature… [that] conformed to their personal standards.'[86] Lakṣmīdhara generally takes an inclusivist view of Purāṇic material, noting that, while:

> In his work, Gopāla, his [= Lakṣmīdhara's] contemporary, sometimes cited the words of Purāṇas and sometimes those of Smṛtis, but composed his own work in the form of prose. This composition, however, will be created in a way that is pleasing to wise people using chiefly the words of the Vedas, Smṛtis, and the like, whose meanings will be crowned by exegesis, so that it will not be too large, yet will have no lacunae to speak of.[87]

In Ballālasena's *Dānasāgara* (12th century), the choice of which Purāṇic materials to include in a digest was inflected by sectarian considerations.[88] Ballālasena lists 'accepted texts' (*saṃgṛhītagranthas*) and unaccepted texts (*asaṃgṛhītagranthas*). He rejects some texts due to their association with 'heretics' (*pāṣaṇḍins*):

> The eighth and ninth chapters (of the Bhaviṣyapurāṇa), which have been devoured by the heretics, have been rejected. Another Purāṇa, the Liṅga, measuring six-thousand (verses) is connected with the initiation and consecration of heretics… The Devīpurāṇa, having been determined to agree with the śāstra of heretics because of its relation with impure practices… is not compiled here.[89]

[85] David Brick (ed. and trans.), *Brahmanical Theories of the Gift A Critical Edition and Annotated Translation of the Dānakānda of the Krtyakalpataru* (Cambridge, MA: Harvard University Press, 2015).

[86] Ibid. 19–20.

[87] Cited in ibid., 12–3: paurāṇīr eva vāṇīḥ kvacid akṛtau kṛtau kvāpi bhūyaḥ smṛtīṇāṃ **gopālas** tadvayasyaḥ svakṛtiviracanaṃ vākyrūpeṇa cakre / śrautasmārtādisārair vibudhajanamanohāri kāriṣyate 'yaṃ mīmāṃsottaṃsitārthair apṛthur atha kathātītarandhraḥ prabandhaḥ.

[88] For Ballālasena's date and works, see Kāṇe, *History of Dharmaśāstra*, Vol. 1, 140–1.

[89] *Dānasāgara of Ballāla Sena*, ed. Bhabatosh Bhattacarya (Calcutta: Asiatic Society, Bibliotecha Indica Vol 273, 1956) /1.59cd (**bhaviṣyasya**) tyaktvāṣṭamīnavamyau kalpau pāṣaṇḍibhir grastau/ 1.64 ṣaṭsahasramitaṃ **laiṅgaṃ purāṇam** aparaṃ tathā / **dīkṣāpratiṣṭhāpāṣaṇḍayukt**i…// & 1.67cd: /pāṣaṇḍaśāstrānumataṃ nirūpya **devīpurāṇaṃ** na nibaddham atra / Ballālasena states at 1.55, that 'gifts of reservoirs and temples are not stated here because that have been explained in full in the *Pratiṣṭhāsāgara*': jalāśayānāṃ dānāni tathā ca suraveśmanām / noktāni samyaguktāni **pratiṣṭhāsāgare** yataḥ //: Granoff argues that Ballālasena's hostility to *some* 'heretical' consecrations was the result of a feud with the Pāñcarātrins or Śaivasiddhāntins over control of a royal temple, rather than a general animosity to image worship. See Phyllis Granoff, 'Reading Between the Lines: Colliding Attitudes Towards Image Worship in Indian Religious Texts', in Gerard Colas and Giles Tarabout (eds), *Hindu Rites, Transfer, and Transformations* (Paris: Ecole de Des Hautes Etudes, 2006): 389–422, 395–7. See ibid., fn. 19 for a discussion of Ānandabhaṭṭa's (16th century) biography of Ballālasena, wherein the royal purohita schemes to take over control of a richly endowed local temple.

In the chapter on giving (*Dānaprakaraṇa*) of Aparārka's (1125 CE) commentary on the *Yājñavalkyasmṛti*, the author cites roughly the equivalent of 150 Purāṇic materials without interruption.[90] Aparārka has a strong penchant for Purāṇic materials. In an elaborate defence of the validity of Tantric and Purāṇic sources as a source of Dharma that appears in his comments on *Yājñavalkya* 1.7., Aparārka argues that 'in reference to consecration also, it is accepted that what is to be done is only that which is stated in the Purāṇas and not anything else'.[91]

Fourth, many Sanskrit jurists took more analytical – as opposed to philological – approaches to harmonising Dharmaśāstric and Purāṇic materials, especially with regard to divine endowments. Drawing on arguments from Śabarasvāmin's *Mīmāṃsāsūtrabhāṣya*, Bhāruci and Medhātithi argued that deities cannot own assets in a primary (*mukhya*) sense. Instead, the cultural usage (*paricāra*) of endowing deities with assets entails a secondary (*gauṇa*) ownership (*svatva*) that reflects a cultural, rather than a śāstrically derived practice. Nevertheless, this secondary ownership's social reality and practical capacity to impose moral and legal restrictions on temple servants is tacitly or explicitly recognised under śāstric principles. Other jurists, including, Aparārka and Devaṇṇabhaṭṭa (13th century) provided accounts of how deities functioned within the wider remit of a Dharmaśāstric model of property law in practice rather than in theory. They explored the analogous legal relationship between deities, minors, women, and the other categories of protected persons discussed in the *Kauṭilīyārthaśāstra* and in early Dharmaśāstric literature.

Another group of Dharmaśāstrins incorporated a wide array of commercial and charitable phenomena – including temples and other Pūrāṇic activities – within the purview of *supplemental* (*pāribhāṣika*) law. In discussions concerning the non-observance of conventions (*samayānapākarma*) commentators such as Vijñāneśvara (11th–12th century CE), Aparārka, and Devaṇṇabhaṭṭa argue that the endowment and maintenance of temples (and related institutions) is regulated through contractual relations (*samvids*), the conventions of guilds, the custom of families, and royal commands.[92] Even though the early Dharmasūtras de-emphasised the secular, royal jurisprudence of the *Arthaśāstra*, Dharmaśāstra commentators explicitly recognised that many legal phenomena – especially Purāṇa-inspired temple-building – that had become ubiquitous in the medieval epigraphic record, could be reconciled with Dharmaśāstric jurisprudence by classifying them as equitable, supplementary laws that were enforceable under the Crown's *parens patriae* jurisdiction.

[90] For Aparārka's date and works see Kāṇe, *History of Dharmaśāstra*, Vol. 1. pp. 328–34.

[91] *Aparārka: Commentary on the Yājñavalkya-dharmaśāstra*, ed. Hari Nārāyaṇa Āpate (Poona: Ānandāśrama Sanskrit Series, no. 46, 1903), 1.7: pratiṣṭhāyām api **purāṇādy**uktaivetikartavyatā grāhyā nānyā.

[92] For the date of Vijñāneśvara, see Kāṇe, *History of Dharmaśāstra*, Vol. 1, 287–93 & 328–34.

Early modern Dharmaśāstrins from Bengal (*Gauḍas*); including Śūlapāṇi Upādhyāya (1375–1460 CE), and Raghunandana Bhaṭṭācārya (1510–80 CE), furnished accounts of deities' artificial (*kalpita*) ownership (*svatva*), imposing fiduciary duties on their trustees (*sevakas*), while Vārāṇasī-based Mahārāṣṭrian Dharmaśāstrins, including Kamalākarabhaṭṭa (active 1610–40 CE), Nīlakaṇṭhabhaṭṭa (1610–50 CE), and Anantadeva (1645–95 CE), argued explicitly – if laconically – that temple deities are distinct legal persons or the source of royal sovereignty.[93] Śūlapāṇi and Raghunandana developed a theory of divine ownership (*devasva*) as the suppositious knowledge (*āropajñāna*) of the deity's ownership by the donor. Raghunandana in particular uses this theory of suppositious, hypothetical, theoretical ownership – similar to that of Medhātithi – to untangle a series of thorny legal issues surrounding 'odd' forms of property including temple endowments, public charities, and the like. Given that Justice Mookerjee cited these Bengali Dharmaśāstrins at length in ***Bhupatinath***, it is also unsurprising that Raghunandana's jurisprudence of divine endowments is so similar to contemporary Indian law.

Finally, at the chronological tail of this tale of the Sanskrit jurisprudence of Equity and Trusts, we find, in the writing of Kamalākarabhaṭṭa and his cousin, Nīlakaṇṭhabhaṭṭa, the fullest Dharmaśāstric endorsement of the juridical personality of Hindu deities. In their discussions of the consecration of temples and charities, both cousins drew on earlier Śaiva and Vaiṣṇava Tantric manuals (*paddhatis*) to argue that the establishment of a temple deity results in the creation of a juridical person – who shares a name with the temple founder. Here, at last, the creation of eponymous deities by temple founders, which is ubiquitous in the epigraphic record, is fully recognised in Sanskrit jurisprudence. Anantadeva, for his part, gestures towards the historical – and still current – practice of king ruling in the name of their tutelary deity when he describes the foundation of a kingdom in his treatise on royal dharma, the *Rājadharmakaustubha*.[94]

The resulting picture is one in which the pre-colonial Sanskrit jurisprudence of Equity and Trusts coheres with pre-colonial legal practices and prefigures colonial and post-colonial developments in non-trivial ways. Equity – in the form of royal guardianship and the supplementation of Dharmaśāstric dicta with meta-legal conventions – and Trusts – in the form of complex forms of non-standard ownership that require fiduciaries to utilise properties for specific beneficiaries – appear, albeit diffusely, in Sanskrit jurisprudential literature.

[93] For the dates and works of these authors, see ibid., 393–6 (Śūlapāṇi), 416–19 (Raghunandana), 432–7 (Kamalākara), 438–40 (Nīlakaṇṭha), and 447–53 (Anantadeva).

[94] The most famous example of divine sovereignty is Virūpākṣa (followed by Veṅkateśvara) in the Vijayanagara Empire (1336–1646). See Sontheimer, 'Religious Endowments', 38 fn. 91, and Chapter 3, §3.3.2, 'The sulṭān among Hindu kings at Vijayanagara'.

To argue, as Derrett, Sontheimer, Davis, Birla, Das Acevedo and others have, that the colonial, Anglo-Hindu law of Equity and Trusts was a foreign imposition in its entirety, presupposes the absence of a similar legal system before the arrival of English hegemony on the subcontinent. This position elides India's rich pre-colonial legal history and, ironically, denies agency to pre-colonial agents while affording it, unjustifiably, to colonial agents. True, the Sanskrit jurisprudence of Equity and Trusts is much less straightforward than other topics in Dharmaśāstra. On the one hand, Dharmaśāstric authors rarely prescribe *specific regulations* regarding divine endowments. In fact, they often argue against interpreting passages from Dharmaśāstric sources as referring to such regulations. On the other hand, however, Dharmaśāstric authors *explicitly* and *repeatedly* argue that a *fundamental principle* of Sanskrit jurisprudence is the Crown's Dharmaśāstric duty, as *parens patriae* to protect the extra-śāstric conventions that regulate divine endowments and other charities. In the following chapters, we shall see that this Dharmaśāstric principle served – and continues to serve – as a touchstone for the practical administration of religious and charitable trusts in India.

1.4 Guardianship

> *A king rescues his people from fear, and protects them. Therefore, being their protector, a king is to his subjects a father. Of this there is no doubt.*
>
> *Brahmavaivartapurāṇa*[95]

In the best of times, kings, across differences of culture, time, and place, protect their subjects in exchange for taxes and feudal service.[96] From Mesopotamia to Mesoamerica, from Tang China to 21st-century Britain, the Crown invariably frames itself as a benevolent parent of the nation (*parens patriae*) which looks after its subjects' welfare as parents look after the welfare of their children.[97] It should, therefore, come as no surprise that the image of the Crown as *parens patriae* runs deep in Sanskrit jurisprudential literature. Robert Lingat argues that, 'the function of the king [in Sanskrit jurisprudence] is fully expressed in the words *prajānāṃ paripālanam*, "protection of his subjects" '.[98]

When the Mughal Emperor Shāh 'Ālam II (r. 1759–1806 CE) awarded the *Dīwānī* (the formal right to collect revenue) of the provinces comprising the Subāh

95 Quoted in Tagore, *Hindu Loyalty*: bhayatrātā ca rājā syāt sarveṣāṃ pālakaḥ sadā / yo rājā sa pitā pātā prājānām eva niścaya //49//

96 For a comparative study of kingship, see Lynette Mitchell and Charles Melville (eds), *Every Inch a King: Comparative Studies on Kings and Kingship in the Ancient and Medieval Worlds* (Leiden: Brill, 2013).

97 For a discussion of English theories of guardianship, see Richard Helmholz, 'Roman Law of Guardianship in England, 1300–1600', *Tulane Law Review* 52 (1978): 223–47.

98 Robert Lingat, *The Classical Law of India*, trans. J. Duncan Derrett (New Delhi: Munshiram Manoharlal, 1973), 222.

(district) of Bengal, Bihar, and Orissa, to the British East India Company in 1765, he also delegated responsibility for administering the civil and criminal justice system.[99] Following Warren Hastings' Judicial Plan of 1772, British judges were obliged to apply Sanskrit jurisprudence – subject to various provisos – when adjudicating cases 'in all suits regarding inheritance, marriage, caste, and other religious usages, or institutions... with respect to the Gentoos'.[100] Over the subsequent century-and-a-half of colonial rule, the agents of the Company and Crown slipped, as it were, into the Sanskrit jurisprudential vestments of a Hindu sovereign when claiming, as *parens patriae*, a right of supervision over temples, monasteries, wards, and feudal succession.[101]

Earlier in this monograph we saw that, according to the *Kauṭilīyārthaśāstra*, the Crown is obliged to protect some of the most vulnerable people in the realm, including women, children, the sick, elderly, priests and deities.[102] Again, many ancient legal systems employed the same analogy between religious institutions and minors/women/dependents in their justification of royal supervision of temples, churches, etc.[103] It is surprising, therefore that while the *Dharmasūtras*, the earliest stratum of Brāhmaṇical treatises on jurisprudence, appropriate *most* of Kauṭilya's jurisprudence concerning royal protection, temples and deities are not included in the *Dharmasūtras*' formulation of these equitable doctrines.

The *Dharmasūtras* argue that the Crown is the legal guardian of the defenceless and that there must be a concomitant abrogation of the laws of taxation, toll, and adverse possession for them. For example, Gautama asserts that a king 'should keep the property of children safe until they reach the legal age or have completed their studies' and 'he should support... non-Brahmins who are unable to work'.[104] Vasiṣṭha links a sovereign's duty of guardianship to his right of escheat to intestate estates when he argues that, 'the king should maintain people who are impotent (*klība*) or mad (*unmatta*) because their estates go to him'.[105] Even Āpastamba shields

[99] For this process and its connection to European philological research on Sanskrit, see Fleming, *Ownership and Inheritance*, 167–73.

[100] Ibid., 167.

[101] For this right as reflected in Sanskrit and Anglo-Hindu Jurisprudence, see Mukherjea, *Hindu Law*, 28–9 ¶1.36. See Pudukota Iyer, *The Law Relating to Hindu and Mahomedan Endowments*, 2nd edn. (Madras: Modern Printing Works, 1918), 23–5, where the author cites Sanskrit theories of royal supervision in connection with the East India Company's seizure of direct management of Hindu religious endowments (Bengal Regulation XIX of 1810, Madras Regulation VII of 1817, Bombay Regulation XVII of 1827).

[102] See Chapter 1, §1.3.1, 'The solution, part 1 – Arthaśāstra'.

[103] For *parens patriae* in the West, see Lawrence Custer, 'Origins of the Doctrine of *Parens Patriae*', *Emory Law Journal* 27.2 (1978): 195–208. For China (and its effect on Germany), see Susan Richter, '*Pater Patriae Sinensis*: The Discovery of Patriarchal Rule in China and Its Significance for German Theories of State in the Eighteenth Century', in A. Flüchter and S. Richter (eds), *Structures on the Move: Technologies of Governance in Transcultural Encounter* (Berlin: Springer, 2012): 61–86.

[104] *Gautamadharmasūtra* 10.48: rakṣyaṃ bāladhanam ā vyavahāraprāpaṇāt; 10.9–11: bibhṛyād brāhmaṇān nirutsāhāṃś. Vasiṣṭha 16.6–9 enjoins the king to protect the property of minors: saṃpannaṃ ca rakṣayet. rājabāladhanāni. aprāptavyavahārāṇām. tu tad yat.

[105] For the royal right of escheat, see ibid.,16.19: prahīṇadravyāṇi rājagāmīni bhavanti; Āpastamba (2.14.2–5); Gautama (28.41–42); Baudhāyana, 1.119–15; Vasiṣṭha (17.81–84).

similarly protected categories of people from taxation, while Vasiṣṭha exempts them from tolls.[106] Finally, while Gautama and Vasiṣṭha outline the legal notion of adverse possession – wherein legal owners lose their rights after a period of time – they both include a list of individuals who are exempt: 'mentally incapacitated' (*jaḍa*) or 'under the age of sixteen' (*apogaṇḍa*) for Gautama, and 'minors' (*bālas*) for Vasiṣṭha.[107] While these references are brief, they are also non-negligible. Vasiṣṭha also offers an evocative description of the trusteeship of 'non-abandoned' property of missing persons when he explains that 'the king, together with ministers and city folk, should administer the property' (on the behalf of the missing person), and we might, with an eye towards Kauṭilya's formulation of the village elders as guardians of deities, ponder whether Vasiṣṭha's dictum might apply to temple property.[108]

The *Dharmasmṛtis* (1st–8th centuries CE) expand and refine the positions of the *Dharmasūtras* and sometimes – but not often – include deities, temples, and monasteries in their lists of categories of legally protected people. A common argument in Dharmaśāstric discussions of land possession (*bhukti*) is that of adverse possession: that individuals who permit others' usage of their assets will forfeit their legal ownership after a stipulated period of time. Take Manu's statements (8.147–8) as a representative example:

> Whatever thing the owner meekly sees being used by others in his presence, for ten years, that thing he does not deserve to recover. If the owner is neither an idiot nor a minor, and the property is used in his own country, it becomes frustrated in law, and the user becomes entitled to the property.[109]

[106] *Āpastambadharmasūtra* 2.26.9–17: dhārmyaṃ śulkam avahārayet. akaraḥ śrotriyaḥ. sarvavarṇānāṃ ca striyaḥ. kumārāś ca prāg vyañjanebhyaḥ.... tapasvinaś ca ye dharmaparāḥ... andhamūkabadhiraro gaviṣṭāś ca. ye vyarthā dravyaparigrahaiḥ. *Vasiṣṭhadharmasūtra* 19.23–24: akaraḥ śrotriyo rājapumān anāthapravrajitabālavṛddhataruṇaprajātāḥ. prāggāmikāḥ kumāryo bhṛtapatnyaś ca.

[107] *Gautamadharmasūtra* 12.37: 12.37: ajaḍāpaugaṇḍadhanaṃ daśavarṣabhuktaṃ paraiḥ saṃnidhau bhoktuḥ. *Vasiṣṭhadharmasūtra* 16.17: tatra bhuktānubhuktadaśavarṣam. anyathāpy udāharanti. ādhiḥ sīmā bāladhano nikṣepopanidhistriyaḥ / rājasvaṃ śrotriyadravyaṃ na saṃbhogena hīyate //

[108] *Vasiṣṭhadharmasūtra*, 16.19–20: prahīṇadravyāṇi rājagāmīni bhavanti. tato 'nyathā rājā mantribhiḥ saha nāgaraiś ca kāryāṇi kuryāt. Cf *Baudhāyanadharmasūtra* 1.18.16: abrāhmaṇasya pranaṣṭasvāmikaṃ rikthaṃ saṃvatsaraṃ paripālya rājā haret.

[109] *Mānavadharmaśāstra*, 8.147–8: yat kiṃ cid daśa varṣāṇi saṃnidhau prekṣate dhanī / bhujyamānaṃ parais tūṣṇīṃ na sa tat labdhum arhati // ajaḍaś ced apogaṇḍo viṣaye cāsya bhujyate / bhagnaṃ tad vyavahāreṇa bhoktā tad dravyam arhati // Compare with *Yājñavalkyasmṛti*, 2.24–5: paśyato 'bruvato bhūmer hānir viṃśativārṣikī / pareṇa bhujyamānāyā dhanasya daśavārṣukī // ādhisīmopanikṣepajaḍ abāladhanair vinā / tathopanidhirājastrīśrotriyāṇām // 'The right (of a person) to land when he, seeing his property encroached by another, does not question, extends over twenty years; for a movable property, ten years. Excepting mortgaged properties, boundaries, deposits, properties of invalids and minors, and, similarly, sealed deposits and the property of the king, women, and śrotriya priests.' Also see *Nāradasmṛti*, edited and translated by Richard Lariviere (Philadephia: University of Pennsylvania, 1989): 1.72–3: ajaḍaś ced apogaṇḍo viṣaye cāsya bhujyate / bhuktaṃ tad vyavahāreṇa bhoktā tad dhanam arhati // ādhiḥ sīmā bāladhanaṃ nikṣepopanidhī striyaḥ / rājasvaṃ śrotriyasvaṃ ca nopabhogena jīryate // 'As long as the owner is not mentally incompetent or a minor, and his property is being used legitimately in his presence, the possessor is entitled to that property. A pledge, boundary, sealed and unsealed deposits, women, the king's property, and learned brāhmaṇa's property are not lost through adverse possession.' Also see 4.8–9 where the legal incapacity of women, children, and 'idiots' ensures that contracts signed by them are void: adattaṃ tu bhayakrodhaśokavegarujānvitaiḥ / tathotko caparīhāsavyatyāsacchalayogataḥ // bālamūḍhāsvatantrārtamattonmattāpavarjitam / kartā mamāyaṃ karmeti pratilābhecchayā ca yat //Bṛhaspati (1.7.29) makes the same argument: na strīṇām upabhogaḥ syād vinā lekhyaṃ kathaṃ cana /rājaśrotriyavitte ca jaḍabāladhanena ca //

The natural exception to adverse possession – besides royal and priestly property – is the property of persons who lack legal capacity and Kātyāyana folds deities into this category: 'One should not put forth possession (as a cause of ownership) with reference to women, deities' and kings' assets. They are like (the assets) of children and priests that have come from the mother and father.'[110] This theme of the Crown as the protector of women, children, and deities is central to the political theology of the Purāṇas as well. The *Agnipurāṇa*, one of the more encyclopedic Purāṇas, extols, the *Dharmasmṛtis*' insistence on the royal protection of women, children, and deities at length: 'From seizing the assets of deities, etc., (a king) would dwell in hell for an eon. The king, devoted to worshipping deities should construct temples. Deities (and) their temples should be established and protected.'[111] A description of the royal duty to protect women (221.19–26) and minors and those without guardians follows: 'He should protect the estate belonging to a minor until he (the minor) completes his study or crosses the state of childhood... [with] the same... followed in the (case of the properties) belonging to widows with children and those not having the guardians.'[112] Sanskrit jurists' arguments trended, in the course of time, towards a theory of royal guardianship in which deities came, increasingly, to be treated as legally analogous to women, children, and other dependents. Part of this trend occurred in concert with a broader incorporation of the Purāṇic themes and passages regarding other aspects of equity, with the result that the treatment of deities bore a greater similarity to that of Kauṭilya than that of the *Dharmasūtras*.

We saw that Kātyāyana included deities within this category of protected persons; this is not an isolated comment. Aparārka, in his commentary on *Yājñavalkyasmṛti* 2.136 (discussing the estate of a man who dies without male issue), records the opinion of Paiṭhīnasi, there author of an as-of-yet undiscovered Dharma treatise:

> The assets of a śrotriya priest (who dies without issue) go to the assembly (*pariṣad*), not the king. The king should not escheat to (assets) belonging to the groups of deities, nor sealed or unsealed deposits, nor what has come in sequence from sacrifices, nor in the assets of minors and women.[113]

[110] *Kātyāyanasmṛtisāroddhāraḥ*, ed. & trans. P.V. Kāṇe (Pune: Oriental Book Agency Reprint for *Hindu Law Quarterly*, 1933): 330: na bhogaṃ kalpayet strīṣu devarājadhaneṣu ca / bālaśrotriyavat te ca mātṛtaḥ pitṛtaḥ kramāt //

[111] *Agnipurāṇa*, edited by Baladeva Upādhyāya (Vārāṇasī: Caukhambā Sanskrit Series, 1966) 222.11–2ab: devadravyādiharaṇāt kalpaṃ tu narake vaset / devālayāni kurvīta devapūjārato nṛpaḥ // surālayāḥ pālanīyāḥ sthāpanīyāś ca devatāḥ /

[112] Ibid., 223.18cd–21: bāladāyādikam ṛkthaṃ tāvad rājānupālayet / yāvat syāt sa samāvṛtto yāvad vātītaśaiśavaḥ / bālaputrāsu caivaṃ syād rakṣaṇaṃ niṣkulāsu ca // pativratāsu ca strīṣu vidhavāsv āturāsu ca //

[113] *Aparārka*, on Yāj. 2.135–6, p. 746: **paiṭhīnasiḥ**: 'pariṣadgāmi vā śrotriyadravyaṃ na rājagāmi, na hāryaṃ rājñā devatāgaṇasaṃsthitaṃ na nikṣepopanidhikriyākramāgataṃ na bālastrīdhanāny evam. For the royal duty of protecting the property of minors and the like, see *Mānavadharmaśāstra* 8.27: bāladāyādikaṃ rikthaṃ tāvad rājānupālayet / yāvat sa syāt samāvṛtto yāvat cātītaśaiśavaḥ // 'The king shall take care of the property owned by a minor, until such time as he may return from the teacher's house, or till he may have passed his minority.'

Other medieval authors of Dharmaśāstra anthologies (*nibandhas*) explained the *reasoning* behind the royal guardianship of women, children, and deities, etc. These authors made it clear that rules governing the assets of minors and other such individuals can be transferred over to deities and their temple endowments. For example, in the *Vyavahārakāṇḍa* of his *Smṛticandrikā*, Devaṇṇabhaṭṭa argues that,

> Kātyāyana says that, 'one should not put forth adverse possession (as a cause of ownership) with reference to women, deities' and kings' assets. They are like (the assets) of children and priests that have come from the mother and father, respectively.' Because deities' intrinsic nature of not rejecting, their assets are not lost when they are used by another.[114]

Finally, in the *Vyavahāracintāmaṇi*'s discussion of 'exemptions from adverse possession' (*anyabhogna hānyapavādaḥ*), Vācaspatimiśra II (1425–80 CE) offers a more-or-less identical list of *smṛti* passages, including Kātyāyana, that weave deities into the wider category of protected individuals.[115] In the aggregate, then, these passages indicate that the legally analogous position between minors and deities – both under the *parens patriae* jurisdiction of the Crown – is a connection made by both the Arthaśāstric and the Dharmaśāstric jurisprudential traditions.

1.5 Equity as supplemental law

> When among villages, guilds, groups, heretics, traders and the like, a time of minor adversity or a matter of dharma such as the repair of old (public spaces) arises, that technical/supplementary (*paribhāṣikī*) act of convention without which the adversity is difficult to solve and the matter of dharma difficult to accomplish, that is known as a technical/supplementary act of convention. Men are made (*kṛtāḥ*) by various characteristics (into) groups expressible by words such as village, etc. An act of convention should be observed by the many associated men who are joined together according to these various characteristics.
>
> Devaṇṇabhaṭṭa (13th century), *Vyavahārakāṇḍa* (*Samayānapākarma*)[116]

[114] *Smṛticandrikā:* Searchable Electronic Edition of the Vyavahārakāṇḍa of the Smṛticandrikā by Devaṇṇabhaṭṭa, transcribed, edited, formatted by Patrick Olivelle. https://docs.google.com/document/d/1pm1UjraMz8O4gkP3hmFv9-ltw1Kx2TvCOtkGGAlNa9o/edit (on bhukti), 73: **kātyāyana**. na bhogaṃ kalpayet strīṣu devarājadhaneṣu ca / bālaśrotriyavitte ca mātṛtaḥ pitṛtaḥ kramāt // devānām anirākartṛsvabhāvatvāt taddhanasyānyabhoge na hāniḥ.

[115] *Vyavahāracintāmaṇi by Vācaspati Miśra: A Digest on Hindu Legal Procedure*, crit. ed. and trans. Ludo Rocher (Gent: Gentse Orientalistiche Bijdragen 1. 1956), Verses 490–9. For the date of Vācaspatimiśra II, see Kāṇe, *History of Dharmaśāstra*, Vol. 1, 399–401.

[116] Donald Davis, 'The Non-Observance of Conventions: A Title of Hindu Law in the Smṛticandrikā', *Zeitschrift der Deutschen Morganländischen Gesellschaft* 157.1 (2007): 103–24, 110. For identical passages, see *Sārasvatīvilāsa*, 27 and the *Pārāśaramādhavīya*, ed. Vāman Śāstri Islāmpurkar (Bombay: Bombay Sanskrit Series, 1893), 122. grāmaśreṇīgaṇapāṣaṇḍanaigamādīnāṃ kṣudropadravakāle jīrṇoddhārādidharmakārye ca yāṃ pāribhāṣikīṃ samayakriyāṃ vinopadravo duṣpariharaḥ dharmakāryaṃ ca duḥsādham, sā pāribhāṣikī samayakriyā yena yenopādhinā narāḥ grāmādiśabdābhilapyajātyā kṛtāḥ tattadupādhyupahitair narair bahubhir militaiḥ kāryeti.

We saw earlier in this chapter that one facet of Equity in English and Anglo-Indian jurisprudence is its capacity to 'augment', 'enhance', or supersede the normal function of statutory law (or, in the English case, the Common Law).[117] In the Civil Law jurisdictions of the European continent, Equity was applied 'geometrically' by judges alongside statutory law. In England, Sir Thomas More's refusal, around 1530, 'to apply henceforth what has been called "geometric equity", meaning "an amendment or correction of the law"' directly led to the Court of Chancery's development as a court of equitable jurisdiction that ran parallel to the Common Law.[118]

In Roman Law, a magistrate's (praetor's) edicts served as equitable supplements to statutory law and, the *Lex Cornelia de iurisdictione* of 67 BC 'attempted to prevent arbitrary decision-making by praetors by turning the *ius praetorium* or *honorarium*, in the shape of the Edict, into a code of the same sort as the XII Tables'.[119] Sanskrit jurisprudence, for its part, enjoins the Crown to identify, protect, and promote a wide variety of supplemental laws (*pāribhāṣikadharmas*) that fill in gaps or errors in Dharmaśāstric dicta. This distinctly Sanskritic theory of Equity explicitly acknowledges the limitations of Sanskrit jurisprudence and enables the Dharmaśāstric tradition to recognise extra-śāstric legal phenomena. All of these theories of Equity share a common theme: the acknowledged need for formal legal systems to be tweaked, from time to time, in order to achieve fairness. It is precisely this broader sense of Equity – as opposed to the formal mechanisms of the Court of Chancery – which English jurists first imported to India as 'Justice Equity and Good Conscience' (from Regulation 60 of Warren Hastings' 1781 *Regulations for the Administration of Justice* to Article 142(1) of the Constitution of the Republic of India).[120]

1.5.1 Conventions (Samayas)

Many Dharmaśāstric discussions of supplemental law occur within the context of the titles of law (*vivādapādas*) called the Non-Observance of Conventions (*samayānapākarma*) or the Transgression of Compacts (*samvidvyatikrama*).[121] Conventions (*samayas*) and compacts (*samvids*) refer to 'the rules and conventions created by corporate groups of various kinds, from religious communities to merchant groups to military units to villages'.[122] As Donald Davis notes:

[117] See Chapter 1, §1.1.1, 'Equity'.
[118] Zwalve and Koops, 'Introduction', 4. For More and 'geometric equity', see J.H. Baker, *The Oxford History of the Laws of England VI: 1483–1558* (Oxford: Oxford University Press, 2003), 46–7.
[119] Mike MacNair, 'Arbitrary Chancellors and the Problem of Predictability', in W.J. Zwalve and E. Koops (eds), *Law & Equity Approaches in Roman Law and Common Law* (Leiden: Brill, 2013): 80–104, 80–1.
[120] See Note 17.
[121] Davis, 'The Non-Observance of Conventions', 103.
[122] Ibid., 103.

> the interest in this title of law seems to have grown over time in the earlier smṛti texts of the Dharmaśāstra tradition: 3 verses in MDh (8.219–221); 7 verses in NS (10.1–7); 8 verses in YS (2.185–192); 15 verses in KS (668–682); 25 verses in BS (17.1–25). The growth of interest in this title can be attributed to an increasing prominence of corporate groups of various groups in the political, religious, and economic landscape of medieval India.[123]

These conventions could be either local (*laukika*) or royal (*rājya*) in origin, but they share a common jurisprudential source of legitimacy due to their inclusion within the category of supplemental law: they 'do not threaten the authority of the Dharmaśāstra itself, but rather operate where the śāstra is silent or ambiguous to supplement or clarify what the dharma is in any given situation.'[124] In fact, this theory of supplemental law – of Equity – is so strong that the sovereign's edict 'is held to be supplementary in nature or technical in its specificity and, therefore, to work in the margins of the Dharmasastra rules.'[125]

In practice, this enabled Sanskrit jurists to incorporate a wide array of otherwise extra-śāstric legal phenomena into the parameters of Sanskrit jurisprudence. Some of these phenomena include temple endowments, public charities, arrangements made for the protection of women, children, and the sick, as well as a host of 'heretical', non-Vedic religious communities such as Jains, Buddhists, and even Muslims.[126] Many of these extra-śāstric phenomena represent post-Vedic Purāṇic innovations that were incorporated into Dharmaśāstra as supplemental laws – paralleling the philological appropriation of Purāṇic material by authors of Sanskrit legal digests in the second millennium CE.

Attending to this uniquely Sanskritic theory of Equity as supplemental law explains the conspicuous paucity of positive legal statements in Dharmaśāstra concerning the regulation of religious endowments. While Sontheimer, Richard Davis, Derrett, or even Justice Mukherjea see a tension between Brāhmaṇical Dharmaśāstra and popular practice, I argue that the data suggests the opposite: the explicit recognition of a wide array of legal and religious practices within the jurisprudential rubric of Dharmaśāstric Equity.

As Davis notes, 'the historiography of law in India has been largely based on technical, often overly legalistic, readings of Dharmasastra or, at the other extreme, on village customs as collected and enumerated by British officials.'[127]

[123] Ibid., 104.

[124] Ibid., 105. Also see Davis, 'Intermediate Realms of Law', 103: 'the connection between settled Brahmin groups and the kings or rulers who provided for their livelihood… [and] this connection, whether real or imagined, between the king and the diversity of associations in his purview including these Brahmin groups helps explain the presence of discussions of royal edicts (*rājaśāsana*) under this title of law'.

[125] Davis, 'The Non-Observance of Conventions', 105.

[126] Ibid., 106. For secularism in ancient India, see Rajeev Bhargava, 'An Ancient Indian Secular Age?', in Akeel Bilgrami (ed.), *Beyond the Secular West* (New York: Columbia University Press, 2016): 188–214.

[127] Davis, 'Intermediate Realms of Law', 111.

This lingering impression accounts, perhaps, for Birla and Das Acevedo's characterisation of the colonial jurisprudence of Hindu religious endowments as the unwarranted imposition of elite, Dharmaśāstric law onto wider popular practices. Dharmaśāstric Equity recognised 'intermediate realms of law' and, in epigraphic records of Hindu temple endowments, 'Dharmaśāstra terms like *samaya*, *samayadharma*... and *śāsana* are not only frequently used but are used in precisely the contexts one would expect from reading the "śāstric" rules regarding the Non-Observance of Conventions'.[128]

In what follows, I outline the evolution of Dharmaśāstric theories of Equity – its origins in the *sūtras* and *smṛtis*, its incorporation of Purāṇic and Tantric social practices, and its delineation of many donative practices that constituted an essential legal feature of classical Temple Hinduism. This approach provides an historical account of the process where 'the realities of legal practice on the ground were translated into the specialized academic idiom of Dharmasastra... [and] these academic textbooks, in turn, were (re)translated into rules governing corporate associations as well as many other legal and religious rule systems'.[129]

Kauṭilya, as we saw above, states that the king, through his Bureau of Official Records (*Akṣapaṭala*), should record and enforce the conventions of guilds and other associations. In the *Arthaśāstra*, conventional laws are, generally, covered by the term *saṃsthāna*, which, 'refers to "fixed" or "established" rules or instructions, probably in specific contrast to *caritra* or customary rules...[and] represent injunctions established and enforced by royal authority'.[130] This reflects, perhaps, a reticence to delineate forms of law-making outside of the purview of the Crown and an insistence on a top-down, centralised administrative jurisprudence.

The *Dharmasūtras* and *Dharmasmṛtis*, in contrast, recognise the *suis iuris* capacity of corporate and religious associations as well as royal edicts (*śāsanas*) through the lens of conventional laws (*sāmayikadharmas*). This reflects a broader shift in Brāhmaṇical jurisprudence in which it 'was, we suggest, unacceptable to... [Brāhmaṇical authors] writing in a later period under different intellectual conditions [than those of the *Arthaśāstra*], that either custom (*caritra/saṃsthā*) or State law (as *vyavahāra/vyāvahārika śāstra*) could overrule Dharmaśāstra'.[131] Dharmaśāstric Equity, then, is *recognised* and *protected* rather than *imposed* by the Crown (as it is in Arthaśāstric Equity).

The *Gautamadharmasūtra*, outlines the duties of kings and notes that: 'The laws of regions, castes, and families are also authoritative if they are not in conflict with the sacred scriptures. Farmers, merchants, herdsmen, moneylenders,

[128] Ibid., 114
[129] Ibid., 115
[130] Olivelle and McClish, 'Four Feet', 40–1.
[131] Ibid., 46

and artisans exercise authority over their respective groups. He [the king] should dispense the Law after he has ascertained the facts from authoritative persons of each group.'[132] Similarly, Vasiṣṭha invokes 'Manu' when he argues that 'when there are no specific rules in Vedic texts, Manu has said that one may follow the Laws of one's region, caste, or family'.[133] These regional, caste or family laws are protected by the Crown in turn: 'After inquiring into all the Laws specific to various regions, castes, and families, the king should make the four classes adhere to the Laws proper to them.'[134] While the *Arthaśāstra* argues that a king should keep a record of regional customs and conventions, Gauatama and Vasiṣṭha enjoin a king to recognise and enforce those regional customs and conventions as well as the other Dharmas outlined in their treatises. Later Dharmaśāstric authors expanded this model of supplemental law and linked it to the maintenance of temples and other forms of charitable endowment, but the core jurisprudential theory of Equity as supplemental law is undeniably present in the *sūtras*.

1.5.2 Temple conventions

The *Dharmasmṛtis* extend the theory of supplementary Dharmas, seen in the *Dharmasūtras*, to include the governance and repair of temples and monasteries. This is part of a wider, ubiquitous promotion of conventional (*sāmayika*) laws in the *smṛtis* which, in the course of time, became a favourite place of commentators to refer to the jurisprudence of Equity. The *Nāradasmṛti*, in its section of the 'Non-Observance of Conventions' (*samayasyānapakarman*), provides a succinct account of these conventional Dharmas (although, sadly, it does not include temples, but, rather, monastic institutions):

> The rules that govern heretics, corporate bodies, and the like are called their conventions; the Nonobservance of Conventions is a title of law. The king must protect the conventions of heretics, corporate bodies, guilds, councils, troops, groups, and the like in towns and in the countryside. Whatever their laws, duties, rules for worship, or modes of livelihood are, he must permit them. He must prohibit them from doing anything that is inimical to the king, offensive to his subjects, or an impediment to his

[132] *Gautamadharmasūtra*, 11.20–2: deśajātikuladharmāś cāmnāyair aviruddhāḥ pramāṇam. karṣak avaṇikpaśupālakusīdikāravaḥ sve sve varge. tebhyo yathādhikāram arthān pratyavahṛtyadharmavya vasthā. See Āpastamba 2.15.1 for his formulation of supplemental Dharma: etena deśakuladharmā vyākhyātāḥ. Baudhāyana 1.2.1–8 outlines a series of northern and southern practices based on 'the authority of the customs of that region (*deśaprāmāṇya*)'.

[133] *Vasiṣṭhadharmasūtra*, 1.17: deśadharmajātidharmakuladharmāñ chrutyabhāvād abravīn **manuḥ**. For discussion of 'Manu' in the *Vasiṣṭhadharmasūtra*, see Kāṇe, *History of Dharmaśāstra*, Vol. 1, 55–6.

[134] *Vasiṣṭhadharmasūtra*, 19.7: deśadharmajātikuladharmān sarvān evaitān anupraviśya rājā caturo varṇān svadharme sthāpayet.

> purposes... Those who sow disharmony among groups should be severely punished, because if such persons are ignored, they spread an epidemic of fear and terror.[135]

Virtually every commentator on this topic expands the already capacious list of legal phenomena to include the preservation of temples. Bṛhaspati gestures in this direction when he notes, in the context of describing various contractual associations, that: 'the head of those making a garden, or a temple and dharmic instruments as a joint partnership is entitled to two shares'.[136] Although Bṛhaspati's dictum is concerned with compensation in, presumably, joint ventures regarding the construction of temples, its application of the rules of *sāmayikadharma* to the phenomenon of temples anticipates the direction of later Dharmaśāstrins who described endowments to deities, explicitly, in terms of supplemental law. Vijñāneśvara's (11th–12th centuries CE) *Ṛjumitākṣarā* (commenting on *Yājñavalkyasmṛti* 2.185–6) provides a representative example:

> The definition of *samaya* is said by Nārada to be the usage (*sthiti*) of heretics (*pākhaṇḍa*) corporate bodies (*naigama*), etc. A *samaya* is an arrangement (in the form of) a supplemental law (*pāribhāṣikadharma*). That Dharma arising from a convention, having the form of the protection of temples (*devagṛhas*) and the guardianship of cattle and water, etc. should also be protected. And (a *samaya*) should be protected by the king.[137]

[135] *Nāradasmṛti*, 10.1–4, & 6: pāṣaṇḍanaigamādīnāṃ sthitiḥ samaya ucyate / samayasyanapākarma tad vivādapadaṃ smṛtam // pāṣaṇḍanaigamaśreṇīpūgavrātagaṇādiṣu / saṃrakṣet samayaṃ rājā durge janapade tathā //yo dharmaḥ karma yac caiṣām upasthānavidhiś ca yaḥ / yac caiṣāṃ vṛttyupādānam anumanyeta tat tathā //pratikūlaṃ ca yad rājñaḥ prakṛtyavamataṃ ca yat / bādhakaṃ ca yad arthānāṃ tat tebhyo vinivartayet // pṛthaggaṇāṃś ca ye bhindyus te vineyā viśeṣataḥ / āvaheyur bhayaṃ ghoraṃ vyādhivat te hy upekṣitāḥ //
See *Yājñavalkyasmṛti*, 1.361 & 2.186–7: kulāni jātīḥ śreṇīś ca gaṇān jānapadān api / svadharmāc calitān rājā vinīya sthāpayet pathi // 'Families, castes, guilds, corporations and the provinces, – when those deviate from the paths of their duty, the King should check them and bring them round to the right path'; nijadharmāvirodhena yas tu sāmayiko bhavet / so 'pi yatnena saṃrakṣyo dharmo rājakṛtaś ca yaḥ //gaṇadravyaṃ hared yas tu saṃvidaṃ laṅghayec ca yaḥ / sarvasvaharaṇaṃ kṛtvā taṃ rāṣṭrād vipravāsayet // 'He (a Brāhmaṇa) should carefully follow, without impeding his own Dharma, a sāmayika dharma that would arise, and, also, a Dharma made by the king. He who would steal the assets of a gaṇa and he who would break a compact, having expropriated all their assets, they should be exiled from the kingdom.' All translations are Lariviere's.
See also *Mānavadharmaśāstra* 8.41 & 8.219: jātijānapadān dharmān śreṇīdharmāṃś ca dharmavit / samīkṣya kuladharmāṃś ca svadharmaṃ pratipādayet // 'The king knowing his duty shall determine the law for each man, after haying duly examined the provincial laws pertaining to each caste, the laws of guilds, as also the laws of families'; yo grāmadeśasaṅghānāṃ kṛtvā satyena saṃvidam /visaṃvaden naro lobhāt taṃ rāṣṭrād vipravāsayet // 'If a man, after having entered into a compact under oath with a village, a country or a confederation, should break it, through greed, – him the king shall banish from his kingdom.'

[136] *Bṛhaspatismṛti*, 1.13.36: harmyaṃ devagṛhaṃ vāpi dhārmikopaskarāṇi ca / saṃbhūya kurvatāṃ caiṣāṃ pramukho dvyaṃśam arhati //

[137] *Yājñvalkyasmṛti with the Mitākṣarā of Vijñāneśvara*, ed. R.K. Panda (Delhi: Bharatiya Kala Prakashan, 2011), 2.185–6: (Prelude to 2.185): tasya ca lakṣaṇaṃ **nāradena**... pākhaṇḍinaigamādīnāṃ sthitiḥ samaya ucyate... pāribhāṣikadharmeṇa vyavasthānaṃ samayas...; (Commentary on 2.186): samayān niṣpanno yo dharmo gocārodakarakṣaṇadevagṛhapālanādirūpaḥ so 'pi yatnena pālanīyaḥ... tathā rājñā ca...

Aparārka, for example, in his commentary on Yāj. 2.186, employs Bṛhaspati's dictum (cited above), to give the following description of conventional laws: 'Having agreed to a conventional law concerning the restoration of dilapidated halls, wells, temples, and tanks, pools, and the consecration rites for poor orphans, etc., it should be carried out with the common property'.[138] Medieval Dharmaśāstrins also framed the conditions of royal and private grants of land to deities – ubiquitous in the epigraphic record of the Middle Ages – in terms of supplemental laws. In his discussion of royal edicts (*rājaśāsanas*) Devaṇṇabhaṭṭa notes that:

> Yājñavalkya (1.313) says that, 'having given land or having made a permanent arrangement the king should have a document made for the information of future good kings.' The meaning is that a permanent arrangement should be obtained as a royal conventional dharma (*prabhusamaya*) (to the effect that): some money, from the assets of each merchant should be given by the head of the merchants each year or each month to that Brāhmaṇa or to that deity. Although the heads of the merchants are the agents of the giving of wealth, nevertheless, the merit belongs to the settlor (of the arrangement) because the former only acts due to the instigation of the latter in specifying the recipient as X.[139]

Devaṇṇabhaṭṭa's examples are explicitly *descriptive*: they are not intended to provide specific positive *law* for judges to apply to any and all religious endowments. Rather, Devaṇṇabhaṭṭa explicates the equitable jurisprudence whereby specific rules and regulations may be included (and enforced) under the Dharmaśāstric rubric of supplemental law.

Through the mechanism of Equity – the ability of various communities, often with approval from the Crown, to create conventional Dharmas that the Crown would enforce – medieval Sanskrit jurists strove to incorporate the internal mores of various religious communities (Tantric, Purāṇic, and Vedāntic) and the financial arrangements between merchants, the Crown, and those communities which are attested in the epigraphic record into their jurisprudence. We will

rakṣaṇīyaḥ. For an analysis of this, and related Dharmaśāstric passages which concern 'medieval India's religious diversity [that] was inextricable from the widespread acceptance of a rather capaciously imagined emic form of legal pluralism', see Jason Schwartz, 'The King Must Protect the Difference: The Juridical Foundations of Tantric Knowledge', *Religions* 9.4 (2018): 1–25. Also see *Sarasvatīvilāsa*, ed. R. Shama Sastry (Mysore: University of Mysore Oriental Library Publications, Sanskrit Series, No. 71, 1927). There, *samayadharma* is applied to Vaiṣṇava and Śaiva religious practices: yadā naigamādīnām āndolikārohaṇaṃ cāmarādivījanādikaṃ saṃbhāvitaṃ karmāstīti samayas tatkarmakāribhir anuṣṭhīyeta tadā rājñaiva vivādaḥ parisamāpyaḥ. tathaiva pāṣaṇḍādīnāṃ vaiṣṇavānām. For the date of Vijñāneśvara, see Kāṇe, *History of Dharmaśāstra*, Vol. 1, 287–93.

[138] Aparārka on Yāj. 2.186: sabhāprapādevakulataḍāgādīnāṃ jīrṇānām uddhāro dīnānāthādīnāṃ ca saṃskāro yajñabhikṣādinimittaṃ ca dānaṃ sādhāraṇadhanenānayā vyavasthayaitat kartavyam. See his comments on Yāj 2.187 where he invokes a litany of Dharmasmṛtis to the effect that the crown must punish those who break these conventional Dharmas.

[139] Smṛticandrikā, p. 65: tatra viśeṣam āha **yājñavalkyaḥ** / dattvā bhūmiṃ nibandhaṃ vā kṛtvā lekhyaṃ tu kārayet / āgāmibhadranṛpatiparijñānāya pārthivaḥ // nibandho vāṇijyādhikāribhiḥ prativarṣaṃ pratimāsaṃ vā svavāṇijyāt dravyāt yat kiṃcid dhanam asmai brāhmaṇāyāsyai devatāyai vā deyam iti prabhusamayas labhyo 'rthaḥ. yady apy atra dhanadātṛtvaṃ vāṇijyādhikāriṇām eva, tathāpi nibandhakartur eva puṇyaṃ taduddeśenaivetarasya pravṛtteḥ.

see in Chapter 2 that innumerable epigraphic records document gifts – royal and secular – to deities and to Brāhmaṇas in more or less precisely the same terms.[140] To be emphatic: there is an identifiable Sanskrit jurisprudence of religious endowments – Equity in the form of *Pāribhāṣikadharma* – that had a significant bearing upon the actual historical practice of law regarding the regulation of these endowments in various periods of Indian history.

1.5.3 The legal personality of deities as a conventional Dharma

Finally, the Sanskrit jurisprudence of Equity as supplemental law provides an effective mechanism for understanding the juridical personality of Hindu deities. As Alexis Sanderson has demonstrated at length, the juridical, as opposed to metaphysical personality of consecrated (*pratiṣṭhāpita*) images in Śaiva (and Vaiṣṇava) temples during the 'Śaiva Age' (6th–13th centuries) is documented in sectarian ritual texts and in scores of epigraphic records.[141] When discussing Rājendravarman's (r. 944–968 CE) eponymous Śiva Liṅgas at Vat Phu (modern Laos), Sanderson observes that:

> The name of the first of these Śivaliṅgas was formed in accordance with the common practice observed in the Indic world for images of deities enshrined by individuals, that is to say, as a compound consisting of the distinctive part of the individual's name, or of that of a person designated for the honour, followed by a term indicating the universal deity invoked into the image for worship: -īśvara for a Śiva, -svāmin, -mādhava or -nārayana for a Viṣṇu.[142]

Sanderson is extremely clear that 'the legal fiction of ownership [on the part of the deity] is the function of the name' and refers to the *Somaśambhupaddhati*'s injunction that a donor, 'should make over all that he can, such as gold, domestic animals and lands "to N-īśvara" to [fund] the singing, instrumental music and other [expenses of the cult]'.[143] Indeed, Sanderson emphasises that, 'the naming

140 See Chapter 2, §2.1.1, 'Theory'.

141 Alexis Sanderson, 'The Śaiva Age: The Rise and Dominance of Śaivism During the Early Medieval Period', in Shingo Einoo (ed.), *Genesis and Development of Tantrism* (Tokyo: University of Tokyo, 2009): 41–350.

142 Alexis Sanderson, 'The Śaiva Religion Among the Khmers (Part 1)', *Bulletin de l'Ecole française d'Extrême-Orient* 90–91 (2003): 349–462, 415.

143 Ibid., 415 fn 250: That the legal fiction of ownership is the function of the name is implicit in *Somaśambhupaddhati* 4:227 (v. 46): hiranyapaśubhūmyadi gītavādyādihetave / amukeśāya tad bhaktyā śaktyā sarvaṃ nivedayet 'With devotion he should make over all that he can, such as gold, domestic animals and lands "to N-īśvara" to [fund] the singing, instrumental music and other [expenses of the cult]'. Sanderson cites a corpus of additional tantric sources in support of this position: *Mohacurottara*, fn. 34v9–35rl: yajamānasya yan nāma yojayed īsvareṇa tu 'he should compound the name of the patron with -īsvara'; Bhojarāja, *Siddhāntasārapaddhati*, f. 76r4: yajamānādyaṃ īsvarāntaṃ bhagavate nāma datvā 'after giving the deity a name that begins with [that of] the patron and ends in -īsvara'; *Somaśambhupaddhati* 4:227 (N-īśvara for a Śiva), 275 (N-īsvarī for a Goddess), 291 (N-svāmin or N-āditya for a Sun), 311 (N-svāmin or N-mādhava for a Viṣṇu); *Īśānaśivagurudevapaddhati* Kriyāpāda, p. 446: yajamānābhidhānādyam *nāmeśvara(em.: nāmaiśvarya ed.)padāntakaṃ 'the name, beginning with the name of the patron and ending with the word -īśvara'

convention is mentioned only in this context' of creating legal personality for the newly consecrated deity.[144]

Sanderson notes that Nīlakaṇṭhabhaṭṭa, the renowned early modern Sanskrit jurist, incorporated this tantra-inflected jurisprudence into a Dharmaśāstric treatise on consecration, the *Pratiṣṭhāmayūkha*. Nīlakaṇṭha enjoins that, when building a new temple:

> the enlivening ceremony [of the image] should be performed as it is stated in the Pūrtakamalākara [of his cousin, Kamalākara, and]... then he should make the name of the deity connected with the name of the agent for the purpose of future legal transactions. For example: so-and-so lord for Viṣṇu; or so-and-so Nārāyaṇa; or so-and-so lord for Śiva; or so-and-so lord for Bhānu; or so-and-so lady for the goddess; or so-and-so leader for Gaṇapati.[145]

However, Kamalākara and Nīlakaṇṭha argue that one only creates a juridical person when establishing a *new* deity. As Kamalākara notes: 'The consecration of temples... should be performed in the case of decrepit Śivaliṅgas or images. When building a new temple only (i.e., where a deity is already consecrated), the rule regarding the relinquishment (*utsarga*) of reservoirs (should be followed).'[146] To my knowledge, Nīlakaṇṭha's brief comment is the only statement – Kamalākara's brief repetition of it in the *Pūrtakamalākara* notwithstanding – of the direct legal personality of Hindu deities in Sanskrit jurisprudence, and it dates to the 17th century. It took a millennium for Sanskrit jurists to make a direct endorsement of divine legal personality, but it did happen, and it likely represents the culmination of the gradual Dharmaśāstric acceptance of Purāṇic and Tantric Temple Hinduism.

Nīlakaṇṭha's passage, quoted above, is possibly the most important dictum discussed in this chapter because it is an unequivocal endorsement of the legal personality of Hindu deities in Sanskrit jurisprudential literature. Alexis Sanderson is emphatic that Nīlakaṇṭha is:

[144] Sanderson, 'The Śaiva Religion'.

[145] *Bhagavantabhāskaraḥ*, ed. by Veṇīmādhava Śāstrī (Delhi: Caukhambā Saṃskṛta Pratiṣṭhāna, Vrajajīvana prācya bhāratī granthamālā no. 9, 1985), Vol 2. (*Pratiṣṭhāmayūkha*), p. 26: prāṇapratiṣṭhāṃ kuryāt. sā yathā **pūrtakamalākaroktāṃ** prāṇapratiṣṭhāṃ; and 31: atha kartṛnāmayu[k]taṃ devasya nāma kuryāt sarvadā vyavahārārtham. tac ca viṣṇor amukasvāmī. amukanārāyaṇa iti vā. śivasyāmukeśvaraḥ. bhānor amukasvāmī. devyā amukeśvarī. gaṇapater amukavināyaka iti. Compare with Kamalākarabhaṭṭa's *Pūrtakamalākara*, Bhandarkar Oriental Research Institute Ms. No 838 fol. 85a: tataḥ kartā svanāmayuktaṃ devasya nāma kuryāt.

[146] *Pūrtakamalākara.*, fol 30a: atha prāsādapratiṣṭhā. sā ca jīrṇe śivaliṅge mūrtau vā jīrṇāyāṃ prāsādamātre nūtane kṛte jalāśayotsargavidhinā kāryā. Also see *Nirṇayasindhu* ed. by Vrajaratna Bhaṭṭācārya (Vārāṇasī: Chaukhambā Vidyābhavana, 1991), 251: prāsādamātre nūtane tu **mātsyokta jalāśayapratiṣṭhāvidhim** eva kuryāt. Nīlakaṇṭha makes a similar argument in the *Pratiṣṭhāmayūkha*, p 25, where he includes 'self-manifest' (svayambhu) images in the list: yatra tu svayambhūdevaḥ, prāg eva vā pratiṣṭhitaḥ prāsādaś ca nūtanas tatrāpi taduttare maṇḍapaṃ kṛtvā.

> pointing to the fact that the apparent individualization of the deity through the giving of this composite name is understood as a device that enables the deity in the principal image of the temple to be treated in law as the owner of the lands and other goods gifted by the founder and any subsequent benefactors. It has no further reality. The Śiva in an image is never worshipped under this name but only as Śiva pure and simple.[147]

One might assume, incorrectly, that Nīlakaṇṭha's dictum is not an endorsement of the direct legal personality of Hindu deities. In this view, Nīlakaṇṭha's injunction is merely for the purpose of forming a deity's name for use in practical speech, rather than for the purpose of conducting legal transactions. This perspective is erroneous because it ignores Sanderson's observation – one informed by a deep immersion in the tantric materials that Nīlakaṇṭha cites throughout the *Pratiṣṭhāmayūkha* at length – that these naming conventions are *not* relevant in a ritual context and have 'no further reality' beyond their *legal* significance. Furthermore, Nīlakaṇṭha's dictum matches precisely the consistent legal practices that one finds in numerous inscriptions and copper-plates over more than a millennium of Indian history.[148] To read this *injunctive* passage as referring *descriptively* to purely non-legal, non-ritual linguistic usage would require us to ignore the numerous tantric sources discussed by Alexis Sanderson, thousands of epigraphic records, and *inter alia*, Devaṇṇabhaṭṭa's description of giving gifts to deities that I discussed earlier in this chapter.

How, though, would Nīlakaṇṭha categorise the creation of an extra-śāstric legal entity (the deity) that provides a nexus for the property rights of a temple? He doesn't state his opinion directly, but, in view of the aforementioned discussion of Equity, it seems probable that he would have described it as a supplemental law – a *pāribhāṣikadharma*. Although not a Dharmaśāstric text, the *Śivāgamaśekhara* links Devaṇṇabhaṭṭa's model of divine endowments as supplemental laws with Nīlakaṇṭha's theory of deities as legal persons: 'Then the patron should go to the king and having prepared a copper-plate or stone edict he should donate gold, villages and the rest down to male and female slaves for the sake of the dancing, singing and other [expenses], saying [that he does so] "to N-īśvara".'[149] This is,

[147] Sanderson, 'The Śaiva Religion', 415 fn 250. Also see Alexis Sanderson, 'How Public was Śaivism?', in Nina Mirnig, Marion Rastelli, and Vincent Eltschinger (eds), *Tantric Communities in Context* (Vienna: Austrian Academy of Sciences Press, 2019): 1–48, 36–7 fn 39, for his ruminations on the legal effects of this process: 'The purpose of such naming was not merely to immortalise the founder. It also served a legal purpose. Giving a personal name to the deity installed in the principal idol of a temple enabled it to be the locus of the foundation's juristic personality. It was then possible to appoint officials who could, when necessary, go to court to defend its legal rights, notably its right to whatever properties and revenues had been gifted to it by the founder, and any later donors, to fund its activities.'

[148] See Chapter 2, §2.4.1, 'Eponymous deities and the law of Trusts'.

[149] Edited by Brunner-Lachaux. Cited by Sanderson in 'The Śaiva Religion', 415 fn 250: tato rājāntikaṃ kartā gatvā hiraṇyagrāmādi dāsadāsīparyantaṃ nrttagītādihetave amukeśvarāyeti svaśaktitas tāmraśilāśāsanaṃ krtvā nivedayet.

of course, more or less exactly the same view taken in Anglo-Hindu jurisprudence: deities are legal persons who may own assets, which, in turn, must be utilised by trustees for the purposes specified by the donor.[150] If the deity's agents do not utilise the assets for these stipulated purposes, then they can be held accountable by the Crown for breach of trust.

1.6 Trusts

> *When someone receives a guardian-less child, along with his assets, with the intention of acting as a guardian (for the child and their wealth), [then] for such assets, this rule (concerning the fiduciary duties of depositees) should be observed.*
>
> Asahāya on *Nāradasmṛti* 2.8[151]

In its simplest formulation, a Trust is a fiduciary duty regarding property: someone is bound, by law or by conscience, to utilise or protect some property for a particular purpose. I discuss the history and legal permutations of the Trust in English jurisprudence in some depth in the introduction to this monograph. The inevitable differences between Indian and English phenomena that were born from the unique history and procedures of the Court of Chancery notwithstanding, one finds many legal phenomena in Sanskrit jurisprudence that reflect complex applications of fiduciary principles and that can be compared analogously to similar phenomena in the English jurisprudence of Equity and Trusts.

For example, from its inception, Sanskrit jurisprudence describes a wide array of deposits (*nikṣepa*/*nidhi*/etc) in which the depositee is explicitly bound to guard the asset or to utilise it for a specific purpose. Some forms of pledge (*ādhi*) allow the pledgee to utilise the asset but nevertheless enjoin them to protect it as if it were their own property. In course of time, Sanskrit jurists deployed Mīmāṃsā-derived theories of ownership to explore the moving parts of fiduciary law and to explain how, legally speaking, someone who *possesses* an object without *owning* it can nevertheless make use of it. Questions included: who owns mortgaged or pledged assets; what duties of care do bailees owe towards bailors' property; and what are the legal implications of the proposition that 'sons become owners by birth' (*janmasvatva*)? In the aggregate, this data demonstrates that Sanskrit jurisprudence developed a sophisticated jurisprudence of fiduciary duties and trusts. But what about divine assets?

We saw earlier in this chapter that, according to Sanskrit jurisprudence, deities and their assets merit special legal guardianship by the Crown and that this royal

[150] See Chapter 4, §4.2.3.i, 'The legal personality of Hindu deities.'

[151] *Nārada* 2.8 (Nikṣepa): yo 'nāthaṃ bālaṃ sapradhanaṃ nāthābuddhyā pratigṛhṇāti tadīyadhanasyāpy ayam evam vidhir draṣṭavyaḥ. For Asahāya's date, textual history and positions in Dharmaśāstra, see Kāṇe, *History of Dharmaśāstra*, Vol. 1, pp. 247–51.

guardianship is analogous to that provided to minors, women, and those who lack legal capacity. We also saw that religious endowments, like charities and commercial guilds, were governed according to conventional laws (*sāmayikadharmas*) that were recognised in Sanskrit jurisprudence as a form of supplementary law (*pāribhāṣikadharma*). Nevertheless, two glaring questions remains concerning divine endowments: 1) does the tutelary deity of a temple *own* its temple's assets? and 2) in either case, are the deity's earthly representatives bound by a fiduciary duty to use the deity's assets for the benefit of the deity?

The answer to both questions, from the perspective of Sanskrit jurisprudential literature, is sometimes ambiguous. Several sources describe deities as possessing a nominal, 'secondary' (*gauṇa*) ownership, which is distinct from the 'primary' (*mukhya*) ownership which vests in the deities' servants (*sevakas*). Does a secondary or figurative ownership impose moral or legal obligations on those who enjoy the primary ownership of an asset? Dharmaśāstra and Mīmāṃsā sources vary in their answers to this question - some say yes, others say no. Nevertheless, all of these authors describe (and many endorse) socio-legal practices wherein deities enjoy a nominal ownership (*svatva*) which enjoins these deities' legal representatives to manage assets for the benefit of the deity - much like the duty of care a pledgee or depositee owes to the pledgor or depositor. When viewed from the ownership-oriented perspective of Sanskrit jurisprudence, deities' endowments can correctly be classified as a species of trust. Whether descriptive or prescriptive, such descriptions in Dharmaśāstric and Mīmāṃsā, offered important jurisprudential principles for the practical legal administration of religious endowments in India over the centuries.

1.6.1 Pledges, deposits, and joint-family trusts

Sanskrit jurisprudence describes many proprietary phenomena that one would associate with security interests in English law: pledges, mortgages, bailments, liens, etc.[152] Generally, these phenomena involve a distinction between the *possession* and *ownership* of an asset and a concomitant fiduciary duty on the part of a creditor towards the owner's asset. For example, the *Arthaśāstra* uses its discussion of deposits (*nikṣepa*) as the archetype for other types of fiduciary relations with regard to property, such as pledges and mortgages. This pattern is followed by subsequent jurists who identified a common thread running through them.[153]

[152] The standard work of reference for Sanskrit (and Islamic) securities law in ancient and colonial India is Rashberhary Ghose, *The Law of Mortgage in India* (Calcutta: Thacker Spink & Co., 1877). Also see P.V. Kāṇe, *History of Dharmaśāstra*, Vol. 3, 2nd edn. (Pune: Bhandarkar Oriental Research Institute, 1973): 411–61; and Priyanath Sen, *The General Principles of Hindu Jurisprudence* (Calcutta: University of Calcutta, 1989), Chapter 6: 176–206.

[153] 3.12.8: tena ādhipraṇāśopabhogavikrayādhānāpahārā vkyākhyātāḥ. 'The above discussion also explains the loss, use, sale, mortgage, and theft of a pledge.'

According to the *Nāradasmṛti*, 'when one deposits his own property out of confidence, and without apprehension, this, according to the wise, is the title of law called Deposits'.[154]

A depositee might have possession and use of an asset, but not ownership and this ensures that they may not sell or mortgage the deposit and, as Nārada notes, 'in case he mortgages or sells the deposit or denies receiving it, the fine is four times one-fifth the amount'.[155] Furthermore, a pledgee or mortgagee (when the mortgagee is in possession of the asset) has a duty of care over the mortgaged asset. As Kauṭilya notes: 'Those who use these [agricultural assets] on lease, on fixed rent, as a pledge, for a share of the crop, or with the permission for use should keep them in repair. For not keeping them in repair, the fine is double the loss.'[156] These terms appear regularly in the *Dharmasūtras* and in the *Dharmasmṛtis* where we encounter the same twinned phenomena: the holder of a mortgaged or pledged asset cannot sell that asset and they must maintain the asset in the condition in which it was received. According to the *Gautamadharmasūtra*: 'As long as a person has a blameless reputation, he is not accountable for an open or sealed deposit, something borrowed or purchased, or a collateral for a loan that is lost without fault.'[157] In his comments on this passage, Haradatta (c. 1200 CE) describes this duty of care in terms of one's own property (*svadravya*):

> The bearer is accountable if he does not protect (that deposit, etc.) like his own property. (For example) if in the case of fire, etc. he saves his own property and neglects the deposit, etc., or (in the case of a calamity) he conceals his own property and leaves the deposit, etc., exposed. When he (the depositee) is accountable (the principal) should be given (to the depositor).[158]

In the *Vyavahāramayūkha*, Nīlakaṇṭha quotes and comments on a passage of the *Bṛhaspatismṛti* that explicitly mentions a depositee's duty of care: 'If the depositee allows the deposit to perish by making a difference (in care in relation to his own property) or by indifference or fails to return the deposit when requested to do so, he shall be made to pay for it together with interest.'[159]

[154] *Nāradasmṛti* 5.1: svadravyaṃ yatra viśrambhān nikṣipaty aviśaṅkitaḥ / nikṣepo nāma tat proktaṃ vyavahārapdaṃ budhaiḥ //1// Lariviere's translation.

[155] *Arthaśāstra* 3.12.6: ādhānavikrayāpvyayaneṣu cāsya caturguṇapañcabandho daṇḍaḥ. Olivelle's translation.

[156] *Arthaśāstra* 3.9.36–7: prakrayāvakrayādhibhoganisṛṣṭopabhoktāraś caiṣāṃ pratikuryuḥ. apratīkāre hīnadviguṇo daṇḍaḥ.

[157] *Gautama*: nidhyanvādhiyācitāvakrītādhayo naṣṭāḥ sarvān aninditān (a)puruṣāparādhena //12.39//

[158] puruṣāparādhas tu yadi dhārayitāraḥ svadravyavan na rakṣayeyuḥ, yady agnibhayādau svadravyaṃ gṛhītvā nidhyādy upekṣeran svadravyaṃ vā guptaṃ nidhāya bahir nidhyādi sthāpayeyuḥ. etasmin puruṣāparādhe sati dadyur eva.

[159] *Bṛhaspati* cited in *Vyavahāramayūkha*, 117: bhedenopekṣayā nyāsaṃ gṛhītvā yadi nāśayet / yācyamāno na dadyād vā dāpyaṃ tatsodayaṃ bhavet // Note Nīlakaṇṭha's gloss of bheda in terms of duty of care: bhedaḥ svadravyatāratamyam.

The *Sarasvatīvilāsa*, which arguably offers the most comprehensive account of deposits, mortgages, and other secular trusts in Sanskrit jurisprudence, characterises the pledgee's duty of care as a conventional law. In a discussion of the difference between usufructuary (*bhogya*) and custodial (*gopya*) pledges (*ādhi*), the author argues that:

> The pledgee should protect the pledge – either as a usufructuary or as a protected pledge via the same method – deposited as usufructuary or protected – that it was deposited by the creditor. Otherwise, if (the deposit) is protected as usufructuary when it is custodial or as custodial when it is usufructuary, then the interest (for the pledgee) is lost (in the case of a custodial deposit treated as a usufructuary deposit) on account of breach of convention (*samayātikramāt*) or the asset's principal is lost (for the depositee in the case of a usufructuary deposit being treated as a custodial deposit).[160]

Creditors with possession of collateral owe fiduciary duties to debtors, but what happens when: 1) a creditor does not have possession of collateral; 2) a debtor attempts to sell a mortgaged asset; or when 3) a creditor sells a security when the creditor defaults on a loan? Sanskrit jurists in the second millennium employed Mīmāṃsā-derived (and, sometimes logic-derived) theories of ownership (*svatva*) to answer these questions. Broadly, jurists beginning with Asahāya argued that ownership could be 'obstructed' (*bādhita/bandhita*) by liens, the co-ownership, and other forms of legal and ethical obligation.[161] Jurists drew on the jurisprudence of mortgage, and on Mīmāṃsā-derived theories of ownership as: 'A quality (*guṇa*) of an asset (*dhana, dravya*), produced by extra-śāstrically established acts of acquisition (*lokasiddhārjanopaya*) and characterized as a fitness for use as desired (*yatheṣṭaviniyogayogyatva*).'[162]

Vijñāneśvara systematised a legal model of patrilineal 'coparcenary' trusts:

> Inheritance is twofold: unobstructed (*apratibandha*) and obstructed (*sapratibandha*). Unobstructed Inheritance is when the assets of fathers and grandfathers become the property of sons and grandsons by virtue of their being sons and grandsons. But obstructed inheritance is (when these same assets) become the property of paternal uncles, brothers, etc in the absence of the owner and in the absence of (their) sons.[163]

[160] *Sarasvatīvilāsa*, 231–2: yathā – yena prakāreṇa gopyatvena bhogyatvena vā sthāpitam – adhamarṇenādhīkṛtam. tathaiva – gopyam ādhiṃ gopyatvenaiva bhojyam ādhiṃ bhogyatvenaiva dhanī pālayet. anyathā – gopyaṃ bhogyatvenaiva bhogyaṃ vā gopyatvenaiva pālitaṃ cet. samayātikramāl lābho naśyati, mūlaṃ vā dravyaṃ naśyati.

[161] Fleming, *Ownership and Inheritance*, 33–4. Asahāya's definition of a deposit is telling. On deposits (Nikṣepa 5.1): 'The deposit of someone who deposits their personal property is bound': svakīyaṃ dravyaṃ yo nikṣīpati tasya nikṣepaḥ saṃbadhyate. Also see Sen, *Hindu Jurisprudence*, 184–5, discussing Ghose, *Law of Mortgage*, 24–48.

[162] Fleming, *Ownership and Inheritance*, 30.

[163] Ibid., 33. *Yājñavalkyasmṛti: with the Mitākṣarā of Vijñāneśvara*, ed. R.K. Panda (Delhi: Bharatiya Kala Prakashan, 2011), 2.168: sa ca dvividhaḥ apratibandhaḥ sapratibandhaś ca. tatra putrāṇām pautrāṇm ca putratvena pautratvena ca pitṛdhanam pitāmahadhanam ca svam bhavatīty apratibandho dāyaḥ pitṛvyabhrātrādīnām tu putrābhāve svāmyabhāve ca svam bhavatīti sapratibandho dāyaḥ.

Sen and Ghose, the two foremost scholars of mortgage in Sanskrit jurisprudence, associate medieval Sanskrit jurists' increasing interest in obstructed ownership as part of a wider shift towards the recognition of hypothecation – the pledge of an asset as collateral without the pledger transferring possession – and other more complicated financial arrangements (*nibandhas/kuṭṭās/nīvīs*) that were used to fund religious endowments.[164] We will see in the next chapter that perpetual endowments (*akṣayanīvīs*) are ubiquitous in medieval epigraphic records of Buddhist, Jain, and Brāhmaṇical endowments. Gregory Schopen has discussed perpetuities in Buddhist disciplinary texts (*vinayas*) and in the epigraphic record.[165] This precise term is absent in Dharmaśāstric texts and Schopen surmises that, 'if… the *aksaya-nīvī* retained a Buddhist smell this may account for the fact that "orthodox" *dharmaśāstra* authors were reluctant to deal with it'.[166] Nevertheless, Viśvarūpa describes 'imperishable treasures' (*akṣayanidhis*) in more or less the same terms as *akṣayanīvīs*.[167] Viśvarūpa probably bases his Brāhmaṇical recasting of an ostensibly Buddhist legal term on *Yājñavalkyasmṛti* 1.310 which states that: '[The king] should give *Vipras* (i.e., Brāhmaṇas) various comestibles and riches. What is presented to *Vipras* is the imperishable treasure of kings.'[168]

In short, Dharmaśāstric discussions of pledges, deposits, and inheritance describe relationships of trust and the legal duties owed by fiduciaries using the language of ownership (*svatva*). Dharmaśāstric discussions of divine endowments are few and far between compared to those involving deposits, joint-family trusts, or mortgages. Nevertheless, Sanskrit jurisprudential discussions of divine endowments share a common language and theory of ownership. This shared conceptual vocabulary is significant because it can enable us to infer (albeit with a healthy measure of caution) certain jurisprudential principles into the often terse passages that I will analyse in the following paragraphs.

[164] Sen, *Hindu Jurisprudence*, 184–5. For definitions and comments on these terms, which, generally speaking, entail 'obstruction' of ownership see Patrick Olivelle, David Brick, and Mark McClish (eds) *A Sanskrit Dictionary of Law and Statecraft* (New Delhi: Primus, 2015): 5 (*akṣayanidhi*), 214–15 (*nibandha*), and 271 (*pratibandha-kraya*). For an overview of these limited forms of ownership, see J. Duncan Derrett, 'The Development of the Concept of Property in India, c. AD 800–1800', in J. Duncan Derrett (ed.), *Essays in Classical and Modern Indian Law*, Vol. 2 (Leiden: Brill, 1977): 8–130, 67–89; and Lubin, 'Theory and Practice', 808–10. For epigraphic records of *nibandhas* and *akṣayanīvīs*, see Kāṇe, *History of Dharmaśāstra*, Vol. 2.2, 860 fn. 2023.

[165] Gregory Schopen, 'Doing Business for the Lord: Lending on Interest and Written Loan Contracts in the Mūlasarvāstivāda-vinaya', *Journal of the American Oriental Society* 114.4 (1994): 527–54.

[166] Ibid., 535, referring to J. Duncan Derrett, 'Nīvī', *Vishveshvaranand Indological Journal* 12.1–2 (1974): 89–5.

[167] *Bālakrīḍā* on Yāj. 1.313, Yāj. 2.124, and 2.189. Viśvarūpa equates nibandhas with akṣayanidhis – nibandho 'kṣayanidhiḥ. nibandho vā akṣayanidhiḥ. tad yuktaṃ vṛttimad grāmagṛhakṣetrākṣayanidhy ādisthāpitam arthaṃ dattvety arthaḥ.

[168] Ibid., bhogāṃś ca dadyād viprebhyo vasūni vividhāni ca / akṣayo 'yaṃ nidhī rājñāṃ yad vipreṣūpapāditam //1.310// Compare with Manu 7.82–3 (Medhātithi's edition).

1.6.2 Deities' property (*devasva*)

One of the most contentious topics in the Sanskrit jurisprudence of Equity and Trusts is deities' property (*devasva*). In Sanskrit jurisprudence and in contemporary Indian case law focuses on a triad of related questions: 1) *what* is a deity; 2) *who* owns assets that are dedicated to a deity; and 3) *how* can the Crown or public ensure that the managers of temple endowments act *bona fide* towards their tutelary deities? We saw earlier that, although the *Arthaśāstra* answers all of these questions in a fashion that is remarkably similar to contemporary Hindu law, the *Dharmasūtras* and *Dharmasmṛtis* had little to say about the matter. Furthermore, early authors of Sanskrit legal commentaries, such as Bhāruci and Medhātithi appear to have adopted the 'iconophobic' perspective of earlier Mīmāṃsakas such as Śabarasvāmin that deities cannot own property because deities are merely phonemes (*śabdamātradevatā*).

Nevertheless, at virtually every level of the chronological development of Sanskrit jurisprudential thought, the jurists tacitly or explicitly acknowledged the existence of the legal and cultural practice of divine endowments. While some of the more 'iconophobic' jurists endeavoured to classify these practices as extra-śāstric (*laukika*), they nevertheless accepted their legal validity (presumably under the rubric of *pāribhāṣikadharma*). Other scholars explicitly assimilated these practices into specific Dharmaśāstric injunctions. The data suggests, in the aggregate, that despite the paucity of passages to analyse, Sanskrit jurists understood and acknowledged that deities' figurative ownership and a concomitant fiduciary duty on the part of deities' guardians was a part of classical Indian jurisprudence. The jurists might differ on the metaphysical niceties of divine endowments and debate whether *particular* rules of Dharmaśāstra applied to them, but deities' figurative, but legally efficacious, ownership as a form of 'divine trust' was a longstanding feature of Sanskrit legal thought.

1.6.2.i Dharmasūtras, Dharmasmṛtis, and the Purāṇas

The *Dharmasūtras* are not completely silent on the possibility of the juridical personality of Hindu deities (and their ownership of temple assets). Gautama explains, in 9.63–4, that a recent Vedic 'graduate' (*snātaka*) 'may approach the king for the sake of a livelihood, but not anyone else except gods, elders, and righteous people'.[169] The meaning of 'deva' ('deity') in this passage is ambiguous, but Olivelle's comment that 'Gods' [deities] here refer to divine images… [and] the meaning may be that a Brahmin in dire straits may go to a temple to obtain

[169] *Gautamadharmasūtra*, 9.63–4: yogakṣemārtham īśvaram adhigacchet. nānyam anyatra devagurudhārmikebhyaḥ.

assistance from the temple funds, which technically are owned by the deity', seems plausible.[170] If so, then this metonymic description of a temple (and its assets) as a 'deva' would be the earliest description of deities as owners in Sanskrit jurisprudence.

The *Dharmasmṛtis* describe, albeit laconically, categories of deities' property (*devasva*) and temple priests (*devalakas*). Manu and Nārada, for example explicitly refer to the 'property of the gods' (*devasva*) and insist on punishment for those who would appropriate it. According to Manu: 'The sinful man who, through covetousness, seizes the property of the deities, or the property of Brāhmaṇas, lives, in the other world, upon the leavings of vultures.'[171] Nārada's statement is equally direct: 'The highest items [in terms of accruing liability for theft] are gold, gems, silk, women, men, cattle, elephants, horses, and items belonging to gods, Brāhmaṇas, or kings.'[172] These statements give no indication that they are figurative or secondary (as Bhāruci and Medhātithi will claim later) and they match Bṛhaspati and Kātyāyana's similar descriptions of deities as owners: 'Men, women, along with the valuables of the gods and silk are known as "the best assets". The punishment (for stealing) them is equal to their worth.' And: 'If one should steal, break, or burn the image of a deity or break its temple (*gṛha*) he would obtain the heaviest punishment.'[173]

The *smṛtis, pace* Kauṭilya, do not furnish an itemised list of divine assets, but Manu, in his discussion of disputes between owners and herdsmen (*svāmipālavivāda*) exempts 'deities' animals' (*devapaśu*) from those punishments prescribed for errant animals.[174] The ownership of deities is unambiguously supported by *smṛti* authors, even though the *smṛti* authors are frustratingly silent on its incidents. To emphasise, even if subsequent authors' commentaries on these dicta (such as those of Bhāruci and Medātithi) interpret them differently, there is no reason to take them, in their initial appearance, as anything other than straightforward descriptions of the longstanding social practice of treating deities as legal persons and endowing them with various kinds of assets.

[170] Olivelle, *Dharmasūtras*, 297.

[171] *Mānavadharmaśāstra* 11.26: devasvaṃ brāhmaṇasvaṃ vā lobhenopahinasti yaḥ /sa pāpātmā pare loke gṛdhraucchiṣṭena jīvati //

[172] *Nāradasmṛti*, 14.15: hiraṇyaratnakauśeyastrīpuṃgogajavājinaḥ / devabrāhmaṇarājñāṃ ca dravyaṃ vijñeyam uttamam //

[173] *Bṛhaspatismṛti*, ed. Rangaswami Aiyangar, Calcutta: Baroda Oriental Institute, 1941), 1.23.7: strīpuṃsau hemaratnāni devavipradhanaṃ tathā / kauśeyaṃ cottamadravyam eṣāṃ mūlyasamo damaḥ // and *Kātyāyanasmṛti* 808: hared bhindyād dahed vāpi devānāṃ pratimāṃ yadi / tadgṛhaṃ caiva yo bhindyāt prāpnuyāt pūrvasāhasam // Also see Manu, 9.280: koṣṭhāgārāyudhāgāradevatāgā rabhedakān / hastyaśvarathahartṝṃś ca hanyād evāvicārayan // 'Those who break into a storehouse, an armoury, or a temple, and those who steal elephants, horses and chariots – he shall put to death without hesitation.'

[174] *Mānavadharmaśāstra*, 8.242: anirdaśāhāṃ gāṃ sūtāṃ vṛṣān devapaśūṃs tathā / sapālān vā vipālān vā na daṇḍyān manur abravīt //

The role of the temple-priest (*devalaka*) is ambiguous.[175] On the one hand, Manu (3.152) and Viṣṇu (82.8) exclude them from participating in funerary rituals (*śrāddhas*), along with doctors, tradesmen and various reprobates.[176] Viṣṇu's inclusion of *devalakas* in his list of individuals that are banned from *śrāddhas* is perplexing given the fact that he also extols manual service to the temple deities: 'By removing the remains of offerings to a deity, a man obtains the fruit of giving a cow, as also by cleaning the temple, [and] by daubing it with cow-dung.'[177] The *devalakas*' status as *persona non grata* has been used, repeatedly, in support of the contemporary scholarly proposition of 'iconophobia' on the part of the Dharmaśāstric tradition but that proposition might be overstated.[178] After all, Medhātithi, who adopts the Mīmāṃsakas' phonetic description of deities' metaphysical status, draws a distinction between acceptable and unacceptable temple-priests: 'There is no sin for doctors and temple priests [who pursue these activities] for the sake of dharma.'[179] Nevertheless, what is strikingly absent from most of these texts are the exhortations to endow temples to the deities that appear ubiquitously in Purāṇic materials.[180] The only Dharmasmṛti to discuss gifts of temples, images, and monasteries at length is the comparatively late *Viṣṇusmṛti* (6th–8th centuries CE). Even here, the author limits himself to a few brief statements.[181] Viṣṇu notes that, 'a man who constructs a temple attains the world of that very god for whom the temple is constructed' and that 'when someone repairs a well, a park, a reservoir, or a temple, he obtains the same fruit as if he had constructed it himself'.[182]

Viṣṇu's inclusion of religious charities (*iṣṭāpūrta/yogakṣema*), especially gifts to temples, anticipates later Sanskrit jurists' efforts to incorporate vast tracts of

[175] For *devalakas*, see Gérard Colas, *Viṣṇù, ses Images et ses Feux* (Paris: EFEO, 1996), 133–40. See also Colas, 'Competing Hermeneutics', 155, and Stietencron, 'Orthodox Attitudes', 129–30, where he discusses the term's derivation from Pāṇini 5.3.99: jīvikārthe cāpaṇye.

[176] *Mānavadharmaśāstra*, 3.152: cikitsakān devalakān māṃsavikrayiṇas tathā / vipaṇena ca jīvanto varjyāḥ syur havyakavyayoḥ //

[177] *Viṣṇu.*, 91.17–8: devanirmālyāpanayanād godānaphalam āpnoti. devagṛhamārjanāt tadupalepanād... ca.

[178] See Note 31.

[179] *Manu-Smṛti with the 'Manubhāṣya' of Medhātithi*, ed. Gaṅgānātha Jha. Vol. 1 (Calcutta: Asiatic Society of Bengal, 1932), 272: dharmārthatve tu cikitsakadevakatvayor adoṣaḥ.

[180] One notable exception is Manu's (4.226) influential invocation of iṣṭāpūrta: śraddhayeṣṭaṃ ca pūrtaṃ ca nityaṃ kuryād atandritaḥ / śraddhākṛte hy akṣaye te bhavataḥ svāgatair dhanaiḥ // 'He shall always diligently perform, with faith, sacrifices and other religious acts; done with faith, and with well-begotten wealth, they become imperishable.' The term *iṣṭāpūrta* is Vedic in origin. See Sarasvati, *Hindu Law*, 18–20 ¶17–19. The term, probably appears first in connection with temples in the *Mahābhārata* (Atri, 44): ekāgnikarma havanaṃ tretāyāṃ yaś ca hūyate / antarvedyāṃ ca yad dānam iṣṭam ity abhidhīyate //vāpīkūpataḍāgādi devatāyatanāni ca / annapradānam ārāmaḥ pūrtam ity abhidhīyate //

[181] Patrick Olivelle, *The Law Code of Viṣṇu: A Critical Edition and Annotated Translation of the Vaiṣṇavadharmaśāstra* (Cambridge MA: Harvard University Press, 2010). For the Pāñcarātra view in and the dating of the text, see p. 15.

[182] Ibid., 91.10: devāyatanakārī yasya devasyāyatanaṃ karoti tasyaiva lokam āpnoti; & 91.19: kūpārāmataḍāgeṣu devatāyataneṣu ca / punaḥsaṃskārakartā ca labhate maulikaṃ phalam//

Purāṇic dicta commending these charities into their treatises. For example, the *Agnipurāṇa* extols temple construction and image consecration (typically under the tutelage of the Pāñcarātras):

> [Constructing] reservoirs, wells, tanks, and temples, giving food and gardens are (known to be) *Pūrtadharma*, that confers emancipation. Performing the *Agnihotra*, penance, truth, protecting scriptures, serving guests, the *Vaiśvadeva* (sacrifices) are said to be *iṣṭa* that takes one to heaven.[183]

The compilers also list assets that should be given to the deity: 'One would get fortune and wealth and would go to heaven by giving a maid-servant, servant, ornaments, cow, land, horse and elephant and other things for the deity.'[184] So, the *Dharmasmṛtis* note that deities own assets, and the Purāṇas list what sorts of assets deities should be endowed with. To take another example, the *Viṣṇudharmottarapurāṇa* (VDhP), provides several comments about the content of divine endowments. In the 93rd Adhyāya of the 3rd Kāṇḍa of the VDhP the compilers note that, 'In the Kali Yuga, Kings desiring heaven should make cities filled with temples… (Deities) should be consecrated by him (the king) in cities built previously (and), O Yādava, other people, also, having obtained the king's permission, should make temples.'[185] The VDhP enjoins the donation, presumably to the deity, of substantial lands:

> Consecrated deities who are worshipped receive (material offerings). Therefore, in the Kali Yuga, a wise man should perform consecration (of deities) with effort. With effort he should always make (the deity) well-endowed through the gift of land, etc. Therefore, in the Kali Yuga, one should install (a deity), with a generous sacrificial fee, having, with effort made (the deity) well-endowed through the gift of land, etc.[186]

The VDhP inveighs against the royal resumption of temple endowments, 'Having overcome another kingdom, he (the king) should not harm previously-given (land

183 The Pāñcarātra elements of the *Agnipurāṇa* are outlined by Marion Rastelli, 'The 'Pāñcarātra Passages in *Agnipurāṇa* 21–70', in *Melanges tantriques a la memoir d'Helene Brunner* (Pondicherry: EFEO, 2007): 187–229. See Chapters 38–67 for descriptions of the merits and techniques for temple construction. *Agnipurāṇa* 209.2–3: vāpīkūpataḍāgāni devatāyatanāni ca / annapradānam ārāmāḥ pūrtaṃ dharmaṃ ca muktidam // agnihotraṃ tapaḥ satyaṃ vedānāṃ cānupālanam / ātithyaṃ vaiśvadevaṃ ca prāhur iṣṭaṃ ca n[o]dakam //

184 *Agnipurāṇa*., 211.72: dāsīdāsam alaṅkāraṃ gobhūmyaśvagajādikaṃ / devāya dattvā saubhāgyaṃ dhanāyuṣmān vrajed divam //

185 *Viṣṇudharmottapurāṇa* (Hyderabad: Sarvodaya Sāhitya Mandira, 1929): 3.93.5cd-6ab: / devatāveśmapūrvāṇi nagarāṇi kalau yuge // kartavyāni mahīpālaiḥ svargalokam abhīpsubhiḥ / & 3.93.14: pratiṣṭhā tena kartavyā nagare pūrvanirmite / anujñāṃ nṛpateḥ prāpya kuryād anyo 'pi yādava //

186 Ibid., 3.93: tasmāt kalau prayatnena pratiṣṭhāṃ kārayed budhaḥ //20cd// arcāgatāś ca gṛhṇanti kṛtadevapratiṣṭhitāḥ /21cd/ tasmāt kalau prayatnena pratiṣṭhākaraṇaṃ hitaṃ / yatnāt suvihitaṃ kuryād bhūmidānādibhis sadā // & 24: tasmāt kalau pratiṣṭhānaṃ kartavyaṃ bhūrīdakṣiṇam / yatnāt suvihitaṃ kṛtvā bhūmidānādibhiḥ śubhā // Note that 3.93.17–8 connects this activity with 'iṣṭāpūrta': kṛtvā suvihitām ārcāṃ pratiṣṭhāpya yathāvidhi / iṣṭāpūrtena dharmeṇa naro yujyaty asaṃśayam // rājasūyāśvamedhānāṃ phalena ca narādhipa /

grants). In his own kingdom and another kingdom, the honored (land endowments of) deities and Brāhmaṇas (should not be harmed).'[187]

So, the VDhP encourages gifts of land to deities and exempts these gifts from royal resumption. What about the terms and conditions attached to these gifts? India's epigraphic corpus contains numerous detailed records of complex legal arrangements for the regulation of religious endowments. These are explored in depth in the next chapter of this monograph. In the present context, however, the VDhP is not completely silent on the issue. The compilers devote over three-hundred verses of the 341st Adhyāya to listing the merits conferred by gifts of hundreds of different assets – instruments, slaves, fans, ritual implements, etc. Within this list, we find statements that a donor's intention when gifting plays a role in shaping that asset's use: 'A pious person (who gives) a measure of grain, corn, seeds (or) golden, silver, or bronze coins, having stipulated that they are for the purpose of the worship (of the deity) obtains the reward of the sacrifice that is full of all desires.'[188] Another example, a narrative drawn from the *Skāndapurāṇa*, which describes the origin of the Somanātha temple at Paribhāsa, should suffice to support my contention that, despite some frustrating silences, the Sūtras, Smṛtis, and Purāṇas articulate a jurisprudence of divine trusts. As Granoff relates, in the *Nāgarakāṇḍa*, 'the moon is told to build a temple and perpetuate the worship of Śiva's liṅga.' The text provides the 'elaborate rituals… of the building ceremonies.'[189] The Moon founds a city nearby and, 'having settled this city near the God Someśvara, the Moon requested the Brahmins to dwell there and carry out their appointed tasks (*svakarmaṇāṃ pracārārthaṃ*)' using funds furnished by 'merchants [who] have been instructed to make over to the Brahmins a portion of their earnings.'[190] The Brāhmaṇas demur, noting that if they 'worship in a professional capacity, making use of the leavings of the offerings to Śiva [*niyogataḥ pūjayatāṃ śivanirmālyasevināṃ*]' then they would lose their caste status, 'a state that is abhorred by the… *śruti* and *smṛti* texts [*śrutismṛtivigarhitam*]'. Subsequently, the Moon appoints an alternative community of sages to manage the temple according to the aforementioned contractual terms.[191]

Granoff reads this passage, in connection with Manu's comments about *devalakas* (3.152) as an unambiguous reflection of Brāhmaṇical ambivalence

[187] Ibid., 3.306.28: paraṃ rāṣṭraṃ samāsādya prāgdattaṃ naiva hiṃsayet / svarāṣṭre pararāṣṭre vā devabrāhmaṇasātkṛtaṃ // Also see 3.326.12 (a discussion of possession, bhukti) where deities and Brāhmaṇas are exempted from royal resumption: prākprasādāḥ pradīyante paścād vāpi na pārthivāḥ / devadvijātivitteṣu na syāt svāmī nṛpaḥ kvacit //3.326.12//

[188] VDhP 3.341.72–3: mātrāṃ tu paricaryārthe nivedya vidhivat tathā / sarvakāmasamṛddhasya yajñasya phalam aśnute //dhānyānāṃ atha sasyānāṃ bījānāṃ dhārmikaḥ / suvarṇaraupyalohānāṃ rūpakāṇāṃ //Please note that the last two sections are not complete pādas.

[189] Granoff, 'Reading Between the Lines', 392

[190] Ibid., 393.

[191] Ibid., 393.

about image worship – wherein they will preside over temple construction but have no part in daily temple management.[192]

Nevertheless, this narrative provides a positive description of the kinds of legal arrangements that are implicit in Purāṇic statements about temple endowment: a founder builds a temple, hires Brāhmaṇas to preside over its consecration, establishes an image, makes a formal arrangement for a regular supply of funds, and employs a community to use those funds (enjoying some of the usufruct to pay for personal expenses) for the stipulated purpose of worshipping the deity. This is exactly what one finds in contemporaneous epigraphic records. This is also the model of deities' property (*devasva*) that Mīmāṃsā literature invokes (albeit as a somewhat disparaged social convention) in wider 'iconophobic' discussions of image worship. The broader point is that even ostensibly *iconophobic* passages provide *descriptive* accounts of divine endowments that entail the imposition of fiduciary duties on those who appropriate assets on behalf of a deity.

As a final example, in the *Pratiṣṭhākāṇḍa* ('Section of Consecration'), Lakṣmīdhara compiles a series of almost entirely Purāṇic verses that outline the consecration of images and temples. Lakṣmīdhara discusses 'gifts of shelter' (*Āśrayadānas*) and quotes the *Kālikāpurāṇa*:

> There is nothing more excellent than Śaṅkara [i.e., Śiva]. Therefore, dedicating it to him, one should construct an ascetics' shelter that is made out of baked bricks.... and that is equipped with a fine hall, lovely residences, attendants, a pavilion for expounding the scriptures, a flower-garden, and water next to a temple of Śaṅkara. One should further appoint a village of servants (*preṣya*), oh Cetanā, to provide lamps, kindling, loincloths, sandals, and the like for the shelter. Then one should honor ascetics with devotion; feed them especially well; worship Īśa with garments; and bestow the shelter upon them.[193]

Lakṣmīdhara only makes one comment here: explaining that 'dedicating' (*vikalpya*) means 'devoting' (*saṃkalpya*). Intention plays a crucial, technical role in Brāhmaṇical theories of gifting, wherein the intentions of the donor frame the nature and benefits of the donation.[194] The wider point is that Sanskrit jurists *adopted* rather than *rejected* Purāṇic dicta concerning the kinds of financial arrangements that donors ought to make when consecrating and endowing temples, monasteries and other forms of charitable trusts.

[192] Ibid., 394.

[193] *Dānakāṇḍa* 22.1.1–4: śaṅkarāt paramaṃ nānyad atas tasmai vikalpya ca / yatīnām āśrayaṃ vāpi kṛtvā pakveṣṭakāmayam // vikalpya saṃkalpya. suśālaṃ cārunirvāsaṃ parivārasamanvitam / vyākhyāmaṇḍapasaṃyuktam āsanair vividhais tathā / puṣpodyānasamāyuktaṃ sodakaṃ śaṅkarālaye // grāmaṃ dīpendhanādyarthaṃ preṣyāṇāṃ caiva cetane / kaupīnopānahādyartham āśraye 'pi niyojayet // tato 'bhyarcya yatīn bhaktyā bhojayitvā viśeṣataḥ / vastraiś caiva prapūjyeśaṃ bhaktyā tebhyo nivedayet //

[194] Axel Michaels, *Homo Ritualis: Hindu Ritual and Its Significance to Ritual Theory* (New York: Oxford University Press, 2016), Chapter 1, 'The Beginning of Rituals'.

1.6.2.ii Divine endowments in Mīmāṃsā and Vedānta

The Sanskrit text-tradition of ritual hermeneutics (*Mīmāṃsā*), beginning with the *sūtras* of Jaimini (2nd century BCE–1st century CE), the commentary of Śabarasvāmin (4th century), and the school-founding works of Kumārilabhaṭṭa (8th century) and Prabhākaramiśra (6th century) provided a legal-hermeneutical philosophy for Sanskrit jurists who wrote commentaries from the late first millennium CE onwards.[195] The Mīmāṃsakas aimed to distil a comprehensive account of the Vedic sacrificial liturgy from a large, unwieldly corpus of Vedic texts. Their analytical techniques provided Sanskrit jurists, many of whom studied and wrote about Mīmāṃsā, with a legal-hermeneutical toolbox. Śabara and Kumārila reject the ownership of deities in the 'primary' (*mukhya*) sense, but they acknowledge the conventional social practice of deities' ownership in a 'secondary' (*gauṇa*) sense. This provided later legal writers with a way of incorporating divine endowments within their jurisprudence of Equity and Trusts.[196]

My broader argument follows Colas' dovetailed assertions that Mīmāṃsakas 'relativized' rather than 'denied' the existence of deities, and that they implicitly 'recognized… the principle of donation of lands to a deity… as an acceptable current socio-religious convention'.[197] Mīmāṃsā authors, followed by Sanskrit jurists, relativised deities by arguing that, while deities' exist *metaphysically* as mere liturgical phonemes (*śabdamātradevatā*), deities exist *legally* as figurative owners of temple property. This relativisation occurred in conversation with the efforts of Vedāntins (whom one might characterise as 'theologians') logicians (*Naiyāyikas*), and even Purāṇic authors who provided metaphysical descriptions of deities that supported the theory that image worship in Temple Hinduism – as in Anglo-Hindu law – primarily benefits the worshippers.

Here is the crucial point: whatever the metaphysical acceptance, rejection, or relativisation of image worship by authors of Mīmāṃsā treatises, these authors acknowledge the existence of divine endowments as an acceptable legal and social practice. The Mīmāṃsā tradition, like the early Dharmaśāstric commentarial tradition, essentially views the legal practices associated with divine endowments as

[195] For Jaimini, see Francis X. Clooney, *Thinking Ritually: Rediscovering the Pūrva Mīmāṃsā of Jaimini* (Vienna: Nobili Research Library, 1990). For the Prābhākara school of Mīmāṃsā, Gaṅgānātha Jha, *The Prābhākara School of Pūrva Mīmāṃsā* (Allahabad: University of Allahabad, 1911). For an overview of the historical evolution of Mīmāṃsā, see Jean-Marie Verpoorten, *Mīmāṃsā Literature* (Wiesbaden: O. Harrassowitz, 1987). For the relationship between Dharmaśāstra and Mīmāṃsā, see McCrea, 'Hindu Jurisprudence and Scriptural Hermeneutics'; P.V. Kāṇe, *A History of Dharmaśāstra*, Vol. 5.2 (Pune: Bhandarkar Oriental Research Institute, 1962), 1283–351; and A.S. Nataraja Ayyar, *Mīmāmsā Jurisprudence: the Sources of Hindu Law* (Allahabad: Gaṅgānātha Jha Research Institute, 1952).

[196] For the relationship between Mīmāṃsā theories of ownership and Sanskrit trusts jurisprudence, see Fleming, *Ownership and Inheritance*, especially Chapter 2, 'Mīmāṃsā and the Mitākṣarā School of Jurisprudence', 29–69.

[197] See Note 32.

an extra-śāstric (*laukika*) cultural practice which can be harmonised with śāstric practices through the paradigm of Equity.

The question of deities' property is as old as the definition of ownership in Sanskrit literature. According to Śabarasvāmin, donation (*dāna*) differs from sacrificing (*yāga*) because the purpose of the former is the creation of ownership for another.[198] The accrual of ownership by a donee, however, requires an act of acceptance (*parigraha*) and herein lies one argument against the proposition of divine ownership:

> In response to the objection 'that which is given to a deity is its share', we reply: that (asset) is abandoned, having stipulated (it is for) the deity, and it is not the case that the deity's ownership arises through mere abandonment. Since the relationship between owner and property (*svasvāmisambandha*) arises through acceptance, and because (that asset) is not accepted by the deity, there is no share (for the deity) Pūṣan.[199]

Nevertheless, Śabara lived in a social milieu where deities were, legally speaking, treated as owners of assets. In a discussion over the entitlement (*adhikāra*) of animals and deities to perform sacrifices, Śabara's *prima facie* opinion (*pūrvapakṣin*) argues that, 'There is acceptance of assets (on the part of deities and animals), because of the convention (*upacāra*), "deities' villages," "elephants' villages," "bull's village." Therefore, there is *adhikāra* (for sacrifices) on the part of non-humans.'[200]

Śabara does *not* reject the conventional practice of treating deities *as if* they are owners. In fact, Śabara is emphatically *not* concerned with the *legal* implications of this conventional practice. Whether such practices are purely linguistic or legally efficacious is irrelevant to Śabara. His sole focus is on denying deities' eligibility for sacrifice on the grounds that such eligibility requires ownership (*svatva*) in its *primary* sense: 'And animals (and, presumably deities) do not accept assets, for they are not observed using those assets as desired (*svecchayopayuñjānāḥ*). Therefore, they are not masters of assets. As for "deities' village"(and) "elephants' village" this is mere convention (*upacāramātra*).'[201]

Śabara's notion that use as desired is an essential quality of ownership influenced the development of Sanskrit jurisprudential theories of ownership (as applied especially to inheritance and trusts) and this notion runs throughout the

[198] *Śābarabhāṣya*, 2.2.4, p. 8: na ca dānam itarayor anuvādaḥ. parasvatvārthatvād dadāter itarayoś ca tyāgārthatvāt.

[199] Ibid., 3.15.44: nanu yad devatāyai dīyate, tat tasyā bhāgo bhavati. ucyate – etad dhi devatām uddiśya tyajyate, na ca tyāgamātreṇa devatāsvatvaṃ bhavati. parigrahaṇena hi svasvāmisaṃbandha āpadyate, na ca parigṛhītaṃ devatayeti… tasmān nāsti pūṣṇo bhāgaḥ.

[200] Ibid., 6.1.4: dravyaparigraho 'pi devagrāmaḥ, hastigrāmaḥ, ṛṣabhasya grāma ity upacārād asty eveti. tasmād amanuṣyāṇām api śaknuvatām adhikāra iti.

[201] Ibid., 6.1.5: na ca tiraścāṃ dravyaparigrahaḥ, na hy ete dravyaṃ svecchayopayuñjānā dṛśyante. tasmād anīśānā dhanasya. yat tu, devagrāmo hastigrāma iti, upacāramātraṃ tat.

Śābarabhāṣya.[202] In the section on deities (*Devatādhikaraṇa* – 9.1.6–10), Śabara outlines the customary practice of divine ownership:

> The convention, 'deities' village' (and) 'deities' field', are mere convention (*upacāramātra*). Something is someone's property (when) someone is eligible to use it according to will. And it is not the case that a deity uses a village or field according to will. Therefore, one can't say 'he bestows (ownership on the deity).' That which is abandoned, having stipulated a deity becomes the wages (*bhṛti*) of the deity's servants (*devaparicārakas*).[203]

The statement that assets given to a deity become the wages (*bhṛti*) of that deity's servants might be taken to support the Dakor temple priests' claims in ***Manohar Ganesh Tambekar*** that their deity's image and assets were 'their property free from any secular obligation'.[204] In my view, however, this stretches Śabara's comments beyond their intended meaning. Śabara does not comment on whether or a deity's servants are obliged, by conventional legal and moral practices, to utilise assets over which they have 'primary' ownership for the support of a deity or other specified purposes. Rather, Śabara limits his argument to rejecting the possibility of using such conventional practices to prove that deities own assets in a primary sense. Śabara's stakes are whether deities have full ownership, not whether equitable legal doctrines impose fiduciary duties on the 'owners' of deities' assets:

> As for (the argument) that deities can make use of their assets through temple priests who act in accordance with the deity's will, this is not right. What is vouched for by direct perception is the will of the temple-priests (in administering those assets). Even those who consider deities as owners (of assets), do not deny the priests' will (in the use of the deities' assets). That person who follows the will of another and who cannot make use of the things according to his own will cannot be an owner (of assets).[205]

Even as Śabara insists that deities are not legal owners, he nevertheless acknowledges the convention (*upacāra*) of treating deities as owners.[206] As Colas notes, epigraphic records from Śabara's time attest to the existence of arrangements wherein deities' endowments were administered by temple priests in favour of

[202] See Fleming, *Ownership and Inheritance*, especially Chapters 1 and 3.

[203] *Śābarabhāṣya*, 9.1.9: upacāro 'pi devagrāmo devakṣetram ity upacāramātram. yo yad abhipretam viniyoktum arhati tat tasya svam. na ca grāmam kṣetram vā yathābhiprāyaṃ viniyuṅkte devatā. tasmān na saṃprayacchatīti. devaparicārakāṇāṃ tu tato bhṛtir bhavati, devatām uddiśya yat tyaktam.

[204] See Note 52.

[205] *Śābarabhāṣya*, 9.1.9: yad devalakā arthān viniyuñjate, tad devatābhiprāyād evety adhyavasyāma iti. tan na. pratyakṣāt pramāṇād devatāparicārakāṇām abhiprāya ity avagamyate. sa na śakyo bādhitum. ye 'pi devatām īśānām varṇayanti, te 'pi nāpahnuvate paricārakāṇām abhiprāyo bhavatīti. na ceśāno bhavati yaḥ parābhiprāyam anurudhyate, yasya na svābhiprāyād viniyogo bhavati.

[206] For Mīmāṃsā theories of deities as phonemes, see Francis X. Clooney, 'Why the Veda Has No Author: Language as Ritual in Early Mīmāṃsā and Post-Modern Theology', *Journal of the American Academy of Religion* 55.4 (1987): 659–84; and Francis X. Clooney, 'What's a God? The Quest for the Right Understanding of Devatā in Brāhmaṇical Ritual Theory (Mīmāṃsā)', *International Journal of Hindu Studies* 1.2 (1997): 337–85.

the deity and in accordance with the stipulated conditions of the grants.[207] Colas' point is crucial for the wider purposes of this monograph because it enables us to appreciate how Śabara and other authors *accommodate* divine endowments as an extra-śāstric social practice even when they might ostensibly appear to downplay their importance within specific śāstric contexts. Śabara's relativisation of divine ownership, by acknowledging its existence as a social practice, is similar to Sanskrit jurists' view of Equity in terms of supplemental law. They recognise the existence of legal phenomena outside the purview of their Sanskrit text traditions while acknowledging that those text traditions can be supplemented by social practices. Drawing such boundaries between śāstric and extra-śāstric (but legally recognised under Dharmaśāstric principles of Equity) phenomena is *not* equivalent to rejecting the existence of extra-śāstric phenomena.

Francis X. Clooney argues that later authors of Mīmāṃsā literature explicitly accepted image worship (even as they relativised its importance vis-à-vis Vedic sacrifice).[208] Kumārilabhaṭṭa, for example, 'Clearly mentions... the "dharmic character" (*dharmatva*) of the rites performed in the temples of deities...[and he argues] that "such actions as the worship of gods... are approved as belonging to the behaviour of a well-educated man (*śiṣṭa*).'[209] Kumārila also describes deities' hypothetical – but perhaps legally efficacious – ownership: 'in a case where we find an injunction wherein the deity is mentioned in the dative case, we must explain it as meaning that 'the offering should be made to that deity, as if creating its right of ownership (*parasvatvam ivāpādayituṃ*) in the object offered'.[210]

In the centuries following Kumārila, Sanskrit jurists deployed theories of theoretical ownership to argue that, even though deities' ownership is not 'true' ownership, that a hypothetical relationship of ownership is sufficient to impose legal restrictions on the deities' 'assets'. Even if Kumārila did not view such hypothetical ownership as being legally efficacious, subsequent authors of Dharmaśāstra treatises did and they applied it to the specific context of temple endowments.

[207] Colas, 'Images and Territory of Gods', 110–17.

[208] For the development of a limited divine realism among Mīmāṃsakas, see Clooney, 'What's a God'. For Mīmāṃsakas' navigation of devotional participation (*bhakti*), see Anand Venkatkrishnan, 'Are There Atheists in Potholes? Mīmāṃsakas Debate the Path of Bhakti', in Gil Ben-Herut *et al.* (eds), *Regional Communities of Devotion in South Asia: Insiders, Outsiders, and Interlopers* (London: Routledge, 2020): 177–191; and Anand Venkatkrishnan, 'Ritual, Reflection, and Religion: The Devas of Banaras', *South Asian History and Culture* 6.1 (2015): 147–71.

[209] *Mīmāṃsādarśana*, vol. 5, p. 1656: upacāro 'pi devagrāmo devakṣetram ity upacāramātram. *Tantravārttika*, ed. by Dhuṇḍhirāja Panta (Benares: Benares Sanskrit Series No 5, 1882), 1.3.7, p. 130: dharmatvena prapannāni śiṣṭair yāni tu kāni cit / vaidikaiḥ kartṛsāmānyāt teṣāṃ dharmatvam iṣyate // pradānāni japo homo mātṛyajñādayas tathā / śakradhvajamahoyātrā devatāyataneṣu ca // & 1.3.7, p. 132: devabrāhmaṇapūjādi yat teṣām api kiṃ cana / tatreṣṭam eva dharmatvaṃ śiṣṭācāramataṃ hi tat //

[210] *Tantravārttika*, 2.2.10, pp. 484–5: yatra saṃpradānatvanirdeśaḥ tatraitad uktaṃ bhavati. parasvatvam ivāpādayituṃ taduddeśena dravyaṃ tyajed iti.

Other contemporaneous philosophical traditions engaged in a similar process of developing metaphysical descriptions of deities that relativised and accommodated the validity of customary ritual and legal practices. For example, while Sontheimer frames the Vedāntin Śaṅkarācārya's (8th century) arguments in the *Brahmasūtrabhāṣya* as a validation of the 'popular theory' of the embodiment of deities against the views of the Mīmāṃsakas, Colas deftly demonstrates that, 'Advaita tends to assimilate the notions of sacrifice and worship and acknowledges the notion of the embodiment of gods, but it also clearly denies the importance of the image as such in worship'.[211]

When discussing deities in his commentary on the *Brahmasūtras* (1.3.26–33), Śaṅkara takes up 'the opinion of Jaimini that deities, etc. have no *adhikāra*'.[212] Śaṅkara argues that the Vedas (*Mantrārthavāda*), history (*Itihāsa*), the *Purāṇas*, and conventional behaviour (*loka*) support the position that deities *do* have bodies.[213] Śaṅkara's stake is the ability of deities to be eligible for knowledge of Brahman, the imperishable absolute: 'And, because it is possible for (deities and the like) to have the "desire" for *Brahmajñāna*, etc., it is appropriate (to affirm) that they also have the *adhikāra* for the knowledge of Brahman.'[214] Sontheimer claims that 'the popular theory may derive its sanction from the Vedānta authority'.[215] This is implausible, because, like Śabara, Śaṅkara does not view a temple image (*pratimā*) as a deity in the true sense of the word. For Śaṅkara, a deity may own property and have an *adhikāra* for sacrifice, but a temple image is *not* a deity. Consequently, Śaṅkara and Śabara accept image worship and divine endowments as a *social* practice (with legal implications) while arguing that a temple image cannot be a legal owner in a primary sense of the word.

Śaṅkara theorises image worship as an activity that is more about the devotee than the deity. He describes the 'superimposition of the idea or cognition (*buddhi*) of Viṣṇu, etc. in images, etc.'.[216] Colas cites a series of further examples of the usage of this '*Viṣṇupratimānyāya*', which attest to the plausibility that Śaṅkara: 'Clearly distinguishes concrete images from the gods they represent in passages where he mentions images. A divine image has no value by itself. It receives value only

[211] For Sontheimer's interpretation of the Vedāntic arguments, see 'Religious Endowments', 21–6. For Colas', see 'Competing Hermeneutics', 155–9. Also see Francis X. Clooney, 'Śaṅkara's Theological Realism: The Meaning and Usefulness of Gods (*Devatā*) in the Uttara Mīmāṃsā Sūtra Bhāṣya', in Bradley J. Malkovsky (ed.), *New Perspectives on Advaita Vedanta: Essays in Commemoration of Professor Richard De Smet, S.J.* (Leiden: Brill, 2000): 30–50.

[212] *Brahmasūtrabhāṣya*, ed. Nārāyan Rām Āchārya (Bombay: Satyabhāmāmābāī Pandurañg, 1948), 1.3.31: devādīnām anadhikāraṃ **jaiminir ācāryo** manyante.

[213] Ibid., 1.3.32: mantrārthavādetihāsapurāṇalokebhyo devādīnāṃ vigrahavattvādyavagamād ayam adoṣa[ḥ].

[214] Ibid., 1.3.33: tataś cārthitvādisaṃbhavād upapanno devādīnām api brahmavidyāyām adhikāraḥ.

[215] Sontheimer, 'Religious Endowments', 26.

[216] *Brahmasūtrabhāṣya*, 3.3.9: yathā vā pratimādiṣu viṣṇvādibuddhyadhyāsaḥ. Cited in Colas, 'Competing Hermeneutics', 157.

through a superimposition, a mental application of the idea of a god to it.'[217] This perspective is similar to the Anglo-Hindu jurisprudential theory that 'the dedication to a deity is a compendious expression of the pious purposes for which the dedication is designed'.[218] The deity, in both perspectives, in an isometric mirror-image of the pious intentions of the worshipper. Śaṅkara, like Śabara, acknowledges the social convention of divine endowments – presumably along with its legal implications – while relativising the metaphysical nature of the deities involved and thereby bringing them into alignment with his wider philosophical project.

Even some Purāṇas take a relativised view of the metaphysical – as opposed to legal – nature of temple deities. The VDhP argues that the invocation (*āvāhana*) of deities in temples is for the benefit of the worshippers:

> God's form is two-fold: one and another. The other (form) is the Pauruṣī form, shines with the five elements. Through that (form) the supreme lord, becomes embodied everywhere. There is nothing in the world where that *Puruṣa* (form) does not exist. The invocation (*āvāhana*) of the *Puruṣa* (into a physical image) so that he is proximate is for one's own satisfaction. Similarly, the worship (of the deity) is for one's own satisfaction, oh fortunate one.[219]

Granoff interprets this and related passages as 'at best… a grudging acceptance of image worship' that reflects a discomfort in the Brāhmaṇical (and Purāṇic) tradition about the legitimacy of image-worship.[220] It also attests, however, to the fact that the Anglo-Hindu jurisprudential view of a deity as the 'compendious expression' of a worshipper's pious intentions is germane to the Purāṇic traditions and *not* a colonial appropriation of Mīmāṃsaka arguments. Even early Purāṇic thinkers believed that a deity's worshipers were the beneficiaries of temple consecration – and, presumably, endowment.

Finally, in his *Nyāyakusumāñjali* (and its auto-commentary), the 11th-century logician (*Naiyāyika*), Udayana, provides another example of the argument that image worship is primarily to the benefit of a deity's devotees.[221] Udayana examines Vedic sacrifices (*iṣṭa*) and charities (*pūrta*). Udayana argues that these rites perfect (*saṃskṛta*) the agent of the rite, rather than the divine object.[222] On the one hand, Udayana endorses a limited presence of a deity in a temple image, but

[217] Colas, 'Competing Hermeneutics', 158–9. The other passages cited are Śaṅkara's commentary on *Brahmasūtras*, 4.1.3 & 5.

[218] See Note 38.

[219] VDhP, 3.108.10–11: devasya dvividhā mūrtiḥ parā caiva tathāparā / pārāyāḥ pauruṣī mūrtiḥ pañcabhūtavirājitā // tayā samūrtir bhavati sarvagaḥ parameśvaraḥ / puruṣeṇa vinā loke na kiñ cid iha vidyate // & 17: āvāhanaṃ svatṛptyarthaṃ puruṣasya yathāsthitam / tathāpy arcā mahābhāga svatuṣṭyarthaṃ prayojanam // Also see Granoff, 'Reading Between the Lines', 401–3, for analysis of this passage and VDhP, 3.46, where similar arguments are made.

[220] See Granoff, 'Reading Between the Lines', 402.

[221] For God (Īśvara) in Nyāya philosophy, see John Vattanky, 'Aspects of Early Nyāya Theism', *Journal of Indian Philosophy* 6.4 (1978): 393–404.

[222] Colas, 'Competing Hermeneutics', 161–2. These translations are Colas'.

he also notes that: 'According to others one must interpret [worshipfulness of the image] as a state of (being) an object of acknowledgement of what has been long worshipped (*pūrvapūrvapūjitapratyabhijñānaviṣaya*) and of [being] an object of acknowledgement of what has been consecrated (*pratiṣṭhitapratyabhijñānaviṣaya*).'[223]

The broad point of all of these examples is that virtually every Sanskrit textual tradition developed theories of divine images that accommodated the legal and cultural reality of divine endowments. Different textual traditions offered metaphysical accounts of deities that aligned with the fundamental principles of their philosophical systems, but they all accepted the socio-legal reality of deities as owners (be that ownership figurative, conventional, or otherwise). For Mīmāṃsakas like Śabara and Kumārila, because deities are merely liturgical phonemes, they cannot 'own' assets in a literal way. Nevertheless, society treats deities *as if* they are owners. While this is an acceptable, even Dharmic practice with legal implications according under a Dharmaśāstric theory of Equity, it doesn't mean that deities are entitled to perform sacrifices.

For Vedāntins like Śaṅkara, deities may own assets, but temple images are not the deities they represent and cannot, therefore, have ownership of endowed assets. Rather, worshipping an image at a temple entails the superimposition of the cognition (*buddhi*) of a deity onto the image by a worshipper. For Śaṅkara, presumably, gifts to deities may therefore be viewed – as they are in Anglo-Hindu jurisprudence – as the gift of an asset that is coloured by the particular intention that they be used to support worship of a particular deity. Alternatively, in some of the Purāṇas, image worship is framed as act of divine grace for the benefit of devotees.

Finally, in Nyāya, one finds a somewhat circuitous view of temple images as being the object of human knowledge of ritual consecration that enables worship. All of these views, however, can and did flourish within the Dharmaśāstric view that, whatever be the metaphysical explanation of temple images, divine endowments are recognised as a form of conventional (*sāmayika*) or supplemental (*pāribhāṣika*) law. The enormous success of Sanskrit jurisprudential theories of Equity as the lynchpin of the practical regulation of religious endowments in pre-colonial India was precisely its ability to accommodate *all* of the metaphysical perspectives of deities that have just been discussed.

In fact, some early modern Dharmaśāstrins also took the view that the worship of deities was primarily of benefit to their devotees. In his discussion of the worship of Viṣṇu during the Ekādaśī festival, Raghunandana quotes 'Jamadagni' to the effect that: 'It is for the sake of rites of the worshippers that the *(para)brahman*,

[223] Ibid., 163–4.

which is made of consciousness, which cannot be measured, which is imperishable, and which has no body, is postulated to have form (in an image).'[224] An almost identical passage to Jamadagni's also appears, unattributed, at the start of Śūlapāṇi's *Devapratiṣṭhātattva*. This passage had a profound impact on the proposition in Anglo-Hindu jurisprudence, beginning with its invocation by Justice Mookerjee that Hindu deities are the legal personification of the pious intentions of their founders and worshippers in in ***Bhupati***.[225] A very similar passage from the *Rāmatāpanīya Upaniṣad* also appears in Kamalākara's *Pūrtakamalākara*.[226] This demonstrates that Sanskrit jurisprudence takes a metaphysical view of deities that is very much in concert with Mīmāṃsā, Vedānta, the Purāṇas, etc.

1.6.2.iii Divine endowments in medieval Dharmaśāstra

Medieval authors of Dharmaśāstric commentaries generally denied that deities owned assets dedicated to them in the primary sense of the word. These authors typically adopted Śabara and Kumārila's Mīmāṃsā theory of deities' ownership as a customary or figurative practice. Although some medieval Sanskrit jurists took ostensibly 'iconophobic' stances that downplayed or rejected the relevance of certain Dharmaśāstric dicta to temple endowments, many jurists accepted that deities' figurative ownership imposes fiduciary duties on those who take possession of deities' assets. Additionally, in the case of deities' animals (*devapaśus*), these authors either accepted deities' ownership in a primary sense, or they described, in limited detail, the legal arrangements of dedicating an animal, in trust, to a deity. Although the jurisprudence of divine endowments in medieval Dharmaśāstra commentarial literature is complex and sometimes uneven, one cannot say that Dharmaśāstric literature endorses temple priests' unrestricted ownership of temple endowments. The *specific* rules that regulated divine endowments fell under the category of Dharmaśāstric Equity while the *general principles* of deities' ownership were *described* (rather than prescribed) as a species of Dharmaśāstric Trust.

[224] *Smṛtitattva*, ed. by Jīvānanda Vidyāsāgara, 2nd edn., Vol. 2 (Calcutta: Siddheśvara Press, 1885) (*Ekādaśītattva*), 58: **jamadagniḥ.** cinmayasyāprameyasya niṣkalasyāśarīriṇaḥ / upāsakāṇāṃ kāryyārthaṃ brahmaṇo rūpakalpanā // The phrase appears in the *Rāmāyaṇatāpanīyopaniṣad* (1.7), a Vaiṣṇava Upaniṣad on the *Artharvaveda* dated, variously, between the 11th and 16th centuries CE. For the text, see Albrecht Weber (ed.), *Die Rāma-Tāpanīya-Upanishad* (Berlin: Königl. Akademie der Wissenschaften, 1864). For an analysis of the influence of this passage in legal history (especially the Ayodhyā dispute), see Christopher T. Fleming, 'Dharmaśāstra and the Legal Personality of Deities in the Ayodhya Verdicts (2010 & 2019)', *Contemporary South Asia* 32.1 (2023): 26–39.

[225] ***Bhupati Nath Smrititirtha v Ram Lal Maitra*** ¶61 [Mookerjee, J].

[226] Kamalākarabhaṭṭa quotes a verse (1.13) from the same text in the *Pūrtakamalāra*, Bhandarkar Oriental Research Institute Ms. No 838 fol. 56a: **rāmatāpanīye**: sarvagasthasya devasya vigraho ya[n]trakalpanā // vinā mantreṇa cet pūjā devatā na prasīdati //

In his comments on Yāj 3.258 (concerning the penance of gifting to Brāhmaṇas), Viśvarūpa considers whether such gifts come with concomitant duties for the recipient. Viśvarūpa invokes Manu 11.20, 'the learned regard the property of persons given to performing sacrifices as the deities' property', and notes that:

> That (*devasva*) is not the property of the deities, for, if that were the case, the sacrifice would not exist. For, a sacrificer could not abandon the deities' property (in favor of the deities). Thus, the sort (of property) which, having been dedicated to the deities (*devān uddiśya*), is abandoned, is '*devasva*.' What is shown by that is that only the ownership in assets for those (Brāhmaṇas who are) devoted to sacrifice is primary/literal (*mukhya*) and (the ownership) is secondary/figurative (*gauṇa*) for others. And, therefore, that (asset) which is acquired merely through acceptance, (which is) a wage (and) whose purpose is merely enjoyment and pleasure (rather than sacrifice) is '*asurasva*' and they (the Brāhmaṇa-recipients) have no ownership in it – this is the intention (of the verse of Manu).[227]

Effectively, Viśvarūpa holds that ownership in a 'primary' or 'literal' (*mukhya*) sense applies *only* to the very limited context of assets held by a Brāhmaṇa for the specified purpose of conducting sacrifices. Every other instance of ownership – the overwhelming majority – is 'secondary' or 'figurative' (*gauṇa*). Under Viśvarūpa's scheme, *all* legal relations regarding assets – purchase, sale, deposit, mortgage, gift, and even divine endowments – entail *secondary*, rather than *primary* ownership. Viśvarūpa acknowledges as much when he notes, in further comments on Yāj 3.258, that, 'because the ownership of unvirtuous Brahmins is merely figurative (*aupacārika*), it does not entail a grievous sin to steal from them.'[228] For Viśvarūpa, it is still a sin (just not a grievous one) and a criminal offence (a grievous one) to steal from an unvirtuous Brāhmaṇa. Furthermore, an unvirtuous Brāhmaṇa is an 'owner' for all practical legal purposes. Therefore, Viśvarūpa, like Śabara the Mīmāṃsaka, concedes that deities' ownership, like other conventional or figurative ownerships are legally efficacious – just not in the specific context of Yāj 3.258.

Bhāruci makes a very similar argument in his commentary on Manu 11.26:

> That (asset) set apart, having appointed it for the purpose of the deity, is '*devasva*.' In the present topic, it is that which is begged for the purpose of sacrifice, not anything else. And that being the case, that well-known use in the world of '*devasva*' (as something actually owned by the deities) is not used here, because it contradicts the present topic and because the deities have no *adhikāra* since they have no 'mine-ness.'

[227] *The Yājñavalkyasmṛti with the Commentary Bālakrīda of Visvarūpāchārya*, two parts., ed. T. Ganapati Sastri (Trivandrum: Government Press, 1922–24), on Yāj 3.258: na tāvad devānāṃ tat svaṃ, tathā sati yāga eva na syāt. na hi devasvaṃ yajamānaḥ śaknuyāt tyaktum. ato yathāvidhaṃ devān uddiśya tyajyate, tathāvidhaṃ devasvam. ato yāgaśīlānām eva dravye svatvaṃ mukhyam, gauṇam itareṣām ity etad evānena darśitam. tataś cāyajvanāṃ yad vittaṃ parigrahamātreṇa sāṃvyavahārikaṃ kāmabhogamātraupayikaṃ tad asurasvam, tatra teṣāṃ svatvaṃ nāstīty abhiprāyaḥ... See Manu, 11.20, for the verse that Viśvarūpa is assuming here: yad dhanaṃ yajñaśīlānāṃ devasvaṃ tad vidur budhāḥ / ayajvanāṃ tu yad vittam asurasvaṃ taducyate //

[228] Ibid.: nirguṇabrāhmaṇānām aupacārikatvāt svatvasya na tadapaharaṇe mahāpātakayogaḥ.

> The (use of) '*devasva*' seen in the śāstra can be said to be '*devasva*' only on account of the dedication (of assets) at the time of offering. And the time of the enjoyment of the deity is momentary. After the enjoyment has ceased (that asset) cannot be called '*devasva*.' Therefore, whatever has been begged for the sake of the sacrifice should be used for sacrifice. Nothing should be set aside for one's own enjoyment. This exhortatory statement with reference to the breaking of a restriction applies to that fool who does not use everything for sacrifice.[229]

Like Viśvarūpa, Bhāruci recognises that, outside of the context of the Dharmaśāstric dictum at hand, people use the term *devasva* to refer to assets owned by deities. Bhāruci gives no indication that this 'well-known', popular usage isn't legally efficacious. For Bhāruci, this legal efficacy derives from Equity rather than from Manu 11.26. Nevertheless, Bhāruci also accepts an additional, purely śāstric (i.e., non-Equitable) view of divine ownership as a real, if momentary ownership in sacrificial assets that imposes clear moral duties on the Brāhmaṇas that appropriate those assets.

In his commentary on the same verse of Manu, Medhātithi offers a similar, but more sophisticated explanation of divine trusts.

> That asset which has been abandoned, having been dedicated to the deities for the purpose of performing sacrifices, etc, is '*devasva*', because of the impossibility of the deities' participating in the relationship of property-and-property-owner in the primary (*mukhya*) sense. For, a deity does not use an asset according to (its) desire and they are not observed in the activity of protecting (their assets). In the world, 'property' (*sva*) is used in this sense. Therefore, that which is dedicated to a deity with the phrase 'this is not mine, this is for the deity', is '*devasva*.' And that (property) is enjoined for deities such as Agni for the (purpose of) sacrifices such as the Darśapūrṇamāsa (and) only through the well-known custom of virtuous people (can it be used for the purpose of) sacrifices to Durgā, which are secondary usages.[230]

Medhātithi invokes what, at the time, was a common, Mīmāṃsā-inflected theory of ownership in terms of 'use as desired' (*yatheṣṭhaviniyoga*), but it is important to note that this definition applies to 'primary' (*mukhya*) ownership only. While

[229] *Manu-Śāstra-Vivaraṇam, a Commentary on the Manusmṛti by Bhāruci*, ed. S. Jagannatha. (Mysuru: Oriental Research Institute, 2020), on Manu 11.26 (11.25 in Bhāruci's text): devatārthaṃ yat prakalpya sthāpyate tad devasvam. prakaraṇasāmarthyād yajñārthaṃ bhikṣitam. nānyat... evaṃ ca sati yad idaṃ loke prasiddhaṃ devasvaṃ tan nehābhidhīyate, prakaraṇavirodhāt. devatānāṃ ca mamatā nāsty anadhikārāt. śāstradṛṣṭaṃ ca yad devasvaṃ tat saṃpradānakāla evoddeśasāmarthyād devasvam iti śakyate vaktum. kṣaṇikaś cāsau devatopabhogakālaḥ, nivṛtte ca tasmin devatopabhoge devasvaṃ tad ity aśakyaṃ vyapadeṣṭum. evaṃ ca sati yajñārthaṃ bhikṣitaṃ sarvaṃ yajña evopayojyam. na kiṃcid ātmopabhogāya sthāpanīyam. yas tu mohān na sarvam upayuṅkte, tasya niyamavyatikrame 'yaṃ nindārthavādaḥ.

[230] *Manubhāṣya* on Manu 11.26: devān uddiśya yāgādikriyārthaṃ dhanaṃ yad utsṛṣṭaṃ tad devasvam, mukhyasya svasvāmisaṃbandhasya devānām asaṃbhavāt. na hi devatā icchayā dhanaṃ niyuñjate. na ca paripālanavyāpāras tāsāṃ dṛśyate. svaṃ ca loke tādṛśam ucyate. tasmād devoddeśena yad uktam 'nedaṃ mama devatāyā idam' iti tad devasvam. tac ca darśapūrṇamāsādiyāgeṣv agnyādidevatābhyaś coditaṃ. śiṣṭasamācāraprasiddhyaiva gauṇopāyadurgāyāgādiṣu.

Medhātithi argues that Manu 11.26 does not apply to temple endowments, he acknowledges, rather than rejects, that customary socio-legal practice involves the dedication of assets to temple images. In the same passage, Medhātithi acknowledges that 'property connected with images of Viṣṇu, etc., is referred to in the world as "*devasva*".'[231] He notes that: 'According to custom (*samācāra*) there may be "*devasva*" (on the part of temple images), but, nevertheless, there is no ownership (*svasvāmibhāva*). And the propriety of using "property" (with regard to temple images) according to the aforesaid manner has been shown in (my commentary on) the second (chapter of Manu).'[232]

Medhātithi connects these jurisprudential themes in his comments on Manu 2.189, where he describes (without rejecting) a customary theory of divine ownership as an artificial (*kalpita*) and secondary (but efficacious) socio-legal practice:

> But (some) desire to use 'deity' to refer to the image (of the deity) with reference to the section on punishment. Otherwise, there would be a breaking of the restriction. The '*devadravya*' in such (Dharmaśāstric statements as *Nāradasmṛti* 14.15), 'the property of deities, Brāhmaṇas, and kings is known as the highest (class of property)' is connected with an artificial state of owner and property on the part of images whose divine form is artificial (*kalpita*). For, deities do not have the state of owner and property. Because of the impossibility of the primary meaning (of property), the secondary meaning (of property with reference to deities) is accepted.[233]

Medhātithi accepts that the ascription of artificial (*kalpita*) ownership and artificial divine personality to temple images is legally efficacious in the context of *Nāradasmṛti* 14.15, but not in the context of Manu 11.26. The key distinction is that *Nāradasmṛti* 14.15 refers to *criminal sanctions* (*daṇḍa*) for the secular crime of theft, whereas Manu 11.26 refers to expiation (*prāyaścitta*) for the moral *sin* of violating a particular śāstric injunction. Effectively, then, Medhātithi accepts that temple images are treated legal persons and legal owners for the purposes of criminal and civil law (in which theories of Equity can play a prominent role) but *not* for the very circumscribed purpose of śāstric dicta such as Manu 11.26, which enjoin expiation on the part of certain Brāhmaṇas.

In short, Medhātithi, like Bhāruci and Śabara, *accommodates* rather than *rejects* the socio-legal practice of divine endowments. Yes, he rejects deities' ownership of assets in the *primary* sense of the word – saving that for expiation in very particular sacrificial contexts – but he explicitly endorses the legal efficacy of deities' artificial ownership in *legal* contexts. Sontheimer is therefore mistaken

[231] Ibid.: nanu caturbhujādipratimāsaṃbandhi loke devasvam ucyate.

[232] Ibid.: atha samācārato devasvaṃ bhavatu, svasvāmibhāvas tāvan nāsti | yathoktena ca prakāreṇa svavyavahāropapattir iti śiṣṭaṃ dvitīye || 11.26 ||

[233] Ibid., on Manu 2.189: daṇḍādhikāre tu pratikṛtiviṣayam eva devatāvyavahāram icchanti. anyathā vyavasthābhaṅgaḥ syāt. kalpitadevatārūpāṇāṃ pratikṛtīnāṃ kalpitenaiva svasvāmibhāvena yat saṃbandhi tad eva 'devabrāhmaṇarājñāṃ tu dravyaṃ vijñeyam uttamam' (*Nāradasmṛti* 14.15) ityādiṣu devadravyam. na hi devatānāṃ svasvāmibhāvo 'sti, mukhyārthāsaṃbhavād gauṇa evārtho grāhyaḥ.

in assuming that Medhātithi's perspective is 'destructive of the popular view' of deities as legal owners.[234] Medhātithi was not, as Sontheimer suggests, protecting Brāhmaṇical entitlements to temple assets. Rather, he protected temple assets through a theory of artificial ownership that preserved the Mīmāṃsā metaphysical view of deities are mere phonemes.

The Bengali commentator, Śūlapāṇi, describes divine ownership in similar terms: 'The state of being a deity is the state of being the dedicatee of abandonment according to the Vedas and the state of being a dedicatee is the state of being the content of a super-imposed cognition: "This is his [i.e., the deity's]"'.[235] Śūlapāṇi's comments were limited to the context of funerary rituals (*śrāddhas*), but they became a touchstone for more substantive legal discussions by subsequent jurists and logicians (*Navya-Naiyāyikas*).[236] Śūlapāṇi's arguments appear repeatedly in the various sections (called *tattvas*) of Raghunandana's comprehensive *Smṛtitattva*. Raghunanda, for his part, employed Śūlapāṇi's theory of divine ownership as a 'suppositious knowledge' to analyse concrete legal instances of trusts. For example, when describing the dedication of a reservoir in his *Ekādaśītattva*, Raghunandana argues that, 'According to the *Śrāddhaviveka*, "sacrifice" is the abandonment of assets with the deity as the dedicatee. "Deity" is the state of the dedicatee of an (act of) abandonment (as) enjoined in the scriptures. The state of being a dedicatee is the state of being the content of a suppositious (cognition): "this is his"'.[237]

Sontheimer asserts that 'Raghunandana makes an exception in the case of the land on which the idol stands' and concedes that the deity was 'the true recipient of land' in accordance with a 'popular view' in that one exceptional case.[238] In fact, Raghunandana acknowledges a wide array of gifting practices in which deities are the primary recipient (*sampradāna*). Raghunandana lists a series of gifts to Viṣṇu (as part of the Ekādaśī festival) but clearly states, in line with Śūlapāṇi, that 'because of the non-production of the deity's ownership, the word "gift" here is secondary, in the sense that they are acquired for their (the deities') Dharmas such as worship and sacrificial fees'.[239] In Raghunandana's estimation these gifts, and those listed in his analysis of 'gifts wherein the deities are the primary recipient', are expropriated

234 Sontheimer, 'Religious Endowments', 29–30.

235 *Śrāddhaviveka*, ed. Mathurānātha Tarkaratna (Calcutta: Prākṛta Press, 1880), 11: devatātvañ ca vedamayatyāgoddeśyatvaṃ uddeśyatvañ ca tasyedam ityāropajñānaviṣayatvam.

236 For Śūlapāṇi's influence in Navya-Nyāya see Ethan Kroll, *A Logical Approach to Law* (PhD Dissertation, University of Chicago, 2010), 167 fn. 49 (Jāyarāma) *Kārakavāda* (*Vyākhyā*), fo. 6a–6b.

237 *Smṛtitattva* (*Ekādaśītattva*), 85: tathā ca **śrāddhavivekaḥ.** devatoddeśyakadravyatyāgo yāgaḥ. devatātvañ ca vedameyatyāgoddeśyatvam. uddeśyatvañ ca tasyedam ity āropaviṣayatvam iti.

238 Sontheimer, 'Religious Endowments', 32.

239 *Smṛtitattva* (*Ekādaśītattva*), 58: devasya s[v]attvānutpādanāt dānapadaṃ gauṇaṃ pūjādidakṣiṇādi taddharmaprāptyartham.

by Brāhmaṇas. He writes, glossing a verse from the *Skāndapurāṇa* (cited in the *Dānaratnākara*) that:

> Something that is fit for donation, after having been abandoned, and having been dedicated to Śiva or to Viṣṇu, should be given to a Brāhmaṇa. According to the *Matsyasūkta*, 'gifts, having been given to the deity and ritual fees that one would give to the deity, all this should be given to a Brāhmaṇa, otherwise they would be useless'.[240]

Raghunandana states that, even when deities are the recipient of a gift, Brāhmaṇas take possession of the gifted asset. Nevertheless, Raghunandana follows this statement with a series of cautionary exhortations that enjoin the recipient not to appropriate the deities' property for their own uses. Furthermore, he uses a passage from the *Pūjāratnākara* to describe the fiduciary duties that these Brāhmaṇas owe to their deity.[241] Additionally, S.C. Bagchi records a passage from the Caṇḍīcaraṇa edition of the *Ekādaśītattva*, wherein Raghunandana justifies the legal efficacy of cautionary statements about appropriating deities' property, by arguing that, '"deities' assets" are assets which possess "propertyness" described by ownership hypothetically attributed to the deity'.[242] The language is abstruse (and tinged with *Navya-Nyāya* terminology), but the meaning is clear: even though Brāhmaṇas take *possession* of assets presented to deities, the deities' hypothetical ownership imposes clear duties on these priests to employ those assets for the deities' benefit. All of this, accords with the views of Śabara, Bhāruci, Viśvarūpa, and Medhātithi.

Furthermore, several medieval and early modern Sanskrit jurists explicitly endorsed the deities' *primary* ownership over particular types of assets. In his analysis of Manu 8.242, a verse exempting 'deities' animals' (*devapaśus*) from noxal liability, Medhātithi argues that:

> They say that 'deities' are images of Viṣṇu, Śiva, etc., that are installed in structures (made of) brick, etc. Their (the deities') animals are (animals) that have been abandoned, having been dedicated to them. Because of the existence of the relationship between owner and property on the part of the deities and animals (and) because of the absence of the state of owner and property on the part of another person, this law applies to (animals that) adorn temples but not to those (animals) kept in temples by their herdsmen for the sake of giving milk, etc. Since the herdsmen use (these

[240] Ibid. (*Maṭhapratiṣṭhātattva*), 630: tatpratipattim āha **dānaratnākare...** yat kaścid deyaṃ dānārhaṃ vastu īśānam uddiśya tyaktaṃ viṣṇave vā tyaktaṃ paścād brāhmaṇāya pradīyate... tathā ca **matsyasūktam:** deve dattvā tu dānāni deve dadyāc ca dakṣiṇām. tatsarvaṃ brāhmaṇe dadyād anyathā niṣphalaṃ bhavet.

[241] Ibid., 631–2. visarjanaṃ tadīyadravyapratipattivyavahāraḥ atra nīrājanavidhim āha **pūjāratnākare devīpurāṇam**.

[242] Bagchi, *Juristic Personality*, 56: devaniṣṭhālīkasvāmitvanirūpitasvatvavad dravyaṃ.

> animals) for the sake of those deities, the herdsmen are the owners with reference (to those animals).[243]

Medhātithi concedes that the otherwise ownerless animals dedicated to temples belong to the resident deity. This is not an isolated instance in Sanskrit jurisprudence. Nīlakaṇṭhabhaṭṭa explains 'deities' animals' in a similar way:

> One should give a milk-cow to Śiva or to Viṣṇu. In gifts to the deities, the deity alone is the primary recipient and not a Brāhmaṇa. And, according to the *Dānasaukhya*, that given (cow) should be placed in this or that deity's temple in the southern portion (of the temple).[244]

So, to the extent that Mīmāṃsā philosophical theories are applied to the phenomenon of deities' ownership, they are employed to *justify*, and to *protect*, as a unique form of *trust*, rather than to *reject* the endowments described in the Purāṇas.

The incorporation of Purāṇic Temple Hinduism culminates in Anantadeva II's *Rājadharmakaustubha* (17th century). Here, Anantadeva offers a legal description of the medieval and modern phenomenon of a sovereign endowing a deity with the ownership of their kingdom and ruling in the name of that deity.[245] Anantadeva inverts the conventional Dharmaśāstric and Purāṇic account: rather than enjoining kings to endow and protect temples, Anantadeva argues that a king is a king by virtue of their building and endowing temples. The Crown's ownership derives from a divine ownership in this system. Anantadeva opens the *Rājadharmakaustubha* not with the coronation (*abhiṣeka*) of the king, but, rather, with the construction of temples and cites as described in the *Viṣṇudharmottarapurāṇa*'s section on temple endowment:

> 'Cities filled with temples should be built in Kaliyuga by kings who wish to obtain heaven.' With reference to this, the definition of cities will be discussed in the fifth

[243] *Manubhāṣya*, on Manu 8.242. devapaśavo… veṣṭakādikūṭasthāpitā hariharādīnāṃ pratikṛtayo devā ucyanti. teṣāṃ paśavaḥ. tān uddiśya kenacid utsṛṣṭāḥ… devānāṃ paśūnāṃ ca svasvāmisaṃbandhasya saṃbhavāt, puruṣasvāmibhāvasyāsaṃbhavāt, devāyatanamaṇḍanānām caiṣa dharmaḥ. na tu tatpālakair vāhadohādyarthaṃ ye devagṛheṣu dhāryante. yataḥ pālakā eva teṣāṃ devānām arthaṃ viniyuñjate. atas tatra pālakā eva svāminaḥ. Devaṇṇabhaṭṭa, in his *Smṛticandrikā* (*Vyavahārakāṇḍa*) acknowledges that deities do not own animals endowed to temples for stipulated purposes, but he notes that such animals can be given (presumably a herdsman) with the stipulation that their milk be used for the deity's benefit: devapaśavo hi devatāpratimādīnāṃ kṣīrasnānādyarthaṃ taduddeśena dattāḥ, na ca tatra vastutaḥ svasvāmibhāvo 'stīti. We find many instances of these types of purpose trusts in epigraphic records.

[244] *Dānamayūkha*, ed. by Ratna Gopal Bhatta (Benares: Chowkhamba Sanskrit Series, Kāśī Saṃskṛta Granthamālā, no. 44, 1909), 186: śivāya viṣṇave vāpi yas tu dadyāt payasvinīm… devatābhyo dāne devatāiva saṃpradānaṃ na brāhmaṇaḥ dattaṃ ca tadtaddevatāyatane dakṣiṇabhāge sthāpyam iti **dānasaukhye**. The *Dānasaukhya* is a section of the *Ṭoḍarānanda*, a digest compiled under the patronage of Toḍaramalla, Akbar's finance minister (and patron of the Kāśīviśveśvara Temple) in the late 16th century. For more information on the text and its patron, see Ludo Rocher, *Vyavahārasaukhya: The Treatise on Legal Procedure in the Ṭodarānanda Composed at the Instance of Ṭoḍaramalla During the Reign of Akbar* (Florence: Società Editrice Fiorentina, 2016).

[245] See Note 94.

> chapter (of this work). And the making of those cities, just as they will be accomplished with a beautiful new form, that very act constitutes a proprietary relationship with it, because: 1) of the use of the verbal root 'to do' in the verbal root of acceptance; and 2) because the authors of śāstras describe only the *utpādya* as the direct object of the verb 'to cause to be' (*bhāvayati*), which is a synonym of 'to do' as well as the *amskara* of something that is immutable.[246]

The *Viṣṇudharmottarapurāṇa* enjoins the king to build cities filled with temples as a sort of divine right of kings over territories. Anantadeva uses this as a segue to discuss the origins of royal sovereignty:

> Thus, in the *Bhāgavata(purāṇa)*, manifold ownership of the world is said to be the reward for the consecration (of deities): 'through consecration lordship of the entire world.' Or else, in the Kaliyuga, the state of having previously built a temple for a deity is enjoined for a king whenever they wish to take ownership of a particular (temple).[247]

Sanskrit jurists tended to view the Crown as possessing ownership over only the usufruct of their kingdoms' lands, rather than owning an unfettered superior interest in all land.[248] Anantadeva's perspective appears to be that all ownership rights enjoyed by Crown stem from the king's participation in Temple Hinduism. We shall see in the following chapter that this was a common practice in medieval and early modern India. Anantadeva enjoins that 'certainly, the construction of temples should be done before coronation by one who desires ownership over the world.'[249] Over more than a millennium of Indian history, numerous kings followed this injunction and founded temples whose deities – often named after their founding king – bestowed ownership and overlordship over South Asia (or portions of it) as a form of divine grace (*prasāda*).

1.7 Conclusion

This chapter demonstrated that we can uncover a more substantial and internally consistent jurisprudence of Equity and Trusts in Sanskrit literature than has been appreciated in previous scholarship. Admittedly, this jurisprudence is spread

246 *Rājadharmakaustubha*, ed. Kamala Kṛṣṇa Smṛtitīrtha (Baroda: Oriental Institute, Gaekwad Oriental Series 122, 1935), 4: devatāveśmapūrāṇi nagarāṇi kalau yuge / kartavyāni mahīpālaiḥ svargalokam abhīpsubhiḥ // tatra nagaralakṣaṇaṃ pañcame prakaraṇe vakṣyate. tatkaraṇañ ca yathābhinavarūpeṇa sampādanaṃ tathā svasvāmikatvenāpi tatrāpi svīkaraṇam iti karoteḥ prayogāt karotiparyyāyasya bhāvayateḥ karmatvenotpādyasyaivāpy avikāryyasaṃskārasyāpi śāstrakṛdbhir nirūpaṇāc ca.

247 Ibid., 4–5: ata eva **śrībhāgavate** pratiṣṭhāphalatvenaiva sarvaprakārakabhūsvāmyam uktam. pratiṣṭhayā sārvabhaumyaṃ. tatra tatra svasvāmikatvaṃ vā cikīrṣuṃ rājānaṃ prati kalau nimittadevatāveśmapūrvakatvaṃ vidhīyate.

248 See Lubin, 'Theory and Practice', 810–14 Also see Kāṇe, *History of Dharmaśāstra*, Vol. 2.2., 865–9.

249 *Rājadharmakaustubha*, 5: abhiṣekeṇa bhuvaḥ svāmyam icchatāpy avaśyaṃ tatpūrvaṃ prāsādādinirmāṇaṃ kartavyam.

diffusely in Sanskrit juridical, philosophical, and devotional texts. Nevertheless, by sifting through these materials I have discovered many hitherto unexplored passages that throw new light on the Sanskrit jurisprudence of Equity and Trusts. Taken collectively and synchronically, these gleanings reveal the existence of several ancient, consistent, and nuanced Sanskrit jurisprudential principles that have been highly relevant to the practical legal administration of religious endowments during many different periods of Indian history. There is, therefore, an identifiable Sanskrit jurisprudence of Hindu temples and such jurisprudence has had and continues to have a substantial bearing upon the actual historical practice of law regarding Hindu temples in various periods of Indian history. This jurisprudence was *neither* at odds with a presupposed 'popular' tradition (as Sontheimer and others argue) or a colonial fabrication (as Birla and others aver). Rather, this jurisprudence was a synthetic accommodation of the socio-legal reality of Purāṇic Temple Hinduism (and its attendant institutional phenomena) within the metaphysical parameters of Mīmāṃsā, Vedānta, and Nyāya.

At its core, these jurisprudential themes are analogous to those which one would associate with Courts of Equity in English jurisprudence: trusts, guardianship, and the administration of the estates of legal incompetents. The core of the Sanskrit jurisprudence of Equity and Trusts, much like the English jurisprudence of Equity and Trusts, is the Crown's duty, as *parens patriae*, to protect the property and legal interests of its most vulnerable subjects (including religious institutions).

In the Sanskrit jurisprudential context, the Crown's *parens patriae* jurisdiction extended to an Indic form of Equity as a form of supplemental law (*pāribhāṣikadharma*). We saw that in Greco-Roman and English jurisprudence, Equity, in its Aristotelian sense, entails corrective, supplemental rules which enable the formal codified system of laws and judicature to promote just outcomes. The precise meaning of Greco-Roman and English Equity has been the subject of continuous debate for centuries, and it would be unfair for me to assert that Sanskrit jurisprudence articulates an exact analogue to those contested theories of Equity. Nevertheless, theories of supplemental law (*pāribhāṣikadharma*) functioned in a similar way to the kind of corrective law administered by the Court of Chancery – they enabled the effective administration of trusts and other legal phenomena that involve fiduciary relationships.

The Sanskrit jurisprudence of divine endowments, however diffuse, is consistent: temples and other religious endowments are consistently afforded royal protection; their assets are managed by guardians who owe fiduciary duties to those institutions; various secular and religious communities have the right to establish the conventional legal rules which govern the management of their endowments (either through writing or through the intentions of a founder); when guardians breach their fiduciary duties, the Crown must hold them accountable for breach of trust; deities share an analogous relationship with women, minors, and other protected categories of individuals; and, whatever the metaphysical explanation used to explain it, deities' juridical personhood (their nominal ownership of assets) is recognised as a customary (and therefore legal) convention.

Recovering this jurisprudence enables us to problematise the common scholarly assumption – typified by Richard Davis and Sontheimer – that popular, customary conventions and elite, Sanskrit jurisprudence were, and are, diametrically opposed. The Dharmaśāstric tradition, at every historical level, *accommodates* image worship within its wider jurisprudence of Equity and Trusts. It is true that several authors of Dharmaśāstra commentaries, such as Bhāruci, Viśvarūpa, and Medhātithi, adopt Mīmāṃsā-inspired arguments about deities' lack of ownership (*svatva*) in the primary (*mukhya*) sense of the word. Sometimes, these authors argue that particular Dharmaśāstric dicta do not apply to deities' property (*devasva*). Nevertheless, all of these authors accept and describe the conventional social practice of creating and regulating divine endowments. Admittedly, many of these authors do not supply specific legal rules that outline the administration of divine endowments. They are, however, consistent in their argument that the specific rules that govern the administration of religious endowments – including deities' assets at temples – are supplemental (*pāribhāṣikadharma*) or conventional (*sāmayika*) laws that fall under the Dharmaśāstric rubric of Equity.

Dharmaśāstra provides jurisprudence (the intellectual principles of law) rather than positive law (discrete rules). Scholars such Sontheimer, Derrett, and Birla seem to have mistakenly taken the Sanskrit jurists' failure to provide positive legal rules for religious endowments as a hostile rejection of temple-based Hindu religiosity. Again, this would be a gross misreading of Sanskrit jurisprudence. On one level, Brāhmaṇical anxiety about image worship appears, perhaps ironically, in the very Purāṇic sources that extol the merits of image worship. On another level, the Mīmāṃsā treatises that purportedly reject the ownership of deities furnish some of the most detailed legal accounts concerning the practical operation of temple trusts (involving servants who enact the wishes of deities in return for compensation). Thus, we can safely dispense with Derrett's (and the Dakor temple priests') argument that gifts to deities are *entirely* free of secular obligation. We can also dispense with Bagchi's insistence that deities' endowments can be assimilated to purpose trusts. Juridical personality for Hindu deities forms a ubiquitous facet of Dharmaśāstra.

Dispensing with this false dichotomy in the context of Sanskrit philology also enables us to attend to Ritu Birla, Deepa Das Acevedo, and Arjun Appadurai's contention that the creation of the Anglo-Hindu jurisprudence of religious and charitable trust involved, through an overemphasis on Mīmāṃsā, a more-or-less complete elision of pre-colonial practices. Undoubtedly, the introduction and evolution of Anglo-Hindu law over the course of the colonial period witnessed considerable distortions of pre-colonial legal practices – especially regarding limitation and the capacity of a fiduciary to alienate temple assets and create derivative tenures. These distortions, however, must be (as we shall see in the fourth chapter of this monograph) ascribed largely to the judicial introduction of English theories of Equity and Trusts and civil procedure to India rather than to the philosophical predilections of Mīmāṃsakas and Dharmaśāstrins. Shifting our search for explanations of these distortions from looking *within* Sanskrit jurisprudence to looking *outwards* towards English theories of Equity and Trusts will enable us to offer greater nuance to a legal history that lies at the heart of some of India's most important contemporary legal cases.

Having outlined the core principles of Equity and Trusts in Sanskrit jurisprudence, I turn to the second core task of this monograph: tracing the application of these jurisprudential principles to the practical legal regulation of religious endowments under a wide array of different political regimes during various epochs of Indian history. What we shall see in the course of this monograph, is that the Sanskrit jurisprudence of Equity and Trusts served an important, even seminal role in India's legal and political history for millennia. Emphatically, then, Dharmaśāstric ideas about the Crown as *parens patriae*, about the guardianship of women, children, and deities, about Equity as supplemental law, and about trusts as fiduciary relationships were absolutely integral to real legal practices in Indian history.

2

Equity and Trusts in Classical Indian Legal History

Only an extensive enquiry into the phraseology of inscriptions would make it possible to define and organize in a historical perspective the various political, social, and religious circumstances of the rise of the concept of deity-image in epigraphy.

Gerard Colas[1]

This chapter follows Colas' desideratum by surveying Indian inscriptions between the reign of Aśoka Maurya (r. 268–223 BCE) and the establishment of the Delhi Sulṭānate (1206). It provides a periodised, phenomenological account of the legal administration of religious endowments in pre-modern Indian history. I aim to demonstrate that this epigraphic survey provides evidence of the practical implementation of the Sanskrit jurisprudence of Equity and Trusts that I discussed in Chapter 1.

A core theme of this chapter is that the emergence of deities as beneficiaries of endowments and as legal persons during the greater Gupta Era (4th–6th centuries CE) coincided, broadly, with the 'Sanskritisation' of epigraphic records concerning religious endowments in pre-modern Indian history. By 'Sanskritisation', I mean a series of related themes that appear in epigraphic records: 1) a linguistic shift from vernacular languages (*prakrits*) into Sanskrit; 2) the explicit invocation of Dharmaśāstric and Purāṇic imprecatory dicta warning against the resumption of grants by future rulers; 3) the use of technical Dharmaśāstric (and Arthaśāstric) legal vocabulary in constructing the terms of particular trusts; and 4) implicit and explicit invocations of Dharmaśāstric jurisprudential principles of Equity and Trusts throughout the legal and rhetorical portions of inscriptions. Chief among these principles of Equity was the secular principle that the conventions and property of any sectarian faith community – be they Jain, Buddhist, Hindu, or any

[1] Colas, 'Images and Territory of Gods', 114.

other – would be recognised and protected by the Crown through its equitable jurisdiction over supplemental (*pāribhāṣika*) laws.

This shift from Prakrit into Sanskrit as the discursive language of law occurred hand-in-glove with the clear use of Sanskrit jurisprudence as the legal theory underlying actual legal practice. More broadly, this chapter demonstrates that there was very much a pan-Indic law of Equity and Trusts that emerged in conversation with Sanskrit jurisprudence. In time, particularly after the turn of the second millennium CE, vernacular languages largely supplanted Sanskrit as the primary language of inscriptions. Nevertheless, the jurisprudential foundations of the law of Equity and Trusts remained Sanskritic. By 'Sanskritic', I mean a *conceptual* connection with Sanskrit jurisprudential principles and texts that often existed even in the absence (or de-emphasis) of the use Sanskrit as the language for expressing specific legal rules. An inscription or copper-plate granting land to a deity, for example, might use Tamil, Kannada, or Telegu for some or all of its specific legal commands, but it might, nonetheless, be suffused with Dharmaśāstric principles regarding, *inter alia*, Equity and Trusts.

Additionally, I advance the bold claim that India developed one of the world's earliest and most sophisticated systems of trusts law. I also want to highlight this legal system's moving pieces and their evolution over the course of time. This will be of great benefit to historians and to contemporary jurists. A focal point of this account is the emergence of deities as beneficiaries of purpose trusts (3rd–4th Centuries CE) and their gradual, although linear, evolution into robust legal persons, especially after the turn of the second millennium CE.

In contrast to the sparse number of *dicta* on temple trusts in Sanskrit jurisprudential literature, India's epigraphic corpus contains thousands of records of endowments in an unbroken tradition beginning with the Edicts of Aśoka in the 3rd century BCE. During the 19th and 20th centuries, the editors and contributors of *Epigraphia Indica* (hereafter EI) and other venues such as *Indian Antiquary*, etc. – under the auspices of the Archaeological Survey of India – performed the herculean task of finding, dating, transcribing, and editing thousands of copper-plate charters, stone inscriptions, and other epigraphic bricolage.[2] Augmented by other series, such as *South Indian Inscriptions* (hereafter SII), *Corpus Inscriptionum Indicarum* (hereafter CII), *Epigraphia Indica* provided a substantial data set for several more recent masters of epigraphy studies, including Dineschandra Sircar and Richard Salomon.[3]

[2] *Epigraphia Indica* ran from 1882–1977 under the editorship of most of the pioneers of scholarship on Indian epigraphic history: James Burgess, Eugen Julius Theodor Hultzsch, Sten Konow, Dineshchandra Sircar, Govind Swamirao Gai; and with contributions from others, such as Aurel Stein, and John Faithfull Fleet.

[3] Now in its 34th volume, *South Indian Inscriptions* began publication in 1890. In seven volumes, *Corpus Inscriptionum Indicarum* began publication in 1877. Dineschandra Sircar, *Indian Epigraphy* (Delhi: Motilal Banarsidass, 1965); Dineschandra Sircar, *Select Inscriptions Bearing on Indian History and Civilization*, 2 vols., 2nd edn. (Calcutta: University of Calcutta: 1965); and Richard Salomon, *Indian Epigraphy: a Guide to the Study of Inscriptions in Sanskrit, Prakrit, and the other Indo-Aryan languages* (New York: Oxford University Press, 1998).

This work enabled scholars to reconstruct royal genealogies, outline the dates and localities of political regimes, and analyse the economic practices of pre-modern, pre-sulṭānate India.[4] Some Indologists, such as Hermann Kulke, Hans Bakker, and James Heitzman, utilised the ever-expanding epigraphic data set to propound and contest various theories of pre-sulṭānate Indian statehood – mostly in relation to Burton Steins' model of the 'segmentary state' and 'ritual sovereignty'.[5] Other prominent epigraphists have focused their analysis on individual dynasties.[6] Still others, notably Alexis Sanderson (Tantric Śaiva), Bihani Sarkar (Śākta), Richard Davis (Śaiva-Siddhānta), Michael Willis (Vaikhānasa-Vaiṣṇava), Ronald Inden (Pañcarātra-Vaiṣṇava), Gregory Schopen (Buddhist), and Peter Bisschop and Elizabeth Cecil (Śaiva and Jain), examined the complex relationships between 'disciplinary orders', the Crown, and various 'political formations'.[7]

[4] See, for example, D. Chattopadhyaya *et. al.* (eds), *Inscriptions and Agrarian Issues in Indian History: Essays in Memory of D.C. Sircar* (Kolkata: The Asiatic Society, 2017); Y. Subbarayalu, *South India Under the Cholas* (New Delhi: Oxford University Press, 2012); Ryosuke Furui, *Land and Society in Early South Asia: Eastern India 400–1250 AD* (New Delhi: Routledge, 2019).

[5] The best overview of this literature is Hermann Kulke, 'Ritual Sovereignty and Ritual Policy: Some Historiographic Reflections', in Margo Kitts *et al.* (eds), *State, Power, and Violence* (Wiesbaden: Harrassowitz Verlag, 2010): 603–26. According to Kulke, ibid., 608: 'Stein distinguishes between ritual sovereignty as a loose and custodial hegemony exercised by the king at the top of the pyramidal segmentary structure on the one hand, and political sovereignty, consisting of the direct rule or control exercised by local authorities and little kings in their immediate localities on the other.' Also see Hermann Kulke, 'The Early and Imperial Kingdom: A Processural Model of Integrative State Formation in Early Medieval India', in Hermann Kulke (ed.), *The State in India, 1000–1700* (New Delhi: Oxford University Press, 1995); Hermann Kulke, 'Fragmentation and Segmentation versus Integration? Reflections on the Concepts of Indian Feudalism and the Segmentary State in Indian History', *Studies in Indian History* 4 (1982): 237–63; Hans Bakker (ed.), *The Vākāṭaka Heritage: Indian Culture at the Crossroads* (Groningen: Egbert Forsten, 2004); Bakker, Hans, 'Royal Patronage and Religious Tolerance The Formative Period of Gupta–Vākāṭaka Culture', *Journal of the Royal Asiatic Society* 20.4 (2010): 461–75; and James Heitzman, *Gifts of Power: Lordship in an Early Indian State* (New Delhi: Oxford University Press, 1997).

[6] Emmanuel Francis, *Le Discours Royal dans l'Inde du Sud Ancienne: Inscriptions et Monuments Pallava, IVème-IXème Siècles* (Louvain-la-Neuve: Université Catholique de Louvain, 2013); Annette Schmiedchen, *Herrschergenealogie und religiöses Patronat: Die Inschriftenkultur der Rāṣṭrakūṭas, Śilāhāras und Yādavas (8. bis 13. Jahrhundert)* (Leiden: Brill, 2014); Dániel Balogh, *Inscriptions of the Aulikaras and Their Associates* (Berlin: Walter de Gruyter, 2019), v: 'So, here is another book on the timeless theme of "Inscriptions of [insert your preferred obscure dynasty here]."' Stefan Baums' online corpus, *Early Inscriptions of Āndhradeśa* is an invaluable resource for one of the most influential times and places in Indian epigraphic history, http://hisoma.huma-num.fr/exist/apps/EIAD/index2.html

[7] For 'disciplinary orders', see Ronald Inden, Jonathan Walters, and Daud Ali (eds), *Querying the Medieval: Texts and the History of Practices in South Asia* (Oxford: Oxford University Press, 2000), 23: 'we use the expression "disciplinary order"... to denote both the societies of adepts who have taken some particular name and the life-transforming practices in which they engage'. For 'imperial formations', see ibid., 24: 'the idea of an imperial formation is... used to theorize India as a complex polity consisting of a hegemonic empire and other subjected, allied and rival kingdoms and allied, and rival empires'. Sanderson, 'The Śaiva Age'; Bihani Sarkar, *Heroic Shāktism: The Cult of Durgā in Ancient Indian Kingship* (Oxford: Oxford University Press, 2017); Davis, *Ritual in an Oscillating Universe*; Willis, *Archaeology*; Inden, 'Imperial Purāṇas'; Schopen, 'The Buddha as an Owner'; Elizabeth Cecil, *Mapping the Pāśupāta Landscape: Narrative, Place, and the Śaiva Imaginary in Early Medieval North India* (Leiden: Brill, 2020); and Peter Bisschop and Elizabeth Cecil, 'Jayati Bhagavāñ Jinendraḥ! Jainism and Royal Representation in the Kadamba Plates of Palāśikā', *Journal of the American Oriental Society* 141.3 (2021): 613–35.

Finally, several scholars, including Günther-Dietz Sontheimer, J. Duncan Derrett, P.V. Kāṇe, Gerard Colas, Dineschandra Sarkar, Donald Davis, and Timothy Lubin produced legal surveys of the epigraphic corpus.[8] Given the vast quantity of primary materials and secondary scholarly commentary on the subject, distilling a concise, jurisprudentially coherent, account of the practical administration of religious and charitable trusts from India's epigraphic corpus is a daunting task.

2.1 The theory and practice of Equity and Trusts in classical Indian law

The Sanskrit jurisprudence of Equity and Trusts as articulated in the *Arthaśāstra* and in the Dharmaśāstric texts discussed in the previous chapter, provide a suturing intellectual thread to the legal practices documented in the India's pre-modern epigraphic records. Broadly, I am interested in how jurisprudential *theories* of Equity Trusts in Sanskrit jurisprudence were translated, *isometrically*, into legal *practices* – and *vice versa*. In his analysis of pre-modern Indian property rights, Timothy Lubin draws a distinction between:

> • A theory, which is developed in the Sanskrit Arthaśāstra and Dharmaśāstra literatures, and developed… almost exclusively by Brahmins, who were also often the beneficiaries of land-grants and other legal dispensations of the types described in their texts; and
>
> • A practice discernible in its traces left in inscriptions on stone and metal, which constitute permanent copies of legal documents, mostly related to property transfers, especially endowments.[9]

I follow Lubin's strategy of considering 'documents from a wide variety of periods and regions of India (and Indian-influenced spheres) with an eye to commonalities as well as differences of context and form'.[10] Like Lubin, I want to 'call attention to patterns across periods, regions, and document types, which point to a diffusion of diplomatic structures and compositional elements'.[11] Given the 'vast purview' of such a task, Lubin focuses on 'older documents' in his studies of property,

[8] Sontheimer, 'Religious Endowments', 33–40; Derrett 'Religious Endowments, Public and Private'; J. Duncan Derrett, 'An Example of Tax-evasion in Medieval India', *Bulletin of the School of Oriental and African Studies* 19.1 (1957): 162–6; Kāṇe, *A History of Dharmaśāstra*, Vol 2., Pt. 2., 856–67; Colas, 'Images and Territory of Gods'; Dineschandra Sircar, *Epochs in Indian Legal History* (Hoshiarpur: Vishveshvaranand Vedic Research Institute, 1958); Davis, 'Intermediate Realms of Law'; Lubin, 'South Asian Diplomatics'; Lubin, 'Theory and Practice'; and Lubin, 'Endowments'.

[9] Lubin, 'Theory and Practice', 804–5.

[10] Lubin, 'South Asian Diplomatics', 39–40.

[11] Ibid., 39–40.

religious endowments, and formal diplomatics, but I survey the moving pieces of Trusts law over several epochs in Indian history.

This chapter queries: 1) what kinds of religious and charitable institutions were endowed; 2) what sorts of financial arrangements were made to support these endowments; 3) who received and/or managed these assets on institutions' behalf; 4) what duty of care trustees owed to their institutions; and 5) how royal and local actors safeguarded temples and the like from maladministration by their trustees. A related line of questioning concerns the juridical personality of Hindu deities in the epigraphic record: 1) when do deities become beneficiaries of divine endowments? 2) what sorts of assets do deities own? and 3) when do deities take on active legal agency? Answering these questions requires us to examine more than one-and-a-half millennia's worth of data. The result, however, is extraordinary. The material surveyed and summarised in this chapter demonstrates that India developed one of most, if not the most sophisticated pre-modern, comprehensive legal systems of Equity and Trusts in the medieval and pre-modern world. In terms of practical law, the epigraphic record contains a diverse array of legal phenomena. These technical legal phenomena were also deeply infused with the jurisprudential principles of Dharmaśāstra – to which we now turn.

2.1.1 Theory

This chapter defends a strident claim: that the Sanskrit jurisprudence (Arthaśāstric and Dharmaśāstric) outlined in Chapter 1 provided the constitutional foundation for much of the legal activities described in India's pre-modern epigraphic records. Chapter 1 demonstrated that the *Arthaśāstra* discusses the Crown's authority to record and to enforce conventional laws among religious and commercial organisations and to guard legal incompetents (as *parens patriae*).[12] The *Arthaśāstra*, in contrast to later Dharmaśāstric literature, outlines a state-centred polity in which the power of the Crown is absolute.[13] The *Arthaśāstra* offers a substantial jurisprudence of Equity and Trusts in which the Crown exercises direct supervision over various guilds, corporations, temples, etc. – via the machinery of the royal bureaucracy. Patrick Olivelle and Mark McClish argue that Brāhmaṇical redactions of earlier recensions of the *Arthaśāstra* and Dharmaśāstric appropriations of Arthaśāstric materials in the early centuries of the Common Era subordinated the centralised state – and the role of the king – to

[12] See Chapter 1, §1.3.1, 'The solution, part 1 – Arthaśāstra.'

[13] See McClish, The History of the Arthaśāstra, 166: 'The *Daṇḍanīti* conceived of no constitutional limits constraining the king's exercise of sovereign power, whether in the form of legal, moral, or religious obligations.'

a Brāhmaṇical political theology in which the Crown served as a guardian of effectively *sui iuris* communities.[14]

Early, pre-Sanskrit inscriptions written in Middle Indic dialects (*prakrits*) under the Mauryan (322–184 BCE), Kuṣāṇa (30–375 CE), Śaka (60 BCE–415 CE), and Sātavāhana (2nd century BCE–early 3rd century CE) polities bear more than a passing resemblance to Arthaśāstric jurisprudence. Given the *Arthaśāstra*'s complex and contested compositional history – perhaps a 3rd-century CE redaction of a 1st-century BCE treatise that was compiled from Mauryan or post-Mauryan materials – it is difficult to parse the precise nature of the relationship between the *Arthaśāstra* and Middle Indic epigraphy.[15] Aśoka's inscriptions share the mature *Arthaśāstra*'s juridical theory of a centralised state, and Kuṣāṇa, Śaka, and Sātavāhana-era inscriptions employ Mauryan and Arthaśāstric terminology.[16]

McClish adamantly argues that 'the scholarly community is best served by discontinuing any presumed connection between the *Arthaśāstra* and the Mauryan period'.[17] Even if the *Arthaśāstra*'s provenance or source material is not Mauryan (although its compilers clearly drew on an ancient tradition of Sanskrit political theory dating to at least the 6th century BCE), the treatise was likely compiled under the aegis of post-Mauryan polities whose epigraphic records frame those polities and their legal practices as the heirs to Aśoka Maurya. The 'Age Between the Empires' was, in a jurisprudential sense, an Arthaśāstric age.[18]

The gradual shift from the use of Middle Indic to the use of literary Sanskrit in the 2nd and 3rd centuries CE – partially evident in Śaka, Sātavāhana and in Ikṣvāku (3rd century–early 4th century) of Vijayapurī (modern Nāgārjuṇikoṇḍa) – culminated in a complete Sanskritisation under the Gupta Empire and its subordinates (4th century CE–late 6th century CE). This linguistic shift coincided with a gradual jurisprudential transition from *Arthaśāstra* to Dharmaśāstra.[19]

[14] Olivelle and McClish, 'Four Feet'; McClish, *The History of the Arthaśāstra*, 216: 'The statecraft tradition had existed since at least the time of the *Chāndogya Upanisad* (ca. sixth century BCE). It was characterized, according to slightly later texts, by its lack of adherence to a moral law. In this light, we can typify the development of *rājadharma* within the Dharmaśāstras as the gradual appropriation of an independent statecraft tradition, an appropriation culminating in the *Mānava Dharmaśāstra*.'

[15] See McClish, *The History of the Arthaśāstra*, 151–3, for his dating the text. For the connection between Kṣatrapa/Sātavāhana inscriptions and the jurisprudence of the *Arthaśāstra*, see S. C. Mishra, *Evolution of Kauṭilya's Arthaśāstra: An Inscriptional Approach* (Delhi: Anamaka Prakashan, 1993), 105–24.

[16] For the relationship between the Arthaśāstra and inscriptions of the Kṣatrapas and Sātavāhanas, see Kelsey Martini, 'The Origin of Akṣayanīvī and the Historical Context of the Arthaśāstra', *Indo-Iranian Journal* 65 (2022): 144–69. For some comparisons between Mauryan, Sātavāhana, Kṣatrapa, and Ikṣvāku terminology, see Michael Skinner, '*Urbanization and Interactions in the Early Historic Deccan: The Sātavāhana, Western Ksatrapa, and Iksvāku Dynasties* (Unpublished MA Dissertation, University of Washington, 2012), 9.

[17] McClish, 'Is the Arthaśāstra a Mauryan Document?', 299.

[18] For this formative epoch, see Patrick Olivelle (ed.), *Between the Empires: Society in India 300 BCE–400 CE* (New York: Oxford University Press, 2006).

[19] Lubin, 'Endowments', 99, argues that this occurred in conjunction with the development of a new Brāhmaṇical socio-legal status.

This shift was not coincidental: the Guptas' and their successors' appropriation of Middle Indic epigraphic legal concepts parallels the Dharmaśāstric appropriation of Arthaśāstric jurisprudence that McClish recounts. A centuries-old tradition of centralised royal sovereignty – along with its attendant legal infrastructure – was subordinated to a Brāmaṇical political theology and, in the process, became the foundation for jurisprudential and practical legal discourse throughout India. Earlier legal instruments, such as the 'perpetual endowment' (*akṣayanīvī*), immunity from taxation, and *parens patriae* jurisdiction, that one finds in Middle Indic epigraphy and in the *Arthaśāstra* were appropriated in Sanskrit epigraphy and recast according to an emergent Dharmaśāstric jurisprudence.

This process was gradual, occurring during a:

> Formative era during which significant innovations in the social and political life of India occurred, including the political and financial solidification of the Buddhist monastic community; the early epigraphical and archeological evidence of maritime trade; the composition of culturally foundational Indic texts such as the *Rāmāyaṇa* and *Mahābhārata* epics, and the *Laws of Manu*, and... the creation of a nonliturgical, literary use of Sanskrit and its close connection to the articulation of a cosmopolitan rulership.[20]

The emergence of these foundational Indic texts enabled the creation of what Donald Davis defines as Hindu law: 'a variegated grouping of local legal systems that had different rules and procedures of law but that were united by a common jurisprudence or legal theory represented in Dharmaśāstra'.[21]

Sheldon Pollock's theory of the 'Sanskrit Cosmopolis' entails the proposition that Mahākṣatrapa Rudradāman's (r. 130–150 CE) Sanskrit Junāgaṛh inscription – chiselled on a boulder on which Aśoka Maurya had inscribed his own edicts four centuries before – inaugurated a new form of kingship 'signaled by an explosion both of secular poetry and drama and of epigraphic panegyric' which 'eschewed administrative centralization' and enabled 'local languages, politics, and laws to coexist within a cosmopolitan discourse of rulership'.[22]

Andrew Ollett's analysis of Middle Indic epigraphy from 50 BCE to 250 CE, however, serves as a salutary reminder that Rudradāman's Junāgaṛh inscription was merely one milestone in 'the centuries-long process by which "languages of power" were continuously fashioned, defined, and contested'.[23] It took a century or more, in the wake of the fall of the Sātavāhana Empire, for Rudradāman's reinvention of Sanskrit into a language of power to become a pan-Indic phenomenon.

[20] Davis, 'Historical Overview', 18.

[21] Donald Davis, 'Law', in S. Mittal and G. Thursby (eds), *Studying Hinduism* (New York: Routledge, 2008), 225.

[22] Davis, 'Historical Overview', 18. Davis is summarizing Pollock's, Language of the Gods.

[23] Andrew Ollett, *The Language of the Snakes: Prakrit, Sanskrit, and the Language Order of Premodern India* (Berkeley: University of California Press, 2017), 26.

By that time, it was intimately connected to a Brāhmaṇical, Dharmaśāstric jurisprudence that included the legal personality of Hindu deities.[24]

Sheldon Pollock's claim that 'no uniform code of law was ever enforced anywhere' in the Sanskrit cosmopolis elides the fact that epigraphic records reveal that Sanskrit jurisprudential principles and terminology were applied almost everywhere in classical India.[25] Sovereigns in the 'Sanskrit cosmopolis... protected and enabled the *dharmas* of the orders of life and caste... [rather than] forcibly legislate or promulgate that law', but this theory of rulership is articulated most clearly in Sanskrit jurisprudential literature.[26] Davis notes that:

> The legal cosmology of Dharmaśāstra thus parallels the replicative cosmopolitanism of literary discourse. Dharma as law was in practice to be negotiated and articulated locally under the control of a ruler... [and] in fact, the cosmopolitan political imagination was partially articulated by means of Hindu jurisprudence and not merely by literary texts or epigraphs.[27]

The broad point is that Sanskrit jurisprudence served as the primary source of pre-Islamic Indian constitutional thought. Constitutional thought is: 'The aggregate of fundamental principles or established precedents that constitute the legal basis of a polity, organisation or other type of entity and commonly determine how that entity is to be governed.'[28]

Every polity has constitutional principles – either codified or uncodified – through which the conferral of political power is contested, authorised, or legitimated, and classical India is no exception.[29] The sovereigns of the Sanskrit Cosmopolis utilised a cosmopolitan Sanskrit literary idiom to articulate their rule, but that rule in its legal, administrative aspect was justified by its relationship with the idealised, cosmopolitan constitutional order discussed in Dharmaśāstra. Pollock's observation that no uniform code of *law* was applied in the Sanskrit cosmopolis belies the fact that a uniform *jurisprudence* – Dharmaśāstra – provided

[24] Ibid., 47: 'The outcome of these processes was the total obsolescence of Middle Indic as an inscriptional language. If it was unthinkable to use Sanskrit to commemorate political power at the beginning of the Sātavāhana empire, it was unthinkable not to use Sanskrit within a few generations of its dissolution.' Ollett warns, p. 47, that: 'The tendency has been to look for Brahmans behind every process of Sanskritization, and to postulate them when they can't be found.' Nevertheless, as Lubin notes, 'Endowments', 102, that 'the use of Sanskrit rather than middle Indic' in a 3rd century temple endowment at Vijayapurī 'is a signal that the temple was in Brahmin hands'.

[25] Pollock, *Language of the Gods*, 277.

[26] Davis, 'Historical Overview', 19.

[27] Ibid., 18–19.

[28] *The New Oxford American Dictionary*, 2nd edn., ed. Erin McKean (Oxford: Oxford University Press, 2005), 2051. For other definitions of the term 'constitution', see Mark Tushnet, 'Constitution' in Michel Rosenfeld and Andras Sajo (eds), *The Oxford Handbook of Comparative Constitutional Law* (Oxford: Oxford University Press, 2012): 217–32.

[29] For an overview of constitutional theory, see Martin Loughlin, 'Constitutional Theory: A 25th Anniversary Essay', *Oxford Journal of Legal Studies* 25 (2005): 183–202.

the theoretical underpinning for the many legal systems that flourished within the Sanskrit cosmopolitan political order.

Arguably, the most important constitutional principal of the Sanskrit Cosmopolis was a Dharmaśāstric model of Equity in which the Crown must investigate and protect the supplemental laws (*pāribhāṣikadharmas*) of its subjects.[30] Furthermore, Sanskrit jurisprudential discussions of Trusts describe the religious and charitable endowments whose financial organisation marked the occasion for the overwhelming majority of inscriptions made in that cosmopolitan political discourse. Many of the inscriptions discussed in this chapter explicitly declare themselves to be discrete supplemental laws who must be protected by the Crown under Equitable Dharmaśāstric principles of, *inter alia*, *parens patriae* jurisdiction. The occasions for codifying these supplemental, Equitable laws were, overwhelmingly, the enactment of Dharmaśāstric and Purāṇic exhortations to build, endow, and protect religious and charitable institutions.

In short, the Sanskrit cosmopolis was a Dharmaśāstric cosmopolis and, if we accept Davis' definition, then the aggregate epigraphic data that I present in this chapter will demonstrate that the legal system of the Sanskrit cosmopolis was constitutionally Hindu (in Donald Davis' view of what makes law 'Hindu').[31] Nevertheless, this Hindu legal system was secular in the theoretical and applied sense: sovereigns who expressly identified as Buddhist, Jain, Vaiṣṇava, Śaiva, Śākta, etc., invoked Dharmaśāstric jurisprudential principles and terminology when endowing an equally diverse array of religious institutions.[32]

The Dharmaśāstric cosmopolis was also pan-Indic: one finds remarkably similar legal forms as far south as Tamil Nadu, as far north as Afghanistan, as far east as Bengal, and as far west as Gujarat. Finally, the Dharmaśāstric cosmopolis was political: the creation, endowment, protection, plundering, and re-founding of religious institutions was intimately connected to the Crown's political authority.[33] The reality that kings removed images and treasures from temples, confiscated, reassigned, or restored land grants, or otherwise engaged in (or warded against) mischief towards endowments is reflected in epigraphic records and in many

[30] This is the thrust of Davis' analysis in 'Intermediate Realms of Law'.

[31] In Donald Davis, *The Spirit of Hindu Law* (Cambridge: Cambridge University Press, 2010), 13 fn. 28, Davis warns that, 'obviously, the propriety of the label Hindu for any particular legal system is a matter for empirical and historical investigation and judgment.'

[32] Pollock, *Language of the Gods*, 89, argues, that the advent of the Sanskrit cosmopolis included 'a new secularization – not too strong a word, and no anachronism – of the god' language [Sanskrit]'. For secularism in ancient India, see Bhargava, 'An Ancient Indian Secular Age?'.

[33] Lubin, 'South Asian Diplomatics', 37–8, argues that, while Davis, 'Toward a History of Documents', 'argues for sharp distinction between "royal documents," which serve strictly political rather than "legal" purposes and "popular documents" which are precisely legal in the sense of justiciable' he does not. According to Lubin, 'in practice the distinction gets blurred'. Even if the confiscation or reassignment of a grant by Crown might not be justiciable, nevertheless the assignation of a royal grant clearly entailed legal *effects* that were very much justiciable.

Dharmaśāstric injunctions against expropriatory practices.[34] Jurisprudence's idealised goal of enacting the rule of law is invariably curtailed by the unprincipled vicissitudes of political power.[35] Sanskrit jurisprudence in India was no exception to this rule. Nevertheless, Sanskrit jurisprudential *ideals* – particularly of kings protecting rather than looting religious and charitable endowments – provided a moral matrix in which political agents acted.

2.1.2 Practice

Although this chapter views epigraphic records as evidence of legal practice, it is salutary to remember Davis' warning that:

> Neither [Dharmaśāstra nor Epigraphic records] presents the law unmediated by questions of theology, politics, status, etc., but both provide partial insights into the nature and importance of… law in medieval India… While epigraphists have helped to demonstrate the limitations of using śāstra texts for historical research, some fail to apply the same level of critical scrutiny to the nature of epigraphical sources. It is, for instance, not at all clear that medieval inscriptions, for all their dates, names, and details, are significantly closer to some historical reality beyond the words of the inscriptional text.[36]

It is true that the eulogistic introductions (*praśastis*) of medieval copper-plate grants contain elaborate rhetorical flourishes and mytho-poetical fancies. Nevertheless, these texts' illocutionary force is oriented towards making practical *legal* interventions – in contradistinction to the more academic intervention of Sanskrit *jurisprudential* texts.[37]

Furthermore, the political and theological distortions of epigraphic records notwithstanding, they serve, generally, as proof that 'śāstric vocabulary and

[34] For the ancient, pre-Islamic practice of the plunder (and re-consecration) of temple images and treasures, see Richard Davis, 'Indian Art Objects as Loot', *The Journal of Asian Studies* 52.1 (1993): 22–48; Davis, *Lives of Indian Images*, especially Chapter 2, 'Trophies of War'.

[35] For the best discussion of this topic, see Thomas (Lord) Bingham, *The Rule of Law* (London: Penguin, 2011), especially p., 19: 'The core of the existing principle [of the Rule of Law] is, I suggest, that all persons and authorities within the state, whether public or private, should be bound by and entitled to the benefit of laws publicly made, taking effect (generally) in the future and publicly administered in the courts. This statement… is not comprehensive, and even the most ardent constitutionalist would not suggest that it could be universally applied without exception or qualification… My formulation owes much to Dicey, but I think it also captures the fundamental truth propounded by the great English philosopher John Locke in 1690 that "Wherever law ends, tyranny begins". The same point was made by Tom Paine in 1776 when he said "that in America THE LAW IS KING. For as in absolute governments the King is law, so in free countries the law ought to be King; and there ought to be no other."'

[36] Davis, 'Intermediate Realms of Law', 113. See ibid., fn. 32 for Dan Arnold's cautionary take on the work of Gregory Schopen.

[37] The best study of the ideology and political significance of *praśastis* is Daud Ali, 'Royal Eulogy as World History: Rethinking Copper-plate Inscriptions in Cōḷa History', in Ronald Inden, Jonathan Walters, and Daud Ali (eds), *Querying the Medieval: Texts and the History of Practices in South Asia* (Oxford: Oxford University Press, 2000): 165–229.

"śāstric conceptions" were used in the "practical" context of medieval inscriptions'.[38] Sometimes, as Lubin notes, 'epigraphy does bear witness to the persistent influence of śāstric categories and terminology related to property rights and legal institutions'.[39] At other times, the relationship between epigraphic and śāstric text is more isometric. For example, as Davis notes in his work on guilds, corporate groups, and other 'intermediary' legal organisations in medieval India:

> Even in the absence of direct citation, persistent parallels between Dharmaśāstra discussions relating to these intermediary groups and the contemporary epigraphical evidence suggest that they are two different witnesses to the same legal tradition each with its own idiosyncrasies of expression, level of abstraction, and scope of (intended) relevance... [wherein] the realities of legal practice on the ground were translated into the specialized academic idiom of Dharmaśāstra. These academic textbooks, in turn, were (re-)translated into rules governing corporate associations as well as many other legal and religious rule systems.[40]

In short, even as I, like other scholars previously, turn to epigraphic records as a source of data about practically oriented legal documents, I recognise that, as *texts*, they have their own idiomatic conceits inflected by time, place, culture, and so forth. Different empires and kingdoms developed idiosyncratic epigraphic legal idioms, but they all drew on a common wellspring of Sanskrit jurisprudential thought. Tracing the emergence and transformation of the building blocks of Sanskrit Trusts law in epigraphy reveals that this śāstric-cum-epigraphic idiom was pan-Indian, multireligious, and, over time, increasingly financially sophisticated.[41]

From the simple financial arrangements of perpetual endowments (*akṣayanīvīs*) and assigned 'monks' land' (*bhikkuhala*) for Buddhist monasteries made by Sātavāhana and Śaka rulers, to the Imperial Cōḷa and Kaḷyāṇi Cālukyas' charters for vast, deity-owned temple cities, we find consistent invocations to the Sanskrit jurisprudence of Equity and Trusts. The story of how the practical legal activities recorded in Indian epigraphy emerged, evolved, and flourished against the backdrop of Sanskrit jurisprudence is also the story of India: of the Buddhist Saṅgha; of deities as legal owners; of the rise of Sanskrit as a language of power; of the establishment of Temple Hinduism; of the birth and death of empires; of

[38] Davis, 'Intermediate Realms of Law', 114. Davis argues against Leslie Orr. For the contrary view, see Leslie Orr, 'Women in the Temple, the Palace, and the Family: The Construction of Women's Identities in Pre-Colonial Tamilnāḍu', in Kenneth Hall (ed.), *Structure and Society in Early South India: Essays in Honour of Noboru Karashima* (New Delhi: Oxford University Press, 2001): 198–234.

[39] Lubin, 'Theory and Practice', 805.

[40] Davis, 'Intermediate Realms of Law', 113–15.

[41] For 'multireligion' as an analytical field, see Jonathan S. Walters, 'Multireligion on the Bus: Beyond "Influence" and "Syncretism" in the Study of Religious Meetings', in Pradeep Jeganathan and Qadri Ismail (eds), *Unmaking the Nation: The Politics of Identity and History in Modern Sri Lanka* (Colombo: Social Scientists' Association, 1995): 25–54. Walters argues that 'multireligious fields have been constituted wherever and whenever adherents of different religions share common space'. One such common space, I argue, is in epigraphic discourse.

daring raids on imperial capitals; of the foundation of ancient universities that rivalled those of Oxford and Cambridge; and of the individuals who lived during these sometimes extraordinary circumstances.

2.2 The Mauryan era and the edicts of Aśoka (322 BCE–184 BCE)

Our story of Equity and Trusts in Indian legal history begins with Aśoka Maurya (r. 268–232 BCE). Aśoka may well be the most famous sovereign in Indian history, and it comes as no surprise that his lion capital from Sāraṅganātha (modern Sarnāth) serves as the model for the State Emblem of India. As Romila Thapar notes, 'to speak of… [Aśoka] in a retrospective vein is to trace virtually the entire span of Indian history'.[42] His empire, based in Pāṭaliputra (modern Patna), stretched over a vast swath of the Indian subcontinent, from Kandahar in the northwest, to Amarāvatī in the southeast.[43] His empire's influence on subsequent religious narrative was as great as its geographical scope: a vast corpus of Buddhist, Jain, and Hindu materials recount various legends concerning the Mauryan Empire and its foundational place in Indian religious and political history.[44]

The broad arc of the core narrative is well-known: Candragupta Maurya (r. 324–297 BCE), with aide of Cāṇakya, the ostensible compiler of the *Arthaśāstra*, defeated Dhana Nanda of Māgadha, before following the Jain preceptor (*ācārya*), Bhadrabāhu (367– c. 298 BCE), to Śravaṇa Beḷagoḷa (in modern Karnataka), and ritually fasting to death (*sallekhanā*).[45] Candragupta's son, Bindusara (r. 297–273) ruled unremarkably – at least according to later accounts – and left his son, Aśoka, in control of a substantial polity. After conquering Kalinga in 261 BCE, Aśoka 'converted' to Buddhist teachings and set about reforming his empire according to the principles of Dhamma (Dharma).[46]

[42] Romila Thapar, 'Aśoka: A Retrospective', in Patrick Olivelle, Janice Leoshko, and Himanshu Prabha Ray (eds), *Reimagining Aśoka* (Oxford: Oxford University Press, 2012): 18–37, 18. For the authoritative biographical overview of Aśoka, see Patrick Olivelle, *Ashoka: Portrait of a Philosopher King* (New Haven: Yale University Press, 2024).

[43] See Himanshu Ray, 'The Mauryan Empire', in Peter Bang, C.A. Bayly, and Walter Scheidel (eds), *The Oxford History of Empire: Volume 2: The History of Empires* (Oxford: Oxford University Press, 2021): 198–217.

[44] For Aśoka's role as a model ruler in Buddhist countries, see Stanley Tambiah, *World Conqueror, World Renouncer* (Cambridge: Cambridge University Press, 2010), Chapter 5, 'Asoka Maurya: The Paradigm'. For Aśokan legends, see John Strong, *The Legend of King Aśoka: A Study and Translation of the Aśokavadana* (Princeton: Princeton University Press, 1984.

[45] For legends of Candragupta, see Radhakumud Mookerji, *Candragupta and His Times* (New Delhi: Motilal Banarsidass, 1966). For a critical appraisal of the connections between Cāṇakya, Candragupta, and the *Arthaśāstra*, see McClish, *The History of the Arthaśāstra*, 39–47.

[46] See Major Rock Edict 13 for an account of the Kaliṅga war.

Aśoka ordered the creation of an number of inscriptions in Greek, Aramaic, and Middle Indic throughout his empire.[47] These inscriptions 'are the earliest firmly datable and localisable set of texts from Ancient India'.[48] They proved to be incredibly influential in Indian history in three key ways: 1) ideologically; 2) spatially; and 3) legally. Ideologically, Aśoka's constitutional model of sovereignty was anchored in the universal political theology of Dharma – a term capable of remarkable semantic flexibility – and inspired countless subsequent South Asian polities, including the current Republic of India.[49] As Patrick Olivelle notes:

> Scholars now take the Sanskrit epics and treatises on dharma, such as the Mānava Dharmaśāstra, as responses to Aśokan reforms. Aśoka is the implicit subtext of these documents. The presentation of Rāma and Yudhiṣṭhira as dharmarajas, kings of righteousness, could be read against the image of Aśoka as the righteous king from a Buddhist perspective.[50]

Spatially, Aśoka's edicts serve as literal political palimpsests: Śaka, Kuṣāṇa, Sātavāhana, Gupta, and even Mughal rulers added their own inscriptions next to – or on top of – those of the Mauryan Emperor.[51] The fact that numerous rulers explicitly oriented their inscriptions in relation to Aśoka's, even after the meaning of the inscriptions was lost, is, as Patrick Olivelle notes, 'a clear testimony of the power of images of texts, rather than simply the content of texts'.[52] As Pollock observes, the overwriting of Aśoka's Junāgaṛh inscription by successive dynasties, speaks to 'the capacity of certain objects, natural or man-made, to embody and preserve political charisma, and… [to instantiate] one form of the historical imitation and emulation that would prove central to the imperial mode across time and space'.[53]

In addition to charism, and most importantly for this study, Aśoka's edicts also introduced several core features of Equity and Trusts in Indian epigraphy. As Lubin notes:

[47] E. Hultzsch, *Corpus Inscriptionum Indicarum Vol 1: Inscriptions of Asoka* (Oxford: Clarendon Press, 1925). For a philological appraisal of the edicts, see K.R. Norman, 'The Languages of the Composition and Transmission of the Aśokan Edicts', in Patrick Olivelle, Janice Leoshko, and Himanshu Prabha Ray (eds), *Reimagining Aśoka* (Oxford: Oxford University Press, 2012): 38–64. Also see Dineschandra Sircar, *Aśokan Studies* (Calcutta: Indian Museum, 1979).

[48] Patrick Olivelle, 'Aśoka's Inscriptions as Text and Ideology', in Patrick Olivelle, Janice Leoshko, and Himanshu Prabha Ray (eds), *Reimagining Aśoka* (Oxford: Oxford University Press, 2012): 157–83, 157.

[49] For Aśoka's Dharma as a model for the newly-independent Republic of India, see Ananya Vajpeyi, *Righteous Republic* (Cambridge, MA: Harvard University Press, 2012), Chapter 4, 'Jawaharlal Nehru: Dharma, the Self's Aspiration, Artha, the Self's Purpose'.

[50] Patrick Olivelle, 'Introduction', in Patrick Olivelle, Janice Leoshko, and Himanshu Prabha Ray (eds), *Reimagining Aśoka* (Oxford: Oxford University Press, 2012): 1–16, 9.

[51] Most notable are the Aśokan pillars. For their importance in Sulṭānate India, see Syed Ali Nadeem Rezavi, 'Antiquarian Interests in Medeival India: The Relocation of Ashokan Pillars by Firuzshah Tughluq', *Proceedings of the Indian History Congress* 70 (2009–10): 994–1010.

[52] Olivelle, 'Introduction', in Reimagining Aśoka, 12.

[53] Pollock, *Language of the Gods*, 68.

> Although in comparison with all later Indian epigraphy the famous edicts of the Maurya emperor Aśoka… have generally (and to a large extent quite correctly) been seen as unique in form and purpose – not least for their intensely personal, even confessional, tone – nonetheless the edicts introduce structural elements and even particular expressions that persist in later epigraphy.[54]

These elements include: 1) the form of a royal command with a king issuing an edict and ordering his successors to enforce it; 2) the assignation of taxable income or other forms of gifts to a diverse array of religious communities (*pāṣaṇḍas*) and secular charities; 3) a theory of the sovereign as *parens patriae* whose agents serve as guardians of defenceless individuals; and 4) the application of this principle of guardianship to the royal supervision of religious institutions and practices. Collectively, this data indicates that Aśoka's edicts articulate a model of Equity and Trusts that, despite some idiosyncratic deviations, is roughly comparable to later Sanskrit jurisprudential theories, and seems to have directly inspired later epigraphic practices.[55]

2.2.1 Typology of an Aśokan edict

Aśoka's edicts introduce a basic theme of: 'Embedding… the content of a royal decree within a statement expressing the issuing of the order and/or its recording in writing… [such that] most versions of the Minor Rock Edict (MRE; the earliest of Aśoka's decrees) formally begin: *devāṇampiye hevaṃ āha* ('The Beloved of the Gods speaks thus).'[56] The pillar edicts' introductions are more complex. These introductions provide regnal years and also serve 'the double role of *intitulatio* and *promulgatio*, that is, providing the name and title of the issuer and his intended purpose (also called the notification)'.[57] This 'order-issuing' form would, as Lubin observes, 'survive as a legalistic reflex in… later inscriptions, which identifies the one issuing the order'.[58]

Furthermore, Aśoka's edicts articulate 'an early prototype of the 'classical' eschatocol, which calls upon later kings to recognise and enforce the order or deed, and includes penalties and/or imprecations directed at those who would violate its terms.'[59] One feature of the eschatocol protocol is a perpetuity clause: that the order should endure for 'as long as the moon and sun' (*ācaṃdamaṣūliyaṃ*).[60]

[54] Lubin, 'South Asian Diplomatics', 40.

[55] On features of Aśokan inscriptions that are not consistent with later inscriptions, see Richard Salomon, 'Aśoka and the "Epigraphic Habit" in India', in Patrick Olivelle (ed.), *Aśoka in History and Historical Memory* (Delhi: Motilal Banarsidass, 2009): 45–52.

[56] Lubin, 'South Asian Diplomatics', 40.

[57] Ibid., 41–2.

[58] Ibid., 44.

[59] Ibid., 43–4.

[60] Ibid., 44.

Later kings would flesh out Aśoka's skeletal facets of imperial command into the elaborate genealogies of kings and Dharmaśāstric injunctions against resumption of royal gifts that typify medieval epigraphic discourse.

2.2.2 Religious endowments and secular charities

The Mauryans also introduced prototypes for the endowment of religious institutions, the gift of caves to ascetic groups, and the construction of public charities. Aśoka's jurisprudence is explicitly ecumenical: 'King Devanampriya Priyadarśin is honouring all sects: ascetics or house holders, with gifts and with honours of various kinds… that a promotion of the essentials of all sects should take place.'[61]

Aśoka's pillar inscription at Lumbinī, the birthplace of Śākyamuṇi Buddha, is, in Lubin's estimation, the 'first example of a king conferring exemption from paying a tax (*bali*) as a form of pious endowment'.[62] The inscription notes that:

> When king Priyadarśin, dear to the gods, had been anointed for twenty years, he came in person and paid reverence. Being aware that the Buddha was born here, he had a stone fencing constructed on the site [of the birth] and a stone pillar erected. Being aware that the Lord was born here, he made the village of Lumbinī tax-free and provided it with a share in eight parts [of the ashes of the Buddha that had originally been divided].[63]

Harry Falk argues that the purport of this edict lay in 'exempting the village from royal jurisdiction and placing it under the rule of those clerics looking after it [as trustees]'.[64] Falk identifies the railing mentioned in the Lumbinī edict with one uncovered in Sāraṅganātha. This railing contains a brace of epigraphs in which the Sarvāstivādin and Sāṃmaitrīyas contested their possession (*parigraha*) of the site and its income by tampering with the original inscription.[65] This is the earliest example of contested possession (or trusteeship of a religious endowment), and it parallels similar patterns of 'fraudulent alteration of property deeds to obscure

[61] 12th Major Rock Edict (Kalsi), CII 1, p. 41: **devānāpiye piyadaṣi** lājā ṣāvāpāṣaṇḍāni pavajitāni gahathāni vā pujeti dānena vividhaye ca. athā kita śalāvaḍhi śiyāti śavapāśaḍāna.

[62] Lubin, 'Theory and Practice', 819.

[63] The translation is from Harry Falk, 'The Fate of Aśoka's Donations at Lumbinī', in Patrick Olivelle, Janice Leoshko, and Himanshu Prabha Ray (eds), *Reimagining Aśoka* (Oxford: Oxford University Press, 2012): 204–16, 215–16: **devānaṃpiyena piyadasina** lājina vīsati-vasābhisitena. atana āgāca mahīyite hida **budhe** jāte **sakyamuni** ti. silā vigaḍabhī cā kālāpita silā-thabhe ca usapāpite. hida **bhagavaṃ** jāte ti **luṃmini**-gāme ubalike kaṭe aṭhabhāgiye ca. Lubin, 'Endowments', 17 fn. 51 notes that the term 'tax free' (*ubalike*) has an early Arthaśāstric cognate, *ucchulka* and that Aśoka's endowment bears a similarity to the *Arthaśāstra*'s exemption of 'customs levies (*śulka*) goods destined for Brahmanical ritual or sacramental uses'. This is, perhaps, an indication of the *Arthaśāstra* Brāhmaṇicalization of a Mauryan-era legal practice.

[64] Falk, 'Aśoka's Donations', 207.

[65] Ibid. 213–14.

or alter the original terms of the grant' in Aśoka's dedication of the Barabar and Narayani caves to the Ājīvikas.[66]

The Mauryans also created secular charities. In his second major rock edict, Aśoka notes that, 'everywhere two (kinds of) medical men were established by king Devanampriya Priyadarsin, (viz.) medical treatment for men and medical treatment for cattle'.[67] The 'Queen's Edict' on the Aśokan pillar at Kosambi lists the various charities donated by the Mauryans: 'Whatever may be the gift of the second queen, whether a mango-grove, a monastery, an institution for dispensing charity or any other donation, it is to be counted to the credit of that queen.'[68] The Sohgaura copper-plate inscription – the first known copper-plate inscription in Indian history – offers an example of the legal regulation of a charitable endowment: 'The order of the High Functionaries of Srāvastī! These two storehouses, (which are situated, one) in Mānavāśītikṛtaśrīmanta (and the other), in Ūṣagrāma, (the provisions of) fodder and wheat, (and) the loads of ladles, canopies, yoke-pins and ropes are used in (times of) urgent need (these are) not to be taken away.'[69]

2.2.3 Aśoka as *parens patriae*

Aśoka's edicts articulate a theory of sovereignty in which the king, as *parens patriae* has a duty to look after the welfare of his most vulnerable subjects – much like in the jurisprudence of the *Arthaśāstra*. Aśoka frames his officers' (*mahāmātras*) legal mandate as an extension of this duty. In his separate rock edicts, Aśoka enjoins his judicial officers (*vihohālakas*) to operate under the sanction of his delegated *parens patriae* jurisdiction. In the first edict, Aśoka notes that: 'All men are my children. As on behalf of (my own) children I desire that they may be provided with complete welfare and happiness in this world and in the other world, the same I desire also on behalf of [all] men.'[70] The same jurisprudential principle appears in Aśoka's second separate rock edict: 'Therefore, acting thus, (you) must fulfil (your) duty and must inspire confidence to them, in order that they may

[66] Lubin, 'South Asian Diplomatics', 44. Also see Richard Salomon, 'The Fine Art of Forgery in India', in Gérard Colas and Gerdi Gerschheimer (eds), *Écrire et transmettre en Inde Classique* (Paris: École Française d'Extrême-Orient, 2009): 107–134.

[67] 2nd Major Rock Edict (Kalsi), CII 1, p. 28: savatā **devānaṃpiyasā piyadasisā** lājine duve cikisakā kaṭā manusacikisā cā pasucikisā cā.

[68] CII 1, p. 159: e hetā dutiyāye devīye dāne aṁbā-vaḍikā vā ālame va dāna-[gah]e [va e vā pi a]mne kīchhi ganīyati tāye deviye ṣe nāni.

[69] B.M. Barua, 'The Sohgaura Copper Plate Inscription', *Journal of the Bhandarkar Oriental Research Institute* 11.1 (1930): 32–48, 48: **sāvatiyānam** mahāma(ttā)naṃ sāsane[:] **mānavāsītikaḍasilimate ussagāme** va ete duve koṭṭāgālāṇi tinayavāni maṃthullocachammādāmabhālakān[i] va laṃ kayiyati atiyāyikāya[;] no gahi(ta)vvāya.

[70] CII 1, pp. 111–2: savamu[n]ā me pajā atha p[jā]ye icchām[i] kiṁ]t[i] me savena hitasukhena y[ū] yeyū ti hi[dal]o[g]ik[a]pālalokikena [he]meva me ichha savamanus[e]su.

learn that Devanampriya is to them like a father, that Devanampriya loves them like himself, and that they are to Devanampriya like (his own) children.'[71]

In the Aśokan jurisprudential discourse, the delegation of royal authority represents an extension of the Crown's duty of guardianship. To offer a final example, in his fourth major pilar edict, Aśoka informs his provincial governors (*rajūkas*) that: 'As one feels confident after having entrusted (his) child to an intelligent nurse, (thinking): "The intelligent nurse will be able to keep my child well", so the *lajūkas* were appointed by me for the welfare and happiness of the country-people.'[72] This sense of the imperial, central bureaucracy as an extension of the Crown's duty of guardianship entails active guardianship. In his fifth major rock edicts, Aśoka outlines the remit of his 'Dharma Agents' (*Dhaṃmamahāmātras*):

> They are occupied with servants and masters, with Brāhmaṇas and Ibhiyas, with the destitute; (and) with the aged, for the welfare and happiness of those who are devoted to morality, (and) in releasing (them) from the fetters (of worldly life). They are occupied in supporting prisoners (with money), in causing (their) fetters to be taken off, and in setting (them) free, if one has children, or is bewitched, or aged, respectively.[73]

2.2.4 Regulating religion

We saw, in Chapter 1 of this monograph, that the *Arthaśāstra* argues that a sovereign should create a Bureau of Official Records (*Akṣapaṭala*) to investigate and to uphold the conventional law of the various commercial, cultural, and religious communities within his realm.[74] Aśoka took an interest in regulating cultural and religious affairs, banning some practices and promoting others. Furthermore, he tasked his agents, as an extension of his *parens patriae* jurisdiction, to supervise these communities actively. In contrast with Dharmaśāstric jurisprudence, in which the Crown protects communities' supplemental (*pāribhāṣika*) laws, Aśoka views himself as the arbiter of acceptable community norms according to a centralised, ostensibly Buddhist political theology. Aśoka's edicts articulate a clear jurisprudential theory of royal supervision of religious practices and institutions.

The first major rock edict, banning animal sacrifice is, *pace* Pollock, evidence of unified *legal* rules being applied in India under the rubric of a unified

[71] CII 1, pp. 115–6: sa hevaṁ [ka]ṭu k[aṁ]me [cha]litaviye asvāsa[n]iyā ch[a] te en[a] te pāpuneyu a[th]ā pita [h]evaṁ [ne] lājā ti atha [a]tānaṁ anukaṁpat[i he]vaṁ a[ph]eni anuka[ṁpa]ti athā pajā hevaṁ [may]e lā[j]ine.

[72] CII 1, p. 123: athā hi pajaṃ biyatāye dhātiye nisijitu asvathe hoti viyata dhāti caghati me pajaṃ sukhaṃ palihaṭave hevaṃ mama lajūkā kaṭā jānapadasa hitasukhāye.

[73] CII 1, p. 32: bhaṭamayesu baṃbhanibhesu anathesu [vu]dhesu hidasukhāye dhaṁmayutāye apalibodhāye viyapaṭā te. baṁdha[nabadha]sā paṭividhānāy[e] apalibodhāye mokh[ā]ye chā eyaṁ anubadh[ā] pajāva ti v[ā] [kaṭābhikā]le ti vā m[ah]ā[la]ke ti v[ā] viy[ā]paṭā te.

[74] See Chapter 1, §1.3.1, 'The solution, part 1 – Arthaśāstra.'

jurisprudence.[75] Aśoka enjoins that: 'Here no living being must be killed and sacrificed. And also, no festival meeting must be held. For king Devanampriya Priyadarsin sees much evil in festival meetings. And there are also some festival meetings which are considered meritorious.'[76] The arbiter of a festival's merits was, of course, Aśoka. In the second minor rock edict, Aśoka asserts his authority over the activities of various guild-like groups when he instructs his agents to: 'Ensure that elephant trainers, clerks, fortune-tellers, and Brahmans instruct their apprentices according to ancient tradition... This is the ancient custom, conducive to long life, and thus it must be carried out.'[77]

Finally, Aśoka took a keen interest in the regulation of religious institutions. In his seventh major pillar edict, Aśoka describes the centralised regulation of religious sects:

> Those my *Mahāmātras* of morality too are occupied with affairs of many kinds which are beneficial to ascetics as well as to householders, and they are occupied also with all sects. Some (*Mahāmātras*) were ordered by me to busy themselves with the affairs of the Saṁgha; likewise, others were ordered by me to busy themselves also with the Brahmanas (and) Ājīvikas; others were ordered by me to busy themselves also with the *Nirgranthas*; others were ordered by me to busy themselves also with various (other) sects; (thus) different *Mahāmātras* (are busying themselves) specially with different (congregations). But my *Mahāmātras* of morality are occupied with these (congregations) as well as with all other sects.[78]

The Aśokan regulation of religion involved direct intervention in institutional and ideological affairs by agents of the Crown. This is evidenced by Aśoka's establishment of an acceptable Buddhist monastic textual canon in his third minor pillar edict, and his instruction to his *Dhaṁmamahāmātras*, in the 'Schism edicts' at Sāñcī, Sāraṅganātha, and Kauśambī, that: 'The monk or nun who shall break up the Saṁgha, must be caused to put on white robes and to reside in a non-residence. For my desire is that the Saṁgha may be united (and) of long duration.'[79]

Mauryan inscriptions provide a seminal, and quite sophisticated model of the law of Equity and Trusts as applied by the Crown. As in the *Arthaśāstra*, the sovereign is framed as the father of the nation, who must protect his subjects'

[75] See Chapter 2, §2.1, 'The theory and practice of Equity and Trusts in classical Indian Law'.

[76] CII 1, p. 27: no pi ch[ā] samāje kaṭaviye. bahuk[ā] hi dosā samājasā devān[aṁ]piye pi[ya]dasī lājā dakhati. athi pi ch[ā e]katiyā samāja sādh[u]matā.

[77] The translation is a conflation that appears in Romila Thapar, *Aśoka and the Decline of the Mauryas*, revised edition (New Delhi: Oxford University Press, 1997), 259.

[78] CII I, pp. 132: dhaṁmamahāmātā pi me te bahivhesu aṭhesu ānugahikseu viyāpaṭāse. saṁghaṭhasi pi me kaṭe ime viyāpaṭā hohaṁti ti nigaṁṭhesu pi me kaṭe ime viyāpaṭā hohaṁti nānāpāsaṁḍesu pi me [kha]ṭe ime viyāpaṭā hohaṁti ti paṭivisiṭhaṁ paṭīvisiṭhaṁ tesu tesu [te] ... mātā. dhaṁmamahāmātā cha me etesu cheva viyā[pa]ṭā savesu cha aṁnesu pāsaṁḍesu.

[79] For the 2nd minor pillar edict, see CII 1, p. 172. The Kosambi pillar, edict, ibid., 159, addresses the injunction to the local Mahāmātras: kosaṁbiyaṁ mahām[ā]ta... [saṁghaṁ bhā]khati bhikh[u] v[ā] bhikh[u]ni vā [se pi] chā [o]dāt[ā]ni dusāni [sa]naṁdhāpayitu a[nāvā]sas[I ā]v[ā]sayiy[e].

interests. The Crown, either directly or indirectly through its agents, enjoys a right of supervision over religious and social affairs – intervening in instances of unjust practices and enjoying the capacity to create and regulate religious endowments. We shall see in the following sections, that the Mauryas' successors appropriated and reshaped these core legal concepts over subsequent centuries into a vastly more sophisticated system of religious and charitable endowments.

2.3 Equity and Trusts between the empires (3rd century BCE–4th century CE)

Within fifty years of Aśoka's death, the Mauryan Empire disintegrated, with 'the political landscape returned to conflict between small, regional states, and invaders from the northwest once again claimed domains across the north'.[80] A series of '*arriviste* warlords', including, the Indo-Greek kings (1st century BCE–2nd century CE), the Northern and Western Śakas (1st century BCE–2nd century CE), and the Kuṣāṇas (1st–3rd centuries CE), 'adapted to the local cultures… [and] brought foreign customs and techniques of rule'.[81] In Southern India, 'the first great… polities arose', including the Sātavāhanas (1st century BCE–3rd century CE) and the Andhra Ikṣvākus (3rd–4th centuries CE).[82]

This era, between the fall of the Mauryan Empire and the rise of the Imperial Guptas in 4th century CE, produced numerous influential developments in Indian society: the consolidation of the Buddhist Saṅgha as a property-owning institution, the compilation of jurisprudential literature such as the *Arthaśāstra* and the *Mānavadharmaśāstra*, the emergence of devotional literation, such as the *Rāmāyaṇa* and the *Mahābhārata*, and, of course, the emergence of Middle Indic and Sanskrit as 'languages of power'.[83]

Alongside these wider social developments, the incipient legal practices of Equity and Trusts that we saw in the context of Aśoka's edicts blossomed. A more sophisticated system of religious endowments arose in the Northern Kṣatrapa and Kuṣāṇa polities, centred around Mathurā in the Gangetic plain (but stretching to Takṣaśilā in the north).[84] Royal and private donors consecrated (*pratiṣṭhā*) images and relics, created 'perpetual endowments' (*akṣayanīvīs*) to maintain religious

[80] McClish, *The History of the Arthaśāstra*, 10.
[81] Ollett, *Language of the Snakes*, 41; McClish, *The History of the Arthaśāstra*, 11.
[82] McClish, *The History of the Arthaśāstra*, 11.
[83] See Note 18. Ollett, *Language of the Snakes*, 26–7: 'A "language of power" can be a language used by political power as well as language that confers power on those that use it.' Also see Harry Falk, 'The Tidal Waves of Indian History: Between the Empires and Beyond', in Patrick Olivelle (ed.) *Between the Empires: Society in India 300 BCE to 400 CE* (Oxford: Oxford University Press, 2006): 145–66.
[84] For the Kuṣāṇas, see Michael Skinner, *Marks of Empire: Extracting a Narrative from the Corpus of Kuṣāṇa Inscriptions* (Unpublished PhD Dissertation: University of Washington, 2017).

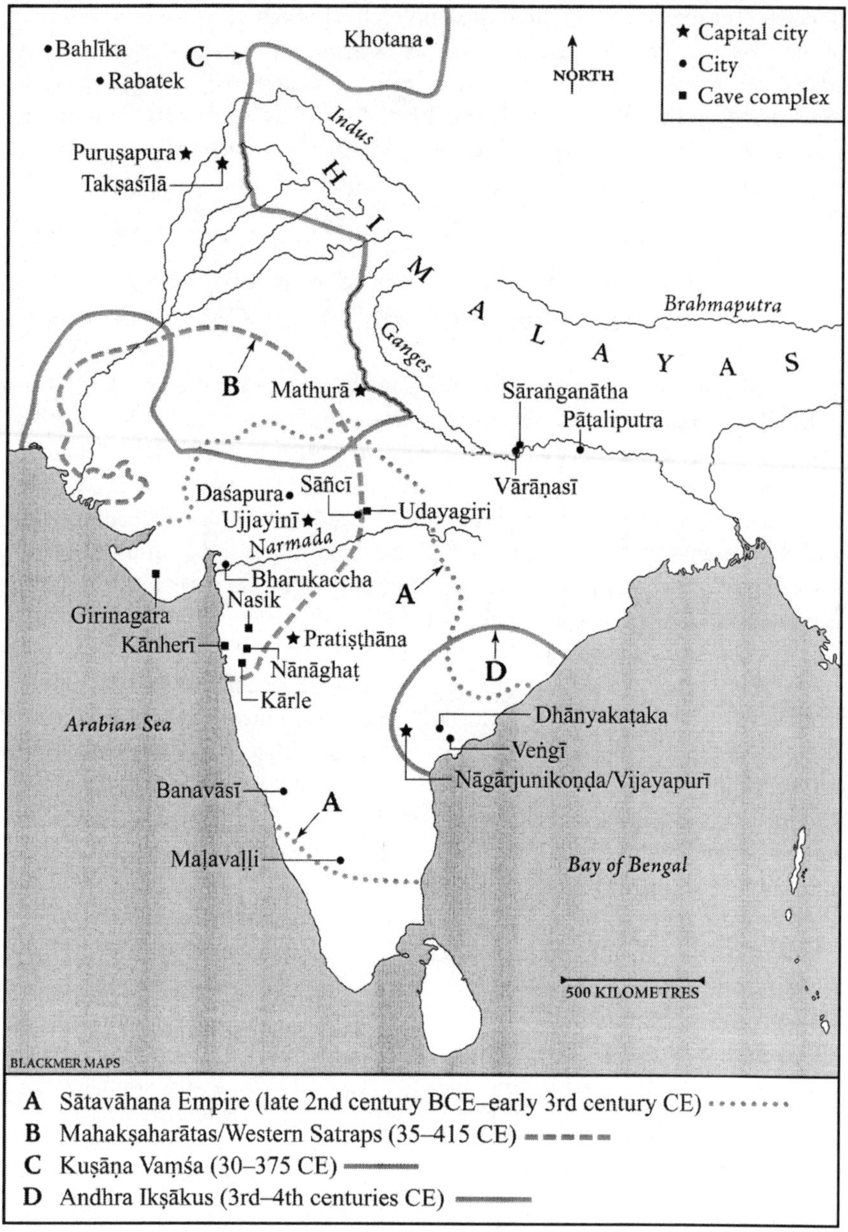

Map 2.1 India between the Empires (~100 BCE–300 CE)

institutions (including temples), and classified such donations as religious gifts (*deyadharma*, *dharmadeya*, etc). No single inscription from the Northern Kṣatrapa or Kuṣāṇa polities contains all of these features. Nevertheless, in the aggregate, this epigraphic milieu contains an early assemblage of the core building blocks of the legal practice of Equity and Trusts in medieval India.

The Sanskritisation of Śaka legal phenomena occurred in the context of the encounter – sometimes hostile, sometimes matrimonial – between the Western Kṣatrapas (the Kṣaharātas) and the Sātavāhanas in western India during the first centuries of the Common Era. Andrew Ollett notes, that: 'The Sātavāhana dynasty, which ruled most of central India between 50 BCE and 250 CE is closely associated both with radical innovations in inscriptional discourse in this period and with the invention of Prakrit literature.'[85] Ollett's account of the Sātavāhanas and Kṣatrapas 'focuses on the centuries-long process by which "languages of power" were continuously fashioned, defined, and contested'.[86] I argue that this centuries-long process coincided with the development of a Sanskrit legal practice of religious endowments.

Broadly, the data suggest that the Kṣaharātas introduced the Sātavāhanas to the legal building blocks of religious endowments, that the Sātavāhanas adopted these building blocks, and that they were partially Sanskritised during the later Sātavāhana period. During the rule of the Andhra Ikṣvākus of Vijayapurī (Nāgārjunikoṇḍa), the Sātavāhanas' direct successors in Andhra Pradesh, these practices were more – although never completely – Sanskritised. Eventually, the rise of the Imperial Guptas in the 4th century CE saw the expansion of Sanskrit epigraphic discourse and Equity and Trusts across the Indian subcontinent that was very much in conversation with Dharmaśāstric jurisprudence.

2.3.1 Northern Kṣatrapas and Kuṣāṇas

Scholars have long noted the importance of Mathurā during the Age Between the Empires as a centre of art, culture, and religion.[87] Alongside these cultural developments, the Śakas and Kuṣāṇas introduced the phenomena of consecrating (*pratiṣṭhā*) images (*pratimās*/*mūrtis*) of Jinas, saints (*arhats*), Buddhas, and Bodhisattvas.[88] Despite their seemingly ritual function, they represent a wider

[85] Ollett, *Language of the Snakes*, 27.

[86] Ibid., 26.

[87] See Doris Srinivasn (ed.), *Mathurā: The Cultural Heritage* (New Delhi: American Institute of Indian Studies, 1989).

[88] See EI 1.14 and Heinrich Lüders, *Mathurā Inscriptions* (Göttingen: Vandenhoeck & Ruprecht, 1961). For an overview of Pratiṣṭhā, see Istvan Keul (ed.), *Consecration Rituals in South Asia* (Leiden: Brill, 2017).

phenomenon in the post-Mauryan world of consecrating the relics of the Buddha, stupas, or monasteries.[89]

The lion capital reliquary from Mathurā, inscribed during the reigns of the Northern Kṣatrapas, Rājūvula (r. 10–15 CE) and Śoḍāsa (1st century CE), further develops the model of Aśoka's Lumbinī inscription: the king establishes a relic, creates a monastery, endows it with land, and passes possession of the complex to the head of a disciplinary order. Like the Lumbinī inscription, the Mathurā lion capital reliquary records a change in monastic custody over a royal endowment. Harry Falk notes that the Mathurā pillar is a palimpsest and contains two inscriptions. Falk attributes the first inscription to the reign of Rājūvula and argues that it was erected originally at a monastery in Jamu. Rājūvula's chief queen, Tasi Kumari, installs relics and gifts a park to the Sarvāstivādin order of monks:

> At this piece of land, outside the monastic border, the relics of the Lord, the Śakyamuni, the Buddha, have been installed on the ground of the king of the Śaka-race in the Bodha-monastery and a *stūpa* and a park for the order (of monks) of the four quarters into the acceptance of the Sarvāstivādins.[90]

Falk argues that, when Rājūvula's successor, Śoḍāsa, shifted his power base from Jamu to Mathurā, Śoḍāsa re-established the pillar, the relics, and the associated order of 'tutelary' Sarvāstivādins in Mathurā at the expense of the local Mahāsaṅghikas:

> (By) the son of the Mahākṣatrapa Rajuvula, Śodāsa, the Kṣatrapa this piece of land… [at] the camp named Vaijayadinna, which is separated from the Victory-camp by the Bodha-hill, was presented, after having taken it out of the *sīmā* (of the community to which it formerly belonged)… to Budhila from Nagara, the monk belonging to the Sarvāstivādins… into the care of the Sarvāstivādins… (it) must not be offered to the Mahāsaṅghikas… (this is) a pious donation in the cave-monastery.[91]

The inscription is fragmentary and opaque, but it connects four practices that would become instrumental in the subsequent practice of Trusts law in Indian epigraphy: 1) a sovereign establishes an image, relic, or building; 2) endows that

[89] For an early instance of the establishment of the relics of the Buddha, see the Swāt Inscription of the Greco-Indian ruler Theodoros (1st century BCE), CII Vol 2. Part 1, A.1: **theūdorena meridarkhena** pratiṭhavid(ra) ime śarira **śakamuṇisa** bha(r)**avato** bahujaṇastitiye.

[90] Harry Falk, 'Ten Thoughts on the Mathura Lion Capital Reliquary', in Shailendra Bhandare and Sanjay Garg (eds), *Felicitas: Essays in Numismatic, Epigraphy and History in Honour of Joe Cribb* (Mumbai: Reesha Books, 2011): 121–42, 123–4: iśa praḍẖavi-pra[ṯe] (A11) śe nisime śarira praūṯeṭhaviṯo (A12) **bhaḵavaṯo śakamuṇisa budhasa** (A13) śaki[mu → X]rayasa śpa[e] bhusavi[ha] (A14) thuva ca sagharama ca caṯ<u>(A15)diśasa saghasa **sarva(A16)stivatana** parigrahe. For the political backdrop of these events, see ibid., 131–3.

[91] Ibid., 126–31: (B1) **mahakṣatravasa** (B2) **vajulasa putra** (B3) **śudase** kṣatrave (M2) imo paḍẖavi (M3) praṯeśo (I1a) veyaaḏirṇa (I2) namo kadha (I3) varo (I4) viyaa (I1b) kadhavaro busapa (J1) rva(take?)[?]na palichina (J2) nis̱imo karita niyaṯṯiṯo… (F1) **budhilasa** naḵaraasa (F2) bhikusa **sarvastivadasa**… (J3) **sarvastivatana** parigrahe… (N3) na **mahasaghiana** pra(N4)ñaviṯave… (H') dhamadana (H) guhavihare.

institution with (the income of) lands or some form of capital; 3) he entrusts that institution to an individual or association to possess and to maintain it; and 4) reserves the right to adjust the legal terms of the grant according to political expediency.

Royal establishments of images, stūpas, and relics occurred in conjunction with charitable endowments of groves, alms houses, hospitals, etc. For example, the Takṣaśilā copper-plate of the Kṣaharāta Patika (1st century BCE–1st century CE) records that the Śaka king 'established a previous non-established body (relic) of the Buddha and a garden for the Saṅgha' through 'Rohiṇimitra, the superintendent of the construction of the Saṅgha's garden'.[92] Perhaps the first record of a temple endowment occurs in a pair of inscriptions by Vima Kalpiśa (r. 113–127 CE) and his grandson Huviṣka (r. 150–180).[93] In the first inscription, Kalpiśa notes that, 'a temple (*devakula*) was caused to be made (as well as) a garden, a tank, a well, an assembly hall, and a gateway'.[94] In the second inscription, Huviṣka, 'having seen that the temple was broken, fallen down, and in a ruinous state', presumably rebuilt it.[95]

Furthermore, Huviṣka created what is probably the first surviving record of a complete Brāhmaṇical endowment in Indian legal history: wherein a donor makes over a perpetual endowment (*akṣayanīvī*) with clear stipulations concerning the use of that endowment for charitable purposes:

> This eastern hall of merit was given a perpetual endowment... [by the king]. From what is cleared off month for month from the interest therefrom [a] hundred Brāhmaṇas should be served in the open hall, and day for day... [various foodstuffs] should be given for the sake of destitute people... The perpetual endowment was given to the rāka-guild [weavers?], 550 purāṇa, and to the flour-maker-guild, 550 purāṇa.[96]

[92] CII 2.1, B.13: patiko apratithavita bhagavata **śakamunisa** shariram (*pra)tithaveti [samgha]ramam ca. **rohiṇimitreṇa** ya ima[mi] saṁgharame navakamika. For the dating of this inscription, see, Stefan Baums, 'Catalog and Revised Texts and Translations of Gandharan Reliquary Inscriptions', in David Jongeward, Elizabeth Errington, Richard Salomon and Stefan Baums (eds), *Gandharan Buddhist Reliquaries* (Seattle: Early Buddhist Manuscripts Project, 2012): 211–12.

[93] While Rājūvala and his son, Śodāsa, refer to temples in several of their inscriptions, they never endow them in clear financial terms. For Śodāsa's 1st-century CE Vāsudeva Inscription of Śodāsa at Mathurā, see Sonya Quintanilla, *History of Early Stone Sculpture at Mathura: Ca. 150 BCE - 100 CE* (Leiden: Brill, 2007), 262–3: '... a stone *torana* [gateway] and railing were caused to be erected by Vasu at the ... of the great temple of lord Vasudeva'. For Śodāsa's 'Mora Well Inscription', see ibid., 260: 'the images of the holy *paṁcavīras* [five heroes] of the Vr̥ṣṇis... the stone shrine... whom the magnificent matchless stone house of Toṣā was erected and maintained'.

[94] Lüders, *Mathurā Inscriptions*, #90, 135: devakula[ṃ] kāritā ārāmo puṣkariṇi udapāna[ṃ] ca sa[bh]ā dā[ra]koṭhako.

[95] Ibid., #99, 139–41: devakal[aṃ bha]gnapatitaviśirṇa[ṃ] d[ṛ]śya... For a discussion of the possibility that the Kuṣāṇa kings were themselves the object of cultic worship at this temple, see Upinder Singh 'Cults and Shrines in Early Historical Mathura (c. 200 BC–AD 200)', *World Archeology* 36.3 (2004): 378–98.

[96] EI 21.10: akshayanīvi dinn[ā] tu[ta]tō vṛi[ddhi]tō māsānumāsaṁ śuddhasya chatudiśi puṇyaśā[lā] yaṁ brāhmaṇaśatataṁ parivishitavyaṁ divasē diva[sē] cha... anādh[ā]nāṁ kṛitēna dātavya[ṁ] babhakshitāna pibasitānaṁ... akshayanivi... [r]ākaśreṇ[ī]yē purāṇaśata 500 50 samitakaraśreṇī[ye cha] purāṇaśata 500 50.

Presumably, these two guilds invested the donated money and bore a fiduciary duty to deliver the interest to someone who was responsible for administering the alms hall.

2.3.2 Kṣaharātas and Sātavāhanas

The reign of the Sātavāhanas (50 BCE–250 CE) in central and western India witnessed three connected events of great importance in Indian history: 1) the emergence of Middle Indic and then Sanskrit as 'languages of power'; 2) the compilation of the *Arthaśāstra*; and 3) the coalescence of a practical jurisprudence of religious endowments in the epigraphic tradition.[97] The Sātavāhanas and their Śaka rivals, the Kṣaharātas, developed precursors to the political, cosmopolitan Sanskrit of Rudradāman (r. 130–150 CE); explicitly invoked terminology from the *Arthaśāstra*; and endowed a series of religious institutions. At this juncture, then, we see the emergence of a practical law of religious endowments at the same time that the *jurisprudence* of Equity and Trusts developed in the Arthaśāstric - and, eventually, the Dharmaśāstric - traditions.

One of the oldest Sātavāhana inscriptions, found in a cave in Nāsik, in modern Mahārāṣṭra, records that the 'Mahāmātra Samaṇa of Nāsika caused a cave to be made during the reign of Kṛṣṇa of the Sātavāhana lineage'.[98] The use of the term Mahāmātra suggests an Aśokan connection.[99] At a cave at Nāṇāghāṭ, the Sātavāhanas, King Śrī Sātakarṇi and Queen Nāganikā (r. 88–42 BCE), inscribed a list of their accomplishments 'in a new kind of language - a poetry of politics, in stark and obvious contrast to the prosaic inscriptions of earlier kings'.[100] This Middle Indic inscription, like those of Aśoka, invokes Dharma, but at Nāṇāghāṭ, the Sātavāhanas associate Dharma with Vedic and post-Vedic deities, with sacrifices, and with the ritual re-distribution of fees to Brāhmaṇas.[101] Although these

[97] Martini, 'Origin of Akṣayanīvī', 148, argues that the *Adhyakṣapracāra* of the *Arthaśāstra*, which is the only śāstric source on the *Akṣayanīvī*, was 'composed ca. 1st C. BCE–1st c. CE in an area somewhere close to the coast of northwest Maharashtra or southern Gujarat'. This is the same area where the Kṣaharātas and Sātavāhanas were creating Akṣayanīvīs. For the dates of the Sātavāhana kings, see Appendix A in Ollett, *Language of the Snakes*.

[98] Vasudev Vishnu Mirashi, *The History and Inscriptions of the Sātavāhanas and the Western Kshatrapas* (Bombay: Government Press, 1981), #1: sādavāhanakule kanhe rājani nāsikakena / samaṇena mahāmāteṇa leṇa kārita //

[99] For this possibility, see Skinner, *Urbanization and Interactions*, 32: 'Furthermore, the *mahāmātra* referenced in this inscription indicates that the early Sātavāhana kings developed a bureaucratic form of government comprised of state officials, possibly an adaptation from the Mauryan period whose rulers also employed *mahāmātras*.'

[100] Ollett, *Language of the Snakes*, 30.

[101] Ibid., 30–1. Ollett, ibid., 32 finds another connection to the *Arthaśāstra*: 'The Sātavāhanas called themselves "those whose wheels are unstoppable" (*apratihata-caka*), an epithet that is condensed and allusive: the 'wheels' in question are those of the royal chariot, but perhaps also the "spheres" of political influence theorized in works such as the *Treatise on Power*.'

early Sātavāhana inscriptions reflect the emergence of a literary form of political discourse tied to a new political theology – of Brāhmaṇical Dharma – they don't describe legal phenomena.

The emergence of legal discussions of religious endowments in Sātavāhana inscriptions stemmed from an interaction with the Kṣaharātas (the Western Kṣatrapas), who 'established a small kingdom in what was now Gujarat in the middle of the first century CE'.[102] King Nahapāna 'wrested a number of key sites from the Sātavāhanas and introduced the region to the use of Sanskrit in political inscriptions'.[103] Nahapāna's son-in-law, Uṣavadāta, also introduced the same sorts of legal phenomena that developed, roughly contemporaneously in Mathurā, in their power base in Western India. At Nāsika (modern Nasik), Uṣavadāta created a legal trust similar to that of Huviṣka at Mathurā:

> He (Uṣavadāta) gave a perpetual endowment of three thousand *Karsāpāṇas* to the Saṁgha... it will be utilized for the expenses of the clothing and the medicines of the monks living in this cave. And these *Karsāpāṇas* have been invested in the guilds at Govardhana... these *Karsāpāṇas* are not to be paid back. Only their interest is to be utilized.[104]

Uṣavadāta stipulates the uses for the interest, and notes that, 'all this has been announced in the town-assembly and has been recorded on wooden tablets according to custom'.[105] He closes his inscription by noting that he also gave seven thousand *Karsāpāṇas* to 'deities and Brāhmaṇas.'[106]

Uṣavadāta made a series of further endowments at Kārle and Nāsika – the latter in Sanskrit – where he describes his liberality to the Buddhist Saṅgha, his donations of villages to 'deities and Brāhmaṇas' and his creation of several secular charities. These parallel those of Huviṣka:

> Who gave sixteen villages to the deities and Brāhmaṇas... who gave four-roomed rest houses in Bharukaccha, Daśapura, Govardhana, and Śūrpāraka, who has made gardens, tanks, and wells, who has established free crossings at the Ibā, Pārādā, Damaṇa, Tāpī, Karabeṇā, Dāhanukā, and Nāvā Rivers.[107]

In time, however, the Sātavāhana, 'Gautamīputra Śrī Sātakarṇi [r. 60–84 CE] retook all of these sites from Nahapāna and the local kings who had thrown in their lots

[102] Ibid., 37.
[103] Ibid., 38–9.
[104] Mirashi, *History*, #38: datta cānena akṣayanivi kāhāpaṇasahasrāṇi trini 3000 saṅghasa... ye imaṃsi leṇe vasaṃtānaṃ bhavisati civarika kuśaṇamūle ca. ete ca kāhāpaṇā prayutā govardhanavāthavāsu śreṇisu... ete ca kāhāpaṇā apaḍidātavā vadhibhojā.
[105] Ibid., ete ca sarvaṃ srāvita nigamasabhāya nibadha ca phalakavāre caritrato ti.
[106] Ibid., devānaṃ brāhmaṇānaṃ ca.
[107] Ollett, *Language of the Snakes*, 40. His translation: devatabhyaḥ brāhmaṇebhyaś ca ṣoḍaśagrāmadena... **bharukacche daśapure govardhane śorpārage** ca catuśālāvasadhaprati śrayapradena ārāmataḍāgaüdapānakareṇa ibāpārādādamaṇatāpīkarabeṇādā hanukānāvāpuṇyatarakareṇa.

with him.'[108] The restoration of Sātavāhana suzerainty coincided with their restoration of the use of Middle Indic (rather than the Kṣaharātas' incipient use of Sanskrit), but the Sātavāhanas' inscriptions appropriated legal phenomena, such as perpetual endowments, from the Kṣaharātas.[109] They also introduced a series of novel developments in the legal practice of religious endowments. For example, Lubin notes that Gautamīputra Śrī Sātakarṇi's Nāsika inscription – which reassigns some of Uṣavadāta's erstwhile land to the Buddhist Saṅgha:

> Exhibits several features of what will become a standard framework of a South Asian land-grant. It begins with an introductory portion announcing the royal order, including further particulars of time or (as in this case) place, and identifying the officer responsible for seeing the order enacted. This is followed by the order itself... which includes a description of the property, followed by a list of five special privileges accorded to the recipient. In this record, each of the five 'exemptions' (*parihāra*) is expressed in a single word or compound; in later epigraphy, the number of such privileges grows, and they are sometimes described at more length.[110]

At Kārle, this financial arrangement was formalised as 'monks' land' (*bhikhuhala*).[111] The notion of assigning land to monks as a form of perpetual endowment eventually extended to Hindu deities. The Kṣaharātas gave villages to deities, but their inscriptions never mentioned the legal implications of these gifts. The Maḷavaḷḷi pillar inscription of Cuṭukulānanda Sātakarṇi (3rd century CE) in Karnataka, is probably the earliest record of a trust in favour of a Hindu deity. In it, the king gives a village: 'To [the Brāhmaṇa] Koṇḍamāṇa of the Kauṇḍinya gotra as a *brāhmadeya* for the enjoyment (*bhoga*) of the deity Maḷapaḷi.'[112]

In short, the conflict between the Kṣaharātas and the Sātavāhanas saw more than just the development of an increasingly sophisticated epigraphic discourse of political power – in Prakrit or in Sanskrit. This interaction between two rival polities also saw the introduction and refinement of religious endowments: kings made over the income of fields or the interest from financial deposits to specified institutions or individuals for specific purposes; listed the legal immunities the trustees of these endowments enjoyed; and recorded the arrangement in the official bureaucracy. The beneficiaries of the grants included the Buddhist Saṅgha, Brāhmaṇas, and, for the first time, deities. This process occurred in tandem, perhaps, with the compilation of the *Arthaśāstra*. It was the successors of the Sātavāhanas, however, who Sanskritised the law of endowments in the sense that the use of Sanskrit as a language of power dovetailed with a full embrace of Dharmaśāstric jurisprudence.

[108] Ibid., 37.
[109] See Mirashi, *History*, #19 & #27 for examples of *akṣayanīvis*.
[110] Lubin, 'South Asian Diplomatics', 49.
[111] Mirashi, *History*, #12.
[112] Ibid., #35: **maḷapaḷidevabhogaṃ**... bahmadejjaṃ diṇṇam kauṇḍinyasagottāya... **koṇḍamāṇāya**.

2.3.3 The Ikṣvākus of Vijayapurī (3rd–4th centuries CE)

The Sātavāhanas' successors in 'the Krishna valley of today's Andhra Pradesh', the Ikṣvākus, followed their predecessors' inscriptional style in form and content. After pursuing 'marital alliances with the Kṣatrapas of Ujjayinī', however, 'there appears to be a trend toward the use of Sanskrit in [their] inscriptions'.[113] From their capital in Vijayapurī (modern Nāgārjunikoṇḍa), the Ikṣvākus endowed a series of Buddhist and Hindu religious institutions. Like the Sātavāhanas and the Kṣaharātas, the Ikṣvākus created perpetual endowments by investing liquid capital and assigning income from land.[114]

The Ikṣvākus, however, created more complex endowments: these listed the legal niceties of their institutions, outlined fiduciary duties, and included arrangements to protect the endowment. Although the Ikṣvākus frequently refer to epic figures such as Rāma, Yuddhiṣṭhira, etc., they do not seem to have adopted Dharmaśāstric jurisprudential language. Furthermore, for the first time in Indian history, the Ikṣvākus made endowments directly to deities – introducing divine legal personality to the subcontinent. Taken collectively, this data suggests that we can date the emergence of divine temple trusts to the 3rd century CE.

An octagonal pillar inscription, written in grammatically correct Sanskrit, from the sixteenth regnal year of Siri-Ehavalacāntamūla (r. 250–300 CE) records that the king: 'Caused to be made (this) temple of the Bhagavant Puṣpabhadrasvāmin, established a flagstaff and gave as perpetual endowment the village Puḍokeḍaṁ'.[115] Another, undated inscription from the reign of Siri-Ehavalacāntamūla explicitly describes the deity as the beneficiary of the trust:

> [The ruler] had a temple and a platform made for the Bhagavant Noḍhagīsarasāmi. And having made a permanent endowment … month after month … *dināris* (are to be deposited?)… Thus, in four guilds… [a] hundred *dināris*… [are deposited]… [and]… the *taithika*, *nākṣatrika* as well as *prāharika* rites and so forth (are to be performed) for the god Noḍha…; the repair of what is damaged and dilapidated and the embellishment are to be made by themselves. And thus, the townsmen… headed by the members of the guild cause to act (accordingly) those who do not act accordingly.[116]

[113] Ollett, *Language of the Snakes*, 45.

[114] For *Akṣyanīvīs* during this time, see Ingo Strauch, 'Money for Rituals: Akṣayanīvī and Related Inscriptions form Āndhradeśa' in Henry Albery, Jens-Uwe Hartmann, and Himanshu Prabha Ray (eds), *Power, Presence and Space South Asian Rituals in Archaeological Context* (London: Routledge, 2020): 193–214.

[115] Arlo Griffiths and Vincent Tournier, 'EIAD 53: Octagonal Pillar from Site 34 at Nagarjunakonda – Reign of Siri-Ehavalacāntamūla, Year 16': **bhagavato puṣpabhadrasvāminaḥ** devakulaṁ kāritaṁ. dhvajastaṁbaś ca pratiṣṭhāpitaḥ grāmaś ca puḍokeḍaṁ akṣayanivī dattaḥ.

[116] EIAD 56, http://hisoma.huma-num.fr/exist/apps/EIAD/works/EIAD0056.xml?&odd=teipublisher.odd: **bhagavato [noḍhagī]saras[ā]misa** devakulaṁ thali[ṁ] [ca] [kāri]tā akhayanīvi[ṁ] ca kat[ū]ṇa mas[anu]mas[ika]sa [vi]dhi? dh[i]kaseni[ya] [dināri]… eva[ṁ] senis[u] catusu dinarisa[ta]… **no[ḍha] [de]va[sa]** [te]thikanakhati[k]āpa[hā]raḍhikā bhagaphulasa[ṁ]ṭhapa apanā ca citanaṁ katavaṁ eva ca akaraṁta seṭhipam⟨u⟩kha nigama karayaṁ.

This purpose trust identifies the deity as the clear beneficiary. The sovereign creates an endowment, deposits the capital with various guilds, appoints priests to serve the deity, arranges for the repair of the temple, and makes the townspeople responsible for correcting any maladministration of the trust.

The introduction of a limited legal personality of deities coincided with efforts to protect deities' assets from spoliation. An inscription by an official of the 4th century Abhīra king, Vasuṣeṇa of Vijayapurī, notes that: 'Lord Aṣṭabhujasvāmin, made from *udumbara* wood, which had never been moved from Sañjayapurī, [that is,] from its [original] place, by the kings Śaka Rudradāman of Avanti and Viṣṇurudraśivānanda Sāṭakakarṇi of Vanavāsa has now been installed on Seḍagiri.'[117] Richard Salomon argues that this 'inscription can be understood in light of this well-attested practice of appropriation of sacred images' by rival kings during the medieval period.[118] Presumably, 'medieval Hindu rulers plac[ed] themselves forthrightly in the center of a redistributive network involving expropriated objects' once temple deities became the beneficiaries of substantial benefices.[119] Spoliation requires the existence of something worth plundering. Therefore, it is expected that deities' emergence as beneficiaries of endowments would coincide with the rise of the political strategy of expropriating the endowments (and temple images) of one's rivals.

At the same time, the Buddha became a legal beneficiary in Ikṣvāku dedications. An early 4th-century donation to a monastery has the intriguing line, 'the own property of the Bhagavant (*bhagavato sākanibaṁdha*)' and a contemporaneous dedication notes that the donor, 'established a wing of the monastery in the splendid chief among monasteries, dwelling of Him (i.e. the Buddha) who got rid of mental afflictions'.[120] Gregory Schopen argues that the emergence of the Buddha as a resident of monasteries and as a legal owner of monastic property coincided with the emergence of an official known as the 'Keeper of the Perfume Chamber' (*Gandhakuṭivārika*), 'the central cell in a Buddhist monastery reserved as the residence of the Buddha himself'.[121] It is no coincidence that at about the same time

[117] Richard Salomon, 'Aṣṭabhujasvāmin: A Reinterpretation of the Ābhīra Inscription from Nagarjunakonda' *Indo-Iranian Journal* 56 (2013): 397–417, 417: **saṃjayapur**[**ī**]**to** yo rājābhi **āva**[**nta**] **kena śakena rudradāmena vānavāsakena** [ca] **viṣṇurudraśivalānanda**[**sāta**]**karṇiṇnā** [s]**thāpito** pi na cālito [e]ṣa **bha**[**gavāṃ**] **ruṃbarabhavo āṣṭaṃjasvāmi** [**ṣeḍa**]**giriya** sth[ā]pito.

[118] Ibid., 405, citing Davis, *Lives of Indian Images*, 51–87. The earliest example of this phenomenon, to my knowledge, is a phrase in Hathigumpha inscription of Khāravela (2nd century BCE–1st century CE, Odisha). See Salomon, 'Aṣṭabhujasvāmin', 405: **naṃdarājanītaṃ** ca **kā**[**li**]**ṃgajinaṃ** saṃnive[sa]. 'And (he) sets up the Jina of Kalinga which had been taken away by King Nanda.' My translation.

[119] Salomon, 'Aṣṭabhujasvāmin', 404. Davis, *Lives of Indian Images*, 28.

[120] EIAD #105, http://hisoma.huma-num.fr/exist/apps/EIAD/works/EIAD0105.xml?&odd=teipublisher.odd & EIAD #77, http://hisoma.huma-num.fr/exist/apps/EIAD/works/EIAD0077.xml?&odd=teipublisher.odd: vihāramukkhye vigatajvarālaye ˘ – ˘ – – – ˘ ˘ – [niveśitā] vihārabā[hā] vipulārtthak āṅkṣiṇā.

[121] Schopen, 'Buddha as an Owner', 187.

as these two aforementioned inscriptions, 'the reverend Saṅghadeva, keeper of the Perfume Chamber of King Govinda's monastery' at Chaitanyapuri (near modern Hyderabad), who 'established the great monastery at Puphagiri' recorded *his* creation of a new residence.[122] The more the Buddha, as a legal person, owned substantial assets, the more influence his legal representatives – his fiduciaries – exercised in his name.

In short, the epoch between the fall of the Mauryan Empire and the rise of the Gupta Empire witnessed the development of fairly sophisticated legal records of religious and charitable endowments. The Kuṣāṇas and Śakas introduced the installation and endowment of images, relics, temples, monasteries, and charitable institutions while devising different financial instruments to maintain them. These arrangements were, of course, subject to political vicissitudes. As time wore on, divine and Buddhist beneficiaries of endowments took on a greater legal personality and received more sophisticated assets. Some of these assets, the *akṣayanīvī* in particular, and the political language described in these inscriptions appear to be Arthaśāstric rather than Dharmaśāstric. A shift in jurisprudence came with the rise of the Imperial Guptas in the 4th century CE.

2.4 Equity and Trust in the greater Gupta era (4th–6th centuries CE)

Like the Mauryan Empire, the Imperial Guptas left an indelible imprint on Indian history. As Bisschop and Cecil note:

> The 'Gupta Period' is a commonly invoked heading used to designate not only an historical period, but also a high point of premodern South Asian culture. It has become synonymous with terms like 'classical' or 'golden age', a period in which artistic production flourished and great works of literature, science, philosophy, architecture, and sculpture were produced, presumably under the patronage or influence of the Gupta rulers and their associates.[123]

While the Gupta period might function 'as a convenient scholarly shorthand for an [sic] significant period of cultural production', the historiographical tendency to credit the Guptas with innovations in art, religion, law, etc., means that

[122] EIAD #173, http://hisoma.huma-num.fr/exist/apps/EIAD/works/EIAD0173.xml?&odd=teipublisher.odd: [bhadaṁ]ta **saṁghadevena govidaṁrājavihārasa** gaṁdhakuṭivārike[na] ima tasela. [sa]ṁvāsa[va]raṁ pa[ti]ṭhāpitaṁ. For the perfume chamber in epigraphy, see Schopen, 'Buddha as an Owner', 182–97.

[123] Peter Bisschop and Elizabeth Cecil, 'Primary Sources and Asian Pasts: Beyond the Boundaries of the "Gupta Period"', in Peter Bisschop and Elizabeth Cecil (eds), *Primary Sources and Asian Pasts* (Berlin: De Grunter, 2021): 1–17, 1.

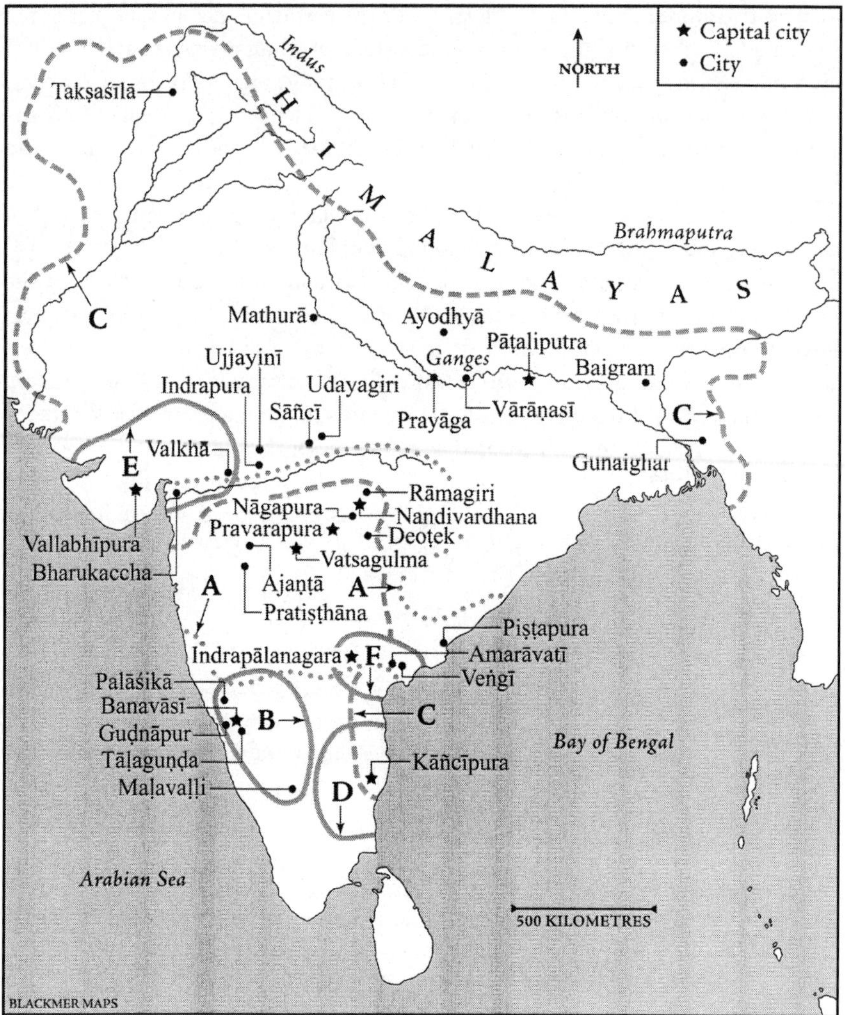

A Vākāṭaka Dynasty (~250–500 CE)
B Kadambas of Banavāsi (345–540 CE)
C Imperial Guptas (4th–6th centuries CE)
D Early Pallavas (~275–500 CE)
E Maitrakas of Vallabhī (475–776 CE)
F Viṣṇukuṇḍina Dynasty (420–624 CE)

Map 2.2 India during the Greater 'Gupta Age' (~4th–6th centuries CE)

'it remains difficult to extricate the Guptas from the grandiose and romanticized estimations of their role in South Asian history'.[124]

Its brilliance notwithstanding, Michael Willis' *The Archaeology of Hindu Ritual* exemplifies the dangers of failing to extricate the Guptas' unique contributions from romanticised estimations of their importance in Indian history. Willis' monograph provides a detailed account of Hindu temple trusts – and attendant theological and jurisprudential theories – within the Gupta era. Willis argues that Candragupta II (r. 375–415 CE) introduced 'a revitalized form of early Hindu kingship in which the ruler was envisaged as a paramount sovereign (*cakravartin*) and supreme devotee of Viṣṇu (*paramabhāgavata*)'.[125]

This novel form of sovereignty involved the application of 'an effective legal system across most of India by the early fifth century.'[126] This legal system is, of course, the cosmopolitan Dharmaśāstra of 'the cadres of specialists in dharma' and it subtended the imperial formations of the Sanskrit cosmopolis.[127] Willis examines, *inter alia*, the 'system of rural development through land-grants to priests and temples' in order to uncover 'the rich matrix of constitutive and distributive acts through which the Guptas, Vākāṭakas, and their subordinates controlled their ritual polity'.[128]

The Gupta era witnessed a transformation of the practical law of Equity and Trusts: purpose trusts in favour of deities became ubiquitous and they invariably involved the invocation of a set series of Sanskrit scriptural verses drawn from the Purāṇas and the *Mahābhārata*.[129] These divine trusts also entailed a standard list of purposes: sacrificial offerings to the deity, almshouses, water tanks, repairs of the temple, etc.[130] Trusts entail fiduciaries and Willis notes that the 'use of trustees suggests that… we can think of the early gods of the Gupta period as minors whose estates had to be managed by guardians before they reached maturity'.[131] Finally, Willis documents the financial instruments used to endow temples and argues, that during this period, deities acquired 'a juridical personality with established rights to offerings and to land'.[132]

Willis' thesis has been widely criticised for its anachronistic assumption that: 'The copper-plate charters of the Gupta age provide the first written evidence of these [Hindu deities as] living images… [and] the records themselves… present us with a mature cult in almost every particular – nothing about them seems formative.'[133]

[124] Ibid., 3.
[125] Willis, *Archaeology*, 2–3.
[126] Ibid., 6.
[127] Ibid., 6–7.
[128] Ibid., 5.
[129] Ibid., 84–8.
[130] See ibid. 96–113, where Willis gives examples of each term.
[131] Ibid., 124.
[132] Ibid., 127.
[133] Ibid., 122–3.

The divine trusts of the Gupta era had clear antecedents during the Mauryan and post-Mauryan ages and Hindu deities became full juridical persons – in the sense of active legal agents holding complex property portfolios – only in the centuries following the Gupta Empire.[134] Furthermore, as Leslie Orr notes, Willis largely ignores contemporaneous developments in donations to Buddhist and Jain institutions during the Gupta age that also utilised Dharmaśāstric jurisprudence.[135]

Taking the long view, we can see that the Gupta era was formative in several ways. First, the law of Equity and Trusts was Sanskritised during the Gupta era and inscriptions and copper-plate grants endowing Hindu, Buddhist, and Jain religious institutions adopted a broadly Dharmaśāstric jurisprudence when compared to inscriptions of earlier eras. Second, this Sanskritisation of religious endowments went hand-in-glove with the development of a cosmopolitan legal, political, and religious model of kingship in which imperial and sub-imperial sovereignty entailed a commitment to the creation and preservation of religious endowments.

Furthermore, the donors of the Gupta era employ Sanskrit almost exclusively, open with clear religious opening praises, describe land ownership practices in more detailed terms (including the formal apparatus of the royal bureaucracy), sometimes invoke formal Dharmaśāstric terminology, outline fiduciaries' duties of care, and quote Purāṇic imprecatory verses (sometimes attributing them to Manu and other *Smṛti* sources). Deities often appear as direct recipients of grants – being expressed in the dative case – and we find the first instances of deities being named after their donors, but they are not yet active legal agents. They are beneficiaries of purpose trusts. Finally, this legal model was applied, almost without variation to Buddhist and to Jain religious institutions in a remarkably secular fashion.

2.4.1 Deities as beneficiaries

While the Sātavāhanas and the Ikṣvākus made a few donations for the support of deities, this practice became ubiquitous only in the Gupta era. Inscriptions from the 4th–7th centuries, however, tend *not* to use the dative case to identify the deity as a beneficiary. Rather, they employ a several idiosyncratic expressions. This suggests that rulers and their jurists were still working out the moving parts of divine trusts.

For example, the Mahārājas of Valkhā (4th–5th centuries CE in Mahārāṣṭra) provide an early example of the experimentation in the legal language of divine

[134] See Lubin, 'Endowments', 104, for this criticism.

[135] Leslie Orr, 'Michael Willis, *The Archaeology of Hindu Ritual: Temples and the Establishment of the Gods*', *South Asian Studies*, 26.2 (2010): 238–242. Willis discusses the Buddhist origins of some features of this tradition at *Archaeology*, 106.

trusts.[136] These kings, likely vassals of the early Imperial Guptas, attempted to domesticate several local cults by formalising their legal relationship to the Crown.[137] The Mahārājas employ Sanskrit exclusively, but they largely eschew Dharmaśāstric juridical vocabulary or imprecatory verses. Nevertheless, their grants describe divine estates (*devāgrahāras*) in precise legal terms. When creating a trust in favour of a deity, the Mahārājas place the deity in the genitive case, express the trustee using the suffix '*pratyaya*' (entrusted with), and stipulate clear fiduciary duties.[138]

In one grant, King Bhuluṇḍa notes that:

> We have granted... until the moon, sun, and stars last and for the performance of the *bali*, *charu*, and *satra* rites, for the Mother goddesses installed by us at Navataṭāka, the village... entrusted with Mūlaśarman... from now onwards... Mahāmātras and temple servants who are engaged in the duties (of the temple)... should endorse this grant.[139]

In a gift to Nārāyaṇa, Bhuluṇḍa states that: 'These three plots of land belong to Lord Nārāyaṇa, which are being cultivated by the deity's servants according to the rules of *devāgrahāras*, should be endorsed by all of our agents.'[140] This suggests that, from Bhuluṇḍa's perspective, his audience would recognise divine estates as distinctive legal arrangements. A grant wherein Bhuluṇḍa formalised a legal trust by converting a village from *devabhukti* (enjoyed by the deity) to a *devāgrahāra* confirms this assumption.[141] The implication is that a *devabhukti* was, perhaps, less legally formal than a proper *devāgrahāra* – and represents a development in the history of divine trusts.

Later Gupta grants contain varied, equally idiosyncratic attempts to describe deities as beneficiaries of purpose trusts. In his Bhitarī pillar inscription (456–57 CE), Skandagupta (r. 455–76 CE) records that: '(Saying to himself that) an image of some kind or other [should be made], he... made this image of that (famous god) Śārṅgin... and having here installed this (god), he, whose commands are well-established, has allotted this village.'[142] While Willis reads this as evidence

[136] K.V. Ramesh and S.P. Tewari (eds), *A Copper-Plate Hoard of the Gupta Period from Bagh, Madhya Pradesh* (New Delhi: Archeological Survey of India, 1990).

[137] Suchandra Ghosh, 'A Hoard of Copper Plates: Patronage and the Early Valkhā State', *Studies in History* 31.1 (2015): 1–29. Also see Ramesh and Tewari, *Copper-Plate*, xiii–xiv.

[138] Ramesh and Tewari, *Copper-Plate*, xvi.

[139] Ibid., #2: vijñātam astu vaḥ samanujānāmy āsām **bhagavatīnām** asmābhiḥ pratiṣṭhāpitikānāṃ **navataṭākamātṛṇāṃ mūlaśarmmapratyayaṃ**... grāmaṃ... balicarusatropayogārttham ācandrārkkatārakālīnena... visṛjāmaḥ... mahāmātṛṇā[ṃ] santakāyuktakadevakarmmiṇaś ca balicharusatropayogādiṣu... upayojyayamānā sarvvair eva... anumantavyam.

[140] Ibid., #4: **bhagavato nārāyaṇasyaitatkṣetrapadatrayaṃ**... devāgrahārakrameṇa devaparicārakaiḥ kṛṣyamāṇaṃ... sarvvair evāsmatpakṣīyaiḥ samanumantavya[ṃ].

[141] Ibid., #5: **bappapiśāchadevasya** pūrvvabhujyamānakaṁ... grāmasyārddhaṁ devāgrahāram... asmābhir anujñātam uch[i]tayā devāgrāhārabhuktyā.

[142] CII 3.13: [karttavyā] pratimā kāchit=pratimāṁ tasya **śārṅgiṇaḥ** s[u]-pratītaś=chakār=ēmāṃ... iha ch=ainaṁ pratishṭhāpya su-pratishṭhita-śāsanaḥ grāmam=ēnaṁ sa vidadh[ē].

of a mature legal personality of Hindu deities, he over-eggs the pudding.[143] Skandagupta assigns a field to a deity whose image has been consecrated, but we find neither the deity in the dative case – as the primary beneficiary – nor a list of trustees, nor a delineation of uses for the income from the field in question.

Skandagupta's later inscription at the imperial Daśāvatāra temple at Prayāga (467–68 CE) utilises the idiom of gifting assets 'at the feet' (*pāda*) of the deity for stipulated purposes:

> Having caused (a temple having) a flat roof to be made… (and) having installed the feet of (the god) Anantasvāmin… for the purpose of repairing whatever may become… torn, there have been given twelve [units of the assets of the endowment] which belong to the entrance of the [the treasury at] the feet of the divine (god) Chitrakūtasvāmin.[144]

This formulation appears in the records of the Vākāṭakas (250 CE–500 CE), vassals of the Guptas in the Deccan.[145] The Vākāṭakas intermarried with the Guptas and the Gupta princess, Prabhāvatīguptā (r. 390–410 CE), then ruled as regent on behalf of her son, Dāmodaraseṇa.[146] Rudraseṇa I's (r. 335–60 CE) Deoṭek inscription was incised on an excised Aśokan inscription that, probably, recorded a *Dharmamahāmātra's* prohibition on animal sacrifice.[147] Rudraseṇa built a Śaiva temple on the site, which he refers to as a 'dharma-site' (*dharmasthāna*). Here, the shift in religion from Buddhism to Śaivism fits hand-in-glove with a shift from Middle Indic to Sanskrit.[148] Prabhāvatīguptā constructed a reservoir and temple at Rāmṭek where she established a deity known as Prabhāvatīsvāmin – in what may well be the first instance of a Vaiṣṇava deity being named after its founder.[149] When Prabhāvatīguptā created an endowment for the worship of Viṣṇu, however, she

[143] Willis, *Archaeology*, 144–9.

[144] CII 3.66: vaḍabhīṁṅ=kārayayitvā **anantasvāmi**-pādāṁ pratishṭhāpya gandha-dhūpa-srag… s[phu]ṭa-pratisaṁskāra-karaṇ-ārthaṁ bhaga[va]ch-chittra[k]ūṭasvāmi-pādīya-koshṭhē(?)ta-praveśya-mati… dattā dvādaśa. Also see the Indor copper-plate, Fleet, #16 for a similar grant to a temple of the sun god.

[145] For the history, politics, and religion of the Vākātakas, see Hans Bakker, 'Throne and Temple: Political Power and Religious Prestige in Vidarbha', in Hans Bakker (ed.), *Holy Ground: Where Art and Text Meet* (Leiden: Brill, 2019): 149–66.

[146] See Hans Bakker, 'The Gupta-Vakataka Relationship: A New Interpretation of the Ramagiri Evidence (2)', *Religions of South Asia* 5.1–2 (2012): 293–302.

[147] CII 5.1. This is Mirashi's opinion, *History*, 1–5.

[148] The Kadamba Ravivarman endowed a Buddhist institution (see EI 31.15), but he did so in accordance with Dharmaśāstric legal paradigms (such as Purāṇic genealogies and imprecatory verses).

[149] For a translation of this fragmentary inscription, see Hans Bakker and Harunaga Isaacson, 'The Ramtek Inscriptions II: The Vākāṭaka Inscription at the Kevala-Narasiṃha Temple', in Hans Bakker (ed.), *Holy Ground: Where Art and Text Meet* (Leiden: Brill, 2019): 113–47. See verse 21: **prabhāvatisvāminam**. ca, lokanā<tha> … / puṇyam akṣayam uddiśya mā… <a>k<ā>raya<t>// This inscription is quite similar to the Aulikara Prakāśadharman's Rīsthal Inscription (515 CE) which also mentions the defeat of a Hūṇa, the construction of a reservoir, and the creation of an eponymous (in this case Śaiva) deity. See Cecil, *Mapping*, 64–7; and Peter Bisschop, 'Śaivism in the Gupta-Vākāṭaka Age', *Journal of the Royal Asiatic Society* 20.4 (2010): 477–88, 481.

framed it, legally, as an estate (*agrahāra*) that was gifted to a Brāhmaṇa 'devoted to the Lord (Viṣṇu)' after 'having offered it at the feet of the Lord'.[150]

Podalic idioms penetrated into the mountainous foothills of Afghanistan, where the goddess Bhīmā was ensconced in a cave in Smast (in Kaśmīra). A copper-plate charter, which Harry Falk dates to the beginning of the 5th century CE, attests to the increasing financial sophistication of temple endowments during the greater Gupta era:

> At the feet of (goddess) Bhīmā, who lives in the great cave on the Śrī-Miñja mountain, Viṣṇuśiri... offers a permanent endowment... His golden Vardhamāneśvara is to be given a bath (ornamented?) with three girdles. And two garland sellers (and) the inhabitant of the Maṭha in charge of the shop business shall eat in (every) eighth (night) of the waxing moon in front of the Vardhamāneśvara... (they) shall eat as long as the waters, cows, moon and sun (will exist).[151]

Like Prabhāvatīguptā, Viṣṇuśiri offers his perpetual endowment 'at the feet' (*pādamūle*) of the deity, whose legal personality appears to be limited to the status of a beneficiary of the grant. Nevertheless, we see evidence of commercial activity in the form of a shop associated with the goddess's monastery. Like the monastic seals discussed by Schopen, a seal from the Smast cave which reads 'of Bhīmā, living in the cave of mount Śrīmiñja', suggests that the goddess's fiduciaries may have executed contracts in the name of their deity.[152]

Finally, this model of deity-as-beneficiary was found within in the grants of virtually all of the Guptas' vassals. Jayanātha (late 5th century) of the Ucchakalpa dynasty (5th–6th century, Madhya Pradesh), followed the Guptas' model of divine purpose trusts in a copper-plate granting a village 'for the benefit of the feet of the Divine One' as a divine estate (*devāgrahāra*) to a scribe (*dvivira*) and his descendants for stipulated religious purposes.[153] In 512–13 CE, Jayanātha's successor,

[150] Mirashi, *History*, #2: grāmo... **bhagavadpādamūle** nivedya **bhagavadbhaktācāryyacanālasvām ine**... [dattaḥ].

[151] Harry Falk, 'A Copper Plate Donation Record and some Seals from the Kashmir Smast', in *Beiträge Zur Allgemeinen und Vergleichenden Archäologie 23* (Mainz am Rhein: Verlag Phillip von Zabern, 2003): 1–19, 5–6: **śrī-miñja-parvva-mahāguhā-nivasiny<ā> bhīmāyāḥ** pādamūle prayacchaty akṣayaṇīyaṃ suvarṇā satera pañca svassa 5 viṣṇ<u>śirir... asya suvarṇasya **vardhamāneśvarasya** tṛbhiś ca paṭṭakaiḥ snāpanaṃ kartavyaṃ puṣpahārika-dvayena ca kuṭivy<ā>p(ā)ramaṭhakena śuklāṣṭamyāṃ bhoktavyaṃ **vardhamāneśvarasyāgratas**... yāvad āpo gāvaś candrādityau tāvad bhoktavyam. Falk argues that the Vardhamāneśvara 'should be a form of an idol'.

[152] Ibid., 7–15: **śīmiñjaparvatag<u>hāvāsinyabhīmaya**. Falk notes the existence of a series of seals bearing the name of Bhīmā. For Buddhist examples, see Schopen, 'Buddha as an Owner', 194–7. Bhīmā's seal is remarkably similar to that of the Buddha at Sarnāth (6th–7th century CE): **śrīsaddharmmacakkre** mūla-gandhakuṭyāṃ **bhagavataḥ** (of/belonging to the Blessed One in the original Perfume Chamber in the Śrīsaddharmacakra (Monastery). Schopen notes, at p. 195, that, 'the two primary uses of such sealings appear to have been either to mark ownership of the property to which they were attached, or to "vouch for the genuineness" of the letters or documents that were sent or circulated under their seal'.

[153] CII 3.27: eṣa grāmo mayā... śāśātaneyasarvvavāḍhadviratatputtrabhāgavatagaṅgata[t]puttraraṅka boṭājagaradās[ā]nāṃ... **bhagavatypād[e]bhyaḥ** dev[ā]grahāro 'tisṛṣṭhaḥ. Note that the deity is in the dative case. and the trustee is in the genitive case.

Śarvanātha, allotted a village, in four shares, to various parties and their descendants, who had agreed to use the income of the donated lands for the benefit of Viṣṇu and the Sun.[154] Likewise, in his Bhamodra plate of 502 CE, another Gupta-vassal, the Maitraka Droṇasimha of Vallabhī (r. 499–519 CE), entrusted a village to a 'deity's attendant' (*devīkarmāntika*) with the stipulation that its income be applied for a variety of standard activities - repair of the temple, *bali*, *caru*, *sattra*, etc. - for the Goddess, Pāṇḍurājā.[155]

Direct gifts to deities appear with regularity only from the 6th century onwards. In the Dāmodarpur inscription from the reign of Bhānugupta (early 6th century CE), a nobleman named Amṛtadeva requested the local administration:

> To make a gift, on accepting from me *dīnāras* (as the price) of some land by means of a copper-plate grant according to the custom of perpetual endowment (*apradā*) for making of repairs of whatever is broken or torn in the shrine of Bhagavān Śvetavarāhasvāmin… and for the continuance of *bali*, *caru*, *sattra*, the supply of cow's milk, incense and flowers, and the maintenance of *madhuparka*, lamps, etc.[156]

The bureaucracy approved the request, noted that the land was 'given to lord Śvetarasvāmin to be enjoyed for all time', and repeated the injunction for future administrators to protect the terms of the grant.[157]

A few decades later, the Viṣṇukuṇḍin, Vikramendravarman II (r. 555–72 CE) used almost the same format in a donation of a village to Śiva (using the dative case to identify the beneficiary).[158]

[154] CII 3.28: eṣa grāmo mayā… caturbhir anśe pratipāditaḥ. ato 'nśa **viṣnunandinaḥ** aparo 'py anśaḥ **svāmināgaputtravaṇijaśaltināgasya**… etatputtra[pauttra]prapauttratatputrādyanukrameṇa tāmraśāsanātisṛṣṭha[ḥ]. ebhir ap[i] mayānumoditakaṃ yathoparilikhitakakkrameṇaiva… **svaṣṭhāpitakabhagavatpādānām aditsābhaṭṭārakapādānāṃ** ca… khaṇḍaphuṭṭapratisaṁskārakaraṇāya… c[ā]tisṛṣṭhaḥ. Also see Śarvanātha's three plates endowing Piṣṭhapurikādevī, CII 3.29–31. In the last plate, the king reassigns the trusteeship of the land and temple which 'were previously bestowed as a mark of favour upon Pulindabhaṭa' to 'Kumārasvāmin.' Here we have evidence of a sovereign exercising their royal right of supervision over religious endowments.

[155] EI 16.4: **śrībhagavatyāḥ pāṇḍurājāyāḥ…** balicaruvaiśvadevādyānāṃ kriyāṇāṃ samutsarppaṇārthaṃ triaṃgamakagrāmo ghandhadhūpadīpatailamālyopayojyaṃ devakulasya ca pati taviśīrṇṇapratisaṃskaraṇārthaṃ satropayojyas sahiraṇyādeyas saḥ… brahmadeyasthittyā… nisṛṣṭaḥ… The 'deity's attendant' appears following several imprecatory verses: **bhiruvakadevīkarmāntikaḥ**.

[156] EI 15.7.5: matto dīnārānupasaṁgṛhya… **bhagavataḥ śvetavarāhasvāmino** devakule khaṇḍaspuṭṭaprati[saṃ]skā[rakra]raṇāya balicarusatrapravarttanagavyaghūpapuṣpaprāpaṇamadhuparkkadīpādyupa[yo]gā[ya] ca apradādharmmeṇa tāmrapaṭṭīkṛtya kṣetras tokan dātum.

[157] Ibid.: **bhaga[va]te śvetavarāhasvāmine** śaśvatkālabhogyā dattāḥ.

[158] EAID.182, http://hisoma.huma-num.fr/exist/apps/EIAD/works/EIAD0182.xml?&odd=teipublisher.odd: **bhavate somagireśvarānāthāya** dattaṁ. For Vikramendravarman's Śaiva predilections see Sanderson, 'The Śaiva Age', 71.

2.4.2 Eponymous deities and the law of Trusts

Eponymous deities first appear during the Gupta era. The Mathurā pillar inscription from the reign of Candragupta II (r. 375–415 CE) provides the earliest evidence of the creation of juridical persons using the formula 'x +*īśvara*' for a *Śivaliṅga*.[159] The inscription, dated to the sixty-first year of the Gupta era (380 CE), records the creation of two *liṅgas* named after, presumably, biologically deceased Kāpālika preceptors: 'Upamiteśvara and Kapileśvara the teachers were installed in the Teachers' Shrine… [The current teachers] thinking them to be (their own) property, they should preserve, worship, and honor (them) as (their own) property.'[160]

The *liṅgas* in this inscription, however, are named after the honouree rather than the *donor* of the endowment. The first instances of eponymous *royal* temple deities come from the Vākāṭakas. We saw, previously, that Prabhāvatīguptā created an eponymous Viṣṇu image in a temple that she founded and that her son, Pravarasena II (r. 420–55), began endowing deities directly. In fact, Pravarasena II, like his mother, Prabhāvatīguptā, created and endowed an eponymous deity, Pravareśvara - this time in his new capital, Pravarapura.[161] Pravarasena issued his Pāṇḍhurṇā plates 'from the place of the temple of Pravareśvara', which he refers to twice as a 'Dharma-site'.[162] In his Paṭṭana plates, Pravarasena II gifts 'four hundred nivartanas of land to be used by the alms house belonging to Viṣṇu'.[163]

Similarly, at the base of a *liṅga* in Karamdanda, near modern Faizabad, Pṛthivīṣeṇa, Kumāragupta's (r. 415–55 CE) minister, created a purpose trust in favour of an eponymous deity, Pṛthivīśvara.[164] Finally, in Kaliṅga, Hastivarman (r. 5th–6th centuries CE) of the Eastern Gaṅgā dynasty, who bore the epithet 'Feared in Battle' (Raṇabhīta), created a *devāgrahāra* and 'granted it to the god Nārāyaṇa… who has the designation Raṇabhītodaya… for the sake of performing… *bali*, *caru* and *satra*… [etc]' before closing his command (*śāsana*) with Purāṇic imprecations.[165] Here we see the practice of kings endowing eponymous deities happening beyond a Śaiva milieu and beyond the central Indian heartland.

159 See Chapter 1, §1.5.3, 'The legal personality of deities as a conventional Dharma'.

160 EI 21.1: **[upamiteśva]rakapileśvarau** gurvvāyatane guru… pratiṣṭhāpito… parigraham iti matvā viśaṅka[ṁ] pūjapuraskāra[ṁ] parigrahapāripālyaṁ kuryyād. See Cecil, *Mapping*, 33–7.

161 For Pravarapura, see Hans Bakker (ed.) *Mansar: The Discovery of Pravareśvara and Pravarapura Temple and Residence of the Vākāṭaka King Pravarasena II* (Groningen: Library of the University of Groningen, 2008).

162 CII 5.14: **pravareśvaradevakulasthānāt**…dharmmasthāne… dharmasthāne ca… Bisschop, 'Śaivism', 480, argues that this plate: 'Is among the first examples of royal sanctuaries dedicated to a chosen deity… incorporating the ruler's name. These temples became a characteristic feature of most early medieval kingdoms, in which Śaivism was the norm.' Of course, Prabhāvatīguptā's eponymous Śaiva deity appears to be an influential antecedent.

163 CII 13: bhūmer nirvartanaśatāni catvāri **mahāpuruṣapādamūlasatropayojyaṃ**… dattam.

164 EI 10.16. Also see Bisschop, 'Śaivism', 478.

165 EI 23.10: **bhagavate… raṇabhītodayābhidhānāya nārāyaṇāya** balicarusatrapravarttanāya… devāgrahāraṃ kṛtvā [bhūmi] dattā…. **raṇabhītasya śāsanaṃ**.

2.4.3 Sanskritisation of Equity and Trusts

Along with the identification of deities as beneficiaries of endowments and the creation of eponymous deities, another major development during the greater Gupta era was the Sanskritisation of the practical law of Equity and Trusts. The wholesale shift from Prakrit into Sanskrit as the discursive language of law coincided with a wholesale adoption of Sanskrit jurisprudence as the legal theory undergirding legal practice.

On the one hand, we find the adoption of earlier forms of financial endowment. The Guptas incorporated *akṣayanīvīs* within a Sanskrit jurisprudential idiom. For example, The Baigram plates (447–48 CE) records the earliest perpetual endowment in Gupta usage. In this private endowment, two brothers created a perpetual endowment for the purpose of protecting and maintaining a temple.[166] Perhaps this served as a model for other royal grants. Skandagupta (r. 455–67 CE) donated a village in Bihar as a perpetual endowment, although the beneficiary of the grant is now lost.[167]

Slightly later, Gupta endowments become more legally complex and adopted elaborate Dharmaśāstric imprecatory statements against resumption.[168] A brace of copper-plate inscriptions from a ruined temple in Dāmodarpur, in modern Bihar, outlines the development of sophisticated legal trusts for temples during the Gupta era. In the first plate, dated to the reign of Buddhagupta (r. 476–95 CE), the 'guild-president' of the town (*nagaraśreṣṭhin*), Ribhupāla, applied to the local government representing the Gupta emperor to purchase land: 'in order to make a pair of temples and a pair of granaries for the two deities Kokāmukhasvāmin and Śvetavarāhasvāmin'.[169] The plate records that the application was approved and enjoins that 'in the future these grants must be preserved by the administering agents out of reverence to the gods'.[170] The grant closes with three imprecatory verses attributed to Vyāsa that appear in most later Gupta grants. An obscure, 5th–6th-century grant from an unknown king, Sīharāja, to the deities of a cave temple near modern Goa warns readers that '[he] who seizes deities' property (*devasva*) becomes afflicted with the five great sins'.[171] Here, we find one of the first instances of the *Mānavadharmaśāstra*'s theory of '*devasva*' being applied in a practical legal context.[172]

166 Ibid. 21.13.

167 CII #12: [ak]shayanīvī grāmakshēttraṁ. Also see the gift by the lay-woman (*upāsikā*) Harisvāminī at Sāñcī (CII #62).

168 For these imprecatory verses, see Appendix II in Sircar, *Indian Epigraphy*.

169 EI 15.7.4: tayor **ādyakokāmukhasvāmi[śvetavarāha]svāminor...** devakuladvayam etatkoṣṭhikādvayañ ca kārayitum.

170 Ibid.: dattāḥ taduttarakālaṃ [saṃ]vyavahāribhir devabha[ktyā]numantavyā.

171 EI 31.50.ii: devasvaṁ harati yaḥ pañcamahāpātaka saṁyukto bhavati.

172 *Mānavadharmaśāstra*, 11.26: devasvaṃ brāhmaṇasvaṃ vā lobhenopahinasti yaḥ /sa pāpātmā pare loke gṛdhraucchiṣṭena jīvati. For similar Dharmaśāstric dicta, see Chapter 1, §1.6.2, 'Deities' property (*devasva*)'.

Alongside the use of Sanskrit imprecatory verses, we also find the technical Dharmaśāstric terminology in inscriptions from the Gupta era. The Kadamba dynasty of Vaijayantī (325–540 CE), which was based in what is now Karṇāṭaka, employed the legal model of divine purpose trusts, with Dharmaśāstric elements, in their gifts to Jain, Buddhist, and Brāhmaṇical institutions.[173] The first recorded Kadamba inscription, from an unknown Kadamba king of the 3rd–4th century CE, re-established a grant of villages for the benefit of Maḷavaḷḷi (endowed by Cuṭukulānanda Sātakarṇi in the 3rd century CE).[174] Later Kadamba grants, written in Sanskrit, extended this model of the deity as a legal beneficiary to a series of other religious institutions.

A pillar inscription at the temple of Kāmadeva at Vaijayantī (modern Banavāsī) records a donation by Ravivarman (r. 465–500 CE) and contains numerous references to Arthaśāstric and Dharmaśāstric jurisprudence.[175] Ravivarman commissioned a temple to Kāmadeva (*tena veśma manmathasyedaṃ raviṇā kṣitīndreṇa kāritam*) and enjoined future kings to protect it as a conventional law (*samayadharma*): 'From now on, future kings who aspire to pleasure, fame, and piety, and who are committed to upholding the terms of the conventional law, are the authorities with regard to its [i.e. the temple's] protection.'[176] Here, Ravivarman explicitly refers to the Dharmaśāstric theory of Equity as an extra-śāstric conventional Dharma and his subsequent donation of several villages 'for the sake of the ceremony of worship at the temple of Kāmadeva' (*kāmadevālayasya pūjāsaṃskārārttham asau mahārājaśrīravivarmmā iḍiūragrāmaṃ... etc*) attests to the increasing use of trust clauses during the Kadambas' suzerainty.[177]

2.4.4 The secularity of the Sanskrit law of Equity and Trusts

Perhaps the most striking development of the law of Equity and Trusts during the Gupta era is the more-or-less wholesale application of this new Sanskritised, Dharmaśāstra-inflected model of deities as beneficiaries of trusts to Buddhist, Jain, and Ajīvika religious institutions. If, during the Age Between the Empires, a largely Buddhist, and Arthaśāstric juridical model was sometimes applied to

[173] For the history of the Kadambas, see G.S. Gai, *Inscriptions of the Early Kadambas* (New Delhi: Pratibha Prakashan, 1996).

[174] Ibid., #1: sampradattaṃ ca tad eva bhogaṃ... **maḷapaḷidevāya**. Note that this is the first recorded instance, to my knowledge, of a gift *directly* to a deity.

[175] Elizabeth Cecil and Mekhola Gomes, 'Kāma at the Kadamba Court: The Guḍnāpur Pillar Inscription of Ravivarman as a Text-Monument', *Indo-Iranian Journal* 64 (2021): 10–50. See fns 26, 29 & 33 for Arthaśāstric references. See fns 26 & 57 for the *Mānavadharmaśāstra*.

[176] Ibid., Verse 30: itaḥ prabhṛtirakṣaṇe 'sya sukhakīrttidharmmaipsavaḥ pramāṇam avanīśvarās samayadharmmarakṣāparāḥ // 30 // See Chapter 1, §1.5, 'Equity as supplemental law' for *samayadharma* and the Sanskrit jurisprudence of Equity.

[177] Ibid., Verse 31.

Brāhmaṇical religious institutions, during the Gupta era, a largely Sanskrit, Dharmaśāstric legal paradigm was often applied to non-Brāhmaṇical religious institutions.

During the Gupta age, even endowments made to Buddhist and Ajīvika institutions utilised Brāhmaṇical imprecations against resumption. An early dedication during the reign of Candragupta II (r. 375–415 CE) records the gift of an endowment (*mūlya*) to the Buddhist community at Sāñcī – with associated financial stipulations – and concludes with the admonition that, 'whosoever shall interfere with this his arrangement – he shall become invested with (the guilt of) the slaughter of a cow or of a Brāhmaṇa.'[178]

Grants from the reign of Vainyagupta (early 6th century CE) attest to the growing importance of Dharmaśāstric jurisprudence at the end of the Gupta era as well as to the development of the Buddha as a juridical person. In the Gunaighar Plate, Vainyagupta states that:

> Eleven *pāṭakas* of uncultivated lands… are granted by me, by means of a copper plate as an *agrahara* in absolute possession; for providing perpetually for perfumes, flowers, lights, incense, etc. thrice a day unto the Lord Buddha in the abode of the Vaivarttika congregation of monks… and also for repairing breaks and cracks in the Vihara… Here again, both Veda and *Smṛti* (texts) are indeed prescribed. Regarding keeping up (in the future), there are again verses sung by the revered Vyāsa, the compiler of the Vedas, and the son of Parāśara…[179]

It is striking that a grant endowing 'Lord Buddha' – himself legally personified – would explicitly invoke *smṛti* (Dharmaśāstra). This demonstrates conclusively that Dharmaśāstra provided the jurisprudential foundation for the practical legal system of medieval India. Vainyagupta employs almost identical Dharmaśāstric terminology in his grant to the Ājīvika order in Bengal:

> The illustrious Vainyagupta… [informs the following:] 'It should be known to you. Those that were given to the ones belonging to *varṇas* and *āśramas* by previous kings… with *akṣayanīvī* (tenure), by copperplate grant, are also approved by me… for the sake of the *saṃgha* of respectable Ājīvika *śramaṇas* as at the abode of the venerable Maṇibhadra in four-faced image… with all the excessive enjoyments and with *akṣayanīvī* tenure, by my own copperplate grant. Thus, they should be preserved by you who desire your own welfare.

[178] Fleet #5: tad=ētat-pravṛittaṁ ya uchchhindyāt=sag ō-brahma-hatyayā saṁyuktō bhavet.

[179] Dinesh Bhattacharyya, 'A newly discovered Copperplate from Tippera [The Gunaighar Grant of Vainyagupta: The Year 188 Current (Gupta Era)]', *The Indian Historical Quarterly* 6:1 (1930): 45–60: mayā… vaivartijabhikṣusaṅghanām parigrahe **bhagavato buddhasya** satataṃ triṣkālaṃ gandha puṣpadīpadhūpādipra[varttāya*]… vihāre [ca] khaṇḍaphuṭṭapratisaṃskārakaraṇāya sarvato bhogen āgrahāratvenaikādaśakhilapāṭakāḥ…. tāmrapaṭṭenātisṛṣṭāḥ. api ca khalu **śrutismṛtīhā**[**sa**]**vihitāṃ**… anupālanam prati ca **bhagavata parāśarātmajena vedavyāsena vyāsena** gītāḥ ślokāḥ bhavanti. See Schopen's discussion of this grant, along with an almost identical one from Valkhā in 'Buddha as an Owner' 184–5.

> With regard to preservation, there are verses sung by the venerable Vedavyāsa, the son of Parāśara: 'For sixty thousand years, the giver of land rejoices in heaven. The one who refuses it and the one approves him would live in hell for the same duration.' '(No matter if it was) given by himself or given by others, the one who appropriates the land will be boiled with his ancestors, after being born a worm in excrement.' 'Protect with effort what was previously given to Brāhmaṇas, oh Yudhiṣṭhira! Oh best of kings! The preservation of land is superior to its donation.'[180]

At Vijayapurī, the Viṣṇukuṇḍins (5th–7th centuries CE), successors to the Ikṣvākus, also adopted a Dharmaśāstric idiom for their grants to Buddhist monasteries and to Hindu deities.[181] In a copper-plate grant to the Buddhist *saṅgha*, Govindavarman I, describes himself as one:

> Who has adorned all directions by repairing and building anew many temples, monasteries, halls, cisterns, tanks, wells, and pleasure-groves (*ārāmas*); whose array of wealth and riches, which he has lawfully acquired, is being enjoyed by monks, brahmins, those without a protector, beggars, the sick, the poor and the wretched people.[182]

This is a clear invocation of Dharmaśāstric and Purāṇic lists of charitable activities and he concludes with a series of imprecatory verses – the same as those of the Guptas – that he attributes to 'Manu' (*manugīta*).[183] His successor, Vikramendravarman uses almost the same format in a donation of a village to Śiva (in the dative).[184]

The Kadambas favoured Jain institutions, but, as in the case of the Ravivarman's Kāmadeva inscription, they employed a Dharmaśāstric idiom to do so. For example, a series of grants to Jain institutions at Palāśikā (modern Halsi) made by successive Kadamba rulers utilise the same legal idiom as in the grant to the Kāma temple discussed previously.[185] Intriguingly, the legal personality of the Jinas

[180] Ryosuke Furui, 'Ājīvikas, Maṇibhadra and Early History of Eastern Bengal: A New Copperplate Inscription of Vainyagupta and its Implications', *Journal of the Royal Asiatic Society* 26.4 (2016): 657–81: **śrīıvainyaguptaḥ**... viditaṃ bhavatām astu pūrvvarājabhir yyāḥ... akṣayanīvyā va-[rṇṇin]āṃ ā[ś]ramiṇāñ ca tāmraśāsanena dattikās tā mayā (')pi... **bhagavatas caturmmukhamūrtter mma[ṇi] bhadrasyāyatana-m-ājīvikabhadantaśramaṇasaṁghāya** sarvvātibhogenākṣayanīvīdharmmeṇṇa svatāmraśāsanenābhyanumoditā yuṣmābhir api svaśreyortttthibhir evam evānupālayitavyāḥ. anu[pā] lanam prati ca **bhagavatā parāśrātmaja vedavyāsena** gītāḥ ślokāḥ / ṣaṣṭiṃ varṣasahasrāṇi svargge modati bhūmidaḥ / ākṣeptā cānumantā ca tāny eva narake vaset // svadattāṃ paradattāṃ vā yo hareta vasundharāṃ / sa viṣṭhāyāṃ kṛmir bhūtvā piṛbhiḥ saha pacyate // pūrvvadattāṃ dvijātibhyo yatnād rakṣo **yudhiṣṭhira** / mahīṃ mahimatāṃ śreṣṭha dānāc chreyo (')nupālanaṃ //

[181] For the history of the Viṣṇukuṇḍins, see S. Sankaranarayana, *The Viṣṇukuṇḍis and their Times: An Epigraphic Study* (Delhi: Agam Prakashan, 1977).

[182] EIAD 174, http://hisoma.huma-num.fr/exist/apps/EIAD/works/EIAD0174.xml?&odd=teipublisher.odd anekadevāyatanavihārasabhāprapātaḍākodupānārām[a]pratisaṁskārapūrvvakaraṇenālaṁkr̥tasakaladigantareṇa bhikṣudvijā[n]ātha[yāca]kavyādhitadīnakr̥paṇajanopabhujyamāna...

[183] Ibid.: bhavanti cātra **manugītā** ślokā...

[184] EIAD 182, http://hisoma.huma-num.fr/exist/apps/EIAD/works/EIAD0182.xml?&odd=teipublisher.odd

[185] Discussed at length in Bisschop and Cecil, 'Jayati'.

in these grants solidifies over time. In the first Kadamba grant at Palāśikā, the crown prince (*yuvarāja*) Kākusthavarman (r. 435–55 CE): 'gave to the general Śrutakīrti... the field called Badovarakṣetra... for the blessed Arhats'.[186] The grant closes with a series of Purāṇic imprecatory verses that, as Willis notes, appear in southern recensions of the Āśvamedhikaparvan of the *Mahābhārata*.[187] In this grant, in which the beneficiary is expressed in the genitive case, Śrutakīrti serves as a trustee for the endowed lands, much like the Valkā grants discussed earlier.

Later, however, the Arhats and Jinas who were the beneficiaries of Kadamba endowments were identified in the dative case. For example, a grant by Ravivarman records a donation of land directly 'to the Jinas' for the specified purpose of bathing the images.[188] Bisschop and Cecil, argue that 'the grant of additional land suggests the expansion of the temple territories overseen by the Jinas or Arhats as juridical personalities'.[189] Another series of plates, issued by Mṛgeśavarman (r. 475–85 CE) from Vaijayantı records that the king: 'gave to the blessed Arhats thirty-three nivartanas [of land]... for the [purpose of supporting] the Yāpanīyas, the Nirgranthas, and the Kūrcakas', and ends with the customary Purāṇic verses.[190]

Bisschop and Cecil note that, like 'the early examples of grants to Brahmanical temples, the deities (Arhats/Jinas) enshrined in Palāśikā's temple(s) were similarly understood as juridical personalities capable of owning land'.[191] My broader point, however, is that it is salutary to remember that the incipience of Jain legal personality took place within the context of the development of a pan-Indic law of Trusts that was very much in conversation with Sanskrit jurisprudential principles of Equity. For example, Mṛgeśavarman's gift of land at Devagiri to the 'supreme arhat deities' for the stipulated purposes of 'cleaning, anointing, worshipping, and repairing broken (parts of the temple)', or his subsequent gift of land to the 'blessed Arhat, the great Jinendra deity' represent an assimilation of Jain legal personality to a Brāhmaṇical, Dharmaśāstric legal idiom.[192] This attests to the fact that Dharmaśāstric principles of Equity of Trusts could accommodate a wide variety of different religious traditions within a common, secular legal paradigm.

Mṛgeśavarman describes 'the riches that comprise that deity's share' as assets 'that are to be used, according to the conventional rule of divine enjoyment (*devabhogasamayena*), for such purposes as *bali*, *caru*, doing sacred work, and

[186] Ibid., 616–17.

[187] Ibid., 617 fn. 20. Also see Willis, *Archeology*, 84–8. Bisschop and Cecil, 'Jayati', argue that these 'verses... show the Kadambas participating in a Brahmanical paradigm, with which the lineage is strongly affiliated'.

[188] Gai, No 17: vasudhā dattā **jinebhyaḥ**... snapanārthaṃ.

[189] Bisschop and Cecil, 'Jayati', 621.

[190] Ibid., 618.

[191] Ibid., 619.

[192] Ibid., 632. Gai Nos 6: **paramārhaddevebhyaḥ** saṃmārjjanopalepanābhyarccanabhagnasaṃskāram ahimātarthaṃ. & 7: **bhagavadarhanmahājinendradevatābhyaḥ**.

undertaking repairs of broken (parts of the temple)'.[193] Note, again, the use of the technical, Dharmaśāstric term '*samaya*' to describe the legal convention imposed on the trustees. This is an explicit appeal to Dharmaśāstric concepts of Equity as conventional, supplemental law as applied in the context of a practical legal document. It is striking, too, that when the Jina become more similar to a Hindu deity in terms of legal personality (being the recipient of endowments and owning assets) the jurisprudential language and principles of the specific grants to Jain institutions became significantly more Dharmaśāstric. Developments in *law* and *jurisprudence* went hand-in-glove in medieval religious endowments, regardless of religious affiliation.

Taken collectively, this data indicates that the practical law of religious endowments changed fundamentally during the Gupta era. Every imperial or sub-imperial polity issued grants to religious institutions from a wide variety of disciplinary traditions. They invariably did so in a Sanskrit literary and jurisprudential idiom. There were, of course, regional variations in style and phrasing but there is a remarkable level of consistency on the core features of the law of trusts: 1) an elaborate introduction of the king and his relation to other rivals; 2) a donation of land or capital for specified religious purposes; 3) an identification of a trustees along with a list of their duties; and 4) a series of imprecatory verses attributed to various Purāṇic and Dharmaśāstric sources. The jurisprudence of Equity and Trusts in the greater Gupta age, however, was explicitly Dharmaśāstric, but in a remarkably secular way. These are major developments, but they are also a far cry from the vast imperial temples of the following centuries in which deities named after rulers – sometimes named as rulers themselves – directly owned vast, intricate property portfolios, lent money at interest, and were, in turn, subject to despoliation as a result of the shifting vicissitudes of imperial rivalries. To that story, this chapter now turns.

2.5 The Pallava/Cālukya rivalry and the politicisation of temple endowments (7th–9th centuries CE)

By the mid-6th century CE, two puissant powers fought over the suzerainty of Southern India: the Pallavas of Kāñcīpuram and the Cālukyas of Vātāpi.[194] These imperial houses fought countless battles, sacked each other's capitals, and, along the way created hundreds of inscriptions that recorded a wide array of religious endowments. In doing so, the Cālukyas and the Pallavas introduced a new

[193] Gai, No 7: devabhāgadhānya... balicarudevakarmmakarabhagnakriyāpravarttanādyartthupabhog āya... devabhogasamayena.

[194] For the Pallavas, see Francis, *Le Discours Royal*. For the Cālukyas, see K.V. Ramesh, *The Cālukyas of Vātāpi* (Delhi: Kala Prakashan, 1984).

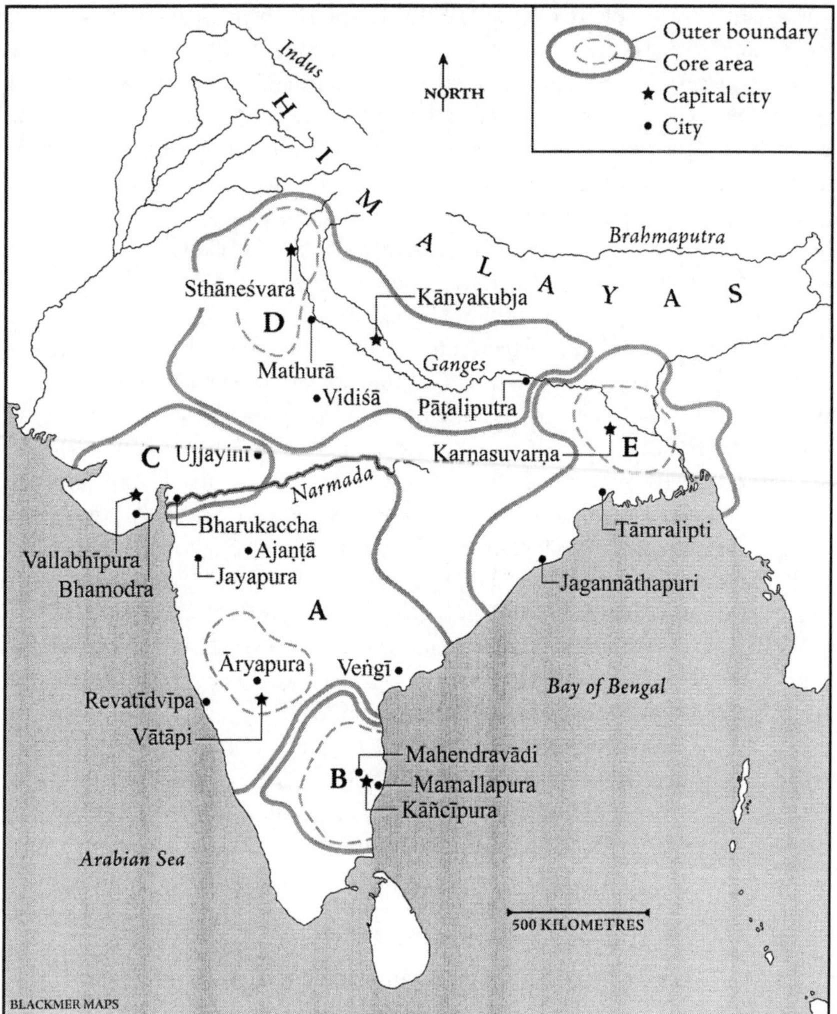

A Cālukyas of Vātāpi (543–753 CE)
B Imperial Pallavas (~575–897 CE)
C Maitrakas of Vallabhī (475–776 CE)
D Puṣyabhūti/Vardhana Dynasties (~6th–7th centuries CE)
E Gauḍa Rājya (~6th–7th centuries CE)

Map 2.3 India after the Guptas (~6th–8th centuries CE)

paradigm of imperial sovereignty – one in which the ruler creates and endows a vast temple complex on behalf of an eponymous deity, from which his own rule emerges. Of course, imperial ambitions invite imperial conflict and it comes as no surprise, then, that politically motivated despoliations of religious endowments became a much more common feature of epigraphic records during this time. As Richard Davis notes:

> With divine images already preponderant participants in the medieval system of authoritative relations, it is not surprising that images were often seized publicly by one ruler from another in circumstances of conflict… royal looters dislodged selected images from their customary positions and employed them to articulate political claims in a rhetoric of objects whose principal themes were victory and defeat, autonomy and subjugation, dominance and subordination.[195]

On a legal level, the Cālukya and Pallava grants became vastly more sophisticated. Deities begin to feature as true legal persons – almost always in the dative case and often bearing the name of the sovereign. Deities are granted more sophisticated and more precisely delineated assets, while the rights, duties, and regulations affecting deities' fiduciary guardians become more explicit. Furthermore, we begin to see bilingual, Tamil/Sanskrit and Sanskrit/Kannada inscriptions – and a more complex approach to the 'language issue' that would define subsequent eras in Indian epigraphic history.

One of the earliest Pallava grants (4th century CE), records a donation of a village by Cārudevī, the Vijayaskandavarman's queen, to the deity Nārāyaṇa.[196] While the grant does not mention any trustees or stipulations on the use of the endowment, it does end with a pair of imprecatory verses in Sanskrit. This is broadly representative of the gradual Sanskritisation of Prakrit Pallava grants before a shift to a bilingual Tamil/Sanskrit usage.[197] This Sanskritisation culminated in the early 6th century, as represented by a series of copper-plates issued by Siṃhavarman III (r. 525–55 CE).[198] This Sanskrit grant records the creation of a '*devabhoga*' (something to be enjoyed by the deity) for the temple of the deity Viṣṇuhāra made by the general Viṣṇuvarma.[199] A series of subsequent grants that explicitly exempt *devabhogas* from new endowments of land demonstrates that these deities' portions became a standard legal phenomena in the Pallava realm by the end of the 6th century.[200]

[195] Davis, 'Indian Art', 23.

[196] EI 8.12: **kūḷimahātarakadevakula**[**ssa**] **bhagavannārāyaṇassa**… bhūminivattaṇā… sampadattā. See EI 32.8b for Siṃhavarman I's (4th century CE) grant to the priests of a temple of 'Bhagavat Jīvaśivasvāmin'.

[197] For the Sanskritisation of epigraphs during this time, see Dineschandra Sircar, *Successor of the Sātavāhanas in Lower Deccan* (Calutta: University of Calcutta, 1939).

[198] Fleet, Indian *Antiquary* Volume 5, 1876, 49–54.

[199] Ibid., 52: nivarttanāni… **viṣṇuvarmmasenāpatikṛtaviṣṇuhāradevakulāya** devabhogaṃ kṛtvā…

[200] See, for example, Vijayaskandavarman's Omgoḍu grants, EI 15.11.A: devabhogahalava. Also see EI 8.23–24.

Mandendravarman's (r. 600–30 CE, alias Śatrumalla) bilingual, Tamil-Sanskrit cave-inscription, records the creation of a temple at Dalavanur for an eponymous 'Śatrumalleśvara'. This inscription also appears to be the earliest record of the construction of imperial Pallava rock-cut temples as well as the use of both Tamil and Sanskrit in inscriptions.[201] Mahendravarman's imperial ambitions attracted the ire of the Pallavas' rapidly expanding northern rivals, the Vātāpi Cālukyas, and he suffered defeat by Pulakeśin II at the Battle of Pullalur around 618–30 CE.[202] Mahendravarman's successor, Narasiṃhavarman I (630–68 CE), avenged his father's defeat by sacking Vātāpi in 642 CE, erecting a pillar of victory (*jayastambha*), adopting the sobriquet 'seizer of Vāṭāpi' (*Vāṭāpikondan*), and re-installing spoliated images in temples in the Pallava heartland.[203] The most famous of these images is the Vātāpigaṇapati (the Vātāpi Gaṇeśa), which was seized from Vātāpi by the Pallava general, Paranjothi, and re-installed in the Uthrapathiswaraswamy temple.[204] The confiscation of one's rivals' temple images (and their endowments) and their reinstallation (and re-endowment) became a regular feature of the politics and practice of religious endowments.[205]

In the wake of this victory, Narasiṃhavarman's successors' land grants grew larger in length, scope, frequency, and juridical complexity, as did their use of Dharmaśāstric terminology (perhaps as a result of encountering the conventions of the Cālukyas and the Viṣṇukuṇḍins). The Sanskrit/Tamil Kūram plates of Parameśvaravarman I (r. 670–95 CE) represent a significant leap forward in the law of Equity and Trusts in early medieval India.

The grant opens with a Sanskrit panegyric in which Parameśvaravarman describes himself as the grandson of Narasiṃhavarman, 'who wrote the syllables of (the word) victory on Pulakeśin's back… and who destroyed the city of Vātāpi'; he also declared that he is the son of Mahendravarman (r. 688–70 CE), 'who thoroughly enforced the sacred law of the castes and the orders'.[206] Here, Parameśvaravarman makes a clear connection between his royal authority and the socially stratified world of Dharmaśāstra. The terms of the grant as expressed in Sanskrit are a clear evolution of the purpose trusts of the greater Gupta era, and

[201] EI 12.27: kāritaḥ **śatrumallena** śaile 'smin **śatrumalleśvarālaya[ḥ]. śattrumalleśvararālaiyam eṉṟaraṇukkiḍamāgavaṅguṟjjaḥ.** For the ideology of Pallava royal endowments, see Michael D. Rabe, 'Royal Temple Dedications', in Donald Lopez (ed.), *Religions of India in Practice* (Princeton: Princeton University Press, 1995): 235–43.

[202] For the Battle of Pullalur, see D.P. Dikshit, *Political History of the Calukyas of Badami* (New Delhi: Abhinav, 1980), 67–112.

[203] Pulakeśin's Vijayastambha remains in Vātāpi, albeit in fragmentary form. See SII 11.1.

[204] See Amy Catlin, '"Vātāpi Gaṇapatim": Sculptural, Poetic, and Musical Text in a Hymn to Gaṇeśa', in Robert Brown (ed.), *Ganesh: Studies of an Asian God* (Albany: SUNY, 1991): 141–70.

[205] For earlier examples of spoliation, see Notes 117–18.

[206] SII 1.151: **pulakeśiṣṭaṣṭhapaṭṭalikhitavijayākrarasya**… **vimathitavātāpeḥ** pautro… mahendrasya… supranītavarṇṇāśramadharmasya putraḥ.

reveal the deity's greater juridical substantiality as well as its closer association with the sovereign and sovereignty:

> This Parameśvara gave, at the command of Vidyāvinīta, the lord of the Pallavas, the village named Parameśvaramaṅgala... as a Brahmadeya delimited by the deity, to the lord of the Pallavas, the blessed lord Pinākapāṇi, established in the temple of Vidyāvinītapallavaparameśvara, in the village of Kūra... for the purpose of worship, bathing, flowers... etc. etc., and the recitation of the Mahābhārata, [and] for (performing) divine rights and the repairs of the temple of Vidyāvinītapallavaparameśvara... Anantaśivāchārya and Phullaśarman were appointed.[207]

The deity is named after the sovereign, is stated to be the overlord (*ādhirāja*) of the Pallava king, and commands that king to donate land on his behalf. Here we have an almost perfect instance of Alexis Sanderson's model of 'Śaiva Kingship'.[208] Two trustees, a *smārta* (follower of the *smṛtis*) Brāhmaṇa and a Śaiva preceptor, are entrusted with the temple, and their duties include not only the standard list of temple ritual activities, but, also, the recitation of the *Mahābhārata* – clearly linking the legal clauses of the donation with the jurisprudence of Dharmaśāstra. The Tamil portion of the grant provides more intricate details of the temple's construction, the various assets of the village given, and the duties and shares entrusted to Anantaśivāchārya, Phullaśarman, and their respective families. The grant ends with a series of fragmentary, Sanskrit imprecatory verses, one of which is a direct citation of *Mānavadharmaśāstra* 11.26: 'Who, out of greed, harms/damages "deities' property" (*devasva*) or Brāhmaṇas' property...'[209]

Installing, endowing, and protecting temple deities' images – according to Dharmaśāstric principles of Equity and Trusts – became a central pillar of imperial sovereignty. For example, Narasiṃhavarman's (r. 695–728 CE) Kailāsanātha temple at Kāñcīpura, the grandest imperial Pallava edifice, represents the apex of the legal personality of eponymous imperial deities in 7th–8th-century India. The temple – which contains the shrines of several deities named after their eponymous Pallava emperors – is wrapped in inscriptions that name these deities and record a wide array of objects dedicated to them.[210] Nandivarman III's (r. 846–69 CE) Velūrpāḷaiyam plates, which record the creation of a legal settlement (*vyavasthā*) that transferred various forms of income (brokerage, bride-tax, etc) from the

[207] Ibid.: tena **parameśvareṇa...** kūragrāmanāmamadhye **vidyāvinītapallavaparameśvaragṛhe** pratiṣṭhāpitatasya **bhagavataḥ parameṣṭhina[ḥ] pinākapāṇe[ḥ]** pujyāsthāpanakusuma... ādipravarttanārthaṃ... **bhāratam** ākhyānanimittārthañ ca... parameśvaramaṅgalanāmagrāmaḥ devatānimitta brahmadeya **vidyāvinītapallavavādirājavijñaptaḥ** dattaḥ... **vidyāvanītaparameśvaragṛha** iha ca devakarma[n]varma (read devanavakarmārtham) **anantaśivācārya[ḥ]**... [phu]llaśarm[ā]... ājñaptaḥ.

[208] See Sanderson, 'The Śaiva Age', 253, for his list.

[209] SII 1.151: devasvam br[ā]hmaṇasvañ ca lobhenopahinasti yaḥ. For Dharmaśāstric dicta concerning deities' property (and commentaries thereon), see Chapter 1, §1.6.2, 'Deities' property (*devasva*)'.

[210] SII 1.24–30.

Crown to 'Yajñeśvara only'[211] also attest to the importance of temple-building to the Pallavas' claims of imperial supremacy. These assets were then 'placed into (the hands of) the assembly (*pariṣad*) as a divine endowment (*devadāna*)'.[212] The plates also recount the genealogy of the Pallava dynasty, including Narasiṃhavarman's creation 'of a stone house from the moon-crested (Śiva) comparable to Mount Kailāsa'.[213] For the later Pallavas, the construction of great imperial temples was as important as the sack of Vātāpi.

We find very similar legal developments in the inscriptions of the Pallavas' rivals, the Cālukyas of Vātāpi (543–753 CE). The Yekkeri inscription from the reign of Pulakeśin II (r. 610–42 CE) records the donation of a village to Mahādeva and closes with Sanskrit imprecatory verses.[214] Pulakeśin's Aihole inscription, written in elaborate, Kālidāsa-influenced Sanskrit, records his conflict with the Pallavas – neglecting to mention, of course, the sack of Vātāpi.[215] According to his Amudaladu plates, Pulakeśin's successor, Vikramāditya I (r. 655–80 CE), re-established Cālukya suzerainty and restored deities' property (*devasva*) that had been lost under the Pallava regime.[216]

Royal despoliation of a rival ruler's temple endowments was, probably, a natural consequence of the increasing association between temple cults and imperial aspirations, but it was not a foregone conclusion. The Cālukyas' improvement in fortune coincided with the establishment of a vast imperial temple at Paṭṭadakal, outside of Vātāpi. According to Kirtivarman II's pillar inscription at Paṭṭadakal, Vijayāditya (r. 696–733 CE) 'established the deity Vijayeśvara in a great stone

[211] SII 2.5.98.

[212] Ibid.: pul̲ar̲koṭṭattu nāyar̲unāṭṭuttirukkāṭṭuppaḷḷippañcavaram āirakkā – [47] ṭi itu kovicaiya nantivarmmar̲ku yāṇṭu ār̲āvatu col̲amahārājar viṇṇappattā [48] l iraiyūr uṭaiyān̲ nampan̲āṇattiyākatt iyākattirukkāṭṭuppaḷḷiccan̲n̲a – [49] kkur̲i yajñabhaṭṭar[e]ṭuppitta **yajñeśvarattu mahādevarkku** nāṭṭ nīṅkalā – [50] y uṭpuravāy tevardān̲amākap per̲r̲atar̲kup per̲r̲a parihāram nāṭāṭciyum [51] ūrāṭciyum puravuṭupān̲n̲um tirumukkāṇamum vaṭṭinā l̲iyum putā l̲iyum taṭṭu – [52] kāyamum īl̲ampūṭciyum iṭaippūṭciyum man̲r̲upāṭumt [11 cancel t] tarakum tar̲ikkūr̲[ai] – [53] yum kūlamum nallāvum nallerutu nallāṭum nāṭukāvalum ūṭupokkum [54] kallāṇakkāṇamum kucakkāṇamum pār̲aikkāṇam paṭṭin̲aceriyum mar̲r̲umivvū – [55] [12 read ellai] raillai u[ḷ]ḷakappaṭṭatu kottoṭṭuṇṇappālatellām ev[vai]kaippaṭṭa – [56] tum kokk[o]ḷḷapper̲āte ivyajñeśvarattu mahādevareyu [13 read rēy] koḷḷappe – [57] r̲r̲atar̲kupper̲r̲a **vyavasthai**[|] cuṭṭoṭṭāl māṭamāḷikai eṭukkapper̲uvatā – [58] kavum taman̲akamum iruveliyum ceṅkal̲unīrum uḷḷiyum naṭapper̲uvatākavum kāvute – [59] ṅkiṭapper̲uvatākavum turavukiṇar̲il̲ittapper̲uvatākavum peruñcakkiṭapper̲u – [60] vatākavum ivvūrellai e[ḷ]ḷiṭṭa teṅkum pan̲aiyum ivarkaḷ man̲amin̲r̲i īl̲avarer̲ap – [61] per̲ātārākavum ivvakaipaṭṭa **vyavasthaiyin̲ūṭu** [14 read n̲ōṭu] yajñeśvarattu mahādevark – [62] kuktevatān̲amāy varmmaparihāramāka paraṭatti cen̲r̲atu [63]

[213] SII 2.5.1: tatputrassūnur **narasiṃhavarmā…** śilamayaṃ veśma śaśāṅkamauleḥ kailāsakatpañ ca mahendrakatpaḥ.

[214] EI 5.2: **bhagavato mahādevasya** nivarttanāni…

[215] EI 6.1.

[216] EI 32.21: tasmin rājyatraye vinaṣṭāni devasvabrahadeyāni… svamukhena sthāpitavān. The Amudaladu plates are famous for recording the king's donation of a village to the Śaivācārya, Sudarśan as a fee (*gurudakṣiṇa*) for initiation in the 'Śivamaṇḍala'. Also see EI 42.1 for another example of the same restoration of lost religious endowments.

temple'.[217] The inscription entrusts Vijayeśvara's priest, Brahmamūrttyāryabhaṭṭa trivikrama, with the income of a village 'as a provision for the discourses' of a Śaivācārya Jñānaśiva, who was 'dwelling in the asylum of the holy Vijayeśvara' and for the training of those who worship the deity'.[218]

When Vikramāditya II (r. 733–746 CE) avenged Pulakeśin and captured Kāñcīpura in 740, he left behind a remarkable record, written in a mixture of Kannada and Sanskrit, in the imperial Rājasiṃheśvara Temple: 'Vikramādityasatyāśraya... having captured Kāñcī and having inspected the riches of Rājasiṃheśvara gave them again to the deity. Those who destroy these letters and the stability of the king's charity which was thus given, shall enter the world of those who have killed the men of the assembly of this city'.[219] Vikramāditya II hedges between respecting Rājasiṃheśvara's property and taking credit for (re)donating that same property. In either case, he appears to have abided by the ubiquitous imprecatory epigraphic injunctions to respect the religious endowments of conquered kingdoms.

What better way for a conquering Cālukya monarch to assert his authority over the Pallavas than by propitiating the tutelary deity of the Pallava dynasty with the very endowment that the Pallavas could not themselves protect? The Pallavas had failed in their duty, under Dharmaśāstric principles of Equity and Trusts, to protect their tutelary deity, his temple, and his endowments. Vikramāditya, in contrast, protected Rājasiṃheśvara and his endowment and proved the Cālukyas' greater moral and political virtue. Protecting religious endowments – even of one's enemies – was such an important quality of kingship that in the Kendur plates, Vikramāditya II's son, and the final Vātāpi Cālukya, Kirtivarman II (r. 746–753 CE), praised his father as one: 'Who had rejoiced Brāhmaṇas, and poor and helpless people by his uninterrupted liberality, [and] who acquired high merit by restoring heaps of gold to the stone temples of Rājasiṃheśvara and other deities.'[220]

There is a clear connection between Vikramāditya's liberality to the helpless and his protection of the deity, Rājasiṃheśvara. This connection speaks to the longstanding influence of Arthaśāstric and Dharmaśāstric theories of the Crown as *parens patriae* on the practical operation of the law of Equity and Trusts in premodern India. Since the time of Aśoka Maurya, the Crown's guardianship of religious institutions went hand-in-glove with equitable principles. As religious

[217] EI 3.1: mahāśailaprāsāda**śrīvijayeśvarabhaṭṭārakas**... Two Kannada inscriptions from Paṭṭadakal identify this temple. See *Indian Antiquary*, Vol 10 (1881), Nos 112–13, p. 170: **śrībhijayēśvarada** mane... & **śribijēśvarada** sūḷe **chalabeyya** kamba muṟu.

[218] EI 3.1: **śrīvijayeśvarabhaṭṭārakasyāśrayāvasthitena**... **(no semantic connection with following line) vrahmamūrttyāryyabhaṭṭatrivikramacaturvvedāya** dattaḥ... ācāryaprasaṅgadevakarmmikāva rttanopāyanimittaṁ devasya pūjāsaṃskārāya [ca]... dattāni rakṣitavyāni.

[219] EI 3.48: **vikramād[it]yasatyāśraya...** kañciyān=koṇḍu **rājasi[ṃ]ghēśvarada** dhanamān=kaṇḍu maguḻdu dēvargge biṭṭār. intu biṭṭa bhaṭārāra dharmmada sthitiyu[m] īy=akṣaraṅgaḷumān=aḻivār=īy= ūrā ghaṭigeyā mahājanamān=kondāra lokakke sandār=appār.

[220] EI 9.21: satatapravṛttadānānditadvijadīnānāthajanaḥ... **rājasiṃheśvarādidevakulasuvarṇarāsipr atyarppaṇopārjitorjitapuṇyaḥ**.

institutions' legal infrastructure grew increasingly sophisticated, their endowments grew more substantial, and they became intimately associated with imperial ambitions, it is understandable that they would fall victim to increased spoliation. Richard Davis emphasises that the *spoliation* of temples, along with their images and treasures, was a reasonably commonplace practice among dynasties with imperial aspirations. It is prudent to remember, however, that the *protection* of temples was the expected, virtuous norm according to the prevailing jurisprudence of the day. Kings often failed to live up to this Dharmaśāstric jurisprudential norm - the rule of law is rarely if ever realised.[221] Nevertheless, spoliation was an effective method for undermining a rivals' claims to imperial sovereignty precisely because such sovereignty was predicated on upholding Dharmaśāstric injunctions to endow and protect religious endowments.

2.6 Deities as active legal agents during the Tripartite Struggle (8th–10th centuries)

During the 8th–10th centuries, the north of the Indian subcontinent was dominated by the 'Tripartite Struggle' over Kānyakubja (modern Kannauj) between three vast empires: the Rāṣṭrakūṭas of Mānyakheṭa (who had overthrown their erstwhile suzerains, the Cālukyas of Vātāpi); the Gurjara-Pratihāras (also former feudatories of the Cālukyas); and the Pālas of Bengal.[222] Alongside this conflict, this epoch also witnessed the arrival of political Islam into the Indian subcontinent: the Umayyad conquest of Sindh in 711 was followed by a series of Caliphal campaigns again the Gurjara-Pratihāra, Nāgabhaṭa I (r. 730–60 CE) and his successors.[223]

The law of Equity and Trusts developed coevally with these political vicissitudes. The capture and reconsecration of deities from imperial competitors became so commonplace that kings took pride in delineating the political provenance of these images. The shifting homes of a temple image reflected the shifting boundaries of royal power. At the same time, kings began to invoke much more

[221] For the Rule of Law see Note 35.

[222] For this era of history, see Dineschandra Sircar, *The Kānyakubja-Gauḍa Struggle: from the Sixth to the Twelfth Century AD* (Calcutta: Asiatic Society, 1985). For the Rāṣṭrakūṭas, see Schmiedchen, *Herrschergenealogie*; for the Gurjara-Pratihāras, see B.N. Puri, *The History of the Gurjara-Pratiharas* (Delhi: Munshiram Manoharlal, 1957); for the Pālas, see Jhunu Bagchi, *The History and Culture of the Pālas of Bengal and Bihar, cir. 750–1200 AD* (Delhi: Abhinav, 1993).

[223] For an overview of Muslims in Sanskrit inscriptions between 736 and 1000 CE, see Truschke, *The Language of History*, 28–34. For the early history of Islam in northwest India, see Andre Wink, *Al-Hind: The Making of the Indo-Islamic World, Vol 1: Early Medieval India and the Expansion of Islam*, 3rd edn. (Leiden: Brill, 2002), 192–218. For the early Gurjara's battles against the Turks (Tājikkas) see verse 2: yenāśeṣalokasaṃ[tā]pakalāpadas tājjikānalo, EI.18.12, for the Gwalior Praśasti of Mihirabhoja, which recounts his conflict with 'Turks' on the northwestern frontier.

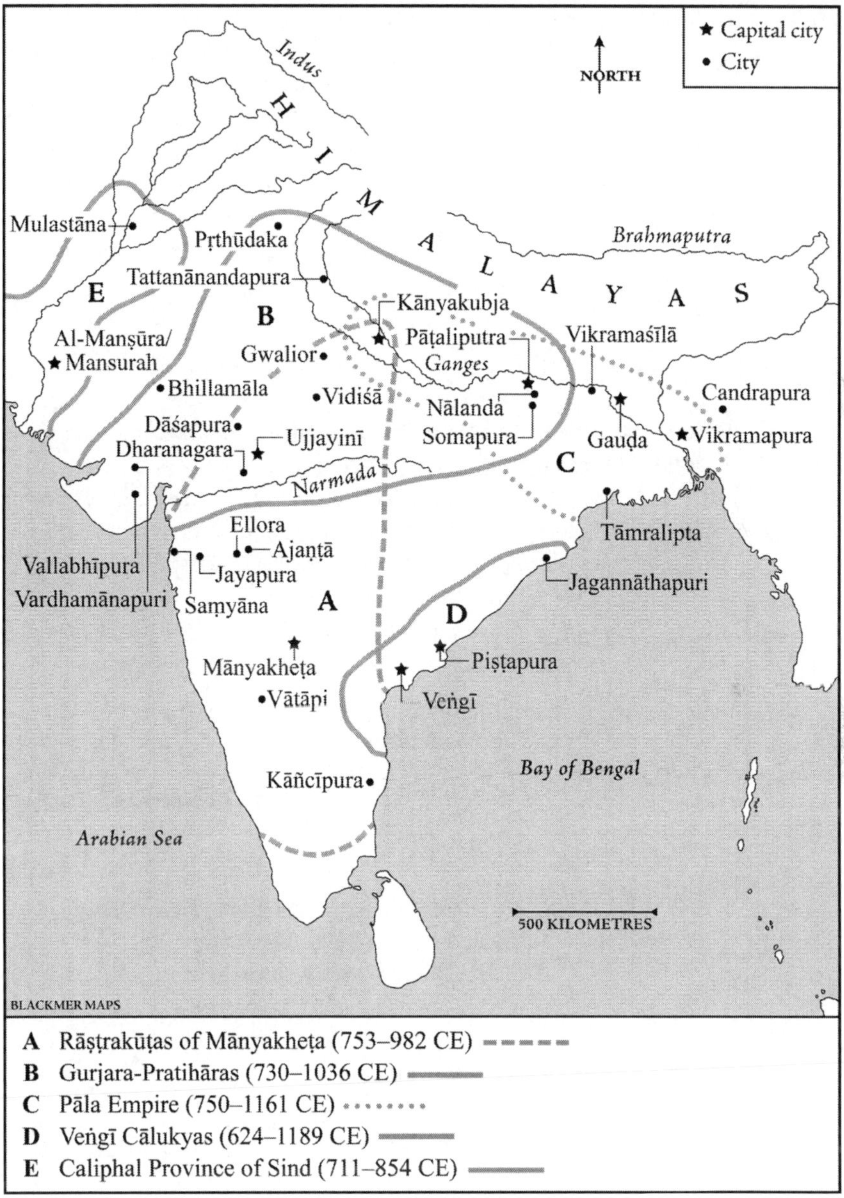

Map 2.4 The Kannauj Triangle (~8th–10th centuries CE)

explicit Dharmaśāstric, Purāṇic, and epic (the *Mahābhārata* and the *Rāmāyaṇa*) terminology in their grants while, endowing deities – now invariably in the dative case – with more complex significant assets such as oil-mills, shops, houses, etc.

Deities, for their part, grew to be much more active legal agents during this period. Deities loaned money at interest, engaged in commercial activity such as executing deeds of sale, and even acted as litigants in legal disputes – all while being represented by their fiduciaries. Taken collectively, this data indicates that the emergence of deities as full, active legal persons in Indian law can be dated to the 8th–10th centuries CE.

2.6.1 Deities as imperial palladia

The imperial temples of the Pallavas and Cālukyas during the 7th century became widespread by the 8th century. Of course, when a temple deity and its treasures became imperial palladia, they inevitably fell victim to the vicissitudes of power politics. Against this religio-political backdrop, indigenous Indian kings also followed the pattern of the Pallavas, Cālukyas, and earlier kings of spoliating temples and reconsecrating images captured from political rivals.

The Nesarika plates of the Rāṣṭrakuṭa Govinda III (r. 793–814 CE) list the royal standards seized from rival kings:

> The fish from the Pāṇḍyas; the bull from the Pallavas; the tiger from the Colas; the elephant from the Gaṅgās; the bowstick from Kerala; the boar from the Andhra, Cālukya, and Mauryas; the board bearing the image of the kettle-drum and snake from the Gūrjaras; the bull from the Pallavas; the names of the rulers from the Kosala, Avanti, and Siṃhala kings, and the celebrated goddess Tārā from the king of Vaṅgala.[224]

Likewise, in his Saṃyāna (modern Sanjan) plates, Amogharvaśa I (r. 814–78 CE) boasts that, 'having brought to Helāpura from Laṅkā two statues of its lord, these, having afterwards proceeded to Kāñcī, were established there in the temple of Śiva.'[225]

Yaśovarman Candella (r. 925–60 CE) provides a political pedigree of a deity that he installed at Khajuraho (953–54 CE):

> [The image of] Vaikunṭha [which]… Yaśovarman… has set up [here], – the Lord of Bhoṭa obtained it from the Kailāsa, and from him Sāhi, the king of Kīra, received

[224] EI 34.19–20: **pāṇḍyadeśādhipān** matsyaṃ vṛṣabhaṃ **pallaveśvarā[t /] colād** vyāghraṃ gajaṃ **gaṅgāc** cāpayaṣṭim ca **keralā[t]** //21// **aṅghracālukyamauryebhyo** va[rā]haṃ **gūrjareśvarā[t /]** phalakaṃ prativadhāryaṃ vṛṣabhaṃ **pallaveśvarā[t** //22//] **kosalāvantināthābhyāṃ siṃhalād** api nāma [/] **tārābhagavatikhyātāṃ dharmmād vaṅgalabhūmipāt** //23//

[225] EI 18.26: **helāpure laṅkāt acchila** tatprabhupratikṛtī **kāñcīm** upetau tataḥ kīrttistambhanibhau **śivāyatanake** yeneha saṁsthāpitau //34//

> it as a token of friendship; from him afterwards Herambapāla [a Pratihāra king] obtained it by a force of elephants and horses; and [Yaśovarman] received it from his son, Devapāla.[226]

Likewise, in his Bilhari inscription, the Tripuri Kalacuri Yuvarajadeva II (r. 980–90 CE) recounts that his father, Lakṣmaṇarāja (r. 940–70 CE), 'worshipped Someśvara with (an image of) Kāliya (the serpent) wrought of jewels and gold, which he had obtained from the prince of Oḍra, after defeating the lord of Kosala'.[227]

Endowing a tutelary temple of one's suzerains could also constitute an act of ritual obeisance. When the Gurjara-Pratihāra Mahendrapāla's (r. 885–910 CE) feudatories, Balavarman and his son Avanivarman, endowed the Sun God (*Tarunādityadeva*) at a temple constructed by their suzerains, they did so in conjunction with an elaborate preamble in which he professed their subordinance to Mahendrapāla.[228] These acts of endowment to the Sun as feudal obeisance helps to explain the Rāṣṭrakūṭa Govinda IV's (r. 930–35 CE) boast that his father, Indra III (r. 914–29 CE) destroyed the Pratihāra capital, Kānyakubja, after having made 'the courtyard of Kālapriya (a temple of the Sun outside of Kānyakubja) uneven by the strokes of the tusks of his rutting elephants'.[229]

2.6.2 Dharmaśāstra and *devāgrahāras*

While the invocation of Dharmaśāstric and related Purāṇic and epic jurisprudential theory began during the Gupta era, it become much more explicit during the 8th–10th centuries. This occurred alongside increasingly elaborate lists of stipulated charitable purposes. Taken collectively, this suggests that once *devadānas* became well-established as a clear legal category, it could accommodate more precisely defined trust conditions. The 8th-century Pūri plates from Kalinga attribute their imprecatory verses to the '*Mānavadharmaśastra*'.[230] Even though these verses don't appear in the *Mānavadharmaśāstra*, their appellation in the

[226] EI 1.19.2: **kailāsāḍ bhoṭanāthaḥ** suhṛd iti ca tataḥ **kīrarājaḥ** prapede **sāhis** tasmād avāpa dvipaturagabalenānu **herambapālaḥ** / tatsunor **devapālāt** tam atha... prāpya ninye pratiṣthāṃ **vaikuṇṭhaṃ... śrīyaśovarmarājaḥ** //43// Discussed by Richard Davis, 'Indian Art', 28–9.

[227] CII 4.1.45: jitvā **kosalanātham o[ḍra]nṛpater** āptas tu yaḥ **kāliyo** ratnasvarṇṇamayaḥ sa yena vihitas **someśvarābhyarccanam**.

[228] EI 9.1.A–B.

[229] EI 7.6: yanmādyadvipadantaghātaviṣamaṃ **kālapriyaprāṅgaṇaṃ** [kṛtaṃ]. Discussed by Michael Willis, 'Religious and Royal Patronage in North India', in Vishakha Desai and Darielle Mason (eds), *Gods, Guardians, and Lovers: Temple Sculptures from North India A.D. 700–1200* (London: Asia Society Galleries, 1993): 48–65, 58. D.R. Bhandarkar, editor of the plates in EI, argues that the Kālapriya temple was dedicated to Śiva. V.V. Mirashi identifies it as a Sun-temple. See Vasudev Vishnu Mirashi, *Bhavabhūti: His Life Date and Works* (Delhi: Motilal Banarsidass, 1974), 102–9; and Vasudev Vishnu Mirashi, 'Three Ancient and Famous Temples of the Sun', *Purāṇa* 8 (1966): 38–51.

[230] EI 23.19: uktañ ca **mānave dharmaśāstre**...

inscription reveals a desire by the grantor to tie the grant to the jurisprudence of Dharmaśāstra.

A local ruler near Nāsik, Bhogaśakti (8th century CE) issued two grants to the eponymous deity Bhogeśvara that employ a wide array of Sanskrit jurisprudential terminology. The panegyrics praise Bhogaśakti as: 'Ever eager to perform acts of charity such as temples, tanks, alms houses, and reservoirs… [and] who is skilled in (knowing) the real imported of the *Mahāhbārata*, the Purāṇas, the *Rāmāyaṇa*, and royal *śāstra*.'[231]

This 'royal *śāstra*' is, presumably, Dharmaśāstra and it comes as no surprise that the charities associated with Bhogaśakti appear in these same texts.[232] We also find extensive Dharmaśāstric vocabulary in the terminology of the dedication itself. Bhogaśakti donated eight villages to 'Bhagavān Nārāyaṇa' at Jayapura for the standard list of charitable purposes (worship, a *sattra*, repairs to the temple). He also adds an elaborate list of taxes (*ādānāni*) payable to the deity and describes these fiscal arrangements as a 'town dharma' (*nagaradharma*), or as a 'convention' (*sthiti*) – which we would term a conventional, equitable Dharma applicable to the townsfolk.[233] Bhogaśakti describes the relationship of trust in concrete terms: 'Since this temple has been entrusted to the town merchants, on them shall devolve the service and custody (*yogakṣema*) of the divine lord.'[234] Here, Bhogaśakti explicitly invokes Dharmaśāstric theories of Equity (conventional Dharma) when establishing a divine endowment owned by the deity.

During this period, the divine endowments and estates (*devadānas* and *devāgrahāras*) became standard legal models that many kings appear to take for granted in their inscriptions. In the 8th century, *devadānas* were common and regularised. In his Kavi plate, the early Gurjara, Jayabhaṭṭa IV (r. 720–37 CE), who repulsed the Umayyad campaigns in northwest India, gave some land as a '*devadāya*' (divine endowment) to the deity 'Āśramadeva', but he excluded 'other previous endowments to deities and Brāhmaṇas'.[235] The ubiquitous use of this clause in Hindu, Buddhist, and Jain inscriptions presumably stems from the practical necessity of distinguishing an increasingly large number of divine endowments from one another during the early medieval period.

In his Cambay plates, the Rāṣṭrakūṭa Govinda IV (r. 930–936 CE) introduces his order by stating that: 'I, who am permanently settled in Mānyakheṭa, am protecting "*devaboga agrahāras*" (estates enjoyed by deities) although they were resumed

[231] EI 25.22: devakulataṭākasattraprapādharmakriyānuṣṭhānavyasanī… **bhāratapurāṇarāmāyaṇarāja śāstrārthatvanipuṇaḥ**.

[232] See, for example, Chapter 1, Note 137.

[233] EI 25.22, lines 35–48: nagaradharmam… sthitim… An addendum, added later, compensated Bhogeśvaradeva (the deity of temple) for the conversion of some of his lands into a public pasture.

[234] Ibid.: yad etatd devakulaṃ tadvaṇiṅnagarāya nirūpitaṃ taiś ca sarvair bhagavato devasya śuśrūṣā yogakṣemaś ca voḍhavyaḥ.

[235] CII IV.23: **āśramadevapādebhyaḥ**… pūrvvāparadevabrahmadāyarahitaṃ… devadāyatvena pratipāditam. Also see Jayabhaṭa III's use of the same phrase in his Anjaneri plates, CII IV.22.

previously, and who am daily issuing new grants of villages to be respected by all.'[236] Govinda frames his royal authority in terms of protection (*pālana*) of religious grants – an application of the *parens patriae* jurisdiction seen in Dharmaśāstra and throughout Indian epigraphic history. Govinda describes giving eight-hundred villages to temples for the benefit of deities – listing various purposes in the process – before granting a large endowment to Brāhmaṇas.[237] This *brahmadeya*, however, entails a long list of highly detailed charitable purposes that include numerous types of sacrifices, and providing the requisite materials for Purāṇic charities of 'alms houses, free water, the release of bulls, wells, tanks, orchards, and temples'.[238]

The Dharmaśāstric *devadāya* model of trusts extended to Buddhist and Jain endowments from the period. In the Konnur Inscription (860 CE), Amoghavarśa I (r. 814–78 CE) gifted the income of a village, specifying it is 'for any new work connected with the sanctuary, for future repairs, for the cleansing, plastering, maintaining of it, and for other acts of piety', to Devendra, a monk, 'appointed to protect the temple of the Jina constructed by (the General) Baṁkeya'. Amoghavarśa describes this financial arrangement as a '*devadāya* custom' (*devadāyasthiti*) and invokes the standard series of Purāṇic verses attributed to Vyāsa.[239] Similarly, in the Bharat Kala Bhavan plates of the Bengali king, Rājyapāladeva, we see that Rājyapāladeva, although professing devotion to the Buddha, could, nevertheless, create a Brāhmaṇical grant – following the standard Dharmaśāstric model – 'in honour of the Buddha'.[240] Whatever be the doctrinal differences between Jains, Brāhmaṇas, and Buddhists during this era, their institutions were regulated by a legal idiom that was intimately tied to Dharmaśāstric jurisprudential principles. Indeed, in the 8th century, kings from the Western Gaṅgā dynasty (4th–11th centuries CE) adopted Manu's category of deities' property (*devasva*) in the imprecatory portion of the endowments.[241]

[236] EI 7.6: **mānyakheṭarājadhānosthiratarāvasthānena**… pūrvvaluptān api devabhogāgrahārān pratipālayatā pratidinaṃ ca niravadhinamasyagrāmaśāsanāni prayacchatā mayā…

[237] Ibid.: devabhogārthaṃ ca devakulebhyaḥ khaṇḍasphuṭitādinimittaṃ… grāmāṇām aṣṭaśatāni.. dattvā.

[238] Ibid.: sattraprapāśrayavṛṣotsargavāpīkūpataḍārāmadevālayādikaraṇopakaraṇārthañ ca. For a Bengali example, see the Nālandā plates of Devapāladeva (9th century), EI 17.17: pūrvvadattabhuktab hujyadevabrahmadeyavarjitāḥ mayā…

[239] EI 6.4: **baṁkeyanirmmāpitajināyatanaparipālananiyuktāya**… **śrīdevendramunīśvaraḥ** [the grammar is defective]. Tadvasatisambandhinavakarmmottarabhāvikhaṇḍasphuṭitasammārjjanopalep anaparipālanādidharmmopayogikarmmakaraṇanimittaṁ… (grāmaḥ dattaḥ)… devadāyasthityā… na paripanthanā kāryā.

[240] **bhagavantaṃ buddhabhaṭārakam** uddiśya. For examples, see Ryosuke Furui, 'Bharat Kala Bhavan Copper Plate Inscription of Rājyapāla, Year 2: Re-edition and Reinterpretation', *Puravritta: Journal of the Directorate of Archaeology & Museums* 1 (2016): 41–56; Ryosuke Furui, 'Rangpur Copper Plate Inscription of Mahīpāla I, Year 5', *Journal of Ancient Indian History* 27 (2011): 232–45.

[241] See, for example, Andrea Schlosser and Pankaj Tandon, 'The Channapatna Plates: A New Set of Copperplates of the Western Gaṅgas', *Studien zur Indologie und Iranistik* 29 (2009): 219–49, 229: devasvaṃ brāhmaṇasvaṃ ca yo lobhenopabhuñjati / sa pāpātmā pare loke gṛdhrocciṣṭena jīvati // Also see Lewis Rice, 'Nagamangala Copper Plate Inscription', *Indian Antiquary* 2 (1873): 155–61, 159: api cātra **manugītā** ślokā… devasvan tu viṣaṃ ghoraḥ na viṣaṃ viṣaṃ ucyate / viṣam ekākinaṃ hanti devasvam putrapautrakaṃ //

Finally, the Śrīcandra plate (930 CE) of the Candra Dynasty (10th-century subordinates of the Pālas) describes the financial constitution of a vast university, a true 'Oxford of the East', through the legal mechanism of a *devadāna* trust. The analogy is productive because, like Oxford – indeed, before Oxford – the 'University of Candrapura' was comprised of several colleges (*maṭhas*) with separate endowments, different student bodies, and diverse curricula. Nevertheless, the entire institution was licensed by a royal charter that assigned collegiate endowments to the tutelary deities of each college.[242] Like most Pāla plates, the Śrīcandra plate invokes the Buddha and issues the donation 'in honour of the Buddha'; however, the grant is made exclusively to Hindu deities.

Śrīcandra transforms a large plot of land into an eponymous '*brahmapura*' named Candrapura and, having subdivided it, transfers it to various deities.[243] Through a legal instrument (niyama), Candra allocates 120 *pāṭakas* of land to Brahman, with the following stipulations:

1. 10 *pāṭakas* for a teacher of Sanskrit grammar (*Vyākaraṇa*)
2. 10 *pāṭakas* for the maintenance and school supplies of 10 students
3. 5 *pāṭakas* for feeding guests
4. 1 *pāṭaka* for the Brāhmaṇa in charge of the temple
5. 2.5 *pāṭakas* for the scribe
6. ½ *pāṭaka* for each of 4 florists, 2 oilmen, 2 potters, 17 musicians, and 22 servants and cobblers
7. 2 *pāṭakas* for each of 1 dancer, 2 carpenters, 2 masons, and 2 blacksmiths
8. ¾ *pāṭaka* for 8 maid servants
9. 47 *pāṭakas* for repairs to the college.[244]

Śrīcandra then assigns 280 *pāṭakas* to four deities worshipped at four foreign (*deśāntarīya*) and at four Bengali (*Vaṅgāla*) *maṭhas*: Vaiśvānara, Yogeśvara, Jaiminī, and Mahākāla. As in the endowment to Brahman, these 280 pāṭakas were allocated for supporting teachers and students of the four Vedas that were attached to each of the eight *maṭhas* – presumably each deity/*maṭha* taught a different Veda – as well as their respective servants, repairment, etc.[245] Śrīcandra's endowment is representative of a wider phenomenon: the capacity of divine trusts

[242] Not dissimilar to the ancient Oxbridge system of dedicating colleges – and their endowments – to Saints John, Hugh, Catherine, Hilda, etc.

[243] EI 38.51: **śrīśrīcandrapurādhidhānabrahmapuram** parikalpya.

[244] Ibid: **brahmaṇe** etanmaṭhapratibaddhacāndravyākhyānopādhyayasya daśadrōṇikadaśapāṭakāḥ. daśacchātrāṇāṁ pālighuṭṭakārthaṃ daśapāṭakāḥ. apūrvvapañcabrāhmaṇānāṃ pratyaham bhaktan datum pañcapāṭakāḥ. etadadhiṣṭhānakārayitur brāhmaṇasya pāṭakaḥ. gaṇakasya pāṭakaḥ. kāyasthasya sārddhapaṭakadvayam. mālākārachatuṣṭayasya. tailikadvayasya. kumbhakāradvayasya. pañcakāhalikānām. śaṅkhavādakadvayasya. ḍhakkāvādakadvayasya. aṣṭadrāgaḍikānām. dvā viṁśatikarmmakaracarmmakārāṇāñ ca. pratyekaṁ pādonapāṭakaḥ. navakarmmanimittañ ca saptacaturviṁśatpāṭakāḥ. evam anena noyamena viṁśatyadhika[ṁ] pātakaśataṁ.

[245] Ibid.: tathā **deśāntarīyamaṭhacatuṣṭaye**. **vaṅgālamaṭhacatuṣṭaye** ca. **vaiśvānarayogeśvarajaimini mahākālebhyaś** ca. eṣām ubheyeṣāṃ maṭhapratibaddhargyajussāmārtharvvopādhyāyānām aṣṭhānām pratyekaṃ daśapāṭakāḥ.

to implement a wider array of highly specific charitable purposes under the wider rubric of Dharmaśāstric theories of Equity and Trusts.

2.6.3 Deities' complex assets

By the mid-9th century CE, deities began to hold increasingly complex financial portfolios. Divine endowments became quite intricate, with multiple deities owning diverse assets in the same villages. Deities also functioned as substantially more active legal agents – suing and being sued, lending money at interest, etc. For example, we find boundary clauses that demarcate one deity's holdings from another's. Deities also began loaning their funds at interest, renting out their buildings and land, and purchasing new assets. Legal disputes inevitably resulted from such financial complexity and we find at least one instance of deities engaging in litigation against one another. These developments in the substantive law of religious endowments coincided with an increasing use of Dharmaśāstric principles and terminology in that law's jurisprudential underpinning.

The Tattānandapura (modern Ahar, UP) inscription from the reign of the Pratihāra king, Mihirabhojadeva (r. 836–85 CE), illustrates the situation. The grant contains ten sequential documents that record various transactions undertaken in the name of the goddess Śrīkañcanaśrīdevī (and other sobriquets). These transactions include gifts *to* the goddess and assets purchased *with the goddess's own funds*. One transaction, from 886 CE, presents a limited form of active legal agency on the part of the deity:

> Having caused a receipt to be written with both of their names, Bhadraprakāśa of the Varkkaṭa caste of merchants who came from Śrī Bhillamāla [and is] residing in Śrī Tattānandapura, as well as Mauṅka, purchased a shop in Pattana with Śrī Kañcana Śrī Devī's drachmas. The boundaries of this shop are… in the southern direction, Nandā Bhavavatī Devī… [and] to the north, Vāmanasvāmi. Now, [this shop] is presented by Bhadra and Mauṅka and by the Saurvarṇika and Merchant Mahājana living in Śrīmat Tattānandapura (for the purpose of)… (*a long, incomplete list of temple activities*). [246]

Śrī Kañcana Devī's assets were far from the only deity-owned assets in these towns. Other deities owned shops of their own. One document notes that: 'The boundaries of this shop are… to the South, the shop belonging to Śrī Gandha Śrī Devī. The West-facing shop was purchased by the Sauvarṇika Mahājana with Śrī

[246] EI 19.7: **śrītattānandapure** prativasamānaḥ śrī**bhillamāla**vinirgatavaṇigvarkkaṭajātīya**bhadrap rakāśa**… tathā… **mauṅkaḥ**… anayoḥ nāmnā patram abhilikhāpya **śrīkañcanaśrīdevyā** drammaiḥ krayakrītāvārīhaiva pattanābhyantare… asyā avāryā āghāṭā… bhavanti… dakṣiṇasyāṃ diśi yā **nandā bhagavatī devī**… uttarato **vāmanasvāmi**…sammārjanopalepanakuṅkumapuṣpadhūpapradīpadhvajā dhavalāpanasindūrakhaṇḍasphuṭita… [22 graphemes missing] pratipāditā.

Kanaka Śrī Devī's funds and presented.'[247] Another document records that: 'The boundaries of this shop are… to the South, the shop belonging to Śrī Daśavatāra Deva [and] to the West, the house belonging to Śrī Nandā Bhagavatī. The shop was purchased by the Sauvarṇika Mahājana with Śrī Kanaka Śrīdevī's funds.'[248]

Kañcana Devī owned more sophisticated assets than the assigned lands and liquid capital we saw during the earlier centuries. In 886, four brothers 'presented a home… to Śrī Kanaka Śrī Devī as surety for the rent (of the house) for the monthly payment of ten Viṃśopakas, with a deed of receipt'.[249] Effectively, the brothers pledged to pay the deity a fixed monthly sum and offered the house (from whose rent the sum was to be paid) as surety for that pledge. In 904, the goddess' agents, the 'Saurvarṇika Mahājana', purchased the home outright, 'with Śrīkanaka Śrī Devī's funds on a 99-year lease, with all of the rent'.[250]

Kañcana Devī's temple trust is vastly more complicated than anything seen before the turn of the 9th century. By the 9th century, however, these sorts of arrangements became more commonplace. The Sīyaḍoṇī inscription (10th century CE), like the Tattānandapura inscription, is a composite document that records several gifts – houses, shops, income from land, foodstuffs, cash, perpetual endowments, by private citizens to Viṣṇu.[251] The inscription was something of a ledger for an elaborate, economically active divine trust.

The increasing financial complexity of divine endowments extended to monasteries (*maṭhas*). The Partabgarh inscription of Mahendrapāla II (r. 944–48 CE), like the Tattānandapura inscription of his forefather Mihirabhojadeva, consolidates several grants to various deities associated with the monastery of Hariṣeśvara.[252] The monastery, located at Daśapura (near modern Mandasor), supervised several separate divine endowments that were each made in the name of a separate deity. In effect, the members of the *maṭha* served as trustees of several different divine endowments – much like Oxbridge dons often supervise multiple endowments.

Likewise, the Tiruvoṟṟiyūr inscription, dated to the reign of the Rāṣṭrakūṭa Emperor, Kṛṣṇa III (r. 939–67 CE), records that the head of a Śaiva monastery:

[247] Ibid.: … asyāḥ avāryāḥ āghāṭā yatra bhavanti… dakṣiṇataḥ **śrīgandhaśrīdevy**āvārī… paścimābhimukhāvārī **śrīkanakaśrīdevyā** dravyeṇa sauvarṇikamahājanena krayakrītā… saṃpradatā ca.

[248] Ibid.: asyā āvāryā āghāṭā yatra bhavanti… dakṣiṇataḥ **śrīdaśavatāradeva**satkāvārī paścimataḥ **śrīnandābhagavatyāḥ** satkagṛhaṃ… āvārī **śrīkanakaśrīdevyāḥ** dravyeṇa sauvarṇikamahājanena krayakrītā.

[249] Ibid.: catvāro… gṛhaṃ… pratigrahapatreṇa daśaviṃśopakāmāsapradeyabhāṭakanyāsena **śrīkanakaśrīdevyai** pradattaṃ.

[250] Ibid.: sarvabhāṭakena navanavatipatreṇa **śrīkanakaśrīdevyā** dravyeṇa sauvarṇikamahājanena krayakrītaṃ.

[251] EI 1.21. Also see EI 1.23 for the Pehowa inscription (9th century). In the Pehowa inscription, several horse traders agree to a tax on equine sales – as a *sthiti*, or conventional Dharma – in order to fund *akṣayanīvīs* for various deities. For an analysis of the Sīyaḍoṇī inscriptions, see Aman Mishra, 'Sīyaḍoṇī: An Unplanned Town of the Gurjara-Pratīhāra Times' *Urban History* 50.4 (2022): 1–18.

[252] EI 14.13: gūrvadattadevabrahmādeyavarjjito… **śrīdaśapuracāturvvedyahariṣeśvaramaṭhasaṃba dhyamānaśrīvaṭayakṣinīdevyai** śasanatvena pratipāditaḥ.

'Caturānana by name and bearing the burden of maintaining the monastery... made the assembly at Narasiṃhamaṁgala receive for eternity, a hundred pieces of Śiva's pure gold with an interest of three *māṣas* per year.'[253] Caturānana follows this Sanskrit statement with a list, in Tamil, of the various activities on which this interest should be spent – such as cooks, temple assistants, etc. In essence, Caturānana created a permanent endowment using the funds of the monastery's tutelary deity.

Of course, the proliferation of complex, multilayered trusts in discreet geographical locations led to legal disputes between deities and their trustees over their assets. Three copper-plates issued by the Rāṣṭrakūṭa Indra III (r. 914–29 CE) in 926 CE recount an inter-deity dispute at Saṃyāna (modern Sanjan).[254] In the first document, an Arab vassal of the Rāṣṭrakūṭas, Madhumati (i.e., Muhammad), 'of the Tājika lineage, by whom the whole of the Saṃyāna maṇḍala was obtained as a gift from King Kṛṣṇa' gave a village: 'For the purpose of the establishment of the *maṭhikā* (little monastery) created by him... (and) similarly for the purpose of the feeding with all accoutrements of the nine persons of the great assembly of eastern Brāhmaṇas dwelling here and of Bhagavatī, as the tenth, the feeding of her done on the principle of *varākāra*.'[255] It is remarkable that one of the first inscriptions made by an Islamic feudatory in India – 'sandwiched between different levels of the indigenous hierarchy' – entailed the construction of a monastery and an endowment made for the worship of the goddess.[256] There were other deities in Saṃyana at the time, and the goddess ran afoul of one of them, Śrī Bhillamāladeva. In 926 CE, Kṛṣṇa III issued two plates recording a legal settlement (*vyavasthā*) between these two parties. After a royal eulogy, the plates introduce the plaintiffs:

> Here, (in Saṃyāna) there is Śrī Bhillamāladeva, the *tilaka*, who removes the fear of the beings of the three worlds, saluted by the praiseworthy, unimpeachable... Here, there is (also) a noble, faultless *maṭhikā*, furnished with a rampart that is difficult to traverse, and free from strife... surrounded with readers. In which (*maṭhikā*) there is Bhagavatī Devī.[257]

[253] EI 27.47: nāmnā **śrīcaturānano** maṭhadhuram bibhrad... **śambhoś** śuddhasuvarṇaniṣkaśatakan niṣkakatrimāṣa[r]ddhikam pratyabdan narasiṃhamaṅgalasabhām ākalpam agrāhayat.

[254] EI 32.4.1–2.

[255] Ibid.: **kṛṣṇarāja**dayāvāptakṛtsna**saṃyāna**maṇḍalaḥ / āsīn **madhumatiḥ** śrīmān nṛpatis **tājikā**nvaye//17//... etatkṛtamaṭhikāsaṃskārārthaṃ... tathātra nivāsi**pañcagauḍīya**mahāparṣado navajanānāṃ daśamyāś ca **bhagavatyā** varākāranyāyena sarvopakaraṇopabhogārthaṃ... grāmo dattas...

[256] For Madhumati, see Annette Schmiedchen, 'Imperial Rulers and Regional Elites in Early Medieval Central India (8th to 13th Centuries)', in Herman Kulke and Bhairabi Sahu (eds), *The Routledge Handbook of the State in Pre-Modern India* (London: Routledge, 2022): 291–308, 300; and Truschke, *The Language of History*, 33.

[257] EI 32.4.2: astīha tilakabhūtas tribhuvanabhavanabhayāpahāraḥ / **śrībhillamāladevaḥ** vandyair abhinandito 'nin[d]yaḥ //12// astīha kautukakṛtir maṭhikānaghārryā durlaṅghyaśālakalitā kalinā vimuktā / svādhyāyikair.... //15//.... parītā / 16a / yasyāṃ **bhagavatī devī** devadānavapūjitā /17ab/

The grant shifts to the voice of Śrī Bhillamāladeva:

> And he, the aforementioned Śrī Bhillamāladeva, accompanied by his servants, offers a legal settlement, pursuant to a (royal) edict, to the Śrī *maṭhikā*, along with its readers belonging to the great assembly and its (servants). Since that little bit of land which is ours has been incorporated into the enclosure situated in the northern portion of the *maṭhikā*, in connection with that, 40 drachmas (minted by) the trader, Gaṃbhuvaka shall, at the end of every festival of lights, be given by the *maṭhikā* to us as a debt (*śrotaka*).[258]

Śrī Bhillamāladeva speaks in the first-person voice and is clearly an active legal agent. He not only spells out the terms of the legal settlement, but also outlines two indemnity clauses:

> a) Now, whosoever, the deity's *vipra* (priest) or merchant, acting as a 'Crow and Palm', through a fraud (aimed at) augmenting the debt or through some other method (aimed at) destroying the rampart (or) kills himself, even though he is dead, he shall be regarded as a dog, an ass, and a Cāṇḍāla. But, (if he be) a merchant, (his) entire estate will be confiscated by the crown.[259]
>
> b) Similarly, if the tax is not given by the deity's (i.e., the Goddess') servants, then, if someone other than a member of the *parṣat* (the members of the monastery) performs *pūjā* to Bhagavatī, opens the Maṭhikā's gate, or kills himself, even though he is dead, he shall be regarded as a dog, an ass, and a Cāṇḍāla (and, assuming they are a merchant, have their estate confiscated by the crown).[260]

Śrī Bhillamāladeva closes the settlement in the legal language we've seen in most divine endowments:

> By this decree, this settlement should be protected by both parties as long as the sun and moon endure... He who would seize the (aforementioned) land to break the payment would be blemished by the five great sins. The giver of the settlement effects my will. This is my will, Śrī Bhillamāla Deva, accompanied by my servants. This edict is clear, with the assent of both (parties).[261]

[258] Ibid.: sa ca pūrvoktaḥ **śrībhillamāladevo** vārikapurassaras tasyāś ca śrīmahāparṣatsvādhyāyikasametaśrīmaṭhikāyāḥ śāsanapūrvaṃ vyavasthāṃ prayacchati... yathā maṭhikottaradigbhāge sthitaprākārābhyantare 'smadīyā kiyanmātrā bhūmir yā praviṣṭā tatsaṃbandhe māṭhikayā 'smākaṃ pratidīpotsavabhaṅgaṃ vyavahārikaśreṣṭi**gaṃbhuvaka**drammāḥ śrotake deyāḥ catvāriṃśad aṅkato 'pi dra 40.

[259] Ibid.: adhunā yaḥ kaścid devakīyavipro vaṇijo vā śrotakasaṃvardhanavyājenānyena vā prakāreṇa prākārabhañjanāya kākatālīyo bhūtvā ātmahananaṃ vyājaṃ vā karoti sa mṛto 'pi śvagardabhacāṇḍālavad draṣṭavyaḥ. vaṇijas tu rājakulena sarvasvāpaharaṇaṃ karaṇīyaṃ.

[260] Ibid.: tathā devavārikāṇāṃ śrotakaṃ na dattaṃ cet tadā maṭhikādvāraṃ dadatāṃ **bhagavatyai** vā pūjāṃ vidhatāṃ parṣanmadhyavarttyanyoḥ vā ātmahananaṃ karoti sa mṛto 'pi śvagardabhacāṇḍālavad [draṣṭavyaḥ]. See Sontheimer, 'Religious Endowments', 39, for an instance of temple devotees self-immolating as a protest against, presumably, the seizing of temple property.

[261] Ibid.: anayā sthityā vyavastheyam ācandrārkakālaṃ yāvad ubhayavargeṇāpi pālanīyā... yas tu punaḥ śrotakollaṅghanavyājena bhūmyapahāraṃ karoti sa pañcabhir mahāpātakaiś ca saṃpṛkto bhavet... vyavasthādātā svamatam āropayati. mataṃ mama **śrībhillamāladevasya** vārikapurassarasya. śāsanaṃ... anumatenobhayo spaṣṭam etat.

The Saṃyāna plates display the full complexity of the theory and practice of premodern Indian trusts law. Kṛṣṇa III follows his Dharmaśāstric duty to intervene when two *sui iuris* trusts come into conflict, and issues a legal settlement in the form of a royal command (*rājaśāsana*). The terms of the settlement, assented to by both deities and their followers, contain specific contractual obligations and specific enforcement clauses – using technical Dharmaśāstric theories of Equity (*sthiti*/*samaya*/etc.).[262] This is a legally sophisticated and thoroughly Dharmaśāstric instance of deities acting as legal owners of assets and as juridical persons for the purpose of lawsuits – the first, perhaps, in Indian history. In the following centuries, even as the vernacular largely supplanted Sanskrit as the primary language of inscriptions, the jurisprudential foundations of the law of Equity and Trusts remained Sanskritic (i.e., Dharmaśāstric).

2.7 Equity and Trusts in the second millennium CE

In 973 CE, the Paramāra King, Sīyaka (r. 949–72 CE) sacked the Rāṣṭrakūṭa capital, Mānyakheṭa.[263] Taking advantage of the chaos, Taila II (r. 957–97 CE), a Cālukya feudatory of the Rāṣṭrakūṭas who ruled from Bījapura, declared his independence and carved out a large domain from the ruins of his erstwhile overlords' empire in the Deccan.[264] By the reign of Someśvara I, who moved the Cālukyas' capital to Kalyāṇa (modern Basavakalyan), the dynasty ruled over a vast central Indian empire.

At the same time in the South, the Cōḷa dynasty, which had suffered a crushing defeat at the hands of Kṛṣṇa III at the Battle of Takkōlam in 948–49 CE, also took advantage of the collapse of Rāṣṭrakūṭa hegemony to carve out their own imperial dominion.[265] Rājarājacōḷa (r. 985–1040 CE), who constructed the glorious Rājarājeśvara temple at the Cōḷa capital, Tañjāvūr (modern Tanjore), conquered a vast imperium: he subjugated Kerala and the Pāṇḍyan realm; invaded Śrīlaṅka; and created a powerful navy that controlled the lucrative spice trade of the Indian Ocean (which also enabled his son, Rājendracōḷa, to conquer the Kingdom of Anurādhapura in 1017 CE and invade Southeast Asia in 1025 CE).[266] Rājarāja's Śaivasaiddhāntika preceptor, Īśānaśiva, who served as the residing priest of the Rājājeśvara temple, also composed a liturgical manual, the *Īśānaśivagurudevapad dhati*, which enjoins the naming of a *liṅga* after the donor.[267]

[262] See Chapter 1, §1.5, 'Equity as supplemental law'.
[263] Ali, 'Royal Eulogy', 192.
[264] Ibid., 192–3.
[265] For an account of this battle and earlier attempts by the Cōḷas to establish hegemony, see Ali, 'Royal Eulogy', 187–93.
[266] Ibid., 193–4 & 197–203.
[267] Ibid., 214. For eponymous deities, see Chapter 1, §1.5.3, 'The legal personality of deities as a conventional Dharma'.

Map 2.5 India in the early second millennium (~11th–12th centuries CE)

Both dynasties ruled, with varying levels of puissance, until the 13th century, when the establishment of the Delhi Sulṭānate fundamentally changed the constitutional basis of law in India: from Dharmaśāstric jurisprudence to Persian-Islamic jurisprudence.[268] This final, culminating epoch of pre-sulṭānate India witnessed significant developments in the practical law of Equity and Trusts and in the relationship between that law and Dharmaśāstric jurisprudence. The most striking was a shift from the use of Sanskrit to vernacular languages (although these vernacular languages were highly Sanskritised). Despite the shift in the language used, the legal practices of Equity and Trusts retained their same contours from times past. Nevertheless, the law also developed further.

First, temple construction, guardianship, and endowment became a much more common form of political domination or of political independence. Ruling a kingdom implied building and maintaining a temple – and, conversely, conquering a kingdom seems to have implied despoiling one's rivals' imperial temples. Second, religious endowments and their associated charitable activities became more complex financially and fiduciarily. On the one hand, deities bought, sold, and redistributed assets in a fashion that resembled modern-day banks. On the other hand, donors used divine trusts to fund a wide array of charitable uses such as the establishment of discipline-specific colleges and academic chairs and the administration of cost-free hospitals for the poor.

Third, donors, royal and common, set up more sophisticated methods for regulating trusts in the event of maladministration by the trustees or by interference from the public. We find morals clauses for monastic trustees, explicit mechanisms for protecting endowments, an increased use of '*devasva*' as an active legal category, and clear instances where either the deity or the king intervenes in cases of breach of trust. Finally, endowments made to Jain and Buddhist temples apply the Dharmaśāstric law of Equity and Trusts to the Jina and to the Buddha as complete legal persons. In the aggregate, this data indicates that, by the 13th century, India had developed a comprehensive law of Equity and Trusts that matches Dharmaśāstric jurisprudence and contemporary law fairly accurately.

2.7.1 Imperial politics and divine endowments

The plunder and preservation of divine endowments was a key vector in inter-regnal politics between the 10th and the 13th centuries CE. In northwestern India, the Solaṅki Cālukyas battled with Maḥmūd of Ghazni over control of the Somanātha

[268] Davis, 'Historical Overview', 22–3. According to Donald Davis, the 'language of political Islam' introduced to India through the Delhi Sulṭāns, 'emanates more from the traditions of rulership associated with Central Asia and Persia than from Islamic political theory, which insists on a rather clear separation of state and law'.

temple, foreshadowing contentious Hindu–Islamic conflicts in which: 'As the frontier of control shifted over the ensuing centuries, nearly every Islamic ruler seeking to establish control over Gujarat felt the compulsion to desecrate the *liṅga* at Somanātha, and every Hindu chieftain seeking independence felt an imperative to restore it.'[269] At the same time, the Cōḷas were on the march.[270] Rājādhirāja (r. 1044–52 CE) defeated the Cālukyas at the Battle of Pūṇṭūr in 1044 and sacked Kalyāṇa.[271] Rājādhirāja seized a door-guardian (*dvarapāla*) statue from a temple in Kalyāṇa and reconsecrated it in Tañjāvūr.[272]

The Cōḷa-Ceylonese conflict during the 11th century brought the Sanskrit law of Equity and Trusts to Śrīlaṅka.[273] When Vijayabāhu (r. 1055–1110 CE) recaptured the island from the Cōḷas he established a trust in favour of the Buddha's tooth relic that, in effect, doubled as a declaration of independence.[274] In his Poḷonnarua inscription, Vijayabāhu re-established Buddhist hegemony over Śrīlaṅka by constructing and endowing a temple to the Buddha's tooth relic (*dalada*). This was, of course, part of his wider articulation of an independent Śrīlaṅkan political identify, but this Sanskrit/Tamiḷ inscription essentially copies the legal form and jurisprudential principles of Cōḷa grants even as it uses the language of its erstwhile overlords. Viajayabāhu notes his construction of 'the dwelling of the tooth-relic of the Buddha', and his assumption of the crown of Śrī Laṅka 'with the approval of the *Saṅgha* for the purpose of protecting the Buddhist religion'.[275] Viajayabāhu bases his sovereignty on his ability to install, endow, and protect the tooth of the Buddha, much like a Hindu sovereign would endow a deity. Toward this end, Vijayabāhu explains that he:

[269] Richard Davis, 'The Rebuilding of a Hindu Temple', in Donald Lopez (ed.), *Religions of India in Practice* (Princeton: Princeton University Press, 1995): 627–48, 628.

[270] See, for example, the Tirumukkudal inscription of Vīracōḷa which describes Cōḷa conflicts with Śrīlaṅka and the Cālukyas, EI 21.38.

[271] Davis, *Lives of Indian Images*, 51–2.

[272] Ibid. The inscription reads: 'This is the door guardian brought by Lord Vijayarājendradeva after burning Kalyāṇapuram' (*ARE* 24 of 1908). Also see Eaton, *Persianate*, 23–9, for Rājendra's capture of a *murti* from the Pālas.

[273] The kingdom of Anurādhapura participated in earlier (especially the Cālukya/Pallava) imperial formations. See Jonathan S. Walters, 'Buddhist History: The Sri Lankan Pāli Vaṃsas and Their Commentary', in Ronald Inden, Jonathan Walters, and Daud Ali (eds), *Querying the Medieval: Texts and the History of Practices in South Asia* (Oxford: Oxford University Press, 2000): 99–164, 132–4. According to the *Cūlavaṃsa* (L-LI), when the Pāṇḍyas conquered Śrīlaṅka in the 9th century, they seized a golden Buddha image from the Ratnapāsāda of the Abhayagirivihāra, which was not returned until Sena II (r. 853–87 CE) supported a Pāṇḍyan rebellion against the Cōḷas. Walters provides an excellent survey of the religio-political situation in Śrīlaṅka before the Cōḷa conquest – drawing in no small part on pre-Cōḷa inscriptions.

[274] EI 18.26b. For the Pāḷi chronicle of the Buddha's tooth relic, the *Dāṭhāvaṃsa*, and its relationship to Śrīlaṅkan history, see Chapter 8 in Alastair Gornall, *Rewriting Buddhism: Pali Literature and Monastic Reform in Sri Lanka, 1157–1270* (London: UCL Press, 2020).

[275] EI 18.26: **laṁkāyāṁ jinadantadhātubhavanaṁ...** 'kārṣīt... **buddhaśāsanaṁ** rakṣikka vēṇḍi saṁghaniyōggattāl tirumuḍiśūḍi.

> Directed his general to erect at Poḷannaruva, (i.e.), Vijayarājapūri, the Temple of the Tooth as a permanent receptacle of the Tooth and Bowl Relic Gods (*daladā pātra dhātu svāmi devarkaḷ*), the crest-gems of the three worlds, whose original chief place of deposit was in the Abhayagiri Mahāvihāra, and as a prosperous edifice for the first consecration of, and as a *Gandhakuṭi* for the handsome large image of God Buddha...[276]

The Vēlaikkāra mercenary company then vows to protect the shrine and endow it with income and servants from villages, before noting that 'for the cruel sinner who misappropriates the property donated to the deities, *bhūtas* (spirits) and priests... becomes an enemy of the Vēlaikkāras'.[277]

Vijayabāhu's use of Tamil/Sanskrit for his declaration of independence from the Cōḷa Empire utilises the legal trusts framework of his erstwhile overlords even as it is applied to quintessentially Siṅhalese phenomena: Buddha-relics described as legal deities. Ironically, at least according to the *Cūlavaṃsa*, Vijayabāhu's successor, Vikramabāhu (r. 1111–32 CE), funded his military misadventures during a brief civil war by expropriating 'the maintenance villages belonging to the Buddha' as well as 'gems, pearls and the like that had been given by the faithful as offerings to the alms-bowl relic and precious tooth relic'.[278]

With the help of the Pāṇḍyas, the Śrīlaṅkans took the fight to the Cōḷa homeland. Parākramabāhu (r. 1153–86 CE) invaded the mainland in support of the Siṅhalese candidate for the contested Pāṇḍyan throne, and Parākramabāhu plundered a Cōḷa Śiva temple at Rāmeśvara.[279] Nevertheless, if plundering temples was a powerful form of destroying the religio-sovereignty of an opposing kingdom, protecting and re-creating the very same temples could be an act of establishing one's own suzerainty. Thus, when Parākramabāhu's successor, Niśśaṅkamalla (r. 1186–96 CE), visited a Siṅhalese garrison at Rāmeśvara while campaigning with the Pāṇḍyas, he left behind an elaborate inscription written in Siṅhala.

Niśśaṅkamalla boasts of having introduced the practice of writing copperplates in Śrīlaṅka and tells his audience that: 'he gave incalculable treasure to repair a dilapidated shrine (*devālaya*) in the ... country and erected here the shrine named Niśśaṅkeśvara... having raised it to the revenue of... he acquired a gift-village and assigned it to the almshouse (*satra*)'.[280] In contrast to Vijayabāhu's use

[276] Ibid.: seṉavirattarkku niyokittup **pulanariyāṇa vijayarājapurattu** eḍupitta mūlasthānamākiya **abhayagiri** mahā vihārattu agra yatanamāṇa... mūvulakukkuñ cikāmaṇi yākiya **daḷadā pātra dhātu svāmi [d]evarkaḷukku** nitya vāsa bhavanamāṇa pratamābhiṣekattukku maṅkala grahamāṇa... **buddha devarkku gandhakūṭiyāṇa**.

[277] Ibid.: tēvar pūtar mātavattōrukkuk kuḍuttaṇa koḷḷum koḍum pāviyum.

[278] Gornall, *Rewriting*, 25–6. Cf. *Cūḷavaṃsa* 61.54–7: **buddhādisantake** bhogagāmake... saddhehi pattadhātussa **dāṭhādhātuvarassa** ca pūjanatthāya dinnāni maṇimuttādikāni ca.

[279] Walters, 'Buddhist History', 143–4. For the destruction of the Rāmeśvara temple, see the Ārpākkam inscription of Rājādhirājacōḷa II (r. 1166–78 CE), *AR Report*, 1899 pp. 8–9.

[280] EI 36.3: pa[vatnā niyāyen tāmraśāsana pavat karavā]... [de]śayehi jīrṇṇa devālaya karana paridden Ananta vastu deva mehi **niśśaṁkeśvara** nam yut devālayak naṁvā... ye ayaṭa nagā gamvarak ut genä satrayaṭa lava vadāra.

of Tamil to endow Buddhist relics – explicitly framed as deities – Niśśaṅkamalla uses Siṅhala to consecrate and endow an eponymous Hindu deity in a prominent Cōḷa temple that had been destroyed by Parākramabāhu. This is a memorable moment in Indian history that demonstrates how the legal paradigm of Equity and Trusts in Sanskrit jurisprudence served as a baseline for rulers across the South Asian subcontinent from a wide variety of linguistic and religious backgrounds. This shared jurisprudential and political baseline enabled Niśśaṅkamalla to articulate his suzerainty over an all-Indian imperial formation by following the great Rājarājacōḷa and his contemporaries in creating and endowing a trust in favour of an eponymous deity.[281]

The Cōḷas' political fortunes declined in the 13th century and their temples became the object of the spoliation that they visited on other kingdom's shrines. The Tiruvendipuram inscriptions of Rājarājacōḷa III (r. 1218–56 CE) relate that the Kāḍava king, Kopperuñjiṅga, with the assistance of a Prākramabāhu, 'King of Īḷam', captured the Cōḷa emperor and imprisoned him in Śendamaṅgalam in 1231–32.[282] Rājarāja's ally, the Hoyśaḷa Vīranarasiṃha II (r. 1220–34 CE), freed him after having heard, *inter alia*, that the Cōḷa realms' 'temple of the god (Śiva) and the places (sacred to) Viṣṇu were destroyed'.[283] Vīranarasiṃha II's indignation at the sack of temples is ironic, given that Cōḷa accounts of their earlier wars with the Hoysaḷas in the 12th century frequently mention the plunder – and subsequent recovery, reinstallation, and re-endowment of lost temple images – in the wake of the conflict.[284]

2.7.2 Complex endowments and complex charitable trusts

Religious and charitable trusts continued to grow more complex during the second millennium CE. On the one hand, the active financial agency of deities and their fiduciaries that we saw in the 9th- and 10th-century Saṃyāna and Tattānandapura records became far more common. Deities bought and sold property, lent money at interest, and took a far more active role in economic affairs. At the same time, endowments made by kings and private citizens became more detailed – both in terms of the various assets gifted and in terms of the allocation of those assets

[281] Walters, 'Buddhist History', 145, makes the plausible claim that Niśśaṅkamalla's efforts were merely a symbolic 'taunting' of the Cōḷas by a dynasty that would soon lose its last toehold on the Indian subcontinent. What makes this 'taunting' so effective, however, is the shared Sanskritic jurisprudential principles of Equity and Trusts.

[282] EI 7.23. Note that in Kopperuñjiṅga's description of the event (EI 23.27) he elides the detail of the temple destruction.

[283] Ibid.: deva[laiyaṅga]lu[m] **viṣṇasthāṇaṅgalum** aḷigaiyāle ippaḍi devaṇ… Also see EI 24.6 for a Kāḍava king in the early 13th century signalling his imperial ambitions by creating an endowment for an eponymous deity.

[284] See EI 32.22 (pp. 191–3) for an account of image-taking during the conflict.

for specific purposes. The end result was that, by the 13th century CE, Sanskrit theories of trusts – expressed in vernacular languages – became the ordering legal model for a significant portion of the political economy of much of India.

In the Cōḷa realm, temple treasuries functioned like commercial banks, and we find many records of deities issuing loans at interest – with other associated duties – to commercial groups.[285] An inscription from the local village assembly in the temple of Tintriniśvara at Tindivanam records that: 'We… having sold the land in this wise, and having received from Śaṇḍeśvaradevar (the deity) the sale amount and tax amount, made this village and the tank a tax-free *devadāna*, drew up a sale deed and gave it to Rājādhirākaviṭaṅkarśaṇḍeśvaradevar (who is) set up in Tiruttiṇḍīśvaram.'[286]

Another contemporaneous inscription records a settlement between a group of villages and the deity of a temple at Kāñcīpura: 'In the 3rd year of Korājakesarivarman, we, the villagers… made this written agreement. We have received from Ādidāsacaṇḍeśvara of the holy stone temple in Kāñcīpuram eighteen *kaṛañjus* of gold… from the interest… we shall pour out daily… one lamp (etc. etc).'[287]

The inscriptions on Rājarājacōḷa's Rājarājeśvara temple at Tañjāvūr, are a vast record of an intricate series of financial relationships between the temple deity, the temple administrative body, the king, and innumerable groups of cowherds, merchants, servants, etc.[288] Rājarāja's imperial inscriptions list the gifts of gold and other precious substances that he made to his eponymous, tutelary deity; some of these treasures having been despoiled from defeated kings.[289] These inscriptions, like many of the Cōḷa dynasty, contain little or no Dharmaśāstric jurisprudential language, but simply list the substantial assets held by the deity.[290] Nevertheless, in his Larger Leiden plates – written in a mixture of Tamil and Sanskrit and with plenty of Dharmaśāstric terminology – Rājarājacōḷa offers a lengthy description of boundaries of his gifted lands. His landmarks, are, almost entirely, the *devadāna*

[285] See, for example, the distribution of temple lands by the god of the Tiruvārūr temple himself, as cited in Sontheimer, 'Religious Endowments', 37–8.

[286] SII 7.842. Transcribed and translated in EI 23.4 (extract 3): viṛṛukkuḍutta nilattil uḷudu kuḍigaḷai epperpaṭṭa… iṛaimaṛṛa…kaṭṭapperādomāgavum ipparišu viṛṛu vilaikāśum **śaṇḍeśvaradevarpakkal** vilaipporuḷum iṛaipporuḷumāgakkoṇḍu ivvūrum eriyum iṛaiyili devadāṇam ākki [vi]ṛṛu vilaiyāvaṇam śeydu kuḍuttom **tiruttiṇḍīśvaratt** eḷundaruḷuvitta **irādh[i]rājaviṭaṅkardevar śaṇḍeśvaradevar[k] ku**… ūrōm.

[287] SII 1, 116: kovirājakecaripanmaṟku yāṇṭu 3 [āvatu] kāliyūrkoṭṭat[tokaḻa]nāṭṭu tiru[kka]-ṟṟaḷippuṟattu meṉalūr ūrom kaiyeḻuttu [||] kāñcīypurattu tirukka-ṟṟaḷi **[ā]-didāsacaṇḍeśvara** pakkal yāṅkaḷ koṇṭu kaṭava poṉ patiṉeṇ[kaḻa-ñcey] munṟu mañcāṭiyum kuṉṟiy [|] ippon patiṉneṇkaḻañcey mu[nṟ mañcā]-[ṭi] kuṉṟikkum palicaiyāṟcantrātit[ta]vaṟa nicatam uḻakkeṇṇai ūraka[muṭaiyār kā]-loṭokkum uḻakkāle aṭṭuvomānom oru nantāviḷakku aṭṭuloma-[ra]no[m] … . .ūrār colla eḻutineṉ ivvūr vicavan alappaṭiyeṉ ivai en eḻut[tu] [||]

[288] See a comprehensive list in SII 2 – Parts 1–4.

[289] See SII 2.1.1. See SII 2.1.3, paragraphs 5 and 6, for treasure taken from the Chera and Pāṇḍya kings.

[290] The Cōḷas use the term '*devadāna*' repeatedly. See SII 2.1.5, paragraph 2, and #22.

holdings of other deities.[291] The Nāndāṇā plates from the reign of the Cāhamāna family of Nāḍol record a series of transactions in the early 13th century. The plates document dozens of transactions between the court, between deities, and between *devadāsīs* (females slaves/servants) and other servants assigned to these deities. The transactions reveal complex, overlapping financial interests (and administration) between these various parties.

The plates mention a deity named Tripuruṣa, who owned *vilāsinīs* (*devadāsīs*) and flute-players, but these human assets of the deity also benefited from direct gifts or from stipulated shares of the deity's income.[292] Another deity, Śrīcandaleśvara, named after the Chāhamāna queen, Candaladevī, had her temple in close proximity to Tripuruṣa. Tripuruṣa's agents (*vārikas*) held a significant measure of control over Candaleśvaradeva's assets. This complex distribution of legal agency led to numerous financially complicated situations. For example, a village granted for Candaleśvara's benefit was entrusted with Tripuruṣa's agents, who would provide for Candaleśvara's students, etc., from a common fund – while retaining a fourth share of the remainder exclusively for Tripuruṣa.[293] Candaladevī's decision to establish and endow the goddess Gaurī *inside* the *maṭha* of Candaleśvara complicated the overlapping ownership of deities at Nāndāṇa further.[294]

As the relationship between deities, their trustees, their endowments, and the public became more sophisticated, the portfolios and charitable purposes attached to these trusts did as well. The Kannada inscriptions at Pūli made by the Kalyāṇa Cālukyas (11th–12th centuries CE) offer a representative example.[295] If the Śrīcandrapūra plates recall the founding of an 'Oxford of India' in Bengal, then Pūli was 'a veritable Cambridge of the late medieval Deccan'.[296] Scholars from a wide variety of religious and pedagogical backgrounds benefited from funds allocated by the 'Pūli One Thousand', that was 'comprised of the "academic faculty" of the *agrahāra*' and who were 'headed by a village superintendent (*ūroḍeya*)'.[297]

[291] EI 22.43, lines 134–66.

[292] EI 33.45, lines 1–2: vilāsin[yāh] **pa[dm]āvatīsutā[yāḥ] Vijalāyā** śodaśamaṃ… pradatta[ṃ]. tathā vāṁśika**lhauḍiyākas tri[puruṣā]ṇā[ṁ]** pradattaḥ. mehari… nikāyāḥ vaśaṁ prati devakīyadānamadhyāt… droṇāḥ pañca… dātavyā[ḥ].

[293] Ibid., lines 3–6: **bhiṁṭalavāḍāgrāmaḥ śrīcaṁdaleśvaradevārthaṃ tripuruṣāṇāṁ** pradattaḥ. asmād grāmād utpattis **tripuruṣāṇāṁ** satkavārikaiḥ samādāya svīyādānasyaika[t]va[ñ ca] vidhāya **śrīca[ṁ]daleśvarīyavi[l]āsin[āṁ]** vidyā[viśaya]bhaktādikam… kārayitavyas **tripuruṣāṇāṁ** ca[turtha]sthāyī… draṣṭavyaḥ.

[294] Ibid., lines 10–16. Dineschandra Sircar, the editor of the plate, notes that construing this section is difficult, but surmises that 'it appears that Chandaleśvara would have to receive one-third of the collection of leaves and wheat made on behalf of the Tripurusha temple or Gaurī would have to receive a similar share out of the collection of the Chandaleśvara shrine'.

[295] See Elaine Fisher, 'A Microhistory of a South Indian Monastery: The Hooli Bṛhanmaṭha and the History of Sanskritic Vīraśaivism', *Journal of Indian Intellectual History* 1 (2018): 13–47 The inscriptions appear in EI 18.22.

[296] Fisher, 'Microhistory', 18.

[297] Ibid., 18–19.

The superintendent was something akin to a chancellor, who allocated the assigned tax revenues of the 'university's' endowed trusts.[298] The analogy is productive, because Oxbridge's financial structure as a series of charitable trusts emerged at the same time in England.[299] Elaine Fisher focuses her analysis of the Pūli epigraphic record on the relationship between an 'ecumenical culture of Sanskritic learning and the institutional culture of a distinct lineage of Kālamukha preceptors' who served as pontiffs of many of the endowed temples and colleges of Pūli.[300] It is, however, advantageous to remember that the economic basis of this pluralistic university town was a Sanskrit trust: Pūli's endowments were dedicated to several deities for a series of stipulated pedagogical and ritual purposes.

Similarly, in his Kotavumachgi inscription, Vikramāditya V (r. 1008–15 CE) created a divine and educational trust:

> Twelve mattars (of land) and one house(site) to the deity Mārakabbe Bhaṭāri, fifty mattars and one house(site) towards *bhaṭṭavṛtti* (priest's wages) to be enjoyed in return for performing the duties of expounding *nyāsa* and Prābhākara (Mīmāṃsā), twenty-five mattars and one house(site) as *akkarigavṛtti* (teacher's wages) to Nāgadesiga who was able to compose and expound mathematics, astronomy, prosody, poetics..., and who had a knowledge of sounds (i.e., *Vyākaraṇa*), to be utilized for his daily requirements in virtue of his services of teaching his pupils, feeding them every day and supplying them with a cloth once a year.[301]

At almost the same time in Piṭhāpura, Vīracōḷa (r. 1065–70 CE) created a vast agrahāra endowment for hundreds of Brāhmaṇas, and included a remarkably similar series of clauses in Sanskrit for his new Brāhmaṇa trustees:

> In this (charter) one share (was assigned) for the maintenance of one who expounds grammar; two to the expounder of Mīmāṃsā; one for the expounder of Vedānta; one to the teacher of the *Ṛgveda*... one to the expounder of the Rūpāvatāra; one to him who teachers the reciting of the Purāṇas; one to the physician... two shares to the deity Viṣṇu who resides in the center of the village; two (shares) also (to Viṣṇu)

[298] Ibid., 19.

[299] For the legal status of the colleges of the universities of Oxford and Cambridge, see Alan Cobban, *The Medieval English Universities: Oxford and Cambridge to C. 1500* (London: Routledge, 1988), 58–63.

[300] Fisher, 'Microhistory', 19.

[301] EI 20.6: **mārakabbe bhaṭārige** matter=ppanneraḍu maney=ondu nyāsaṁ **prābhākaravuvaṁ** vakkhāṇisi guṇaśāsanadin=uṇba bhaṭṭavṛtti mattar=ayvattu maney=ondu chchhaṭṭargge matter=irppattaydu gaṇitam jōyisachchhandavaḷaṁkāravuvan=ābhaya... veyuvaṁ bareyaluṁ bājisaluṁ balla śabdasaṁskāravuḷḷāta **nāgadēsigargge** nityasthitiy=ondu po<u>l</u>ta<u>l</u>=āhāramuṁ varishakk=ondu kappaḍavuvan=ikkiy=ōdisi guṇaśāssanadin=āḷv=akkarigavṛtti. Compare with the Kondguli inscription (1126 CE) from the reign of Someśvara III (EI 37.34) in which the king creates an endowment for educational purposes (*vidyādānananimitta*) that entails teaching pupils the *Sūtasaṃhitā* of the *Skāndapurāṇa*, Vedic *saṃhitās*, *kāvya*, *nāṭakas*, the *Yājñavalkyasmṛti* (Vijñāneśvara's *Mitākṣarā* commentary having been composed under Cālukya patronage), and Vyākaraṇa.

> who resides on the western side; two to Śrīkailāsadeva; (and) one to the other local deities. These (are) the seven shares of the deities.'[302]

Vīracōḷa used almost identical language in the Tamil Tirumukkudal inscription, where he also makes provisions for the endowment of a hospital, including lists of eligible patients and required medicines, before he enjoins that 'this charity (dharma) shall be under the protection of the great assembly (*mahāsabhā*) of Śrī madurāntakacaturvedimaṅgalam'.[303]

2.7.3 Protection from breach of trust

Perhaps as a result of the greater financial complexity of the religious and charitable trusts of the second millennium CE, or perhaps because of the greater number of trustees responsible for administering these trusts, there is a marked increase in epigraphic statements pertaining to the legal protection of endowments in case of maladministration or other sorts of mischief.[304] While the imprecatory, Purāṇic Sanskrit verses warning against resumption that appear ubiquitously in the medieval epigraphic record are largely *moralising*, the mostly vernacular protective clauses in the second millennium have a practical, *legal* force.

At the same time, we find evidence of kings and, in one instance, a deity, intervening when fiduciaries violate the terms of an endowment. For example, the Cāḷukya Taila II's (r. 973–97 CE) Sogal inscription records an elaborate donation of 500 *kammas* of land to 'the seigniors of Solu' for the benefit of Śiva, his ascetics, an alms house, and tank. Taila notes that: 'The priors of the establishment and the town jointly shall protect (the foundation) if princes do harm; if the town harm it, the prior of the establishment shall protect it; if the head of the establishment do harm, the thirty shall protect it.' [305] Similarly, the Tumbagi inscription of the Cālukya subordinate, Satyāśraya, dating to 1004 CE, records the donation of land to Brahmeśvara and the ascetics living in the attached monastery. It adds an enforcement clause in case of breach of trust: 'In the case of any superiors of this place, if there should be committed a breach of celibacy or the like in conducting the highest offices, they shall expel them. The leading men shall be such. They shall preserve this pious foundation under the constitution.'[306]

[302] EI 5.10: atra **vyākaraṇaṃ** vyācakṣānasya vṛtyarthaṃ bhāga ekaḥ **mīmāṃs[ā]vyākhyātre** dvau. **vedāṅtaṃ** vyākhyātur ekaḥ **ṛgvedam** adhyāpayitur eka[ḥ]… **rūpāvat[ā]raṃ** vyācakṣāṇasyaikaḥ **purāṇavācayitur** ekaḥ vaidyasyaikaḥ… grāmamadhyavadhivasat[e] **viṣṇubhaṭṭ[ā]rakāya** bhāgau dvau. paścimaṃ digbhāgamadhivasate ca dvau **śrīkailāsadevāya** dvau itarābhya **vāstude[vat]ābhyaḥ** eka iti sapta devabhāgāḥ.

[303] EI 21.39: idharmam **śrīmadhurāntakachchatu[rvedimaṅga]lattu** mahāsabhaiyār rakṣai.

[304] For other examples, see Sontheimer, 'Religious Endowments, 38–40.

[305] EI 16.1: sthānācāryyarum=ūruṁ bhūnāthar=kkiḍise kāvar=ūr=kkiḍisalk=ā [sthānā]charyyaṁ kāvaṁ sthān-ēśaṁ kiḍise mūvadiṁbar=kkāvaru //29//

[306] EI 17.2: alliy=orvvar=pradhānar=appavargge uttamāgra[ṁ] naḍeyisuva[r] brahmacharyyādilopam=ādaḍe poṛavaḍisuvar=[u]ttamar=appar=aṁt=appar=ī sthitiyoḷ=ī dharmmamaṁ pratipāḷisuvar=ūroḍeyaruṁ.

Similarly, an 11th-century donation at Pūli enjoins a temple endowment's trustees to 'religiously protect this monastery and field in respect of any minor claims to possession that may arise'.[307] In his Sūṇḍi inscription (1160 CE), Nāgadeva, a Cāḷukya general, endowed an eponymous deity, Nāgeśvara, and assigned the income of lands to the Kāḷāmukha Śaiva Ācaryya, Someśvarapaṇḍitadeva, as 'a sacred estate administered for Nāgadeveśvara'.[308] On the one hand, Nāgadeva created legal constraints on the local seigniors: 'In order that the seigniors... should continue to apply the revenues of lordship... for all time to the god Nāgeśvara, they laved Someśvarapaṇḍitadeva's feet and... made over (to him) the revenues of lordships... taking charge of this pious foundation, (they) shall maintain it according to its proper rule.' [309] On the other hand, Nāgadeva enjoins the seigniors to ensure that the Kāḷamukha Śaivas entrusted with the temple be held accountable for a breach of trust:

> If the Goravas (Śaiva asectics) who are Kāḷamukhas should not be devout, [and] if they should be so neglectful that the company of women should not come for three days for enjoyment [i.e., not serve the deity], or if all the students should fail to study actively always, the worthy superintendents must never allow them to stay: to this effect has Nāgadeva established and regulated this pious foundation at Sūṇḍi.[310]

In his dedication of a vast, temple-city, Śivapura at Ehūr, Vikramāditya VI's general, Ravideva (1077 CE) invokes the Dharmaśāstric concept of conventional law (*sāmayikadharma*) to frame his warning against breach of trust by the custodial Śaiva monks:

> Whether they are Ācāryas of this establishment of ascetics, it is not open to any persons except such as observe strict celibacy to abide in the monastery: the villagers, the burghers, and the king, in concert, shall expel those who do not observe celibacy: if being unwilling to go forth, they shall attempt contumacy... moreover: whether it be the head of the establishment, or the Gorava, or such as are under the rules (*samaya*) of this establishment; if there should be a man who lusts for venery in this establishment, the establishment and the king must expel him.[311]

[307] EI 18.22.L: int=ī maṭhamumaṁ keyyuman=āv=avāntaravasatenyāyaṁgaḷu puṭṭidaḍaṁ sāsirvvaruṁ sa[d]dharmmadiṁ pratipāḷipar.

[308] EI 15.6.F: **śrīmadnāgadeveśvarakk=āḷva** devabhogaṃ. See EI12.37.C for an inscription from Yewur (1105 CE) in which Satyaprachārabhaṭṭārakadeva, the pontiff of a maṭha, used his monastery's property to endow another deity.

[309] Ibid. See lines 46–9.

[310] Ibid.: **goravar=kāḷāmukhar=**nnaishṭhikar=enisadoḍaṁ bhōgadoḷ mūṟu porttuṁ varakāntā-saṁkuḷaṁ bandirade taḍevaḍaṁ viśvavidyārtthigaḷ bittaradiṁd=ā porttum=ōduttiradoḍam=irisalk=āgad=enduṁ varādhīśvarar=end=ī dharmmamaṁ nirmmisi niyamisidaṁ **sūṇḍiyoḷ nāgadēvaṁ** //14//

[311] EI 12.32.B: ī sthānada āchāryyar=akke tapōdhanar=ak[k]e naishṭhikabrahmachārigaḷg=allade maṭhadoḷ=iral=salladu brahmacharyam=illadavaran=ūruṁ nakaramum=arasum=iḻdu poṛamaḍisi kaḷevar poṛamaḍal=ollade moṇḍuyatanaṁ geydar=appoḍe...|| kandaṁ || sthānapati goravan=akk=ī sthānada samayaṁgaḷ=akke ratilaṁpaṭan=ī sthānadoḷ=iralāg=avanaṁ sthānamum=arasugaḷum=iḻdu kaḷeyalu-vēḻkuṁ.

A Sūṇḍi inscription of Someśvara I from 1058 CE describes the terms of a divine endowment as a 'statutory constitution' (*śāsanamaryyāda*).[312]

The Kadamba vassal of Someśvara I, Harikesarin enjoined that 'the establishment of the five monasteries (associated with the deity) and the sixteen (burgesses) thus shall protect this pious foundation' when he endowed the tutelary deity of the Kadamba line, Kadambeśvara and Baṅkāpura.[313] Likewise, when Vikramacōḷa donated fifty sheep to Keśavasvāmin at Chebrōlu (under the custody of a local family of herdsmen) in VS 1049, he enjoined that 'the three-hundred temple servants (and) the three-hundred dancing girls of this place shall protect (this grant)'.[314]

Cōḷa records reveal concrete instances of the king intervening to protect the financial interests of deities and their servants from internal or external issues. For example, Rājādhirāja Cōḷa's 1167 inscription in the Tyāgarājasvāmin temple in Tiruvarūr records that, after the local Cheṭṭis (merchants) encroached on the house-sites of the deity's servants, the king exercised his right of supervision and restored the divine endowment – while levying a fine of the Cheṭṭis.[315] In a subsequent inscription from the same temple during the reign of Kulōttuṅga III, the deity Vīdiviḍaṅgapperumāḷ gave his formal assent to the temple servants' purchase of land.[316] In a remarkable inscription from 1201 CE, a deity of the same temple, Śrīpūrvvārūrvāsi, speaking in the first person voice, voided his servants' inappropriate distribution of lands allocated to them, and delineated a new allocation of lands.[317]

Finally, the Kalyāṇa Cālukyas' inscriptions use an imprecatory verse that explicitly refers to *devasva*. Taila II's Sogal inscription ends with a direct reference to deity's property: 'food is unfit to eat if touched by dust from the feet of the sinner who should have appropriated the estates of gods and Brāhmaṇas: hence are any more degraded than he who infringes a god's estate?'[318] This same verse also appears in Nāgadeva's Sūṇḍi inscription.[319] Harikesarin closes his Bakāpura endowment with a brace of verses that invoke the legal category of *devasva*.[320]

[312] EI 15.6.E.2

[313] EI.13.14: biṭṭar=idaṁ paṁchamaṭhasthānamuṁ padinaṛuvaṛuṁ nakaramum=int=ī dharmmamaṁ pratipāḷisuvudu.

[314] EI 6.21: iṅdula sthānapatulu sunnūrvvuru sānulu munnūrvvuruyyalu bratipāliṅpaṅgalavāru.

[315] SII 17.588.

[316] SII 17.596. Also see #598 for the deity's purchase of land using temple funds.

[317] SII 17.599.

[318] EI 16.1: devasvaṁ brahmasvaman=āvu *** nda pātakana pādarajaṁ bhāvisal=abhojyam=enal= ā devasvaman=aḷivaniṁ nikṛiṣṭarum=oḷare //33// Also see the Bichapalli Inscription (1074 CE) of Bhuvanaikamalladeva EI 36.9: devasvaṁ viṣam ucyate. viṣam ekākinaṁ hanti devasvaṁ putrapautrikam. Cf Sircar's 'Stanzas on Bhūmidāna' #'s 44–8 where the vast majority of imprecatory verses involving *devasva* are from the records of the Kalyāṇa Cāḷukyas.

[319] EI 15.6.F: Verse 21.

[320] EI 15.14: devadvijagatā[ṁ] bhūmī[ṁ] pūrvvabhuktāṁ haret[a] yaḥ [/] praṇaṣṭam api kālena tam āhu[r] brahmaghātakaṁ // na vi[ṣ]aṁ vi[ṣ]am ity āhu[r] devasva[ṁ] vi[ṣ]am uchyate / vi[ṣ]am ekākina[ṁ] haṁti devasvaṁ putrapautr[a]kaṁ //

2.7.4 Jinas and Buddhas as deities

During the second millennium CE, endowments for Jain and Buddhist purposes assimilated the Dharmaśāstric model of divine endowments. For example, in the Arasibidi inscription from the reign of Someśvara I (r. 1042–68 CE) a gift of land to a Jain temple is described as a gift to the god (*dēvargge koṭ[ṭa] bhūmi*).[321] Likewise, the Tirumalai rock inscription of Rājendracōḷa (r. 1014–44 CE) records a gift by a merchant's wife to 'the god of the Śrīkundavai Jina temple on the holy mountain'.[322] Similarly, when the Raṭṭa Prince Kārtavīrya IV endowed the 'Raṭṭa Jain Temple' (*raṭṭajinālaya*) at Beḷgaum in 1204 CE, he ended with a warning against 'seizing the property of deities and Brāhmaṇas'.[323] Clearly, a Jina and its endowment could be folded into the legal category of a deity (as a juridical person) and benefit from Dharmaśāstric protections of divine endowments (*devasva*).

In the Buddhist milieu, when Queen Kumaradevī of Kannauj (12th century CE) re-established and refurbished a monastery at Sarnāth, she restored an image of 'Śrīdharmacakrajina so that he was protected according to the rule from the time of King Aśoka', created a copper-plate grant, and placed this image in a *vihāra* that she had constructed for him.[324] The deification and legal personification of the Buddha is best represented in a 12th-century pillar inscription at Amarāvatī. The donor, Keṭa II, assimilates the Buddha to a Dharmaśāstric theory of Hindu deities as legal persons (along with concomitant protections from spoliation).

Keṭa introduces his capital as the abode of Śiva: 'There is a city named Śrīdhānyakaṭaka wherein Amareśvara Śiva is worshipped.'[325] Keṭa and Ameśvara have a symbiotic relationship of mutual protection and Keṭa lauds his various endeavours in Purāṇic charitable activities.[326] At this same city, however, there is 'God Buddha [and] a well-decorated Shrine (*caitya*)'.[327] Keṭa donates several fields, two lamps, and 110 sheep directly to 'God Buddha' before closing with a Purāṇic imprecatory verse.[328]

[321] EI 17.10: dēvargge koṭ[ṭa] bhūmi. Also see EI 37.54, where the Palāśikā Kadamba Guhalladeva, a subordinate of Vikramāditya VI used Purāṇic imprecatory verses when endowing a Jain temple.
[322] EI 9.31: **śrīkundavaijinālayattu devaṛku**.
[323] EI 13.3.A: api gaṅgāditīrtthеṣu hantur gām athavā dvijam / niṣkṛtis syān na devasvabrahmasvaharaṇe nṛṇām //
[324] EI 9.51: **śrīdharmacakrajinaśāsannivaddhaṃ**... tattāmraśāsanavara[ṃ] pravidhāya... **dharmāśokanarādhipasya** samaya **śrīdharmacakro jino** yādṛk tannayarakṣitaḥ punar ayañ cakre. vihāraḥ sthavirasya... kāritas tasminn eva samarpitaś ca... The editor, Sten Konow surmises (p. 320) that 'it seems necessary to infer that... the vihara built by... Queen Kumaradevī... was a shrine, a *gandhakuṭī*'.
[325] EI 6.15.A: asti **śrīdhā[nya]kaṭakaṃ** [puraṃ]... yatr**āmeśvaraśaṃbhur amareśvarapūjitaḥ**.
[326] Ibid.: **amareśvaradevena** rakṣitaṃ rakṣakaṃ nṛṇāṃ. See verses 40–3 for his list of alms houses, reservoirs, gardens, and temples. For Purāṇic and Dharmaśāstric lists of similar charities, see Chapter 1, §1.3.2, 'The solution, part 2 – a synchronic account of Equity and Trusts'.
[327] Ibid: **buddho deva...** caityam... [ca] nānācitrasucitritaṃ.
[328] Ibid.: grāmān vareṇyān bahūn saṃprādāt **sugateśvarāya**... dīpau **buddhāya** dattavān... guruvāramunaṃ damaku dharmmārthamugā **śrībuddhadevara**kunakhaṁḍavarttidīpamulu...

Finally, the larger Leiden plates of Rājarājacōḷa record the donation of villages 'to the Buddha rising in the surpassingly beautiful Chūḷāmaṇivarmavihāra'.

2.8 Conclusion

This survey of roughly two thousand years' worth of Indian epigraphs sought to fulfil Gerard Colas' recommendation of using an 'extensive enquiry into the phraseology of inscriptions' to provide an historical perspective on the rise of the concept of the deity-image in classical Indian law. More than that, however, this chapter sought to provide an account of the origin and development of a comprehensive law of Equity and Trusts in pre-modern, pre-Islamic India. One core argument was that Sanskrit theories of Equity and Trusts – articulated in Arthaśāstric and in Dharmaśāstric literature – provided the jurisprudential bedrock for practical legal activities.

In the aggregate, the data strongly suggests a linear evolution of trusts from the Mauryan Empire to the establishment of the Delhi Sulṭānate. At various strata in the historical record, trusts become more sophisticated. Aśoka's simple allocation of income to the Buddhist monks in possession of the Buddha's relics at Lumbinī became the template for more elaborate dedications of perpetual endowments by the Kuṣāṇas, Śakas, and Sātavāhanas during the Age Between the Empires. The *Arthaśāstra* was compiled during the same period, and it therefore comes as no surprise that the theory of sovereignty (a centralised state unbeholden to Brāhmaṇical theology), as well as the legal phenomena articulated in this treatise appear in contemporaneous epigraphic records.

By the advent of the Gupta era, these legal instruments – which had been used extensively, but not exclusively, for Buddhist institutions, were applied to the deities of Brāhmaṇical temples and folded into a Brāhmaṇical, Dharmaśāstric jurisprudential framework. In Dharmaśāstric jurisprudence, the Crown acted as an administrator and guarantor of *sui iuris* communities under its wider, equitable jurisdiction over supplemental laws (*pāribhāṣikadharmas*). This effectively inaugurated the constitutional order of the Sanskrit cosmopolis, in which a common linguistic and jurisprudential idiom anchored a stable, pan-Indic model of sovereign power that involved a series of porous, layered political polities.

At the same time, divine endowments became a legal mechanism for creating additional subordinate charitable purposes, such as running alms houses. Additionally, divine trusts of this era display an incipient model of the legal personality of Hindu deities. We rarely find the deity as a direct owner of endowed assets. Rather, various linguistic idioms – placing at the feet of the deity, or entrusting assets to fiduciaries for stipulated purposes – were employed to describe legal relationships of trust.

During the Cālukya/Pallava feuds of the 6th–9th centuries CE, deities and their endowments were pulled into grand, pan-Indic imperial politics. Imperially aspirational sovereigns built grand edifices for the eponymous deities that they established, allocated significant resources for these deities' benefit, and, sometimes despoiled the endowments of rival rulers and their tutelary deities. At the same time, the panegyric and legal language of these grants grew increasingly Sanskritic, even as the regional vernaculars (such as Kannada and Tamil) were used for the first time.

By the 8th century and the rise of the 'Tripartite Struggle' between the Rāṣṭrakūṭas, Pālas, and Gurjara-Pratihāras, deities owned intricate property portfolios and their trustees held increasingly sophisticated rights over divine endowments. On the one hand, deities shifted from largely passive beneficiaries to active agents in lending money at interest, buying and selling assets, and even acting as litigants in proprietary disputes between deities. After all, a world replete with different deities holding assets – shops, houses, fields, etc. – in close proximity to one another is also a world in which the kinds of property disputes that are ubiquitous in any society will involve those same deities.

On the other hand, we see a greater number of more diverse charitable purposes associated with divine endowments emerging at this time. Perhaps because divine endowments – *devadānas, devadāyas, devāgrahāras* – had become a universal and well-established legal category, they now had the capacity to serve as the archetype for more complex trusts. The most interesting example of that is the University of Śrīcandrapura, a vast pedagogical institution which trained scholars in a wide variety of traditional Sanskrit disciplines.

The theory and practice of the law of Equity and Trusts reached its pre-Islamic zenith around the turn of the second millennium, CE. While the great Cālukya and Cōḷa empires battled for subcontinental supremacy, they, their subordinates, and their occasionally overambitious rivals, left behind elaborate records of divine and charitable trusts. The charters for these endowments, although often written in Kannada and in Tamil, nevertheless utilised the jurisprudential theories of Dharmaśāstra and the legal instruments of earlier eras.

Royal and popular donors added additional features, however, such as elaborate clauses for the protection of endowments, some of which were clearly enforced. A notable feature of this era was also the despoliation of rival temples and, occasionally, their destruction as an act of political domination. Certainly, the battle between Śrīlaṅka and the Cōḷa mainland involved the destruction, re-endowment, and preservation of deities of both parties according to the legal paradigms of Equity and Trusts in Sanskrit jurisprudence.

This chapter has offered more insight into the history and moving parts of India's longstanding and intricate law of Equity and Trusts, as well as its relationship to religion, political power, and other historical vicissitudes. The constitutional system of the Sanskrit legal cosmopolis dramatically changed by the establishment of the Delhi Sulṭānate in 1206. Although the Umayyad Caliphate conquered Sindh in 711, and although India had seen numerous raids by Maḥmūd of Ghazni and others before this, the establishment of the Sulṭānate effectively changed the constitutional order from a Brāhmaṇical/Sanskritic one, to a Persio-Islamic one. The next chapter of this monograph attends to that story and its contested, controversial legacy.

3

Hindu Temple Trusts in Islamic India

There is not in the countries of India and Sind, though widely separated by distance and by religion, a king or a subject who hath not given to this idol the most precious portion of his wealth: hence, the wakfs settled on it consisted in ten thousand considerable villages of those countries, and its treasury was filled with all kinds of riches. It was served by one thousand bramins; three hundred youths and five hundred females sang and danced at its gate, and each individual of these classes received a fixed sum out of the wakfs settled on the idol.

Sulṭān Maḥmūd of Ghazni (r. 998–1030 CE) describing the Somanātha temple in a letter to Caliph Abu'l-ʿAbbās Aḥmad ibn Isḥāq (r. 991–1031 CE)[1]

3.1 Introduction

When Maḥmūd of Ghazni described his 1025 CE sack of the Somanātha temple on the Gujarati coast to the Caliph of Baghdad, he boasted of having annihilated what Maḥmūd's scholar-slave, al-Bīrūnī, the 'father of Indology', described as 'the most famous' of the 'idol houses' in al-Hind.[2] Maḥmūd's iconophobia notwithstanding, his report to the Caliph accurately describes Sanskrit models of Equity and Trusts in pre-Islamic India.

Maḥmūd notes that the temple deity (the 'idol') is the owner of trust properties settled on it by kings *of all religions*, and that the deity's fiduciaries *serve* the temple according to a fixed financial scheme. Maḥmūd describes this financial

[1] *Ibn Khallikan's Biographical Dictionary*, edited and translated by Baron MacGukin de Slane, Vol 3 (Paris: Oriental Translation Fund, 1868), 332.

[2] *Alberuni's India: An Account of the Religion, Philosophy, Literature, Chronology, Astronomy, Customs, Laws, and Astrology of India.* Edward Sachau (ed.) (London: Trübner & Co, 1887/1888), *l-Bīrūnī, Kitāb al-Hind*, Vol. 2, 104.

arrangement using the term *waqf*, a distinctly Islamic form of 'trust'.[3] Maḥmūd's attempt to understand the Somanātha temple through Islamic theological and legal categories, even as his army desecrated it, introduces the core problem discussed in this chapter: how do we distil a legal history of the application of Sanskrit principles of Equity and Trusts in Islamic India from historical sources that often describe the *destruction* rather than the *preservation* of Hindu (and Jain and Buddhist) religious endowments?[4]

This chapter examines the transformation of Sanskrit theories and practices regarding Equity and Trusts in Islamic India between 711 and 1765 CE. These dates correspond, respectively, to the advent of Islamic rule in a small portion of northwestern India under the Umayyad Governor Muḥammad ibn al-Qāsim al-Thaqafī (r. 712–15 CE), to Robert Clive's receipt of the *Dīwānī* of Bengal, Bihar, and Orissa (along with the Northern Sarkars) from Emperor Shāh 'Ālam II (r. 1759–1806 CE). The millennium in question witnessed profound changes to India's religious, political, linguistic, and legal landscapes: Muslim communities immigrated to India; a series of Islamic dynasties established sulṭānates over parts of the subcontinent, especially in the north; Persian largely supplanted Sanskrit as the predominate language of literature and administration; and highly centralised bureaucratic regimes replaced the decentralised, administrative polities of the Sanskrit cosmopolis.

[3] For *awqāf* (plural of *waqf*), see Gregory Kozlowski, *Muslim Endowments and Society in British India* (Cambridge: Cambridge University Press, 1985), 1: '*Awqaf* are "endowments" in the general sense that they are gifts made to individuals as well as institutions… funds derived from endowments built and sustained places of worship, established schools and hospitals, supported scholars and preachers, provided paupers with graves, and supplied weapons to warriors fighting in the cause of the faith… Euro-American legal lexicons do not supply a single technical term which is exactly the equivalent to "*waqf*." Sometimes a *waqf* serves as a "trust" sustaining some "public" religious or charitable institution. At other times, a *waqf*'s provisions resemble those of a "will" or "entailment" and therefore have a "private" dimension.'

[4] For the long and contentious history of 'Hindu' as a descriptive term, see Audrey Truschke, 'Hindu: A History', *Comparative Studies in Society and History* 65.2 (2023): 246–71. In using the term 'Hindu' in the sense of the indigenous, non-Muslim people of the Indian subcontinent during the Islamic age, I follow Wink, *Al-Hind, Vol. 1*, 5: 'In a political-geographical sense, "India" or al-Hind, throughout the medieval period, was an Arab or Muslim conception. The Arabs, like the Greeks, adopted a pre-existing Persian term, but they were the first to extend its application to the entire Indianized region… it therefore appears to us as if the Indians or Hindus acquired a collective identity in interaction with Islam.' I follow Truschke, *The Language of History*, 3, in the 'use [of] the general categories of "Hindu" and "Muslim" throughout this book, in part, because they do not offer strong interpretive frameworks for premodernity. Such categories are broad enough to enable us to recover the highly variegated identities expressed by premodern Sanskrit [and Persian] intellectuals.' I also follow Truschke's eschewal of the term 'Islamicate'; see ibid., 10: 'you cannot study Islam outside of Islamic cultures. I see neither sense nor purchase in distinguishing between two things that are one and the same. And so, I reject a theology- centric definition of Islam, along with all vocabulary distinctions – "Muslim" versus "Islamic" versus "Islamicate" – premised on that bias. Once we take this step of clarifying that studying Islam in history is the study of Islamic cultures, no separate vocabulary… [is required].'

Richard Eaton describes this new constitutional paradigm as the 'Persian cosmopolis'.[5] The Mughal emperors (1526–1857 CE) and the Marāṭhās (1674–1818 CE), endowed many Hindu temples within the parameters of a Sanskritised-Persianate chancery practice of revenue allocation.[6] In the Mughal context, state patronage, protection, and legal supervision of Hindu religious trusts under an Islamic, Persianate legal regime was integral to an effort to build an inclusive state in which substantial ecumenical imperial patronage went hand-in-glove with Mughal authority.

When the British East India Company acquired sovereign authority over Bengal, Bihar, and Orissa in 1765 – inaugurating the legal forebear of contemporary India's constitutional order – they did so via a decree (*farmān*) from the Mughal Emperor Shāh 'Ālam II.[7] The Company stepped into Persianate Mughal administrative vestments as a nominal agent of the emperor. Initially, the fiscal arrangements and juridical systems that governed Hindu religious endowments were Persian and Islamic – even if the jurisprudence was Sanskritic.[8] That is to say that while the technical legal instruments might be Persian/Islamic, the *principles* underlying the application of those legal instruments (i.e., the jurisprudence) were often Sanskritic. This observation invites this chapter's core question: how did the transition from a Sanskritic to an Persianate constitutional order in the second millennium CE transform the theory and practice of Hindu Equity and Trusts?

On the one hand, I explore the reception of Sanskritic phenomena within Islamic political culture: how did Muslim rulers understand Hindu temple trusts and charities according to Islamic theological and legal categories; and how did these conceptualisations inform Muslim rulers' decisions to plunder, tolerate, or even support Hindu religious institutions – and vice versa? On the other hand, I examine the reception of Islamic phenomena within Sanskritic political culture: how did Sanskritic – i.e., Brāhmaṇical, Jain, and even Buddhist – authors and political agents understand Islamic religious institutions (mosques and madrassas) and practices according to Sanskritic theological and legal categories; and how did Hindu conceptualisations of Islamic polities transform the pre-Islamic, Sanskritic model of Dharmic kingship that I explored in the previous chapter?

[5] Richard Eaton, 'The Persian Cosmopolis (900–1900) and the Sanskrit Cosmopolis (400–1400)', in Abbas Amanat and Assef Ashraf (eds), *The Persianate World: Rethinking a Shared Sphere* (Leiden: Brill, 2018): 63–83.

[6] For an overview of Persianate chancery practices, see Nile Green, 'Introduction: The Frontiers of the Persianate World (800–1900)', in Nile Green (ed.), *The Persianate World: Frontiers of a Eurasian Lingua Franca* (Oakland: University of California Press, 2019): 1–74. Also see Said Arjomand, 'Evolution of the Persianate Polity and its Transmission to India', *Journal of Persianate Studies* 2 (2009): 115–36.

[7] See Fleming, *Ownership and Inheritance*, 158–73.

[8] For the property system of early East India Company rule, see J. Albert Rorabacher, *Property, Land, Revenue, and Policy: The East India Company, c. 1757–1825* (London: Routledge, 2016).

3.1.1 The theory and practice of iconoclasm in Islamic India

3.1.1.i Theory

From the incept of their sovereignty over the Indian subcontinent, many early Muslim rulers (or, as Truschke puts it, 'people who happened to be Muslim') generally – although far from exclusively – viewed image worship in Indian temples negatively: as idolatry/polytheism (*širk*) and Hindus as polytheists (*mušrikūn*).[9] Andre Wink observes, that, 'there is nothing more striking in the Arabic literature on Sind and Hind than its constant obsession with the idol worship and the polytheism of the Indians.'[10] Numerous Islamic legends either associate the genesis of idolatry with India or claim that Indian image worship stemmed from an idol of Manāt from al-Kaʿba that escaped the Prophet Muḥammad's iconoclastic cleansing of Mecca in 630 CE (although Indian idolatry and polytheism are spoken about vibrantly and positively in much Islamic poetry).[11]

This perhaps accounts for the fact that Arabic and Persian authors recounted the plunder of Hindu (and Jain and Buddhist) religious institutions, and the erection of mosques from the despoiled remnants of these desecrated sanctuaries, with approbation. Eaton and Wagoner note that:

> One of the most contentious issues in the writing of India's pre-modern history centres on the fate of Hindu temples under the sway of Muslim conquerors or rulers. School textbooks, not to mention more popular forms of mass media, are replete with tales of scores, hundreds, even thousands of Hindu temples desecrated or destroyed by conquerors or rulers between about 1000 and 1757, India's so-called Muslim era.[12]

Somanātha typifies this contested legacy.[13] Richard Davis observes that, while 'Islamic chronicles… reduced the complex world of Indian images, with their varied iconographic forms and complicated mythological backgrounds, to a single interpretive criterion… "idols,"… [Somanātha's] idol received special treatment

[9] Truschke, *The Language of History*, 2.

[10] Andre Wink, *Al-Hind: The Making of the Islamic World, Vol 2: The Slave Kings and the Islamic Conquest 11th–13th Centuries* (Leiden: Brill, 2002), 319.

[11] For both accounts, see Davis, *Lives of Indian Images*, 95. According to Ibn al-Kalbī's (737–819 CE) *Kitāb al-Asnām*, 'Adam, after leaving Paradise, descended onto an Indian mountain, and the children of Seth later came to worship his deceased body. One of Cain's sons subsequently carved an idol so that they too would have an object of worship.' The best overview of Islamic sources on image-worship in India is Yohanan Friedmann, 'Medieval Muslim Views of Indian Religions', *Journal of the American Oriental Society* 95.2 (1975): 214–21. Friedman explores the existence of a 'conciliatory trend in mediaeval Muslim thought in India' regarding non-Islamic religious practices.

[12] Richard Eaton and Phillip Wagoner, *Power, Memory, Architecture: Contested Sites on India's Deccan Plateau, 1300–1600* (Oxford: Oxford University Press, 2017), 39.

[13] For the contested legacy of Somanātha, see Romilla Thapar, *Somnath, the Many Voices of a History* (New Delhi: Penguin, 2004).

in accord with his special status as the "lord of all idols"'.[14] Al-Bīrūnī records Maḥmūd's 'special treatment' of the Somanātha *liṅga*: 'He [Maḥmūd] ordered the upper part to be broken and the remainder to be transported to his residence with all its coverings and trappings of gold, jewels, and embroidered garments. Part of it has been thrown in the hippodrome of the town.'[15] According to the Mughal-era historian, ʿAbd al-Qādir al-Badāyūni (1540–1615 CE), the broken Śiva *liṅga* was transported to the courtyard of Maḥmūd's triumphal mosque in Ghazni (created and endowed with assets plundered from India), where the deity was 'trodden under foot' by the community of the faithful.[16]

These distressing narratives of bloody conquests and humiliating iconoclastic depredations against religious institutions require a disclaimer. Richard Davis, among other scholars, cautions that, as these religiously charged accounts of temple desecration were written by Islamic authors – Maḥmūd's letter aimed to justify the semi-independent authority of the Ghaznavids within the sovereign umbrella of the distant Abbasid Caliphate – for Islamic audiences, they ought to be viewed within the genre of heroic epics.[17] Davis draws on the seminal work of Aziz Ahmad, who posited the existence of largely separate 'epic' and 'counter-epic' traditions of conquest and resistance by medieval Muslim and Hindu authors, respectively.[18] Ahmad explores the 'irrepressible bravado of iconoclasm' in the *qaṣīdas* (panegyrics), *razmiya* (martial epics), and historical narratives of Islamic authors in India and concludes that 'all this makes sense as a historical attitude rather than as history'.[19]

Notwithstanding its possible historical inaccuracy, this iconoclastic narrative bombast provides insight into the *ideological theory* behind early Islamic kingship in India. In sharp contrast to Dharmaśāstric models of kingship in which the Crown's claims to sovereignty lay in the protection and endowment of religious trusts from many confessional backgrounds, Maḥmūd and his successors explicitly leveraged their iconoclastic activities (whatever be their motivation in desecrating temples) to buttress their claims to royal status as representatives of Allah.

[14] Davis, *Lives of Indian Images*, 108.

[15] Edward Sachau (ed. & trans.), *Alberuni's India: an Account of the Religion, Philosophy, Literature, Geography, Chronlogy, Astronomy, Customs, Laws and Astrology of India about A.D.1030*, Vol. 1 (Delhi: S. Chand, 1964), 107, cited in Davis, *Lives of Indian Images*, 108. For Al-Bīrūnī, see M.S. Khan, 'al-Bīrūnī and the Political History of India', *Oriens* 25/26 (1976): 86–115.

[16] George Ranking (ed. & trans.), *Muntak͟habu-t-tawārīk͟h*, Vol. 1 (Calcutta: Asiatic Society of Bengal, 1898), 28. Cited in Davis, *Lives of Indian Images*, 108.

[17] Davis, *Lives of Indian Images*, 89–91.

[18] Aziz Ahmad, 'Epic and Counter-Epic in Medieval India', *Journal of the American Oriental Society* 83.4 (1963): 470–6.

[19] Ibid., 470.

3.1.1.ii Practice

Ideological rhetoric aside, the destruction of Hindu religious institutions served practical functions to Islamic rulers who, unlike Maḥmūd, established permanent suzerainty within the Indian subcontinent. If Hindu temples, particularly imperial temples, served as a font of sovereignty for kings who followed a Dharmaśāstric model of rulership, then the establishment of a new political order necessitated their destruction. Although he leveraged his iconoclastic plunder of Somanātha, Mathurā, and Kānyakubja, to shore up political support with the Abbasid caliphate, Maḥmūd of Ghazni had no territorial ambitions in India. Instead, he operated out of a practical venality borne from a pressing need to fund the military adventures of him and his catamite, Malik Ayaz's, in Central Asia.[20] Nevertheless, Maḥmūd's exploits served as a model for Islamic rulers, such as the Ghūrids, who established sovereignty over the Indian subcontinent. The answer, I argue, lies in a desire to supplant one constitutional order (a Dharmaśāstric one) with another (an Persio-Islamic one). According to Richard Davis:

> Muslim warriors correctly surmised, [that] the Indian temple cult was closely tied to the political order, with kings and ruling groups sponsoring and participating ostentatiously in the building and grand festivities of royal temples and images. So, it was important for Muslim conquerors not only to denounce Hindu images for theological reasons, but also to act against them as a statement of conquest. Muslim chronicles of the medieval period repeatedly portray the destruction of politically significant images and temples, coupled with the establishment of mosques, as a conversion, a transformation of the land of the heathens into the land of Islam.[21]

We saw in the previous chapter that the establishment and preservation of divine trusts was *the* central pillar of royal sovereignty in the Sanskrit cosmopolis. Contemporary scholars of Indo-Islamic history often draw direct or partial analogies between the despoliation of temples and their images within a Sanskrit cosmopolitan context and the Ghaznavid/Ghūrid/Sulṭānate demolition of Hindu temples within an Islamic context. For example, Eaton and Wagoner note that: 'Ever since the seventh century, when royal temples were first perceived as objects of political contestation, states throughout India – including the Chalukyas of Kalyana… routinely engaged in desecrating the temples of their enemies as a matter of policy.'[22] Both contexts share similar features such as the destruction of temples and the

[20] For the Maḥmūd-Ayāz theme, see Davis, *Lives of Indian Images*, 97. As Wink, *Al-Hind*, 302, notes: 'The Turkish conquest of Northern India was, in the final analysis, a goldrush.'

[21] Davis, *Lives of Indian Images*, 88.

[22] Eaton & Wagoner, *Power, Memory*, 40 & 44: 'For centuries, states in the Deccan – as in India generally – had desecrated royal temples of defeated enemies by way of delegitimizing the latter's authority. This they did on the premise that a royal temple contained the image of a ruling dynasty's state deity, who was considered responsible for protecting a king's sovereign territory.' Eaton, *Persianate*, 29, argues that, 'Rajendra Chola's seizure of the Śiva image from the Palas of Bengal in 1022, then, was hardly unique. In order to sever the links between a defeated king and the visible manifestation

spoliation of their endowed assets in the interests of supplanting one hegemonic polity with another. These contexts differ, however, in the core constitutional principles underlying this spoliation.

India's epigraphic record between the 7th and 13th centuries contains several descriptions of the spoliation of imperial temples, along with their endowments and consecrated images. *Desecration*, however, does not seem to be an appropriate word, for example, for the Pallava general, Paranjothi's re-endowment of the Vātāpi Gaṇeśa, or for the Cālukya Vikramāditya II's (r. 733–46 CE) decision to return Rājasiṃheśvara's endowment after conquering Kāñcīpura. Some sovereigns who operated under a Dharmaśāstric paradigm boasted of burning their opponents' capitals or of capturing – and re-consecrating – images seized from their rivals' temples, but the overwhelming majority of the pre-Islamic epigraphic records take the Dharmaśāstric view (in their panegyric, legal, and imprecatory portions), that a just king must *protect* religious endowments within the domains of conquered kingdoms.[23] Richard Davis supplies several examples of instances in which these ideals were flagrantly ignored, but, more often than not, looted temple endowments were re-dedicated to one's own tutelary deities.[24] The constitutional principle of the Crown as *parens patriae* and a wider Sanskrit jurisprudence of Equity and Trusts was the animating force behind the example just described.

Early Islamic raiders and sovereigns, in contrast, may have an appreciation for the intimate connection between temple trusts and political authority, but their *practical* and *constitutional* relationship to these trusts differed markedly. Davis' distinction between the Cōḷa and Ghaznavids' treatment of plundered temple images is telling:

of his divine patron, it was necessary to carry off images or in other ways desecrate his royal temples. Consequently, a high level of inter-state violence between the ninth and thirteenth centuries inevitably accompanied efforts to create idealized mandalas and to transform neighbouring enemies into subordinate vassals. Conquest of the quarters was built into the politics of the day.' Also see Truschke, *The Language of History*, 39: 'Perhaps the event [at Somanātha] was unremarkable to local Brahmins, who were accustomed to temple raids from Indian kings across the board. For instance, only three years earlier, in 1022, the army of Rajendra Chola I (r. 1014– 44) had sacked another Shiva temple, in the Pala kingdom of Bengal in that case, and carted off its central image as a war trophy'; & 111: 'people might be tempted to make something out of Jinaprabha's citation of Muslim political violence, whose iconoclasm followed on earlier examples of 'Hindu' kings desecrating the icons and temples of rival rulers.'

[23] See Chapter 2, §2.5. 'The Pallava/Cālukya rivalry and the politicisation of temple endowments (7th–9th centuries CE)'.

[24] See Davis, *Lives of Indian Images*, 65: '[For Hindu sovereigns] appropriated images are, nevertheless, still also divine images… [and] we do not hear of the intentional humiliation of divine images, nor very often of their public mutilation, by those who seize them. Often looters made a considerable effort to erect new temples to house appropriated images in the manner to which they were accustomed.' Davis explains that when the Vijayanagara Emperor Kṛṣṇadevaraya (r. 1509–29 CE) captured the Gajapati capital, Udayagiri, he appropriated an image of Bālakṛṣṇa, which he re-installed and re-endowed in a specially constructed temple at the imperial capital of Hampi.

> Lying at the gate of the Bride of Heaven mosque, the Saiva icon from Somanatha in its new situation echoed the Hindu trope by which defeated enemies were subordinated into door guardians, but in a rather more humiliating mode… the new audience was encouraged to interact with the appropriated object. Far from offering worship to the looted deity as a subordinate member of a hierarchized pantheon, however, the faithful of Ghazna could tread on the idol of another religious community with their bare feet as they went to prayer, repudiating the polytheism it represented and reenacting as they did Mahmud's own victory at Somanath.[25]

Medieval Islamic authors did not laud Maḥmūd's iconoclastic treatment of the Somanātha temple because it followed the appropriative paradigms of the Sanskrit imperial cosmopolis, they lauded it because it *overturned them* and enabled the foundation of a new political order. To the extent that Maḥmūd cared about the Sanskritic world order, he probably viewed it, correctly, as a hinderance to his ambitions in India. This distinction is *not* concerned with making moral judgements about the use of state violence against religious institutions a thousand years ago. Tragically, of course, narratives concerning Islamic rulers' desecration of Hindu temples have and continue to fuel communal violence in South Asia. Noting the *similarity* between Sanskrit cosmopolitan and early Islamic rulers' plundering of temple trusts probably helps to ensure that the representation of past iniquities doesn't catalyse contemporary inequities, but it is important to remember that Islamic and Hindu temple plundering had different motivations and consequences.[26]

Nevertheless, over-emphasising continuities between Sanskritic and Persianate (and before that, Arabic) political orders in India elides their notable differences. Andrew Wink's rejoinder to Davis is timely:

> Iconoclastic motives can be distinguished from economic and political motives only with the greatest difficulty, if at all. Iconoclasm escalated, no doubt, because the Indian temple cities still contained vast amounts of immobilized treasure. But the Ghaznavid reputation throughout the Islamic world was based on two interrelated accomplishments: the 'breaking of the idols' and the de-hoarding of the temple treasure of al-Hind.[27]

Early Islamic rulers in the Indian subcontinent operated according to their own theological and legal paradigms and the establishment of this new constitutional

[25] Davis, *Lives of Indian Images*, 108–9.

[26] See James Laine, 'The *Dharma* of Islam and the *Dīn* of Hinduism: Hindus and Muslims in the Age of Śivājī', *International Journal of Hindu Studies* 3.3 (1999): 299–318, 299 for an elegant summary of the position: 'There are some dominant models for understanding religious communities of Hindus and Muslims which produce a sort of knowledge that replicates contemporary patterns of identity construction and occludes real insight into premodern identities. This replication occurs among modern communalists who read history teleologically, finding in the past all the ingredients for a future subcontinent divided into two or more political states by religion.' The best overview of the stakes remains Richard Eaton, 'Temple Desecration and Indo-Muslim States', *Journal of Islamic Studies* 11.3 (2000): 283–319.

[27] Wink, *Al-Hind, Vol 2*, 321.

order necessitated the extirpation of the pre-existing Sanskrit cosmopolis. Iconoclasm and political sovereignty were initially inseparable. Imperial and sub-imperial temples posed a *constitutional* threat to the establishment of Indo-Muslim rule and this explains, as Richard Eaton argues in his seminal 'Temple Desecration and Indo-Muslim States', why 'the original data associates temple desecration with the annexation of newly conquered territories' on the shifting political frontiers of Islamic polities.[28]

This approach to the practical, political elements of iconoclasm in Indo-Islamic history also enables us to appreciate Indo-Muslim rulers' reasonable concern 'that a temple's latent political significance might be activated and serve as a power-base to further its patron's political aspirations'.[29] That this happened, repeatedly, under the Delhi Sulṭānate and Mughal Empire, also explains why many Hindu temples were left alone.[30] Nevertheless, causality is always layered, and trying to figure out if Maḥmūd was really iconoclastic or just avaricious is probably a fool's game. Instead, Maḥmūd and other Muslim iconoclasts in medieval India were almost certainly motivated by a layered, complex set of factors, that included material gain, political domination, and ideological legitimacy.

3.1.2 Accommodative trends in Islamic and Sanskritic governance

3.1.2.i Islamic

Amid the contemporary strife concerning the contested historiographical approach to temple desecration in medieval India, it is salutary to remember that, beginning with the Umayyad conquest of Sindh in 711, Muslim rulers accommodated temples and appropriated Sanskrit theories of Equity and Trusts in a variety of remarkable ways. Most importantly, from the inception of Islamic sovereignty in portions of India, many rulers and Islamic jurists treated Hindus as 'protected subjects' (*ahl aḏ-ḏimmah*) who were free to practice their religion, however idolatrous, provided they pay the (sometimes collected) poll-tax (*jizya*).[31] Although debates within the rich and variegated schools of Islamic jurisprudence (*fiqh*) took widely divergent views on the exact status of Hindus, Muslim rulers, in *practice*, operated, on the assumption that Hindus were *ḏhimmī, de jure* or *de facto*.[32]

[28] Eaton, 'Temple Desecration', 314.

[29] Ibid., 305–6.

[30] Ibid., 306–9

[31] See Wink, *Al-Hind, Vol. 1*, 193. Also see Yohanan Friedmann, 'The Temple of Multān: A Note on Early Muslim Attitudes to Idolatry', *Israel Oriental Studies* 2 (1972): 176–82, 180–2.

[32] See Wink, *Al-Hind, Vol. 1*, 193–4: 'such debates did not change the fact that Hindus in practical ways remained dhimmīs'. The best study of Islamic jurisprudential debates is Friedmann, 'Medieval Muslim Views'.

Furthermore, the incorporation of different areas of the Indian subcontinent into Caliphal or Persianate political formations meant that emirs and sulṭāns found themselves responsible for the supervision of Hindu religious endowments and other local trusts – as the British would discover centuries later. Responses to this responsibility varied considerably. These responses often defy communalist narratives that attribute rulers' actions to their personal religious sentiments. Four of India's most ostensibly iconoclastic rulers – Muḥammad ibn al-Qāsim al-Thaqafī (Ummayad Sind), Maḥmūd of Ghazni (technically not a ruler *of* India, but a central Asian ruler *in* India), Muḥammad bin Tughluq (Delhi Sulṭānate), and Aurangzeb (Mughal Empire) – passively or actively protected or supported Hindu temple endowments.

Some rulers served as custodians of temple deities and their endowments – sometimes for pecuniary or political advantage. For example, according to several medieval chronicles, when al-Qāsim conquered Multān, in Sindh, he spared the city's renowned Sun temple.[33] While sources vary considerably, Ibn al-Jawzī (1116–1201 CE), in his *Talbīs Iblīs*, claims that the Multānese locals convinced al-Qāsim to agree to a financial settlement in which the deity's income was split into three portions: one going to al-Qāsim (in exchange for the protection of the temple); one going to support the temple and its attendants; and one going to secular charitable purposes such as the relief of poverty and the improvement of the city's defences.[34] In a substantially less venal vein, the Mughal Emperor Aurangzeb issued a series of decrees (*farmāns*) in the 17th century that explicitly enjoined the protection of Hindu temples and their fiduciaries.[35] Whatever be their theological orientations, these rulers performed the practical Dharmaśāstric model of the Crown as the guardian of deities and their endowments.

Other rulers took a far less active approach of *tolerating* indigenous trusts, although often with the proviso that non-Muslim communities pay the *jizya*. For example, several 'temple tokens' from the temple complex of the goddess Bhīmā in Smast – a divine trust discussed in Chapter 2 – bear the imprimatur of the Ghaznavid sulṭāns.[36] Furthermore, 'while [these temple] coins were issued independently for use in the Kashmir Smast complex, the local temple authorities nominally acknowledged their lords in Gandhara, who may have conferred on the temple mint the right to mint coins'.[37]

[33] Friedman, 'The Temple of Multān'.
[34] Ibid., 178.
[35] For a sample, see Audrey Truschke, *Aurangzeb: The Life and Legacy of India's Most Controversial King* (Palo Alto: Stanford University Press, 2017), 78–83
[36] For the Smast temple in classical times, see Chapter 2, Notes 151–2. For Smast in Islamic times, see Waleed Ziad, '"Islamic Coins" from a Hindu Temple', *Journal of the Economic and Social History of the Orient* 59 (2016): 618–59. Ziad, 622–3, hypothesises that these small, copper coins, 'may have served as temple offerings or facilitated daily transactions to facilitate a temple economy'.
[37] Ibid., 624.

Considering the region's wider importance as a linkage between Maḥmūd's central Asian domains and India, and 'given its administrative, economic, and commercial utility… the, wanton desecration of the Kashmir Smast or the expulsion of the deities that resided there would have had drastic repercussions' for the Ghaznavids' wider political ambitions.[38] Similarly, Eaton notes that, 'at the centre of power in Delhi, meanwhile, ultra-conservative thinkers such as Ziya al-Din Barani (d. c.1357 CE)' inveighed against Firuz Shah Tughlaq's (r. 1351–88 CE) financially conditional tolerance of Hindus' image worship:

> In their capital [Delhi] and in the cities of the Musalmans the customs of infidelity are openly practiced, idols are publicly worshipped … they also adorn their idols and celebrate their rejoicings during their festivals with the beat of drums and dhols [a two-sided drum] and with singing and dancing. By merely paying a few tankas and the poll-tax [jizya] they are able to continue the traditions of infidelity.[39]

However, Barani's reactionary lambasting of the overly tolerant disposition of the Delhi Sulṭānate towards Hindus (in his opinion) does *not* include active patronage of Hindu religious institutions. If Firuz Shah Tughlaq had patronised Hindu institutions, or if such a claim were credible, it stands to reason that Barani would have included it in his invective. Some exceptions notwithstanding, it was only under the Mughal regime that the central government of an Islamic realm actively and substantially endowed and protected Hindu deities and Jain sanctuaries. The decades' worth of donations to and legal rulings concerning Govindadevajī of the Vṛndāvana is probably the most studied instance of direct Mughal patronage, but other examples are legion.[40] Last, but far from least, Tipu Sulṭān (r. 1782–99 CE) made elaborate gifts to illustrious temples within his domain such as Raṅganātha,

[38] Ibid., 654.

[39] Eaton, *Persianate*, 54.

[40] For Govindadevajī, see Monika Horstmann, 'Govindadevjī of Vrindaban and Jaipur and its Kachvāhā Patrons from the Mid-Seventeenth to the Mid-Eighteenth Century', in Alan W. Entwistle and Françoise Mallinson (eds), *Studies in South Asian Devotional Literature: Research Papers, 1988–1991 presented at the Fifth Conference on Devotional Literature in New Indo-Aryan Languages* (New Delhi & Paris: Manohar & École Française d'Extrême-Orient, 1994): 82–93; Monika Horstmann, 'Govindadeva and His Custodians from 1643 through the Time of Jaya Siṃha II (1700–1743)', in Margaret Case (ed.), *Govindadeva: A Dialogue in Stone* (New Delhi: Indira Gandhi National Centre for the Arts, 1996): 185–93; and Monika Horstmann, *In Favour of Govindadevjī: Historical Documents Relating to a Deity of Vrindaban and Eastern Rajasthan* (New Delhi: Indira Gandhi National Centre for the Arts & Manohar Publishers & Distributors, 1999). Also see Tarapada Mukherjee and Irfan Habib, 'Akbar and the Temples of Mathura and its Environs', *Proceedings of the Indian History Congress* 48 (1987): 234–50; Tarapada Mukherjee and Irfan Habib, 'The Mughal Administration and the Vrindaban During the Reigns of Jahangir and Shah Jahan' *Proceedings of the Indian History Congress* 49 (1988): 287–300; and Tarapada Mukherjee and Irfan Habib, 'Land Rights in the Reign of Akbar (the Evidence of the Sale-Deeds of Vrindaban and Ariṭha', *Proceedings of the Indian History Congress* 50 (1989): 236–55. Also see Rembert Lutjeharms, 'A Temple of Stone and a Temple of Love: Govindadeva in the Religious Imagination of Early Gauḍīya Vaiṣṇavas', in Kiyokazu Okita and Rembert Lutjeharms (eds), *The Building of Vṛndāvana: Architecture, Theology, and Practice in an Early Modern Pilgrimage Town* (Leiden: Brill, 2024): 149–96.

the Śaṅkarite *maṭha* at Śrīraṅgam, and the Nārāyaṇasvāmi temple Melukote.[41] Tipu Sulṭān's location deep in south India, and his desperately needing Hindu support in his conflict with the English, may have played a role in his largesse. Nevertheless, a circular that Tipu Sulṭān sent to his district officers in 1790–91 exemplifies the substantial adoption of Sanskrit models of Equity and Trusts by a Muslim ruler:

> The temples are under your management: you are… to see that the offerings of the gods… are duly regulated, as directed out of the government grants. The offerings are to be subsequently distributed among the poor, but they ought not be partaken of by the Pujaris. You are to take care that the money and provisions belonging to temples are not stolen; and you are further to prepare a list of all the jewels of the temples… and hand over the jewels under your seal to the charge of the temple Parpattegar. You are to allow (the temple authorities) to use the jewels during the festivals and them carefully preserve them in the temple under your seal. This procedure will prevent the pujaris from stealing the jewels of the temple.
>
> A certain amount of money is set apart and given out on interest for the purpose of conducting the worship, etc., of the gods; and this money being paid to the temple is called Puduvat money. You are to enter both the principal and the interest in the temple accounts, and also to preserve in the temple the document executed by the person who received the money on interest. You are to order both the Pujaris and the Parpattegars to make use of the jewels, cloths, etc., during… festivals, and then to preserve them as before.[42]

3.1.2.ii Sanskritic

From the inception of Islam in India, the Sanskrit archive records numerous instances of the accommodation of Islamic political and religious activities – far more instances, in fact, than harshly negative views. Sanskrit jurisprudence, epigraphy, and narrative all attest to the incorporation of political Islam within a Sanskritic milieu – even as that incorporation prompted transformations in the Sanskritic thought. Consequently, even as the political theology of the Persian cosmopolis supplanted the hegemony of the Sanskrit cosmopolis it also elicited changes within that tradition.

One of the most striking features of Islamic rulers – the Umayyads, Ghaznavid, and the Ghūrids, for example – in early medieval Sanskrit epigraphic records is

[41] A. Subbarraya Chetty, 'Tipu's Endowments to Hindus and Hindu Institutions', *Proceedings of the Indian History Congress* 7 (1944): 416–19; and B.A. Saletore, 'Tipu Sultan as Defender of the Hindu *Dharma*', in Irfan Habib (ed.), *Confronting Colonialism: Resistance and Modernization under Haider Ali and Tipu Sultan* (London: Anthem Press, 2002): 115–30.

[42] Translated in J. Jemi Merlin Rani, 'The Religious Legacy of Tipu Sultan', *IOSR Journal of Humanities and Social Science* 23.4 (2018): 84–8, 85–6.

the relative ease with which they slot into political panegyrics. As Truschke notes, 'during this initial five hundred years in which Muslims entered the Indian subcontinent, roughly the late seventh century until the late twelfth century, they appear somewhat infrequently in Sanskrit inscriptions and texts'.[43] We saw in the previous chapter that the sovereigns of the Sanskrit cosmopolis usually opened their endowments with genealogies of their dynasties that entailed, *inter alia*, their conflicts with imperial competitors.

Muslim rulers appear in these 'governance contexts' in Gurjara-Pratihāra, Solaṅki Cālukya, and Rāṣṭrakuṭa epigraphs, but almost universally 'with vague ethnonyms, especially turuṣka and tājika ["Turk"]'.[44] Truschke notes that these epigraphic authors 'showed limited interest in the cultural, much less religious, practices of these new communities' but the opaque Sanskrit view of early Islamic rulers as 'foes on the frontlines of battle' attests to far more than the absence of religious communalism on the part of Sanskrit-writing rulers.[45] The Tājikas, whatever their ethnic origins or devotional affinities, could be incorporated into the secular political-theological model of the Sanskrit cosmopolis – just like Śakas, Kuṣāṇas, and Drāviḍians, or Buddhists, Jains, Tantrikas, Śāktas, etc.

This accommodative tendency explains the remarkably (from a modern sensibility) unremarkable treatment of Madhumati Sugati, the 10th-century Tājika feudatory of the Rāṣṭrakūṭa, Indra III, who administered Saṃyāna on the Gujarati Coast and who endowed a collegiate *maṭhikā* (little monastery) of the goddess.[46] As with other neighbouring kings, the Gurjaras or Rāṣṭrakūṭas might do battle with or incorporate Tājikas into their political formations, but the representation of these Tājikas followed the political parameters of the Sanskrit cosmopolis. Even after the advent of the Delhi Sulṭānate and the supplanting of the Sanskrit cosmopolis by the conventions of the Persian cosmopolis, Jain and Hindu records of charitable endowments – mostly step-wells and 'secular' charities in the Hindu context – provide political genealogies that 'integrated Indo-Muslim rulers into the tradition of Indian kingship by positioning them as successors to earlier, non-Muslim lineages… [with] the Tomars, Chauhans, and early Delhi Sulṭānate rulers [listed] as successive kings of Delhi and surrounding areas'.[47]

While this small sample attests to the capacity of Sanskrit epigraphic discursive practices to integrate the rulers of the Delhi Sulṭānate 'in a matter of decades, into Sanskrit representations of political authority in the present and the past' as well as 'Sanskrit into the robust world of Indian kingship' it also attests to the vastly more

[43] Truschke, *The Language of History*, 28.
[44] Ibid., 29.
[45] Ibid.
[46] See Chapter 2, Notes 254–6.
[47] EI 34.21. Truschke, *The Language of History*, 70.

circumscribed domain of Sanskrit jurisprudence.[48] Local donors incorporated the Delhi Sulṭānate into their political histories in a local, benedictory context, but this highly localised use – absent any endorsement by the Crown – attests to the collapse of the Dharmaśāstric epigraphic genre's use as a *legal* language within the sulṭānate. A local donor might follow Dharmaśāstric conventions in recording the ruling dynasty when creating a well, but there is little indication that the ruling dynasty – the sulṭānate – was aware of the dedication or felt any duty to protect it.

Inscriptions from polities under Hindu suzerainty reveal that Muslim religious institutions found easy accommodation within the paradigms of Sanskrit jurisprudence. As Truschke notes, 'Muslim communities slotted easily into pre-existing transreligious patronage practices on the subcontinent and the tradition of praising such generosity in Sanskrit'.[49] Most famously, an inscription from 1264 CE records the construction and endowment of a mosque in Veraval, near Somanatha on the Gujarati coastline 'by Nuruddin Firuz (*Noradīnapīroja*, in Sanskrit), a trader from Hormuz, and was accompanied by a Sanskrit inscription and a shorter Arabic summary dating two months later'.[50] Veraval, then under the administration of the Vaghela Dynasty (1244–1304 CE), was a multicultural entrepot and despite Maḥmūd of Ghazni's raid, the authorities of the Somanātha temple, whose deity owned much of the local land, assented to the construction of the mosque.[51] On the one hand, the inscription praises the: '"Lord of the world" (Viśvanātha), described as "omnipresent, formless, and both visible and invisible" (*viśvarūpa*, *śūnyarūpa*, *lakṣālakṣa*)... [such that] the reader cannot fully tell whether the opening lines refer to Shiva or to Allah [and this] signals the possibility of cultural similitude.'[52] Alongside this *theological* accommodation, the Veraval inscription describes Islam, the donor, and the financial arrangements using Dharmaśāstric terminology. The authors of the inscription incorporate Islamic religious trusts according to a quintessentially Dharmaśāstric theory of Equity: this community, like other ethnic and religious communities, has its own group-specific Dharmas which can coexist with other communities' supplemental laws within the overarching rubric of the Sanskrit cosmopolitan legal order.

An earlier, 12th-century inscription from the reign of the Varman ruler Bhoja of Bengal, records the dissolution of an endowment 'intended for the repair of the *vihāra* under the protection of *Allahabhaṭṭārakasvāmin*', as well as the endowment's replacement with state-allocated funds.[53] Like the Gujarati coast, the Bay

[48] Ibid., 73. Eaton, *Persianate*, 54, notes that, these inscriptions 'were not patronized by the sultanate, or even known to its officers'.

[49] Truschke, *The Language of History*, 74. Truschke provides numerous additional examples of Jain and Hindu donors supporting the construction and endowments of mosques.

[50] Ibid., 74.

[51] Cited in Eaton, *Persianate*, 93–4.

[52] Truschke, *The Language of History*, 74.

[53] Ryosuke Furui, 'Sujanagar Stone Inscription of the Time of Bhojavarman, Year 7', *Pratna Samiksha: A Journal of Archeology* 10 (2019): 115–22.

of Bengal was an active hub for Arab merchant seafarers, and it appears that these merchants' religious institutions could be incorporated within the parameters of the Sanskrit jurisprudence of Equity and Trusts *when Dharmaśāstra was the hegemonic constitutional jurisprudence*.

The advent of Islamic rule on the Indian subcontinent markedly changed the paradigms of Dharmaśāstric kingship in three ways: 1) Dharmaśāstric rulers framed their sovereignty much more explicitly in terms of protecting Hindu temples from the spoliative penchants of Islamic rulers (real or imagined); 2) rulers operating under a Dharmaśāstric rubric nevertheless adopted many of the courtly manners and centralised bureaucratic structures of the Persian cosmopolis; and 3) rulers made the hitherto unheard of but subsequently commonplace decision to donate their entire realm to their tutelary deities and to rule *in the name of these deities*. These trends were undoubtedly linked. The sulṭānate's forcible suppression of imperial Hindu temple cults ensured that, *ideologically*, the promotion of such cults became the *conditio sine qua non* for asserting political legitimacy.[54]

The centralisation of power in Delhi and the introduction of Persianate systems of governance across virtually the entire subcontinent under the Tughlaq dynasty (1320–1413 CE) essentially eliminated the practical utility of the decentralised administrative systems of earlier pre-Islamic rulers. Finally, the increased importance of royal protection of deities and the centralisation of administrative control probably led to the culmination of the legal personality of Hindu deities as the legal owners of entire kingdoms with rulers serving as fiduciaries.[55]

[54] Truschke, *The Language of History*, devotes an entire chapter (pp. 44–65) to the *Pṛthvīrājavijaya* (Victory of Prithviraj Chauhan; c. 1191–1200 CE), an influential Sanskrit text that, 'projected the Ghurids as hazardous to an established ritual and social order and that they – by virtue of being a new danger – allowed Jayanaka [the text's author] to imagine his own political and cultural traditions, alongside their royal protectors, with renewed potency.' Central to this narrative is the Ghurids' violence to temples and Brahmaṇical estates (*devagṛhāgrahārahiṃsā*) and a wider assault on the Dharmaśāstric model of society as bound by the rules of caste and class – *varṇāśramadharma*. Similarly, Gaṅgādevī's *Madhurāvijaya* (Victory at Madurai; c. 1380), which recounts her husband Kampan's defeat of the Ma'bar Sulṭānate of Madurai in 1371, frames its protagonist's conquests as the culmination of a divine plan to restore, *inter alia*, the deities of the Mīnākṣī temple of Madhurai and the Raṅganāthasvāmi temple of Śrīraṅgam to their pre-sulṭānate glory.

[55] For the Islamicisation of the courtly culture of the Vijayanagara Empire, see P.B. Wagoner, '"Sultan among Hindu Kings": Dress, Titles, and the Islamicization of Hindu culture at Vijayanagara', *The Journal of Asian Studies* 55.4 (1996): 851–80. For the Islamicisation of Vijayanagara's feudal administrative structure, see Phillip Wagoner, 'India c. 1200–c. 1500' in Anne Curry and David Graff (eds), *The Cambridge History of War*, Vol. 2 (Cambridge: Cambridge University Press, 2020): 470–506, 500: 'Vijayanagara's response to sultanate military culture was not limited to the areas of technology and tactics alone. There is also evidence suggesting that Vijayanagara adopted the sultanate institution of the *iqta*ʿ, although the military service tenures it granted are referred to not as *iqta*ʿ but as *nayamkara*. Although the terminology differs, it is clear from these sources that the *nayamkara* functioned in a manner that was strikingly similar to the iqtaʿ.' Also see Phillip Wagoner, *Tidings of the King: A Translation and Ethnohistorical Analysis of the Rāyavācakamu* (Honolulu: University of Hawaiʿi Press, 1993), 100–7, & 198–200.

3.1.3 Outline of sections

The following sections examine the relationship between Indo-Islamic rulers and pre-Islamic religious endowments during three epochs in Indian history: 1) the establishment of Islamic hegemony in limited portions of South Asia between 711 and 1206 CE; 2) the introduction of the sulṭānate system of rule between 1206 and 1526; and 3) the reign of the Mughal emperors and the Hindu Marāṭhā rulers between 1526 and the rise of the British East India Company in 1765. For each epoch, I examine how prominent rulers and dynasties – Hindu and Muslim – understood the wider politics and theological import of the Hindu-Muslim encounter within the specific context of the management (or plunder) of temples, monasteries and mosques.

Initially, Indo-Islamic rulers viewed Hindu religious endowments as idolatrous treasuries filled with immobilised wealth that was ripe for seizure according to the tenets of Islam. Muḥammads Qāsim, Ghazni, and Ghōri, generally – but not exclusively – viewed temple treasures as banks to be robbed in their efforts to fund wars in Central Asia or Islamic institutions in India. Nevertheless, all three rulers also protected or tolerated some Hindu and Jain institutions when it was to their direct benefit. Hindu rulers, for their part, saw these activities as a profound, existential threat to the established Dharmaśāstric principles of the Sanskrit cosmopolis, and viewed the advent of Indo-Islamic ruler as the unfolding of a decline of Dharma in the Kali Yuga.

With the establishment of the Delhi Sulṭānate in 1206, Indo-Islamic rulers largely shifted their approach towards Hindu temples and other charitable trusts from spoliation to political re-appropriation. Several prominent temples (at Warangal and across the Deccan) were converted into mosques – capturing the cache of these erstwhile Hindu or Jain establishments – while others seem to have been tolerated so long as their devotees remained loyal to the Crown. Rebellion by Hindu subjects or the conquest of new realms probably served as a catalyst for the destruction of temples. Hindu commoners and rulers, for their part, largely accepted and adapted to Indo-Islamic rule. The Delhi sulṭāns were added to political histories in Sanskrit inscriptions and the Vijayanagara emperors (among other dynasties) adopted the technologies, cultural symbols, and language of the sulṭāns, even as they Sanskritised them in the process.

Finally, the rise of the Mughal Empire in 1526 and the Marāṭhā Confederacy in 1674 witnessed a harmonisation of Indo-Islamic and Hindu systems of government, particularly with regard to Equity and Trusts. Beginning with Akbar, Mughal emperors actively patronised and protected Hindu and Jain endowments. The are hundreds of *farmāns* from the Mughal emperors and their subordinates that assign income to temples and their fiduciaries, intervene in cases of breach of trust, and issue specific injunctions when other individuals infringed on the liberties of religious communities.

Nevertheless, sedition still warranted temple desecration and the Rajpūt and Marāṭhās' assertions of independence against their quondam suzerains in Agra resulted in Aurangzeb's demolition of many magnificent temples such as the Kāśīviśvanātha temple in Vārāṇasī. In establishing sovereignty within and against the Mughal realm, however, the Rajpūts and Marāṭhās developed their own, highly Persianised chancery practices for the administration of temple trusts in accordance with the Sanskrit jurisprudence of Equity and Trusts.

3.2 A tale of three Muḥammads (711–1206 CE)

This section covers the advent of Islamic rule in the Indian subcontinent: from the Umayyad conquest of Sind in 711 CE to the establishment of the Delhi Sulṭānate in 1206. Three Muḥammads, from very different backgrounds and with very different personalities, played a central role in this time period. The first, Muḥammad ibn al-Qāsim al-Thaqafī, ruled Arab Sind 712–15 CE. Al-Qāsim, ruled briefly, but he is remembered positively as a guardian of Brāhmaṇical and Buddhist religious institutions and practices in the narrow band of northwest India that he administered.

In contrast, Maḥmūd of Ghazni (r. 998–1030 CE) invoked bombastic iconoclastic rhetoric to justify exploitative raids on northwest India and its temples. Although Maḥmūd used his plundered treasures to develop a sophisticated sulṭānate bureaucracy in Ghazni – one that would be adopted throughout India in the centuries to come – and although he patronised scholars (such as al-Bīrūnī who developed an early, if idiosyncratic approach to Islamic-Sanskritic intellectual exchange), Maḥmūd is portrayed in Sanskrit sources in a highly negative fashion.

Finally, Mu'izz ad-Din Muḥammad ibn Sam (r. 1173–1206 CE) combined aspects of the rules of Muḥammads Qāsim and Ghazni. He plundered and raided throughout India, sacking temples and seizing treasure, but he also established permanent sovereignty and government over these lands – often building new mosques or converting Jain and Hindu temples into mosques. Muḥammad Ghori is also remembered negatively in Sanskritic sources, but, and this is a crucial difference, his introduction of Indo-Islamic rule as an enduring phenomenon promoted the emergence, if only seminally at first, of a new paradigm of Sanskritic kingship in which the preservation of temple deities was foregrounded more than ever.

All three Muḥammads contributed to the wider history of the transformation of Sanskrit theories and practices of Equity and Trusts under Indo-Islamic rule and to that story, this chapter now turns.

3.2.1 al-Qāsim al-Sindī

Early Islamic rule in al-Sind provides an early (and largely idiosyncratic) example of the administration of Hindu temple trusts under early Indo-Muslim rulers. Centuries before Maḥmūd of Ghazni's raids or the emergence of Persianate models of rulership, a small portion of South Asia, largely congruous with modern Pakistan, fell under the yoke of Muslim rulers – first as a Caliphal province (711–≈850s CE), and then as a brace of semi-independent Emirates in Manṣūra and Multān (≈850–≈1000 CE). Despite, or perhaps because of, al-Sind's linguistic and temporal isolation from the Persianate rulership of later Indo-Islamic India, it provides a unique example of Islamic rule in which Arabic-oriented rulers exercised authority over Hindu populations and religious institutions.[56]

The sources for this era are Arabic narratives of conquest, with the exception of the *Chachnāma*, a 13th-century Persian history of the campaigns in Sind, ostensibly based on a lost Arabic original.[57] Their view of India and its religious institutions is very much from the perspective of the wider Caliphal world, stretching from al-Andalus (the Iberian Peninsula) in the West, to al-Sind (modern Sindh) in the East, with Damascus, and later, Baghdad at its political heart. While these historians' descriptions of the management – or destruction – of Sindhi religious institutions vary considerably on the details, they are, generally consistent in the broad brushstrokes with which they paint the gestalt of life in al-Sind. In the 8th century, Umayyad armies overthrew the Brāhmaṇa Dynasty of Brahmanābād (subsequently al-Maṣūra) and established Islamic hegemony in Sindh.

This was accompanied, of course, with the widespread, but not universal, destruction of indigenous religious institutions (Buddhist and Hindu temples, for example), the decimation of the male fighting-age population, the enslavement of women and children, and the construction of triumphal mosques. Alongside these atrocities, however, the rulers of al-Sind also protected indigenous religious institutions (often for explicit financial advantage), confirmed the customary rights of Brāhmaṇas, and even permitted the construction of new temples.[58] In no small way, then, we might see al-Sind as something of a microcosm of Indo-Muslim

[56] For a history of Sind (the Arabic spelling of Sindh), see Finbarr Flood, 'Conflict and Cosmopolitanism in Arab Sind', in Deborah Hutton and Rebecca Brown (eds), *A Companion to Asian Art and Architecture* (Oxford: Blackwell, 2011): 365–97.

[57] Arabic sources include 'Aḥmad ibn Yaḥyā ibn Jābir al-Balādhurī's 9th-century *Kitāb Futūḥ al-Buldān* (*Book of the Conquest of the Countries*), Muḥammad Abū'l-Qāsim Ibn Ḥawqal's 10th-century *Ṣūrat al-'Arḍ* (*Face of the Earth*), al-Bīrūnī's 11th-century *Taḥqīq mā li-'l-Hind*, Ibn al-Jawzī's 12th-century, polemical *Talbīs Iblīs* (*The Devil's Delusion*), and al-Shaṭībī's 14th-century *al-jumān fī akhbār al-zamān* (*History of Time*). For the *Chachnāma*, see Manan Ahmed, *A Book of Conquest: The Chachnama and Muslim Origins in South Asia* (Cambridge, MA: Harvard University Press, 2016).

[58] Flood, 'Conflict and Cosmopolitanism', addresses the archeological evidence of Buddhist and Hindu religious practices throughout the history of Arab Sind.

approaches to the Sanskrit jurisprudence of Equity and Trusts: iconoclasm and desecration give way to practical accommodation and even recognition of Hindu religious institutions.

3.2.1.i al-Qāsim in the Arabic chronicles

In 712, Muḥammad ibn al-Qāsim al-Thaqafī, the teenage son-in-law of Abū Muḥammad al-Ḥajjāj, the Umayyad governor of Irāq and Hind and Sind (694–714 CE), sailed from Širâz with an army of six thousand Syrian cavalrymen on a punitive expedition to Dēbal (near modern Karachi).[59] According to Arab chroniclers, al-Qāsim's original mandate was to destroy Dēbal in retaliation for a piratical attack on Muslim women making the Haj along the western coast of India.[60] After capturing and destroying Dēbal and capturing Nīrūn and Sadūsān, al-Qāsim confronted and killed Raja Dahir (r. 695–712 CE) of the Brāhmaṇa Dynasty of Sindh (632–712 CE) in a pitched battle on the banks of the river Mihrān, before culminating his conquest of Sindh with the subsequent capture of Brahmanābād, Alor, and Multān.[61] When al-Ḥajjāj died in 714, followed by the Caliph al-Walīd ibn ʿAbd al-Malik ibn Marwān (r. 705–15 CE), al-Qāsim ran afoul of Sulaymān ibn ʿAbd al-Malik (r. 715–17 CE) and was tortured to death in Mosul, Iraq.[62] Despite al-Qāsim's brief tenure, al-Balādhurī records that 'the people of al-Hind deplored the loss of Muḥammad, and set up a portrait of him at al-Kiraj [perhaps the Kangra Valley]'.[63] This might be surprising, given the plunder of Dēbal, its temple and its populace, but al-Qāsim's governorship of Sind was also marked by a somewhat ambiguous guardianship of religious institutions.

Balādhurī's account of al-Qāsim's siege of Dēbal focuses on its temple:

> Qasim... arrived at Daybul on a Friday. In Daybul was a great temple (*budd*) with a tall mast, and on that mast was a red flag, which covered the city when it blew in the wind. And they report that the temple had a great minaret built in the midst of the city, which housed their idols (*sanam*). The temple was known by the name of the idols... The fight lasted for three days, as Muḥammad killed many soldiers there. The governor of Dahar fled, and the custodian (*saadni*) of their house of gods was killed. After the capture of the city, Muḥammad measured the quarters for Muslims and built a mosque and settled four thousand men.[64]

[59] Wink, *Al-Hind, Vol. 1*, 202–3. According to Ahmed, *Book of Conquest*, 37: 'The Umayyad State was interested in the region for several reasons: to secure a frontier region against rebels, to address the financial affairs of the Marwanid branch of the Umayyad, and to consolidate mercantile routes.'

[60] Wink, *Al-Hind, Vol. 1*, 203.

[61] Ibid., 204–5.

[62] Ibid., 206–7.

[63] Ibid., 207.

[64] *Futūh al-Buldān*, p. 420. Translated by Ahmed, *Book of Conquest*, 40–1. Note that '*budd*', in Islamic accounts is a general term for all indigenous non-Islamic practices. See ibid., 42–3.

This event occurred in conjunction with a massacre of the city's inhabitants that lasted three days – precisely as a result of al-Ḥajjāj's command that al-Qāsim 'not grant *amān* (peace) to any of them'.[65] According to Balādhurī, a similar pattern of temple destruction, massacre, and mosque foundation occurred in Brahmanābād.[66] However, Balādhurī notes two key features of the Sanskrit jurisprudence of Equity and Trusts when describing the sack of the temple of Dēbal: the juridical personality of Hindu deities (an eponymous temple); and an individual who served the temple deity as a fiduciary. In fact, Balādhurī's description of the custodian of the temple – (*saadni*), appears to be a variation of *sādin*, an Arabic term for the custodians of the pre-Islamic shrines as well as the Ka'ba.[67]

When al-Qāsim reached Al-Rūr, however, Balādhurī records that,

> He besieged the city and conquered it by treaty with the condition that he would neither kill them nor enter their temple. He said, 'The *budd* are like the churches of the Christians and the Jews and the fire houses of the Magians.' And he imposed tax (*kharaj*) on them and in Aror he built a mosque.[68]

Friedmann argues that the statement above is far more than a theological analogy. It follows, more or less exactly, the Ḥanafī school of jurisprudence's (*madhhab*) opinion that idolators who are not Arab (*'ajam*) may be allowed to pay the *jizīya* tax and practise their non-Islamic religious customs.[69] According to Friedmann, Balādhurī's decision to place this argument in al-Qāsim's mouth at the time he captured a Hindu temple is an explicit 'projection into the past of the legal doctrine' of the Ḥanafī school, whereby: 'The inclusion of the Hindūs and of the other idolators in the category of *ahl al-dhimma* constitutes the final stage in the gradual extension of the concept, which originally involved Jews and Christians only, was soon extended to the Zoroastrians and finally came to denote practically all

[65] See Derryl Maclean, *Religion and Society in Arab Sind* (Leiden: Brill, 1989), 37. Also see Friedmann, 'The Temple of Multān', 176–7. Reading against other interpretations, Friedmann insists that the temple was destroyed during the invasion. Also see Flood, 'Conflict and Cosmopolitanism', 384, where he notes that, 'excavations of the congregational mosque at Banbhore/Daybul, the port city of Mansura, revealed that a linga (an aniconic sign of the Hindu deity Shiva) was set at its main entrance, to be trampled by those entering, a common practice of monotheist polemicists'. Cf. Fazal Ahmad Khan, 'Excavations at Banbhore', *Pakistan Archaeology* 1 (1964): 48–55, 53, pls. XVIB, XVIIA; Ashfaque, S.M., 'The Grand Mosque of Banbhore', *Pakistan Archaeology* 6 (1969): 182–209, 198–9.

[66] Friedmann, 'The Temple of Multān', 177

[67] See, for example, Francesco Grande, 'Definiteness Marking in Earlier Stages of Arabic Areal Evidence from Classical Arabic Idols' Names', *Annali di Ca' Foscari Serie Orientale* 57 (2021): 19–52, 39: 'The pre-Islamic religious practice of *sidāna*, which literally means "shrine-keeping". In basic terms, a sādin was at once the minister of an idol's shrine and an older inhabitant of the area in which that idol was located.' The same verb is used in the context of Qusayy ibn Kilāb ibn Murrah (400–80), the ancestor of the Prophet Muḥammad and the guardian of the Ka'aba in Mecca. See Brannon Wheeler, *Mecca and Eden: Ritual, Relics, and Territory in Islam* (Chicago: University of Chicago Press, 2006), 27–8.

[68] Ahmed, *Book of Conquest*, 40. Compare with Friedmann, 'The Temple of Multān', 181: mā al-budd illā ka-kanā'is **al-naṣārā** wa **al-yahūd** wa buyūt nīrān **al-majūs**.

[69] Friedmann, 'The Temple of Multān', 180–1. Friedmann discusses the issue within different school of jurisprudence in some depth.

unbelievers living under Muslim rule.'[70] In short, whatever the precise historical veracity of Balādhurī's account of al-Qāsim's conquest of Sindh, it articulates a very clear effort to understand Hindu religious trusts and to incorporate them within the parameters of Islamic jurisprudence – even if that requires the use of anachronistic timeframes. The caliphal province of Sind served, at the very least, as a fertile source for the creative imagination of Islamic historians centuries later.

Al-Qāsim is perhaps best known for his questionable stewardship of the renowned Sun temple in Multān. During his visit to Multān in 641 CE, the Chinese traveller Xuanzang (602–64 CE) described the Sun temple and its associated charities:

> The image of the Surya-deva is cast in yellow gold and ornamented with rare gems... The kings and high families of the five Indies never fail to make their offerings of gems and precious stones. They have founded a house of mercy, in which they provide food and drink, and medicines for the poor and sick, affording succor and sustenance.[71]

Balādhurī's account also contains 'theological commingling' between Islam and Hinduism in its description of the sun temple as: 'a great temple. Great gifts were brought for it, offerings were given, and the people of Sind made pilgrimage here. They circumambulated it and shaved their heads and beards. They claim that the idol (*sanam*) inside is in the likeness of the prophet Job, may Allah bless him.'[72]

Although Balādhurī narrates that al-Qāsim plundered the temple's treasures and imprisoned its custodians, every other Arabic account describes, in some depth, al-Qāsim's accommodation of the temple cult and his re-arrangement of its finances.[73] Al-Birūnī records that al-Qāsim hung a piece of beef around the idol's neck as a sign of humiliation, but otherwise left the temple alone.[74] As discussed above, Ibn al-Jawzī described a tri-partite division of the deity's assets wherein the temple, the poor, and the Amīr each received shares.[75] Al-Shaṭbībī emphasises that al-Qāsim was motived out of pecuniary desire (*raghbatan fī almāl*), and Ibn Ḥawqal relates that the temple custodians were paid a fixed sum out of the total collections, which were appropriated by the Amīr.[76]

It would probably be overly generous to characterise al-Qāsim's approach to the Sun temple of Multān as the fulfilment of the fiduciary duties outlined for sovereigns in Dharmaśāstric jurisprudence, but it was a form of custodianship, nonetheless. Furthermore, al-Qāsim, at least according to his Arab chroniclers,

[70] Ibid., 181.
[71] Maclean, *Religion*, 18–20.
[72] Ahmed, *Book of Conquest*, 40–1.
[73] Friedmann, 'The Temple of Multān', 177.
[74] Ibid., 178.
[75] See Note 34.
[76] Friedmann, 'The Temple of Multān', 178–9.

understood Hindu religious institutions and their financial endowments within their own paradigms and within the categories of Islamic jurisprudence. Nevertheless, as Ibn Ḥawqal and several other sources note, when Hindu rulers attempted to invade Multān, 'the Muslims threatened to break and burn the idol', using it as something of a divine hostage and as a stratagem for retaining control of the city.[77] Eventually, when Sind fell under Ismā'īlī control in the 10th century, Ḥalam b. Shaybān obliterated the temple, killed its guardians and transformed the site into a mosque.[78]

3.2.1.ii Political accommodation in Chachnāma

The *Chachnāma* (The Book of Chach), is a Persian prose work – ostensibly based on an anonymous Arabic predecessor – that was written by `Ali Kufi in 1226 at Uch (near modern Karachi), under the aegis of Nasir-ud-Dīn Qabacha, Maḥmūd of Ghōr's governor in Multān.[79] The full name of the text is 'The Book of Stories of the King Dahir bin Chach bin Sila'ij and His Death at the Hands of Muḥammad bin Qasim'. The full title is important because it establishes the productive narrative juxtaposition of the work. `Ali Kufi recounts the adventures of two great rulers of Sindh, one Hindu and the other Muslim: Chach (631–71 CE) of the Brāhmaṇa Dynasty and Muḥammad al-Qāsim. At its heart, the *Chachnāma* 'is the tale of Chach and Qasim, two young men who strive to establish an ethical polity in Sind but whose work is undone by the greed and lust of others'.[80]

Ideologically, the *Chachnāma*'s overarching theme lies in its explication of a model of just rulership across religious and cultural boundaries. `Ali Kufi shows us, in intricate detail, Chach and al-Qāsim's conquests, administration, and political jockeying with an eye towards showing the reader that, despite their differences of time, dynasty, and religion, they drew on a common wellspring of virtuous rulership: protecting religious institutions; promoting the hereditary rights and restrictions of various castes; and honouring treaties and pledges. From a Sanskritic perspective, this shared theory of good governance bears a remarkable similarity to Dharmaśāstric jurisprudence. A Hindu reader can see that Kufi's al-Qāsim listens to the political advice – often drawn from the *Hitopadeśa* – given by the Brāhmaṇas whom he meets and follows some Dharmaśāstric political values – particularly in relation to Equity and Trusts. Likewise, a Muslim reader can see in Chach many of the same moral virtues of al-Qāsim.

77 Ibid., 179.
78 Ibid., 179.
79 Ahmed, *Book of Conquest*, 12–13.
80 Ibid., 14.

While scholars of past generations have tended to view the *Chachnāma* as more historical 'romance' than history, Manan Ahmed Asif's definitive monograph on the text demonstrates that the *Chachnāma* is valuable not *despite*, but *because* of its ideological distortions.[81] The *Chachnāma*'s 'political vision', articulated after the establishment of the Delhi Sulṭānate in 1206 CE, is one in which pre-Islamic and Islamic models of rulership can coexist, but only through the efforts of virtuous rulers to understand and to adapt to the cultural conditions of India.

Ahmed argues that, 'as [an] Indic text of political theory, *Chachnama* also draws upon literary traditions that are normatively understood to be outside of particularly "Muslim" political theory… [namely] *Arthasastra* and *Hitopadesha*'.[82] I agree 'that [the] Chachnama is a fully Indic text influenced by texts and genres from Persian as well as Sanskrit, reflecting the intertwined world of thirteenth-century Sind'.[83] In contrast to the Arabic chronicles which sought to understand and accommodate – to an extent – indigenous religious practices according to Islamic jurisprudential categories, the *Chachnāma* is markedly synthetic. As Ahmed notes, the *Chachnāma* is not a tale of conquest, but, rather, a work of political theory.[84]

3.2.1.iii Chach: a Dharmaśāstric king in a Persian idiom

The *Chachnāma* opens with Chach arriving at the court of Rai Sihasi in Aror, 'the capital of Hind and Sind', where he tells the chamberlain that he, along with his father and brother live and serve at the temple at the outskirts of Aror in order to obtain a position in the royal bureaucracy.[85] Our hero's first political virtue is his status as a temple trustee. When Chach ascends the throne he appoints his brother as his viceroy, noting that:

> Our nearest relations are ascetics, and have always been faithful worshippers of idols in their temples. Their custom of worshipping fire and devotion to God are widely known. Our father Selaij acts on the saying, – 'But we saw our fathers doing the same' and this is approved by all our learned men… You can assist in the administration of the country by practising religiousness, faithfulness, abstinence and piety here also.[86]

Chach describes his congenital law (*kuladharma*) as serving temple deities using Qur'an 26.74. The connection between the Qur'anic and Dharmaśāstric theories

[81] Ibid., 14–15. For 'source-critical' aspersions cast on the *Chachnāma*, see Wink, *Al-Hind, Vol. 1*, 195.
[82] Ahmed, *Book of Conquest*, 96.
[83] Ibid., 21.
[84] Ibid., 20.
[85] Mirza Fredungberg, *The Chachnamah: An Ancient History of Sind* (Karachi: Commissioner's Press, 1900), 27.
[86] Ibid., 23–4.

of Equity – in which individual communities are subject to community-based supplemental Dharmas – is striking.

When appointing his brother, Chach articulates a theory of sovereignty which extends the fiduciary relationship between the temple priests to their deity to the people of the kingdom. This represents a classic example of the Sanskrit jurisprudential model of *parens patriae*:

> To treat kindly the innumerable subjects under our sway, who are a trust (committed to our care) by the Creator, and to keep them contented and happy by administering justice and equity in such a manner that the strong should not oppress the weak, and we might not be reprehended in the august court of God for lack of judgment or denial of redress.[87]

Kufi offers a similar description of Chach's encounter with the caretaker (*samani*) of the Budd temple in Brahmānābād. Chach finds this monk busily engaged in making idols, and, 'when he finished all his idols', Chach requests the monk to join his royal administration. Although the monk denies Chach's request and fears that Brahmanābād fort might cause 'injury and mischief to the sown fields of Budh' (the legal personality of 'Budh' as an owner of fields is highly relevant here), he nevertheless notes that: 'Owing to the vicissitudes of time, some parts of the structure have suffered injury. It should, therefore, be built anew, and you should spend your own funds in laying a fresh foundation.'[88]

In short, Kufi offers a highly positive portrayal of Chach as a virtuous Dharmaśāstric sovereign: a humble, learned Brāhmaṇa who served his kingdom and its inhabitants with the same fidelity that he served his tutelary deity according to his congenital Dharma. All of this is assimilated to a Persian-Islamic cultural milieu.

3.2.1.iv al-Qāsim as Dharmaśāstric sovereign

Kufi follows a similar paradigm in his characterisation of al-Qāsim. On the advice on Brāhmaṇas, he becomes a patron and protector of temples and the caste-based order of pre-conquest Sind. Initially, al-Qāsim raids the temple at Dēbal:

> Those who had taken shelter in the temple wanted to close the door, and burn themselves to death. The two door-keepers, however, were dragged out and killed, and entry was then made. 700 beautiful females, who were under the protection of Budh, were all captured with their valuable ornaments, and clothes adorned with jewels.[89]

[87] Ibid., 24.

[88] Ibid., 36–7. After Chach captured Multān, 'he himself went to an idol temple, which stood in a retired and solitary place, prostrated himself before the idol, offered sacrifices, and then proceeded on his forward journey'.

[89] Ibid., 84.

After capturing Brahmanābād, however, al-Qāsim encounters the Brāhmaṇas of the city, who effectively transfer the Chach dynasties Dharmaśāstric mandate to him:

> About 1,000 men from amongst the Brahmins of the place came to the court of Muḥammad Kasim with their heads and beards clean shaved. When Muḥammad Kasim saw them, he enquired: 'To what army does this body of men, who have come here in this shape, belong?' The men themselves replied: 'O Commander, who are a faithful observer of promises, our king was a Brahmin. When he was killed and the reins of the kingdom were taken away from him, some of his subjects killed themselves out of excessive love and loyalty towards him, and others shaved their heads and beards. Now that the great and omnipotent God has entrusted this kingdom to your charge, we have come here to pay our respects to the just commander and to know his will as to the survivors.'[90]

This positive relationship prompts al-Qāsm to assign the collection of the *jizīya* to non-Muslims of Brahmanābād as a precondition of being able to 'retain the religion of their fathers and grandfathers'. Al-Qāsm, following a classic Dharmaśāstric paradigm of supporting Brāhmaṇas and protecting community conventions, tells the Brāhmaṇas: 'I confirm you in your previous posts. The management of all the affairs of State, and its administration, I leave in your able hands, and this (right) I grant (also) to your children and descendants hereditarily, and you need fear no alteration or cancellation of the order thus issued.'[91] Furthermore, after hearing that the conquest had left several Budd temples desolate, al-Qāsm ordered that 3 per cent of the *jiziya* tax should be paid to the priests and monks of these temples.[92]

Like Chach, al-Qāsm patronises indigenous religious institutions and confirms hereditary caste rights in perpetuity but he does so on the basis of Islamic jurisprudence. The result of this narrative is, in Kufi's handling, a vision of a political order in which Islamic and Sanskritic constitutional orders can and should coexist. After his encounter with the Brāhmaṇas, al-Qāsm protects a temple image at Aror when he conquers the city:

> Then, as Muḥammad bin Qasim entered the fort, he heard that all the inhabitants were gathered at the temple of Naubahar (*nava-vihar*), praying… Then he entered it and saw a figure (*surati*) sitting on a horse. On its hands were bracelets of gold and rubies. Muḥammad bin Qasim reached out and with his hand took the bracelet from the idol. Then he called the caretaker priest and said, 'Is this your idol?' He replied, 'Yes. But he had two bracelets and now has only one.' Muḥammad bin Qasim said, 'Why does your god not know that his bracelet is gone?' The priest bowed his head, and Muḥammad bin Qasim smiled and returned the bracelet.[93]

[90] Ibid., 164–5.
[91] Ibid., 165
[92] Maclean, *Religion*, 44–5.
[93] Ahmed, *Book of Conquest*, 113.

This scene echoes Vikramāditya II's decision to return Rājasiṃheśvara's endowment after conquering Kāñcīpura: a triumphant king enters his defeated rivals' sanctum, inspects the deity's assets, and returns them in an act of pious domination. As Ahmed notes, 'the taking and return of the bracelet asserts the dominance of Islam, and the speechless priest bears witness of this dominance'.[94]

A final episode brings the parallel journeys of Chach and al-Qāsim into critical relief: al-Qāsim's protection of the great temple of Multān. After capturing Multān, al-Qāsim:

> Entered that temple… [and] saw a gold idol with two bright ruby eyes, glowing red. Muḥammad bin Qasim thought that this was a man. He unsheathed his sword to strike the idol, but the Brahmin caretaker exclaimed, 'Oh just Commander! This is an idol that the king of Multan, Juban, created and under which they sequestered riches and treasures.'[95]

After consultation with the idol's caretaker, al-Qāsm: 'Gathered the noble and the public of Multan and entered into a pact with them, safeguarded the idol, built a central mosque, and appointed as the city's commander Daud bin Nasr bin Walid `Umani.'[96]

Kufi portrays the culmination of al-Qāsm's political career in Sind in part in terms of his gradual acceptance of a similar, if Islamic, version of the Chach's political paradigm: safeguarding the people of the nation; confirming Brāhmaṇical authority; allocating public funds for the repair of Budd temples, and protecting Hindu temple images. Ahmed's conclusion encapsulates the political theory articulated in the *Chachnāma*: 'Like Chach agreeing to rebuild the Buddhist temple, Qasim, under the advisement of the caretaker, commits to the public good by protecting the idol and the temple… and to create a just political order for the city that is based in the politics of accommodation.'[97]

Amid the backdrop of medieval and contemporary communitarian narratives of harsh iconoclasm and conflict between essentialised categories of 'Hindus' and 'Muslims' it is intriguing to hear that al-Qāsim, a teenage warlord, was able to protect the sun temple in Multān. He anticipated accommodative developments in Indo-Islamic rule by several centuries. The *Chachnāma*'s political vision of a just world in which Persianate and Sanskritic approaches to Equity and Trusts – and kingship more generally – can coexist was realised, to some extent, by the 14th century, but the path of destruction carved by Maḥmūd of Ghazni in northern India stands between al-Qāsim and it.

[94] Ibid., 114.
[95] Ibid.
[96] Ibid.
[97] Ibid.

3.2.2 Maḥmūd and the Ghaznavid period (977–1186 CE)

The Ghaznavids were a slave dynasty of Central Asian Turkish extraction who served the Persian Sāmānid Dynasty (819–999 CE) as governors of eastern and southern Afghanistan.[98] After shaking off the yoke their erstwhile suzerains, the Ghaznavid sulṭāns rapidly carved out a vast central Asian empire that stretched, at its zenith, from Tehran in the west, to Lahore in the east. This empire did not last long and was overthrown in 1186 by the equally ambitious Ghūrid Dynasty (1186–1206 CE), who like their former overlords, were a slave dynasty. The Ghaznavids, especially Maḥmūd (998–1030 CE), played an important role in Indian history for two reasons. First, as Richard Eaton observes, 'the Ghaznavids brought to the Punjab the entire gamut of Persianate institutions and practices that would define the political economy of much of India for centuries to come'.[99] Second:

> What gave the Ghaznavid Turks their special character, and perhaps their clearest contrast with contemporary Indian states, were the geostrategic forces driving their continued raids on north India in the early eleventh century. Those raids aimed not at appropriating territory but at plundering wealthy cities and their temples, especially for gold or silver.[100]

These two trends – the establishment of a strong, Persianised sulṭānate and the plunder of immobilised wealth from Hindu, Jain, and Buddhist religious institutions – were linked. To fund their territorial ambitions in Central Asia, the Ghaznavid sulṭāns had to repeatedly maraud through the Panjabi and Gangetic plains, sacking temples, extracting tribute, and, generally, making no substantive attempts at establishing permanent political authority over these Indian territories. Maḥmūd infamously raided northwest India seventeen times during his thirty-two-year reign.

With the sole exception of his apparent toleration of the strategically important and financially lucrative temple complex at Kaśmīri Smast, the Ghaznavids are probably unique in the history of Indo-Muslim rule in their essentially entirely antagonistic relationship with indigenous religious institutions. One might wonder if the Ghaznavids' contribution to the history of Indo-Muslim engagements with Sanskrit theories of Equity and Trusts lies in illustrating, *via negativa*, the positive qualities of subsequent rulers.

Perhaps not. Unlike the Arabic chronicles of al-Sind, the Ghaznavid era archive offers little substantive information on the protection of Dharmaśāstric Trusts. Nevertheless, their rule inaugurated several political and theoretical trends that would, in the course of time, provide frameworks within which Indo-Muslim

[98] Wink, *Al-Hind, Vol. 2*, 72.
[99] Eaton, *Persianate*, 33.
[100] Ibid., 32.

and Dharmaśāstric rulers would frame their relationships to Dharmaśāstric trusts and with each other. In what follows, this chapter explores four themes: 1) the Ghaznavids' Persianised sulṭānate as the model for subsequent Islamic and Hindu rulers in South Asia; 2) the Ghaznavids' plunder of numerous Indian religious institutions as a religiously *justified*, financially *motivated* transfer of capital; 3) al-Bīrūnī's *Kitāb al-Hind* (*History of India*) as the first effort to understand the Sanskrit jurisprudence of Equity and Trusts from an Islamic perspective; and 4) Buddhist and Jain efforts to understand Islam and the Ghaznavid incursions from traditionally Sanskritic perspectives.

In the aggregate, the Ghaznavids contributed far more to the history of Dharmaśāstric trusts than a trail of devastated temple complexes. Rather, they set the political and theoretical stages for subsequent individuals to build what would become the model for the relationship between Crown and temple in Islamic India.

3.2.2.i From Turkish ʿamīrs to Persianised sulṭāns

Before Maḥmūd's conquest of Sindh and the Punjab in the early 11th century, Islamic rule in India was limited to emirates – Muḥammad al-Qāsm ruled as an ʿamīr. By the turn of the 11th century, al-Sind was home to the Habari Emirate (854–1011 CE) centred in Manṣūra (formerly Brahmanābād) and the Emirate of Multān (855–1010 CE). As Eaton notes:

> [A new political] legacy was realized in the idea of a transregional, sovereign state under the authority of a supreme ruler, the sultan. While such a figure theoretically governed as a deputy appointed by the caliph in Baghdad, in fact the scope of a sultan's authority progressively grew, filling the political space vacated first by the Samanid amirs when they were eclipsed in 999, and then by the Abbasid caliphs when the Mongols overthrew them in 1258.[101]

Administratively, the Ghaznavids 'inherited from the creative ferment of tenth-century Khurasan and Central Asia under the Samanid rulers of Bukhara' the phenomenon of a 'ranked and salaried bureaucracy tied to the state's land revenue and military systems', alongside 'the institution of elite, or military, slavery'.[102] It is difficult to overstate the importance of the Ghaznavids' introduction of 'a salaried bureaucracy… based on the principle of state-run revenue assignments known as *Iqta*ʿs, which were defined units of land whose revenues were collected by the assignee, or *iqtaʿdar*'.[103] The *Iqṭā*ʿ system, essentially a form a feudal land tenure, became *the* normative system of political governance in Islamic India, and was,

[101] Eaton, 'Persian Cosmopolis', 71.
[102] Eaton, *Persianate*, 35.
[103] Ibid.

with cosmetic Sanskrit nomenclative changes, adopted by Hindu polities like the Vijayanagara Empire.[104]

In this system, *Iqṭā'* lands were 'assigned to free nobles as well as to high-ranking slaves who enjoyed the special confidence of the sultan' effectively fusing 'the state's revenue and military systems'.[105] However, the Ghaznavids only shifted to a feudal tenurial system in the 'late eleventh century, when they could no longer rely on war booty' from plundered temples 'to finance government operations, as they had done in the dynasty's early days'.[106] The Sulṭānate system of governance was, therefore, causally connected with the cessation of temple-raiding.

These administrative developments occurred hand-in-glove with the Persianisation of the Ghaznavid Empire. The Ghaznavids were of Turkish extraction, but as Wink notes, 'in so far as there is any emphasis on the Turkishness of the Ghaznavids… it always comes from the very early years of the dynasty… [and] the dynasty spoke Turkish (Turki) up to the time of Mas'ud (1031–41)'.[107] However, 'with the aid of Persian chroniclers, secretaries and officials, the transformation of a congeries of pagan Turkish slaves into a Perso-Islamic ruling elite which could put to use the administrative nomenclature and political rhetoric of the eastern caliphate seems to have been effected almost overnight'.[108]

Of course, this erasure of the dynasty's 'pagan Turkish past' through a dubious 'Persian pedigree harking back to pre-Islamic times' recast the Ghaznavids 'in the role of defenders of Sunnī orthodoxy against the Shī'ite Buyids', and gave the sulṭāns 'the historic mission… to raid and conquer "the infidels of al-Hind"'.[109] In short, the Ghaznavids used the plundered treasure of Indian religious institutions to finance their Persianisation, and, as Eaton notes: 'the production of a revived Persian language, literature, and culture gravitated with the Ghaznavids eastward – first to Ghazni in eastern Afghanistan, home to Ferdowsi, Bayhaqi, and al-Biruni (d. 1048) during the reign of Sultan Mahmud (d. 1030 CE), and then to Lahore in the Punjab'.[110] For example, Abū l-Qāsim Firdawsī's (931–1025 CE) *Šāhnāme* (*Book of Kings*) portrays Maḥmūd 'as combining the virtues of both Iranian and Islamic sovereignty', as well as 'the warrior ethos of Central Asian Turks and the heritage of Greek civilization'.[111]

[104] For Iqṭā' generally, see Chapter 1, 'The Origins and Development of the Iqṭā' System: An Introduction', in Tsugitaka Sato's *State and Rural Society in Medieval Islam Sultans, Muqta's and Fallahun* (Ledien: Brill, 1997): 1–17. For *Iqṭā'* in India, see Hussain Khan, 'The Institution of Iqṭā' and it Impact on Muslim Rule in India', *Islamic Studies* 22.1 (1983): 1–9.

[105] Eaton, *Persianate*, 35.

[106] Ibid.

[107] Wink, *Al-Hind, Vol. 2*, 112.

[108] Ibid.

[109] Ibid.

[110] Eaton, 'Persian Cosmopolis', 71.

[111] Ibid., 70

3.2.2.ii The Ghaznavid raids

The early Ghaznavids were, whatever be their subsequent iconoclastic ideological justifications, rapacious plunderers. Eaton provides an illustrative view on the 'expansive and predatory… self-catalysing cycle' at the heart of the Ghaznavid regime wherein the:

> Bullion [seized from Indian temples] was… melted down into coins to finance campaigns in Central Asia and Iran… for purchasing war-horses, slaves and manufactured goods, and for paying the salaries of Mahmud's army and administrative hierarchy. As… the size of the army grew… ever more cash was needed to pay them.[112]

In effect, Ghaznavid raids converted the accumulated capital of Dharmaśāstric temple trusts – the foundation and expression of Dharmaśāstric sovereignty – into a puissant military power. Truschke notes, and Chapter 2 of this monograph explores in detail, how Hindu temple trusts 'served, among other functions, as banks in ancient India'.[113] Their systematic plunder – a sustained bank robbery as it were – of these engines of the economy attenuated the Dharmaśāstric political networks in which it had circulated for centuries.

Although the Ghaznavids directed their puissance towards territorial gains in Central Asia, the astonishingly high financial cost of their raids weakened the political strength of the Sanskrit cosmopolitan order and paved the way for the Ghūrids' establishment of Persianate sovereignty in the 12th century.

Maḥmūd's father, Sabuktigin (r. 977–97 CE), raided Lamghan and Multān as a general in the 960s, defeated 'a coalition of Indian kings' headed by Jayapāla (r. 964–1001 CE) of the Śāhi Dynasty in 991, and 'established [Ghaznavid sovereignty] in virtually all areas to the west of the Indus'.[114] The tempo of conquest escalated significantly when Maḥmūd acquired official 'caliphal sanction (*mauqif-i-khilāfat*) for his actions'.[115] Maḥmūd overthrew the Sindhī 'Amīrates (1004–5 CE), broke Śāhi resistance by 1010 and set about initiating a 'huge transfer of wealth' from Indian temples to the court in Ghazni.[116]

Wink notes that 'the sources repeat ad nauseam that from the destroyed temples and sacred sites, and as booty or tribute obtained from vanquished Indian rulers, the "army of Islam" obtained abundant wealth and unlimited riches'.[117] These financial

[112] Eaton, *Persianate*, 32

[113] See Truschke, *The Language of History*, 27 for the bank comment. Perhaps *the* essential distinction between royal spoliation of temples in the Sanskrit cosmopolis and in the Ghaznavid epoch lies in the subsequent use of plundered treasure. Sanskrit cosmopolitan rulers invariably *reinvested* plundered treasures in local temple economies. The redistribution of plundered funds was as much a *financial* act as it was a *political* act.

[114] Wink, *Al-Hind, Vol. 2*, 129.

[115] Ibid., 130.

[116] Ibid., 124.

[117] Ibid.

peculations coincided with the mass enslavement of the local population. For example, according to Muḥammad Qāsim Hindū Shāh Astarābādī's *Ta'rikh-i-Firishta* (17th century): 'After the capture of Thanesar in 1014 AD, 'the army of Islam brought to Ghazna about 200,000 captives (*qarib do sīt hazār banda*), and much wealth, so that the capital appeared like an Indian city, no soldier of the camp being without wealth, or without many slaves.'[118]

The rhetorical *justification* for this widespread plundering was, of course, iconoclastic. Certainly 'from the time of Sabuktigin onwards' the raids in India were framed as 'a jihad against the inhabitants of Hind who are all "worshipers of images and idols" (*mu'abbid-i-ausān-o-asnām*)' with the ultimate objective being 'to humiliate the sinners, Hindu unbelievers, the idol-worshipers... to spread the carpet of Islam... [and] to cleanse the country of the odiousness of the idolatrous.'[119] Iconoclasm served the political purpose of justifying the rapacious plunder of millions of dirhams' worth of immobilised treasure from India which was concentrated in temples at India's major pilgrimage sites.

Given the context, it would have been surprising if the Ghaznavids *had not* acted as they did. As Wink notes, 'the Turkish invaders were certainly familiar with Hindu sacred geography... [and] the main religious sites were easily identified and taken out serially in the first quarter of the eleventh century.'[120] In 1008, Maḥmūd defeated the Śāhi ruler Anandapāla and plundered 'the storehouse of a great idol' (the legal personality of the 'idol' in the description is noteworthy) at 'Bhīmnagar' (near modern Nagarkot).[121] In 1011 Maḥmūd captured Sthāneśvara (modern Thanesar), whose chief deity, Cakrasvāmin, according to Astarābādī, was 'held in the same veneration by idolaters, as Mecca by the faithful.'[122] Maḥmūd sacked the city and carted Cakrasvāmin off to Ghazni, where it was thrown into the hippodrome – soon to be joined by Somanātha. In 1018, Maḥmūd burnt Mathurā to the ground, where, according to Astarābādī, 'Maḥmūd broke down or burned all the idols, and amassed a vast quantity of gold and silver, of which the idols were mostly composed.'[123] Kānyakubja was sacked the same year – with similar results – and Somanātha (discussed previously) fell in 1025.

Maḥmūd's raids didn't put an end to Indian temple-building or the creation of religious endowments by Hindu sovereigns – probably because, as so many authors have pointed out, Hindu rulers would, by necessity, build and maintain temples as *the* method for establishing sovereignty. The Ghaznavids' iconoclastic raids, unaccompanied by attempts (outside of the Panjab) to develop territorial

[118] Ibid., 126 fn. 76.
[119] Ibid., 328.
[120] Ibid.
[121] Ibid., 329
[122] Ibid.
[123] Ibid., 124.

hegemony, ensured a more-or-less endless supply of capital and slaves for their territorial ambitions in Central Asia.

In short, Maḥmūd and his successors viewed Dharmaśāstric temple trusts as capital reserves for a Sanskritic, image-worshipping political order. Those capital reserves, divine banks, so to speak, were free for the taking due to their association with image worship. At the very least, remembering Maḥmūd as India's most famous iconoclastic *bank-robber* helps us to foreground one key element of the history of Equity and Trusts in Sanskrit jurisprudence: that deities' endowments served as politically essential financial nodes in ancient and medieval India.

3.2.2.iii Al-Bīrūnī on image worship

The noted polymath, Abū Rayḥān al-Bīrūnī (973–1048 CE), a scholar-slave in Maḥmūd's employ and a court astronomer, followed his sulṭān on his Indian raids from 1017 onwards.[124] His history of India, *Kitāb taḥqīq mā lil-Hind min maqūla maqbūla fi'l-'aql aw mardhūla*, completed in 1030 after the death of Maḥmūd, presents what Mario Kozah describes as an 'Islamisation' of Hinduism, in the sense that it 'may very well be the very first systematization of "Indian" beliefs into one "Indian religion", as al-Bīrūnī calls it'.[125]

In his travels, al-Bīrūnī collected Sanskrit manuscripts, collaborated with Brāhmaṇas, and sought to weave together a theory of Indian religion, culture, and history, using a comparative method that included Greek, Hebrew, Arabic, and Persian sources.[126] Astonishingly, al-Bīrūnī took the opportunity afforded by Maḥmūd's death to criticise his former patron: 'He [Maḥmūd] utterly ruined the prosperity of the country [of India], and performed those unheard-of things by which the Hindus became like atoms of dust scattered in all directions, and like a tale of old in the mouth of the people.'[127]

Although al-Bīrūnī took a negative view of Hindu image worship, he nevertheless provides the earliest Islamic explication of image worship's metaphysics, history, and legal form (albeit briefly), while also adumbrating the earliest Brāhmaṇical account of temple desecration by Muslim rulers. This latter point has gone largely unnoticed and it provides a notable exception to Truschke's observation that, 'contemporary Brahmin thinkers did not, so far as we know, write about Ghaznavid-led assaults'.[128] Taken in the aggregate, al-Bīrūnī's descriptions of

[124] For the life and works of al-Bīrūnī, see Bill Scheppler, *Al-Biruni: Master Astronomer and Muslim Scholar of the Eleventh Century* (New York: Rosen Publishing, 2006).

[125] Mario Kozah, *The Birth of Indology as an Islamic Science: Al-Bīrūnī's Treatise on Yoga Psychology* (Leiden: Brill, 2015), 1.

[126] For al-Bīrūnī's method, see ibid., 23–32.

[127] Ibid., 27.

[128] Truschke, *The Language of History*, 39.

Indian image worship provide an evocative, early perspective on the reception of Hinduism in Islamic thought as well as providing a Brāhmaṇical perspective on the arrival of Islam in India – particularly in relation to Hindu temples.

Al-Bīrūnī argues that, at its heart, Hinduism is monotheistic. In the second chapter of the *Hind*, entitled, 'a description of their [the Hindus] belief in God, may He be exalted', al-Bīrūnī opines that: 'The belief of the Hindus in God… is that He is the eternal one with neither beginning nor end, who is free in His actions, omnipotent, all wise, living and life giving, ruling and preserving, alone in His kingdom without likeness or unlikeness, resembling nothing and nothing resembling Him.'[129] But what about image-worship? Al-Bīrūnī argues that image worship has as its origins, 'monuments [made] in honour of certain much venerated persons, prophets, sages, angels, destined to keep alive their memory when they are absent or dead, to create for them a lasting place of grateful veneration in the hearts of men when they die'.[130]

Unlike 'the heathen Greeks, before the rise of Christianity' whose 'common people held the same idolatrous views as those of the Hindus', however, 'the Hindus had no men of this stamp both capable and willing to bring sciences to a classical perfection'.[131] Unable, or unwilling to dispel the 'superstitions' of the masses, al-Bīrūnī attributes the lack of unity between 'the educated among the Hindus' who 'abhor anthropomorphisms' and 'the crowd and the members of the single sects [who] use them most extensively' to the defective state of Indian scientific knowledge.[132]

Al-Bīrūnī draws a dichotomy between *philosophers* and the *general public* on the issue of image worship. Nevertheless, al-Bīrūnī is clear that, notwithstanding this distinction, there was a common *legal* understanding of image worship among Hindus. Chapter 1 of this monograph demonstrated that philosophical theories that downplayed the metaphysical identification of temple deities as conscious beings nevertheless accommodated jurisprudential theories of deities as legal persons (and figurative owners of property).[133] Al-Bīrūnī follows a similar line of thought and this likely reflects the view of his native Hindu informants. He invokes Patañjali's *Yogasūtras* and the *Bhagavadgītā* to articulate a sophisticated Advaitavedāntic view of a monotheistic Hindu god that can be assimilated to an Islamic monotheistic deity.[134] Al-Bīrūnī also provides a detailed account of the

[129] Kozah, *Birth of Indology*, 41.

[130] *Al-Beruni's India*, Vol. 1, 111.

[131] Ibid., 24–5.

[132] Ibid., 24–5 & 39. See page 25 for al-Bīrūnī's description of Indian science: 'You mostly find that even the so-called scientific theorems of the Hindus are in a state of utter confusion, devoid of any logical order, and in the last instance always mixed up with the silly notions of the crowd… as far as I know it, to a mixture of pearl shells and sour dates, or of pearls and dung, or of costly crystals and common pebbles.'

[133] See Chapter 1, §1.6.2.ii, 'Divine endowments in Mīmāṃsā and Vedānta'.

[134] See, for example, Kozah, *Birth of Indology*, 34–72.

alternative view, and translates a 'whole chapter from the book [*Bṛhat*] *Saṃhitā* relating to the construction of idols, which will help the student… to comprehend the… subject'.[135] Al-Bīrūnī's passage offers detailed descriptions of various images and how to construct them, but it ends with a description of the custody of images in temples.

It is unfortunate that al-Bīrūnī skips over many of these 'very long and tedious instructions', but the fact that he mentions them is significant: the statement demonstrates that there *were* long and tedious trust laws active at Hindu religious institutions according to al-Bīrūnī's Brāhmaṇa informants.[136] Although al-Bīrūnī doesn't elaborate on the fiduciary duties of temple servants, he briefly summarises Dharmaśāstric theories of Equity – conventional Dharmas among different religious communities that were in charge of the temple – when he notes that, according to Hindu doctrine:

> Servants and priests to minister to the idols should be nominated from different classes of the people. To the idol of Vishnu are devoted the class called Bhagavata; to the idol of the Sun, the Maga, i.e. the Magians; to the idol of Mahadeva, a class of saints, anchorites with long hair, who cover their skin with ashes, hang on their persons the bones of dead people, and swim in the pools. The Brahmana are devoted to the Eight Mothers, the Shamanians to Buddha, to Arhant the class called Nagna. On the whole, to each idol certain people are devoted who constructed it, for those know best how to serve it.[137]

This is a straightforward account of the creation and regulation of Hindu temples from the highly paraphrased perspective of Dharmaśāstra. Despite the ostensible aniconic philosophical predilections of his Brāhmaṇa informants, they provided al-Bīrūnī with an accurate understanding of Dharmaśāstric perspectives on temples and other religious endowments.

Finally, and perhaps most importantly, al-Bīrūnī records the first Brāhmaṇical Sanskrit account of temple desecration by Muslims. Numerous scholars have noted that medieval Sanskrit (and Prakrit) accounts of temple desecration and the Islamic conquests of India involve two interrelated theories: 1) the decline of Dharma during the 'Age of Strife' (*Kaliyuga*); and 2) the moral and martial decline of those tasked with protecting a Dharmically ordered society.[138] Al-Bīrūnī's account of the Kaliyuga is as follows:

[135] *Al-Beruni's India*, Vol. 1, 117–21.

[136] Ibid., 121.

[137] Ibid.

[138] See, for example Truschke, *The Language of History*, 109, 180. Davis, *Lives of Indian Images*, 110 (Kumārapāla's reconstruction of the Somanātha temple after Maḥmūd's raid), 117–19 (the *Madhurāvijaya*), & 191–2 (the *Kānhaḍade Prabandha*). Also see Phyllis Granoff, 'Tales of Broken Limbs and Bleeding Wounds: Responses to Muslim Iconoclasm in Medieval India', *East and West* 41.1 (1991): 189–203, 190: '[The *Ekaliṅgamāhātmya*] suggests that a king in his lack of faith may bring disaster upon his kingdom in the form of invading and pillaging hordes.' For Jain perspectives on the weakness of the Solaṅki Cālukyas, see Andrew Ollett, 'Attempted Iconoclasm: Mahmud of Ghazna, King Yoga, and the Poet Dhanapāla', *Comparative Studies of South Asia, Africa and the Middle East*, 42.2 (2022): 309–24. Finally, see Prithvi Datta Chandra Shobhi, 'Kalyāṇa Is Wrecked: The Remaking of

> In the story of Saunaka which Venus received from Brahman, God speaks to him in the following words: 'When the Kaliyuga comes, I send Buddhodana, the son of Suddhodana the pious, to spread the good in the creation. But then the Muḥammira, i.e. the red-wearing ones, who derive their origin from him, will change everything that he has brought, and the dignity of the Brahmans will be gone... Men will entirely be occupied with gathering wealth by crimes, with hoarding up, not refraining from committing horrid and sinful crimes... the four castes will be abolished... the temples will be destroyed and the schools will lie waste.'[139]

It is a dark vision but it also a thoroughly Dharmaśāstric and Brāhmaṇical explanation for the destruction of temples. Whatever Maḥmūd's motives, the understanding of temple desecration according to al-Bīrūnī's informants lay in a general decline of a Dharmic ordering of society.

3.2.2.iv Mleccha Dharma in the Kālacakratantra

The *Kālacakratantra* (*Tantra of the Wheel of Time)* and its *Vimalaprabhā* commentary was completed between 1025 and 1040 CE.[140] As Truschke notes, the *Kālacakratantra* tradition 'is perhaps the single most important pre-1190 CE Sanskrit source that talks about Islam', because it 'projected Islam as central to its own self- articulation, and numerous texts proffer extensive information about Muslim social and religious practices and Islamic theology'.[141] The *Kālacakratantra* belongs to a richly hybrid Mahāyāna Buddhist tradition that incorporates many Brāhmaṇical aspects, including Sāmkhyan metaphysics and the Purāṇic scheme of the ten Avatāras – the Buddha's ten emanations being named after the ten Avatāras of Viṣṇu.[142]

The *Kālacakratantra* tradition articulates a theory of Islam in essentially Dharmaśāstric and Purāṇic terms, even as it takes a generally negative view of Islam (and Brāhmaṇical orthodoxy) in relation to its moral endorsement of its vision of Buddhist flourishing. What the *Kālacakratantra* tradition provides, then, is a doxographic model of a competing system of Dharma – one that, despite its similarity to Buddhist Dharma, is hostile toward Indian temples. Of note, the *Kālacakratantra* was far from the only tradition to frame Islamic history in terms of the *Avatāra* system.

a Medieval Capital in Popular Imagination', *South Asian Studies* 32.1 (2006): 90–8, where it is observed that medieval authors often attributed the collapse of Kalyāṇa to Islamic forces as the result of the moral collapse of the Śaivas associated with the Kālacūri court.

139 *Al-Beruni's India*, Vol. 2, 831.

140 Truschke, *The Language of History*, 36. For a detailed study of the text, see John Newman, 'Islam in the *Kālacakratantra*', *Journal of the International Association of Buddhist Studies* 21.2 (1998): 311–72.

141 Ibid., 36.

142 Sara Cappalletti, 'The Avatāra in Medieval South Asian Contexts: Dynamic Translation Across Hindu, Buddhist and Islamic Traditions in the Ghaznavid Period', in Blain Auer and Ingo Strauch (eds), *Encountering Buddhism and Islam in Premodern Central and South Asia* (Berlin: De Grunter, 2019): 161–76, 165.

Sara Cappelletti argues persuasively, based on a close examination of numismatic and textual evidence that the Ismāʿīlī traditions in Sind and Multān, who aligned themselves with 'the Fāṭimids of North Africa and the Buyids of Iran', struck coins which presented 'the Prophet Muḥammad… as following the pantheon of Hindu deities, who are, perhaps, treated as prophets of Hinduism'.[143] Likewise, several bilingual, Sanskrit/Arabic coins struck by Maḥmūd of Ghazna, translate the *shahada*, the Islamic profession of faith (*lā ilāh illā Allāh Muḥammad rasūl Allāh* – there is none worthy of worship except Allāh: Muḥammad is the Prophet of Allāh) in a Saṅkhyan, Purāṇic vein: 'The unmanifest is one: Mahammad is the *Avatāra* (*avyaktam eka muḥammada avatāra*).'[144]

In this competitive multireligious milieu, the *avatāra* model was a shared conceptual vocabulary among Hindus, Muslims, and Buddhists. Even though they shared this vocabulary, the *Kālacakratantra* tradition presents Islam pejoratively. According to John Newman, 'the Kalacakra literature uniformly refers to Muslims as *mlecchas* – barbarians, and Islam is called the *mleccha-dharma*, the barbarian religion'.[145] The *Vimalaprabhā*, however, describes these *mlecchas* 'as *tāyin* (Arabs)', while their teacher-master is identified as 'Madhumati, the *avatāra* of *Rahmaṇa*'.[146] The full passage presents Muḥammad in unambiguously Dharmaśāstric terms: 'Muḥammad, the divine manifestation of the Islamic God, the teacher of the barbarian dharma, the guru and master of the barbarian Arabs'.[147] The *Laghukālacakratantra* describes Muḥammad as the seventh Avatāra of Allāh, who 'will clearly be born in the city of Baghdād (*vāgadā*) in the land of Makka (*makha*), where the demonic incarnation – the mighty, merciless idol of the barbarians – lives in the world.'[148]

Allāh is, in this estimation, a deity described, violently, as a deity of death, '*maradevatā*' whose image is housed in the land of *Makka* (Mecca).[149] The *Kālacakratantra* describes the Dharmas associated with this deity in terms of violence '(*hiṃsādharma*) that inspires savage behavior (*raudrakarman*)', or as demonic (*daitya/asura*).[150] The *Kālacakratantra* notes that:

> Using the mantra of the barbarian deity Bismillah, they will slit the throats of animals with cleavers. Then they will prescribe eating the flesh of those beasts killed with the mantra of their own deity, and will prohibit eating the flesh of those that die

[143] Ibid., 164.
[144] Ibid., 167–8.
[145] Newman, 'Islam', 316.
[146] Cappalletti, 'Avatāra', 165.
[147] Ibid., 166 fn. 19: **madhumatī rahmaṇāvatāro mlecchadharmadeśako mlecchānāṃ tāyināṃ** guruḥ svāmī.
[148] Ibid., 165–6 fn. 18. For the Sanskrit, see Newman, 'Islam', 43: sambhūtih saptamasya sphuṭa **makhaviṣaye vāgadādau** nagaryām yasyām loke 'surāṃśī nivasati balavān nirdayo mlecchamūrtiḥ // 1.155//
[149] Newman, 'Islam', 323 fn. 21.
[150] Truschke, *The Language of History*, 38; Newman, 'Islam', 318.

> due to their own karma. That very dharma is authoritative for you [brahman sages] because of the statement in the *smṛti*: 'Beasts are created for sacrifice' (*Manusmrti* 5.39a). With regard to killing there is no difference between the barbarian dharma and the Vedic dharma... In the barbarian dharma as well as in the Vedic dharma one must kill for the sake of the deities and the ancestors, and the same is true in the dharma of the kshatriyas. For the brahman sages say: 'Having satisfied the ancestors and the gods, there is no fault in eating flesh' (*Yājnavalkyasmṛti* 1.5.178cd).[151]

The argument draws a comparison between Dharmaśāstric and Islamic systems of ritual animal slaughter by using a shared Dharmaśāstric vocabulary. In the *Kālacakratantra*'s estimation, Islam is, at least on this point, almost identical to Brāhmaṇism.

The *Kālacakratantra* tradition's view of the messianic Kalkin draws a key distinction between Islam and Brāhmaṇical thought in relation to temples. The *Kālacakratantra* relates that at the end of the Kaliyuga, the Buddhist Kalkin will 're-establish the Buddha Dharma, and will reign over a new golden age of happiness, prosperity, and righteousness' with the aid of 'the brahmanical gods' after defeating the *mlecchas*.[152] Before this, however, 'the cavalry of the *Tayin*, engaged in war, will entirely destroy shrines (*devālaya*...) that display buddhas, *bhairavas*, men, women, and snakes' and 'sixty-eight temples of the sacred sites'.[153] This is a dark vision, certainly, but it demonstrates that, as with al-Bīrūnī's informants, the destruction of Hindu and Buddhist temples during the Ghaznavids' rule was discussed from Dharmaśāstric and Purāṇic perspectives. It would take some time – and the consolidation of Islamic rule in India for these visions of Islam to become substantially brighter.

3.2.3 The Ghūrids and their Mamluk successors

Towards the end of the 12th century, Ghaznavid power steadily declined in Central Asia. In 1040, Maḥmūd's son Mas'ud (r. 1030–40 CE) was defeated decisively by the Seljuq Turks at the Battle of Dandanaqan outside of Merv (modern Turkmenistan).[154] Mas'ud was quickly assassinated and a much-attenuated Ghaznavid polity regrouped at Lahore. The Ghaznavids' retreat created a power vacuum in which their erstwhile feudatories, the Šansabānīs of Ghur, 'a

[151] Newman, 'Islam', 334–5. For the Sanskrit see ibid., 346–7: **mlecchadevatāviṣavimlāmantreṇa** kartrikayā grīvāyāṃ paśūṃ hatvā tatas teṣām svadevatāmantreṇāhatānāṃ paśūnāṃ māṃsam bhakṣayiṣyanti svakarmaṇā mṛtānāṃ māṃsam abhakṣyaṃ kariṣyanti. so 'pi dharmo yuṣmākaṃ pramānaṃ yāgārthe pagavah sṛṣṭā iti smṛtivacanāt **mlecchadharmavedadharmayor** viṣeso nāsti prāṇātipatatah... iha **mlecchadharme vedadharme** 'pi devatāpitrarthaṁ prāṇātipataḥ kartavyaḥ **kṣatradharme** 'pi ca tarpayitvā pitṛn devān khādan māṃsam na dosabhāg iti **brahmarṣivacanāt**.

[152] Newman, 'Islam', 328–9.

[153] Ibid., 344–5.

[154] Wink, *Al-Hind, Vol. 2*, 135.

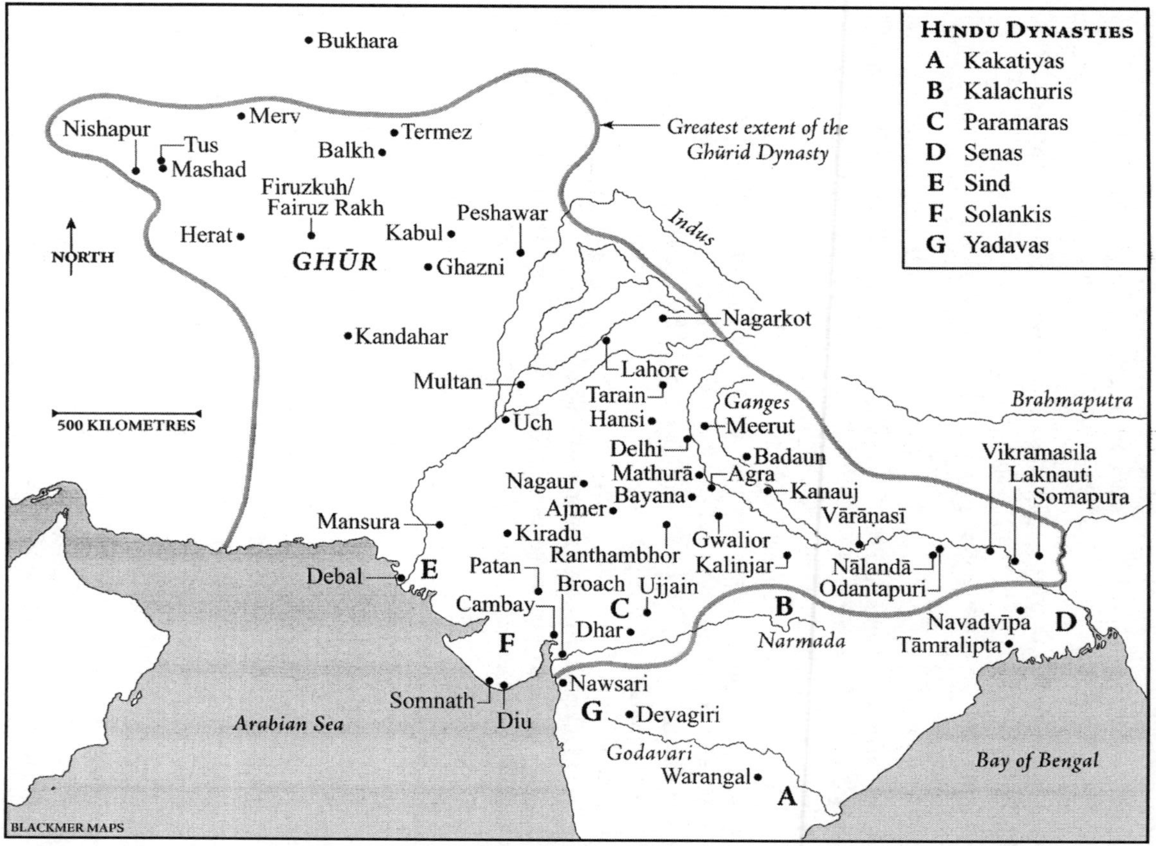

Map 3.1 The Ghūrids and their Mamluk successors (12th–13th centuries CE)

kingdom centred in the remote and rugged heart of Afghanistan's Hindu Kush Mountains', emerged from obscurity.[155] The Ghūrids, under the fraternal diarchy of Ghiyassuddin Ghori (r. 1163–1203 CE) and Mu'izz al-Dīn Muḥammad bin Sām (r. 1173–1206 CE) overran 'the Ghaznavids on their way to defeating the dominant martial lineage of northern Rajasthan, the Chauhans, thereby paving the way for the establishment of the Delhi sultanate (1206–1526 CE)'.[156]

Bursting onto the world stage in the mid-12th century, the Ghori brothers, 'assumed the use of the title *alsulṭān al-mu'aẓẓam* (the Great Sulṭān), a title also held by the Ghaznavids and Seljuqs', and divided and conquered.[157] Ghiyassuddin, reigning from 'Firuzkuh in west-central Afghanistan', went west, focusing 'on conquering and then governing the great Khurasani cities long associated with urban Persian culture: Herat, Nishapur, Tus and Merv'.[158] Muḥammad, who ruled from Ghazni, turned East, to India: between 1175 and 1191, he captured and held Multān, Peshawar, Dēbal, and Lahore. In 1191, however, Muḥammad was defeated at the Battle of Tarain (near Delhi) by Pṛthivīrāja III (r. 1177–92 CE), the Cāhamāna ruler of Ajmer.[159]

In 1192, Muḥammad won a second battle at Tarain, 'an event that paved the way for their seizure of Delhi later that same year and marked the inauguration of over five hundred years of Indo-Persian dynasties ruling over parts of northern India'.[160] Rather than returning to Ghazni, Muḥammad ventured further into northern India (plundering temples along the way) and established a new power base in Delhi, a city that would quickly become India's political centre.[161] Muḥammad's conquests were astonishing: 'Over the next ten years Muḥammad Ghuri's armies attacked and annexed political centres across the whole of north India – Meerut, Hansi, Delhi, Kol (modern Aligarh), Benares, Ajmer, Bayana, Ujjain, Badaun, Kanauj, Gwalior and Kalinjar.'[162] Ghiyath died in 1203 and, following a crushing defeat at the hands of the Khwarazmians (1077–1231 CE) at the Battle of Andkhud, Muḥammad lost almost the entirety of the Ghūrid Sulṭānate's Central Asian domains.[163]

After suppressing a rebellion by the Hindu Khokhars at the Battle of Jhelum, Muḥammad was assassinated, and his slave generals fought a bloody civil war in which Quṭb ud-Dīn Aibak (r. 1206–10 CE) ultimately prevailed.[164] Despite its

[155] Eaton, *Persianate*, 37–9.
[156] Ibid., 39.
[157] Philip Wagoner, *Objects of Translation: Material Culture and Medieval 'Hindu-Muslim' Encounter* (Princeton: Princeton University Press, 2009), 94.
[158] Eaton, *Persianate*, 39.
[159] Wink, *Al-Hind, Vol. 2*, 144–5.
[160] Truschke, *The Language of History*, 44.
[161] Ibid., 44, Wink, *Al-Hind, Vol. 2*, 146.
[162] Eaton, *Persianate*, 40.
[163] Ibid., 44.
[164] Ibid. It was, however, only under Aibak's successor, Shams ud-Dīn Iltutmish (r. 1211–36), that the supremacy of the Delhi Sulṭānate was established.

brevity, Ghūrid hegemony ushered in dramatic changes in India: the establishment of Islamic dominion over a substantial portion of the subcontinent; the erection of triumphal mosques in areas of newly established Islamic control; and the shift of the Indian political centre of gravity out of central Asia and into Delhi. Alongside these events, Sanskrit authors began to write in real time about these new, permanent Islamic rulers and what the incipient Sulṭānate meant for the Dharmaśāstric legal paradigms that their overlords supplanted.

3.2.3.i From temples into mosques

As in the days of Maḥmūd of Ghazni, 'Sunni royal rhetoric in this period was as concerned with the promotion of orthodoxy and the extirpation of heterodoxy as it was with the punishment of unbelief and polytheism.'[165] The rhetoric also coincided with the systematic plunder of indigenous religious institutions in the Indian kingdoms that were conquered by Ghūrid armies.

After defeating the Cāhamānas of Ajmer, the Ghūrids raided Jain and Hindu temples. When Muḥammad's slave general and eventual successor, Quṭb ud-Dīn Aibak captured Vārāṇasī, the chronicles record that, 'after breaking the idols in above 1000 temples, he purified and consecrated the latter to the worship of the true God'.[166] Another slave general-cum-successor, Ikhtiyār al-Dīn Muḥammad Bakhtiyār Khaljī (1150–1206 CE), who founded the Bengal Sulṭānate, conquered Awadh, Bihar and Bengal in the early 13th Century. After taking Uddandapura (modern Odantapuri), a centre of Buddhist learning, the Ghūrid historian Minhaj al-Siraj Juzjani described:

> The whole of this fortress and city as a *vihāra*, which, he explains, is 'a madrasa' or 'place of learning in the *Hindwī* language', inhabited largely by 'shaven headed brahmans', that is by Buddhist monks. These were all slain, he continues, so that when a great number of books was discovered in this monastery town 'there was no-one left who could explain their content'.[167]

Alongside this expected iconoclasm, the Ghūrids built numerous mosques, either on top of plundered religious sites, from the spoliated remnants of pre-existing structures, or *ex nihilo* in accordance with pre-conquest stylistic conventions.[168] For example, in Ajmer, 'a Jain college, built in 1153… was turned into a mosque by putting a massive screen of seven arches in front of the pillared hall which was left standing'.[169] The Ghūrids' efforts to build grand, triumphal mosques in conquered

[165] Wagoner, *Objects of Translation*, 96.
[166] Wink, *Al-Hind, Vol. 2*, 333.
[167] Ibid., 147.
[168] See, for example, Wagoner, *Objects of Translation*, 137–226.
[169] Wink, *Al-Hind, Vol. 2*, 325.

territories – and in long-held territories – was integral to their efforts to establish a permanent dominion in India. As Flood notes, 'the erection of congregational mosques in the newly conquered territories also bolstered the credentials of the Ghurid sultans as promoters of Sunni orthodoxy'.[170]

Chief among these mosques was the great Quṭb Mosque at Delhi, founded in 1191–92 by Aibak. It typifies a key difference between mosques erected before and after Ghūrid expansion: the reuse of structural components from Hindu temples.[171] Similarly, the congregational mosque at Ajmer, incorporates stone slabs containing Cāhamāna eulogies to Hindu deities that were undoubtedly plundered from pre-exiting temples.[172] Nevertheless, Wagoner's broader point – one worth keeping in mind – is that the Ghūrid mosques of post-conquest India *intentionally* adopted the stylistic features of pre-conquest architectural paradigms in order to articulate their sovereignty over these newly acquired territories.[173]

The Ghūrids forcibly plundered and spoliated Hindu and Jain religious institutions. Nevertheless, plunder and spoliation are not what made the Ghūrid dynasty epoch-changing in Indian political history. Rather, the Ghūrids transformed that plundering and conquest into a positive, constructive model for Islamic rule in India – albeit one that forcibly assimilated and supplanted the temple-based sovereignty of the Sanskrit cosmopolis. For example, as Flood notes:

> Just as closer inspection of the postconquest administrative arrangements reveals both continuities and discontinuities in the political life of northern India – the reinstatement of ruling houses and continued operation of coin mints alongside the appropriation of conquered lands and their redistribution according to the alien *iqṭā'* system – so the mosques are marked by a dialectical interplay between continuity and discontinuity, tradition and innovation.[174]

One explanation for this dialectical approach to administration is that, 'having violently annexed so much north Indian territory, Muḥammad Ghuri sought to minimize the disruption of the conquest by establishing continuities with the pre-conquest order'.[175] Muḥammad minted coins in the Cāhamāna style with Sanskrit inscriptions, retained conquered Hindu kings as subordinate rulers in his empire, and possibly gifted signet rings of power to the vassal chieftains. In our efforts to acknowledge that the advent of Sulṭānate administration in India required some incorporation of pre-conquest Indic paradigms of kingship, however, it is equally

[170] Wagoner, *Objects of Translation*, 189.
[171] For reuse, Finbarr Flood, 'Pillars, Palimpsests, and Princely Practices: Translating the Past in Sultanate India', *Res: Anthropology and Aesthetics* 43 (2003): 95–116.
[172] See EI 29.25.
[173] See, for example, Finnbar Flood, 'Refiguring Iconoclasm in the Early Indian Mosque', in Anne McClanan and Jeff Johnson (eds), *Negating the Image: Case Studies in Iconoclasm* (London: Routledge, 2016): 15–40.
[174] Wagoner, *Objects of Translation*, 152.
[175] Eaton, *Persianate*, 42.

important to stress that, from the Sanskritic perspective, these events were radically disruptive to the *status quo.*

3.2.3.ii Sanskrit perspectives on the Ghūrid conquest

Contemporary scholars might laud the Ghūrids' assimilation of Indic political conventions – of architecture, coinage, etc. – as a shift from Maḥmūd of Ghazni's blatant marauding to a genuine interest in ruling India, but, if anything, indigenous rulers and Sanskrit authors almost universally saw this as a profoundly dangerous shift that threatened the very existence of pre-Islamic, Dharmaśāstric paradigms of rulership. While the Rāṣṭrakūṭas and Gurjaras were content to see Islamic Sind as yet another polity at the edges of the Sanskrit cosmopolis and while Maḥmūd's raids could be largely ignored as an ephemeral, if vexing annoyance, the Ghūrid conquests introduced 'a culture of rulership that was markedly different from the Sanskrit-based one shared by most Indian rulers of the time' as a permanent fixture of political life in the Indian heartland.[176] It is understandable, then, that Sanskrit sources from the period articulate two consistent themes: danger and resistance.

Here, I follow Truschke's analysis of the *Pṛthivīrājavijaya* (*The Victory of King Pṛthivī*), a Sanskrit romance written by Jayanaka in the 1190s under Cāhamāna patronage to celebrate Pṛthivīrāja III. As Truschke notes: 'Jayanaka did not merely record what he saw happening around him but also synthesized and reflected upon Ghurid identity, using the conventions of Sanskrit literary discourse. In so doing, he considered how the identities of himself and his patron might be reconstituted against the backdrop of this new rival.'[177] Jayanaka offers a Sanskritic perspective on what the advent of Ghūrid hegemony meant in a traditional cultural milieux. Jayanaka does *not* write from an ideologically neutral perspective, and he asks the reader rhetorically: 'How could the likes of me, who has been honored by the king, possibly be dispassionate regarding poetry?'[178] This defect of objectivity is an ideological merit: Jayanaka's political constraint enables us to gauge the Ghūrids' impact on the Cāhamānas' polity. This means that 'Jayanaka unpacks the Ghurid threat in terms of their ritual impurity, outcaste status, and linguistic limitations, rather than focusing exclusively on military might'.[179]

Jayanaka's core criticism of the Ghūrids is their 'spoiling sacred places within Chauhan territory, and this discussion ought to be read against the backdrop of the

[176] Truschke, *The Language of History*, 44.

[177] Ibid., 46. For a comprehensive analysis of Pṛthivīrāja in Indian history – with special reference to his imbrication in contemporary identity politics, see Cynthia Talbot, *The Last Hindu Emperor: Prithviraj and the Indian Past 1200–2000* (Cambridge: Cambridge University Press, 2016).

[178] Truschke, *The Language of History*, 47.

[179] Ibid., 48–9.

Ghurid penchant for altering the built religious landscape of areas under their control.'[180] Jayanaka opens his story with the Ghūrid desecration of Puṣkara, a prominent pilgrimage site just outside of Pṛthivīrāja's capital of Ajmer. Purāṇic sources extoll the connection between Puṣkara and Brahmā, so it is unsurprising the Jayanaka recounts its sack from Brahmā's perspective.[181] In the *Pṛthivīrājavijaya*, Brahmā laments the dismal state of Puṣkara:

> Before this place was full of sacrifices to me.
> Where once there were three pits full of fire,
> with the passage of time,
> those very pits are full of water...
> my homeland, Pushkar, has been overrun by the terror of the
> Ghurids [*mātaṅga*]
> as if being trampled by elephants.[182]

According to Brahmā, the Ghūrids' desecration of Puṣkara is part of a broader assault on the Brāhmaṇcal ritual order and he bemoans the, 'violent assaults on temples and Brahmin lands'.[183]

The Ghūrid threat is couched in terms of disrupting a Dharmaśāstric ordering of society, where divine and Brāhmaṇical endowments are endangered:

> Pushkar's shores used to be warmed by fire from Shiva's third eye
>
> when the eleven Rudras bowed low to bathe in the waters.
>
> Now those shores are warmed by the tears of Brahmins
>
> imprisoned by the Ghurids.[184]

Jayanaka's Brahmā relates that, moreover, the deities who dwell at Puṣkara are themselves at risk. As with al-Bīrūnī's Brāhmaṇa informants, the cause of this pollution is *not* the Ghūrids themselves or their personal religious commitments, but the decline of Dharma due to advent of the Kaliyuga.[185]

Brahmā convinces Viṣṇu to incarnate as Pṛthivīrāja for the purpose of cleansing Puṣkara and protecting the Brāhmaṇas and deities who dwell there from the abuses of the Ghūrids.[186] In Jayanaka's view, Pṛthivīrāja/Viṣṇu's mandate is the Dharmaśāstric duty of the sovereign to act as the protector of religious institutions.

[180] Ibid., 49.
[181] Ibid., 50. See *Padmapurāṇa*, translated by N.A. Deshpande (Delhi: Motilal Banarsidass, 1988–92), Chapter 15, Section 1, Verse 20.
[182] Truschke, *The Language of History*, 50–1.
[183] Ibid., 51.
[184] Ibid., 226.
[185] Ibid., 225: 'In this Age of Darkness, when Brahmins have ceased to perform sacrifices and sacrificial offerings are not received, Indra finds his strength sapped.' The same pattern follows the other deities who are unable to vanquish the Ghūrids.
[186] Ibid., 52–3.

The Ghūrid destabilisation of the Dharmaśāstric system of Equity and Trusts is the genesis of the divine mandate. As Truschke notes:

> Jayanaka rejoices that the newborn Prithviraj is a 'man with a cause' (*kāraṇamānuṣa*), and the commentator Jonaraja clarifies that this cause is 'killing the Ghurids' (*mlecchavadhena*). In the same scene of Prithviraj's birth, Jayanaka highlights the future king's role in restoring sacrifice to the earth (*dharmakarmakriyāvighnahare*), an act that will prompt sacrificers (*yajamānas*) to rejoice.[187]

Pṛthivīrāja's mission is to maintain a Dharmaśāstric order of society. His opponents and Jayanaka give 'no indication that he saw the Ghurids, primarily, in terms of their religious tradition.'[188] Instead, the Ghūrids were viewed primarily in terms of their threat to a sacred landscape, to caste institutions, to linguistic hierarchies, and to religious trusts. All of these features were, of course, central to the Sanskrit cosmopolis that I discussed in the previous chapter. Indeed, according to Truschke 'the crucial distinction was between Kshatriya kings who upheld the specific requirements of Brahminical ritual purity versus polluted outcastes who undercut them.'[189]

If Jayanaka provides a narrative poetic vision of the disruption of Sanskrit cosmopolitan kingship in the wake of the Ghūrid invasions, an inscription from Etawah fort outside of Kānyakubja, dated to around 1194, attests to its effects on the practical administration of Hindu trusts.[190] In 1194, Jayacandra (r. 1170–1194 CE), the Gāhaḍavāla king of, *inter alia*, Vārāṇasī, fell to a Ghūrid army at the Battle of Chandawar.[191] Kānyakubja and Vārāṇasī were plundered, and, in the ensuing iconoclastic chaos, it appears that the priests of Etawah, in conjunction with Jayacandra's brother Harīścandra (r. 1194–7 CE), attempted to protect an image of the goddess, Durgā. The inscription reads:

> Homage to the Goddess. In honour of the images of Caṇḍikā, Durgā, and Śiva (in the city) installed by the wise Mahārāja Ajayasiṃha who performed the sacrifice after his father's brother Jayacandra of Kannauj. Today, I, his *ācārya* (religious preceptor) as well as his priest, performed the Mahāyoga of Caṇḍikā. The statue of Durgā was previously installed on the boundary, or outer wall of the fort. My rationality has been destroyed out of fear of the *mlecchas*. With great sorrow, touching her with my head, I place this Durgā, the dweller of the fort and destroyer of bad luck, into this pit until Skanda turns their (the Yavanas') glory to dust. When ill fate meets the Yavanas, she might re-appear or manifest herself again amidst uproar. Until that

[187] Ibid., 52–3.
[188] Ibid., 57.
[189] Ibid., 58.
[190] See Pushpa Prasad, *Inscriptions of the Delhi Sultanate 1191–1526* (Delhi: Oxford University Press, 1990), 2.18.
[191] For his portrayal in the Braj-language *Pṛthvīrāja Rāso*, see Talbot, *Last Hindu Emperor*, 13–21.

time I am a fool like a drunkard. Let not fear enter you: the gods will quickly return along with you.[192]

In short, the initial Sanskritic response to the Ghūrid incursions and the establishment of Sulṭānate rule in India was to paint a bleak, eschatological picture in which the advent of the Kaliyuga has led to a collapse of the Dharmic ordering of society. The agents in this story were neither 'Hindus' nor 'Muslims'. Instead, the theo-political narrative was one in which the decline of sovereigns' capacity to uphold the established, Dharmaśāstric moral-political order of the Sanskrit cosmopolis enabled foreign, *mleccha* forces to ransack India. These foreign barbarians acted, to no small extent, as destructive agents of the broader, but equally Sanskritic cosmological force of decline that characterises the Kali Yuga. The decline of Dharma ensured that sovereigns could no longer perform their duties as *parens patriae* – to protect deities, Brāhmaṇas, women, children, and the dispossessed. Without a strong *parens patriae*, there is no enforcement of Dharmaśāstric principles of Equity and, inevitably, religious endowments will be despoiled by internal and external forces. The advent of Islamic hegemony in India from the Sanskritic perspective was, therefore, a decline of Dharmaśātric jurisprudential principles of Equity and Trusts.

Without this protection it is understandable, from the perspective of these Sanskrit authors, that barbarian forces would then extirpate the existing theo-political order. Nevertheless, every Sanskrit source from the epoch of the Ghaznavids and the Ghūrids holds out hope for a better future – proximate or distant – in which a revival of Dharma will enable Dharmaśāstric kings to once again uphold their duties and protect their subjects. We shall see in the next section that, within two centuries, Hindu rulers articulated a positive political theology of the king as trustee of a sovereign deity – and a practical administrative system that Sanskritised Sulṭānate feudal systems. Effectively, Dharmaśāstric *jurisprudential* principles of Equity and Trusts adapted to the new, hegemonic Persianate *legal* system.

[192] Prasad, *Inscriptions*, 2.18: namau **devyai.** pratiṣṭhā pratimānāṃ ca **caṅḍikā purāre durgādhi** mahārā(ja) **ā(ja)ya siṃhena** dhīmatā **kannojasy[ā]jjayacandrasya** pitṛvyasyānvavāyajaḥ. divasam ati (tasya) dhasvāham ācāryas tatpurohitaḥ. mayā saṃpāditaḥ (i) **caṅḍī** mahāyogasta ki vā **durga** sīmā sthale durga sthāpanaṃ cāmavatapurā. kiṃ cāham eva **mlecchānaṃ** [bh]ayena vastimajaya (naṣṭa mānasaḥ)… jātinā… sma bubadaṅḍī…. bhā(nu) drutadayati **sakāndena** tasye tasye vāsi tehāni (śī) sanā cāpi visarjanaṃ karomi. duraga sthitāṃ **durgāṃ** durgatināsinī ca tamayā prakṣipya garte hantā. **yavanānāṃ** yadāyenā bhaviṣyati viniḥsṛtiḥ prādurbhāva svyaṃ tāvac **caṅḍikāyā** bhaviṣyati. garjana jarghanaṃ mūḍha **madhuyāvatpibāmy aham**. mayā tadīya sa te 'yaiva garjaṣyantyāṣu devatā(ḥ).

3.3 Sultāṇates, Muslim and Hindu

The establishment of the Delhi Sulṭānate in 1206 dramatically reconfigured the balance of power in the Indian subcontinent. Indo-Islamic rule became permanent and vastly more organised than the sporadic raids of the Ghaznavid and Ghūrid eras. The Delhi Sulṭānates, their subordinates and their successors introduced new cultures, new linguistic paradigms, new military technologies, and new administrative systems to India. This involved the imposition of rule by force on many Hindu sovereigns who adhered to the older Dharmaśāstric paradigm of decentralised rule, and it also involved the destruction of many temples and their conversion into mosques.

Additionally, the permanence and efficiency of Indo-Islamic rule under the sulṭānate prompted a dramatic reconfiguration of Hindu modes of rule and the Sanskrit jurisprudence of Equity and Trusts. On the one hand, many rulers, especially the emperors of Vijayanagara, embraced Persianate political culture, recruiting Muslim mercenaries, adopting pen-and-paper chancery practices, instituting Sanskritised analogues to Islamic feudal tenure, and engaging actively in political jockeying within the wider Islamic world.

All of this proved highly effective and culturally unproblematic. On the other hand, the Hindu polities embraced a new version of temple trusts in which tutelary deities became the legal owner of the kingdom and rulers acted as trustees to these deities. The centralisation of political power also centralised trust management, and we find a new, unprecedented level of state involvement in the administration of temple and monastic trusts – even as Hindu political theology became vested in narratives of protecting (or restoring) deities from Islamic deprivations.

3.3.1 Delhi and the expansion of the sulṭānate system

While scholars typically date the foundation of the Delhi Sulṭānate to 1206, when Quṭb ud-Dīn Aibak (r. 1206–10 CE), Muḥammad Ghūri's slave general, was crowned in Lahore, Delhi did not become the capital of the sulṭānate until 1214.[193] Before that, several former Ghūrid slave generals carved out regional power centres and fought for the supremacy of Hindustān. In 1205–06, Muḥammad of Ghūri's nephew, Ghiyāth ad-Dīn Mahmūd, 'became the Ghurid suzerain at Firuzkuh' where he appointed three of Muḥammad's slave generals – Aibak, Taj al-Din Yildiz, and Nasir-ud-Dīn Qabacha – to the thrones of Lahore, Ghazna, and Multān, respectively.[194] Additionally in 1204, Khtiyār al-Dan

[193] Wink, *Al-Hind, Vol. 2*, 150.
[194] Ibid.

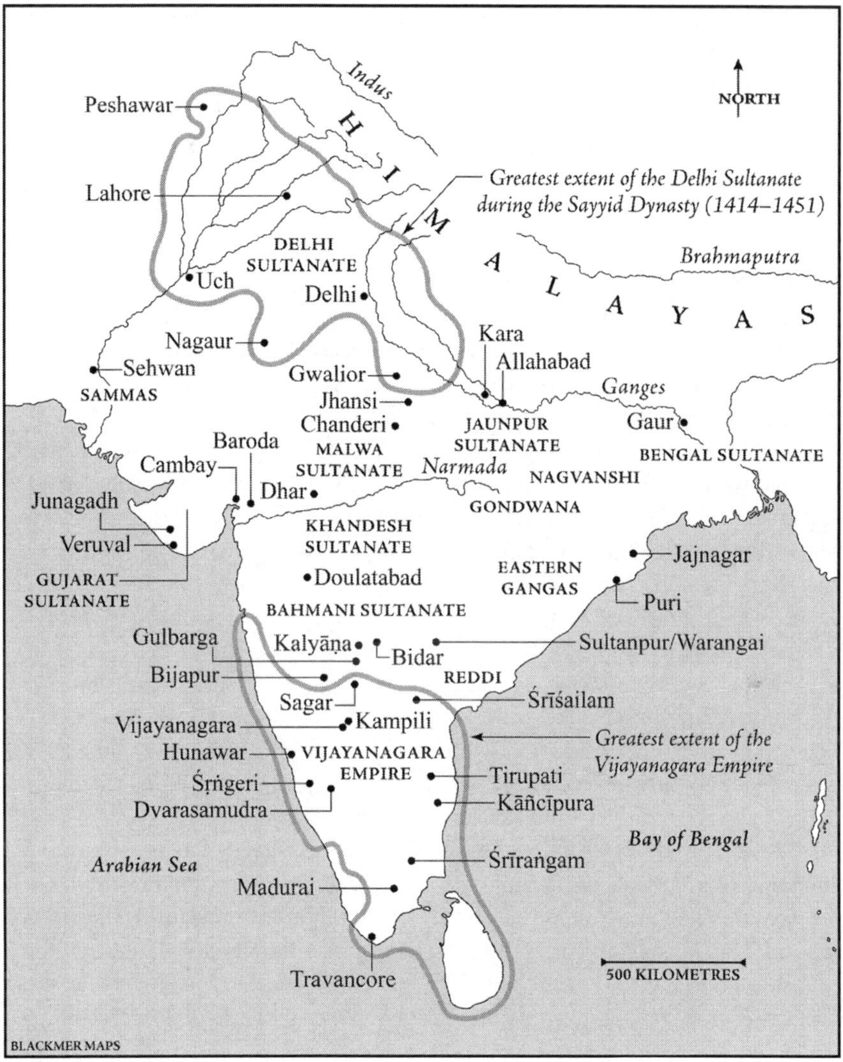

Map 3.2 The Delhi Sulṭānate and the Hindu sulṭāns (India, c. 1450)

Muḥammad Bakhtiyār Khaljī (r. 1203–06 CE) defeated the Sena Dynasty and carved out a semi-independent emirate in Bengal.[195] Aibak died in 1211, followed by Giyāth in 1212, and Shams ud-Dīn Iltutmish (r. 1211–36 CE), Aibak's slave and successor, ultimately won the 'contest for primacy' among the various

[195] Eaton, *Persianate*, 76.
[196] Wink, *Al-Hind, Vol. 2*, 152.

sulṭāns.[196] Iltutmish shifted his capital to Delhi in 1214, and it has remained the political centre of India ever since.

Over the following centuries, the dynasties of the Delhi Sulṭānate conquered – and lost – virtually the entirety of the Indian subcontinent, including Bengal, the Deccan, Gujarat, and southern India, until its supplanting by the Mughal emperor, Babur in 1528. The sulṭānate reached its zenith during the reign of Muḥammad bin Tughluq (r. 1325–51 CE), before different regional subordinates rebelled and claimed independent sulṭānate status: Bengal (1332); Madhura/Ma'bar (1335); Deccan/Bahmani (1347); and Gujarat (1407). In effect, the Delhi Sulṭānate and its regional successors introduced the political and cultural conventions of the Persian cosmopolis to the whole of India, forever changing the constitutional structure of the subcontinent. Virtually every subsequent ruler – Hindu or Muslim – adopted sulṭānate political structures even if they Sanskritised them.

The introduction of the sulṭānate system to India's disparate regions went hand-in-glove with the widespread destruction of pre-existing religious institutions, the construction of Islamic religious and charitable institutions on their ruins, and the settling of administrative colonies of Muslims within these conquered territories. Temples were dismantled and/or re-created as mosques, and their endowed assets were appropriated and rededicated as *waqfs* for the support of mosques. Richard Eaton's record of thirty-seven instances of Hindu temple destruction during the sulṭānate is probably not comprehensive.[197] In his 1328 *Mirabilia Descripta*, the French Dominican missionary Jourdain Catalani de Séverac (1280–1330 CE) notes that: 'The Turkish Saracens, who came forth from Multan, and conquered... destroyed an infinity of idol temples... of which they made mosques for Mahomet, taking possession of their endowments and property.'[198]

These acts of destruction, appropriation, and re-endowment advanced sulṭānate rule in two key ways: 1) they extirpated the pre-sulṭānate temples and monasteries that subtended the political sovereignty of the Sanskrit cosmopolis; and 2) they enacted a new, Islamic paradigm of Equity and Trusts in which mosques and madrassas supplanted temples (and deities) as the nexus of trust properties that were employed for charitable purposes.[199] Take, for example, the

[197] See Eaton's chart in 'Temple Desecration', 316–18.

[198] See Meera Juncu, *India in the Italian Renaissance: Visions of a Contemporary Pagan World 1300* (London: Routledge, 2015), 85.

[199] For sulṭānate *waqfs*, see Gregory Kozlowski, 'The Changing Political and Social Contexts of Muslim Endowments (*waqfs*)', in R. Deguilhem (ed.), *Le waqfdans l'espace islamique, Outil depouvoir socio-économique* (Damascus: Institut Français d'Etudes Arabes de Damas 1995): 355–70. Also see Surinder Singh, 'Dynamics of Statecraft in the Delhi Sultanate: A Reconstruction from the Letters of Ainul Mulk Mahru', *Proceedings of the Indian History Congress* 61.1 (2000–1): 285–93. For sulṭānate *waqfs* in Bengal, see Mohammad Siddiq, *Epigraphy and Islamic Culture: Inscriptions of the Early Muslim Rulers of Bengal (1205–1494)* (London: Routledge, 2015).

chronicler Minhaj al-Siraj's account of Muḥammad Bakhtiyār's 1204 capture of Bengal:

> he left the city of Nudiah in desolation, and the place which is (now) Lakhnauti he made the seat of government. He brought the different parts of the territory under his sway, and instituted therein, in every part, the reading of the khutbah, and the coining of money; and, through his praiseworthy endeavours, and those of his Amirs, masjids [mosques], colleges, and monasteries (for Dervishes), were founded in those parts.[200]

The story is confirmed in the 13th-century chronicle *Siyar al-ʿārifīn*, which records that when the Sūfi Jalal al-Din Tabrizi arrived in Bengal in 1235:

> There he built a hospice and a public kitchen, and bought several gardens and lands as an endowment for the kitchen. These increased. There was also... a (river) port called Deva Mahal, where an infidel had built a temple at great cost. The shaikh destroyed that temple and in its place constructed a (Sufi) rest-house [*takya*]... his holy tomb is located at the very site of that temple, and half the income of that port is dedicated to the upkeep of the public kitchen there.[201]

This pattern of destroying temples, converting their building materials into mosques, and re-allocating divine trust property into Islamic charitable trust property was as important in the establishment of sulṭānate hegemony as the defeat of rival armies. An excellent, well-documented example of this paradigm is the Deccan, where 'in the early fourteenth century, each of the great successor states to the Chalukyas – the Yadavas, Kakatiyas, and Hoysalas – was in turn violently overthrown by armies of the Delhi Sultanate'.[202] In the early 14th century, much of the Deccan was ruled by the Kākatīya Dynasty, whose capital, Warangal, housed a grand imperial temple of the tutelary deity Śvayambhūśiva. Sulṭānate incursions, beginning with Malik Kāfūr's 1309 raid, targeted temples associated with Kākatīya hegemony. An inscription from 1357 at Pillalamarri records the repair and re-consecration of a temple that had been damaged 'during the troubles (*viḍvarālu*) of that time and place'.[203]

In 1318, Sultan Quṭb ud-Dīn Mubarak (r. 1316–20 CE), captured Devagiri (modern Doulatabad) from the last Yādava Dynasty and built a grand Friday mosque from the spoliated ruins of local Hindu and Jain temples.[204] As Eaton and

[200] Richard Eaton, *The Rise of Islam and the Bengal Frontier, 1204–1760* (Berkeley: University of California Press, 1993), 32–3. For a study of *waqfs* in Bengal, see Salim Zaweed, 'The Waqf Estates of Pāṇḍūa: Historical Analysis (from Fifteenth to Twentieth Centuries)', *Indian Historical Review* 48.2 (2021): 273–91.

[201] Eaton, *Rise of Islam*, 73.

[202] Eaton and Wagoner, *Power, Memory*, 18.

[203] Ibid., 42.

[204] Ibid., 43–4. For sulṭānate patronage of Islamic institutions in Bijapur, see Richard Eaton, *The Sufis of Bijapur, 1300–1700: Social Roles of Sufis in Medieval India* (Princeton: Princeton University Press, 1972).

Wagoner note, 'the new mosque simultaneously liquidated and absorbed most if not all the religious monuments that had theretofore defined the city... [and] Devagiri's great Khalaji mosque nearly precisely replicated the metropolitan style of mosques that had been patronized by earlier Delhi sultans in Ajmer, Kaman, Khatu, and in Delhi's Quṭb complex itself'.[205]

In Bijapur, however, when the sulṭānate's agents built a mosque using components from despoiled Yādava-era temples in 1320, they 'appear to have deliberately identified points of commensurability between mosque and temple, between Islam and Hinduism, and ultimately, between the newly arrived Persian cultural order and the older, established Indic cultural order'.[206]

In 1321, Ghiyath al-Din Tughluq (r. 1320–05 CE) dispatched his son – and eventual successor – 'Ulugh Khan, to Warangal, with a view to destroying the Kākatiya dynasty and annexing its territory'.[207] During his three-year campaign, Ulugh followed the familiar pattern of plundering and transforming the temples of rivals into mosques, expropriating their endowments, and transferring them to Islamic charities. For example, Bodhan's hundred-pillared temple became the Deval Masjid.[208] At Warangal, which fell in 1323, Khan transformed the imperial Kākatīyas' Svayambhūśiva temple – the object of considerable trust endowments – into a mosque as well.[209] The 14th-century Vilāsa grant of Prolayanayaka (a minor Deccan chief) records that, after the fall of Warangal, 'all the deities images were destroyed and all the agrahāras were confiscated'.[210] Tughluq followed the same pattern of iconoclastic plundering at Kalyāṇa in the same year and at Rajahmundry in 1324.[211]

Eaton and Wagoner argue for a scholarly analytic beyond the binary of whether 'a given structure was destroyed or it was not' and towards an appreciation of the variety of ways in which temples were re-assembled into mosques instead.[212] Architectural re-assembly – in concert with the establishment of Persianate, sulṭānate political hegemony – also occurred alongside *financial* shifts away from pre-existing systems of religious trusts. These trusts, that had supported temples, Sanskritic pedagogical practices (and charities) were re-allocated to Islamic religious institutions and charities.

This flow of funds was unidirectional – from Sanskritic institutions to Islamic institutions. Eaton and Wagoner's sole, ostensible example of a sulṭānate grant to a non-Islamic religious institution – a 1326 Cālukyan-style inscription from

[205] Eaton and Wagoner, *Power, Memory*, 44.
[206] Ibid., 46.
[207] Ibid., 48–9.
[208] Ibid., 49–51.
[209] Ibid., 52–6.
[210] EI 32.30: bhagnāś ca devapratimās samastāḥ... sarve 'py apāhāriṣat agrahārāḥ.
[211] Eaton and Wagoner, *Power, Memory*, 58–9.
[212] Ibid., 68–9.

Kalyāṇa – was probably made by a Hindu subordinate in the area with the mere sanction (perhaps only implicit) of Delhi.[213] The focus on the architectural reuse or toleration of temples belies the financial and legal implications of sulṭānate conquest. Take, for example, the dedicatory inscription of the Tribeni (a major site of Hindu pilgrimage) mosque, built or restored in 1298 by Alā' al-Dīn Khaljī's (r. 1296–1316 CE) general Zafar Khan. It declares that: 'Zafar Khan… by conquering the towns of India in every expedition, and by restoring the decayed charitable institutions… has destroyed the obdurate among infidels with his sword and spear, and lavished the treasures of his wealth in (helping) the miserable.'[214]

3.3.1.i Sanskrit inscriptions under the sulṭānate

The scholarly consensus is that Hindus, Jains, and Buddhists living under Sulṭānate rule were free to follow their religion and customs provided that they pay the *jizya* tax. In a letter to the emperor of China, who had requested authorisation to build a temple in sulṭānate India, Muḥammad bin Tughluq replied that 'permission to build a temple (*kanīsa*) in a Muslim country can be accorded only to those who pay the *jizya* [poll-tax]. If you agree to pay it, permission for building the temple can be given.'[215] To my knowledge, there is no evidence of the sulṭānate Crown ever directly financing Hindu religious institutions, nor – one notable exception notwithstanding – any evidence of Hindus endowing temples under the aegis of the sulṭānate Crown. At best, the Delhi Sulṭānate pursued legal *toleration* of temples without actively participating in their financial regulation. The sulṭāns did, of course plunder the temples and religious institutions that were maintained by underlings who had rebelled. In this sense, Sanskritic trusts existed in a legal realm of Equity outside of state purview – but always subject to arbitrary peculation.

The corpus of Sanskrit inscriptions composed within the Delhi Sulṭānate reveals a marked denudation of Sanskrit cosmopolitan paradigms. These inscriptions were *private* in the sense that, while acknowledging the political reality of the sulṭānate suzerainty using a prototypically Sanskrit royal panegyric idiom, they never involve the legal apparatuses of the state. This contrasts sharply with the treatment of Islamic religious institutions in contemporaneous inscriptions from Hindu polities – particularly those in Gujarat.

Take, for example, three well inscriptions dated to 1276, 1316, and 1327. All three wells were dug and dedicated near Delhi, and they all include a history of the ruling dynasty. In the first inscription, 'a Hindu landholder, Thakur Udadhara' constructed a well 'to benefit local villagers and to accumulate religious merit

[213] Ibid., 57–61; EI 32.19 & 33.11.

[214] Eaton, *Rise of Islam*, 37–8

[215] Eaton and Wagoner, *Power, Memory*, 60–1.

for himself'. He hired a 'Brahmin author, Pandit Yogishvara' to craft an elaborate Sanskrit inscription.[216] This inscription neatly slots Indo-Islamic rulers into its political genealogy:

> Salutation to Ganapati. Om. Salutation to Śiva ...The land of Hariyanaka [upper India] was first enjoyed by the Tomaras and then by the Cauhanas. It is now ruled by the Shaka ['Scythian', or Central Asian] kings. First came Shahabadina [Shihab al-Din (i.e. Muḥammad) Ghuri], then Khudavadina [Quṭb ud-Dīn Aibak], master of the earth... In his [Sulṭān Balban's] kingdom, abounding in benign rule, extending from Gauda [Bengal] to Gajjana [Ghazni], from the Dravida region [south India] and from the Setubandha [to the north] where the entire region was filled with inner content.[217]

This is a pretty standard political history, but the inscription makes no legal intervention. It does not lay down any rules and regulations regarding the use of the well. The same holds true with the 1316 dedication, which contains almost the exact same political genealogy, but adds Alāvadīna (Alā-ud-dīn Khiljī) as the current ruler of Ḍhillī (Delhi).[218] The donor, Sādhāraṇa, had a well created using 'funds acquired by his own arms' and quotes a Purāṇic verse extolling the dedication of, *inter alia*, wells.[219] As with the previous inscription, 'the state took no part in authorizing or financing the well' and 'it was presumably not intended to be read by government officials'.[220]

The last well inscription, adds 'Śrīmahaṃmadaśāhi' (Muḥammad-bin-Tughlaq) to its royal genealogy, but otherwise follows the pattern of incorporating the sulṭānate rulers in its view of history without making any legal intervention.[221] However, the donors, a pair of brothers, twice note that their ancestors had 'minds ever bent on propitiating gods and Brāhmaṇas' (*devadvijārādhananiṣṭhacittaḥ*), and we might infer that the worship of Hindus deities was a practicable activity during the sulṭānate.[222] While the genealogical element of this inscription seems to be in accordance with earlier inscriptions from the Sanskrit cosmopolis, it is entirely denuded of legal force. One imagines that 'Śrīmahaṃmadaśāhi' was added to the inscription's royal genealogy as a matter of formulaic necessity rather than as an attempt to signal the specific royal guarantor of the safety of the dedication.

A copper-plate dating to 1227 (during the reign of Iltutmish) typifies the circumscribed use of Sanskrit jurisprudential inscriptions during the sulṭānate.[223] This

[216] Prasad, *Inscriptions*, #1.2. Eaton, *Persianate*, 54–6.
[217] Translated in Eaton, *Persianate* 55–6.
[218] EI 12.5.
[219] Ibid., sādhāraṇena... vāpī... kāritā... svabhujopārjjitadrav[y]air...vāpīkūpatāḍāgaughdevaṣa[tā] dikārakāḥ / i[ha] bhuktvā bahūn bhogān indravaddivi modate // In line 31 this act is described as a consecration: vāpīpratiṣṭhā.
[220] Eaton, *Persianate*, 54.
[221] EI 1.14.
[222] Ibid.
[223] Prasad, *Inscriptions*, #2.11.

copper-plate records a series of mortgages made by local cultivators using the reign of the sulṭān for the purposes of dating the transactions.[224] The document lists only the name of the current ruler – for dating purposes – and supplies no other genealogical information. The document was clearly intended to be read as a financial ledger for the parties involved – and not by the central or local government. The broader point is that, while Sanskrit documentary practices readily incorporated the political reality of the Delhi Sulṭānate, the sulṭāns themselves appear to have played no role in the actual execution or enforcement of these documents. Three Jain inscriptions from near Delhi also incorporate the sulṭāns in their political genealogies, but, once again, they do not involve the active participation of the State. Rather, the ruling house is used for the purposes of fixing the date of the dedication.[225]

The famous 1236 Kalyāṇa inscription from the reign of Muḥammad Tughluq typifies the interpretive danger of mistaking the *toleration* of Hindu religious trusts with the active *patronage* of temple institutions. This inscription records the re-consecration (*punar pratiṣṭhā*) of a *liṅga* of Madhukeśvara whose worship had been interrupted during Bahāuddīn Gurshāsp's rebellion against the sulṭān.[226] Eaton and Wagoner, reading P.B. Desai's philologically defective edition of the inscription, arrive at the conclusion that the sulṭān: 'Directly intervened to restore a temple to regular worship by overseeing physical repairs to it.... [thereby] underwriting the entire social order in which the temple's institutional structure – its devotees, trustees, and manager – had traditionally functioned.'[227] Eaton and Wagoner claim that, because 'we do not hear of any chieftain whose authority or legitimacy might have depended on the temple's well-being', the 'governing authorities acted in such a manner that the sultan himself, having assumed proprietary rights over the institution, adopted the role of the temple's *de facto* if not *de jure* patron'.[228]

This inscription is commonly cited as the *sole* example in support of the claim that the Delhi sulṭāns actively patronised Hindu temples. Unfortunately, neither of Eaton and Wagoner's core claims are supported by a careful reading of Dineschandra Sircar's more polished edition of the inscription.[229] In truth, the re-consecration of the *liṅga* appears to have been funded by a local Hindu subordinate of the sulṭān, named Vaijāditya, who was *authorised* to do so by the sulṭān's local administrator. The sulṭān's administrators made the decision to authorise the resumption of Madhukeśvara's cult on the basis of Dharmaśāstric theories of Equity. That is significant even if it does not amount to formal state patronage.

[224] The financial terms are highly technical and the document is described as a 'guḍāṁtapatra'.

[225] The three Jain inscriptions are not available to me, nor were they available to Prasad, who records them as #'s 2.78,84, & 85 in *Inscriptions*.

[226] See Eaton and Wagoner, *Power, Memory*, 59 fn. 48, for an account of the rebellion.

[227] Ibid., 66. Desai's edition is EI 32.19.

[228] Eaton and Wagoner, *Power, Memory*, 66.

[229] EI 33.11.

In my estimation, the Kalyāṇa inscription demonstrates that the sulṭānate could intervene to *allow* Hindu subordinates to create religious trusts in the face of local – probably Muslim – opposition to preserve alliances with local Hindu chieftains.

Much of the interpretive issue is that, as Sircar notes, the text is 'very difficult to decipher and interpret' on account of many typographical and grammatical errors.[230] Nevertheless, Sircar provides a very nicely emendated text that tells a coherent and relatively succinct story. The inscription, like many Sanskrit inscriptions from the sulṭānate period, opens with a description of the ruling government that assimilates the Persian administrative system into a Sanskrit idiom:

> In the reign of Śrī Sulṭān Muḥammad, the resplendent ornament of the entire garland of royal lineage, when Mallika Kāmadīna (i.e., Malīk Qivāmuddīn Qutlugh Khān), the Viceroy (*Mahāpradhāna*) of the Mahārāṣṭra, whose whole task was dependent on his (the Sulṭān's) lotus feet, was carrying out all of the activities of the seal (of state), Khoja Ahamada (i.e., Khwāja Aḥmad), Jadaṁḍamalaṁtara (being his surname or title) was, at that time, appointed by him (Kāmadīna) to be the tax collector (Syāramallika/Sāīr Malīk) of Kalyāṇa.[231]

Next, the inscription states the issue presented before Aḥmad: 'During the rebellion of Bāhavadīnnu (i.e., Bahāuddīn), worship in the presence of Madhukeśvara was blocked by the people of Karṇāṭaka. (They) debated: "Should the deity be purified (for re-installation) there? Certainly not." '[232] Presumably, Bahāuddīn's rebellion caused some disruption in Madhukeśvara's worship, but we do not know the reason, beyond the statement that the people of Karṇāṭaka blocked it. Did Bahāuddīn disrupt the temple or its endowment himself? Did the local Muslim community (Sircar states that this is what he believes) attempt to stop local image worship?[233] Did the local Hindus fear that such worship would incur Bahāuddīn or Delhi's wrath? We simply don't know, but these are all possibilities.

What we do know, however, is how the local government reacted. A man of rank – probably the deity's fiduciary – named Māla, the son of Saṭṭhakkuranainapāla, 'appeared before Khoja and made an effort in regard to the re-installation and worship of the deity in his own place [i.e., his former temple]'.[234] Perhaps the population had, as in many instances of potential desecration, removed the image of their deity from his temple in an effort to protect him from iconoclastic forces and now

[230] Ibid., 71.

[231] Ibid: ady eha samastarājāvalīmālālaṃkṛtavirājitamahārājādhirāja**śrīsuratāṇamahamada**rājye tatpādapadmopajīvitasarvabhāranirūpitamahāpradhāna**mallikakāmadīne mahārāṣṭramaṇḍale** samastamudrāvyāpārān paripaṁthayati. ity evaṁkāle varttamāne **kalyāṇapure** tannirūpita**khojāham ajadaṁḍamalaṁtare** syāramallikatvaṁ gate.

[232] Ibid: **bāhavadīnnu**viparyaye **madhukeśvaradeva**sāṃnidhye kārṇāṭalokaiḥ aṁjanaṃ baddhīkṛtaṃ. jalpanti devaḥ śodhanīyaḥ tatra kim na hi.

[233] Ibid., 71.

[234] Ibid: tatra tasmin nijasthāne punar api devasthāpanapūjanaviṣaye **saṭṭhakkuranainapālasutaṭhāk uramālena khoja**samakṣam udyāsaḥ kṛtaḥ.

sought *permission* to return him. No effort for state funding or for an intervention from Delhi is recorded – merely the desire for Khoja to permit a local action.

Khoja grants Māla's request on the basis of Dharmaśāstric Equity: 'This is your congenital law (*kuladharma*) and it should be followed.'[235] In Sircar's estimation, 'the controversy was really between the local Hindus and Musalmans… and Khoja was on the side of justice and fairplay in giving this permission against the feeling of the local Musalmans'.[236] This may be the case, but it may not be. In the absence of more data, we can say, at the very least, that the inscription suggests that Khoja viewed Madhukeśvara's cult as a congenital custom or legal convention of the local Hindu community. That is significant, because it demonstrates that a Muslim administrator accepted the core theory of Equity underlying Hindu religious trusts: the capacity for communities to create legal covenants among themselves with the permission of the State.[237]

Khoja played a relatively modest role in the sulṭānate's administration, and there is no indication that he consulted Delhi's opinion on the matter. By all accounts, the inscription, like the other Sanskrit inscriptions from the period, was written for a local audience. The closing fragments of the inscription, overlooked by Eaton and Wagoner, give credence to this view. This fragmentary section 'speaks of a *śāsana* or grant (probably of land) which was made in favour of Madhukeśvara by a person named Vaijāditya and states that this grant was honoured by certain rulers including one Usyarasiṁha who was probably a local chief'.[238] If so, then this document's legal purport was *not* to record the singular occurrence of a Delhi sulṭān – one famed for iconoclasm in Warangal – actively patronising a Hindu temple. Rather, the purport of the document was to record a donation of land by a local Hindu subordinate of Delhi to support a deity's newly restored cult, with the *permission* of the local tax-collector after a period of political instability.

The early Delhi sulṭāns appear to have tolerated – but not actively supported – Hindu and Jain religious institutions in some cases and plundered them in others. Whatever be the justice of that political climate, authors of Sanskrit inscriptions appear to have had no significant trouble in incorporating the sulṭānate into their genealogies of the contemporaneous government. Nevertheless, with the exception of the Kalyāṇa inscription above, the legal functions of Sanskrit inscriptions were highly circumscribed.

[235] Ibid: **khojena** prasādaḥ dattaḥ. yuṣmākaṃ kuladharmo varttate. tatkaraṇīyam ca.

[236] Ibid., 73.

[237] See Chapter 1, §1.5, 'Equity as supplemental law'.

[238] Ibid., 74: **śrīma[du]syarasi[ṁ]hādyarājapūjitadaiva[tam]. vaijādityasya** likhita[ṁ] śāsanaṁ **mādhukeśvara[m].** Sircar argues, fn. 6, that 'the intended word for *likhita* may be *vihita*'.

3.3.1.ii The Veraval counterfactual

In 1264, Nuruddin Firuz, a trader from Hormuz, constructed and endowed a mosque at Veraval, near the great Somanātha temple on the Gujarati coast, with the support of the Vaghela Dynasty. The Vaghelas were the last Hindu dynasty of Gujarat before being conquered by the Delhi Sulṭānate in 1304. Nuruddin Firuz commissioned two inscriptions – one in Sanskrit and one in Arabic – that offer a counterfactual to the Sanskrit inscriptions of the Delhi Sulṭānate. That counterfactual concerns how Islamic religious institutions would have been accommodated within Sanskrit jurisprudential principles of Equity and Trusts if the Sanskrit cosmopolis had not been supplanted by the Persian cosmopolis.

The Sanskrit Veraval inscription is not a true counterfactual because it records events that *did* occur, if only briefly, but it is certainly an outlier in the history of Equity and Trusts in Indian legal history. Mosque and Madrassa endowments made under the Vijayanagara Empire bear the imprimatur of the empire's embrace of sulṭānate political structures (and this is discussed in the next section).

The Sanskrit Veraval inscription articulates a vision of Equity as the conventional Dharma of disciplinary and congenital groups. It also articulates a theory of divine trusts in which deities own property that is, in turn, administered by trustees. Nuruddin Firuz purchased properties from the fiduciaries of various local deities, uses these properties to endow his mosque, stipulates the use of these trust funds, and makes arrangements for the protection of the endowment from breaches of trust – all using technical Dharmaśāstric vocabulary.

The Sanskrit inscription praises Viśvanātha, the 'Lord of the Universe', in language that appears to blend Śiva with Allāh.[239] The inscription is dated in the Vikrama, Valabhī, Siṃha and Hijri eras, with the latter being expressed as, 'Year 662 of the Rasūlamumahammad, the preceptor of the boatmen who are devoted to Śrī Viśvanātha'.[240] This is an elegant description of Islam in purely Sanskritic terminology. Next, the inscription introduces the reigning government in terms that are almost identical to the Kalyāṇa inscription discussed earlier: 'During the reign of the glorious Cālukya Cakravartin, Mahārājādhirāja Arjjunadeva in victorious, prosperous Kalyāṇa, the great minister at his feet, Śrī Māladeva, the Rāṇaka, carried out all the activities of the seal (of state) such as (writing) Śrī Śrī (at the beginning of grants), etc.'[241] A description of the local administration of the Somanātha temple, organised as a Pañcakula (group of five lineages), follows.[242]

[239] EI 34.21. See Note 52.

[240] **śrīviśvanātha**pratibaddhanaujanānāṃ bodhaka**rasūlamahammada**saṃvat 662.

[241] Ibid.: **caulukyacakravarti**mahārājādhirājaśrīmad**arjunadeva**pravardhamāna**kalyāṇa**vijayarājye tadpādapadmopajīvini mahāmātyarāṇakaśrī**māladeve** śrīśrīkaraṇādisamastamudrāvyāpārān paripaṁthayatity…

[242] Ibid.: evaṃ kāle parvarttamāne iha śrīsomanāthadevapattane paramapāśupatācāryamahāpaṇḍitamahattaradharmmamūrttigaṇḍaśrīpara**vīrabhadra**pārimahamśrī**abhayaśīha**prabhṛtipañcakulapratipattau.

The inscription relates that Noradīna Pīroja, the son of Khoja Nau Abū Brāhima of the land of Hormuz, came to Somanātha City on business when Amīra Rakanadīna was governing his chiefdom at the harbour of Hormuz.[243] In the presence of the local chief, Chāḍa, and in the presence of various fiduciaries attached to the estate of Somanātha (*somanāthadevadroṇīpratibaddha*), Noradīna acquired a parcel of land, for use at will, outside Somanātha City.[244]

On this parcel, Noradīna, 'having become very Dharmic in accordance with the opinion of his own Dharmaśāstra, and a friend of Dharma, caused an east-facing mosque, a Dharmasthāna, to be constructed'.[245] The description of Islamic law as 'his own Dharmaśāstra' and the repeated use of the word 'Dharma' makes it clear that Noradīna unambiguously embraced Dharmaśāstric jurisprudence when assimilating Islam into a Sanskrit epigraphic idiom. Like the Kalyāṇa inscription, there is a shared sense of Equity as a system of supplemental law (*pāribhāṣikadharma*) applicable to one's community.

An important, often overlooked detail from this inscription is the fact that Noradīna endowed his mosque – effectively creating a Sanskritic *waqf* – with assets that he purchased *from the deities at Somanāthapura*. This may be the only known instance in history where a Muslim purchased properties from deities (via their agents) and re-endowed them as *waqf* property. The inscription states 'the entire estate (*palladikā*) of Śrī Vauleśvara in the city of Śrī Somanātha was acquired' for the creation of the mosque.[246] In essence, the property of one deity, Śrī Vauleśvara, was purchased for the benefit of another deity, Viśvanātha (i.e., Allāh). Deity-to-deity transactions of this sort are fairly commonplace in the epigraphic records discussed in Chapter 2, but given the location – Somanātha – and the deities involved in the present inscription, it is remarkable.[247]

This estate and other productive assets, including shops and fields, were endowed for stipulated purposes that included: 1) the maintenance of the mosque; 2) the daily provision of oil for worship and drink for the congregants; 3) the hiring of an instructor (*mālima*/*muallim*), a crier (*modina*/*muazzim*); and a monthly reader of the Koran; 4) the observance of festivals (*pūjāmahotsava*); and 5) various charities and repairs.[248] All of this, is expressed in a traditional Sanskrit idiom with each clause ending in '*artham*' ('for the purpose of'). Finally, Noradīna stipulates that any surplus funds from the endowment, after satisfying the stipulated

[243] Ibid.: tathā hurmujavelākūle **amīraśrīrukanadīne** rājyaṃ paripaṁthayati sati kāryavaśāt śrīsomanāthadevanagaraṃ samāyāta hurmujadeśīyakhojānau**abūbrāhimasutanākhūnoradīnapīrojena**.

[244] Ibid.: **somanāthadevadroṇī**pratibaddhamahājana**...**rāja**śrīchāḍā**prabhṛtisamastamahaṇalokapratyakṣaṃ... śrī**somanāthadevanagara**bāhye... saṃtiṣṭhamānabhūkhaṇḍaṃ... yatheṣṭakarmakaraṇīyatvena... samupāttam.

[245] Ibid.: **nākhūpīrojena** svadharmmaśāstrābhiprāyeṇa paramadharmmikeṇa bhūtvā... sthāne pūrvābhimukhamijigitidharmmasthānaṃ bṛharājaśrīchāḍāsahāyatvena dharmmabāṁdhavena kāritaṃ.

[246] Ibid: **śrīsomanāthadevanagara**madhye **śrīvauleśvaradevīyapalladikā...** upetā.

[247] See Chapter 2, §2.6.3, 'Deities' complex assets'.

[248] Ibid., 144, for Sircar's outline of the various trust purposes.

purposes, should be dispatched to the *dharmasthānas* (holy places) of Mecca and Medīna.[249] Noradīna closes by entrusting the endowment with the local Muslim population, and issuing a warning that those who rescind the *dharmasthāna* would be guilty of the five major (Hindu) sins.[250]

The Sanskrit Veraval inscription reflects a broader trend during the twilight of the pre-conquest Sanskrit cosmopolis where 'Muslim communities slotted easily into pre-existing trans-religious patronage practices on the subcontinent and the tradition of praising such generosity in Sanskrit'.[251] Truschke notes that, 'Jagadu, a thirteenth century Gujarati trader and a Jain, bankrolled the construction or repair of a mosque used by Ismaili Muslims… [and] likewise, writing in 1349, Rajashekhara says that the thirteenth-century Vaghela ministers Vastupala and Tejahpala gave money to support sixty-four mosques (*maśīti*)'.[252]

All of these dedications occurred, however, in the period preceding the sulṭānate conquest. If the counterfactual is a world in which the jurisprudence that subtended the Sanskrit cosmopolis incorporated Islamic political and religious structures without ceding political power, then the factual that occurred was the pious hope expressed in the Arabic summary of the Veraval endowment that Noradīna had placed at his mosque: 'In the city of *Sūmnāt*, may God make it one of the cities of Islām and purify it from the infidelity and the idols.'[253] When Alā' al-Dīn Khaljī sacked the Somanātha temple in 1299, he carted the temple deity's image – the same deity that had sold some its assets to accommodate Noradīna's mosque – off to Delhi to be broken up and used as paving stones for the Jami Masjid.[254]

3.3.2 The sulṭān among Hindu kings at Vijayanagara

In the early 14th century, Muḥammad bin Tughluq's crushing of the Kākaṭīya Dynasty created a power vacuum that was soon filled by two ambitious brothers, Harihara I (r. 1336–56 CE), and Bukka Raya I (r. 1356–77 CE), who founded the city of Vijayanagara (modern Hampi) and its eponymous empire in 1336.[255] Over the course of its illustrious history, the empire 'encompassed most of the south

[249] Ibid.: yat kiṃcit śeṣadravyam udgirati tat sarvaṃ dravyaṃ **makhāmadīnādharmmasthāne** prasthāpanīyaṃ.
[250] Ibid.: **muśalamānajamāthaprabhṛtibhiḥ** samastair api… pālāpanīyaṃ dharmmasthānam idaṃ varttāpanīyaṃ ca… yaḥ ko 'pi dharmmasthānam idaṃ… lopayati… sa pāpātmā pañcamahāpātakadoṣeṇa lipyate.
[251] Truschke, *The Language of History*, 74.
[252] Ibid.
[253] EI 34.21, p. 150.
[254] Kishori Saran Lal, *History of the Khaljis (1290–1320)* (Allahabad: The Indian Press, 1950), 85.
[255] For the history of Vijayanagara, see Burton Stein, *The New Cambridge History of India: Vijayanagara* (Cambridge: Cambridge University Press, 2008). For the power vacuum, see 18–19.

Indian peninsula between ca. 1336 and 1565 CE and was ruled by three successive dynasties, the Saṅgama (1336–1485 CE),the Sāḷuva (1485–1505 CE), and the Tuḷuva (1505–65 CE)'.[256] Following the sack of Hampi in the wake of the disastrous Battle of Talikota in 1565, a fourth dynasty, the Aravidus, ruled a much attenuated rump state in Adhra Pradesh until 1646. The Vijayanagara Empire was a hitherto unique polity. As Eaton notes:

> From the moment of its launching... Vijayanagara was a culturally hybridized kingdom. Its religious origins and legal foundations were embedded in a state cult focused on a local form of the great god Śiva, just as the Kakatiya kingdom had been grounded on one devoted to another form of that deity. On the other hand, the kingdom's ruling institutions, architecture and its wider, transregional posture suggest a desire to assimilate the ideals and idioms of the Persianate world.[257]

On the one hand, the emperors presented the 'Vijayanagara state as deriving directly *from that of the* [Delhi] *Sultanate*... alongside a host of regional sultanates'.[258] Harihara and Bukka probably started their kingdom as Tughluq vassals. According to most later political foundation myths, they and their successors styled themselves, *inter alia*, as 'Sulṭāns among the Hindu Kings' (*hindurāyasuratrāṇa*).[259] In many respects, the Vijayanagara emperors followed quintessentially Persianate, sulṭānate conventions of administration, architecture, dress, and diplomatics. Wagoner describes the Islamicisation of the Vijayanagara Empire as the 'adoption of certain Islamic cultural forms and practices, which – given the political nature of the process – largely pertain to the broad sphere of secular culture, as opposed to the narrower domain of formal religion'.[260] The Vijayanagara Empire operated, *politically* as a sulṭānate.

On the other hand, the Vijayanagara Empire also operated according to the paradigms of Dharmaśāstric kingship – especially endowing and protecting religious institutions – of the earlier Sanskrit cosmopolis. The same foundation myths that attribute Tughluq suzerainty to Harihara and Bukka also claim that the Saṅgama brothers' meeting with Vidyārayaṇa, the renowned Advaitavedāntin

[256] Valerie Stoker, 'Polemics and Patronage in Sixteenth-Century Vijayanagara: Vyāsatīrtha and the Dynamics of Hindu Sectarian Relations', *Journal of the American Academy of Religion* 51.2 (2011): 129–55, 129.

[257] Eaton, *Persianate*, 88 .

[258] Phillip Wagoner, 'Harihara, Bukka, and the Sultan: The Delhi Sultanate in the Political Imagination of Vijayanagara', in David Gilmartin and Bruce Lawrence (eds), *Beyond Turk and Hindu: Rethinking Religious Identities in Islamicate South Asia* (Gainesville: University of Florida Press, 2000): 300–26, 304–5.

[259] See Wagoner, 'Sultan'. See 862 fn. 8 for Bukka – also called a sulṭān (*suratālu*) in two inscriptions, and 863 for Bukka's successors. Also see Truschke, *The Language of History*, 69: 'In an inscription at a Jain temple in Rajasthan circa 1440, Rana Kumbha of Mewar is said to have been given the title (biruda) of hiṃdusuratrāṇa, "sultan of Hindus," by virtue of his association with the "sultan (suratrāṇa) of Gujarat and Delhi"'.

[260] Wagoner, 'Sultan', 854.

Mahant, 'inspired not only the founding of the empire but [also] the location of its capital in the region of the Virūpākṣa temple in Hampi'.[261] While the establishment of the Empire was gradual – hardly the product of one encounter – Stoker notes that: 'Inscriptional, legendary, and literary sources consistently link the empire's founding dynasty, the Saṅgamas, to… [the Sṛṇgeri] maṭha. Intellectually affiliated with Śaṅkara's Advaita Vedānta, this Brahmin community is famous for its involvement in the Vedic commentarial project undertaken or, perhaps, overseen by Sāyaṇa'.[262]

Virūpākṣa, ensconced in his temple at the heart of the empire, and closely associated with the Smārta Brāhmaṇas of the Śṛṇgeri Maṭha, became the effective legal owner of the entire empire by 1354. As Eaton notes:

> Important state documents now bore the 'signature' of this deity, while the Sangama kings heaped lavish architectural patronage on his temple complex by the banks of the Tungabhadra. Hundreds of copperplate inscriptions recording land grants state that the donation was carried out 'in the presence of Virupaksha on the banks of the Tungabhadra River' and conclude with a large 'signature' of the god 'Śri Virupaksha', written in Kannada script. As owner of all state land within his kingdom, the deity in this way participated in formal transactions and attested to their validity.[263]

In effect, the empire was a political sulṭānate ruled according to the legal framework of an intricate Hindu temple trust in which the land was vested in Virūpākṣa (and, later, Veṅkateśvara). The emperor, acting as an agent of Virūpākṣa, created derivative tenures for feudal vassals, for other deities, for monastic institutions, and even for Jain, Muslim, and Christian communities. Vijayanagara was the ultimate culmination of the Sanskrit jurisprudence of Equity and Trusts' model of the deity as a legal person.

3.3.2.i Persianate political systems

The Vijayanagara emperors' establishment of 'conceptual links between Vijayanagara and Delhi', especially in their efforts to 'trace the origin of their state to the Sultan's gift of territory and authority', was the product of an 'intense and creative interaction with the Islamic world'.[264] The Vijayanagara emperors actively engaged in Islamic political discourse. For example, Devaraya II (r. 1422–46 CE) 'eagerly sought out an emissary from Shah Rukh, his Timurid contemporary in Herat, who had been sent on a mission to Calicut on the Malabar coast'.[265]

[261] Valerie Stoker, *Polemics and Patronage in the City of Victory: Vyasatirtha, Hindu Sectarianism, and the Sixteenth-Century Vijayanagara Court* (Oakland: University of California Press, 2016), 50–1.
[262] Ibid., 50.
[263] Eaton, *Persianate*, 87–8.
[264] Wagoner, 'Delhi Sultanate', 315.
[265] Wagoner, 'Sultan', 864.

These efforts proved invaluable in forging alliances and navigating shifting inter-sulṭānate political rivalries until the ambitious regent, Rāma Rāya (regent 1542–1565), 'overplayed his hand' and led to the Ahmadnagar, Bijapur, Golconda and Bidar Sulṭānates uniting against Vijayanagara.[266] Following the battle of Talikota in 1565, 'the victorious allies spent the next six months looting the Vijayanagara metropolis.'[267]

Furthermore, Islamic military (horsemanship, archery, and gunpowder) and administrative systems (feudal tenure and a paper-based bureaucracy) were 'clearly far more effective than the previously available techniques had been as instruments of political control.'[268] The most important of these technologies, by far, was the *iqṭā'* system of feudal military tenure. Introduced by the Saljuqs, *iqṭā'* tenure entailed the assignment of land-revenue collection rights in exchange for an obligation to 'provide a military contingent of a fixed size'.[269] This, in turn, required 'precise record keeping and the maintenance of registers recording the details relating to each *iqṭā*".[270] (Islamic) paper and pen, rather than (Hindu) palm-leaf and stylus was much better suited to these bureaucratic requirements. The Vijayanagara emperors adopted both techniques (calling their system of feudal tenure *nāyaṃkara* tenure) and Wagoner argues 'in the strongest possible terms that the Vijayanagara arrangement was developed as a direct adaptation from an Islamicate model'.[271]

Militarily, the Vijayanagara emperors recruited Muslim soldiers, trained their armies along Turkic lines, and incorporate Muslims within their feudal *nāyaka* system. For example, the historian Muḥammad Qasim Hindu Shah Astarabadi records that 'Devaraya [II] gave orders to enlist Mussulmans in his service, allotting them estates, and erecting a mosque for their use in the city of Beejanuggur [Vijayanagara]'.[272] A mosque at Vijayanagara – called a 'hall of Dharma' (*dharmaśāla*) in its Kannada dedicatory inscription, which was donated by one Aḥmad Khān. attests to the practical reality of Astarabadi's description of the Vijayanagara emperors as patrons of Islamic religious institutions.[273]

Ironically, 'for many years art historians refused to believe that another structure located in Vijayanagara, a self-styled "*dharmaśāla*" built in 1439, was actually a mosque', despite the fact that it had a '*mehrab*, faced Mecca, and bore an inscription identifying its patron as one Ahmad Khan' because it lacked 'vaulting, domes,

[266] Eaton, *Persianate*, 166–7.
[267] Ibid., 167.
[268] Wagoner, 'Delhi Sultanate', 317.
[269] Ibid., 318.
[270] Ibid.
[271] Ibid.
[272] Ibid., 317.
[273] Discussed at length in Phillip Wagoner, 'Fortuitous Convergences and Essential Ambiguities: Transcultural Political Elites in the Medieval Deccan', *International Journal of Hindu Studies* 3.3 (1998): 241–64.

or arches'.[274] Ironically, this misidentification attests to the success of Vijayanagara in establishing a hybrid political culture in which, looking outwards, the emperors often constructed royal and diplomatic buildings in a Persianate style and, looking inwards, local religious institutions were crafted in classical South Indian styles. A unique imprecatory clause in the Koṇḍavīḍu inscription of Kṛṣṇarāya (r. 1509–29 CE) attests to the hybridisation of Islamic and Dharmaśāstric culture in Vijayanagara-era legal discourse: 'If (any) Oḍḍa (Orissan) kings and Teluṅgu kings shall violate this charity, they shall incur the sin of killing cows on (the banks of) the Gaṅgā; if (any) Turuka (Turkish/i.e. Sulṭānate) kings shall violate (this charity) they shall incur the sin of eating pigs.'[275]

Given this evidence, a communalist narrative that Vijayanagara was, essentially, a traditional Hindu bulwark against aggressive Islamic incursions into the Deccan and Southern India is untenable. Certainly, during the 14th century, defeating the 'Turkish' sulṭān of Madhurai and restoring deities' images to religious sites – Kāñcīpura, Śrīraṅgam, Madhurai, etc. – that had been desecrated by Muslim armies in the earlier decades, formed a key component of the empire's claim to legitimacy.

Nevertheless, the empire supported Muslim religious institutions, enlisted Muslim soldiers in its armies, engaged in extensive trade with the wider Islamic world, and built a Sanskrit-veneered version of an Islamic polity. The stability of that Islamic (or Islamicate depending on preferred nomenclature) polity provided a safe haven for a renaissance of Dharmaśāstric jurisprudence and innumerable Hindu temples whose deities reached the zenith of the legal personality – all under the protective aegis of Virūpākṣa and his fiduciary, the emperor.

3.3.2.ii The deity as sovereign in Vijayanagara

From its inception the Vijayanagara Empire was intimately associated with the preservation and restoration of temple deities. Although the empire utilised Persianate political apparatuses, they applied them in the service of a quintessentially Dharmaśāstric theory of Equity and Trusts. The empire was founded at the shrine of Virūpākṣa at Hampi. Virūpākṣa, a form of Śiva appeared in the epigraphic records of Hampi in the 12th century, when 'the three-eyed god comes to the site, and, by marrying the river goddess Pampa, usurps her position as the dominant deity of the site'.[276] Over the next two hundred years, Virūpākṣa came

[274] Eaton, 'Persian Cosmopolis', 64.

[275] EI 6.22: ī dharmānaku **oḍerājulu teluṅgurājulu** ta[pi]rā gaṅggalonu gohatya ceśina doṣāna bovuvāru / **turukarājulu** tappirā paṅddi diṅ[nna] doṣāna bovuvāru //

[276] Phillip B. Wagoner, 'From "Pampa's Crossing" to "The Place of Lord Virupaksa": Architecture, Cult, and Patronage at Hampi before the Founding of Vijayanagara', in D. Devaraj and C.S. Patil (eds), *Vijayanagara: Progress of Research, 1988–1991* (Mysore: Directorate of Archaeology and Museums, 1996): 141–74, 163.

to be the legal owner of the empire's lands, with successive rulers allocating land grants in the name of the deity as subordinate feudal rights.

The Vijayanagara emperors may have acquired their deity-as-sovereign model of kingship from the Eastern Gaṅgā/Gajapati Dynasty of Orissa. In 1230, Anaṅgabhīma III (r. 1211–38 CE) ritually dedicated his kingdom to Puruṣottama/Jagannāth of the great temple of Puri 'as state deity of Orissa and as his divine overlord'.[277] Later, 'Anaṅgabhīma and his successors claimed to rule under divine order (*ādeśa*) and as son (*putra*) and vassal (*rāuta*) of the Lord of Puri', dating their order to the regnal year of Jagannātha, the tutelary deity that they served as fiduciaries.[278] According to the *Mādalā Pañji*, the traditional record of the Jagannātha temple, the elevation of Jagannātha to the status of state deity (*rāṣṭra devatā*) and king of Orissa (*oḍiśa rājya rajā śrī jagannātha mahāprabhu*) stemmed, in no small part, from Anaṅgabhīma's success in defeating the semi-independent ruler of Bengal, Ghiyāth ad-Dīn ʿIwaz Shāh (r. 1212–27 CE), during a protracted invasion of Orissa between 1223 and 1225.

The Vijayanagara emperors expanded the Gajapati model of deity-as-sovereign. The Virūpākṣa temple (under the guardianship of a satellite branch of the Smārta Maṭha at Śṛṇgeri) lay in the heart of an elaborate sacred precinct in Hampi, surrounded by temples to other subordinate deities – usually tutelary deities of subordinate regions of the empire. In effect, the sacred precinct encapsulated and enacted the ritual, legal, and political constitution of the Empire. Virūpākṣa was enthroned in Hampi at the centre of the imperial formation, surrounded by various vassal kings and deities.

Land ownership vested in Virūpākṣa and was distributed by Virūpākṣa's fiduciary – the emperor – to subordinate kings and deities who, in turn, distributed it to their subordinates. In essence, the Vijayanagara emperors recast the feudal hierarchy of the sulṭānate's *iqṭā*ʿ system as a centralised divine feudalism of Sanskrit trusts. As Eaton notes: 'the state's imperial pantheon, made visual in its capital's built landscape… fused its theology with its sovereign territory'.[279]

[277] Herman Kulke, 'King Anaṅgabhīma III, the Veritable Founder of the Gajapati Kingship and of the Jagannātha Trinity at Puri', *Journal of the Royal Asiatic Society of Great Britain and Ireland* 1 (1989): 26–39, 26.

[278] Ibid., 26–9.

[279] Eaton, *Persianate*, 160. In 1515, Kṛṣṇadevarāya built the first Vaiṣṇava temple in Vijayanagara in order to install an image of Bālakṛṣṇa that he had seized from the Gajapatis in Orissa. As Stoker, *Polemics*, 58, notes, 'he seems to have sought the protection and blessing of Virūpākṣa for what was to be a new cult in the city'. Bālakṛṣṇa was *subordinate* to the empire's tutelary deity. See Eaton and Wagoner, *Power, Memory*, 84, where they note that when Rāma Rāya defeated Sulṭān Husain Nizam Shāh of Ahmadnagar in 1559 and acquired Kalyāṇa, he installed an image of Bhuvaneśvarī as Virūpākṣa's consort (in addition to Pampā) in the capital city. Drawing on the rich legacy of Kalyāṇa and attempting to restore its lost glory in Vijayanagara, Rāya constructed Bhuvaneśvarī's shrine using materials from the Kalyāṇa Cālukyan temple's remains (that had been despoiled under Sulṭānate raids) while his successors adopted Cālukyan titles in their epigraphic records.

Take, for example, the 1466 Śrīśailam plates of the Emperor Virūpākṣarāya II (r. 1465–85 CE). The emperor, named after his tutelary deity, describes himself as 'the sulṭān among the Hindu kings, by whom the sulṭān (of Delhi) was made powerless, king Virūpākṣa, the lord protector of Virūpākṣa.'[280] The emperor, surrounded by pious people belonging to the various sacred sites, issued a land grant to Mallikārjunadeva of Śrīśailam, and signed the grant 'Śrīvirūpākṣa.'[281] Virtually every land grant in the Vijayanagara Empire followed this pattern of Virūpākṣa authenticating the transfer of property – until the Saṅgama house was overthrown by the Saluva Dynasty (1485–1505 CE), which 'openly favoured the Vaishnava deity Venkateśvara, the lord of the popular shrine at Tirupati in southern Andhra.'[282] During the reign of Kṛṣṇadevarāya (r. 1509–29) of the following Tuluva Dynasty, Veṅkaṭeśvara replaced Virūpākṣa as the authenticator of land grants – and, presumably as the tutelary deity of the empire.[283]

The 1613 Kandukuru plates of Veṅkaṭapatideva I (r. 1585–1614 CE) represent the apotheosis of the juridical personality of Hindu deities as imperial sovereigns. The grant records a gift of land and capital *from* Veṅkaṭeśvara *to* Veṅkaṭeśvara (for the purposes of festivals and a garden) that was executed by the king in the name of Veṅkaṭeśvara. The grant reads:

> In the vicinity of the lotus feet of Śrīveṅkaṭeśa, King Śrīvīraveṅkaṭapati gave to Śrīmad Veṅkaṭanātha Viṣṇu (various assets) as a *devabhoga*… Śrīveṅkaṭeśvarasvāmi (also) ordained (the payment of) 23 *varāhas* (a sum) every year to the Dharmakartā (the trustee) Senamodalārikṛṣṇayagāru. For the watershed at the entrance of the garden and for the maintenance of the gardeners, (he, the deity) was pleased to command (payment from) the cash from the above *kālvā* (field). (Signed) Śrīveṅkaṭeśa.[284]

The deity-as-ruler became a normative model of Hindu kingship during the 16th and 17th centuries, with the Gajapatis of Orissa ruling on behalf of Jagannātha, the Kachavāhās of Jaipur ruling on behalf of Govindadevajī, the Mahārājas of Mewar serving as custodians of Ekaliṅgajī, the rulers of Nāthadvara serving as hereditary custodians of Śrīnāthajī, the Mahārājas of Koṭā ruling on behalf of Brijnāthjī, the Rajpūt ruler of Kullu in faraway Himanchel Pradesh as viceroys to an image of Rāma retrieved from Ayodhyā in the 17th century; and the royal house of Travancore,

[280] EI 15.2: **khilīkṛtasuratrāṇo… hindurāyasutrāṇaḥ… virūpākṣakṣitīśvaraḥ… virūpākṣakṣitīpālo.**

[281] Ibid.: dharmasthānagataiḥ sadbhiḥ saṃyuto… śrīvirūpākṣa. See EI 17.8 for Devarāya II's donation to Raṅganātha of Śrīraṅgam in the name of Virūpākṣa.

[282] Eaton, *Persianate*, 159.

[283] Ibid., 159. See EI 9.52, 12.162, 16.18 & 22 for examples of the change in cypher.

[284] EI 19.14: **śrīveṅkaṭeśapādāpadmasannidhau**… **śrīmadveṅkaṭanāthāya**… **viṣṇave**… devabhogyaṃ… **śrīvīraveṅkaṭapatimahārāyamahīpatiḥ**… dattavān. **śrīveṅkaṭeśvarasvāmulu** kaṭṭaḍa śeśinadi dharmakarta **senāmodalāri kṛṣṇayagāriki** pratisaṃvatsarānakunnū ga 24 varahālu. toṭavākiṭa calividrakunnu toṭa śeśevārlaku grāsālunnu ī kālvarokhkhaṃlonu kaṭṭaḍa śāyanavadhariṁcināru. **śrīveṅkaṭeśa**.

served as vassals of their tutelary deity, Padmanābhasvāmi, after Anizham Thirunal Marthanda Varma's (r. 1729–58 CE) donation of the kingdom to the deity in 1750.[285] Today, these deities remain as rulers of their respective, if nominal kingdoms and their endowments are managed by complex committees of trustees. The shift to the deity as ruler, first in Orissa and then, most extravagantly in Vijayanagara heralded a tectonic shift in the history of Equity and Trusts in Sanskrit jurisprudence.

3.3.2.iii Restoration, re-endowment, and state supervision of religious endowments

Vijayanagara's centralisation of political authority on a sulṭānate model enabled the emperors to field puissant military powers that could compete with and overthrow Islamic and Hindu rulers in southern India. As a result, the empire captured, *inter alia*, Kāñcīpura, Śrīraṅgam, and Madhurai, in the mid-14th century, and Kalyāṇa and Orissa in the 16th century. The emperors' conquests coincide with the *restoration* of deities' images to the temples whence they had been evacuated during Islamic iconoclastic rule, or the *relocation* of deities' images from captured Hindu imperial temples to Vijayanagara (where they were reconsecrated and endowed), and, in both cases, the *direct supervision* of divine endowments by agents of the Crown. The emperors' territorial sovereignty went hand-in-glove with their legal right of supervision of deities' trusts – expressed in classical Dharmaśāstric jurisprudential theories of *parens patriae* jurisdiction and Equity.

Furthermore, this centralised system of empire as an integrated feudal hierarchy of divine endowments – with deities enjoying substantial legal personality – enabled two further developments: 1) deities created various forms of sub-tenure in which they allocated funds to other deities or to monasteries; and 2) monastic and priestly communities jockeyed to secure trusteeship positions within this byzantine legal system – in order to promote their own sect and to establish their authority vis-à-vis other sects.[286] For example, in 1359, while Śrīraṅganātha was still in exile, the deity of

[285] For these deities and their cults, see, for example, Jagannātha, O.M. Starza, *The Jagannatha Temple at Puri: Its Architecture, Art, and Cult* (Leiden: Brill, 1993); for Govinddevjī, Horstmann, *In Favour of Govinddevjī*; for Ekaliṅgajī, Deborah Stein, *The Hegemony of Heritage: Ritual and Record in Stone* (Oakland: University of California Press, 2018), 186–242; for Śrīnāthajī, Paolo Pacciolla, *The Indian Drum of the King-God and the Pakhāvaj of Nathdwara* (London: Routledge, 2020); for Brijnāthjī, Nortbert Peabody, *Hindu Kingship and Polity in Pre-Colonial India* (Cambridge: Cambridge University Press, 2003); for Rāma of Ayodhya, Daniela Berti, 'Ritual Kingship, Divine Bureaucracy and Electoral Politics in Kullu', *European Bulletin of Himalayan Research* 29–30 (2006): 39–61; Daniela Berti, 'Fighting Enemies and Protecting Territory: Deities as Local Rulers in Kullu, Himachal Pradesh', *European Bulletin of Himalayan Research* 29–30 (2006): 62–81; for Padmanābhasvāmi, Das Acevedo, 'Divine Sovereignty'.

[286] Initially, the dominant sect was the Śāṅkarite Smārtas of the Śṛṅgeri Maṭha (who operated subordinate *maṭhas* at Kāñcīpura and Vijayanagara). By the 16th century, the Śrīvaiṣṇavas of the Rāmānuja tradition based at Śrīraṅgam, supplanted the Smārtas until, later in the 16th century, when the Mādhvas under Vyāsatīrtha gained control over, *inter alia*, the imperial Veṅkateśva temple – and its vast network of trust properties.

the Hastigiri temple at Kāñcīpura (later subordinate to Raṅganātha) issued a sacred order to its priests:

> On the representation (made) by Perumāḷtātaṉ, who supervises the (sacred) business of our temple, and by our Bhaṭṭas, We are pleased to assign to a Vaiṣṇavadāsa on whom We have bestowed the name of Brahmatantrasvatantrajīyaṉ, the *maṭha* which had been set apart for him, the lands belonging thereto, the worship to be conducted therein and the expenses therefore, the books which he had accumulated and the accessories required for them, so that he may propagate Our Rāmānujadarśan, and after him, the disciples selected by him may, in succession, take possession of these and continue. We directed that the followers of Rāmānuja and those of our Vaiṣṇava *samaya* shall accept him and carry on.[287]

If property rights flowed from Virūpākṣa, to Śrīraṅganātha, to Hastigiri, and to the *maṭhas*, control over a superior divine trust (or a shift in the hierarchy of trusts) could result in significant shifts in the balance of prominence for the various monastic communities that served as trustees of temples. Valerie Stoker's *Polemics and Patronage in the City of Victory* remains the definitive work on the subject of inter-monastic rivalries at Vijayanagara and their role in shaping the emergence of many modern south Indian *maṭhas* as discrete legal institutions with a set lineage, theology, and legal status.[288] In 1524, the Mādhva Ācārya Vyāsatīrtha (1460–1539 CE) appears to have taken over effective control of the Veṅkateśa temple at Tirupati on the basis of a claim that the Śrīvaiṣṇava trustees were expropriating Veṅkateśa's assets.[289] At the time, Veṅkateśa was the tutelary deity of the kingdom in whose name grants were authenticated, so this was a highly significant event beyond the confines of the Tirupati.

The restoration of plundered Hindu religious sites figured prominently in contemporaneous accounts of the Vijayanagara conquest of the Madhurai Sulṭānate. Bukka Rāya's son, Kumāra Kampaṇa, led these assaults and his wife, Gaṅgādevī, composed the *Madhurāvijaya* (*Victory at Madhurai*) in 1380 to commemorate this achievement. The incomplete poem recounts Kumāra's adventures in an epic literary style that evokes other great biographies (*caritas*) of Indian

[287] EI 25.34: **śrīmathastigirīśasya** devadevasya śāsanam. nam vīḍu karumam kēṭkum **perumāḷtātaṉum nam** bhaṭṭa[r]kaḷum śollakkeṭṭu **brahmatantrasvatantrajjīyaṉ** eṉru nām perkuḍutta **vaiṣṇavadāsaṉukku** nām kuḍuttapaḍi. ivaṉukku uṇḍāna maṭhamum maṭhattai nokki varum kṣetramum samārādhanamum adukku veṇḍum muṭṭukkaḷum ivaṉ teḍiṇa postakaṅgaḷum idukku veṇḍum upakaraṇaṅgaḷum nam **rāmānujandarśanam** maḍakkaikkāga ivaṉukku pīṇbum ivaṉ niyamitta ivaṉuḍaiya śiṣyargaḷ paramparaiy āga ivaiyiṟṟaikkaikkoṇḍu naḍattippodakkaḍavargaḷ āgavum. ivaṉai nam **rāmānijamuḍaiyārum** nam samayattil uḷḷārum kaikkoṇḍu naḍattippodacchoṇṇom. iccheydiyai kkallilum śembilum veṭṭikkoḷḷumbaḍī ivaṉukku nām muḍittapaḍiyum pūśiṇapaḍiyum kuḍuttōm.

[288] Stoker, *Polemics*.

[289] Valerie Stoker, 'Polemics and Patronage in Sixteenth-Century Vijayanagara', 150

heroes.[290] It recounts Kumāra's route from Vijayanaraga to Madhurai and, at each stop – Kāñcīpura, Śrīraṅgam, and Madhurai – the young prince restores deities' temple trusts. First, Kumāra follows his father's advice to lay 'waste to the battle-ready troops of Champa [the Sambuvarāya ruler of Kāñcīpura]. Then rule Kanchi as per the will of the people.'[291]

In 1369, Kampaṇa intervened in the administration of the ancient Rājasiṃheśvara temple (Rājasiṃheśvara was the tutelary deity of the Pallava Empire).[292] Kampaṇa ordered that the deity's lands, which had been sold or transferred by the previous regime, were to be restored, that the deity's worship would be renewed, that the deity would enjoy a fresh endowment, and that a Śaiva monastery would be created with some of the deity's assets in order to train priests for the deity's worship.[293] Clearly, Kampaṇa took the idea of sovereignty and supervision of religious endowments very seriously. Additionally, in the case of Kāñcīpura, Kampaṇa also viewed the maladministration of the deity's endowment was the result of poor Dharmic governance on the part of the non-Islamic Sambuvarāya ruler.

According to the *Madhurāvijaya*, while our hero, Kampaṇa, was staying at Kāñcīpura, the goddess Durgā appears to him in a dream; she enjoins him to overthrow the sulṭān of Madhurai by describing the 'Turkish' oppression of the city's temples and religious institutions. As Truschke notes, 'several verses… invoke the historical memory of Muslim-led campaigns that laid the groundwork for the Sultanate of Madurai' and that resulted in the desecration of sacred sites.[294] Durgā tells Kumāra that:

> I am anguished to see many temples of the various other gods –
> their doors eaten away by woodworms,
> their halls overgrown with wild weeds,
> their inner sanctums in disarray.[295]

The goddess refers to Malik Kāfūr's 1313 sack of Chidambaram and Śrīraṅgam (both on the route from Kāñcīpura to Madhurai), outlines the sulṭān's corruption of a Dharmaśāstric political and social order, and entrusts Kampaṇa with a sacred sword. Kampaṇa would eventually use that very sword to kill the sulṭān and restore the Mīnākṣī temple.[296] There is obviously a great deal of rhetorical conceit

[290] See Truschke, *The Language of History*, 75–7, for a discussion of the work's literary elements.
[291] Ibid., 78.
[292] SII 1.88.
[293] Ibid.
[294] Truschke, *The Language of History*, 79. For Islamic accounts of the sack of these temples, see Davis, *Lives of Indian Images*, 112–14.
[295] Truschke, *The Language of History*, 80.
[296] Ibid., 80–1. For this temple, see Crispin Branfoot, 'Remaking the Past: Tamil Sacred Landscape and Temple Renovations', *Bulletin of SAOS* 76.1 (2013): 21–47, 23–32.

in Gaṅgādevī's description of Kumāra Kampaṇa's campaign, but its thrust – in descriptions of victories over 'Hindu' or 'Islamic' opponents – is that 'the new rulers [will] purify the lands from contamination... recover dharma... overturn [the] Kali-yuga and return society to the former golden age'.[297] At the heart of this narrative, however, is the Sanskrit jurisprudence of Equity and Trusts. The restoration, endowment, and protection of religious endowments from Islamic oppression and from Hindu maladministration is the basis of Kampaṇa's sovereignty.

As Richard Davis notes:

> Inscriptions throughout Tamilnad record Kampaṇa's many benefactions to temples. He intervened in local temple affairs by adjudicating disputes and replacing old administrators with new ones. More than this, Kampaṇa also reopened key temples that had been converted or closed over the previous decades. At Kannanur, the former regional capital of the Hoysalas in Tamilnad, the Turks had converted the royal temple built by Vīra Someśvara in the mid-thirteenth century into a mosque; Kampaṇa reconverted it into a temple in 1372 (ARE 162 of 1936–1937). He reopened the great temple at the center of Madurai. Kampaṇa's officer Gopana restored the image of Viṣṇu Govindarāja to the Saiva temple at Cidambaram and, as we shall see, Gopaṇa also brought the portable image of Viṣṇu Raṅganātha back from its place of hiding and had it reinstalled in the sanctum of the temple at Śrīraṅgam, thereby (claims the verse commemorating the event) 'reuniting the ground of Sri Rangam with the Golden Age.[298]

Restoration of deities entailed *control* over their assets. This is most evident in the case of Śrīraṅgam. An inscription from 1371 records Kampaṇa's general, Goppaṇa, restored the image of Śrīraṅganātha to his temple – an image that had spent decades in exile in Delhi, or in Tirupati, depending on the source.[299] An inscription on the temple – a variation on a brace of verses ostensibly composed by Vedānta Deśika (Raṅganātha's trustee) – records the re-installation of the deity:

> Having brought (the deity) from the Añjanādri (mountain), the splendor of whose darkish peaks gives delight to the world, having worshipped (him) at Cheñchi for some time, then having slain the Tulushkas whose bows were raised, Goppaṇārya, the mirror of fame, placing Raṅganātha, together with both Lakṣmī and the Earth in his own town, again duly performed excellent worship.[300]

[297] Davis, *Lives of Indian Images*, 120.

[298] Ibid., 121–2. For a list of the inscriptions, see A. Krishnaswami, *The Tamil Country Under Vijayanagara* (Annamalainagar: Annamalai University, 1964), 43–4 & 49–51.

[299] EI 6.33. For descriptions of Raṅganātha's exile, see Davis, *Lives of Indian Images*, 123–37.

[300] Ibid.: ānīyānīlaśṛṅgadyutiracitajagadrañjanādañjanādreścañjyāmārāddhya kaṁcit samayatha nihatyoḍvanuṣkāns **turuṣkān** / **lakṣmīkṣmābhyāmubhābhyāṃ** saha nijanagare sthāpayan **raṅganāthaṃ** samyagvaryyāṃ saparyyām punar kṛta yaśodarppaṇo **goppaṇāryaḥ** //

While this act was celebrated in the *Kōyil Oḻugu*, the chronicle of the Śrīraṅgam temple, the temple trustees did not, it seems, appreciate the Vijayanagara court's sense of control over the restored temple trust.[301] According to the *Oḻugu*, the great Rāmānuja (1017–1137 CE) had devised an elaborate system for the management of the deity's trust assets – one that largely excluded non-Brāhmaṇas – that was, as a result of a Cōḷa dispensation, largely independent of royal supervision.[302] The *Oḻugu* complains about the despoliations of sulṭānate rulers at length, but it also criticises the Gajapati dynasty for assuming direct control over the temple in the 13th century and argues that the Vijayanagara court overturned Rāmānuja's trust model:

> Originally there was one ruler over the lands of the Cēra, Cōḷa and Pāṇḍya *maṇḍalas*… in fact, until the Śaka year 1249… the kings did not control the *devadāya* and *brahmadāya* lands but left them under the control of the Brāhmans and only enquired into complaints received regarding their administration and meted our justice duly. Then the Muḥammadans came, laid waste the *devadāya* and the deity had to seek refuge in… other places till he came back to Śrīraṅgam in Śaka 1293 (1371 CE)… then all these *maṇḍalas* came under the Rāya… [who] made gifts of many villages… and began to administer the… *devadānas* in the same way as they administered the palace lands (*araṇmanaicaīrmai*) by appointing in Śrīraṅgam… their own servants.[303]

Centralised political authority thus resulted in a centralised supervision of religious endowments – even as the empire's conquests enabled the restoration of deities, the reconstruction of temples, and the concentration of significant financial endowments. According to Raṅganātha's trustees, the old Dharmaśāstric system of Equity in the form of 'the cordial but distant relationship between court and temple which had prevailed prior to the fourteenth century' was gone.[304] Deities still owned property – perhaps more than at any point previously – property rights still vested in these deities, and these assets were in turn administered by trustees according to conventional (*sāmayika*) Dharma. Nevertheless, the Crown (a divine Crown administered by a human ruler as the deity's fiduciary) had a vested interest in a more active supervision in the administration of religious trusts. This development foreshadows the development of Devaswom administrative boards in the 19th and 20th centuries by the East India Company presidencies and by the princely states.[305]

[301] See George W. Spencer, 'Crisis of Authority in a Hindu Temple under the Impact of Islam: Śrīraṅgam in the Fourteenth Century', in B.L. Smith (ed.), *Religion and the Legitimation of Power South Asia* (Leiden: Brill, 1978): 14–27.

[302] Ibid., 16–18.

[303] Sontheimer, 'Religious Endowments', 39–40.

[304] Spencer, 'Crisis', 24.

[305] I discuss this at length in the following chapter. For a quick overview, see Das Acevedo, 'Divine Sovereignty' 845–50.

3.4 Mughals, Rajpūts, and Marāṭhās

The Mughal emperors were active patrons of Hindu and Jain religious endowments. For the first time in history, Indo-Islamic rulers acted as true patrons and protectors of Hindu religious trusts. This is a remarkable achievement – one tied to the desire of Akbar and his successors to cultivate a political alliance with the Rajpūts – and one that ought to be lauded. Hundreds of documents from the Mughal chancery attest to the keen interest that the empire's administrators took in not only in providing pecuniary advantage to Hindu religious organisations, but also in ensuring that they were efficiently run, protected from external harassment, and contributing to a wider ecumenical spirit within the realm.

This camaraderie came to an end, however. Ironically, the Mughal emperor most infamous for destroying Hindu temples, Aurangzeb, was, before the rebellion of Śivāji in the 1660s, an enthusiastic patron of religious institutions. Sedition from the Rajpūts and the Marāṭhās, *inter alia*, prompted Aurangzeb to turn away, although not entirely, from the accommodative practices of his ancestors and destroy several prominent temples that are the subject of considerable communal conflict even to this day: Kāśīviśveśvara (in 1699) and Mathurākeśavajanmabhūmi (1770).

Nevertheless, when the Marāṭhās and Rajpūts asserted their independence and developed their own legal systems for administering Hindu, Jain, and Islamic religious trusts, they incorporated many features of the old Mughal bureaucracy (often giving them a Sanskritic flair). The British jurists of the 18th and 19th centuries inherited these Persianate legal systems when they stepped into the administrative slippers of the decaying Mughal Empire and began the long process of developing the modern law of Hindu religious and charitable trusts that is still in force today.

3.4.1 Equity and Trusts in the Mughal Empire

In 1526, Ẓahīr ud-Dīn Muḥammad (r. 1526–30 CE), or Bābur, a descendent of Timur and Genghis Khan, entered India from Central Asia and defeated the last Delhi Sulṭān, Ibrahim Khan Lodi, at the First Battle of Panipat. This victory ushered in the hegemony of arguably the most famous dynasty in Indian history: the Mughal Empire (1526–1857 CE). It is difficult to overestimate the Mughals' importance to Indian history, culture, arts, and religion. For my purposes, it is necessary to note that the legal system of the Mughal Empire, particularly its chancery practices with regard to revenue allocation and religious endowments, formed the foundation for colonial-era legal practices that survive, although in a much-changed form, to this day.

Map 3.3 India, 1526–1760, the Mughal Empire and the Marāṭhā Confederacy

Between the reigns of Akbar (r. 1556–1605 CE) and his great-grandson, Muhi al-Din Muḥammad (Aurangzeb/Alamgir I, r. 1658–1707 CE), the Mughal Empire developed a sophisticated legal regime that endowed and managed Hindu and Jain religious trusts. For the first time in Indian history, we have evidence of significant patronage of Hindu temples by Islamic rulers. The Mughals – including Aurangzeb issued hundreds of *farmāns* that granted *ʿinām* rights (a share of produce from a taxable jurisdiction), issued specific injunctions protecting (or limiting) Hindu religious practices from external harassment, and directly adjudicated instances of contested trusteeship within religious communities. Much of this legal activity occurred within the 'department of pious foundations and religious affairs' (*daftar-i divān-i saʿadat*) and other associated branches of the Mughal bureaucracy which not only endured until the advent of colonialism in the 18th century, but also provided the core practices and principles for the colonial-era law of Hindu religious trusts.[306]

Bābur's contribution to the history of Equity and Trusts in Sanskrit jurisprudence is, unfortunately, speculative (our data is quite limited) and negative (what data we do have frames him in an iconoclastic light). Bābur patronised Sufi shrines and, 'on entering Delhi in 1526… [he] prayed at the shrine of… [the] great Chishtī shaykh, Bakhtyār Kakī (d. 1235), while the new emperor's brother-in-law rebuilt the tomb of Nizām al-Dīn- Awliyā'.[307] Negatively, Bābur perhaps ordered his officer, Mīr Bāqī, to erect a mosque – the infamous Bābrī Masjid – at Ayodhyā, on what was, perhaps, the site of a temple dedicated to Rāma at his birthplace.[308] A dedicatory inscription found at the mosque before its demolition in 1992 records: 'By the command of the Emperor Babur, whose justice is an edifice reaching up to the very height of the heavens, the good-hearted Mir Baqi built this alighting-place of angels. May this goodness last forever. The year of building… was… (935 AH, i.e., 1528).'[309]

The dating of this inscription and the assessment of the historical veracity of any data from the erstwhile Bābrī Masjid in Ayodhyā is highly controversial in the polarised political environment of contemporary India.[310] A veritable ocean of ink

[306] For the Daftar, see Heidi Pauwels, 'A Tale of Two Temples: Mathurā's Keśavadeva and Orcchā's Caturbhujadeva', in Rosalind O'Hanlon and David Washbroom (eds), *Religious Cultures in Early Modern India* (London: Routledge, 2012): 278–99, 278. Also see Rafat Bilfrāmī, *Religious and Quasi-Religious Departments of the Mughal Period (1556–1707)* (New Delhi: Munshiram Manoharlal, 1984), #'s 1 & 198.

[307] Eaton, 'Temple Desecration', 292.

[308] Peter van der Veer, '"God Must be Liberated!" A Hindu Liberation Movement in Ayodhya', *Modern Asian Studies* 21.2 (1987): 283–301. For the importance of this event in the modern Ayodhyā legal dispute, see Chapter 5, §5.1.4.i, 'A timeline of the Ayodhyā dispute: 1856–2010'.

[309] Van der Veer, 'God Must be Liberated!', 286.

[310] See, for example, Kishore Kunal, *Ayodhyā Revisited* (New Delhi: Ocean Books, 2016), 119–210, where he argues that the Bābrī inscription was an *ex post facto* justification for a mosque erected by Aurangzeb.

and blood has been spilt over this issue. With this in mind, this chapter brackets the Bābrī Masjid historiographical debate for the time being – Chapter 5 of this monograph examines the issue in depth – in order to focus on more strongly attested Mughal legal practices regarding Hindu and Jain religious endowments.

Bābur only ruled India for a brief period and was succeeded by his son, Mirza Nasir-ud-Dīn Muḥammad (Humāyūn, r. 1530–40 and 1555–56 CE). Humāyūn suffered from the dual afflictions of a fondness for intoxicants and the bad luck of having the inimitable Afghan commander Sher Shāh Sūrī (r. 1537–45 CE) as a puissant foe in the eastern Gangetic valley.[311] Sūrī consolidated the remnants of the Lodi Dynasty's nobles and retainers and toppled the Delhi regime in 1537, proclaiming himself the sulṭān of Bengal.

In 1540, he drove Humāyūn from India and declared the founding of the Pashtun Sur Empire (1540–55 CE), which governed northern India with great stability for fifteen years. Humāyūn, however, fled to the court of the Ṭahmāsb I (r. 1524–76 CE), the great Safavid Shāh, where he converted to Shiʿism (becoming a great patron of Sufi institutions), assembled an army and set out to reclaim the throne of Delhi. In 1555, he recaptured Delhi, but died soon afterwards in 1556, leaving his thirteen-year-old son, Abu'l-Fath Jalal-ud-Dūn Muḥammad Akbar, as the heir to a restored, secure empire.

3.4.1.i Akbar and the patronage of sub-imperial temples

The great success of the Mughal Empire, at least in comparison to the Delhi Sulṭānate, lay in its rulers' pursuit of matrimonial alliances with the powerful Rajpūt clans of western India. Akbar inherited an empire that was: 'still surrounded by enemies', such as the 'powerful Afghan chiefs who held considerable territory from the central Ganges valley through Bihar to Bengal and in Malwa… Rajpūt lineages [that] dominated Rajasthan' and 'the rich and powerful state of Gujarat'. Through the shrewd, open-minded conversion of 'Delhi's obdurate foes' into Mughal vassals – beginning with the Kachavāhā clan in 1562 – Akbar created a powerful, centralised state in which Hindus rose to positions of great prominence in the imperial administration.[312] The granting of *jāgīrs* (a form of feudal tenure like the *iqṭā'*), revenue farming (*ijārah*), and grants (*'inām*) was the key to this system.[313] In exchange for fealty and military service to the court in Agra, the Rajpūt clans were conferred limited autonomy, imperial grants, and, most importantly, religious autonomy.

[311] For Humāyūn's career, see Eaton, *Persianate*, 206–14.
[312] For Akbar, see ibid., 215–38.
[313] The best overview of Mughal tenurial rights is Sudev Seth, 'Revenue Farming Reconsidered: Tenurial Rights and Tenurial Duties in Early Modern India, ca. 1556–1818', *Journal of the Economic and Social History of the Orient* 61 (2018): 878–918.

During Akbar's reign, high-profile Rajpūt leaders constructed several prominent Hindu (and Jain) temples with formal financial support from the Mughal Empire. Every Hindu temple discussed below was constructed by a Rajpūt retainer of Agra during Akbar's reign and subsequently demolished during Aurangzeb's reign. The explanation for this lies in the politics of the empire rather than in religious sensibilities: when the Rajpūt were loyal to the Mughals, their suzerains tolerated, supported, and protected their subordinates' sub-imperial temples; and when the Rajpūts rebelled (as they did *en masse* in 1669), Agra's agents swiftly plundered these same temples.

Take, for example Akbar's finance minister (*Dīwān-i-Ashraf*), Rājā Ṭoḍaramalla (c. 1560–89 CE), who, perhaps more than any other individual, was responsible for the institution of an efficient, centralised revenue system in the empire.[314] Ṭoḍaramalla had a vast influence in the Mughal administration and he used it to accomplish, *inter alia*, two key acts of traditional Sanskritic charity: 1) he patronised the compilation of a Dharmaśāstric digest, the *Vyavahārasaukhya*, by leading Brāhmaṇical scholars; and 2) patronised the (re)construction of the Kāśīviśvanātha temple in concert with the famed Mahārāṣṭrian Brāhmaṇa, Nārāyaṇabhaṭṭa (1514–70 CE).[315] Nārāyaṇabhaṭṭa was one of the compilers of the *Vyavahārasaukhya*, and the Kāśīviśvanātha temple provided an assembly place and financial nexus for a large community of Brāhmaṇical scholars from a pan-Indian 'Brahman Ecumene' who were actively involved in adjudicating inter-Hindu religio-legal disputes in the 16th and 17th centuries.[316]

Ṭoḍaramalla also supported the Govindadevajī temple of the Gauḍiya Vaiṣṇavas in Vṛṇḍāvana. A 1568 *farmān* from Agra records that he requested that Akbar grant 'Jīva Gosvāmī, "a poor man, praying for His Majesty", the custodianship (*adhikāra*) of the temples of Govindadeva and Madanamohana, which had been given to him by Rūpa, as well as "the right to claim all offerings (*khairāt)* at the temples"'. A 1584 *farmān* records Ṭoḍaramalla's direct allocation of land to the temple when he served as the *jāgīrdar* (holder of a revenue assignment) of Vṛṇḍāvana.[317] Akbar had already patronised the temple, as early as 1565, at the request of his Rajpūt brother-in-law, Rājā Bhār Malla, of Amber.[318] In 1598, Akbar granted land to at least thirty-five different temples in the area.[319]

Other Mughal subordinates obtained imperial consent and funding for a series of grand temples in some of India's holiest Hindu religious sites. Mānasiṃha I, Kachavāhā king of Amber (r. 1589–1614 CE) and *Sūbedār* of Bengal, Bihar, and

[314] See Rocher, *Vyavahārasaukhya*.

[315] For Nārāyaṇabhaṭṭa and his relationship to Ṭoḍaramalla, see Fleming, *Ownership and Inheritance*, 122–4.

[316] Ibid., 124–30.

[317] Lutjeharms, 'A Temple', 183–4. Also see Mukherjee and Habib, 'Akbar and the Temples', 236–7.

[318] Horstmann, *In Favour of Govindadevjī*, 2.

[319] Ibid., 12 & 238–45.

Orissa (1594–1606 CE), completed his father's construction of a glorious temple for Govindadevajī at Vṛndāvana around 1590.[320] His fellow Rajpūt-cum-Mughal vassal, Vīra Siṃha, the Bundelā King of Orcchā (r. 1605–27 CE) arranged for the construction of a new Keśavadeva temple at Mathurā (the subject of the current Kṛṣṇajanmabhūmi dispute) and either completed or restored the Kāśīviśvanātha temple begun by Ṭoḍaramalla.[321]

Like Ṭoḍaramalla, Vīra Siṃha sponsored the compilation of a vast digest of Dharmaśāstra treatises, the *Vīramitrodaya* of Mitramiśra (active 1610–40 CE).[322] Heidi Pauwels associates these building developments with an expression of 'dharmic kingship' by newly ascendent Rajpūts such as Vīra Siṃha, whose 'grandscale religious sponsorship, of temples and other pious public building, and of works of literature and dharmaśāstra... presented... [them] as a dharmic king' within the wider framework of the Mughal Empire.[323] Hindu rulers' participation in Mughal political life entailed a freedom to articulate their circumscribed sovereignty through a Dharmaśāstric idiom (one that entailed an appeal to the Sanskrit jurisprudential principles of Equity and Trusts).

3.4.1.ii The Mughal regulation of religious endowments under Jahāngīr and Shāh Jahān

Akbar secured the support of the Rajpūt clans by enabling their construction and patronage of Hindu religious endowments – and this led to enormous political success for Akbar. It also created a series of regulatory and political issues for his successors. Akbar had intervened in the regulation of the Govindadevajī temple with his 1568 *farmān* granting Jīva Gosvāmi the trusteeship of the temple. His successors continued to issue grants that patronised Hindu religious institutions, but they also found themselves increasingly responsible for adjudicating disputes regarding religious endowments, issuing injunctions against interference with Hindu religious practices, and, as time passed, suppressing temple cults associated with politically rebellious Rajpūts.

Most documentary evidence concerning the Mughal administration's adjudication of intra-Hindu religious disputes comes from the Govindadevajī temple in Vṛndāvana, where, as Mukherjee and Habid note, Agra's 'authority was... indispensable for the protection of any installed management against pretentious

[320] Pauwels, 'A Tale of Two Temples'.
[321] Ibid., 284–8. For the Kṛṣṇajanmabhūmi dispute, see Conclusion, §6.1.1, 'Communitarian concerns'.
[322] Fleming, *Ownership and Inheritance*, 201–2. Note that, the *Vīramitrodaya* shares many of the same jurisprudential arguments as Nārāyaṇabhaṭṭa and other Mahārāṣṭrian Brāhmaṇa scholars who were funded by Agra-backed Rajpūts. Nārāyaṇabhaṭṭa's grandson, Nīlakaṇṭhabhaṭṭa, was patronised by Vīrasiṃha's kinsman, Bhagvanta Deva of the Sengar clan at Bhareha.
[323] Pauwels, 'Tale of Two Temples', 290.

usurpers'.[324] In 1613, Jahāngīr converted Ṭoḍaramalla's grant – issued in his capacity as *Sūbedār* – into an imperial grant, and formalised the administration of the temple.[325] In 1633, however, Shāh Jahān transferred the *'inām* (grant) from the temple to Jayasiṃha I of Amber (r. 1621–67 CE), on the technical legal basis that 'it is not the rule to make grants in the name of temples'.[326]

This effectively set up a legal regime in which the grant vested in the kings of Amber, but the custodianship (*adhikāra*) of the temple (and Govindadevajī) vested in Jīvagosvāmi's successors. Both Delhi and Agra had vested interests in the supervision of the temple. Jīva Gosvāmi died in 1618, leaving behind a will (dated to 1608) that left behind his property to Vilāsadāsa, who in turn bequeathed it to Kṛṣṇadāsa Gosvāmī.[327] When Jīva died, however, a different disciple, Haridāsa Gosvāmī, was the custodian of Govindadevajī's temple. Kṛṣṇadāsa and his successors engaged in a decades-long legal-cum-theological feud with Vilāsadāsa and his successors over Jīva's will and the custodianship of the Govindadevajī's temples.[328] The dispute went first to Amber in 1643, and then to Agra, where both parties supported Kṛṣṇadāsa – repeatedly, over the decades.[329]

Alongside these disputes about trusteeship, there are numerous other instances in which the local administration of Agra intervened in more mundane property disputes and issued injunctions that protected the Govindadevajī community's freedom to follow their religious practices. For example, the local administration repeatedly intervened between 1645 and 1654 in cases involving trees being cut down in temple lands, and even sent a judge (*qāḍī*), to adjudicate and have both parties sign a binding agreement.[330]

In 1634, Shāh Jahān intervened to prevent local Mughal authorities from prohibiting the sounding of a time-gong (*gharial*) at the Madanamohana temple (associated with Govindadevajī) on the basis of it conforming to 'divine worship according to their own religion and custom'.[331] Likewise, in 1644, Jayasiṃha's *wakil* (legal representative) obtained a binding injunction from the local administration that banned Bengalis from entering the temple of Govindadevajī.[332] Cutting trees, evicting trespassing neighbours, and making the local population accept the annoyance of midnight monastic bells for the sake of religious freedom are

[324] Mukherjee and Habib, 'Mughal Administration', 291.

[325] Ibid., 294.

[326] Ibid., 295 #17.

[327] Lutjeharms, 'A Temple', 184–5. For a translation of this will, see Tarapada Mukherjee and J.C. Wright, 'An Early Testamentary Document in Sanskrit', *Bulletin of the School of Oriental and African Studies* 42.2 (1979): 297–320.

[328] Lutjeharms, 'A Temple', 185–6.

[329] Ibid., 185–7. For the 1644 *farmān*, see Mukherjee and Habib, 'Mughal Administration', 295 #18. Subsequent imperial interventions are noted in documents #'s 26, 30, & 32.

[330] Mukherjee and Habib, 'Mughal Administration', 297–8, #s 33–4 & 39.

[331] Ibid., 299, #21.

[332] Ibid., 296, #27.

exactly the kinds of quotidian legal issues – alongside broader questions of breach of trusts, etc. – that make up the day-to-day of the contemporary court system. That Mughal administrators busied themselves with these issues, rather than simply ignore them, attests to the substantial integration of Hindu religious trusts within Indo-Islamic law.

Of course, the Mughal Empire was an autocratic empire and there were clear limits on its tolerance of religious freedom by seditious elements. If the Rajpūts earned the right to build and endow temples through serving the empire, their decision to throw off the yoke of Agra warranted their tutelary deities' destruction. For example, when Vīrasiṃha's son, Jhujhar Singh (r. 1626–35 CE) rebelled against Agra in 1635, Shāh Jahān dispatched his son, the future Aurangzeb, to sack Orcchā. The court chronicle, the *Pādshāh Nāmāh*, describes this punitive expedition as setting an example for vassals who might stray from their imperial orbit.[333] Michael Calabria attributes Shāh Jahān's 1633 order to destroy seventy-six temples in Vārāṇasī (whose foundations had been laid during the reign of Jahāngīr) to 'Benaras' lack of support for Shah Jahan during his rebellion against' his father.[334]

3.4.1.iii *The ambiguous position of Aurangzeb*

Emperor Aurangzeb occupies a contradictory, but analytically fertile, place in the history of Equity and Trusts in Sanskrit jurisprudence. On the one hand, Aurangzeb's record of Hindu (and Jain) temple endowment and protection may be unmatched among Indo-Islamic rulers. We have a vast quantity of *farmāns* issued by Aurangzeb and his agents that grant *'ināms* to various temples and monastic institutions, and that enjoin the protection of Brāhmaṇas and temple custodians from harassment from Muslims.[335] Take, for example, a *farmān* from 1659, in which the emperor noted that:

> Information has reached our court that several people have… harassed the Hindu residents of Benares and nearby places, including a group of Brahmans who are in charge of ancient temples there. These people want to remove those Brahmans from their charge of temple-keeping, which has caused them considerable distress. Therefore, upon receiving this order, you must see that nobody unlawfully disturbs the Brahmans or other Hindus of that region… according to the Holy Law (*sharī'at*)

[333] Pauwels, 'Tale of Two Temples', 288.

[334] Michael Calabria, 'The Unorthodox "Orthodoxy" of Shah Jahan: A Reassessment of His Religiosity', *South Asia: Journal of South Asian Studies* 41.3 (2018): 579–600, 592.

[335] Any excellent list appears in Jnan Chandra, 'Aurangzib and Hindu Temples', *Journal of the Pakistan Historical Society* 5.4 (1957): 247–54; Jnan Chandra, 'Alamgir's Tolerance in Light of Contemporary Jain Literature', *Journal of Pakistan Historical Society* 6.4 (1958): 269–72. Also see Satish Chandra, 'Some Religious Grants of Aurangzeb to "Maths" in the State of Marwar', *Proceedings of the Indian History Congress* 32.1 (1970): 405–7; and Truschke, *Aurangzeb*, 81–3. For donations to support a Śaiva *maṭha* in Vārāṇasī, see Nirmala Gupta, 'Land Grants of Mughal Emperors to Jangamavadi Matha of Benares, A Centre of Veershaivism', Quarterly *Journal of the Pakistan Historical Society* 57.1 (2009): 29–40.

> and the exalted creed, it has been established that ancient temples should not be torn down.[336]

Furthermore, the chronicle (*vārtā*) literature of the Vallabhasampradāya (the Puṣṭimārga), a Vaiṣṇava sect that arose in the Braj region alongside the Gauḍīya Vaiṣṇavas in the 15th and 16th centuries, describe Aurangzeb as a devotee and protector rather than as a persecutor of their deities.[337] Aurangzeb even mediated a contentious dispute between the third and sixth 'houses' (*gaddīs*) over the custody and trusteeship of Śrīdvārakādhīśajī and Śrībālakṛṣṇajī (two deities that would end up as the nominal sovereigns of Rajpūt kingdoms).[338]

Aurangzeb's monumental digest of Ḥanafī *fiqh* (Islamic jurisprudence), the *Fatawa-i 'Alamgiri*, completed between 1667 and 1675, standardised the legal system of the realm, or at least its constitutional foundations, and provided *qāḍīs* with something akin to a uniform, codified Islamic law.[339] In this legal environment, Hindu authors produced an Islamic jurisprudential theory of Equity in which Dharmaśāstra was recognised as a 'school' (*madhhab/mazhab*) of jurisprudence applicable to Hindus.[340] In 1658, a Kāyastha (member of the scribal caste) named Lāl Bihārī Bhojpurī, who was employed in the Mughal administration, dedicated the *Aḥkām-i Awāmir o Nawāhī-yi Mazhab-i Hunūd* ('The Legal Rulings on Commanding Right and Forbidding Wrong of the *Mazhab* of the Hindus') to ʿĀlamgīr.[341]

The *Aḥkām* translated the *Yājñavalkyasmṛti* and the *Mitākṣarā* commentary into Persian, perhaps with the intent of providing a legal justification for Aurangzeb ʿĀlamgīr's overtures to the Brāhmaṇical community within the wider remit of the empire's governing principles of Islamic jurisprudence. Considering this evidence, Aurangzeb might well be *the* paradigmatic example of an Indo-Muslim ruler acting as a Dharmaśāstric sovereign who endows and protects a diverse array of religious communities within his realm.

On the other hand, for much of the contemporary world, Aurangzeb might also be *the* paradigmatic example of an intolerant Indo-Muslim ruler who

[336] Eaton, 'Temple Desecration', 305.

[337] Heidi Pauwels and Emilia Bachrach, 'Aurangzeb as Iconoclast? Vaishnava Accounts of the Krishna images' Exodus from Braj', *Journal of the Royal Asiatic Society* 28.3 (2018): 485–508.

[338] Ibid., 503–4.

[339] A.M. Guenther, 'Ḥanafī fiqh in Mughal India: The *Fatawa-i 'Alamgiri*', in Richard Eaton (ed.), *India's Islamic Traditions, 711–1750* (New Delhi: Oxford University Press, 2003): 209–33. The *Fatawa-i 'Alamgiri* was intended to have a generally universal scope – with exceptions made for other schools of Islamic jurisprudence. It became the basis for a codified Muslim personal law in colonial India with the passage of William Hastings' Judicial Plan of 1772. For the colonial adaptation, see Michael Anderson, 'Islamic Law and the Colonial Encounter in British India', in David Arnold and Peter Robb (eds), *Institutions and Ideologies: A SOAS South Asia Reader* (London: Routledge, 1993): 165–85.

[340] Supriya Gandhi, '*Dharmaśāstra* in Aurangzeb's India: A Persian Translation of the *Yājñavalkya Smṛti* and *Mitākṣarā*', *Journal of Hindu Studies* 16 (2023): 33–56.

[341] Ibid., 34.

favoured conservative elements of the *Ulamā* (the Islamic scholarly community), destroyed Hindu temples, re-imposed the *jizya* tax (enlisting the *Ulamā* as tax collectors), issued a series of *farmāns* prohibiting Hindu religious practices, and mortally wounding the power of the Mughal Empire by alienating the Rajpūt vassals whose martial prowess had supported it.[342] The three most contentious, communal court cases involving Hindu temple trusts – at Ayodhyā, Vārāṇasī, and Mathurā – in contemporary India all involve Hindu temples that were destroyed and converted into mosques by order of Aurangzeb. In 1665, Aurangzeb doubled the customs duties for Hindu merchants from 2.5 per cent to 5 per cent; in 1668, he banned Hindu religious fairs; and in 1669, just months before destroying the Kāśīviśvanātha temple, he ordered that 'that the schools and places of worship of the irreligious be subject to demolition and that with the utmost urgency the manner of teaching and the public practices of the sects of these misbelievers be suppressed'.[343] Finally, in 1679, Aurangzeb: 'Issued an order reinstating the discriminatory *jizya* tax, effectively a property tax levied on all non- Muslim males except those in imperial service… [and] it has been suggested that the emperor felt the need to make some dramatic move to rally the empire's Muslims around major political and military initiatives.'[344]

Whatever be their origin – a newfound religious conviction, economic necessity, suspicions about the Brāhmaṇas' loyalty, Śivājī's treason (and his escape from imperial detention at Agra in 1666), a desire to ingratiate himself with the *Ulamā*, or some combination of all of these factors – Aurangzeb's discriminatory policies occurred in concert with the assertion of independence by the Marāṭhās and the Rajpūts against the Mughal Crown.[345] Whether these rebellions were triggered by Aurangzeb's discriminatory policies or vice versa, the result was that the great temples founded during Akbar's reign were dismantled and the deities of Braj were relocated to Rajpūt courts.[346]

Aurangzeb had good reason to question the loyalties of the Brāhmaṇas of the Kāśīviśvanātha temple. Members of the influential Bhaṭṭa family – whose ancestor Nārāyaṇabhaṭṭa had worked with Ṭoḍaramalla to reconstruct the temple under Akbar's reign – had deep and longstanding associations with the Marāṭhā court,

[342] A classic example of decline theory is Stanley Lane-Pool, *Aurangzīb and the Decay of the Mughal Empire* (Oxford: Oxford University Press, 1908). Also see Jamal Malik, 'From Universal Dominion to Principalities (approx. 1650–1800)', in Jamal Malik (ed.), *Islam in South Asia* (Leiden: Brill, 2020): 255–92.

[343] Eaton, 'Temple Desecration', 308.

[344] Eaton, *Persianate*, 330. Also see Malik, 'From Universal Dominion', 256–7.

[345] For Aurangzeb and Śivājī's relationship, see Truschke, *Aurangzeb*, 59–64.

[346] Pauwels and Bachrach, 'Aurangzeb', 485–6, add nuance to the transfer of deities from Braj to Rājasthān, and note that Rup Singh (r. 1643–48), the fifth ruler of Kishangarh state, brough the Puṣṭimārg deity, Śrī Govarddhananāthajī, to Rupnagar in 1646 – well before Aurangzeb's shift in policy towards Hindus.

serving in judicial assemblies (*Dharmasabhās*) on behalf of their royal patrons.[347] In 1669, 'there arose a rebellion in Benares among landholders, some of whom were suspected of having helped Shivājī... escape from imperial detention in 1666' and Aurangzeb responded by ordering the destruction of the temple and the erection of the (now standing) Jñānvāpī mosque on its ruins.[348] The temple-deprived Brāhmaṇas of Vārāṇasī responded by elevating Śivājī to full Kṣatriya status and coronating him as an independent, universal Hindu sovereign (*Chatrapati*) in an elaborate ceremony in 1674.[349] Likewise, in 1670, 'serious Jat rebellions broke out in the area around Mathura, in which the patron of that city's congregational mosque had been killed'; and Aurangzeb responded by destroying the great Keśavadeva temple and erecting the (now standing) Shahi Eidgah mosque.[350]

Aurangzeb's controversial reign was the high-water mark of the Mughal Empire. Although Aurangzeb ruled a vast empire of 150 million people and subsumed 'most of the Indian subcontinent under a single imperial power for the first time in human history', he left his successors an empire divided by rebellion, internal strife, and religious disunion.[351] His deathbed confession, that he 'entirely lacked in rulership and protecting the people', seems unfairly self-critical, given the remarkable inclusivity of his early reign.[352] Aurangzeb's policies were controversial in his time and they will likely remain controversial. Nevertheless, these policies were complex, and that complexity speaks to the ways in which Hindu religious endowments – and Dharmaśāstric principles of Equity and Trusts – were accepted or rejected by Aurangzeb political regime.

In some ways, the Mughal Empire was a victim of its own success. Akbar created a vast, powerful state by including Rajpūts within the imperial administration and by protecting and endowing their sub-imperial Hindu temples. Nevertheless, if Hindu temples served as fonts of political sovereignty for Dharmaśāstric sovereigns in pre-Islamic India, and if the destruction of Hindu temples during the Islamic period is viewed as a form of political domination, then it seems reasonable to understand why, once the Rajpūts (and Marāṭhās) re-established their own tutelary deities under Mughal rule, they subsequently broke away from their vassalage. The horses had bolted and all the Mughals could do was try to lock the barn after the fact.

[347] Fleming, *Ownership and Inheritance*, 127–30. For the contemporary legal dispute involving temple/mosques from the reign of Aurangzeb, see Conclusion, §6.1.1, 'Communitarian concerns'.

[348] Easton, 'Temple Destruction', 307. Eaton notes that 'it was also believed that Shivajī's escape had been initially facilitated by Jai Singh, the great-grandson of Raja Man Singh (one of the founders of the temple)'. That Jai Singh's Kachāvahā family were the imperially sanctioned guardians of Govindadevajī also explains Aurangzeb's dismantling of the Braj temple in 1669 along with Kāśīviśvanātha.

[349] Fleming, *Ownership and Inheritance*, 127–30.

[350] Ibid., 307–8.

[351] Truschke, *Aurangzeb*, 1–2.

[352] Ibid.

3.4.2 Rajpūts and Marāṭhās as Dharmaśāstric sovereigns

In 1674, a group of Mahārāṣṭrian Brāhmaṇas associated with the former Kāśīviśvanātha temple of Vārāṇasī consecrated Śivājī Bhonsle as an independent Dharmaśāstric sovereign; Śivājī soon found himself in a state of semi-permanent rebellion against the Mughal throne. Śivājī was joined in 1679, by two powerful Rajpūt kingdoms, Marwar and Mewar, followed by Amber in 1708. By the mid-18th century, Mughal power was vastly attenuated – although the Marāṭhās continued to rule as nominal vassals of the emperor. The result was a series of regional polities and, among the Marāṭhās and Rajpūts, the development of regionalised, Sanskrit-influenced versions of Mughal administrative practices.

In terms of Equity and Trusts, both the Rajpūt and Marāṭhā polities adopted Dharmaśāstric *theory* and *practice* regarding Equity and Trusts. Court narratives frame these independent sovereigns as protectors of deities and of Hindu Dharma from the destructive raids of the Mughals, while administrative practices show a strong preference for endowing and regulating a wide array of religious trusts. The end result, then, is the full culmination of the history of Equity and Trusts in pre-colonial India, in which deities with strong juridical personalities were endowed and protected according to Mughal-inspired legal regimes (whatever be the Sanskritisation of their technical terminology). Although the practical, bureaucratic machinery of the Rajpūt and Marāṭhā law of Hindu religious trusts was Mughal in origin, the *jurisprudential* ideology behind that law was explicitly Dharmaśāstric.

3.4.2.i Rajpūt kingdoms as divine trusts

Much like Vijayanagara, many Rajpūt kingdoms articulated their sovereignty and their partial or full break from the Mughals by consecrating tutelary deities in their capitals and ruling on their behalf as trustees. The most prominent example of this is the Kachāvahā kings, who overthrew the Mughal yoke under Jayasiṃha II (1699–1743 CE). Jayasiṃha II founded a new capital, Jaipur, performed a pair of Aśvamedha sacrifices – an ancient ritual of royal sovereignty – and installed the deity, Govindadevajī, in the city's palace as the sovereign of the kingdom.[353] Govindadevajī retains his position as ruler of Jaipur to this day.

All nine deities of the Vallabhasampradāya also found their way into Rājasthān, where they were endowed by the royal houses of Mewar, Jaipur,

[353] Horstman, *In Favour of Govindadevjī*, 8–9. Govindadevjī's royal status also brought the Kachāvahās many responsibilities for adjudicating intra-religious arguments among the Gauḍīya Vaiṣṇava. See, for example, Rameshwar Prasad Bahuguna, 'Religion and State in Eighteenth Century Rajasthan: Sawai Jai Singh and "Reformed" Vaishnavism', *Proceedings of the Indian Historical Congress* 74 (2013): 353–62.

and Koṭa.[354] Rajpūt kings' control over these palladia – whether from potential usurpers, Muslim rulers in Delhi, or from local Rajpūts – became *the* means of articulating the sovereignty (or paramountcy) of their respective kingdoms.[355] Unlike the Marāṭhās, or even Vijayanagara, however, Rajpūt deity-based sovereignty was remarkably circumscribed. Power projection was limited to attempts to establish regional hegemony – gaining custody of a few rivals' images at most – rather than creating the constellation of captured deities seen at Vijayanagara.

Rajpūt sovereignty went hand-in-glove with courtly narrative production that depicted these rulers as paragons of Dharmaśāstric royal virtue in opposition to the adharmic rule of the Mughals. For example, Lāl Kavi's 1710 Brajbhāṣā (a precursor to Hindi) *Chatraprakāś* praises his patron, the Bendelā ruler Chatrasal (r. 1675–1731 CE) as the embodiment of *Kṣatriya* Dharma, an opponent of temple-destroying Mughals, and a fierce devotee of the deity Rāma.[356]

Not all Rajpūt narratives frame Aurangzeb and the Mughals in a pejorative light, but many do, and virtually all employ Aurangzeb's conquest and Rajpūt rebellions as spring-boards for the articulation of a Dharmaśāstric model of Rajpūt royal sovereignty. Take for example, the following scene from Mān Kavi's 1680 *Rāj-Vilāsa*, a panegyric poem dedicated to his patron, Rana Raj Singh of Mewar (r. 1652–80 CE), the custodian of Ekaliṅgajī.[357] After giving safe haven to his relative, Ajit Singh of Jodhpur, Rana Raj, described 'as the lord of Hindus (*hindūpati*), maintainer of *kṣatriya* dharma... and the like' vows:

> I spread the superior Veda and will preserve on earth the Puranas,
> The *qazi's* books and all the Qurans, I reduce all these to ashes,
> I will grind down the Chagatai and establish my own garrison in Delhi,
> I maintain Hindu customs and uproot the demonic (*āsurī*) ways,
> I will raise up the best holy temples and tear down the *mlecca* sites.[358]

[354] For this period of Vallabha history, see Isabella Nardi, 'Mobility and Festivity: Krishna Icons and the Reunion of the Seven Svarūps of 1739–1740', *South Asian Studies* 39.1 (2023): 21–34.

[355] For several examples, see Norbert Peabody, 'In Whose Turban Does the Lord Reside? The Objectification of Charisma and the Fetishization of Objects in the Hindu Kingdom of Kota', *Comparative Studies in Society and History* 33.4 (1991): 726–54.

[356] Allison Busch, '"Unhitching the Oxcart of Delhi": A Mughal-Period Hindi Account of Political Insurgency', *JRAS* 27.3 (2018): 415–39. For other examples of the same phenomenon see Allison Busch, 'Literary Responses to the Mughal Imperium: The Historical Poems of Keśavdās', *South Asia Research* 25.1 (2005): 34–7; and Heidi Pauwels, 'The Saint, the Warlord, and the Emperor: Discourses of Braj Bhakti and Bundelā Loyalty', *Journal of the Economic and Social History of the Orient* 52: 2 (2009): 187–228.

[357] Cynthia Talbot, 'A Poetic Record of the Rajpūt Rebellion, c. 1680', *JRAS* 3.28 (2018): 461–83.

[358] Ibid., 472.

Ironically, even though these and similar Rajpūt narratives portray the Mughals in a pejorative light, Rajpūt courts utilised Mughal systems of administration even after they issued documents in Rājasthānī.[359] As Elizabeth Thelen notes:

> [Even after,] the Rajpūt kingdoms relied almost exclusively on local Rajasthani administrative idioms, they and their officials had to deal with Persian documents produced in earlier periods, especially regarding rights and property held by their subjects. The plurality of languages, document types, and administrative and judicial frameworks found within their recently expanded territories presented a challenge these rulers had to address in creative ways.[360]

Even though the numerous documents concerning the cult of Govindadevajī from the Jaipur chancery were printed in Rājasthānī by the mid-18th century, the effective legal terminology bears the imprimatur of the Persianate administrative system of the Mughal Empire from which Jaipur had ostensibly split.[361] In short, even as Rajpūt polities shifted out of Delhi's orbit and into their custodial relationship with local deities, they nevertheless adopted much of Delhi's administrative techniques in protecting those deities – even as they Sanskritised (or vernacularised) the terminology and jurisprudential theory involved in that protection.

3.4.2.ii Equity and Trusts in the Marāṭhā Confederacy

In 1674, Śivājī Bhosle was crowned as a *Kṣatriya* Chatrapati in an elaborate, fortnight-long ceremony by Gāgābhaṭṭa and Anantadevabhaṭṭa, two consummate Brāhmaṇa scholars of Dharmaśāstra (among other śāstric disciplines) from Vārāṇasī. This inaugurated what many view as a Hindu *svarājya* against the authority of the Mughals.[362] Śivājī's rise was meteoric: Śivājī started his career as the *jāgīrdār* of Pune, 'a position assigned to him by his father Śāhajī, who was employed by the 'Ādil Shāh of Bijapur as a prominent general and governor of Bangalore'.[363] Taking advantage of the decline of the Bījapur Sulṭānate, Śivājī slowly built up a power base in the Deccan – and raided sulṭānate holdings – until the sulṭān dispatched Afḍal Khān, to contain Śivjājī in 1659. Khān desecrated the temple of the Bhonsle clan's tutelary deity, the goddess Bhavāni, at Tuljapur.[364]

[359] See, for example, Arik Moran, 'Rajpūt Kingship', in *Oxford Research Encyclopedia of Asian History* (Oxford: Oxford University Press, 2023).
[360] Elizabeth Thelen, 'Disputed Transactions: Documents, Language, and Authority in Eighteenth Century Marwar', *Journal of the Economic and Social History of the Orient* 64 (2021): 792–825, 793.
[361] See Horstmann, *In Favour of Govindadevjī*.
[362] For the coronation of Śivājī, see Rosalind O'Hanlon, 'The Social Worth of Scribes: Brahmins, Kāyasthas, and the Social Order in Early Modern India', *Indian Economic and Social History Review* 47.4 (2010): 563–95.
[363] Laine, '*Dharma*', 302.
[364] Eaton, 'Temple Desecration', 306

On Bhavānī's instruction, Śivājī assassinated Khān at a diplomatic meeting (Khān had intended to assassinate Śivājī as well), bringing his severed head back to Bhavānī's temple as a grisly trophy.[365] This narrative encapsulates Śivājī's self-representation as a dashing *Kṣatriya* king who fights the iconoclastic forces of the sulṭānates and the Mughals in order to protect temples and Brāhmaṇas from oppression.

Alarmed by Śivājī's daring raids, Aurangzeb dispatched Rāja Jayasiṃha (guardian of the Govindadevajī temple) to capture Śivājī in 1665, and, after surrendering to Jayasiṃha, Śivājī came to Agra to pay homage to Aurangzeb.[366] Śivājī 'caused a ruckus at open court', and was promptly imprisoned, but he quickly escaped and returned to the Deccan to wage an insurrection.[367] Jayasiṃha's responsibility for keeping Śivājī in line earned him Aurangzeb's ire and this probably led to Aurangzeb's decision to destroy the Govindadevajī temple.[368] After Śivājī's coronation in 1674 and the final defeat of the *Peshwa* (prime minister, but effective ruler) Baji Rao II (r. 1796–1818 CE) in the Third Anglo-Mysore War, the Marāṭhās carved out a massive realm that stretched, at its peak in 1758, from Rājasthan, to Tamil Nadu, and east to Puri. Śivājī's half-brother, Vyankoji, established Marāṭhā lordship in Tanjavur in 1676 and took over the trusteeship of the Rājarājeśvara temple and other deities' endowment (a position held by his descendants).[369]

Ideologically, the Marāṭhās, like the Rajpūts, to whom they assimilated culturally over the course of time, presented themselves as rejuvenators of Dharmaśāstric kingship. The protection of religious institutions and Brāhmaṇas from Muslim oppression – real or rhetorical – lay at the very heart of this political identity. Truschke notes that, 'in less than twenty years, Sanskrit poets wrote at least five historical works for members of the Maratha Bhonsle clan: the *Sūryavaṃśa* (also known as the *Śivabhārata*); the *Śambhurājacarita*; the *Rājārāmacarita*; *Parṇālaparvatagrahaṇākhyāna* (sponsored by Ekojī, Śivājī's brother who ruled Tanjavur); and the *Paramānandakāvya*.[370]

Śivājī commissioned the *Sūryavaṃśa* from his court poet, Kavīndra Paramānanda, to celebrate his coronation and elevation to full *Kṣatriya* status in 1674 – performed by prominent Vārāṇasī-based Brāhmaṇas – and it is unsurprising that the poem's narrative frame is an explanation of Śivājī's glorious deeds to those very same Vārāṇasī-based Brāhmaṇas.[371] Paramānanda praises Śivājī as Viṣṇu incarnate, as a protector of Dharma, deities, Brāhmaṇas, and cows, who is

[365] Laine, '*Dharma*', 306–7.
[366] Truschke, *Aurangzeb*, 60–1.
[367] Ibid., 61–2.
[368] Ibid.
[369] The work on the Tanjore Marāṭhās is written by a Tanjore Marāṭhā. See Prince Pratap Sinh Serfoji Raje Bhosle, *Contributions of Thanjavur Maratha Kings*, 2nd edn. (Channai: Notion Press, 2017).
[370] Truschke, *The Language of History*, 177–8.
[371] Ibid., 178–9.

engaged in a Purāṇic struggle against *Yāvanas* (who, ironically, were sometimes Rajpūts in Mughal employ).[372] The politics of the Mughal world are transposed into a neo-Dharmaśāstric, Sanskrit idiom. In short, Śivājī's strong patronage and protection of Vārāṇasī's Brāhmaṇas enabled him to transform from a local *jāgīrdār* of ambiguous caste status under sulṭānate subordination into a glorious Kṣatriya revivor of the Dharmic order of the pre-Islamic Sanskrit cosmopolis.

The *administrative* system of the Marāṭhā Empire parallels this ideological transformation. Like Vijayanagara, the Marāṭhās Sanskritised their administrative *vocabulary* (in concert with their Dharmaśāstric politico-theology), but the *form* of the bureaucracy remained Persianate in several respects. Śivājī's attempts to 'subvert Mughal ruling culture… [by replacing] Indo-Persian political norms with Sanskrit based ones' flourished through his sponsorship of 'the *Rajavyavaharakosha* (Lexicon of royal institutes), which provided Sanskrit synonyms for fifteen hundred Indo-Persian administrative terms.'[373]

Wink notes that, 'a rudimentary body of officials with Persian titles which had already been constituted in 1669 when the Bhonsles were formally still *jāgirdārs* of Bijapur was given a Sanskrit nomenclature and converted into a regular *rājmaṇḍal* or *aṣṭapradhān* council of 'eight ministers' modelled upon the ancient examples.'[374] Of course, Eaton observes that 'the very attempt to compile this lexicon only revealed the extent to which Persian terms had already penetrated vernacular Marathi… [and] the effort recalls the futile attempts by the Academie Francaise to prevent hotdogs or supermarkets from infiltrating French.'[375]

Śivājī described his kingdom as a *Hiṇḍvīsvarājya* (a 'Hindu government') and the Dharmaśāstra treatises of the Bhaṭṭa family of Vārāṇasī – the same Brāhmaṇas who crowned him as a *Kṣatriya* sovereign in 1674 – became authoritative sources of jurisprudence for the evolving Marāṭhā legal system.[376] Although the Marāṭhā legal system had a decidedly Dharmaśāstric and Brāhmaṇical jurisprudential foundation, it nevertheless employed Persianate-style techniques and, perhaps most importantly, the Marāṭhās continued to patronise mosques and other Islamic institutions 'according to their importance.'[377] Śivājī and his successors'

[372] Laine, '*Dharma*', 302–8; Truschke, *The Language of History*, 183–6.

[373] Truschke, *Aurangzeb*, 62.

[374] Andre Wink, *Land and Sovereignty in India: Agrarian Society and Politics Under the Eighteenth-century Maratha Svarājya* (Cambridge: Cambridge University Press, 1986), 37.

[375] Eaton, 'Persian Cosmopolis', 82. For the Persianate elements of Marāṭhā chancery, also see Prachi Deshpande, 'The Marathi *Kaulnāmā:* Property, Sovereignty and Documentation in a Persianate Form', *Journal of the Economic and Social History of the Orient* 64 (2021): 583–614.

[376] For the *svarājya*, see Wink, *Land and Sovereignty*, 230–1.

[377] Ibid., 231. See V.T. Gune, *The Judicial System of the Marathas* (Poona: Deccan College, 1953), 69: 'Sanskrit Law Books were very often referred to in suits falling under personal law, such as, inheritance, partition, and marriage [and] the "*Vyavaharamayukha*" attained an equal position with the *Mitaksara*, during the Peshwa period.' In reference to *criminal*, rather than *civil* law, Sumit Guha, 'An Indian Penal Regime: Maharasthra in the Eighteenth Century', *Past and Present* 147.1 (1995): 101–26, 104, argues that, 'even though the *peshwas* were Brahmans, members of the priestly caste, yet their criminal jurisprudence seems to have been little influenced by the Sanskrit scriptures on these matters'.

Hiṇḍvīsvarājya was also known as 'the *rājya* which is beneficent to gods and brahmans' and the *Ājñāpatra*, a quasi-proto-constitution of the Marāṭhā state, extolls the protection of religious institutions as one of the foremost duties of a Dharmaśāstric sovereign.[378]

Given the Brāhmaṇical bent of the realm – the *Peshwas* were Brāhmaṇas after all – it unsurprising that the *Ājñāpatra* enjoins endowments made for 'family men' (*kuṭuṃbvatsal*) 'very well versed in the Veda and Shastra' and proscribes gifts to 'heretics opposed to their own Dharma' (*svadharmavirodhī pāṣaṇḍī*).[379] Several court cases from Peshwa court in the 18th century reveal that the *Ājñāpatra*'s statements were not merely rhetoric: individuals who were not recognised as full Brāhmaṇas could not hold *inā'm*, *agrahāra*, or *devāgrahāra* grants, and religious disputes concerning caste status (adjudicated by Brāhmaṇa courts) had tremendous practical legal implications.[380] Likewise, the Marāṭhā state exercised greater supervisory rights of visitation over religious endowments. The state appointed supervisors for royal grants, while private settlors of religious trusts were afforded greater rights of supervision over temple trustees, and the local population were granted the right to petition the court in cases of breach of trust by temple functionaries.[381]

In short, the Marāṭhās developed the most comprehensive legal system for the administration of Hindu religious trusts in pre-colonial history using a mixture of Mughal financial instruments and the Sanskrit jurisprudential principles of Equity and Trusts. Rulers under this system endowed temples and other religious institutions, exercised a supervisory right of visitation over them – according to a Dharmaśāstric theory of *parens patriae* jurisdiction, and frequently intervened in the administration of specific religious endowments.

3.5 Conclusion

The nominal legality of British East India Company's Indian holdings stemmed from an appeal to Indo-Islamic legal systems. When the British East India Company began its shift from a mostly mercantile organisation that operated out of a series of factories on the Indian coastline to a territorial power in the mid-18th century, it took on the responsibility of adjudicating legal disputes (criminal and civil) among the population in the areas that it held on behalf of the Mughal Crown. When Robert Clive obtained the *Dīwānī* (the formal right to collect revenue) for the provinces (*Subāhs*) of Bengal, Bihar, and Orissa, from the Mughal Emperor Shāh 'Ālam II on behalf of the British East India Company, the

[378] Wink, *Land and Sovereignty*, 231–2.
[379] Ibid., 232.
[380] Ibid., 233–4.
[381] Ibid., 235–6.

Company's agents assumed responsibility for overseeing the administrative complexities of the Mughal revenue system. It was in this administrative role that the Company found itself responsible for supervising Hindu, Muslim, Jain, Buddhist, and Sikh religious endowments.

Likewise, when the Company expanded its western dominion around Bombay after the Anglo-Maratha Wars (1772–1818 CE) it found itself responsible for adjudicating property disputes involving the complex administrative systems of the Marāṭhā Empire. In the south, the Madras presidency acquired *Dīwānī* rights in the Carnatic from the Nawābs of Arcot (undersigned by the Nizāms of Hyderabad). In the course of time, British administrators and jurists applied English theories of Equity and Trusts (and Dharmaśāstra) to the Indo-Islamic legal phenomena that they encountered in their exercise of *Dīwānī* rights. The result, as Chapter 4 discusses, was the colonial jurisprudence of Hindu religious and charitable trusts.

Considering the great importance of Indo-Islamic law to the history of colonial and post-colonial Indian law, it is surprising that much of the past and contemporary scholarly literature on Hindu (and Jain and Buddhist) religious trusts under Indo-Islamic rule focuses on condemning or explaining the destruction of religious institutions. Certainly, the survey presented in this chapter contains numerous instances in which Hindu temples were plundered by venal, iconoclastic rulers who boasted of their transgression of Dharmaśāstric norms. This chapter also examined numerous examples of rulers who punished rebellious subjects by desecrating their temples. These desecrations – particularly those performed by Aurangzeb's agents – left deep wounds that remain unhealed even to this day. Some of those wounds have fuelled significant communal tension in modern India (and are the subject of current legal disputes).

Nevertheless, alongside these darker aspects of Hindu–Muslim relations, we find fascinating instances of the accommodation, protection, and endowment of Hindu trusts by Muslims rulers and the accommodation, protection, and endowment of Islamic trusts by Hindu rulers. That legacy is of vital importance, not only because it attenuates communalistic narratives of a clash of civilisations, but also because it formed the basis of legal institutions that survive to this day. For modern courts to adjudicate temple trust disputes involving deeds of trust from Mughal or Marāṭhā times, it is crucial for judges to have a solid understanding of these Persianate legal systems. Indo-Islamic rulers left an indelible Persianate stamp on the Sanskrit jurisprudence of Equity and Trusts. Effectively, the Sanskrit *jurisprudence* of Equity and Trusts absorbed Indo-Islamic *legal phenomena* in much the same way that it absorbed Arthaśāstric and Buddhist legal instruments more than a thousand years before. Having garnered an appreciation of that Indo-Islamic contribution to the history of Equity and Trusts in Sanskrit jurisprudence, this monograph turns to a jurisprudential sea-change: the advent of British colonial rule and their introduction of English Equity into the equation.

4

Equity and Trusts in Anglo-Hindu Jurisprudence

I wish to explain briefly how the matter presents itself to me, relying on my brothers Mookerjee and Chatterjee for the contents of Hindu texts, which are of prime importance in the decision of the question before us… There is no doubt… that dedication by a Hindu of property to a deity is not only lawful, but commendable in a high decree… [and] a dedication to a deity… has a legal effect…. It is the duty of the Sovereign to see that the purposes of the dedication are carried out.

On… this basis of general principles, modern law has arrived at certain conclusions. Of these the most important… is that an idol after it has been duly constituted is a juridical person in an ideal sense. The practical meaning of this somewhat elusive expression is that the ministers of an idol have over the property dedicated to the idol, which is the same thing as the deity inspiring the idol, the same rights that they would have if they were trustees for his benefit, or if he was an infant and they managers on his behalf, being at the same time liable to corresponding duties legally enforceable.

Stephen, J., ***Bhupati Nath Smrititirtha v Ram Lal Maitra***,
Calcutta High Court (1909)[1]

4.1 Introduction

This chapter examines the development of a comprehensive jurisprudence of Equity and Trusts in Anglo-Hindu law, from its inception in 1772 to the introduction of the Constitution of the Republic of India on 26 January, 1950. During this nearly two-hundred-year period, jurists in the colonial judiciary – staffed by Indians and Europeans – developed a sophisticated, if somewhat abstruse,

[1] (1910) ILR 37 Cal 128 ¶19–22 [Stephen, J.].

corpus of case law regarding Hindu: 1) inheritance; 2) guardianship; 3) marriage; 4) adoption; and 5) religious endowments.[2] Alongside the efforts of the judiciary, Indologists (often judges themselves) codified and translated vast tracts of Dharmaśāstric literature and government administrators passed a series of statutory acts that regulated and refined the nuances of this system of personal law.[3]

Justice Sir Harry Stephen's (1860–1945) opinion from ***Bhupati Nath Smrititirtha*** summarises the theory and practice of Equity and Trusts in Sanskrit jurisprudence nicely: the deity (not just their image) is a juridical person who 'owns' property in a secondary (but legally efficacious) sense; the deity's servants serve as fiduciaries (called *shebaits* or *dharmakartas*) of their deity's property (called *debutter*), just as they would guard the property of a minor or other ward in their care; and in cases of breach of trust by these fiduciaries, the Crown (through the courts) must intervene to secure the interests of the deity and its assets.[4] In my estimation, Justice Stephen's description accords substantially with the theory and practice of Equity and Trusts (and divine endowments in particular) as articulated in the Dharmaśāstric and epigraphic sources that were discussed in Chapters 1, 2, and 3 of this monograph. Nevertheless, the story of how the courts arrived at this perspective on Hindu endowments is also the story of the establishment of European hegemony over the subcontinent; of the formation of colonial courts; of the contestation of sovereignty and jurisdiction of these courts, the Company, and the Crown; of temple functionaries' sometimes questionable and sometimes laudable management of divine endowments; and of the deities caught in between these developments.

Even after Indian independence in 1947 and the introduction of the Constitution (and Supreme Court) of the Republic of India in 1950, Anglo-Hindu judgments – subject to refinement – continue to provide ample authoritative

[2] Some of the most important monographs were born from the Tagore Law Lectures (instituted in 1880) at the University of Calcutta. See, on inheritance, Julius Jolly, *Outlines of an History of the Hindu Law of Partition, Inheritance, and Adoption, as Contained in the Original Sanskrit Treatises* (Calcutta: Thacker, Spink, & Co., 1885); on guardianship, Ernest Trevelyan, *The Law Relating to Minors: As Administered in the Provinces Subject to the High Courts of British India: Together with the Practice of the Courts of Wards in Bengal, Bihar and Orissa, Madras, Bombay, and the United Provinces of Agra and Oudh*, 5th edn. (Calcutta: W. Thacker & Company, 1916); on marriage, Gooroodass Banerjee, *The Hindu Law of Marriage and Stridhan* (Calcutta: Thacker, Spink & Co, 1879); on adoption, Golapchandra Sarkar, *The Hindu Law of Adoption* (Calcutta: Thacker, Spink, & Co., 1891); and on religious and charitable trusts, Sarasvati, *Hindu Law of Endowments*; and B.K. Mukherjea, *Hindu Law*.

[3] Initially, statutory enactments occurred at a presidency level, with varied legislation in the Bengal, Bombay, and Madras presidencies. In 1834, the first Law Commission of India began its appointed task of recommending various statutory reforms to the Indian legal system at a national level. For the Law Commission of India, see George Rankin, *Background to Indian Law* (Cambridge: Cambridge University Press, 1946), 22–45.

[4] For Justice Stephen, see C Hayavadano Rao 'Stephen, Sir Harry Lushington', in *The Indian Biographical Dictionary* (Madras: Pillar & Co., 1915), 414.

material case law for the practice of modern Hindu law.[5] This chapter attends specifically to the regulation of Hindu temple trusts, alongside other related phenomena such as monasteries and public charities, with an eye towards explaining how Dharmaśāstric theories of Equity and Trusts were reconfigured into the progenitor of the modern law of Hindu religious and charitable endowments. I examine these developments within collections of judgments from key time periods: 1) early cases from the *Ṣadr Dīwānī 'Adālats* (Superior Civil Courts) and Supreme Courts of the Bengal, Madras and Bombay presidencies when the Revenue Boards of the East India Company assumed direct control over Hindu religious endowments (1772–1863); 2) cases from the High Courts (established 1862), when the judiciary regulated religious endowments in accordance with the Religious Endowments Act of 1863 (1863–1900); and 3) cases from the early 20th century in which the High Courts (and Judicial Committee of the Privy Council) articulated the nuances of the legal personality of Hindu deities within the wider remit of codified civil procedure (1900–50).

My core contention is that colonial-era jurists (many of whom were Indians who had an exposure to the Sanskrit language and to Dharmaśāstric jurisprudence) drew deeply on Sanskritic principles of Equity and Trusts when fashioning the Anglo-Hindu law regarding religious and charitable endowments. The process was gradual, and was justified on the basis of the belief that Sanskrit jurisprudence articulated a theory Equity in which the sovereign holds *parens patriae* jurisdiction over, *inter alia*, the supplemental (*pāribhāṣika*), conventional (*sāmayika*) Dharmas of the realm's diverse population. Foremost among those conventional Dharmas were the rules and regulations that governed the administration of Hindu religious and charitable trusts.

A Dharmaśāstric theory of Equity and Trusts enabled the agents of the East India Company to exercise a general supervisory administration of Hindu religious endowments until the enactment of the Religious Endowments Act 1863. The 1863 Act was followed by a flurry of statutory enactments and the Anglo-Hindu Law of Equity and Trusts changed significantly as a result. Instead of adopting a *general* theory of a flexible, Equitable, *parens patriae* jurisdiction over religious endowments, the courts developed (and applied) highly *specific* rules for trusts, guardianship, legal personality, etc. Some of these rules were influenced by the Sanskrit jurisprudential principles that were analysed in Chapter 1 of this monograph, but many were explicitly imported from English jurisprudence.

By the turn of the 20th century, however, the increasingly Indianised courts drew on Mīmāṃsā-inflected Dharmaśāstra literature to describe Hindu deities' legal personality as the representation of a pious religious *purpose*. Certainly,

[5] For case law reports, see M.P. Jain, 'Law Reporting in India', *Journal of the Indian Law Institute* 24.2/3 (1982): 560–74.

many of the details, processes, and language of pre-colonial temple management changed with the advent of an English-style judiciary in India, but I argue that the core jurisprudential foundations remained constant – just as they had during the trials and tribulations of the last thousand-plus years beforehand. Effectively, the Anglo-Hindu law of religious and charitable trusts developed, slowly but inexorably, into a rich jurisprudential mélange of English and Sanskrit traditions concerning Equity and Trusts.

4.1.1 The theory and practice of Anglo-Hindu law

Contemporary scholars, particularly anthropologists, have spilt oceans of ink in debating the extent of epistemic continuities and ruptures between pre-colonial and colonial Hindu law. Oftentimes, these debates involve a more limited understanding of Sanskrit jurisprudential literature (discussed in Chapter 1) or medieval legal epigraphic records (discussed in Chapter 2) than has been presented in this monograph.[6] This chapter uses the more nuanced, synchronic account of Sanskrit jurisprudential principles of Equity and Trusts and the diachronic narrative of their application in historical Indian legal practice to provide a new account of the development of the Anglo-Hindu law of religious and charitable trusts. Broadly, this chapter argues that British jurists (assisted by Indian scholars and jurists) crafted a hybrid jurisprudence for the practical administration of Hindu, Jain, and Buddhist religious endowments. This novel, hybrid jurisprudence incorporated elements of both Sanskrit and English jurisprudence. Effectively, the Anglo-Hindu jurisprudence of religious and charitable trusts was neither wholly Sanskritic (in a Dharmaśāstric sense) nor English: it combined elements of both.

The standard argument avers that British colonial administrators, either due to an overly deferential fondness for the primacy of Brāhmaṇical textual traditions or due to the assumption of the universality of the unitary, Christian-centred social norms of the English Courts Ecclesiae, arbitrarily imposed Dharmaśāstric *jurisprudence* as codified *positive law* on the Hindu population.[7] According to this account,

[6] The argument arises in the work of Bernard Cohn and his students. See Bernard Cohn, *Colonialism and Its Forms of Knowledge: The British in India* (Princeton, NJ: Princeton University Press, 1996); Bernard Cohn, *The Bernard Cohn Omnibus* (New Delhi: Oxford University Press, 2004); Neeladri Bhattacharya, 'Remaking Custom: the Discourse and Practice of Colonial Codification', in R. Champakalakshmi and S. Gopal (eds), *Tradition, Dissent and Ideology: Essays in Honour of Romila Thapar* (New Delhi: Oxford University Press, 1996), 20–51; Lingat, *Classical Law*; and Nicolas Dirks, *The Hollow Crown: Ethnohistory of an Indian Kingdom*, 2nd edn. (Cambridge: Cambridge University Press, 1993).

[7] For the regulation and reform of the 'Joint Hindu Family' (also called the 'Hindu Undivided Family', or HUF) in relation to evolving patterns of family, state, and gender, see Eleanor Newbigin, *The Hindu Family and the Emergence of Modern India: Law, Citizenship and Community* (Cambridge: Cambridge

the imposition of Dharmaśāstra as Hindu positive law occurred in concert with several ruptures to pre-colonial Indian society: 1) the creation of a flattened, generic, and universal 'Hindu' cultural and legal identity; 2) the use of statute to 'reform' the Joint Hindu Family as a property-owning institution; 3) the introduction of the courts as the arbiters of religious and family matters; and 4) the shift from local, *ad hoc*, and flexible dispute resolution through community arbitration towards centralised, professional, and replicable binding decisions by a pyramidal court system.[8]

Whatever be their veracity, scholarly narratives about the extent of epistemic rupture between pre-colonial and colonial perspectives on Dharmaśāstra do not infringe on the facticity, however idiosyncratic, of modern Hindu law or Anglo-Hindu law before it.[9] To be emphatic, Anglo-Hindu law was born from a heady mixture of Dharmaśāstric treatises, community customs, statutes, and English law concocted by the legal bureaucracy of the Company and Crown courts that sought to promote the welfare and practices of colonial subjects by forcibly imposing many European legal conventions onto Indian phenomena. Whatever be the justice of that process – *Imperium et Libertas* is oxymoronic to coloniser and colonised alike – it is, nevertheless, necessary to plumb its historic nuances if we are to understand and improve the current legal landscape.[10]

Ironically, I believe that the relative dearth of positive legal dicta concerning divine endowment law in Dharmaśāstric literature, ubiquitously lamented by writers on the subject, resulted in a greater jurisprudential fidelity between pre-colonial and colonial approaches to the administration of Hindu religious trusts. For example, the existence of elaborate, voluminous, and highly polemical discussions of ownership and inheritance in early modern Sanskrit jurisprudential and philosophical literature led colonial jurists to impose these largely *academic*

University Press, 2013); Eleanor Newbigin, 'The Codification of Personal Law and Secular Citizenship: Revisiting the History of Law Reform in Late Colonial India', *Indian Economic and Social History Review* 46.1 (2009): 83–104; and Rachel Sturman, 'Property and Attachments: Defining Autonomy and the Claims of Family in Nineteenth-Century Western India', *Comparative Studies in Society and History* 47.3 (2005–07): 611–37. For the false analogy between Indian and English courts ecclesiae, see Christi Merrill, 'The Afterlives of Panditry: Rethinking Fidelity in Sacred Texts with Multiple Origins', in Judy Wakabayashi and Rita Kothari (eds), *Decentering Translation Studies* (Amsterdam: John Benjamin, 2009): 75–94, 79: 'Hastings made the straightforward assumption that there were sacred texts in India that would offer a source for interpretation comparable to ecclesiastical authorities in British law.'

8 For this process see Fleming, *Ownership and Inheritance*, 208–26.

9 For an extensive discussion and criticism of this narrative of epistemic rupture, see Fleming, *Ownership and Inheritance*, 158–207.

10 See Raymond Betts, 'The Allusion to Rome in British Imperialist Thought of the Late Nineteenth and Early Twentieth Centuries', *Victorian Studies* 15.2 (1972): 149–59, 153: 'The despotic example of Imperial Rome and the not more enlightening examples of subsequent imperial endeavors were bound to provoke concerned consideration among men who believed the chief virtue of the Anglo-Saxon race to be liberty.' For the definitive work on this maxim, see Bernard Holland, *Imperium Et Libertas: A Study In History And Politics* (London: Edward Arnold, 1901).

arguments as practical schools of Hindu law, resulting in the *Dāyabhāga* and *Mitākṣarā* schools of law with which modern lawyers are so well acquainted.[11]

In contrast, colonial jurists and Indologists encountered general *principles* of Equity and Trusts in Sanskrit jurisprudential literature: the Crown as *parens patriae*; Equity as the supplemental, conventional and customary laws of individual communities; and the analogous relationship between deities, women, minors, and other classes of legally incompetent individuals. Although colonial courts in the 18th and 19th centuries cite some Dharmaśāstric statements on *parens patriae* and on conventional laws (*sāmayikadharmas*), complex Dharmaśāstric statements on the legal personality of Hindu deities only emerge in early 20th century – ***Bhupati*** being the most notable example. The *theory* of the Anglo-Hindu law of religious and charitable trusts was, therefore, very much in the *spirit* of Sanskrit jurisprudence.

Robert Lingat and Arjun Appadurai argue for a *practical* disjuncture between pre-colonial and colonial legal approaches to temple management. They argue that the pre-colonial Crown fulfilled an *administrative* rather than a *legislative* role in the legal arena in the sense that 'the commands of Hindu kings... were addressed to specific individuals and groups, were not of general applicability, and were subject to alteration and appeal according to the pragmatic needs to kingship'.[12] Appadurai, following Lingat, claims that the introduction of statute and *stare decisis* (binding precedent) during the colonial period 'created rules and precedents of general applicability, so that decisions made in one context had, under certain conditions, automatic application in other contexts'.[13] Furthermore, Appadurai argues that, pre-colonial Indian kings, 'could only stimulate, ratify, and render authoritative reasonable local agreements'.[14] Thus, 'the administrative actions of the king... did not imply a centralized bureaucratic staff on the Weberian model of legal-bureaucratic authority'.[15]

I think that this distinction ought to be viewed as one of *degree* rather than *kind*. Perhaps in the medieval, pre-Islamic period the sovereigns of the Sanskrit cosmopolis exercised a decentralised administrative supervision over largely autonomous corporate and religious institutions. However, by the early modern period, Islamic and Hindu rulers such as the Vijayanagara emperors, the Mughals,

[11] See Donald Davis, '*Ownership and Inheritance in Sanskrit Jurisprudence* by Christopher T. Fleming (Review)', *Philosophy East and West* 72.3 (2022): 1–6, 4: 'A school of law might deny you inheritance rights in a way that a school of jurisprudence or thought cannot. The reception and application of the two-schools scheme in colonial courts did just that.' For a critique of schools of Hindu law, see Ludo Rocher, 'Schools of Hindu Law', in Donald Davis (ed.), *Studies in Hindu Law and Dharmaśāstra* (London: Anthem, 2014): 119–28.

[12] Appadurai, *Worship*, 68–71; and Robert Lingat, *The Classical Law of India*, trans. J. Duncan Derrett (Berkeley: University of California Press,1973), 229 fn. 54.

[13] Appadurai, *Worship*, 69.

[14] Ibid., 70.

[15] Ibid., 69.

Marāṭhās, and even Tipu Sulṭān oversaw highly centralised bureaucratic regimes which exercised direct legal authority over temple endowments.[16] The *Kōyil Oḻugu*, the record of the Śrīraṅgam temple, for example, mentions that the Vijayanagara Emperors 'began to administer the… *devadānas* in the same way as they administered the palace lands (*araṇmanaicaīrmai*) by appointing in Śrīraṅgam… their own servants'.[17]

The Śrīraṅgam temple functionaries' complaints against the Vijayanagara Empire mirror those that Appadurai makes on behalf of the Pārthasārathi temple against the British East India Company: the imposition of bureaucratic control by a powerful, centralised state. The Śrīraṅgam example anticipates Donald Davis' description of 'a massive transformation of legal practice in India' between 1500 and 1750, which was precipitated by the Persianate administrative systems of the Sulṭānates and 'followed by every major polity in India'.[18] This shift saw 'law gradually move away from the domain of corporate groups and temples into the purview of political states… [and] some ideas of Dharmaśāstra were… consciously adopted by state-based institutions'.[19] Hindu successors to the sulṭānates certainly framed themselves politically and theologically as pious Dharmaśāstric sovereigns executing their duty to endow, protect, and adjudicate disputes at temples, but they nevertheless adopted the direct managerial strategies of the sulṭānate states.

The British colonial state was the direct constitutional heir to the Mughals, who established a centralised 'department of pious foundations and religious affairs' (*daftar-i divān-i sa'adat*) and to the Marāṭhās, rather than the medieval polities discussed by Lingat and Appadurai.[20] It is unfair, then, to ignore early modern technologies of legal regulation by drawing distinctions between the medieval and colonial periods. Doing so not only elides the importance of Indo-Islamic polities to India's legal history (along with Hindu successors to Indo-Islamic polities) but also delegitimises efforts by state and judicial authorities in post-colonial India to regulate temple endowments in the spirit of the pre-colonial and colonial bureaucracies.

When colonial Revenue Boards or courts of law exercised direct supervision of religious trusts or passed related statutes, they invariably appealed to a theory of *parens patriae* and the practice of pre-colonial authorities in ages past. State and federal efforts in post-colonial India follow the same line of reasoning – accurate reasoning in my estimation.[21] The Dharmaśāstric jurisprudence of Equity and

[16] For Tipu sulṭān, see Chapter 3, Notes 41–2.

[17] See Chapter 3, Notes 301–3.

[18] Davis, 'A Historical Overview', 23–4.

[19] Ibid., 24.

[20] See Chapter 3, Note 306.

[21] For the Madras State Government's invocation of a continuity of *parens patriae* from pre-colonial Hindu rulers to independent India (including the Company and English Crown), see Chandra Mudaliar, *The Secular State and Religious Institutions in India: A Study of the Administration of Hindu Public Religious Trusts in Madras* (Wiesbaden: Franz Steiner Verlag, 1974), 149–63.

Trusts has provided the guiding principles for many different polities' administration of religious endowments and the centralised model of the post-Islamic age is no less Dharmaśāstric than that of the Sanskrit cosmopolis.

Finally, it is important to note that the advent of Anglo-Hindu law, like the advent of Indo-Islamic rule, brought profound changes to the legal regulation of religious and charitable endowments. Even though British jurists, working with traditional scholars of Sanskrit (*paṇḍitas*), invoked the core Sanskritic principles of Equity and Trusts when adjudicating, *inter alia*, temple disputes, the British court system introduced many novel features: 1) the concept of binding precedent wherein the outcome of one case provides the determinative principles for another case; 2) the model of a tiered, pyramidal judiciary ranging from courts of first instance to supreme courts of appeal; 3) the reporting of notable cases in comprehensive, chronological records; 4) the creation of scientific legal digests that index relevant case law; and 5) the adjustment of relevant law through statutory *fiat*.

While precedent and statute applied *universally* within certain jurisdictional constraints – within the presidencies of Bengal, Madras, and Bombay, for example – colonial courts repeatedly applied these universal principles to the *specific* practices and customs of specific contexts, and did so by invoking Dharmaśāstric theories of Equity. The review of case law in this chapter reveals that the Anglo-Hindu law concerning temple endowments was largely faithful to the core principles of Equity and Trusts in Sanskrit jurisprudence, even as it introduced novel judicial practices that survive to this day. The Anglo-Hindu law of religious and charitable trusts emerged in conversation and imbued with Dharmaśāstric principles of Equity and Trusts. Even as this body of law evolved through case law and statute to incorporate more and more English principles of Trusts, it retained its Sanskritic roots.

4.1.2 A brief constitutional history of Anglo-Hindu law

The evolution of the Anglo-Hindu law of Equity and Trusts was intimately connected with the development of the legal system of colonial India. Colonial India had a unique constitutional history in which the British East India Company operated as both a sovereign power under the nominal aegis of the Mughal Empire and as a joint stock company operating under a royal charter.[22] As Lauren Benton notes, Britain's colonial geography in India was 'politically fragmented; legally differentiated; and encased in irregular, porous, and sometimes undefined borders'

[22] See, for example, Phillip Stern, *The Company-State: Corporate Sovereignty and the Early Modern Foundations of the British Empire in India* (Oxford: Oxford University Press, 2011).

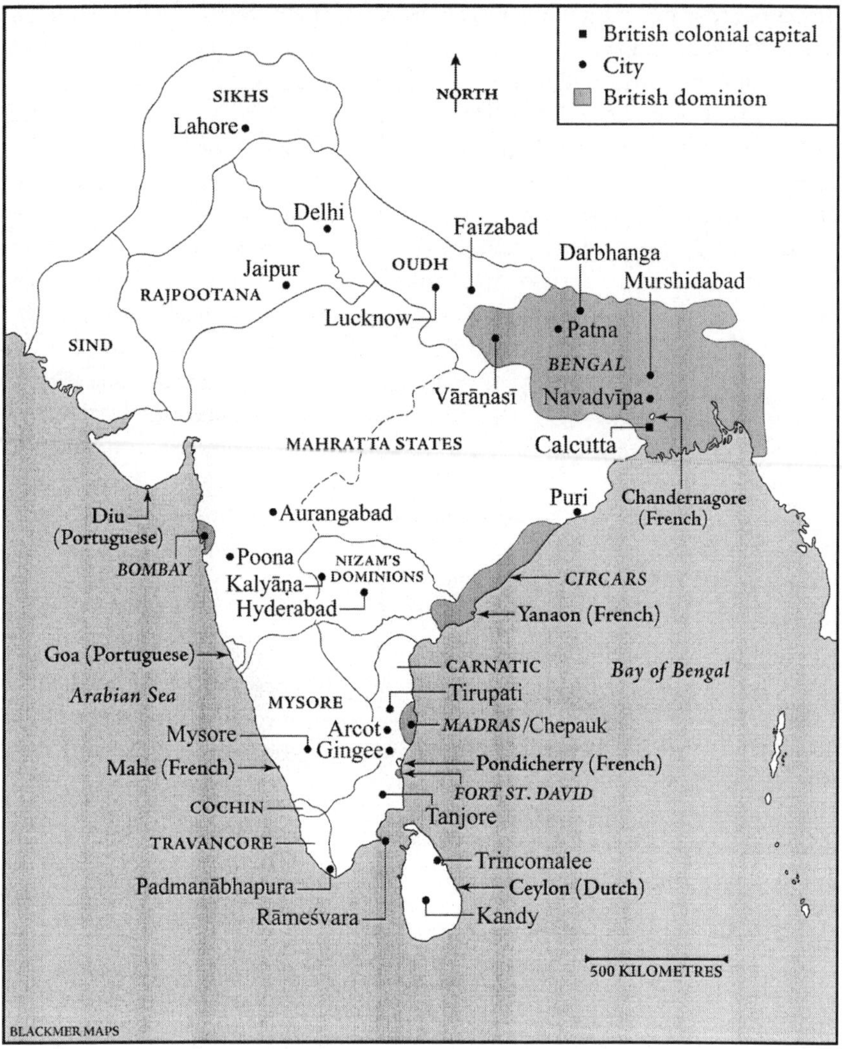

Map 4.1 India at the time of Warren Hastings, c. 1785

just like the jurisdiction of the early colonial Indian judiciary.[23] As the great constitutional historian of India, M.P. Jain notes, 'the [legal] system of today… represents the fruits of the cumulative endeavor… of a multitude of administrators through the generations'.[24] Consequently, in order to understand how and why

[23] Lauren Benton, *A Search for Sovereignty: Law and Geography in European Empires, 1400–1900* (New York: Cambridge University Press, 2010), 2.

[24] M.P. Jain, *Outlines of Indian Legal History* (New Delhi: University of Delhi Press, 1952), xii.

the law evolved as it has, we need to plumb the depths of India's intricate colonial legal history.

Initially, during the Company's early days in the 17th and early 18th centuries, legal disputes within the towns of Bombay, Madras, and Calcutta were adjudicated by Company officials under royal charters, or, by the late 17th century, a series of Mayoral Courts which had jurisdiction over English and native subjects within these towns.[25] In 1765, Robert Clive obtained the *Dīwānī* (the formal right to collect revenue) for the provinces comprising the *Subāh* of Bengal, Bihar, and Orissa, from the Mughal Emperor Shāh 'Ālam II (r. 1759–1806). Clive did this on behalf of the British East India Company through the Treaty of Allahabad.[26] The acquisition of the *Dīwānī* of Bengal, Bihar, and Orissa (followed by a *de facto* acquisition of the same in Madras by the Treaty of the Carnatic in 1801) inaugurated the Company's shift from a primarily trading entity under English royal charter to a semi-sovereign territorial power under nominal Mughal suzerainty.[27] This territorial expansion and acquisition of sovereign rights as Company power 'spread to the interior of India from coastal enclaves at Surat, Bombay, Madras, and Calcutta' meant that the somewhat primitive judicial systems proved insufficient to meet the growing need for adjudicating cases amongst the native population (or holding the Company's executives to account).[28]

Early colonial India contained a vast, somewhat uneven legal landscape populated by different court structures, directions of travel in presidency politics, local customs, inherited pre-colonial systems of land tenure, among other things. Hindu religious endowments were caught up in and buffeted by this diverse legal

[25] For law in company towns during the 17th century, see Jain, *Outlines*, 1–9 (Surat), 10–21 (Madras), 22–30 (Bombay), & 32–5 (Calcutta). The 1600 and 1609 charters for the EIC granted the Company limited legal powers 'not contrary... or repugnant to the laws, statutes, and customs of the English Kingdom'. This was initially exercised in an *ad hoc* fashion by the president and council of the Company towns before the introduction of more formalised Mayoral Courts under royal charter in 1726–27. These courts were reformed by the Charter of 1753. Pre-Mayoral Courts included the 1687 Company Mayoral Court in Madras, the 1718 Company Court of Judicature in Bombay, and in Calcutta, the Collector, exercising the company's role as a Zamindar, operated civil and criminal courts of first interest (under the suzerainty of the Nawāb).

[26] Fleming, *Ownership and Inheritance*, 167.

[27] C.U. Aitchison, *A Collection of Treaties, Engagements, and Sanads Relating to India and Neighboring Countries*, Vol 8: Madras Presidency (Calcutta: Government Press, 1892), #9. The Company's constitutional status was more complicated in the Bombay presidency. Bombay Island was the property of the Crown of England – the dowry of Catherine of Braganza when she married Charles II of England in 1662 – which the outlying territories were held by the Company on behalf of the Mughal emperor.

[28] Benton, *Search*, 240. For the committee, see P.A. Howell, *The Judicial Committee of the Privy Council: 1833–1876* (Cambridge: Cambridge University Press, 1979); and Rohit De, '"A Peripatetic World Court": Cosmopolitan Courts, Nationalist Judges and the Indian Appeal to the Privy Council', *Law and History Review* 32.4 (2014): 821–51. For legal pluralism in the Mayoral Courts, see Leonard Hodges, 'Between Litigation and Arbitration: Administering Legal Pluralism in Eighteenth-Century Bombay', *Itinerario* 42.3 (2018): 490–515; and Niels Brimnes, 'Beyond Colonial Law: Indigenous Litigation and the Contestation of Property in the Mayor's Court in Late Eighteenth-Century Madras', *Modern Asian Studies* 37.3 (2003): 513–50.

ecology, with uniformity emerging with the establishment of the High Courts in 1862 – following the introduction of Crown rule in 1858 and the passage of the all-Indian Religious Endowments Act in 1863. The semi-independent princely states, with their own judicial structures – often modelled on the practices of the presidencies – and the bevy of hereditary aristocrats within the presidencies (with their own contested relationships with the temples they formerly oversaw as sovereigns) only adds to the complexity of this issue.[29] Consequently, it is vital to adumbrate the constitutional framework in which the Anglo-Hindu law developed before examining the essential case law relating to Equity and Trusts in detail.

4.1.2.i Company and Crown Courts (1772–1800)

Anglo-Hindu law 'was born in Calcutta on August 21, 1772' when the Bengal government adopted Governor Warren Hastings' 'Plan for the Administration of Justice in Bengal'.[30] After seven dysfunctional years of mismanagement under the 'dual system' in Bengal – in which the Company delegated responsibility for civil and criminal law to the titular Nawāb while taking on responsibility for revenue collection – the House of Commons appointed a 'Committee of Secrecy to go into the affairs of the Company'.[31] London's efforts to rein in the Company's disorganised rapacity led to decisive constitutional developments that laid the foundation for modern Indian law. The Company, through the mixture of a genuine desire to secure their tenuous sovereignty by supporting the laws and conventions of the native population and a credible fear of the metropole imposing English law in India *in toto*, adopted Hastings' Judicial Plan.[32]

The plan 'established an integrated hierarchy of civil courts (*Dīwānī 'Adālats*), culminating in the *Ṣadr Dīwānī 'Adālat*, to which Hindus and Muslims could appeal', alongside criminal courts (*Nizāmat 'Adālats*, with the *Ṣadr Nizāmat 'Adālat* as the court of appeal) – all of which applied 'Islamic' criminal law.[33] This system, reformed by Governor-General Cornwallis (of Yorktown infamy) in 1793, was adopted by the Bombay and Madras presidencies in 1799 and 1802, respectively. The Judicial Plan gave rise to Anglo-Hindu and Anglo-Islamic law in its stipulation that 'in all suits regarding inheritance, marriage, caste, and other

[29] For Travancore's regulation of religious endowments along the lines of the Madras presidency, see Das Acevedo, 'Divine Sovereignty'. Much of this was attributable to the presence of the 'British Resident… John Munro, [who] served double duty as diwan or prime minister'.

[30] Rosane Rocher, 'The Creation of Anglo-Hindu Law', in Timothy Lubin, Donald Davis, and Jayanth Krishnan (eds), *Hinduism and Law: an Introduction* (Cambridge: Cambridge University Press, 2010): 78–104, 78. Also see Jain, *Outlines*, 64–8.

[31] Jain, *Outlines*, 55. Of note, approximately one fifth of the population of Bengal died in a famine in 1770.

[32] Fleming, *Ownership and Inheritance*, 168–9.

[33] Ibid., 167.

religious usages, or institutions, the laws of the Koran with respect to Mahometans and those of the Shaster with respect to the Gentoos shall be invariably adhered to'.[34] As colonial justices lacked knowledge of Sanskrit or Islamic jurisprudence, the Company hired traditional scholars of Sanskrit (*paṇḍitas*) and scholars of Islamic jurisprudence (*maulvis*) as 'law officers' to assist the courts in determining the complexities of Dharmaśāstra and *Fiqh* for the purposes of developing a consistent personal law for the native population.[35] We have several collections of *responsa* (*vyavasthās*) generated by *paṇḍitas* in early cases involving Hindu law.[36]

Concerns over the reliability (or predictability) of the law officers prompted early jurists-cum-orientalists such as William Jones (1746–94) and H.T. Colebrooke (1765–1837), to codify and translate Dharmaśāstric and Shariatic texts for judicial purposes.[37] Notable in these early efforts were Hastings' commission of the *Vivādārṇavasetu* ('A Bridge Over the Ocean of Litigation'), by a team of eleven Bengali Paṇḍitas from Navadvīpa, Bengal in 1773, William Jones' translation of the *Mānavadharmaśāstra* in 1794; and Jones' overseeing of the compilation of the *Vivādabhaṅgārṇava* between 1788 and 1794 and Henry Colebrooke's translations of the *Vivādabhaṅgārṇava* (published as *A Code of Hindus Law* in 1797–98), the *Mitākṣarā*, and the *Dāyabhāga* (with the latter two published together as *Two Treatises on the Hindu Law of Inheritance* in 1810).[38] The translation of vast quantities of Dharmaśāstric treatises in the following decades went hand-in-glove with the expansion of the *'Adālat* system in the Company's growing Indian realm, the creation of regionally specific 'schools' of Hindu law, and the accumulation of a significant corpus of case law from the presidencies' supreme courts.[39]

Although these philological endeavours provided the courts with vast quantities of useful Dharmaśāstric *dicta* concerning the Hindu law of marriage, adoption, and, above all, inheritance, they produced effectively no positive legal statements regarding the administration of religious endowments beyond the general

[34] Ibid.

[35] Ibid.

[36] See, for example, Shyāmācharan Sarkār (ed.), *Vyavasthādarpana: Digest of Hindu Law as Current in Bengal*, 3rd edn. (Calcutta: I.C. Bose & Co., 1883); and Shyāmācharan Sarkār (ed.), *Vyavasthāchandrikā: A Digest of Hindu Law, as Current in all the Provinces of India, Except Bengal Proper* (Calcutta: I.C. Bose & Co., 1878).

[37] Fleming, *Ownership and Inheritance*, 158–207 (for Sanskrit jurisprudence). For Islamic law, see Anderson, 'Islamic Law'.

[38] Fleming, *Ownership and Inheritance*, 164–7. For British patronage of Dharmaśāstrins, see J. Duncan Derrett, 'The British as Patrons of the Śāstra', in J. Duncan Derrett (ed.), *Religion, Law and the State in India* (London: Faber & Faber, 1968): 225–73; Rosane Rocher, 'Weaving Knowledge: Sir William Jones and Indian Pandits', in Garland Cannon and Kevin Brine (eds), *Objects of Enquiry: The Life, Contributions, and Influences of Sir William Jones, 1746–1794* (New York: New York University Press, 1995): 51–79; Rosane Rocher, 'The Career of Rādhākānta Tarkavāgīśa, an Eighteenth-Century Pandit in British Employ', *Journal of the American Oriental Society* 109.4 (1989): 627–33; and Asheesh Siddique, 'William Jones, Esq.' *Global Intellectual History* (2023): 1–7.

[39] Fleming, *Ownership and Inheritance*, 209–11.

principle of the Crown as *parens patriae* and the Dharmaśāstric doctrine of Equity as the supplementary, customary and conventional laws of guilds, families, and religious associations.[40] While the Dharmaśāstric jurisprudence available to the courts clearly granted the Crown a right of visitation over religious endowments and drew analogical connections between deities, minors, women, and other legal independents, it offered none of the detailed intricacy observed in discussions of ownership (*svatva*) and inheritance (*dāya*).[41]

We saw in Chapter 1 that the principles of Equity and Trusts (and divine endowments in particular) are spread very diffusely throughout Sanskrit jurisprudential literature. Some of the most important *dicta* on divine endowments (especially in the *Arthaśāstra*) were not yet discovered. In order to fill this legal lacuna, the courts and the Company Government adopted different strategies. For example, the courts relied on the doctrine of 'Justice, Equity, and Good Conscience', introduced in Bengal through the Administration of Justice Regulation (Bengal) in 1781 and introduced to the Bombay Presidency in Section 26 of the Regulation of 1827.[42] This rather broad doctrine allowed the introduction of English legal concepts to contexts in which native – i.e., Dharmaśāstric – laws were silent. Ironically, however, many English principles of Equity (that were adopted to fill lacunae in the colonial knowledge of Sanskrit jurisprudence) align well with the Sanskritic, pre-colonial principles and practices that were discussed in Chapters 1, 2, and 3.

While the *Dīwānī 'Adālat* courts were operated under the auspices of the East India Company and followed indigenous jurisprudence – as interpreted by English justices and native informants – the Regulating Act of 1773 established a Supreme Court of Judicature in Calcutta in 1774 that was entirely independent of the Company. Legally speaking, the Regulating Act viewed the city of Calcutta as vesting in the English Crown and the *Diwānī* lands of Bengal, Bihar, and Orissa as vesting *de jure* in the Mughal Crown, with the governor general and council of the presidency of Fort William in Calcutta exercising the administrative duties of the *Diwān*.[43] According to its royal charter, the Supreme Court, 'was to consist of both the Common Law and the Equity Jurisdictions' the first such fusion of Equity and Common Law in English history.[44] During the mid-19th century, the Supreme Courts began to exercise – sometimes reluctantly – their formal equitable jurisdiction to cases involving Hindu religious endowments and charitable trusts. Unfortunately, the precise relationship between the jurisdictions of the *Diwānī*

[40] Strange, *Hindu Law*, 32. Also see Kāṇe *History of Dharmaśāstra*, Vol. 2.2, 910.
[41] See Fleming, *Ownership and Inheritance*, Chapter 4.
[42] See Derrett, 'Justice, Equity'.
[43] Jain, *Outlines*, 73.
[44] Ibid., 84–5.

courts and the Supreme Court were ill defined and 'many difficulties arose due to this confusing and perplexing situation'.[45]

Some of these issues were addressed by the Act of Settlement in 1781 – carving out the scope for the *Ṣadr Dīwānī ʿAdālat* and the Supreme Court to operate as courts of record. As we will see later, questions of sovereignty and jurisdiction continued to vex the Supreme Courts, which were also established in Madras and in Bombay in 1800 and 1823, respectively.[46] In answering these vexed questions – about the relationship between the Company, the Mughal Empire, the Crown of England, and Hindu religious endowments, that Supreme Courts reflected (sometimes deeply and sometimes idiosyncratically) on the Sanskrit jurisprudence of Equity and Trusts.

4.1.2.ii Regulations and the Privy Council (1800–62)

Given India's vast size, diverse population, and the proclivity of *paṇḍitas* to produce a multiplicity of opinions on controversial Dharmaśāstric subjects, its comes as no surprise that the Company and Crown's tangled, overlapping, and unified judicial network produced uneven decisions and uncertainty about the specifics of Hindu law.[47] India was not immune to the Benthamite wave sweeping over England, and the Charter Act of 1833 sought to standardise India's legal system – including Hindu law – through the creation of an All India Legislature and the appointment of a Law Commission for India.[48] The ethos of this plan, as summarised by Lord Macaulay was: 'uniformity where you can have it – diversity where you must have it – but in all cases certainty'.[49] A series of important, all Indian acts followed, including the drafting of a penal code (completed in 1850 but not introduced until 1860), the Dower Act (1839), the Caste Disabilities Removal Act (1850), the Hindu Widows' Remarriage Act (1856), the Code of Civil Procedure (1859), the Law of Limitation (1859), and the Income Tax Act (1860).

The legal regulation of Hindu religious endowments occurred by statute at the presidency level and explicitly invoked theories of trust, *parens patriae* jurisdiction, and Dharmaśāstric theories of Equity as the conventional laws and maxims of

[45] Ibid., 85–92. Also see Chittaranjan Sinha, 'A Judiciary at Odds with the Executive: the Calcutta Supreme Court and the Bengal Administration 1781–1833', *Journal of the Indian Law Institute* 10.3 (1968): 499–519.

[46] Jain, *Outlines*, 125–6.

[47] Rocher, 'Creation', 82–8. For a legal history of this period, see Ramesh Srivastava, *Development of Judicial System in India Under the East India Company, 1833–1858* (Lucknow: Lucknow Publishing House, 1971).

[48] Jain, *Outlines*, 452–3. When debating the bill, Lord Macaulay argued that, 'no country ever stood so much in need of a code of law as India… [and] it is the work which especially belongs to a Government like that of India – to an enlightened and paternal despotism'.

[49] Jain, *Outlines*, 453.

Civil Law	Constitutional Law	Hindu Law
	Introduction of the Constitution and the Supreme Court of India (1950)	
	Indian Independence (1947)	
	Government of India Act (1935)	Hindu Women's Rights to Property Acts (1937, 1938, & 1940)
Indian Partnership Act (1932) Charitable and Religious Trusts Act (1920)		Orissa Hindu Religious Endowments Act (1939) Hindu Gains of Learning Act (1930) Hindu Inheritance Act (1929) Hindu Inheritance (Removal of Disabilities) Act (1928) Madras Hindu Religious Endowments Act (1923)
1908 Civil Procedure Code 1908 Indian Limitation Act	Government of India Act (1919)	Hindu Disposition of Property Act (1916)
Charitable Endowments Act (1890) Guardians and Wards Act (1890)		
Income Tax Act (1886) Indian Trusts Act (1882) Companies Act (1882) Probate and Administration Act (1881)		
	Fourth Indian Law Commission (1879)	
Contract Act (1872)		Hindu Wills Act (1870)
Companies Act (1866) Indian Succession Act (1865)		
Religious Endowments Act (1863)	High Courts Act/Third Indian Law Commission (1861)	
Income Tax Act (1860) Code of Civil Procedure (1859) Law of Limitation (1859)	Second Indian Law Commission (1853)	Hindu Widows' Remarriage Act (1856) Caste Disabilities Removal Act (1850)

Civil Law	Constitutional Law	Hindu Law
	Privy Council Established as Court of Appeal (1833) First Indian Law Commission (1834) Bombay Supreme Court Established (1823)	**Direct Regulation of Temples** Bombay Reg. 17 (1827) Madras Reg. 7 (1817) Bengal Reg. 19 (1810)
Early Development (1765–1803) Madras Permanent Settlement (1803) ʿAdālat System Expanded to Territories Subject to Madras Government (1801) Madras Supreme Court Established (1800) ʿAdālat System Expanded to Territories Subject to Bombay Government (1799) Bengal Permanent Settlement (1793) Calcutta Supreme Court Established (1774) Hastings' Judicial Plan (1772) East India Company acquires the Dīwānī of Bengal, Bihar, and Orissa (1765)		

Table 4.1 Legal legislation in India 1772–1950

specific institutions. Although the regulations do not invoke Dharmaśāstra *explicitly* – they are statutes, not case law – they invoke Dharmaśāstric concepts *implicitly*. In 1810, 'on account of the scandalous mismanagement of certain temples… Reg. 19 of 1810 was passed in Bengal, placing these endowments under the direct supervision of the Board of Revenue'.[50] Equally important to the Government's calculus was its mixed success in resuming the tax-free, charitably-assigned *lehkiraj* lands that continued to multiply even after the Permanent Settlement in 1793.[51] The Act invoked the *parens patriae* principle, according to which 'it is an important duty of every Government to provide that all such endowments be applied according to the real intent and will of the grantor', when justifying its right of supervision over 'the present trustees, managers or superintendents of the several institutions, foundations or establishments' covered by the Act.[52]

Madras Regulation 7 of 1817 adopted similar *parens patriae* language in its efforts to ensure 'the due appropriation of the rents and produce of lands granted for the support of mosques, Hindu temples and colleges, or other public purposes'.[53] The Madras Regulation also added a clause for the punishment of breach of trust by 'all trustees, managers or superintendents employed in, or charged with, the settlement, custody or appropriation of the revenues, funds or other

[50] Mukherjea, *Hindu Law*, 546–7.

[51] For Lehkiraj lands, see Saugata Mukherji, 'A Note on Lekhiraj Lands', *Proceedings of the Indian Historical Congress* 21 (1958): 426–30. For the Bengal Government's rapacious efforts to resume them, see S. Sen Gupta, 'A Note on Resumption of Lekheraj Lands in Bengal and the Landholders Society', *Proceedings of the Indian Historical Society* 43 (1982): 487–93.

[52] Bengal Regulation 19 of 1810. Available here: http://bdlaws.minlaw.gov.bd/act-details-1316.html.

[53] Madras Regulation 7 of 1817. Available here: http://www.bareactslive.com/TN/tn421.htm.

property of the public institution'.[54] Crucially, the criteria for the determination of a trustee's adherence to his fiduciary duties were 'the special provisions of the original endowment and appropriation by the founder or under any general rules or maxims applicable to such institutions and foundations'.[55] This model may be the analogous application of English trusts theory to Indian charities, but it is also, undeniably, in sync with pre-colonial Dharmaśāstric theories of Equity and Trusts. These acts applied *only* to public religious trusts (wherein worship was open to the general Hindu public), and private religious trusts remained, as they always have, under juridical supervision on the basis of Hindu personal law and the courts' equitable jurisdiction.[56]

Finally, the early 19th century saw the introduction of the Judicial Committee of the Privy Council in 1833 as a final court of appeal from the Supreme Courts and *'Adālat* courts in India. The ancient prerogative of the King in Council dates back to the Norman Conquest, when the sovereign 'was regarded as the *fountain of justice*'.[57] While this role was replaced in England by the king in Parliament (i.e., the House of Lords), the king 'enjoyed a prerogative right to hear appeals from any colonial court'.[58] British and Indian subjects enjoyed a right to appeal from the Mayoral, Supreme, and *'Adālat* courts before 1833, but, generally, those appeals were rarely heard (although I will discuss several important constitutional cases, below) and in 1826, Sir Alexander Johnston (1755–1849), a privy counsellor, discovered a vast quantity of important, underheard cases in the council lumber room.[59]

[54] Ibid.
[55] Ibid.
[56] For the public/private distinction see Mukherjea, *Hindu Law*, ¶4.49–54. Also see Michael C. Baltutis, 'Recognition and Legislation of Private Religious Endowments in Indian Law', in Robert Baird (ed.), *Religion and Law in Independent India* (New Delhi: Manoharlal Banarsidass, 2005): 443–68. Private religious endowments have never been directly legislated, but a substantial body of case law recognises that the courts have jurisdiction over private religious endowments. See https://advocatetanmoy.com/2018/09/19/law-of-hindu-debattar-property/ for a list of case law, including: ***Narayanaswami Naidu v Balasundaram Naidu*** (1953) AIR Madras 750, where it was held that: 'even in the case of private trusts, it is open to any member of the founder's family where his rights are impugned to seek redress in Courts of law.... The Court cannot refuse to frame a scheme in the matter of a private trust. So far as the members of the family are concerned who are interested in the trust, if the trustee for the time being mismanages or acts in breach of trust, it is a civil right which is infringed and under S. 9 CPC, they are entitled to seek redress in Court for the purpose of remedying the mischief'; ***Chellam Pillai v Chatham Pillai*** (1953) AIR 1953 Trav-Co. 198, where it was held that, 'though S. 92 CPC, in terms does not apply because it relates specifically and definitely to the case of public trusts, in the case of a private family trust the Court has got jurisdiction to frame a scheme for the management of the trust'; and ***Vaithinatha Aiyar v Thyagaraja Aiyar*** (1921) 41 Mad LJ 20, where it was held that: 'the fact that the plaintiffs belong to the family of the founder would naturally give them an interest in the family charity so as to enable them to bring a suit under S. 92 of the CPC'.
[57] Jain, *Outlines*, 359. For an excellent history of pre-1833 Privy Council appeals, see Loren Beth, 'The Judicial Committee as Constitutional Court for the British Empire 1833–1971', *Georgia Journal of International and Comparative Law* 7.1 (1977): 47–84, 47–8 fn. 1.
[58] Jain, *Outlines*, 360.
[59] Ibid., 368.

To address this backlog, and other inefficiencies of the *ad hoc* nature of the King in Council, Acts 3 and 4, William IV created a professionalised Judicial Committee of the Privy Council to serve as a final court of appeal for the Empire.[60] The Council was extremely important to the development of a cohesive legal system in India, especially in relation to Hindu law, because it could serve as an authoritative (if typically unexpert) arbiter for the often-divergent interpretations of ambiguous Sanskrit treatises by colonial justices, and the constitutional ambiguities between the Company, the Courts, and the Crown.

4.1.2.iii Statutes and the High Court (1862–1950)

After the Indian Rebellion of 1857–58, Parliament passed the Government of India Act, which dissolved the British East India Company and transferred the Company's governmental rights to the Crown. As a result, the distinction between Crown and Company courts became an unnecessary impracticality, and the Indian High Courts Act (1861) rearranged the Indian court system in 1862. The Dīwānī *'Adālat* and Supreme Courts were merged into High Courts in each presidency, while the Judicial Committee of the Privy Council remained as the apex appellate court.[61]

Several new high courts joined this judicial triumvirate: the Agra High Court (1866 for the Northwestern Provinces and shifted to Allahabad in 1875); the Patna High Court (1916 for the newly separated territories of Bihar and Orissa); the Lahore High Court (1919 for Panjab and Delhi); and the High Court at Nagpur (1936 for Central Provinces).[62] The *paṇḍita* and *maulvi* court officers were dismissed in 1864 as the courts took over judicial knowledge of Hindu and Islamic law (the result of decades of accumulated case law and translations of Sanskrit and Arabic treatises).[63] This was, effectively, the final iteration of the judicial structure for India until independence in 1947 and the introduction of the Constitution in 1950. There were a series of High Courts (with civil, criminal, and equitable jurisdiction) of equal standing with the Privy Council as the single court of appeal and numerous lower courts in each presidency.

At the same time, the new central government, in conjunction with the Law Commission, issued dozens of statutes aimed at codifying and unifying the commercial, criminal, and personal law of India alongside civil procedure. These included the Religious Endowments Act (1863), the Indian Trustees Act (1866),

[60] Ibid., 371.
[61] Ibid., 330. For a positive evaluation of the Act, see Prema Natarajan, 'High Courts in India as Palladium of People's Rights Against Administrative Discretion (1861–1900)', *Proceedings of the Indian History Congress* 39.2 (1978): 691–9.
[62] Jain, *Outlines*, 338–45.
[63] Fleming, *Ownership and Inheritance*, 27.

Map 4.2 India, c. 1892

the Contract Act (1872), the Probate and Administration Act (1881), the Indian Companies Act (1882), the Indian Trusts Act (1882 – this governed secular private trusts only), the Indian Income Tax Act (1886), the Civil Procedure Code (1882 and 1887), the Charitable Endowments Act 1890 (this excluded temples), the Civil Procedure Code (1908), the Charitable and Religious Trusts Act (1920), and the

Hindu Disposition of Property Act (1921), among many others.[64] In her seminal monograph, *Stages of Capital*, Ritu Birla describes these acts as part of a process where 'colonial sovereignty sought aggressively to standardize market practice and organization'.[65] At the heart of Birla's argument lies the concept of 'market governance' as a colonial tool whereby:

> An ideology of free trade legitimized an economic system intended to profit Britain, law directed at the free circulation of capital referred first and foremost to the releasing of capital from the binds of tradition and customary codes. But despite these concerns, new legal measures... did not simply render indigenous market norms unilaterally illegal by abolishing them summarily. Even as statutes and jurisprudence established universal models for modern market practice, they regularly insisted on establishing exceptions for vernacular capitalism... kinship-based firms [especially the Joint Hindu Family] were placed under the purview of the personal law that governed what were considered 'private concerns...' [Therefore,] colonial authorities regulated vernacular capitalism exactly by coding it as a rarefied cultural formation.[66]

Birla draws a distinction between colonial law's treatment of the 'invisible hand' of the free market and the 'dead hand' of religious endowments and the 'Joint Hindu Family'. She argues, at length, that late 19th-century judicial approaches to divine endowments stifled the active mercantile activities of pre-colonial religious charities by recoding them as trusts and thereby classifying their properties as *res extra commercium* (outside of commercial circulation).[67] Whatever be the truth of Birla's argument – I attend to its erroneous reading of the relevant case law later in this chapter – the late 19th century witnessed an explosion of cases involving Hindu (and Muslim) religious endowments, wherein the High Courts and the Privy Council debated the intricacies of Hindu trusts law in relation to civil procedure, tax, and secular trusts law. In doing so, the courts clarified many of the ambiguities of the Hindu law of religious and charitable trusts from the Company era, and provided the core case law that is relevant today. Nothing is as conducive to generating a highly refined jurisprudence for an abstruse area of law than a flurry of high profile, high court judgments.

In my opinion, the most proximate cause for this torrent of statutory and judicial regulation of divine endowments was the Company's decision, beginning in the 1830s, to retreat from its legal (and Dharmaśāstric) duty to supervise Hindu religious endowments. As T.T. Arvind notes:

> In 1833, in part as a result of pressure brought by Protestant churches, the Court of Directors of the East India Company ordered the Supreme Government in Calcutta to require servants of the Company to withdraw from all 'arrangements which

[64] See Fleming, *Ownership and Inheritance*, 413, Table C.1 for a chart of the acts.
[65] Birla, *Stages of Capital*, 3.
[66] Ibid., 5, cited in Fleming, *Ownership and Inheritance*, 211–12.
[67] Birla, *Stages of Capital*, 85–7.

> implicate the Government, be it in a greater or lesser degree, in the ministrations of the local superstitions of the Natives', on the basis that they 'exhibit the British power in such intimate connexion with the unhappy and debasing superstitions' and lead to the belief 'that we admit the divine origin of those superstitions, or at least, that we ascribe to them some peculiar and venerable authority'.[68]

The result of such actions (repeated soon after in Madras and Bombay) was to 'usher in a government policy of seeking a single identifiable Indian "trustee" for each religious institution, to whom an endowment, usually in the form of rent-free lands, could be transferred'.[69] By 1841, the Company divested itself almost entirely of the trusteeship of a vast number of temples (there were 7,600 Hindu shrines under government administration in Madras alone in 1833) in an *ad hoc* fashion *with no legal mechanism for remedying cases of maladministration*.[70]

If the present monograph has proven anything, it is that every sovereign power in Indian history has borne some measure of responsibility for the maintenance and administration of Hindu religious endowments. The British Government of India's religiously motivated (as a result of the influence of English Christian missionary iconoclasm) abandonment of deities and their assets to the rapacity of hastily identified 'trustees' constituted a fundamental breach of one of India's core theories of suzerainty: the protection of women, minors, deities, and religious institutions under the principles of the Sanskrit jurisprudence of Equity. An 1858 circular issued by the Chief Commissioner of the Punjab typifies the indifferent attitude towards these new trustees' breaches of trust: 'Our officers will have nothing to do with the management or administration of these institutions… the people must manage their own institutions. If such institutions suffer from internal disputes, that is their business, not ours.'[71]

The Religious Endowments Act (1863) was a landmark piece of legislation which not only formally repealed the 1810 and 1817 regulations in Bengal and Madras respectively (Bombay passed a similar act at the presidency level in 1863), but also created a series of new legal mechanisms to enable the courts to supervise public religious charities and trusts more effectively.[72] The Act created provisions for the appointment of trustees for religious endowments; for the creation of supervisory committees by the Government for the management

[68] T.T. Arvind, 'Religious Endowments and Trusts Law in Colonial India', in Liew Ying Khai and Wu Ying-Chieh (eds), *Asia-Pacific Trusts Law* (London: Bloomsbury, 2022): 55–76.

[69] Chatterjee, *Secularism*, 60.

[70] Ibid., 61.

[71] Dispatch No. 23, dated 25 August 1858 from R. Temple, secretary to chief commissioner for the Punjab, to all commissioners in the Punjab. Cited in Muhammad Abbasi, 'Colonial state and Muslim Institutions: History of Regulatory Framework for Awqāf (Religious Endowment) in British India', in Rajeswary Brown and Justin Pierce (eds), *Charities in the Non-Western World* (Abingdon: Routledge, 2013): 311–32, 314.

[72] Mukherjea, *Hindu Law*, 546–8.

of temples, etc.; and, under §15, for the removal of for 'any misfeasance, breach of trust or neglect of duty, committed by such trustee, manager, superintendent or member of such committee, in respect of the trusts vested in, or confided to, them respectively'.[73]

There was considerable debate concerning the effectiveness of the 1863 Act for replacing trustees in cases of maladministration and concerning the applicability of the Civil Procedure Code of 1877 to religious (as opposed to charitable) trusts. The situation was largely remedied, however, by §539 of the Civil Procedure Code 1882 and the by §92(2) of the Civil Procedure Code of 1888.[74] Having outlined the constitutional backdrop of Anglo-Hindu law, we may now proceed to examine the influential cases decided within that judicial framework that developed the core principles of the colonial and post-colonial law of Hindu religious and charitable trusts.

4.2 The Sanskrit jurisprudence of Equity and Trusts in Anglo-Hindu case law

Justice Mukherjea provides a lucid introduction to this chapter's present task in *The Hindu Law of Religious and Charitable Trusts*, when he notes that, 'it goes without saying that the law which is found administered today in India, is to a large extent the creation of Judges'.[75] Consequently, in order to trace the evolution of Anglo-Hindu trusts law, and to assess 'how this judge-made law fits in and harmonises with the original Hindu ideas' in the Sanskrit jurisprudence of Equity and Trusts, it is necessary to examine the relevant case law from various colonial courts in detail.[76] Mukherjea provides the core story:

> Ever since the establishment of British Courts in India, an array of eminent Judges both English and Indian brought their legal learning and strong common sense to bear upon this delicate and somewhat abstruse branch of Hindu law, and attempted to evolve out of the few cryptic writings of ancient Hindu sages, a sufficiently well-developed body or rules and principles. This development was in a sense necessitated by the demands of the time and the prevalent social and moral ideas, and it cannot be denied that it was influenced to a great extent by the notions and principles of English law.[77]

[73] Religious Endowments Act 1863. Available here: www.indiacode.nic.in/bitstream/123456789/2266/1/A1863-20.pdf

[74] For civil procedure and public Hindu religious trusts, see P. Ishwara Bhat, 'The Parens Patriae Role of the Courts in the Matter of Public Trusts Under §92 of the Civil Procedure Code: Expectations, Contributions, Limitations', *NUJS Law Review* 7.3–4 (2014): 205–24.

[75] Mukherjea, *Hindu Law*, 3.

[76] Ibid.

[77] Ibid.

The Anglo-Hindu law of Equity and Trusts was very much a mélange of English Equity, Dharmaśāstric theory, and other procedural elements, but that observation warrants an analysis of *how*, *when*, and *why* those various components came together. In doing so, I want to look backward and forward. Looking backwards, I'm interested in looking for continuities and ruptures between pre-colonial and colonial theory and practice. Looking forwards, I explore how colonial judgments and legislation gave rise to legal doctrine that lie at the heart of some of the most momentous cases in post-colonial Indian history.

My analysis traces the evolution of Anglo-Hindu trusts law during three formative periods of judicial history: 1) the foundational period between 1772 and 1863 when the *Ṣadr Dīwānī 'Adālats* and Supreme Courts of Judicature examined the government's right to supervise religious endowments against the wider backdrop of major questions of *sovereignty* and *jurisdiction*; 2) the post-rebellion period (1862–1900) when the High Courts and Judicial Committee of the Privy Council articulated the duties, responsibilities, and liability of temple trustees (*shebaits/dharmakartṛs*) against the backdrop of a series of regulatory statutes; and 3) the late imperial period (1900–50), when an increasingly Indianised judiciary applied their formidable knowledge of Sanskrit jurisprudence to articulate a comprehensive account of the legal personality of Hindu deities. The end result, then, is to garner a greater appreciation for the many individuals – judges, litigants, scholars – who contributed to the formation of the Hindu law of trusts as well as the core concerns and social developments that shaped their efforts. Trusteeship lay at the heart of colonial Indian legal history.

4.2.1 The Company and the Crowns: sovereignty, jurisdiction, and trusteeship (1772–1863)

Even before William Hastings' judicial plan in 1772, the East India Company exercised direct supervision of many prominent 'public' temples within their expanding remit in an *ad hoc* fashion. The Company's justification for this direct interference – sometimes a reluctant interference – lay in the argument that pre-colonial governments (typically the Marāṭhās and the Mughals) had a duty of care, on the basis of *parens patriae* jurisdiction, to ensure the proper administration of religious endowments. As early as 1754, for example, the Government in Madras intervened in an intra-Brāhmaṇa disputes concerning the Śrīpārthasārathisvāmi temple in Triplicane (in Madras).[78]

Towards the close of the 18th century, however, the Company's relationship towards Hindu religious and charitable endowments changed in three key respects: 1) the subordination of religious institutions under the supervision of

[78] Appadurai, *Worship*, 106–10. Chatterjee, *Indian*, 57–8 gives several other early examples.

the Presidency Governments' Boards of Revenue (on the basis of *parens patriae* jurisdiction) became increasingly commonplace and legally formalised; 2) the Company civil courts (the *Ṣadr Dīwānī 'Adālats*) built up a substantial body of case law that disentangled the relationship between religious endowments, newly generated Anglo-Hindu law and the revenue system; and 3) the Supreme Court of Judicature in Bengal, Madras, and Bombay, through a series of challenges to the actions of the Government with respect to religious trusts (of many religious backgrounds), elicited several judgments from the King in Council, which clarified the Governments' *parens patriae* jurisdictions and the Supreme Courts' equitable jurisdiction.

In all of this, the legal nature of divine Hindu endowments was rarely, if ever, questioned. It seems to have been taken for granted that land assigned to temple images (public or private) was the legal property of the image, and this divine property (*debutter*) had to be employed for the benefit of the deity by the individuals who held that property as trustees. The juridical personality of Hindu deities or the analogous relationship between temple fiduciaries and English trustees were decidedly *not* an issue for the courts. Rather the core questions that concerned the courts were issues of sovereignty, revenue, and jurisdiction. *Why* were Presidency Governments, rather than local *Zamīndārs* (or formerly independent rulers under various other states of vassalhood), empowered to supervise religious endowments? *When* could members of Joint Hindu Families (fathers, widows, undivided brothers) create endowments using joint family assets according to the paradigms of Hindu law and the Permanent Settlements of 1793 and 1803 (Bengal and Madras)?[79] Finally, *who* was empowered to hold the Government or trustees accountable when they overstepped the boundaries of conscionable behaviour?

In answering the questions – posed in the context of decades' worth of court cases – Government agents, the judiciary, and the Privy Council articulated the initial, Sanskrit jurisprudence-inspired, Anglo-Hindu jurisprudence of divine endowments. First, the Company, in acquiring indigenous forms of sovereignty (as a trustee for the Crown of England) also acquired the sovereign right of supervision over religious institutions within the realms of the native vassals (who, at best, were reduced to the right of being trustees of these endowments). The Government thus had a feudal right, sanctioned by Dharmaśāstra and the force of the Company, to act as previous Dharmaśāstric sovereigns had. Second, the Company's civil courts determined that members of Joint Hindu Families could, with property over which they held powers of alienation according to the

[79] For an overview of the Permanent Settlements in Bengal and Madras, see David Washbrook, 'Law, State, and Agrarian Society in Colonial India', *Modern Asian Studies,* 15:3 (1981): 649–741; and Nicholas Dirks, 'From Little King to Landlord: Property, Law, and the Gift Under the Madras Permanent Settlement', *Comparative Studies in Society and History* 28.2 (1986): 307–33.

Anglo-Hindu law of inheritance (a body of jurisprudence built on idiosyncratic readings of Dharmaśāstra treatises), could create religious endowments (usually private ones). This power of creating endowments, was, however, contingent on not using said endowment as a device for defrauding the revenue system, and a series of legal tests were developed to determine which tax-free endowments were valid or not.

Third, the King in Council delineated the respective jurisdiction of the Government and the Supreme Courts over charities, religious endowments, and other forms of trust. The Company held its sovereign tenure in India in trust for the Crown and the Advocate General in each presidency had, through *parens patriae* jurisdiction, the right to initiate suits involving charities and trusts.

The Supreme Courts, however, by virtue of their royal charters, enjoyed a capacious equitable jurisdiction (the same jurisdiction as the English Court of Chancery). These courts, therefore, had the duty to hear suits brought by the Advocate Generals, by beneficiaries of private religious trusts, and by public trustees against the Government. All of this demonstrates the early history of the Anglo-Hindu jurisprudence of religious and charitable trusts involved the creation of a complex mixture of Sanskrit jurisprudence, English Equity, and the complicated administrative and legal structures of early colonial India. Although this mixture was complex, it is crucial to note that one element was constant, if not always predominate: Sanskrit jurisprudential principles of Equity and Trusts.

4.2.1.i The sovereign Company as parens patriae

Long before Regulation 19 of 1810 and Regulation 7 of 1817 vested the administration of religious endowments in the Boards of Revenue of Bengal and Madras, respectively, the Company Government took an active role in the supervision of several notable temples within their realm. Similarly, the Company began to establish specialised Courts of Wards (for *Zamīndārs*) in the Bengal, Madras, and Bombay presidencies and to empower the civil courts to appoint and to regulate guardians of minors, women, the infirm, etc.

The *ideological* justification for these interventions was, naturally, the capacity of the Company, as the holder of various sovereign titles (the *Dīwānī* of the *Subāh* of Bengal, Bihar, and Orissa, for example) to 'to stand forth as *Dīwān*', and assume the role of previous governments as *parens patriae*.[80] The *practical* justification for

[80] Ranjit Sen, 'The Emergence of a Service Elite in Bengal in the Second Half of the Eighteenth Century: A New Dimension of Collaboration', *Proceeding of the Indian History Congress* 36 (1975): 511–22, 519 fn. 3. On 28 August 1771, the Court of Directors signed the letter in which they ordered the president and Council 'to stand forth as *Diwan*'. Also see Ranajit Guha, *A Rule of Property for Bengal: An Essay on the Idea of Permanent Settlement* (Paris: Mouton, 1964), Chapter 4, specifically §4 under the title 'Who is King of Bengal?'.

these interventions was a desire to ensure an efficient, centralised revenue system that maximised profit for the Company. The Madras presidency, for example, centralised 'the collection... [and] distribution of all temple revenues in the limited territories under their control' in 1796.[81]

We saw in Chapter 3 that Dharmaśāstric theories of Equity and Trusts played a key role in the Vijayanagara and Marāṭhā Empires' administration of religious endowments. Unsurprisingly, the Company acted in this jurisprudential vein when they took control of temples within these erstwhile empires' realms. In essence, as the Company grew in strength and territory, it became vastly more assertive in its usurpation of sovereign rights of visitation and revenue collection from local leaders. This disruption in temple supervision became, then, an index of the rising sovereignty of the British East India Company.

For example, during the chaos of the Carṇātac Wars of the mid-18th Century, French, English, Marāṭhā, and indigenous armies contested the right to supervision over the famed Veṅkaṭeśvara of Tirupati, with the British ultimately securing permanent control of the region and temple by 1801.[82] The British, in turn, took over direct management of the temple's funds, with the collector distributing them to a group of trustees.[83] A series of reports by the collector led, in 1821, to Colonel Bruce, the collector of Chittor, instituting 'Bruce's Code', a forty-two-part series of regulations – which one might compare analogically to any number of medieval Sanskrit endowments governing the income and function of Hindu temples.[84]

The justification for this intervention, seemingly identical to the practices of earlier, pre-Islamic sovereigns, was none other than the right of the Company (and its agents) as a sovereign power to promote Dharmaśāstric theories of Equity. They did so by inquiring into the conventions of local institutions upon conquest of new territory, codifying them in formal grants, and protecting them through the Crown's bureaucracy (at the time, this was the executive branch of the Government). It was precisely this active role as guardian and, occasionally, endower, of this magnificent temple which attracted the ire of Christian missionaries and the Court of Directors.[85]

Similarly, when the British conquered Orissa in 1803, Marquis Wellesley instructed Lt. Colonel Campbell, that, on his arrival to the great Jagannātha temple:

> You will... preserve the respect due to the Pagoda, and to the religious prejudices of the Brahmins and pilgrims. You will furnish the Brahmins with such guards as shall

[81] Appadurai, *Worship*, 109, citing Mudaliar, *Secular State*, 8.

[82] Chatterjee, *Secularism*, 57–8; and S Krishnaswami Aiyangar, *A History of Tirupati*, 2 vols (Madras: Tirumalai Tirupati Devasthanam Committee, 1940–41), Vol. 2, 512–53.

[83] For the British administration of the temple, see T.K.T. Viraraghavacharya, *History of Tirupati*, Vol 2. (Tirupati: Tirumala Tirupati Devasthanam Committee, 2003): 641–3.

[84] Ibid., 642. These regulations were the subject of a legal challenge over the following decades.

[85] See Koutha Kumari, *History of Religious Endowments in Andhra Pradesh* (New Delhi: Northern Book Centre, 1998), 19–35.

> afford perfect security to their persons, rites and ceremonials, and to the sanctity of their religious edifices, and you will strictly enjoin those under your command to observe your orders on this important subject, with the utmost degree of accuracy and vigilance… they will not be required to pay any other revenue or tribute to the British Government, than that which they may have been in the habit of paying to the Mahratta Government, and they will be protected in the exercise of their religious duties.[86]

Wellesley clearly understood something that W.W. Hunter described explicitly seventy years later: '[that] the possession of the god had always given the dominion of Orissa'.[87] Strikingly, the decision to come into British possession – or 'protection' – was the decision of none other than Lord Jagannātha himself. Shortly before the British troops entered Puri, the local Brāhmaṇas informed them that: 'the Brahmins at the holy temple had consulted… Juggernaut to inform them what power was now to have his temple under their protection and that he had given a decided answer that the English Government was in the future to be his guardian.'[88] Once the British took control of Puri, the functionaries of the Jagannātha temple dispatched a letter to Wellesley, which praised him for his support of the deity, the temple, and its associated properties in elaborate Dharmaśāstra-inflected language. The letter offers salutations from the temple residents, including 'the attendants of the deity' (*sevakānāṃ*) whose 'predominance has been established in the holy temple of our Divine Master Jagannātha partly through the grace of the Supreme Lord… and partly through the desire of the esteemed ruler (the English)'.[89]

The letter praises Wellesley as, *inter alia*, one who has 'taken the vow of protecting the gods, the Brāhmaṇas and the Vaiṣṇavas'.[90] The temple inhabitants, pleased by Wellesley's protection during the war, assert that they desire his supervisory authority (*adhikāra*) over them to continue indefinitely.[91] Furthermore, the letter requests that Wellesley use his superintendence to 'establish Dharma just as

[86] *The Despatches, Minutes and Correspondence of the Marquess Wellesley, K.G. During His Administration in India* (London: John Murray, 1836–37), Vol. 3, 269, cited in K.M. Patra, 'The Temple of Jagannath and Pilgrim Tax (1803–1840)', *Proceedings of the Indian History Congress* 30 (1968): 92–301, 292.

[87] Herman Kulke, '"Juggernaut" Under British Supremacy and the Resurgence of the Kurda Rājās as "Rājās of Puri"', in Anncharlott Eschmann, Hermann Kulke, and G.C. Tripathi (eds), *The Cult of Jagannatha and the Regional Tradition of Orissa* (New Delhi: Manorharlal, 1978): 345–57.

[88] Ibid., 326. Melville to Gov. General, 11 September 1803.

[89] Surendranath Sen and Umesha Mishra (ed. & trans.), *Sanskrit Documents: Being Sanskrit Letters and Other Documents Preserved in the Oriental Collection at the National Archives of India* (Allahabad: Ganganatha Jha Research Institute, 1951), #9 (text on 26–9, translation on 90–2), 27: **śrīgagannāthasya mahāprabhor icchānusāreṇa** navāvasāhevasyājñayā ca śrīmaṅdire **śrījagannāt hasvāminaḥ…** asmākaṃ saṃprati prāvalyam āsīt.

[90] Ibid., 90 & 26: devavaiṣṇavabrāhmaṇarakṣādīkṣiteṣu (using the honorific plural). Sen's translation isn't completely accurate.

[91] Ibid.: āsmākaṃ naiścityaṃ sukhaṃ ca bhāgyānusāreṇāgataṃ tasmāt… sarvadā bhavatām adhikāraḥ syāt.

Brahmā, etc. did (in days of old).'[92] This, expectedly, entails 'the protection of the property and lives of all.'[93]

This pair of documents reveals how the Company and the Jagannātha temple viewed the newly established relationship between each other: the Company, in exercising a supervisory role over the temple finances saw itself as simply continuing the right of visitation enjoyed by the Marāṭhā Empire (and the Gajapatis before them); the temple, for its part, expressed its fealty to the new secular authority in highly Dharmaśāstric language that emphasised the legal personality of the tutelary deity, the positions of the deity's servants, and the expected role of the Crown as protector of the institution and its assets.

Although the Company was happy to slip into the Marāṭhās' slippers when asserting its right to supervise the Jagannātha temple – among many others – this nevertheless created a great deal of administrative hassle for the collectors and their superiors who were quickly flooded with innumerable petitions regarding all manner of financial disagreements among the Hindu population.[94] As Nandini Chatterjee notes, 'the British Government soon discovered [that] involvement with Hindu religious institutions could be a very expensive and harassing proposition.'[95]

At Puri, the question of the pilgrim tax repeatedly vexed colonial administrators, who initially revoked the tax only to reinstitute it in various forms under a colonial officer with the title 'Collector of Tax on Pilgrims' through the Bengal Regulation IV of 1809.[96] The same regulation also appointed the raja of Khurda (the Gajapati Scion) as the trustee of the temple – despite his claims to owning the temple in a personal capacity.[97] In fact, the raja and his family would spend the next several decades locked in extensive litigation with the Government of Bengal over the precise relationship between the raja, the Company, and Lord Jagannātha.[98]

These early efforts at regulating temple endowments directly, perhaps because of their *ad hoc* nature, or perhaps because of the ambiguous relationships between native rulers, the company, and the native rulers' erstwhile tutelary temple, prompted the Company Government to pass its presidency-based regulations in

[92] Ibid.: **brahmādibhir** dharmasthāpanam akāri tathaiva bhavān karotu.

[93] Ibid.: sarveṣāṃ prāṇānāṃ dhānānāṃ ca rakṣām.

[94] See, for example, Appadurai, *Worship*, 111–33, for a detailed analysis of the intricate squabbles that sucked in the Śrīpārthasārathisvāmi temple in Madras, the collector, the advocate general, the Government, and the Supreme Court.

[95] Chatterjee, *Secularism*, 57.

[96] Patra, 'Temple of Jagannath', 295; Chatterjee, *Secularism*, 58.

[97] Chatterjee, *Secularism*, 58.

[98] Ibid., 63. Also see Prabhat Mukherjee and Nancy Gardner Cassels (eds), *Pilgrim Tax and Temple Scandals: A Critical Study of the Important Jagannath Temple Records During British Rule* (Bangkok: Orchid Press, 2000); and Hermann Kulke, 'Kings without a Kingdom: The Rajas of Khurda and the Jagannatha Cult', *South Asia: Journal of South Asian Studies* 4.1 (1974): 60–77.

Bengal and Madras in 1810 and 1817, respectively.[99] These regulations formalised the relationship between the Company, the local aristocracy, and the temples: the Company, like the 'previous governments' of the Marāṭhās and Mughals, was framed as the superior sovereign, supervisory power, while the local aristocrats were framed as *trustees* who managed public temples for the benefit of the wider Hindu religious community.

A similar theory of *Zamīndārs* as merely subordinate feudatories rather than kings – implicitly framing the Company in the role of Dharmaśāstric sovereign – appears in Jagannātha Tarkapañcānana's *Vivādabhaṅgārṇava*, compiled between 1788 and 1794 and translated by H.T. Colebrooke as *A Code of Hindus Law* in 1797–98.[100] The compilers of the digest note that: 'From apprehension of offending very great persons, it is not here examined whether some modern princes, who are not independent in the government (*rājeśvara*) of their subjects, but merely employed in levying the revenue of the paramount, should, or should not, be acknowledged as kings.'[101] This passage was widely read by early colonial courts as establishing: 1) that *Zamīndārs* were tributary princes of the Company; and 2) that, according to Dharmaśāstric theories of Equity, the *kulācāra* (family custom, or family Dharma) of heritability by one's eldest son was an acceptable 'exception to the general rule of law'.[102]

This Dharmaśāstric theory of the Company as the sovereign power and the *Zamīndārs* as subordinate princes, also provided ideological justification for the infamous Courts of Wards that the Company established, beginning in the late 18th century, to control the persons and estates of their feudal subordinates.[103] As Benjamin Cohen notes, 'the Court of Wards in India came into existence by an act of

[99] See Notes 52–6.
[100] See Notes 37–9.
[101] atra idānīntanānāṃ rājñāṃ prajāpālane 'svatantryāṇām api rājeśvarakaroddhāramātravyāpārakāṇ āṃ keṣāñcid rājatvam aṅgīkāryaṃ na veti na vivecitam atyantamahājanavirodhabhayād iti brūmaḥ. Colebrooke's note here is fascinating: 'This digression is not altogether misplaced; for the great possessions, called Zemindaries in official language, are considered by modern Hindu lawyers as tributary principalities: and it might seem necessary to determine whether they be alienable and hereditary by the same rules with other landed property.' The importance of this passage to Colebrooke's wider ouvre on Indian land tenure is discussed in Rosane Rocher and Ludo Rocher, *The Making of Western Indology: Henry Thomas Colebrooke and the East India Company* (London: Routledge, 2012), 39.
[102] *Vyavastādarpana*, 18–19. The passage was cited by Jagannātha and other *paṇḍitas* in ***Īshānchander Roy v (Rājā) Īshwar-chander Roy*** (SDAR, Vol. 1, p. 2).
[103] Very little is written about the Courts of Wards in India. The complete list, excluding references in legal digests, is as follows: Benjamin Cohen, 'The Court of Wards in a Princely State: Bank Robber or Babysitter?', *Modern Asian Studies*, 41.2 (2007), 395–420; Benjamin Cohen, *Kingship and Colonialism in India's Deccan 1850–1948* (New York: Palgrave MacMillan, 2007), 101–22; Anand Yang, 'An Institutional Shelter: The Court of Wards in Late Nineteenth-Century Bihar', *Modern Asian Studies 13.2* (1979): 247–64; and Stephen Hemmingham, 'The Raj Darbhanga and the Court of Wards, 1860–1879: Managerial Reorganization and Elite Education', *Indian Economic and Social History Review* 19.3–4 (1982): 347–63. For the English Court of Wards and Liveries, founded by King Henry VIII in 1540, see H. E. Bell, *An Introduction to the History and Records of the Court of Wards and Liveries* (Cambridge: Cambridge University Press, 1953).

Sir John Shore, governor general in Council, on 28 August 1797... [although] earlier references to the establishment of the Court come from Philip Francis, appointed to the Bengal council in 1773'.[104] Francis intended the Courts, to provide 'for the care of estates, of which the incumbents are minors, idiots, or females; and to have the care of the education of minors, now usually committed to servants or relations, who have an obvious interest in bringing up the children in ignorance and stupidity'.[105]

Crucially, the Court of Wards was justified on the basis of an 'overlay [of colonial practices]... onto Indian traditions of child rearing and protection', that were articulated in Sanskrit sources as the jurisprudential theory of the king as *parens patriae*.[106] The application of *parens patriae* jurisprudential principles to justify the Court of Wards' jurisdiction went hand-in-glove with Wellesley's aggressive subordination of independent princely states (subjecting local rulers to guardianship by the Company's agents). It also went hand-in-glove with the court's extension of general principles of guardianship to the civil courts in the Madras presidency in 1804 and, soon thereafter, to the rest of Company India.[107]

In fact, 'soon after the establishment of the Court of Wards in Bengal, it was found necessary to give the Civil Courts powers to nominate [legal] guardians' and this was established by Regulations 1 of 1800, 5 of 1804, and 10 of 1831 in the Bengal, Madras, and Bombay presidencies, respectively.[108] As Ernest John Trevelyan, noted (writing in 1916 after the passage of the Guardians and Wards Act, 1890), 'by the Hindu Law, the ruling power is in every instance, whether the natural guardian be living or dead, recognized to be the supreme guardian of the property of all minors, whether male or female... [and] the ruling power is now represented by the Court of Law'.[109] Trevelyan clearly draws on Dharmaśāstric

[104] Cohen, *Kingship*, 104.
[105] Ibid., 104.
[106] Cohen, 'The Court of Wards', 398.
[107] Cohen, *Kingship*, 104.
[108] Trevelyan, *Law Relating to Minors*, 75.
[109] Ibid., 49. Naturally, Trevelyan cites MacNaughten, Colebrooke, and Manu on this part. The definitive case on this principle is ***Ram Bunsee Koonwaree (Maharanee) v Soobh Koonwaree (Maharanee)*** (1867) 7 WRCR Mayne, for his part, is more extensive in his citation of Sanskrit and case law: 'See (e) Manu, viii. § 27; ix. § 146, 190, 191; 3 Dig. 542–544; F. MacN. 25; 1 Stra. H L.71; 2 Stra. H. L. 72–75; ***Gungama v Chendrappa***, Mad. Dec. of 1859, 100; 1 W. MacN. 103; ***Mooddookrishna v Tandavaroy***, Mad. Dec. of 1852, 105; ***Muhtaboo v Gunesh***, 8. D. of 1854, 329. Under Mithila law, however, it has been held that the mother is entitled to be guardian of the person of her minor son in preference to the father. ***Jussoda v Lallah Nettya*** (1879) 5 Cal. 43. As to the claim of the step-mother, see ***Lukmee v Umurchund***, 2 Bor. 144 [163]; ***Ram Bunsee v Soobh Koonwaree***, 7 Suth. 321; 8. C. 3 Wym. 219; S. C. 2 In. Jur. 193, ***Baee Sheo v Ruttonjee***, Morris, Pt. I. 103.' One notable example of the complexity of multiple layers of guardianship is the relationship between the Company and, the mahārājas of Jaipur, and Rāmānandī sect during the 19th century. The kingdom was a Company protectorate, the mahārāja was a ward of his mother, the mahārāja held a right of supervision over the Rāmānandī sect, who, in turn, were the custodians of a series of deities in temples in 'Lohārgal in the Jhunjhunun district of Shekhawati in Rajasthan'. See Monika Horstmann, 'The Mālik in Rāmānandī Documents of the 18th and 19th Centuries', in Simon Cubelic, Axel Michaels, and Astrid Zotter (eds), *Studies in Historical Documents from Nepal and India* (Heidelberg: Heidelberg University Publishing, 2018): 401–44.

theories of the Crown as *parens patriae*, and argues that the courts (as delegated agents of the Crown of India) now exercise that power – much like the Aśokan legal agents (*mahāmātras*) that were discussed in Chapter 2.[110]

At first blush, the invocation of just a few Dharmaśāstric passages to justify the direct supervision of religious endowments, the creation of a court of wards, the use of hereditary custom in judicial decisions regarding the partibility of landed estates, and the court's regulation of guardians seems like a paltry fig leaf for the wholesale imposition of Company control over their newly subordinate Indian territory – and it may well be.

Ironically, however, we've seen throughout this monograph that virtually every previous ruler power in India utilised Dharmaśāstric theories of *parens patriae* to justify *their* intervention in temple administration, the guardianship of vassal princes, and the family life of their subjects. To be an Indian sovereign was to be entrusted with these powers. Even if the Company abused these powers for their own pecuniary advantage – a breach of trust that does against the paradigms of good kingship in Sanskrit jurisprudence – they nevertheless incorporated Sanskrit theories of Equity and Trusts in their articulation of their venal government.

4.2.1.ii Religious endowments and the Hindu law of inheritance in the Ṣadr Dīwānī 'Adālats

While the Boards of Revenue and the Governments of the Presidency held jurisdiction over the trustees of endowments, the *Ṣadr Dīwānī 'Adālats* held jurisdiction over temple donors within the wider remit of the Anglo-Hindu law of ownership and inheritance. The Government was concerned with *who* could do *what* with endowed assets, while the *'Adālats* were concerned with *what* property could be endowed.

In these early cases, the jurisprudence of divine endowments, *debutter*, as well as the position of a trustee for these endowments (*shebait* in Bengal and Bombay and *dharmakarta* in Madras) are almost always taken for granted. The courts, almost invariably, describe a deity (an 'idol' in legal parlance) as the owner of assigned properties, with the *shebait* serving as a trustee (often with pecuniary advantage), in an unproblematic way. The early *Ṣadr Dīwānī 'Adālat* cases are, however, much more concerned with *debutter* in relation to the public revenue system and with the intricate property relations spelt out in the evolving system of Hindu family law. This lack of judicial interest in the trust element of Hindu religious endowments was probably due to the combination of the Government's assumption of supervisory rights over religious and charitable endowments and

[110] For the Aśokan period, see Chapter 2, §2.2.4, 'Regulating religion'.

the absence of statutory mechanisms formally granting the Courts jurisdiction over native trusts.

An early case from the Bengal *Ṣadr Dīwānī 'Adālat*, ***Collector of Moorshedabad v Bishennath Rai and Sheonath Rai***, presided over by H.T. Colebrooke in 1807, concerned 4,536 *beegas* of land, yielding an estimated 2,468 rupees *per annum*, that had been assigned by a local *Zamīndār*, Ranee Bhuwani, to a series of deities as *debutter*.[111] The Collector sued the Ranee's descendant (the current *shebait* of the deities) for an assessment of the land for tax on two bases: 1) that Bengal Regulation 19 of 1793 (part of the Cornwallis Code) invalidated grants of tax-free (*lekhirāj*) land made without Government sanction since the Company's acquisition of the *Dīwānī* in 1765; and 2) that Ranee Bhuwani, 'in retaining to herself and family the superintendence and management (of the *debutter* as *shebaits*), was in fact both the grantor and the grantee: under which circumstances the grants could not be deemed valid'.[112]

The first contention was merely a question of fact and the *'Adālat*, having distinguished those lands which were assigned before 1765 from those afterwards, held the latter to be resumable under Regulation 19 and ordered a settlement with the current '*shewayut* (*shebait*)'.[113] In answering the second contention, the Court effectively endorsed the notion of a private religious trust. The court ruled that: 'Although the rents of the greater part of the lands might have been remitted to the Ranee, there was sufficient proof… that the religious expenses for which they were appropriated, had been defrayed out of them; and there was no proof adduced of their having been misapplied.'[114] In the following decades, the courts, alongside the Government, strenuously attempted to resume *debutter* lands – for obvious pecuniary advantages – but, it must be said, that the use of religious endowments as a device for defrauding the public treasury is a venerable and universal facet of the global history of Equity and Trusts.[115]

That same year, Colebrooke and the Bengal *Ṣadr Dīwānī 'Adālat* ruled in ***Elder Widow of Raja Chutter Sein v Younger Widow of Raja Chutter Sein***, that

[111] 6 Ind. Dec. (Old Series), 170.

[112] Ibid., 174.

[113] Ibid., 175.

[114] Ibid.

[115] For the Company and Courts' efforts at resumption, see S. Sen Gupta, 'A Note on Resumption'; Abu Mohammad Waheeduzzaman, *Land Resumption in Bengal: 1819–1846* (Unpublished PhD Dissertation, SOAS, 1969); H.R. Ghosal, 'Resumption of Rent-Free Tenures for Assessment by the Company's Government (1819–1850)', *Proceedings of the Indian History Congress*, 13 (1950): 316–19; Mariam Dossal, 'The Bombay Revenue Survey (1865–1872) and the Need for State Empowerment', *Proceedings of the Indian History Congress* 56 (1995): 594–60; Michael Mann, 'A Permanent Settlement for the Ceded and Conquered Provinces: Revenue Administration in North India 1801–33', *Indian Economic and Social History Review* 32.2 (1995): 245–69; and Mohammed Mustafa, 'The Shaping of Land Revenue Policy in Madras Presidency: Revenue Experiments – the Case of Chittoor District', *Indian Economic and Social History Review* 42.2 (2007): 111–267, esp. 214–6. For an ancient example of a religious trust as a tax-avoidance scheme, see Derrett, 'Example'.

debutter lands were both impartible and unconvertable to private use.[116] Two widows of a *Zamīndār* had divided *debutter* lands settled by their deceased husband's mother (also deceased) and created two separate religious endowments – for the benefit of the family's two principal deities – which each managed as *shebait*. The elder widow appears to have been dissolute, and, having illegally sold the lands assigned to her deity, sued the younger widow for a share of the other deity's *debutter* property, on the basis that all of the *debutter* lands were joint heritable property under Hindu law.[117] The Court's Paṇḍitas issued a *vyavasthā* that averred that:

> *debutter* lands are not heritable property: the management of them, along, for religious purposes, devolves on the heirs of the person who made the endowment. It is lawful for heirs to separate by mutual consent, and form distinct religious endowments; and, should one of the heirs sell the portion of endowed land under his management, it is not lawful for such heir to claim a share of the portion managed by the other.[118]

While the Court rejected the elder widow's claim, it also found that, 'in selling the lands under her charge, [she] had illegally converted to private use what was endowed for purposes of religion'.[119] Sadly, the Court had no remedy for this breach of trusts and this typifies the *Ṣadr Dīwānī 'Adālats'* limitations with regard to Hindu religious endowments: the absence of a clear jurisdiction for intervening in cases of breach of trust – something reserved by the Government in its capacity as the delegated agent of the Crown.[120]

Finally, the Courts were probably most concerned with determining when members of joint Hindu families – the central legal entity of Hindu law – from the sundry schools of Hindu law (*Dāyabhāga*, *Mitākṣarā*, *Maithilā*, etc.) could lawfully convert personal and family funds into *debutter* property.[121] As Nandini Chatterjee notes, during the reformation of Hindu inheritance law in the 1870s, Hindus 'claimed that private religious endowments were an inviolable religious right for themselves, an invaluable tool for disciplining errant heirs'.[122]

From this perspective, the assignation of *shebaitship* could, in many circumstances effectively bypass the operation of the Hindu law of inheritance – especially

[116] SDAR, Vol. 1, 180.
[117] Ibid., 180.
[118] Ibid., 181.
[119] Ibid.
[120] In ***Manohar Mukherkee v Bhupendra Nath Mukerjee*** (1932) 37 CWN 29 (FB), www.casemine.com/judgement/in/56e10d6e607dba3896613f91, the court listed several similar cases from the Bengal *Ṣadr Dīwānī 'Adālat*: ***Jagat Chunder Sein v Krishwananda*** [1814] 2 Sel. Rep. SDA, 126; ***Radha Bullab Chandra v Juggat Chinder Chowdre*** [1826] 4 Sel Rep. SDA, 151; and ***Kessnanund v Nursingh*** [1863] 1 Marsh, 485.
[121] For a chart of rights of alienation in different Anglo-Hindu schools of inheritance, see Fleming, *Ownership and Inheritance*, 162–3. Mukherjea, *Hindu Law*, discusses the Joint Hindu Family in reference to endowments on pp. 90–8.
[122] Chatterjee, *Secularism*, 265–6 fn. 260, citing Government of India Legislative Proceedings, August, 1870, Nos. 93, 95, P/436/58, APAC, British Library.

the agnatic coparcenary rights of the male line – and many cases questioned the ability of fathers to endow deities with the patrilineal estate and of widows to endow deities with their life-estates. One crucial division in the courts' approach to the creation of religious endowments by members of joint Hindu families was the distinction between the *Dāyabhāga* and *Mitākṣarā* schools of law. In the former, the Joint Hindu Family held property in something akin to a tenancy-in-common (with each holding alienable, separable shares) and the father held near-unlimited powers of alienation. In the latter school, the family held property in a coparcenary, something akin to a joint family trust, and members only enjoyed limited – but non-negligible – powers of alienation.[123]

Regarding the *Dāyabhāga* school, the courts quickly determined that a father's alienation of the entire estate as *debutter* property was permissible under the doctrine of *factum valet*. Under this doctrine, Dharmaśāstric statements prohibiting a father's alienation of the *entire* estate – even for religious purposes – merely held *moral* rather than *legal* scope.[124] The standard early case for this is ***Juggomohun Roy v Sreemutty Neemoo Dossee*** (1831), from the Supreme Court at Calcutta, which confirmed a decision of the *Ṣadr Dīwānī 'Adālat*.[125] Regarding the *Mitākṣarā* school, the *Ṣadr Dīwānī 'Adālat*'s decision in the 1830 case, ***Gopal Chand Pande v Bahari Lal Pande***, clarified a father's powers of alienation over the coparcenary estate. While a father, generally, was prohibited from alienating joint assets without the consent of the coparceners, other than for the direct benefit of the coparcenary, he might, nevertheless, make 'a gift of a small portion of land, for the sake of piety, even without the assent of his son'.[126]

Two cases from the Bombay *Ṣadr Dīwānī 'Adālat* typify the issue of widows' rights to create *debutter*. In 1812, the Court ruled in ***Jugjeevun Nuthoojee and five ors. v Deosunkur Kaseram***, concerning a widow who had endowed her deceased husband's self-acquired assets as *debutter* (described as '*krishnarpun*', i.e., Kṛṣṇa worship) to her sisters' sons as a device for frustrating the claims of her husband's sisters' sons to the property.[127] The Court ruled in favour of the widow's nephews

[123] See Mukherjea, *Hindu Law*, 90–2.

[124] For the importance of the principle of *factum valet* in Anglo-Hindu law, see Ludo Rocher, 'Jīmūtavāhana's Dāyabhāga and the Maxim Factum Valet', in Donald Davis (ed.), *Studies in Hindu Law and Dharmaśāstra* (New York: Anthem Press, 2014): 305–13. High court case law is discussed in J.C. Ghose, *The Hindu Law of Impartible Property* (Calcutta: S.C. Auddy, 1908), 267–9.

[125] T.C. Morton, *Decisions of the Supreme Court of Judicature at Fort William in Bengal. On the Plea, Equity, Ecclesiastical, Admiralty and Crown Sides, from the Date of the Charter of 1774 to 1841* (Calcutta: Samuel Smith & Co., 1841), 90–1.

[126] (1830) 5 SDAR 33, https://books.google.co.uk/books?id=wkY1AQAAMAAJ&printsec=frontcover&source=gbs_ge_summary_r&cad=0#v=onepage&q&f=false. Followed in ***Muddun Gopal v Rumbuksh*** (1863) 6 WR and ***Raghunath Prosad v Gobind Prosad*** 8 All. 76.

[127] (1812) 1 SDAR (Bombay) No. 27, p. 436, https://books.google.co.uk/books?id=bY8rAQAAMAAJ&printsec=frontcover&source=gbs_ge_summary_r&cad=0#v=onepage&q&f=false

on the basis that Hindu law enabled a widow to assign her husband's estate for religious purposes.[128]

In the 1814 case, ***Kupoor Bhuwanee v Sevukram Sheoshunker***, the Bombay *Ṣadr Dīwānī 'Adālat* ruled similarly. The court denied a natural heir's right to inheritance on the basis of a widow's dedication of property as *debutter* and cited a *vyavasthā* which referred to Nīlakaṇṭhabhaṭṭa's *Vyavahāramayūkha*.[129] These and similar cases granted widows considerable power over their deceased husbands' estates, to the detriment of their husbands' natural heirs. The High Courts subsequently limited widows to endowing only a small fraction of her husband's estate.[130]

Taken collectively, this data indicates that the early Company (and Crown) courts in India took an interest in Hindu religious endowments. They did so largely through the standpoint of endowed property under the Hindu law and jurisprudence of *inheritance* rather than through *Equity*. There are many references to grantees' inability to convert endowed property to secular uses, but these generally tend to be *obiter dicta* rather than *ratio decidendi*. This is because, until the passage of the Religious Endowments Act in 1863, the fiduciary relations involved in public and private religious trusts were arbitrated by the executive government, rather than the courts.

4.2.1.iii Contesting jurisdiction between the Supreme Courts, the Government, and the Crown

Before the advent of Crown rule in 1858 and the implementation of the 1861 High Courts Act, the relative jurisdiction of the Government, the Supreme Courts, the *Ṣadr Dīwānī 'Adālats*, and the Crown remained an open and contested question. The introduction of Crown rule and an integrated judicial hierarchy did much to assuage the issue of competing jurisdictions. Before this, however, conflict between the Government and the various courts led to a series of cases which plumbed major constitutional issues. These proved to be of great importance to the legal administration of Hindu religious endowments during the following decades. Broadly, we can divide these cases into the two constitutional questions which they probe: 1) what was the role of the British East India Company in

[128] Ironically, that same year, the Court rejected another widow's similar efforts in ***Umbashunker Mungulram and the rest of the Nagur Brahmun Caste v Tooljaram Duyaram, and Oomalukmee*** (1812) 1 SDAR (Bombay) No. 30, on the basis that the Court had, in an earlier case, granted her only a life estate in her deceased husband's property.

[129] Ibid., (1814) 1 SDAR (Bombay) No. 32, 446.

[130] For the subsequent limitations, see Ghose, *Impartible Property*, 269–70. These include: ***Lakshminaranya v Das*** 11 Mad. 288; ***Rama v Ranga*** 8 Mad 582; ***Puran Bai v Jainarayan*** 4 All. 482; and ***Collector of Maslipatam v Savalo Vencata*** 8 Mad. 482.

relation to the Crown of England and the Mughal Empire; and 2) how far did the equitable jurisdiction of the Supreme Courts of Judicature extend when they came into conflict with the Governments' statutory rights of supervision of religious endowments?

In answering both questions, the Privy Council (first as the King in Council and then as the Judicial Committee of the Privy Council) developed two related constitutional principles: 1) that the British East India Company was a *trustee* of the Crown of England in the former's exercising sovereign rights that were acquired from the Mughal Empire; and 2) as a sovereign power serving as *parens patriae* in India under the aegis of the English Crown, the Company Government had a duty to protect the interest of minors, women, charities (analogised to perpetual minors), and property held in trust. The Supreme Court, for its part, had a statutory duty to exercise their equitable jurisdiction in hearing cases brought on behalf of legal incompetents by the advocate generals of the presidencies. While this solution may seem eminently sensible to modern sensibilities, it was by no means an established fact during the late 18th and early 19th centuries. In working out this settlement, however, the Supreme Court turned to a familiar source: Dharmaśāstric jurisprudential principles of Equity and Trusts.

As M.B. Hooker notes, Shāh 'Alām's grant of the *Dīwānī* of Bengal Bihar and Orissa to the Company in 1765 'had immediate consequences in England including questions about the right of a trading company to acquire on its own account sovereignty… [and] in the period 1772 up until the Company's dissolution this became one of the main topics for both parties and of immediate concern to English legal history'.[131] While none of these cases directly pertain to Hindu religious endowments *per se*, they nevertheless laid the jurisprudential groundwork for many of the principles which would be employed in the regulation of Hindu religious and charitable trusts in the 1860s and onwards.

The first constitutional case of this kind to emerge from colonial India was ***Commaul Ali Khan v Goring***, decided by the Supreme Court of Judicature in Calcutta in 1777.[132] The case concerned the application of English law to Calcutta (rather than the *Mofussil*) and the judges, Elijah Impey (chief justice) and John Hyde (puisne judge) came to different conclusions. Impey argued that, 'the Company was merely Diwani though he admitted that de facto territorial government lay in the Company'; while Hyde argued 'that the Company cannot be sovereign alone and was also prepared to ignore the formal effect of Diwani'.[133] This

[131] M.B. Hooker, 'The East India Company and the Crown: 1773–1858' *Malaya Law Review* 11.1 (1969): 1–37, 4. For this time period, also see B.B. Misra, *The Judicial Administration of the East India Company in Bengal, 1765–1782* (London: SOAS, 1947). Hooker discusses some pre-1765 cases involving English conquests more generally on pages 6–7.
[132] Morton, *Decisions*, Vol. 1, 63–4.
[133] Hooker, 'East India Company', 7.

hardly settled matters, and in 1793, the issue arose again in ***Nabob of the Carnatic v East India Company***.[134] For decades, as the Nawāb of the Carnātic, Muhammad Ali Khan, grew increasingly indebted to the Company, he signed a number of treaties which either directly ceded power to the Company (as in the case of the Tirupati temple in 1801) or he pledged his lands as collateral for predatory, usurious loans that were offered by the Company.[135]

In 1791, the Nawāb 'filed a bill in the Court of Chancery seeking an accounting of rents and profits from the Company, which possessed part of his territory in southeastern India as security for a loan'.[136] The Company's usurious behaviour, seizure of mortgaged assets, and general unjust enrichment at the Nawāb's (and his people's) expense would undoubtedly fall under the Court of Chancery's equitable jurisdiction if the Nawāb's relations with the Company had been between a merchant company and an English subject. The Court of Chancery, however, ruled that:

> It is a case of mutual treaty between persons acting in that instance as states independent of each other ; and the circumstance, that the East India Company are mere subjects with relation to this country, has nothing to do with that. That treaty was entered into with them, not as subjects, but as a neighbouring independent state, and is the same, as if it was a treaty between two sovereigns; and consequently, is not a subject of private, municipal, jurisdiction.[137]

At the heart of the judgment was the observation that the usurious relations between the Company and the Nawāb were 'not mercantile in… nature, but political'.[138] In the wider Common Law world, ***Nabob of the Carnatic*** established the general principle that political relations were free from the jurisdiction of Equity, but in India, it had the effect of beginning the long process of delineating the legal relationship between the Company, the Crown, and their Indian subjects.[139]

Complicating the situation were a pair of cases in which the Supreme Courts in Calcutta and Madras ruled that English law governed English and Indian subjects within Calcutta and Madras: ***Doe Dem. Savage v Bancharam Tagore***

[134] 30 Eng. Rep. 521.

[135] For the relationship between the Nawāb and the Company, see Jim Phillips, 'A Successor to the Moguls: The Nawab of the Garnatic and the East India Company, 1763–1785', *International History Review* 7.3 (1985): 364–89. For the ruinous effects of these debts on the agrarian population of the Carnatic, see Parvathi Menon, 'The Carnatic Debts and the Agrarian Crisis of the Eighteenth Century' *Review of Agrarian Studies* 9.1 (2019): 10–32.

[136] Seth Davis, 'Empire in Equity', *Notre Dame Law Review* 97.5 (2022): 1985–2017.

[137] 30 Eng. Rep. 523, citing ***Barclay v Russell***, 3 Ves. 424 and ***Dolder v Lord Huntingfield*** 9 Ves. 283.

[138] Ibid.

[139] See Davis, 'Empire' for a thorough account of this case's afterlife in common law. Oddly, as Hooker notes, the Court of Chancery made no reference to two cases, both decided in 1779, in which the Supreme Court in Calcutta ruled that Company held a non-political sovereignty: ***Doe dem. Rajah Huzzoree Mull v Gossinauth*** 1 Ind. D. 1035; and ***Dutturam Turrufdar v The United Company and Watson*** 1 Ind. D. 1037.

(1785, Calcutta) and ***Re Govindo Lalla*** (1801, Madras).[140] In the first case, the Court ruled that, 'the lands of British subjects must descend as in England, except in so far as the descent is interrupted... by Statute or Charter'.[141] The second case, ***Re Govindo Lalla***, concerned the Company's right to escheat to the estate of a person who died by suicide.[142] Under the old English law, the Court noted that 'the goods and chattels of the *felo de se* were forfeited to the King, for whose security it directed the coroner... to deliver them over to the township, to be answerable to the Crown'.[143] In more modern times, however, the Court ruled that, 'the practice of the Crown in such a case now was, to consider itself trustee, first for creditors, and then for the next of kin of the deceased... [and] *the Company here stood for the purpose in the place of the King;* and that it would be fit to preserve the property'.[144]

Unlike the Court of Chancery in England, the Supreme Courts of Judicature in India increasingly took the view in the early 1800s that the Company, despite its pretensions to sovereign political authority, could, nevertheless, have its actions and agents held accountable to the courts. For example, in 1826, the Supreme Court in Bombay held, in ***Amerchund Burdeechund v East India Company, Elphinstone & Robertson*** (the Deccan Prize Money Case), that 'acts of the government, i.e., by the Governor-General in Council, are subject to the jurisdiction of the Court'.[145]

Likewise, in ***Bank of Bengal v The United Company*** (1831), the Supreme Court of Bengal argued that, 'that the Company had no sovereign character such as to prevent an action being brought against it'.[146] Furthermore, in 1820 the Supreme Court in Madras granted the poor Nawāb of Arcot's descendant title to a property resumed by the Company, in ***East India Company v Syed Ally***, but this was overturned on appeal to the King in Council in 1827, when the Privy Council ruled that the Supreme Court in Madras had overstepped its jurisdiction by intervening in the Company's acts as a sovereign power.[147]

By 1833, the introduction of the Judicial Committee of the Privy Council provided an efficient mechanism for resolving these contentious disputes between an ever-increasingly sovereign Company and the Supreme Courts that sought to rein in its excesses. In serving as a referee, the Judicial Committee finally put an end to this judicial confusion by delineating the Supreme Courts' jurisdictional

[140] 1 Ind. D. 65 & 5 Ind. D. 34.
[141] Morton, *Decisions*, 72.
[142] Thomas Strange, *Notes of Cases in the Court of the Recorder and in the Supreme Court of Judicature at Madras: 1798–1816*, Vol. 1 (Madras: Asylum Press, 1816), 74.
[143] Ibid., 75, emphasis added. For suicide and property forfeiture in the Common Law, see John Vincent Barry, 'Suicide and the Law', *Melbourne University Law Review* 5.1 (1965): 1–16.
[144] Strange, *Notes*, 75–6.
[145] 4 Ind. D. 547. Discussed in Hooker, 'East India Company', 8.
[146] Hooker, 'East India Company', 8–9.
[147] Ibid. ***The East India Company v Syed Ally, Habiboon Nissa Begum, Syed Ahmed, Syed Yahyah, and Nagaboon Nissa Begum*** (1827) E.R 552; (1827) 7 Moo Ind App 555; 19 E.R. 417 (1827).

boundaries – particularly their equitable jurisdiction – and by framing the Company as a public trustee of the Government of India on behalf of the Crown of England. In doing so, the Committee provided a model of Company sovereignty centred on a model of *parens patriae* and fiduciary duties.

Three cases involving appeals of Supreme Court decisions to the Committee (one from each presidency's Supreme Court) delineated the role of the company as *parens patriae* (in trust for the Crown) and the Supreme Court's equitable jurisdiction. In the ***Mayor of the City of Lyons v East India Company*** (decided by the Privy Council in 1836), the Committee weighed in, for the first time, on the operation of trusts law in India.[148] The case is usually cited in support of the proposition that the English Mortmain Act of 1736 (9 George II 36) – generally limiting deathbed charitable alienations – was inapplicable in India.[149] The facts of the case are extraordinary in their global connections. Major-General Claude Martin, a Frenchman, served as a captain in the British East India Company and, with Company sanction, as a general for the independent Nawāb of Oudh until his death in 1801.

At the time of his death, Martin possessed a 'very considerable personal estate of every description' in French, British, and native Indian territories.[150] Martin's elaborate will allocated funds for charities of virtually every religious group in India, a series of trusts for the benefit of loved ones, and a school to educate 'children of any sex'; he requested that 'the Government or the Supreme Court' give effect to his deathbed wishes.[151]

In response, the Advocate-General of Bengal filed several suits in the Supreme Court 'for the purpose of having the several charities… established, and for carrying into execution the trusts of his [Martin's] will'.[152] As a Wes Anderson film memorably notes, 'when the destiny of a great fortune is at stake, men's greed spreads like a poison in the bloodstream', and various interested parties, including the governor-general, the Crown, and the mayor of the city of Lyons (Martin's hometown) filed suit for their share of the deceased's largesse.[153]

The case passed through the Supreme Court of Calcutta to the Privy Council, where in 1836, the Judicial Committee determined, *inter alia*, that in Mukherjea's terms, 'the British Government by virtue of its sovereign power possesses, as the former rulers of the country did, the right to control all public religious endowments and all charities… [because] the King is to be considered *parens patriae*,

148 1 Moore 175, www.commonlii.org/uk/cases/EngR/1836/1154.pdf

149 For the act and its political/religious context in Hanoverian England, see Jones, History, 2nd edn., 109–119.

150 Ibid., 172.

151 Ibid., 173.

152 Ibid.

153 Ibid., 174. Wes Anderson, *The Grand Budapest Hotel*. Fox Searchlight Pictures, 2014.

protector of part of his subject[s]'.[154] This, of course, was a statement of a core principle of the Sanskrit jurisprudence of Equity.

Specifically, the Judicial Committee elucidated four key propositions in ***Mayor of Lyons v East India Company*** and its sequel, ***Mayor of Lyons v Advocate General of Bengal*** (1876): 1) that the Crown, as *parens patriae* had a right of supervision over charities; 2) that this jurisdiction was delegated to the Company, as the Crown's agent in India; 3) that the Advocate-General of Bengal, like the attorney-general of England had the delegated responsibility to represent charities – analogised to minors; and 4) that the Supreme Court of Calcutta, as a Court of Equity, had jurisdiction over the Advocate-General's efforts to frame schemes for giving effect to and protecting charitable trusts.[155]

Similar cases reached the Judicial Committee of the Privy Council from the Madras Supreme Court and Bombay High Court in 1846 and 1880, respectively: ***Attorney General v Brodie***, and ***Kahandas Narrandas, In Re.***[156] In ***Attorney General v Brodie***, an Armenian merchant in India had died after making a deathbed bequest of the sizeable sum of 1,200 *pagodas* for the repair of a bridge and steps at St Thomas' mount in Madras. When the trustees made no effort to give effect to this charity, the Advocate-General of Madras, acting as a representative of the Crown as *parens patriae*, filed suit at the Supreme Court of Madras for the settlement of a scheme to give effect to the charity.

Surprisingly, the Supreme Court ruled that it had no jurisdiction over charitable trusts – despite the Court's charter giving it a clear equitable jurisdiction – and that the Advocate-General had no standing to appear as a representative of the Crown as *parens patriae*.[157] The Judicial Committee, citing ***Mayor of Lyons v Attorney General***, ruled that: 'the Supreme Court [of Madras] has jurisdiction over charities… [and] we are surprised that there could be any doubt'.[158] In the

[154] Mukherjea, *Hindu Law*, 546.

[155] ILR 1 Cal 303 PC. Available here: www.casemine.com/judgement/in/5779f2f3e561096c9312fa11. See Mukherjea, *Hindu Law*, 127–32, for a discussion of this case in relation to the establishment of the *cy pres* doctrine in India (a wholly English imposition). For the *parens patriae* rights of the Crown and their delegation to the Attorney-General in English charities law, see Jones, *History*, 2nd edn., 55: 'Lord Nottingham confirmed that the Court of Chancery could cure defective charitable uses and uphold them as valid appointments *inter vivos*, even though the matter had come before the Court by way of information. For "the King as *Pater patriae* may and ought to be the great protector of all charities which were not within the regulation of the statute of 43 Eliz., for he was so at Common Law before that statute." ***Att.-Gen. v Peacock*** (1675), Selden Society, LXXIII, case 300, p. 20)'; and 160: 'the authority of the Crown, acting through the Attorney-General, in whose name the information was presented [in cases involving charities]: … "the King is to be considered as the *parens patriae*… the protector of every part of his subjects, and… therefore, it is the duty of his officer, the Attorney-General, to see that justice is done to every part of those subjects" ***Corporation of Ludlow v Greenhouse*** (1817), 1 Bli. N.S. 17, 48, *per* Lord Eldon. Cf. ***Att.-Gen v Hewitt*** (1804), 9 Ves. 232).'

[156] 4 Moore, 190, https://archive.org/details/in.ernet.dli.2015.213464/page/n203/mode/2up; and ILR 5 Bom 154.

[157] 4 Moore, 193.

[158] Ibid., 193 [Lord Brougham].

Committee's estimation, the supervision of charities 'is part of the general equitable jurisdiction' of the Crown and its delegates as *parens patriae*.' Furthermore: 'The Advocate-General... [is for] all intents and purposes, as His Majesty's Attorney-General, for the time being, is, by law, authorised to exhibit any such information or informations in any of His Majesty's Courts of Equity in this country.'[159]

Putting the Advocate-General of Madras into an analogous position with the Attorney-General of Great Britain (an entirely reasonable position to take) prompted the court to make an unambiguous statement about the nature of the sovereignty of the British East India Company vis-à-vis the Crown:

> It is a fallacy to view the Crown as the present *parens patriae* in India. The delegated Government, the East India Company, is *parens patriae*. By the present charter, 3 & 4 Will. IV., c [17]85 the entire Government of India is... placed under the direction of the East India Company... [and] they are lessees under the Crown...and stand, for the period of the lease, in the place of the Crown, as *parens patriae*.[160]

Finally, Lord Lushington added that, 'under the Charter [of William IV] the East India Company can have no right in anything except as trustees of the Crown'.[161]

While ***Mayor of Lyons*** and ***Attorney General v Brodie*** involved the charitable bequests of non-native, non-British Christians in India, ***Kahandas Narrandas, In Re*** reveals how the principles established in these earlier cases were applied in the context of Hindu religious and charitable trusts after the passage of the Religious Endowments Act in 1863 and the Indian Trustees Act in 1866. The facts of the case were simple: a settlor petitioned the Bombay High Court to appoint a new trustee – one of the two original trustees having died – against the wishes of the remaining sole trustee of a religious endowment. The issue was that the Indian Trustees Act provided a remedy only in 'cases to which English law is applicable'.[162]

In order to circumvent this loophole – later solved by §539 of the Civil Procedure Code of 1882 and the by §92(2) of the Civil Procedure Code of 1888 – Justice West first observed that: 'In India... a system of equity in the English sense... was not intended that the substantive native laws should in their essence be changed, but... [rather provide]... a remedy... wherein that [native] law failed to provide a remedy which the Court could apply.'[163] In Justice West's estimation:

> While the substantive Hindu law insists as strongly as any on the suppression of fraud and the fulfilment of promises, it fails to furnish the detailed rules by which effect is to be given to its principles in cases of trusts... [and] it contemplates no such

[159] Ibid., 195 [Lord Langdale].
[160] Ibid., 196–7 [Lord Langdale].
[161] Ibid., 197 [Lord Langdale].
[162] 5 I.L.R. (Bombay) 157.
[163] Ibid., 172.

> power and flexibility in the legal machinery as are an integral element of the English equity system.[164]

The broad contention of this monograph is that, *pace* Justice West, the Hindu law articulated theoretically in Dharmaśāstra and practically in the epigraphic record contemplates a power and flexibility in the legal machinery that are broadly analogous to the English system of Equity in a general sense. Justice West may be forgiven for not comprehending the intricacies of Sanskrit jurisprudential thought, but, ironically, his application of English Equity to Hindu trusts winds up, more or less, reproducing a Dharmaśāstric model of trusts. As West puts it:

> If the Court is called on to give effect to a trust in a given case it looks to the Hindu law of property to determine the estate of the trustee, but with reference to the duties of the trustee and the rights of the beneficiaries it is governed by the rule of English equity… [but the Court] has to take care, in applying them, not to violate the "laws, manners, customs, and usages" of the native community as these may subsist.[165]

This is, to reiterate, the general substance of the Dharmaśāstric jurisprudence of Equity and Trusts. The Crown is responsible for adjudicating cases of breach of communities' conventional laws that govern their trusts. The application of English Equity in this case was merely to support the jurisdiction of the Court and the Advocate-General (acting as *parens patriae*) to intervene to protect a charitable religious trust from maladministration by appointing a new trustee. We saw in Chapters 1, 2, and 3 that this behaviour was a common pre-colonial practice that was supported by Sanskrit jurisprudential principles of Equity and Trusts. We will also see in the following section, how the Courts explored the intricacies of the analogy between Hindu and English trusts in depth during the 19th century.

The period between 1772 and 1863 was a formative epoch in history of the Anglo-Hindu law of Equity and Trusts. The executive Government actively asserted its sovereign rights as *parens patriae* to take over direct administration of major public temples such as the Jagannātha temple in Orissa and the Tirupati temple in Tamil Nadu. In doing so, they invoked indigenous theories of Dharmaśāstric kingship which portrayed the ruling sovereign as the protector of temple deities. They also invoked elements of English trusts law concerning the courts' giving effect to the pious wishes of the founders of public charities. The Government, of course, also had a clear pecuniary advantage in placing temple management under the supervision of the district collectors who could carefully monitor income and expenditure – and prevent 'fraud' on the public treasury.

At the same time, the *Ṣadr Dīwānī 'Adālat* courts endeavoured to distinguish between valid and invalid religious endowments on the basis of Hindu personal law.

[164] Ibid., 174.
[165] Ibid., 174.

On the one hand, this involved concerns about the property relations between members of Joint Hindu Families that were governed by increasingly complicated 'schools' of Hindu inheritance law. On the other hand, the Courts were interested in identifying invalid religious alienations for the purposes of resuming them or assigning them for tax. In these courts, there was little, if any discussion about the fiduciary duties of trustees or what to do in cases of breach of trust.

Finally, the Supreme Courts of Judicature and the Privy Council examined broader constitutional questions about the limits of the Company's sovereign power and the jurisdiction of the Courts. Although the Supreme Courts of Judicature often acted to curtail the sovereign rights of the Government, it was the Privy Council who intervened to protect the Company as a *trustee* of the Crown of England. As a trustee of the Government of India acting on behalf of the Crown, the Company acquired *parens patriae* jurisdiction in India. The Advocate-General, like the Attorney-General of England, held a visitorial right over charities, and could file suit on their behalf in the Supreme Courts. The Supreme Courts' equitable jurisdiction, however, seemed to be somewhat forced on them by the Privy Council – despite its clear existence in their founding charters.

Nevertheless, before 1863, the charities involved in these cases were Christian, rather than Hindu. It was only after the Rebellion of 1857, the enactment of the High Courts Act in 1861, and the Religious Endowments Act in 1863, that the High Courts combined these sundry judicial strands into a comprehensive Anglo-Hindu trusts law.

4.2.2 Hindu religious endowments and the Indian High Courts (1863–1900)

By 1863, the legal and constitutional landscape of India had changed dramatically. The Government of India Act 1858 (16 & 17 Victoria, C. 95) transferred the Government of India from the British East India Company to the Crown; the High Courts Act of 1861 unified the civil, criminal, and Supreme appellate courts of the presidencies into a series of High Courts; and the 1863 Religious Endowments Act formally divested the Government of direct administration of public religious endowments.[166] A key feature of the 1863 Act was Section 4, which stipulated that:

> In the case of every such mosque, temple or other religious establishment which, at the time of the passing of this Act, shall be under the management of any trustee, manager or superintendent, whose nomination shall not vest in, nor be exercised by, nor be subject to the confirmation of, the Government, or any public officer,

[166] For some discussion on the wider politics of these developments, see Donovan Williams, 'The Council of India and the Relationship between the Home and Supreme Governments, 1858–1870' *The English Historical* 81.318 (1966): 56–73.

> the State Government shall, as soon as possible after the passing of this Act, transfer to such trustee, manager or superintendent, all the landed or other property which, at the time of the passing of this Act, shall be under the superintendence or in the possession of the Board of Revenue, or any local agent, and belonging to such mosque, temple of other religious establishment, except such property as is hereinafter provided.[167]

In place of the Government, a series of committees and trustees would look after the interests of religious endowments. Section 13 of the Act stated that:

> It shall be the duty of every trustee, manager and superintendent of a mosque, temple or religious establishment of which the provisions of this Act shall apply to keep regular accounts of his receipts and disbursements in respect of the endowments and expenses of such mosque, temple or other religious establishment.... [and, according to Section 14] Any person or persons interested in any mosque, temple or religious establishment, or in the performance of the worship or of the service thereof, or the trusts relating thereto, may, without joining as plaintiff any of the other persons interested therein, sue before the Civil Court the trustee, manager or superintendent of such mosque, temple or religious establishment or the member of any committee appointed under this Act, for any misfeasance, breach of trust or neglect of duty, committed by such trustee, manager, superintendent or member of such committee, in respect of the trusts vested in, or confided to, them respectively.[168]

In effect, the Religious Endowments Act made the newly-founded High Courts, rather than the Government, responsible for supervising religious endowments, by serving as a check against breaches of fiduciary duty by temple trustees. Before the passing of the Act, the Government had justified its direct supervision of public religious endowments on the basis of its sovereign prerogative as *parens patriae*, while the courts focused on the issue of religious endowments from the perspective of the powers of alienation in Anglo-Hindu law. After 1863, the courts combined these two jurisprudential trends in order to craft a comprehensive Anglo-Hindu jurisprudence of religious and charitable trusts.

The key themes in this jurisprudence were: 1) the deity owns temple or monastic property; 2) due to the deity's legal incompetence, they require fiduciaries to regulate their property; 3) these fiduciaries, or trustees in the general sense, have powers over the endowed property equivalent to that of a guardian over a ward; 4) in cases of breach of fiduciary duty, the Crown, through the Attorney-General for India and the courts, has a duty to intervene; and 5) the specific financial and organisational structures of religious endowments are determined by the established customs and usages of the individual institutions.

[167] The Religious Endowments Act, 1863. Available online: www.indiacode.nic.in/bitstream/123456789/2266/1/A1863-20.pdf

[168] Ibid.

While all of this appears to be a harmonious fusion of the English and Sanskritic theories of Equity and Trusts, several scholars, most notably Ritu Birla, argue that the High Courts' jurisprudence of Hindu religious and charitable trusts (that developed after 1863) favoured 'Mīmāṃsā', 'Vedic', or 'Brāhmaṇical' theories of the 'figurative', or 'ideal' legal personality of Hindu deities, at the cost of 'popular', pre-colonial ideas and practices.[169] This analysis is defective for two reasons. First, Sanskrit jurisprudential arguments in Mīmāṃsā and Dharmaśāstric literature that discuss the deities' ownership (*devasvatva*) – as opposed to general arguments concerning the royal supervision of conventional laws – do not appear in Anglo-Hindu court cases until ***Bhupatinath*** in 1909.

This was long after the core principles of the Anglo-Hindu jurisprudence of religious and charitable endowments had been established on the basis of Dharmaśāstric theories of Equity. Second, many of the cases cited by Birla and others in support of the contention that British jurists imposed English concepts of trusts onto indigenous Indian endowments actually entail jurists enforcing the specific, historically well-documented regulatory regimes of the Mughals and Marāṭhās. In short, there was little, if any 'Mīmāṃsā' in late 19th-century Anglo-Hindu trusts jurisprudence and the practical actions taken by the court in holding temple officials accountable for breaches of trust were often a direct continuation of pre-colonial administrative practices.

In what follows, I take up two key themes in the development of the Anglo-Hindu law of religious and charitable trusts during the late 19th century: 1) the construal of divine endowments as *trusts* in which the guardianship of deities' property is analogised to the guardianship of wards; and 2) the emphasis on *custom* and *usage* (Dharmaśāstric Equity) in determining the religious norms and legal structure of religious endowments.

4.2.2.i Divine endowments as trusts

In post-1863 cases, the courts examined into the vexed question of whether religious endowments were 'trusts' in the peculiarly English sense of the word ('a confidence reposed in a person with respect to property').[170] In many of these cases after 1863, however, the courts emphasised the existence and enforcement of duties imposed on trustees rather than on the legal personality and rights of temple deities. Analysis of the juridical personality of a deity – rather than simply assuming it as fact – would come only in the context of extensive discussions of Sanskrit sources that begin to appear after 1900. Furthermore, these suits never

[169] Birla, *Stages of Capital*, 83–5. Cited with approval in Das Acevedo, 'Divine Sovereignty', 860–2. The argument also appears in Davis, 'Temples, Deities, and the Law', 204–6.
[170] See Chapter 1, §1.1.2, 'Trusts'.

feature the *deity* as plaintiff or defendant, but are made in the name of or against the trustees. Broadly, at this juncture in time – the late 19th century – the colonial courts framed the legal relationships involved in the administration of religious endowments as fiduciary duties (in English Equity) and justified this framing on the basis of Dharmaśāstric theories of Equity as supplemental, conventional Dharmas.

An early and influential case which reached the Privy Council was ***Maharani Shibessouree v Mothooranath Acharjo*** (1869).[171] The case concerned the alienation of *debutter* lands by a previous *shebait* and a subsequent suit for recovery by the present *shebait*. The core question was whether a *shebait* could alienate *debutter* lands in perpetuity. The Court ruled that the alienated lands were 'dedicated to the religious services of the Idol… [and] the rents constituted, therefore, *in legal contemplation*, its property [emphasis added]'.[172] The *shebait*, for their part, 'had not the legal property, but only the title of manager of a religious endowment'.[173]

While the *shebait could* create 'proper derivative tenures and estates conformable to usage… to create a new and fixed rent for all time… in lieu of giving the endowment the benefit of an augmentation of the variable rent from time to time, would be a breach of [fiduciary] duty in a *shebait*, and is not permissible'.[174] To emphasize, the deity's nominal legal ownership was not problematic for the Privy Council in ***Maharani Shibessouree***. Instead, it was a question of the duty of care on the part of the *shebait* (a fiduciary duty) that concerned the Privy Council.

Ritua Birla argues that ***Maharani Shibessouree*** 'inaugurated the status of the deity as the *owner*' of *debutter* property and the general proposition that a deity's assets are inalienable.[175] Deities were long-established as nominal owners in pre-colonial and colonial law before 1869, however. The crux of the Court's judgment was not the general inability of a *shebait* to use a deity's assets for commercial activity, but rather, their duty to act in the best *interests* of the endowment. We saw, in Chapter 2, that deities often engaged in commercial activity through their agents, but this activity was almost always to the financial benefit of the deity and their endowment. In short, ***Maharani Shibessouree*** established, rather than rejected, the proposition that *shebaits* could utilize the endowment – just as most trusts and charities do – provided that it is not used a fraudulent means for enriching preferred parties at the cost of the endowment.

Soon afterward, the Privy Council clarified many of the underlying assumptions from ***Maharani Shibessouree*** in their judgment in ***Prosunno Kumari Debya***

[171] 13 M.I.A. 270, www.casemine.com/judgement/in/5779f269e561096c9312f81b
[172] Ibid., 483.
[173] Ibid.
[174] Ibid.
[175] Birla, *Stages of Capital*, 82–4. Cited in Das Acevedo, 'Divine Sovereignty', 860–2; and Davis, 'Temples, Deities, and the Law'.

v Golab Chand Babu (1875).[176] The case involved *debutter* lands that had been offered as security for a loan made for the benefit of the proprietary deity. The Court had to determine: 1) if this action was to the benefit of the deity – and therefore legally valid; and 2) if the action of a previous *shebait* was binding on his successor. In answering in the affirmative to both queries, the Court, citing ***Maharani Shibessouree***, ruled that:

> Notwithstanding that property devoted to religious purposes is, as a rule, inalienable, it is… competent for the *Shevait* of property dedicated to the worship of an idol, in the capacity as *Shevait* and manager of the estate, to incur debts and borrow money for the proper expenses of keeping up the religious worship, repairing the temples or other possessions of the idol, defending against hostile litigious attacks, and other like objects. *The power, however, to incur such debts must be measured by the existing necessity for incurring them. The authority of the Shevait of an idol's estate would appear to be in this respect analogous to that of the manager for an infant heir.*[177]

This effectively introduced the ancient Sanskrit analogy between a Hindu deity and a minor into Anglo-Hindu law, and the legal 'minority' of a Hindu deity would vex the court over the following centuries.[178]

Furthermore the Court acknowledged that

> it is only in an ideal sense that property can be said to belong to an idol; and the possession and management of it must in the nature of things be entrusted to some person as *Shevait*… the person so entrusted must of necessity be empowered to do whatever may be required for the service of the idol… if this were not so, the estate of the idol might be destroyed or wasted… for want of the necessary funds to preserve and maintain them.[179]

Birla argues that this 'exquisite equivocation… both limited and reconfirmed' Mīmāṃsā theories of divine legal personality 'which gave precedence to the managerial rights of the *shebait* to the extent that the deity's property became his property'.[180]

[176] LR 2 IA 145, www.casemine.com/judgement/in/5779f2dee561096c9312f9c7 Also see ***Collector of Thana v Hari Sitaram*** (1882) ILR 6 Bom 546.

[177] Ibid., emphasis added. A similar, although less cited case is ***Doorga Proshad Dass v Sheo Proshad Pandah*** (1880) 7 CLR 278, wherein a son sued for recovery of *debutter* properties when both the *debutter* and the idol had been illegally alienated by his father. The son, having created a false replacement idol, was found to be in breach of trust with the deity and his suit for recovery failed.

[178] For a discussion of the 'extravagant doctrine contrary to the decision of the Judicial Committee in such cases as ***Damodar Das v Lakhan Das*** [(1910) ILR 60 Cal 54]' of treating deities as minors under the Limitation Act and the Civil Procedure Code, see Mukherjea, *Hindu Law*, 256–7. The PC cited an early case on the legal duties of Hindu guardians with respect to the property of their wards: ***Hunooman Persand Pauday v Mussumat Babooee Munraj Koonweree*** (1856) 6 MIA 243.

[179] Ibid., 203.

[180] Birla, *Stages of Capital*, 84–5. Birla fn. 59 cites several later cases that follow this precedent: ***Seena Peena Reena v Choklingam*** (1904) 31 LRIA 83; ***Abhiram Goswami v Syama Charan*** (1909) 36 LRIA 148; and ***Palanippa v Devasikamony*** (1916) 44 LRIA 147.

This position is untenable, however. First, Mīmāṃsā is wholly absent from the judicial record until the 20th century, so the judgment in ***Prosunno Kumari*** – or in any trusts case from this period – has no reasonable connection to the claimed argument. Second, we saw in Chapter 1 that Mīmāṃsā and related Dharmaśāstric theories of divine ownership actually emphasise the opposite position to what Birla claims: deities own property in an *ideal* but legally efficacious sense. Deities' *ideal*, figurative (*aupacārika*), or secondary (*gauṇa*) ownership binds the holders of that property to utilise it for stipulated purposes.[181] Third, the analogy between deities and minors – specifically in relation to the fiduciary duties owed by their guardians – is an ancient well-attested practice in Sanskrit jurisprudential literature and in the medieval epigraphic record. The Privy Council's decision in ***Prosunno Kumari*** accords strongly with pre-colonial theories and practices regarding religious endowments.

The final case in this section, ***Manohar Ganesh Tambekar and Ors. v Lakhmiram Govindram*** (1887), the famous 'Dakor Temple Case', involved a serious breach of trust by a deity's servants, and elicited an exemplary delineation of the Anglo-Hindu law of trusts by the Bombay High Court.[182] Manohar Ganesh, a trustee of the great temple of Kṛṣṇa Śrī Ranchhodraijī filed suit against the temple *shebaits* on the grounds that they had appropriated offerings to the deity for their personal benefit and prayed:

> That the Court will make the defendants, as recipients of the offerings at the idol's shrine, accountable, as trustees, for the right disposal of the property thus acquired… for the appointment of a receiver for the exaction from the defendants of accounts of their management, for the delivery up by them of all property appertaining to the temple, for an inquiry into their conduct as ministers of the idol, and for the construction of a scheme of future management.[183]

In response to this reasonable request, the *shebaits* averred that:

> They, as a body, are the owners, for all secular purposes, of the idol, whom, in the spiritual sense, they serve. The offerings made at the shrine, the cattle, and even the land presented by devotees are, they assert, their property free from any secular obligation, as none has ever in practice or in the intention of the donors been annexed to the gifts by which religious merit was sought and gained. They hold the property thus acquired, and have for centuries held it, as a sort of sacred guild, with hereditary succession to the several members. It is not held on any trust for the support of ceremonies or with any obligation annexed to it that can be enforced in a secular Court. The duty of providing a regular worship for the deity is of a purely moral kind, which they discharge merely to satisfy their consciences, one the nature and limits of which have never been settled otherwise than by their own will and judgment.[184]

[181] See Chapter 1, §1.6.2.ii, 'Divine endowments in Mīmāṃsā and Vedānta'.
[182] ILR 12 Bom 247.
[183] Ibid., ¶2.
[184] Ibid., ¶3.

While Birla calls this a 'daring defense… reflecting the tenor of Brahmanic jurisprudence', a more appropriate description of the *shebaits*' argument would be that it was an appalling admission of gross venality. This 'defence' was more brazen than daring and it completely ignores more than two thousand years' worth of Brāhmaṇical jurisprudence and legal practice.[185] The Dakor priests' breach of trust with the deity that they served would have been as indefensible in the Gupta Empire as it was during the British Rāj. Perhaps its only virtue is the learned response that it elicited from the incredulous judges who rejected it – largely on the grounds of a robust consideration of the principles of Equity and Trusts in Sanskrit jurisprudence.

In defending the jurisdiction of the courts over the endowment, the Court noted two documents from the Marāṭhā period, dated to 1772 and 1793, respectively, in which the *shebaits* openly admitted to their fiduciary duties, and in which the 'native governor of the fort of Pavghar exercised a visitorial power to prevent waste of the temple property by either the Tambekar managing the dedicated villages, or the *shevaks* holding the accumulated offerings at the shrine'.[186]

Furthermore, the Court noted several instances of the English collector exercising his supervisory right under Bombay Regulation 17 of 1827 to restrain the *shebaits*' misappropriation of temple funds. In 1861, the *shebaits* petitioned the government for a remission of income tax on the basis that, 'the offerings were primarily the property of the idol', a position that 'derives force from its conformity with the previous history of the institution and with the religious system of the Hindus'.[187] The *shebaits* were clearly on the wrong side of the law and in breach of trust with the deity they claimed to serve.

In response to this 'daring' duplicity, the Court reviewed the jurisprudence of charitable and religious endowments in Roman, English, and Hindu law – the inalienability of endowed property, the juridical personality of the foundation, and the duty of the sovereign to intervene in cases of breach of trust – and concluded that it 'is consistent with the grants having been made to the juridical person symbolized or personified in the idol at Dakor. It is not consistent with this juridical person's being conceived as a mere slave or property of the shevaks whose very title implies not ownership, but service of the god.'[188] Concluding that, 'the law which protects the foundation against external violence guards it also internally against maladministration, and regulates, conformably to the central principle

[185] Birla, *Stages of Capital*, 85–6. Also see Appadurai, *Worship*, 214, where he inveighs against the Madras High Court's castigation of the temple administrators, whose internecine litigation over shares of temple income led to a near collapse of the temple worship that they were responsible for as trustees. ***S. Veeraraghava Achariar And Ors. v Parthasarathy Iyengar And Ors*** (1925) AIR MAD 1070. Available here: https://indiankanoon.org/doc/500523/

[186] ILR 12 Bom 247 ¶10.

[187] Ibid., ¶10.

[188] Ibid., ¶11 [West, J]. Also see ***Rupa Jagset v Krishnaji Govind*** (1885) ILR, 9 Bom.

of the institution, the use of its augmented funds' the court ordered the district judge to place the temple into receivership, to take an account of the endowed funds and to draw up a scheme for the management of the temple.[189] In doing so, the Court was simply following the longstanding, pre-colonial cultural, legal, and political precedent of protecting deities and their endowments from maladministration. The jurisprudential justification invoked by the Bombay High Court was the Dharmaśāstric principle of Equity.

In the aggregate, ***Maharani Shibessouree***, ***Prosunno Kumari***, and ***Manohar Ganesh*** demonstrate that, after 1863, the Courts took an active interest in guarding religious and charitable endowments from the harmful actions of trustees by delineating the fiduciary duties owed by *shebaits* to their deities. The courts justified this act of supervision on the basis of the right of visitation of the Crown in Sanskrit jurisprudence and in English law. In the absence of direct supervision by the government, the duty of looking after deities fell to the Courts, but the principles by which they exercised this right of supervision were ancient. The Sanskritic principles behind these decisions were limited: merely the Crown's right of visitation over religious endowments and the general inalienability of endowed property. Nevertheless, this core Dharmaśāstric theory of Equity – of the Crown as protector of supplemental, customary laws and of otherwise orphaned deities, was consistently present.[190] There was, to reiterate *no Mīmāṃsā theory involved*. When Mīmāṃsā entered the judicial record, it was only to *confirm* the jurisprudence of divine endowments rather than to *invent* it.

4.2.2.ii Customary usage and Dharmaśāstric Equity in Anglo-Hindu Trusts law

The ubiquitous refrain among Indian jurists is the paucity of positive legal statements in Hindu legal treatises concerning the regulation of religious endowments.[191] The *emic* explanation for this, as I explained in Chapters 1 and 2, is that Dharmaśāstric jurisprudence articulates a theory of Equity in which the specific rules and regulations for religious endowments are a form of conventional (*sāmayika*) Dharma that supplements the general rules and provisions of Dharmaśāstra proper – and that endowments to deities are explicitly described in these juridical contexts.[192]

Medieval epigraphic records contain thousands of charters in which local communities, often with royal sanction, established commercial, religious, and

[189] Ibid., ¶12.
[190] See Chapter 1, §1.5, 'Equity as supplemental law'.
[191] See, for example, the epigraph to Chapter 1.
[192] See Chapter 1, §1.1.1.ii, 'Supplemental law'.

political conventions that were justiciable by the Crown. Chapter 2 explored these records. Furthermore, the agents in medieval epigraphic records explicitly invoked Dharmaśāstric theories of Equity in their charters and we find numerous instances in which the Crown intervened to rectify the situation in instances of breach of trust.[193] During the late medieval and early modern periods, Islamic and Hindu rulers followed this medieval practice to varying extents, but the close association between Dharmaśāstric theory and legal practice endured.

The British, for their part, also embraced a Dharmaśāstric theory of Equity, albeit from the standpoint of 'custom and usage'. Rosane Rocher notes that 'differences between commentaries on, and compendia of, *smṛti* texts largely reflected local customs', and 'the fact that *smṛti* texts, commentaries, and compendia all recognized the customs of families, castes, guilds, and corporations as valid sources of law' led colonial-era British judges to give significant judicial credence given to social custom.[194] In ***Collector of Madura v Moottoo Ramalinga*** (1868), for example, the Privy Council, when examining the succession of a *Zumīndārī* in Ramnād, ruled that:

> The duty... of a European Judge who is under the obligation to administer Hindoo Law, is... to inquire whether a disputed doctrine... has been received by the particular school which governs the District with which he has to deal, and has there been sanctioned by usage. For, under the Hindoo system of law, clear proof of usage will outweigh the written text of the law.[195]

The Court followed this emphasis on custom in their treatment of Hindu religious endowments, particularly monasteries. In ***Greedharee Doss v Nundokissore Doss, Mohunt*** (1867), the Privy Council examined the disputed succession of a monastery (*maṭha*) in Burdwan.[196] In evaluating the strength of two rival claims to the Mahantship (abbotship/leadership/trusteeship) of the monastery, the Court observed that:

> Numerous cases have been cited to show what is the usage; but the law to be laid down by this Court must be as to what is the usage of each *Mohuntee*. We apprehend that if a person endows a College or Religious institution, the endower has a right to lay down the rule of succession. But when no such rule has been laid down it must be proved by evidence what is the usage, in order to carry out the intention of the original endower. Each case much be governed by the usage of the particular *Mohuntee*.[197]

The principles were quickly applied to temple trusts in the famous 'Rameshwar Pagoda Case', ***Rajah Muttu Ramalinga v P. Perianayagum Pillai*** (PC, 1874).[198]

[193] See Chapter 2, §2.6.3, 'Deities' complex assets', for royal intervention in trust disputes.
[194] Rocher, 'Creation', 85.
[195] 12 MIA 397, 436, cited in Rocher, 'Creation', 85.
[196] 11 MIA. 405.
[197] Ibid., 421.
[198] LR 1 IA 209.

In this case, discussed at length by Carol Appadurai Breckenridge, the erstwhile independent Setupati Rāja of Ramnād, now reduced to the status of *Zamīndār* of the Madras Presidency, petitioned the Court for the removal of the *Pandaram* (head functionary) of the Rāmeśvara temple, alleging that he, the *Zamīndār*, was 'the *Dharmarkharta* or trustee of the pagoda and had the right to conduct the management of it'.[199] The case essentially turned on Dharmaśāstric theories of Equity and Trusts. The Court, as the legal representative of the Crown, was duty bound to investigate the peculiar legal constitution of the temple trust, and to uphold it against the interference of the Setupati.

For his part, the *Pandaram* made what essentially amounted to a Dharmaśāstric argument: that the Rajas Setupati had only 'the general authority they assumed as the rightful or *de facto* rulers of the district, to prevent abuses in the management of it [the temple], and to see that its laws and usages were properly observed'.[200] The Court agreed with this general principle, and citing ***Greedharee Doss***, observed that:

> The constitution and rules of religious brotherhoods attached to Hindoo temples are by no means uniform in their character, and the important principle to be observed by the Courts is to ascertain… *the special laws and usages governing the particular community whose affairs have become the subject of litigation and to be guided by them.*[201]

Although the Setupatis were *once* the sovereign power of the region and 'in the days of their power exercised control over the pagoda… as the rightful or *de facto* rulers of the district', nevertheless, these sovereign powers, 'whatever they may have been, have now passed to the British Government'.[202] Consequently, the Privy Council dismissed the suit. Appadurai Breckenridge argues that:

> [This] decision of the courts undermined the constitutive capacity of the Setupati as king and as protector of transactions in his domain. In demanding fixity with respect to their interpretation of custom and usage, the court deprived the Setupati of his role as grantor of privileges, a role which permitted innovation and alteration in the distribution of temple honors.[203]

While true, this observation does nothing to discredit the *Pandaram*'s argument – supported by the Privy Council – that the Setupati's interference in temple affairs was predicated on his *erstwhile* sovereign right (a right appropriated by the British Crown) and that, on the extinction of that sovereignty, his rights of supervision

[199] Ibid. www.casemine.com/judgement/in/5779f2cbe561096c9312f983 Cf. Carol Appadurai Breckenridge, 'From Protector to Litigant: Changing Relations Between Hindu Temples and the Rājā of Ramnad', *Indian Economic and Social History Review* 14.1 (1977): 75–106.

[200] LR 1 IA 209, 2.

[201] Ibid., 4, emphasis added.

[202] Ibid., 10.

[203] Appadurai Breckenridge 'From Protector', 99.

had terminated. The *Pandaram* and the Court, rather than the Setupati, were in line with pre-colonial, Sanskrit jurisprudence, and with the legal practice of Equity and Trusts, where a supervisory sovereign might change but the conventional Dharmas of a temple would remain unchanged.

Ironically, in a legal dispute involving the Śrīmīnākṣī temple in Kamudhi between 1897 and 1908, the Courts recognised the Setupatis' heritable right to the trusteeship (*dharmakarta*) of the temple in a way that, once again, worked to the erstwhile king's disadvantage.[204] The case is most widely known as the first to involve the right of entry for low-caste individuals.[205] In 1897, the Nadars, a community of 'former toddy-tappers', forcibly entered the Śrīmīnākṣī temple, worshipped the goddess, and outraged the Brāhmaṇas, other higher-caste communities, and the Setupati himself.[206] In 1901, the Setupati and the Nadars arrived at a settlement by which the Nadars would be permitted to worship in the temple. The Court, however, found that this action: 'would be to ignore and alter the fundamental character and uses of the temple as ascertained by judicial authority… [and] it is not in the power of the trustees to do this'.[207] The power to alter (or preserve) the already-established conventional Dharmas of the temple vested in the sovereign (the Crown) in this case (as it did in Sanskrit jurisprudence), rather than with the fiduciary of the temple (the Setupati).

The Court supported the quashing of the compromise on the basis of ***Attorney-General v Pearson*** (1817) which involved the disposal of the trust property of a protestant congregation split by schism.[208] The core principle of the case was that:

> Where an institution exists for the purpose of religious worship and it cannot be discovered from the deed declaring the trust what form… of religious worship was intended, the Court can find no other means of deciding the question than through the medium of an inquiry into what has been the usage of the congregation… [it is] the duty of the Court to administer the trust in such a manner as best to establish the usage… [and] it is [not] in the power of individuals having the management of that institution at any time to alter the purpose for which it was founded.[209]

The Setupati was bound, as the trustee of the Mīnākṣī temple, to protect the ancient custom barring the Nadars' entry into the temple. Appadurai Breckenridge argues that, while 'custom would have permitted the Setupati to find Nadars appropriate to enter the temple… the Judge made the courts the arbitrators of custom, if

[204] Ibid., 99–100. ***Shankaralinga Nadan v Raja Rajeswara Dorai*** (1908) LR 35 IA 176.

[205] For the early temple-entry movement, see Shabnum Tejani, 'Untouchable Demands for Justice or the Problem of Religious "Non-Interference": The Case of Temple Entry Movements in Late-Colonial India', *Journal of Colonialism and Colonial History* 14.3 (2013).

[206] Appadurai Breckenridge, 'From Protector', 99–100.

[207] ***Shankaralinga Nadan v Raja Rajeswara Dorai***, 179.

[208] 3 Mer 353.

[209] ***Shankaralinga Nadan v Raja Rajeswara Dorai***, 179.

not the innovators of it.'[210] In her analysis of ***Rajah Muttu Ramalinga***, Appadurai Breckenridge conflates the role of the Setupati as *sovereign* with his role as *trustee.* In the former role, the Setupati would very much be entitled to alter a temple trust as a *political* act – despite Dharmaśāstric statements warning against this common royal proclivity in the medieval era – but as a mere *trustee*, he had a fiduciary duty to maintain the conventions of the temple trust.

In short, the introduction of the High Courts and the Religious Endowments Act in the 1860s brought about profound changes in the Anglo-Hindu law of Equity and Trusts. With the Government's retreat from direct supervision of religious and charitable endowments, the courts stepped into this role by exercising a judicial right of supervision of temple trustees. This necessitated the development of a jurisprudence of Equity and Trusts. Much of this jurisprudence was imported from England, but, ironically, English theories of trusteeship essentially matched Dharmaśāstric theories of Equity and Trusts.

Furthermore, the courts' interest in the 'custom and usage' of temples as a credible source of judicial knowledge about an institution's legal arrangements and trust purposes also matched Dharmaśāstric theories of Equity.[211] However, beyond the general principle of the Crown as *parens patriae* and the legal validity of conventional laws (Dharmaśāstric Equity), the colonial courts at this time appear to have drawn few deeper connections to Sanskrit jurisprudence. The overlap between English and Sanskritic jurisprudence in this instance was largely coincidental. It was only with the turn of the 20th century and the widespread appointment of native Indians to the High Courts that the Anglo-Hindu law of religious and charitable endowments began to engage more substantively with Sanskrit theories of divine ownership as a secondary (*gauṇa*), figurative (*aupacārika*) form of ownership.

4.2.3 The Juridical personality of deities in late-colonial Anglo-Hindu law (1900–50)

The 20th century witnessed significant changes in the Anglo-Hindu law of religious and charitable endowments, and in the legal system more widely. First, the Government passed a series of statutes that standardised India's code of civil procedure, formalised the duties of trustees, reformed religious trusts, and added progressive elements to various aspects of Hindu and Muslim personal law. Alongside these developments, state governments began to exercise direct supervision over religious endowments, with the most famous legislation being the Madras Hindu

[210] Breckenridge Appadurai, 'From Protector', 103. Also see Appadurai, *Worship*, 182–9 for a similar case involving the Śrī Pārthasārathi Svāmi temple.
[211] See Chapter 1, §1.5, 'Equity as supplemental law'.

Religious Endowments Act of 1923, which placed all public temples under the purview of a Hindu Religious and Charitable Endowments (HRCE) Board.[212] Furthermore, the 20th century saw the 'Indianisation' of the judiciary, the civil service, and the army.[213]

These wider developments precipitated several innovations in the Anglo-Hindu law of religious and charitable endowments. First, native Indian judges with significant legal and Sanskritic acumen began to provide Dharmaśāstric justifications for the rulings on issues related to Hindu religious endowments. For the first time, judges delved into the intricate details of Dharmaśāstra and Mīmāṃsā concerning the legal personality of Hindu deities and the fiduciary duties of trustees under Hindu law. Second, the courts began to explore the legal personality of Hindu deities in depth. In earlier decades, the courts had focused on *trustees* in their analysis of religious endowments – an expected result of the framing of the 1863 Religious Endowments Act.

In the 20th century, however, the *deity* and its property rights drew significant juridical attention. Third, the courts examined the right of suit in relation to deities at length. Deities *themselves* became litigants in suits filed by their fiduciaries, their devotees, or 'next friends'.[214] Fourth, the courts took divergent views on the question of a deity's 'minority' with respect to the Limitation Acts of 1887 and 1908, thereby setting up one of the vexing issues in the Ayodhyā judgment in 2019.[215] These developments, taken collectively, effectively established the modern law of Hindu religious and charitable trusts which, although modified in accordance with the Constitution of India after independence, is still operable in contemporary India.

4.2.3.i The legal personality of Hindu deities

Before the 20th century, the courts commented on the legal personality of deities in passing, but rarely went beyond mentioning the fact that property dedicated

[212] For the Act, see Mukherjea, *Hindu Law*, 548–9.

[213] According to Rohit De, 'A Peripatetic', 835 fn. 51: 'Partha Chatterjee suggests that the "Indianization" of the judiciary and the other branches of government in the 1920s and 1930s led to the dismantling of structures of colonial rule from within.' See Partha Chatterjee, *A Princely Impostor? The Kumar of Bhawal and the Secret History of Indian Nationalism* (New Delhi: Orient Blackswan, 2004). For the Indianisation of the Bombay High Court, see Abhinav Chandrachud, *An Independent, Colonial Judiciary: A History of the Bombay High Court during the British Raj, 1862–1947* (New York: Oxford University Press, 2015). For the civil service and army, see Murray Hogben, 'An Imperial Dilemma: The Reluctant Indianization of the Indian Political Service', *Modern Asian Studies* 15.4 (1981): 751–69; and Chandar Sundaram, *Indianization, the Officer Corps, and the Indian Army: The Forgotten Debate, 1817–1917* (Lanham: Lexington Books, 2019), respectively.

[214] For an early look at 'next friends' (*prochein amis*) in the Common Law, see Cyrus Wood, 'The New Friend-Extent of Authority to Compromise Suit', *Central Law Journal* 41 (1895): 342–4.

[215] ***M. Siddiq v Suresh Das*** 1 SCC 1 (2020).

to a deity was 'in legal contemplation' the deity's property.[216] Instead, the courts focused on the duties of trustees or on the capacity of members of a Joint Hindu Family to make an endowment in the first place. In the 20th century, however, the judicial focus shifted considerably and we find a flurry of cases in the early 20th century wherein judges entered into detailed discussions of a deity's legal personality. One explanation for this shift is the arrival of Indian judges on the courts.

While *paṇḍitas* had *assisted* early colonial courts before their dismissal in 1864, these *paṇḍitas* did not have the rigorous training in the Common Law that expert Indians (with notable but not specialised Sanskrit training) would have. Furthermore, by the early 20th century, the academic study of Sanskrit had advanced considerably, with a vastly greater corpus of Sanskrit legal and philosophical literature being edited and/or translated. This created a fertile environment for the elucidation of Hindu trusts law.

The most important case, by far, from this period is ***Bhupati Nath Smrititirtha v Ram Lal Maitra***, decided by the Calcutta High Court in 1909.[217] The case examined a deathbed conveyance of property to a trustee for the purpose of establishing an image of a deity and for providing it with regular worship. The issue for the Court was that the famous 1872 case, ***G.M. Tagore v Woopendermohun Tagore*** established that 'the rule against a gift to a person not in existence and capable of taking from the donor at the time when the gift is to take effect.'[218] ***Tagore v Tagore*** involved a deathbed bequest to a *human* not yet in existence at the time of the conveyance in trust. ***Tagore v Tagore*** was cited with approval in three Calcutta High Court cases which established 'the proposition that a gift to a Hindu deity, whose image is to be established and consecrated in future, is void.'[219] In ***Bhupati Nath Smrititirtha***, the Court ruled that the conveyance of property in trust for the establishment and maintenance of a deity whose image and temple is not yet in existence is valid and that the earlier cases were decided incorrectly. The reasoning behind this ruling, however, involved a substantial amount of Sanskrit jurisprudential principles that provided the canonical corpus of Sanskrit legal maxims for virtually all subsequent cases involving Hindu religious endowments.

[216] See Notes 171–4 (discussing ***Maharani Shibessouree v Mothooranath Acharjo*** (1869)).

[217] ILR 37 Cal. 128.

[218] (1872) 9 BLR 377; 47 LRIA. Discussed by Justice Jenkins in ***Bhupatinath*** ¶13.

[219] Ibid., Jenkins at ¶1.ii. The cases are: ***Upendra Lal Boral v Hem Chundra Boral*** (1897) ILR 25 Calc. 405, ***Rojomoyee Dassee v Troylukho Mohiney Basset*** (1901) ILR 29 Calc. 200 and ***Nogendra-Nandini Dassi v Benoy Krishna Deb*** (1902) ILR 30 Calc. 521. For the details of ***Tagore v Tagore***, see Tarender Chatterjee & Bhujendro Bhushan Chatterjee, *G.M. Tagore, versus Woopendermohun Tagore, and Others: Being a Full Report of the Proceedings in the Above Containing the Qill of the Late Honorable Prosonocoomar Tagore, C.S.I., the Judgment of the High Court both of Original and Appellate, Sides, Grounds of Appeal of Parties in the Privy Council, Brief Extract of Argument in the Privy Council During Hearing, and Judgment of the Lords Justices of the Privy Council* (Calcutta: Indian Mirror Press, 1872).

The judicial panel for ***Bhupatinath*** included the celebrated academic and jurist, Sir Ashutosh Mukherjee, a descendent of several prominent Sanskritists and a pupil of the legendary Sanskritist and social reformer, Ishwar Chandra Bandopadhyay.[220] In his verdict, Mukherjee warns that, 'we must not… assume… that a Hindu deity is a juridical person for all purposes, and stands on precisely the same footing, capable of the same rights, and subject to the same liabilities, as an ordinary sentient being.'[221] Mukherjee draws on a sizable corpus of Sanskrit texts – mostly from the Bengal School of jurisprudence – to support his conclusion that, 'according to strict Hindu juridical notions there can be no gift in favour of the Gods.'[222]

Rather, according to Mukherjee: 'The true Hindu conception of dedication for the establishment of the image of the deity and for the maintenance thereof is that the owner divests himself of all rights in the property; the King, as the ultimate protector of the State, undertakes the supervision of all endowments.'[223] This is a fairly conventional description of the Sanskrit jurisprudence of Equity and Trusts in which the Crown exercises a *parens patriae* jurisdiction over the supplemental laws that govern religious institutions.[224] Mukherjee adds a reference to Raghunandana Bhaṭṭācārya's 16th-century *Ekādaśītattva*, which would arguably prove to be the most important Sanskrit passage on the legal personality of Hindu deities:

> In support of this view reliance has been placed upon the following passage quoted by Raghunandan: 'It is for the benefit of the worshippers or devotees that there is manifestation in male and female forms of the supreme being, which is bodiless, which has no attribute, which consists of pure spirit, and which is without a second being.'[225]

[220] Asutosh Mukherjee is an extraordinary figure in Indian history, and decidedly deserves a modern scholarly monograph that covers his polymathic life. For more information, see Syama Prasad Mookerjee, *A Diary of Sir Asutosh Mookerjee, with his Life Sketch* (Calcutta: Asutosh Mookerjee Memorial Institute, 1998). Also see Asutosh Mukherjee, *The Law of Perpetuities in British India* (Calcutta: Thacker, Spink, & Co, 1902).

[221] ***Bhupatinath***, ¶28.

[222] Ibid., ¶56. Intriguingly, the judgment in ***Bhupati*** refers to the *Mahānirvāṇatantra*, a treatise that, while purporting to be ancient, probably dates to the 18th century. According to J. Duncan Derrett, 'A Juridical Fabrication of Early British India: The *Mahānirvāṇa Tantra*', in J. Duncan Derrett (ed.), *Essays in Classical and Modern Hindu Law*, V.II (Leiden: Brill, 1977), the treatise was probably composed by Bengali Brāhmaṇas with the intention of having it used by British Courts. See *Mahānirvāṇa Tantra* 12.92–4: 'The giver is competent to take care of the wealth or property endowed for religious purposes. He can no longer resume it, because Dharma is the then master or owner of such property. Let the owner himself or his representative, O Goddess appropriate to pious purposes the corpus of a property or its income according as it may have been resolved.'

[223] ***Bhupatinath***, ¶58.

[224] See Chapter 1, §1.5.2, 'Temple conventions'.

[225] ***Bhupatinath***, ¶61. See Chapter 1, Notes 224–5. For an analysis of the influence of this passage in legal history (especially the Ayodhyā dispute), see Fleming, 'Dharmaśāstra'.

In his opinion, Justice Chatterjee reviews the same body of Sanskrit literature and comes to the conclusion, based in part on the *dictum* of Raghunandana, that the true beneficiaries of a Hindu temple are the worshippers.[226] Chatterjee, however, makes what I consider to be a jurisprudentially unsound argument when he argues that:

> I have stated above that in the case of a gift to a God, the relation of an owner to the thing owned in its primary sense is considered to be wanting. Who then is the owner of the property? In a secondary sense, no doubt, the deity is the owner, but the shastras lay down i.e., 'Gifts are to be given to the deity and the fee for the acceptance of the gift also is to be given to the deity, but all these are to be (ultimately) given to a Brahman, otherwise the gift would be useless'... Every gift, therefore, in favour of a deity is a gift *for the ultimate benefit of a Brahman or Brahmans*, and may, therefore, be looked upon as a charitable gift.[227]

Chatterjee correctly observes that Sanskrit jurisprudence recognises the ownership of deities in a *secondary* or *hypothetical* sense, but this secondary sense, as we saw in Chapter 1, nevertheless imposes fiduciary duties on the Brāhmaṇas or other temple functionaries who take possession of deities' property.[228] I think that it is fair to say that while Chatterjee gets some of the Sanskrit jurisprudence of divine trusts correct, his greatest contribution, along with Mookherjee is the introduction of a corpus of Sanskrit *dicta* on the subject for future jurists to untangle.

Chief Justice Lawrence Jenkins' opinion, informed by Mookerjee and Chatterjee's explication of Sanskrit juridical treatises, notes that ***Shibessouree Debia*** established the principle that a deity is an owner in 'ideal sense', and queries 'whether this... means more than that the dedication to a deity is a compendious expression of the pious purposes for which the dedication is designed'.[229] Justice Stephen, however, provides a succinct – and later, highly influential – summary of the propositions expounded in Sanskrit jurisprudence texts – cited as the epigraph to this chapter. Taken collectively, the opinions in ***Bhupatinath*** begin the juridical process of recognising a Hindu deity as the personification of the pious charitable purpose for which the property of the endowment was conveyed.

The Privy Council, for its part, expanded on the justices' observations in ***Bhupatinath*** and expanded the juridical personality of Hindu deities. In ***Pramatha Nath Mullick v Pardyumna Kumar Mullick***, decided in 1925, the Court examined a dispute in which several *shebaits* wished to move the deity's image to their own home during the period of their individual, sequential tenure as *shebait*.[230] Their lordships made the observation that, 'the will of the idol in regard to location must

[226] ***Bhupatinath***, ¶83.
[227] Ibid., ¶81–3, emphasis added.
[228] See Chapter 1, §1.6.2.iii, 'Divine endowments in medieval Dharmaśāstra'.
[229] ***Bhupatinath***, ¶15 [Jenkins, J].
[230] LR 52A AP 245.

be respected… [and] in the proper and unassailable administration of the worship of the idol by the *shebait*, it be thought that a family idol should change its location the will of the idol itself, expressed though his guardian, must be given effect to.'[231]

In an effort to protect the interests of the deity in this instance, the Court also advised that 'it would be in the interests of all concerned that the idol should appear by a disinterested next friend appointed by the Court'.[232] The Court entrenched a strong juridical view of the deity and introduced the notion that suits could be filed *in the name of the deity*:

> A Hindu idol is, according to long-established authority… a 'juristic entity.' It has juridical status, *with the power of suing and being sued*. Its interests are attended to by the person who has the deity in his charge and who in law is its manager, with all the powers which would, in such circumstances, on analogy, be given to the manager of the estate of an infant heir.[233]

Although ***Pramatha Nath Mullick***, took a more capacious view of the legal personality of Hindu deities than that taken by the Calcutta High Court in ***Bhupatinath***, the precise nature of what the deity itself *represented* as a juridical person remained unresolved. In the following decade, a series of cases established the principle that deities represent the *pious purpose* of worship. The most notable of these, ***Board of Commissioners for Hindu Religious Endowments, Madras, v Parasaram Veeraraghavacharlu*** (1937), turned on the question of whether the replacement of one deity with another extinguished a religious endowment assigned to the first deity.[234]

When the Commissioners for the newly founded Madras Hindu Religious Endowments Committee attempted to establish a scheme for the regulation of the endowment for a small Viṣṇu temple in the Kistna District, under the auspices of the Madras Hindu Religious Endowments Act of 1923, the local Brāhmaṇas who served as priests in the temple averred that: 1) the current temple was dedicated to a different deity than the deity whose endowments were recorded by the committee; and 2) given the extinction of the former deity, the Brāhmaṇas had appropriated the deity's endowment for their own secular purposes. As in ***Ganesh Tambekar***, the temple priests were clearly of an avaricious demeanour, but the question remained: what was the legal consequence, vis-à-vis a divine endowment, of the extinction of one local deity and its replacement with another, differently named deity?

In response to the Brāhmaṇas' contention that 'this [the new] idol cannot claim to be the owner of properties which once belonged to the other idol', the Madras High Court reasoned, on the basis of ***Bhupatinath***, that:

[231] Ibid., 259 [Lord Shaw].
[232] Ibid., 261.
[233] Ibid., emphasis added.
[234] AIR 1937 Mad 750.

> The principle of the legal personality of an idol cannot be taken quite literally. Observations to that effect were made... only with a view to emphasize the idea that the endowments of a temple are not vested in the trustees, but are only managed by him [sic]... The purpose of making a gift to a temple is... to confer a benefit on those who worship in that temple.[235]

In the Court's estimation, this *purpose* of public worship, whatever its name or physical substratum, could survive a shift in name and image while remaining a nominal legal owner of its endowment. It was, however, only after independence and the introduction of the Constitution of India that the Supreme Court of India resolved the issue definitively in ***Deoki Nandan v Muralidhar*** in 1956.[236]

B.K. Mukherjea offers the most succinct description of this principle in his monograph on Hindu religious and charitable endowments:

> [The juridical personality of a deity] is not only a compendious expression but a material embodiment of the pious purpose and though there is difficulty in holding that property can reside in the aim or purpose itself, it would be quite consistent with sound principles of Jurisprudence to say that a material object which represents or symbolizes a particular purpose can be given the status of a legal person and regarded as the owner of the property which is dedicated to it.[237]

In short, the early 20th century witnessed judicial *exploration* of the juridical personality of Hindu deities, and *not* the *invention* of the concept of the Hindu deity as the figurative (but legally efficacious) owner of endowed assets. Before the Indianisation of the judiciary – and the concomitant introduction of jurists learned in Common Law and in Sanskrit jurisprudence – the legal personality of Hindu deities and the fiduciary duties of their trustees was accepted as legal fact without much metaphysical or jurisprudential speculation about exactly what that entailed (it did not make a substantial difference in the administration of temples and other religious trusts). ***Bhupatinath*** was a fairly narrow ruling – limiting the application of ***Tagore v Tagore*** to bequests for deities – but it provided a rich corpus of Dharmaśāstric language for subsequent jurists to *describe* the complexity of jural relations involved in divine endowments. In the 20th century, the codification of civil procedure, the introduction of income tax codes, and eventually, the Constitution of the Republic of India, made disentangling the intricacies of the juridical personality of Hindu deities an absolute necessity.

[235] Ibid., 754.
[236] 1956 SCR 756; AIR 1957 SC 133.
[237] Mukherjea, *Hindu Law*, 37–8.

4.2.3.ii Filing suit in the name of the deity

Even those who have, at most, a cursory knowledge of the modern Hindu law of divine endowments know that in most cases, the *deity* appears as a litigant, represented by either their 'next friend' or their *shebait*. To my knowledge, deities, rather than their representatives, did not begin to appear as litigants in lawsuits until the 20th century: at which point this practice became ubiquitous. The catalyst for the development of the doctrine that a deity should be the primary litigant in cases involving their assets arose from the courts' consideration of several legal questions during the first half of the 20th century. As Mukherjea notes:

> A distinction undoubtedly exists between a suit by a *Shebait* and one by [a] deity, but what legal consequence[s], if any, flow from this distinction can be considered when I discuss the broader and the more general question, viz., in whom is the right of suit in respect of the deity's property vested? Is the deity to be regarded as a sort of perpetual infant who must act through a guardian in the same manner as persons under disability? Has the *Shebait* any right in him to conduct a suit or proceeding in his own name apart from the rights of the deity? What other persons besides the *Shebait* can represent the deity in suits or proceedings and, if so, under what circumstances and with what results?[238]

Following the Court's description of filing suit on behalf of a deity – and the possibility of a 'disinterested next friend' representing the deity – in ***Pramatha Nath Mullick*** in 1925, ***Sri Sri Kalimata Debi and Anr. v Nagendra Nath Chuckerbutty*** (1927) introduced the now-commonplace phenomenon of deities appearing as litigants.[239] The case involved a 'next friend' and worshipper, Srimati Basanta Kumari Debi, on behalf of Sri Kalimata Devi, a deity established in Calcutta. Sri Kalimata Devi's property had been fraudulently mortgaged and, at the time, her *shebait* was incapable of filing suit for their subsequent recovery. Justice Crozner agreed with the plaintiff, citing ***Pramatha Nath*** with approval, that, 'that the idol is a juristic person and is therefore competent to sue and though in the ordinary way the *Shebait* is the proper parson to represent the idol in any litigation'.[240] However, Justice Crozner, in Mukherjea's estimation, 'certainly misapplied… the facts of the case', and concluded that:

> It would appear therefore that the proper person to have instituted the suit was the *Shebait* and nobody else. Had the position been that Nagendra in his capacity of *Shebait* had definitely declined to institute the suit, it might perhaps have been open to Basanta as the next friend of the idol to have taken his place but in the absence of any such refusal it seems to me that neither Basanta nor the idol are competent. The suit is therefore bad.[241]

238 Ibid., 256.
239 AIR 1927 Cal 244, https://indiankanoon.org/doc/1105045/
240 Ibid., ¶6 [Crozner, J].
241 Ibid., ¶11 [Crozner, J].

It is highly surprising that the case was not overturned on appeal to the Privy Council, but Srimati's unsuccessful argument aligns with the position of the courts in subsequent cases: suits for a deity's property should be filed by the *shebait* in the name of the deity, and, in cases in which the *shebait* is either hostile to the interests of the deity or legally incapable of exercising their right to suit, an interested next friend may file suit on the deity's behalf.

A flurry of cases, mostly in the Calcutta High Court, were filed on behalf of deities by either their *shebaits* or by next friends in the following decades: ***Sharat Chandra v Dwarkanath*** (1931); ***Surendra Krishna v Ishwar Bhubaneshwari*** (1933); ***Radha Charan Saha v Sree Sree Iswar Joykali Bigraha*** (1941); ***Tarit Bhushan Rai v Sri Sri Iswar Sridhar Salagram Shila Thakur*** (1942); ***Annapurna Debi v Shiva Sundari Dasi*** (1944); and ***Sree Sree Sridhar Jew v Kanta Mihan Mullick*** (1947).[242] Several of these cases set important precedents concerning the analogous relationship between deities, minors, and their guardians – and they are discussed in the next section.

In particular, ***Sree Sree Sridhar Jew***, provides a succinct account of the mature, pre-independence jurisprudence of deities as litigants. The case involved the private religious trust of a Śūdra family. All five defendants were family members – and *shebaits* of the family deity – and the wife of one of the defendants (who, along with two other defendants also supported the claim of the deity) filed the case in the name of the deity for recovery of *debutter* property. Justice Gentle ruled that:

> A *thakur* has legal rights which are enforceable by suit and, if the present suit is properly constituted, it cannot be dismissed because the plaintiffs' claims are supported by some of the defendants… A Hindu idol has a judicial status and the capacity to own property but this is only in an ideal sense… It has the power of suing and being sued and its interests are attended to by the person who has the deity in his charge and who is in law its manager … The possession and management of a Thakur's property belong to the *sebait* together with the right to bring whatever suits are necessary for protection of the property, which right is vested in the *sebait* and not in the idol… [but] in spite of being so vested, the procedure of the Courts allows a suit to be brought in the name of the Thakur… In special circumstance, one or some of the *sebaits* can institute a suit and, in such instance, the other *sebaits* must be made defendants.[243]

Nevertheless, Justice Gentle argued that in the present case, while 'the proper course would have been for the first group of defendants to have instituted a suit in the name of the thakurs against the second group as defendants… [instead] the suit was instituted with the wife of defendant 3 as next friend of the thakurs and all the *sebaits* being made defendants'.[244] The issue was, in his estimation, that the next friend had 'not been appointed by the Court as next friend but the suit

[242] AIR 1931 Cal 558; AIR 1933 Cal 295 (https://indiankanoon.org/doc/728860/); AIR 1942 Cal 295 (https://indiankanoon.org/doc/827528/); AIR Cal 1942 99; AIR 1945 Cal 376; and AIR Cal 1947 213.
[243] AIR Cal 1947 213, ¶32 [Gentle, J] citing most of the cases mentioned above.
[244] Ibid., ¶36 [Gentle, J].

was instituted without such appointment having been sought or made'. Gentle acknowledges that, 'the question of the institution of a suit in the name of a thakur by a next friend, who is not appointed by the Court' had been accepted in ***Annapurna Debi,*** but notes that ***Tarit Bhushan*** rejected this perspective.[245] He agrees with the Court in ***Tarit Bhushan*** and rejects the plaintiff deity's case on the basis that:

> Defendants 3, 4 and 5 in substance and in fact are the plaintiffs and have used the name of defendant 3's wife Rani Moni Dassi merely as machinery to institute the proceedings most likely with a hope that in the event of the suit being unsuccessful, they would be able to avoid the ordinary liability as to costs which follow such an event.[246]

The shift from *shebaits* suing in their own name to *shebaits* – and next friends – suing in the name of the deity elicited a series of cases that probed the question of who, when, and why different individuals could sue in the name of the deity. Generally, it was only the *shebaits*– or *dharmakartas* – who could file suit in the name of the deity, but in many circumstances, a deity's fiduciaries were in breach of trust, not *sui juris*, or in contention among themselves concerning the proper course of legal action.

In these instances, next friends could be appointed by the court – and a different strand of legal reasoning eventually expanded the remit of interested and disinterested parties who could file suit on behalf of a deity. This set the stage for vastly more complicated litigation in which next friends, fiduciaries, private third parties, the state, and the courts all became involved in deities' cases. In 1947, however, the precise boundaries of who could file suit for a deity, and when, were still relatively unclear. It would take the Supreme Court of India in ***V.R. Reddy v K.S. Reddy*** (1967) to iron out the details.[247]

4.2.3.iii Deities, minors, and the law of limitation

During the first half of the 20th century, Indian courts examined the analogous relationship between Hindu deities and legal minors in greater detail. This analogy is ancient – appearing in the earliest strata of Sanskrit jurisprudential texts – and was explored at length in 19th-century Anglo-Hindu legal judgments largely

[245] He also ignores Justice B.K. Mukherjea's judgment in ***Nirmal Chandra Banerjee and Anr. v Jyoti Prosad Bandopadhya*** (1941) AIR Cal 562, ¶9: 'The right to sue in such a case is vested in the deity and not in the shebait, the deity can certainly sue through any person as next friend who has no in-interest adverse to it, and it is immaterial that the next friend happens to be one of its shebaits': vide ***Jodhi Rai v Basdeo Prosad*** (1911) 33 ALL 735.

[246] AIR Cal 1947 213, ¶46.

[247] AIR 1967 SC 437.

from the angle of framing deities' fiduciaries as legal guardians.[248] In the 20th century, the courts' focus shifted from outlining the duties and constraints incumbent on guardians towards delineating deities' rights in instances where their *shebaits/dharmakartas* failed to fulfil their fiduciary duties.

One catalyst for the greater judicial interest in the analogous jurisprudential relationship between wards and deities was the codification of India's Code of Civil Procedure during the late 19th and early 20th centuries, particularly with reference to the law of limitation. The law of limitation – in its 1877 and 1908 iterations – exempts minors from limitation during their minority.[249] The salient juridical question, given the longstanding association between deities and minors, was if and when the legal protections afforded to minors, women, and other categories of similarly protected persons could be extended to deities. We saw, earlier, that the courts took the view that while *debutter* vested in the deity (in an ideal sense), the right of suit vested in the *shebait*. This raised numerous legal questions into various aspects of the law, including: 1) does limitation run against the deity or the *shebait*; and 2) can a *shebait* or a third party establish a proprietary right adverse to a deity?

An early case from the Privy Council, ***Maharaja Jagadindra Nath Roy Bahadur v Rani Hemanta Kumari Debi*** (1904) examined the proprietary nature of *shebaitship* in relation to the law of limitation (established first in the Limitation Act of 1877).[250] The cases involved a *shebait* who sued for the recovery of *debutter* assets that had been unlawfully alienated when he was a minor. The court ruled that:

> The possession and management of the dedicated property belong to the *shebait*. And this carries with it the right to bring whatever suits are necessary for the protection of the property. Every such right is vested in the *shebait*, not the idol. And in the present case the right to sue accrued to the plaintiff when he was under age… [and] therefore falls within the clear language of s. 7 of the Limitation Act, which says that… he may institute the suit after coming of age.[251]

The judgment did not weigh in on the status of the deity, but on the status of the *shebait* and it was the minority of the *shebait*, coupled with the framing of his right to sue on behalf of the deity as a quasi-proprietary right that afforded him the protection of the Limitation Act.

[248] See the discussion of ***Prosunno Kumari Debya v Golab Chand Babu*** in Note 176.

[249] For the 1877 Limitation Act, see M.H. Starling, *The Indian Limitation Act, 1877*, 4th edn. (Bombay: Education Society Press, 1900). Note that the Indian Limitation (Amdt.) Act, 1929 (1 of 1929), S.2 assimilated divine endowments to purpose trusts for the purposes of limitation: 'For the purposes of this section any property comprised in a Hindu, Muhammadan or Buddhist religious or charitable endowment shall be deemed to be property vested in trust for a specific purpose, and the manager of any such property shall be deemed to be the trustee thereof.' See Mukherjea, *Hindu Law*, 298–314, for a comprehensive summary of limitation in relation to Hindu deities.

[250] LR 31 IA 203.

[251] Ibid., 210 [Wilson, J.].

In 1910, the Privy Council ruled in ***Mahant Damodar Das v Adhikari Lakhan Das***, that because *debutter* (or *maṭha*) property 'vested not in the Mahant but in the legal entity, the idol', therefore, possession 'adverse to the right of the idol', by a third party would, after the requisite period of time, bar a suit on the grounds of limitation.[252] This seems straightforward enough, but it led to the question of whether a *shebait*'s proprietary right could be adverse to the deity they served. In 1925 the Madras High Court ruled in ***Rama Reddy v Rangadasan*** that a deity is shielded from limitation on account of its 'perpetual minority' and that a *shebait* could not claim adverse possession as a bar to a suit for recovery of a deity's assets.[253]

The case involved a *shebait* who sued for recovery of assets that had been unlawfully alienated by his predecessor more than twelve years after the window of time stipulated by Article 144 of the Limitation Act of 1908.[254] According to the Madras High Court, however:

> In the case of a minor whose property has been improperly alienated by the guardian he has the right of suit within three years after attaining his majority. The legal fiction is that an idol is a minor for all time and it has to be under perpetual tutelage and that being so, it cannot be said that the idol can ever acquire majority, and a person who acquires title form a trustee of a temple cannot acquire any title adverse to the idol, for the idol is an infant for all time and the succeeding trustee could recover the property for the idol at any time… his [the vendee's] possession is that of the trustee [the vendor] and a trustee's possession can never be adverse to the idol… [but] if a person takes possession of the immovable property belonging to a temple and keeps the trustee… out of possession for over 12 years, he could acquire a valid title under section 28 of the Limitation Act.[255]

While Justice Devadoss' reasoning in ***Rama Reddy*** accords with the strong analogous relationship between deities and minors in Sanskrit jurisprudence, the proposition that deities are *wholly* immune to limitation was the subject of scathing judicial critique in subsequent judgments.[256] In ***Surendra Krishna v Ishwar Bhubaneshwari*** (1933), Justice Rankin ruled that, 'the doctrine that an idol is a perpetual minor is, in my judgment, an extravagant doctrine contrary to the decision of the Judicial Committee in such cases as *Damodar Das v. Lakhan Das*'.[257] Yet, in ***Damodar Das*** and in ***Surendra***, unlike in ***Rama Reddy***, however, the parties pleading adverse possession were not doing so on the basis of an alienation that had been made unlawfully by a deity's fiduciary. Rather, both

[252] LR 37 IA 147.

[253] (1925) ILR 49 Mad 543.

[254] In ***Vidya Varuthi Thirtha v Balusami Ayyar*** (1921) 48 IA 302, the Privy Council held that *shebaits* were not *trustees* under article 134 of the Limitation Act of 1908, and that article 144 governed suits for the recovery of possession of property improperly alienated by a manager.

[255] ***Rama Reddy***, 550 [Devadoss, J].

[256] For this analogy between deities and minors, etc., see Chapter 1, §1.4, 'Guardianship'.

[257] AIR 1933 Cal 295 ¶22 [Rankin, J].

cases involved possession held adversely to a deity against the efforts of the deities' fiduciaries – precisely the hypothetical scenario entertained by Justice Devadoss in ***Rama Reddy***.

Despite his indictment of the decision in ***Rama Reddy***, Justice Rankin also draws a legal analogy between minors and deities. In ***Surendra Krishna***, both *shebaits* of the deity *and* a non-*shebait* attempted to establish claims of adverse possession against the deity. While Rankin allowed the claim of the non-*shebait*, he noted that 'there could be no adverse possession by the *shebaits*'.[258] Rankin's justification for this observation was ***Seetaramaraju v Subbaraju***, a 1922 judgment by the Madras High Court which argued that the claim of adverse possession against 'a lunatic… would depend upon whether any fiduciary relation subsisted between the parties'.[259] In essence, Justice Rankin's judgment *limits*, rather than *rejects*, the analogy between deities and minors and uses the shared concept of guardians as fiduciaries to bring the legal personality of deities into accord with the operation of civil procedure.

Justice Ali's judgment in ***Tarit Bhusan Rai and Anr. v Sri Sri Iswar Sridhar Salagram*** (1942) offers a detailed exploration of the analogous relationship between deities and minors under Anglo-Hindu law.[260] Justice Ali notes that:

> 12. The points of similarity between a minor and a Hindu idol are: (1) Both have the capacity of owning property. (2)Both are incapable of managing their properties and protecting their own interests, (a) The properties of both are managed and protected by another human being. The manager of a minor is his legal guardian and the manager of an idol is its *shebait*. (4) The powers of their managers are similar. (5) Both have got the right to sue. (6) The bar of Section 11 and Order 9, Rule 9, Civil P.C, applies to both of them.
> 13. The points of difference between the two are : (1) A Hindu idol is a juristic or artificial person but a minor is a natural person. (2) A Hindu idol exists for its own interest as well as for the interests of its worshippers but a minor does not exist for the interests of anybody else. (3) The Contract Act (Substantive law) has taken away the legal capacity of a minor to contract but the legal capacity of a Hindu idol to contract has not been affected by this Act or by any other statute. (4) The Limitation Act (an adjective law) has exempted a minor from the operation of the bar of limitation but this protection has not been extended to a Hindu idol.
> 14. From the above it is clear that there is some analogy between a minor and a Hindu idol but the latter is neither a minor nor a perpetual minor.[261]

Justice Ali's summary is succinct and accurate. En route to the verdict in ***Tarit Bhusan Rai***, however, the courts worked diligently and successively to narrow

[258] AIR 1933 Cal 295 ¶28 [Rankin, J].
[259] AIR 1922 Mad 12.
[260] AIR 1942 Cal 99.
[261] Ibid. [Ali, J].

down the precise limits of the legal comparison between deities and minors. Nevertheless, this analogy – however imperfect – lay at the heart of the Sanskrit jurisprudence of Equity and Trusts; of the British justification of its *parens patriae* jurisdiction over Indian religious endowments; of the partial legal assimilation of divine endowments to purpose trusts; and, ultimately, of the alignment of the legal personality of Hindu deities with the provisions of India's codified codes of civil procedure. The question, then, was not *whether* deities were analogous to minors, etc., in Sanskrit jurisprudence and Anglo-Hindu law. Rather, the question was, and is, *how far* that analogous relationship should extend in law.

In short, it was only at the turn of the 20th century that Sanskrit jurisprudential theories of divine ownership – especially those which were repurposed in Dharmaśāstra from a Mīmāṃsā context – came to be applied to the specific context of Hindu deities. Sanskrit jurisprudential principles of Equity – as customary, supplemental law and as the Crown's *parens patriae* right of visitation over charities, etc. – had been a longstanding feature of the Anglo-Hindu law of religious and charitable trusts. On the one hand, the Indianisation of the judiciary and the advancement of Indology as an academic discipline allowed judges to draw on a significantly greater level of expertise in Sanskrit jurisprudence in their exploration of technical questions concerning the Hindu law of religious and charitable trusts. On the other hand, the codification of civil procedure and other secular aspects of Indian civil law through enactments of the Central Government meant that justices had to examine specific aspects of Hindu deities' legal personality – particularly their analogous status with minors – within these extremely technical areas of law, rather than in the more general sense of trusteeship (as was the case in the late 19th century).

4.3 Conclusion

Anglo-Hindu law and Company rule were marked by several contradictions. The Government of the British East India Company justified its legal regulation of the native population on the basis of the exercise of sovereign rights that were acquired within the Mughal and Marāṭhā administrative systems. Nevertheless, the Company was subordinate to the Crown of England as a chartered company. Although Hastings' and Cornwallis' Judicial Plans *sprang* from the noble enough intention of ensuring that the native population would be governed by its own laws and conventions (at least in matters of civil law), they were nevertheless *enacted* by a cadre of foreign-born and foreign-trained jurists. Furthermore, colonial jurists endeavoured to ascertain native laws with the help of indigenous experts. Nevertheless, colonial jurists increasingly came to rely on English translations of early jurisprudential treatises (the *Mānavadharmaśāstra*, the *Yājñavalkyasmṛti*, and Vijñāneśvara's *Mitākṣarā*) that probably never functioned as codes of positive law before. The courts attempted to enforce these *jurisprudential* treatises as positive *law*, and, even as they did so, they were quick to introduce plenty of juridical principles from English Chancery law when the opportunity (or need) presented itself.

Anglo-Hindu law was also marked by extraordinary constitutional complexity. The British East Indian Company operated as both a chartered merchant company under the Crown of England, and as a feudal subordinate within the decaying Mughal Empire. This dual sovereignty was reflected in the judicial system within British India. *Within* the Company cities of Calcutta, Madras, and Bombay, Mayoral and Crown courts that largely operated according the English jurisprudence held jurisdiction over the European population, while in the *Mofussil* (the territory governed by the Company in the name of the Mughal emperor) *Ṣadr Dīwānī 'Adālats* held civil jurisdiction, and meted out justice to the native population on the basis of Hindu and Muslim personal law.

Adding to the complexity was the fact that the Governments of the Calcutta, Madras, and Bombay presidencies had the authority to pass legislation for their own territories, while Parliament and the Central Government of India had the authority to pass laws that applied to the entirety of India (excepting the independent princely states). These jurisdictional and jurisprudential distinctions were contested and explored over the course of the 18th and 19th centuries, and were eliminated with the introduction of Crown rule in 1858 and the unification of the *Dīwānī* and Crown Courts through the High Courts Act of 1861.

The Anglo-Hindu law of religious and charitable trusts was shaped, in large part, by these wider constitutional issues between 1772 and 1862, as well as by the principles of Sanskrit jurisprudence and English practices from the Court of Chancery. At first, the Government assumed the power of regulating religious endowments – especially temples – on the basis of their *parens patriae* rights as the *Dīwān* of Bengal, Bihar, and Orissa, and other native titles of sovereignty. These actions, especially as we saw in the context of the Jagannātha temple in Puri, were largely the practices of pre-colonial sovereigns and the jurisprudential theory of Dharmaśāstra, but they also relegated earlier kings to the status of mere trustee, rather than sovereign.

In this sense, British suzerainty over India's galaxy of princes and kings, was *enacted* through its assumption (or usurpation) of the right of visitation over temple and other charitable trusts that they had previously enjoyed. While this represented a rupture between the native princes and their erstwhile prerogatives, it also represented a continuity with pre-colonial patterns of sovereignty.

While the Government busied itself with directly supervising the *management* of religious endowments, the *Ṣadr Dīwānī 'Adālats* focused on delineating the conditions within which individuals could *create* religious and charitable endowments. Many of these conditions focused on the revenue systems after the Permanent Settlements. The Courts sought to disentangle valid from invalid grants of tax-free land to religious institutions by native actors in attempts to ensure a steady supply of revenue to the Company. As expected, this meant that the rights of *Zamīndārs* to alienate land became increasingly restricted and resumption by the Government (with the courts' abetment) became increasingly common.

Furthermore, the *Dīwānī 'Adālats* were instrumental in crafting a comprehensive Anglo-Hindu law of inheritance on the basis of regionally-distinct 'schools' of Hindu law (generally divided into the *Mitākṣarā* and *Dāyabhāga* Schools). The Anglo-Hindu law of inheritance generally limited Joint Hindu Family members' powers of alienation over joint family property and the testamentary powers of family members. This meant that religious and charitable donations – especially 'private' religious endowments – served as a device through which members of a Joint Hindu Family could bypass the restrictions the Hindu law of inheritance. As expected, the *Dīwānī* courts make significant efforts to delineate the validity of bequests made within the wider matrix of Hindu property law. Nevertheless, the courts largely accepted the legal personality and management of Hindu deities as an unproblematic fact, and made little inquiry into *what* Hindu deities were legally, or precisely what duties of care their fiduciaries owed to them.

The era of Crown rule changed India's legal landscape dramatically. The High Courts Act of 1861 led to the creation of unified High Courts within each presidency. The Religious Endowments Act of 1863 formally dissociated the Central Government from its role as administrator of religious endowments (a *de facto* dissociation had been in effect since the 1840s), and shifted responsibility for the supervision of temple trustees to the courts. In 1864, the courts assumed judicial knowledge of Hindu jurisprudence and dismissed their *paṇḍita* court officers. Soon afterwards, the central Government enacted a wide array of legislation which established a unified code of civil procedure, and formalised, *inter alia*, the law of trusts, guardianship, and contract. All of this vastly expanded the responsibilities of the courts and it therefore comes as no surprise that the decades immediately afterwards witnessed an explosive growth in the number and complexity of cases concerning the Anglo-Hindu law of religious and charitable trusts.

The main concern for the courts between 1863 and c. 1900 was the fiduciary duties of trustees in public and private Hindu religious institutions. *Shebaits*, *dharmakartas*, mahants, and other categories of agents who managed endowed assets on behalf of deities, did not assimilate *precisely* to the English concept of a trustee – in which property vested *in the trustee* rather than in the beneficiary. The Government's prior abdication of its supervisory role in temple affairs prompted many trustees to abuse their positions grossly, and it thus fell to the courts to hold those persons responsible for their breaches of trust with their deities.

Contemporary scholars' sympathy for arguments like those made by the temple priests in ***Manohar Ganesh*** – that *shebaits* might appropriate or alienate their deity's assets without compunction or consequence – is unjustifiable on historical or jurisprudential grounds. Every previous government of India, native or foreign, enacted policies to prevent temple functionaries from appropriating religious endowments to their own purposes, and Dharmaśāstra explicitly describes temple functionaries as being beholden to observe the legal clauses of trusts settled on Hindu deities. Only an *extremely* superficial reading of Dharmaśāstra or Mīmāṃsā theories of the legal personality of Hindu deities would lead one to support the abject theft of deities' property. Furthermore, in holding fiduciaries accountable for their malfeasance, the courts also delineated *shebaits*' and *dharmakartas*' positive right as trustees, including the use of endowed assets for the commercial benefit of the deity and its endowment.

Finally, the turn of the 20th century saw the courts turn the focus of their legal analysis to the question of deities' status under the law. The codification of civil procedure and a significant portion of substantive law by the legislature meant that the courts had to resolve several ambiguities in the judicial precedents governing Hindu religious endowments within the wider remit of civil law. In essence, this meant testing earlier rulings concerning the legal personhood of Hindu deities (and the fiduciary duties of their guardians) within the context of the right to suit, the law of limitation, adverse possession, and even taxation.

In pre-20th-century cases, the courts employed the ancient and well-established analogy between deities and minors to explore the duty of care owed by *shebaits* to their deities. While the analogy was unproblematic in that context, it created significant issues when applied in other contexts. Normally, a right to sue on behalf of the deity vests in the *shebait*, but in the many instances in which a *shebait* acts in bad faith, a third party, 'a next friend', was enabled to file suit on the deity's behalf – as is the case in the context of minors.

This had the effect of suits increasingly being filed *with the deity as the primary plaintiff or defendant* – a novel development for Anglo-Hindu law. In teasing out *who* could serve as a 'next friend' – usually on the basis of having a beneficial interest in the endowment – the courts began to frame the legal personality of Hindu deities as a 'compendious expression' of the pious purpose of the worshipper to worship the deity. This effectively reframed divine endowments as purpose.

Nevertheless, the courts emphasised the limits of taking the analogous relationship between deities and minors too literally, especially in the context of limitation. Deities, like minors, could be shielded from adverse possession claimed by their guardians, but to extend the immunity that minors enjoy *during their minority* to deities (who are perpetually *non sui juris*) would lead to the recognition of a legal entity perpetually shielded from any limitation in suit – with a deleterious effect on the confidence of any party transacting with that deity's representative.

Nevertheless, even as the court *limited* the analogous relationship between deities and minors in some respects, they *reinforced* it in many others.

In short, the Anglo-Hindu law of religious and charitable trusts produced a complex, sophisticated hybrid system of jurisprudence that combined features of Sanskrit legal discourse and practice with the characteristic features of the Common Law, including binding judicial precedent and universally applicable statutes. The jurisprudence supporting this hybrid law, however, remained largely faithful to Dharmaśāstric principles even when it took its cue from English Equity. Ironically, in my estimation, the absence of significantly detailed formal rules governing trusts in Sanskrit jurisprudential literature – a feature discussed in Chapter 1 – led British jurists away from the issue which vexed them in the context of inheritance law: the misconstrual of scholastic jurisprudential *theory* as practical positive law. In effect, limiting their use of Dharmaśāstric resources to general principles led British jurists to take a more authentically indigenous approach, *jurisprudentially* and practically, to the supervision of Hindu religious endowments.

When the British 'quit' India in 1947, they left behind a vast administrative and legal bureaucracy that had already been heavily Indianised in the preceding decades. The Judicial Committee of the Privy Council would remain India's apex court of appeal until 1950, with the introduction of the Constitution of the Republic of India and the Supreme Court of India. We will see in the following chapter that Indian independence and the advent of the Constitution led to significant further developments in the Hindu law of religious and charitable trusts.

The Supreme Court found itself responsible for interpreting the principles and precedents of Anglo-Hindu law within the remit of the newly established constitution. Key issues included the status of formerly independent or semi-independent princes within the new Indian Union, the limits of rights to religious freedom when those rights clash with provisions against caste and gender-based discrimination, and communal conflicts over contested religious sites. In approaching all of these questions, however, the Supreme Court has relied, and will continue to rely, on the Anglo-Hindu jurisprudence surveyed in this chapter. It is salutary to remember where that jurisprudence came from before arguing about its future direction of travel. The Anglo-Hindu jurisprudence of religious and charitable trusts came from different sources – some domestic and some colonial – but one important (if idiosyncratically applied) source was the Sanskrit jurisprudence of Equity and Trusts.

5

The Supreme Court of India and Hindu Religious Trusts

Three legal concepts are well settled: (1) An idol of a Hindu temple is a juridical person; (2) when there is a Shebait, ordinarily no person other than the Shebait can represent the idol; and (3) worshippers of an idol are its beneficiaries, though only in a spiritual sense. It has also been held that persons who go in only for the purpose of devotion have, according to Hindu law and religion, a greater and deeper interest in temples than mere servants who serve there for some pecuniary advantage…

The question is, can such a person represent the idol when the Shebait acts adversely to its interest and fails to take action to safeguard its interest. On principle we do not see any justification for denying such a right to the worshipper. An idol is in the position of a minor; when the person representing it leaves it in the lurch, a person interested in the worship of the idol can certainly be clothed with an ad hoc power of representation to protect its interest. It is a pragmatic, yet a legal solution to a difficult situation.

Should it be held that a Shebait, who transferred the Property, can only bring a suit for recovery, in most of the cases it will be an indirect approval of the dereliction of the Shebait's duty, for more often than not he will not admit his default and take steps to recover the property, apart from other technical pleas that may be open to the transferee in a suit.

Should it be held that a worshipper can file only a suit for the removal of a Shebait and for the appointment of another in order to enable him to take steps. to recover the property, such a procedure will be rather a prolonged and a complicated one and the interest of the idol may irreparably suffer. That is why decisions have permitted a worshipper in such circumstances to represent the idol and to recover the Property for the idol.'

Chief Justice of the Supreme Court of India, Koka Subba Rao (served 1966–67), in ***Bishwanath And Anr v Shri Thakur Radhaballabhji & Ors*** (SC 1967)[1]

[1] 1967 AIR 1044, 1967 SCR (2) 618.

5.1 Introduction

This chapter examines the development of the law of Hindu religious and charitable endowments from India's transition to independence in 1947 up until the present. Specifically, I examine how the Supreme Court of India drew, and continues to draw upon the principles articulated in colonial-era Anglo-Hindu legal judgments (from the High Courts, the Judicial Committee of the Privy Council), while balancing these precedents against the fundamental rights enshrined in the Constitution of the Republic of India. The result of this process, I argue, is the transformation of the Anglo-Hindu jurisprudence of divine ownership within a constitutional framework. The description of divine legal personality in the ***Bishwanath*** judgment quoted at the beginning of this chapter is vitally important in the contemporary Hindu law of religious and charitable trusts: a deity is a juridical person who owns assets and whose interests must be looked after by fiduciaries; and when a deity's servant breaks his relationship of trust, a worshipper or other third party can appeal to the Crown to intercede on the deity's behalf. Undergirding this legal personality, I argue, are several Sanskrit principles of Equity and Trusts (alongside principles from the Constitution of the Republic of India).

In modern India, however, the *State* replaced the *Crown* as *parens patriae* – a completely understandable development – and stepped into the slippers of the British Crown (who had, it should be noted, stepped into the slippers of a thousand years' worth of previous sovereigns). This was justified on the basis of the constitution's explicit framing of the Republic of India as the legal heir to the Dominion of India (1947–50), and to colonial India in Articles 296 and 372.[2] As with virtually all previous sovereigns of India, the assumption of sovereignty entailed a concomitant duty to look after the welfare of non *sui iuris* persons: minors, the mentally unfit, charities, and, of course, Hindu deities.[3]

While the State and Courts' right of visitation over endowments stemmed from sovereignty and statute, the juridical personality of deities increasingly came to be expressed in the language of the constitutional rights enshrined under

[2] See Articles 296 and 372 of the Constitution: **Article 296**: 'Subject as hereinafter provided, any property in the territory of India which, if this Constitution had not come into operation, would have accrued to His Majesty or, as the case may be, to the Ruler of an Indian State by escheat or lapse, or as *bona vacantia* for want of a rightful owner, shall, if it is property situate in a State, vest in such State, and shall, in any other case, vest in the Union'; and **Article 372(1)**: '1) Notwithstanding the repeal by this Constitution of the enactments referred to in article 395 but subject to the other provisions of this Constitution, all the law in force in the territory of India immediately before the commencement of this Constitution shall continue in force therein until altered or repealed or amended by a competent Legislature or other competent authority.'

[3] See Chapter 1, §1.4, 'Guardianship'.

Articles 25 and 26 (discussed later).[4] Under the old Anglo-Hindu jurisprudence, deities tended to be viewed primarily within the rubric of private property rights. Donors, fiduciaries, and beneficiaries were all bound by contract or by trust to utilise deities' assets (*devasva*) for stipulated purposes. Under the Constitution, however, deities' juridical personality increasingly functioned as a legal cypher for the right to worship: belief and faith became as important as contract in assessing the relationship between deities and their human co-agents.

While the shift towards constitutional jurisprudence entailed a departure from the paradigms of Anglo-Hindu law, it nevertheless involved new approaches to the Sanskrit jurisprudential maxims and principles that featured in Anglo-Hindu law. Just as the Supreme Court re-examined the cases and doctrines of the colonial judiciary within a constitutional framework, they also examined, expanded, or re-framed Sanskrit jurisprudential theories within the context of fundamental rights. For example, Raghunandana Bhaṭṭācārya's maxim from the 16th-century *Ekādaśītattva* that 'it is for the sake of rites of the worshippers that the (para) brahman, which is made of consciousness, which cannot be measured, which is imperishable, and which has no body, is postulated to have form (in an image)', found a new lease on life when the Supreme Court examined the sorts of religious phenomena that could be recognised as juridical persons.[5] What we find, therefore, is a new post-colonial *refashioning* of the law of Hindu religious and charitable trusts that involves extended juridical interactions between the Sanskrit and Constitutional jurisprudential principles.

At the same time, however, the Court has endeavoured to define the limits of the application of Dharmaśāstric jurisprudence. Sanskrit jurisprudential maxims and principles have been read in conversation with constitutional provisions that protect the freedom of religion. One result has been cases where Dharmaśāstric principles that challenge elements of the civil law – notably in the context of the

[4] The Supreme Court strongly defended the State's status as *parens patriae* in the context of the 1984 Bhopal disaster in ***Charan Lal Sahu Etc. v Union of India and Ors*** (1990) AIR 1480: (C.J. Mukharji ¶3.2): 'The connotation of the term "*parens patria*" differs from country to country, for instance, in England it is the King, in America it is the people, etc. According to [the] Indian concept [of the] *parens patria* doctrine [what is] recognized [is the] King as the protector of all citizens as parent. The Government is within its duty to protect and to control persons under disability. Conceptually, the *parens patriae theory* is the obligation of the State to protect and take into custody the rights and privileges of its citizens for discharging its obligations. Our Constitution makes it imperative for the State to secure to all its citizens the rights guaranteed by the Constitution and where the citizens are not in a position to assert and secure their rights, the State must come into the picture and protect and fight for the right of the citizens. The Preamble to the Constitution, read with the Directive Principles contained in Articles 38, 39 and 39A enjoins the State to take up these responsibilities.' See Lisa Hawkes, '*Parens Patriae* and the Union Carbide Case: The Disaster at Bhopal Continues', *Cornell International Law Journal* 21 (1988): 181–200.

[5] See Chapter 1, Notes 224–5 for the Sanskrit passage. See Chapter 4, Note 225 for its use in ***Bhupati Nath Smrititirtha v Ram Lal Maitra***. For an analysis of the influence of this passage in legal history (especially the Ayodhyā dispute), see Fleming, 'Dharmaśāstra'.

minority-status of deities and their suits' subjection to the law of limitation – have been protected under Articles 25 and 26 of the Constitution. In each of these instances, however, the Supreme Court has engaged in an active process of reinterpretation of past principles and precedents with eyes on the Constitution, prior precedent, and Sanskrit jurisprudence. The contemporary jurisprudence of Hindu religious and charitable trusts is, in effect, a balancing act between these different, sometimes competing threads.

5.1.1 A quick history of the Constitution of the Republic of India

In 1949, Prime Minister Jawaharlal Nehru delivered his 'tryst with destiny' speech, stating that 'all of us, to whatever religion we may belong, are equally the children of India with equal rights, privileges and obligations'. As the clock struck midnight in Edwin Lutyens' Old Parliament House in New Delhi, the Union of India (1947–50) came into being.[6] As Pandit Nehru cautioned, however, on this 'day appointed by destiny', when 'India stands forth again, after long slumber and struggle, awake, vital, free and independent', the Indian people faced a new challenge 'to build up a prosperous, democratic and progressive nation, and to create social, economic and political institutions which will ensure justice and fullness of life to every man and woman'.[7] While Nehru lauded the 'birth of freedom', he also noted that the 'pains of labour... continue even now'.[8]

It took several years' worth of consequential 'pains of labour' to bring the Republic of India into being. The Union of India, the child of that midnight tryst with destiny, is hardly recognisable as the Republic of India of today. India became independent as a self-governing British dominion, with Lord Mountbatten remaining the governor-general, with the Judicial Committee of the Privy Council continuing to serve as the apex Court of Appeal, and with the Crown, rather than

[6] Jawaharlal Nehru, 'Speech On the Granting of Indian Independence, August 14, 1947', *Modern History Sourcebook* (Fordham University, October 1998). Archived from the original on 18 August 2012. The Government of India Act 1935 (26 George V. & 1 Edward. 8. C.2) created an appellate Federal Court (established 1937) that stood between the High Courts and the Judicial Committee of the Privy Council in the juridical pyramid. See George Gadbois, 'The Federal Court of India: 1937–1950'. *Journal of the Indian Law Institute* 6.2/3 (1964): 253–315. For the relationship between the Federal Court and the executive Government, see Rohit De, 'The Federal Court and Civil Liberties in Late Colonial India', in T. Halliday, L. Karpik, and M. Feeley (eds), *Fates of Political Liberalism in the British Post-Colony: The Politics of the Legal Complex* (Cambridge: Cambridge University Press, 2012): 59–90. One notable decision from the Federal Court regarding endowments is ***Umayal Achi v Lakshmi Achi*** (1945) AIR 1945 FC 25 (A), wherein Justice Varadachariar held that the trusteeship of religious or charitable trusts, without a beneficial interest in the property, would not be 'property' for the purpose of the Hindu Women's Right to Property Act 1937.

[7] Nehru, 'Speech'.

[8] Ibid.

Map 5.1 India, c. 1950

the citizens of India as the font of sovereignty.[9] This juridical and political continuity belied the astonishingly complex territorial disunity of the erstwhile British Raj in 1947. Most notably, Mountbatten's scheme for the partition of India led to vast, psychologically scarring communal conflicts that laid waste to much of the Punjab and Bengal, killed at least two lakhs (200,000) of people, and left another half crore (5,000,000) homeless.[10]

Furthermore, in abolishing the title of 'Emperor of India' along with British feudal suzerainty over the semi-independent princely states (more than 560 of which existed in 1947), and in insisting that the princely realms accede to the Union of India or the Dominion of Pakistan, the Indian Independence Act (1947 – 10 & 11 George VI C.30) left vast swathes of the subcontinent open for contestation between India and Pakistan.[11] The twin legacies of Partition; the trauma of communal violence; and the complicated legal legacy of the princely states' accession to the Union, would in time, precipitate some of independent India's most contentious Supreme Court cases involving the contemporary Hindu law of religious and charitable trusts.

While the politics of the human catastrophe of Partition played out, the Constituent Assembly of India, serving as the 'Provisional Parliament of India' appointed a constitutional drafting committee on 9 August 1947, consisting of B.R. Ambedkar, K.M. Munshi, Muhammed Sadulla, Alladi Krishnaswamy Iyer, N. Gopalaswami

[9] In Pakistan, the first governor-general was Jinnah. See Ayesha Jalal, 'Inheriting the Raj: Jinnah and the Governor-Generalship Issue', *Modern Asian Studies* 19.1 (2008): 29–53. For the decision of India, Pakistan, and Ceylon to become British dominions, rather than republics on their achieving independence, see Harshan Kumarasingham, '"The Tropical Dominions": The Appeal of Dominion Status in the Decolonization of India, Pakistan, and Ceylon', *Transactions of the Royal Historical Society* 23 (2013): 223–45, 237: 'Dominion status offered an opportunity to maintain the traditions of the laws and conventions of Britain… [and] the same status could also be sold as an idea to the Congress leadership as a transitional period that gave political independence before the republic could be formed.'

[10] For partition and Mountbatten, see Ian Talbot, 'Mountbatten and the Partition of India: A Rejoinder', *History* 69.225 (1984): 29–35; and Ian Talbot, 'Partition of India: The Human Dimension', *Journal of the Social History Society* 6.4 (2009): 403–10. For a regional approach to the study of Partition, see Ian Talbot and Gurharpal Singh (eds) *Partition and Region: Bengal, Punjab and the Partition of the Subcontinent* (Karachi: Oxford University Press, 1999). For the Punjab during partition, see Yaqoob Bangash, 'Implementing Partition: Proceedings of the Punjab Partition Committee, July–August, 1947', *Modern Asian Studies* 55.6 (2021): 1883–1925; and Swarna Aiyar, '"August Anarchy": The Partition Massacres in Punjab, 1947' *South Asia: Journal of South Asian Studies* (2007): 13–36.

[11] For Partition and princely states, see Ian Copland, 'The Princely States, the Muslim League, and the Partition of India in 1947', *The International History Review* 13.1 (1991): 38–69, esp. 38: 'During the 1930s, the British government tried, and failed, to persuade the princely states to link themselves organically with the provinces in an all-India federation. The princes preferred quasi-independence under the Crown to taking their chances in the hurly of electoral politics.' The Nizām of Hyderabad was a notable holdout, and it was inconceivable that India would tolerate the Nizām's accession to Pakistan. See Sunil Purushotham, 'Federating the Raj: Hyderabad, Sovereign Kingship, and Partition', *Modern Asian Studies* 54.1 (2020): 157–98. The other, equally infamous story of accession is that of the princely state of Kashmir. See Adarsh Anand, 'Accession of Jammu and Kashmir State: Historical and Legal Perspective', *Journal of the Indian Law Institute* 43.4 (2001): 455–68; and Robert Huttenback, 'The Emasculation of a Princely State: The Case of Kashmir' *Journal of Asian History* 7.1 (1973): 1–29.

Ayyangar, Devi Prasad Khaitan and B.L. Mitter.[12] The fruit of their two-year labour, the Constitution of the Republic of India, was approved on 26 November 1949, and came into effect on 26 January 1950. At 146,385 words (in its English iteration), the Constitution of India is the longest in the history of the world.[13]

5.1.2 The Supreme Court of India and the freedom of religion

While comparative, historical, and philosophical studies of the Constitution of India present fertile opportunities for scholarly research, in this chapter, I shall instead examine how the principles enshrined in the Constitution have shaped the development of the post-colonial Hindu law of religious and charitable trusts.[14] According to Article 141 of the Constitution, the Supreme Court of India replaced the Judicial Committee of the Privy Council as the apex court of appeal for India but, in assuming the Privy Council's spot atop the integrated pyramid of India's judicial system, the Supreme Court also introduced the principles of *constitutional jurisprudence* to this role: popular sovereignty; fundamental rights and freedom; secularism; and federalism.[15]

[12] The best work on the Constitution of Indian remains H.R. Khanna, *Making of India's Constitution*, 2nd edn. (Lucknow: Eastern Book Company, 2008). For the Assembly, see James Chiriyankandath, '"Creating a Secular State in a Religious Country': The Debate in the Indian Constituent Assembly', *Commonwealth & Comparative Politics* 38.2 (2000): 1–28. For a general introduction, see M.V. Pylee, *An Introduction to the Constitution of India*, 5th edn. (Noida: Vikas, 2007). For Ambedkar, see Bidyut Chakrabarty, 'B.R. Ambedkar and the History of Constitutionalizing India', *Contemporary South Asia* 24 (2016): 133–48; K.H. Cheluva Raju, 'Dr. B.R. Ambedkar and Making of the Constitution', *Indian Journal of Political Science* 52.2 (1991): 153–64; and Keya Maita, 'Ambedkar and the Constitution of India: A Deweyan Experiment' *Contemporary Pragmatism* 9.2 (2012): 301–20.

[13] Burt Neuborne, 'The Supreme Court of India', *International Journal of Constitutional Law* 1.3 (2003): 476–510, 466 fn 1, notes that, 'the length and complexity of the document is somewhat mitigated by the fact that approximately two-thirds of its provisions are technical, functioning more like organic statutes than constitutional provisions'.

[14] For contemporary scholastic approaches to the Constitution, see Sujit Choudhry, Madhav Khosla, and Pratap Bhanu Mehta (eds), *The Oxford Handbook of the Indian Constitution* (Oxford: Oxford University Press, 2016). For the history of the Supreme Court of India, see George Gadbois, *Supreme Court of India: The Beginnings*, edited and introduced by Vikram Raghavan and Vasujith Ram (New Delhi: Oxford University Press, 2017).

[15] For popular sovereignty, see Sarbani Sen, *The Constitution of India: Popular Sovereignty and Democratic Transformations* (Oxford: Oxford University Press, 2011); for equal protection, see Jagat Narain, 'Equal Protection Guarantee and the Right of Property Under the Indian Constitution', *International and Comparative Law Quarterly* 15.1 (1966): 199–230; and (dissenting) Catharine MacKinnon, 'Sex Equality under the Constitution of India: Problems, Prospects, and "Personal Laws"', *International Journal of Constitutional Law* 4.2 (2006): 181–202. For secularism, see Ronojoy Sen, *Articles of Faith: Religion, Secularism, and the Indian Supreme Court*, updated and revised edition (New Delhi: Oxford University Press, 2019); Ronojoy Sen, *Legalizing Religion: The Indian Supreme Court and Secularism* (Washington, DC: East West Center, 2007); Marc Galanter, 'Hinduism, Secularism, and the Indian Judiciary', *Philosophy East and West* 21.4 (1971): 467–87. For Indian federalism, see Louise Tillin, 'United in Diversity? Asymmetry in Indian Federalism', *Publius: The Journal of Federalism* 37.1 (2007): 45–67; and Ashutosh Varshney, 'How has Indian Federalism Done?', *Studies in Indian Politics* 1.1 (2013): 43–63.

Articles 25–28 of the Constitution enshrine the freedoms of religion in the Republic of India:

(25) Freedom of conscience and free profession, practice and propagation of religion;[16]
(26) Freedom to manage religious affairs;[17]
(27) Freedom as to payment of taxes for promotion of any particular religion;[18] and
(28) Freedom as to attendance at religious instruction or religious worship in certain educational institutions.[19]

As Deepa Das Acevedo notes, much of the courts' post-Independence task involved thinking 'creatively in order to reconcile competing impulses in the Indian Constitution.' In Das Acevedo's estimation: 'The most common clashes are between articles 25(1) and 26 on the one hand (which protect various aspects of religious freedom for individuals and groups) and articles 25(2)(a) and 25(2)(b) on the other hand (which authorize various forms of state involvement in regulating religious institutions and religious life more broadly).'[20] Alongside balancing the benefits of religious freedom and state involvement within the context of Articles 25 and 26, the courts have also weighed Articles 14 (equality before

[16] www.constitutionofindia.net/articles/article-25-freedom-of-conscience-and-free-profession-practice-and-propagation-of-religion/: '(1) Subject to public order, morality and health and to the other provisions of this Part, all persons are equally entitled to freedom of conscience and the right freely to profess, practice and propagate religion. (2) Nothing in this article shall affect the operation of any existing law or prevent the State from making any law – (a) regulating or restricting any economic, financial, political or other secular activity which may be associated with religious practice; (b) providing for social welfare and reform or the throwing open of Hindu religious institutions of a public character to all classes and sections of Hindus.'

[17] www.constitutionofindia.net/articles/article-26-freedom-to-manage-religious-affairs/: 'Subject to public order, morality and health, every religious denomination or any section thereof shall have the right (a) to establish and maintain institutions for religious and charitable purposes; (b) to manage its own affairs in matters of religion; (c) to own and acquire movable and immovable property; and (d) to administer such property in accordance with law.'

[18] www.constitutionofindia.net/articles/article-27-freedom-as-to-payment-of-taxes-for-promotion-of-any-particular-religion/: 'No person shall be compelled to pay any taxes, the proceeds of which are specifically appropriated in payment of expenses for the promotion or maintenance of any particular religion or religious denomination.'

[19] www.constitutionofindia.net/articles/article-28-freedom-as-to-attendance-at-religious-instruction-or-religious-worship-in-certain-educational-institutions/: '(1) No religious instruction shall be provided in any educational institution wholly maintained out of State funds. (2) Nothing in clause (1) shall apply to an educational institution which is administered by the State but has been established under any endowment or trust which requires that religious instruction shall be imparted in such institution. (3) No person attending any educational institution recognised by the State or receiving aid out of State funds shall be required to take part in any religious instruction that may be imparted in such institution or to attend any religious worship that may be conducted in such institution or in any premises attached thereto unless such person or, if such person is a minor, his guardian has given his consent thereto.'

[20] Deepa Das Acevedo, 'Gods' Homes, Men's Courts, Women's Rights', *International Journal of Constitutional Law* 16.2 (2018): 552–73, 554.

the law), Article 15 (prohibition of discrimination on the basis of membership in several protected categories), and Article 17 (abolition of untouchability).[21] In bringing the competing demands of these different – and sometimes conflicting – constitutional principles into alignment, if not harmony, the Supreme Court developed an 'essential practices' test. This test enabled the Court to evaluate – largely on a case-by-case basis – and protect, 'only those practices which form an essential and integral part of the religion'.[22]

Justice Mukherjea notes that 'the attempt of the courts to determine judicially what are or are not the essential parts of a religion may raise difficult questions about whose justiciability is doubtful'. Such questions have vexed the court and observers ever since the introduction of the doctrine in ***The Commissioner, Hindu Religious Endowments, Madras v Sri Lakshmindra Thirtha Swamiar of Sri Shirur Mutt*** in 1954.[23] Regarding Hindu temples, the essential practices test become instrumental in cases involving the denial of women and low-caste individuals access to worship and in protecting the financial arrangements of the endowment from state regulation.[24] Essentially, the Supreme Court has endeavoured to balance the sometimes competing interests of freedom of religion and freedom from discrimination.

Although the Constitution introduced proper constitutional jurisprudence to the Indian judiciary, the Supreme Court, in particular was also heir to the vast corpus of judge-made law from colonial India (some of which I explored in Chapter 4). Generally, the Supreme Court has taken the view that the decisions of the Judicial Committee of the Privy Council are binding on lower courts unless and until the Supreme Court ruled otherwise.[25] Much of the Supreme Court's task with regard to Hindu religious endowments in particular involved bringing the judgments of the Privy Council, which were decided almost entirely on the principles of property and trusts (in their hybrid, Anglo-Sanskrit iterations) into alignment with the principles of the Court's new constitutional jurisprudence. Rajeev Dhawan notes that:

> A very important section of the case law [of the Supreme Court on religious endowments] has been constitutional. Religious rights which under Anglo-Hindu law had been translated into proprietary interests had to be re-translated into constitutional

[21] Ibid. For these and other articles affecting non-discrimination, see Kalpana Kannabiran, *Tools of Justice: Non-discrimination and the Indian Constitution* (Abingdon: Routledge, 2012). For Article 15, see Gautam Bhatia, 'Horizontal Discrimination and Article 15(2) of the Indian Constitution: A Transformative Approach' *Asian Journal of Comparative Law* 11.1 (2016): 87–109.

[22] Mukherjea, *Hindu Law*, 391. For criticism of the courts' acting as 'clergy', see Faizan Mustafa and Jagteshwar Sohi, 'Freedom of Religion in India: Current Issues and Supreme Court Acting as Clergy', *BYU Law Review* (2017): 915–56.

[23] Mukherjea, *Hindu Law*, 391.

[24] Most recently and notably, at the temple of Sabarimala in Kerala. See Das Acevedo, 'Celibate Gods', 103–7.

[25] See A. Lakshminath, *Precedent in the Indian Legal System*, 2nd edn. (Lucknow: Eastern Book House, 2005).

terminology and adjusted into the framework of constitutional limitations. Apart from this proprietary facet, religious rights were protected by the Constitution. Thus, constitutional claims could be made by those that made worship possible and the worshipper.[26]

5.1.3 Outline of the chapter

In what follows, I take up two related, but discrete tasks: 1) outlining a jurisprudential 'toolbox' of core legal themes and concepts in the Court's judgments regarding Hindu endowments (and related phenomena); and 2) exploring the Court's application and transformation of these themes and concepts in the seminal, 1,000-plus page unanimous verdict in the infamous Ayodhyā dispute, ***M. Siddiq v Suresh Das*** delivered in 2019.[27] In pursuing these tasks, I aim to provide the reader with an historical context that reveals deep continuities that exist between the pre-colonial, colonial, and post-colonial Hindu jurisprudence of Equity and Trusts.

The first task assumes that, although the Supreme Court of India frames many of its verdicts in a constitutional language of fundamental rights, it nevertheless embraces several core features of Sanskrit and Anglo-Hindu jurisprudence: 1) the State (as heir to the Crown) as *parens patriae*; 2) the State's duty (assigned to the courts) to inquire into and to protect the customs and conventions of religious institutions (subject to limitation); 3) the figurative, but legally efficacious, juridical personality of Hindu deities and the fiduciary duties which this figurative ownership imposes on these deities' legal representatives; and 4) the construal of *shebaitship* as a form of quasi-proprietary right. Constitutional protections for women, low-caste individuals and other protected classes of people, along with principles of the modern tax regime are entirely novel facets of the modern judiciary.

Nevertheless, as with every political regime during every epoch analysed in this work, the Republic of India and its Supreme Court have stamped the unique legal imprimatur of its constitutional system onto a millennia-old legal practice of divine personhood. The task, then, is to explain how, when, and why the Supreme Court has developed the Hindu law of religious and charitable trusts even further. I work thematically and historically, focusing on individual themes and then tracing their evolution through case law and statute from 1950 to the present. The final result, then, is an index of case law, arranged chronologically, of the core jurisprudential building blocks that would be applied to or clarified in ***M. Siddiq v Suresh Das***.

26 Dhawan, 'The Supreme Court'.
27 ***M. Siddiq v Suresh Das*** 1 SCC 1 (2020).

5.1.4 Introduction to the Ayodhyā dispute

The second task, examining the application of Supreme Court jurisprudence in ***M. Siddiq v Suresh Das***, involves tackling, arguably, the most controversial court case in modern Indian legal history.[28]

5.1.4.i A timeline of the Ayodhyā dispute: 1856–2010

The Allahabad High Court, the Supreme Court, the popular press, and historians have explored the twinned narratives of a Hindu temple built by Vikramāditya (c. 57 BCE according to the Vikram Samvat calendar) and a mosque constructed by Bābur's lieutenant, Mīr Bāqī (c. 1528 CE), but these narratives never pass from *communal account* into *legal title*.[29] The Supreme Court notes that the Ayodhyā dispute is one 'whose origins are as old as the idea of India itself', spanning 'the Mughal empire, colonial rule and the present constitutional regime', but identifies the annexation of Oudh by British East India Company in 1856 as the starting point for legal rights to the disputed site.[30]

In 1856–57, riots between Hindus and Muslims led the colonial government 'to raise a buffer between the two communities to maintain law and order by setting up a grill-brick wall having a height of six or seven feet' dividing the disputed site into two parts: the inner courtyard (containing a three-domed mosque, the 'Bābrī Masjid') for the Muslim community; and the outer courtyard (containing the 'Rām Chabutra', a raised platform that held the images of Rāma, etc.) for the Hindu community.[31] These Solomonic efforts proved to be Sisyphean.[32]

In 1885, Raghubar Das, 'claiming to be the Mahant of Ram Janmasthan', filed a suit before the sub-judge of Faizabad, seeking to build a permanent temple on the Rām Chabutra.[33] In response, Mohd Asghar, the *Mutawalli* of the mosque, was made a party to the suit and 'set up a plea that the mosque was constructed by

[28] I take the view that, despite the difficulties presented by the Emergency, ***D.M. Jabalpur v Shivkant Shukla*** (1976) AIR SC 1207, which effectively suspended *habeas corpus*, was the nadir of the Supreme Court's generally laudable efforts to protect and to promote the constitutional rights of the Indian people. See Kalyani Ramnath, 'ADM Jabalpur's Antecedents: Political Emergencies, Civil Liberties, and Arguments from Colonial Continuities in India', *American University International Law Review* 31.2 (2016): 209–252.

[29] For Hindu temples under the Mughal Empire, see Chapter 3, §3.4.1, 'Equity and Trusts in the Mughal Empire'.

[30] SC ¶2, p. 6. The key juridical moments for the Supreme Court are 7 February 1856 (the annexation of Oudh) and 15 March 1858, when, by the proclamation of Lord Canning, most land was confiscated and vested in the government.

[31] Ibid., ¶10, pp. 9–10.

[32] Ibid., ¶10, p. 10,

[33] Ibid., ¶11, p. 10 (OS No. 61/280 of 1885)

1528: A mosque is ostensibly built by an agent of the Mughal emperor, Babur, at the site of a temple to Rāma.
1856: Annexation of Oudh by British East India Company.
1856–7: Communal riots, grill/brick wall separating disputed site established.
1885: 'Mahant' Raghubar Das, files and loses suit for construction of temple at Rām Chabutra.
1936: Mosque damaged in communal riots.
1949: The image of Rāma moved from the outer courtyard to the space under the central dome. Disputed site attached by local magistrate.
1950: Gopal Singh Visharad and Paramhans Ramchandra Das file suit seeking access to the dispute site for worshipping Rāma.
1959: Nirmohi Akhara files suit for 'a decree to hand over the management and charge of the temple' to them.
1961: The Sunni Central Board of Waqfs, Uttar Pradesh, files suit for recovery of the Babri Masjid.
1989: Retired Allahabad High Court Justice Deoki Nandan Agarwal files suit on behalf of Rāma Lalla Virajman and Asthan Śrī Rām Janmabhūmi for title to the disputed site.
1991: Parliament passes Places of Worship (Special Provisions) Act, 1991.
1992: Babri Masjid forcibly demolished by mob of Kar Sevakas.
1993: Parliament passes Acquisition of Certain Areas at Ayodhya Act, 1993.
1994: Supreme Court delivers verdict in ***Dr M Ismail Faruqui v Union of India***.
2002: Train of Kar Sevakas from Ayodhya burned at Godhra. Gujarat riots.
2005: Islamic Jihadists attack Rām Janmabhūmi.
2010: Allahabad High Court delivers verdict trifurcating the disputed site between litigants.
2019: Supreme Court of India deliver verdict awarding title to the disputed site to Rām Lalla Virajman.

Table 5.1 Timeline of the Ayodhyā dispute

Babur [in 1528 and]... that ownership could not be claimed by the plaintiff [Das] who had not produced any material originating in... the ruler of the time in support of the plea'.[34] The court refused Das' suit, as 'granting permission to construct [a] temple would amount to laying down foundation of riot between the two communities'.[35] Afterwards, the district judge, F.E.A. Chamier, denied Das' appeal, citing limitation: 'It is most unfortunate that a masjid should have been built on land specially held sacred by the Hindus, but as that event occurred 356 years ago it is

[34] Ibid., ¶432, p. 485. For mutawallis as the fiduciary guardians of mosques, see the (Indian) Waqf Act, 1995, at 3.i: https://indiankanoon.org/doc/631210/

[35] AHC (Khan, J) p. 19.

too late now to remedy the grievance. All that can be done is to maintain the parties in status quo.'[36] In the 2010 and 2019 judgments of the Allahabad and Supreme Courts, the question arose as to whether, as a result of Mahant Raghubar Das' 1885 case, the Hindu parties in later suits were estopped by the bar of *res judicata* (both courts found that they were not).[37]

After the 1885 suit, the *status quo* appears to have remained relatively unchanged (with the notable caveat of a 1936 riot in which the mosque was damaged and then repaired by the colonial Government), until the night of 22–23 December, 1949, 'when the mosque was desecrated by a group… who broke open its locks and placed idols of Lord Ram under the central dome'.[38] Three legal consequences followed: 1) a First Information Report (FIR) was filed; 2) the Additional City Magistrate of Faizabad-cum-Ayodhyā issued a preliminary order under Section 145 of the Code of Criminal Procedure 1898, treating the situation to be of an 'emergent nature'; and 3) the Chairman of the Municipal Board of Faizabad was appointed as the receiver of the inner courtyard under an attachment order.[39] The district manager refused a government order to remove the idols, as 'it would lead to slaughter'.[40]

The local magistrate issued a preliminary order, whereby 'two or three Pujaris [ritual experts] were permitted to go inside' the mosque and 'perform religious ceremonies like *bhog* and *puja*' for the idols of Rāma and the Hindu community were restricted to viewing the idols from within the outer courtyard.[41] Furthermore, the magistrate ordered that 'the stakeholders [in the disputed site] were allowed to file their written statements'.[42] Rāma's image would remain in that precise spot, carefully shepherded by his court-appointed guardians, for the next seventy years, during which numerous suits were filed, the conflict became a national issue, the

[36] Ibid. (Khan, J.), pp. 9–20. Civil Appeal No. 27/1885.

[37] When a litigant attempts to file suit on a matter involving the same parties after having received a judgment in a previous case then they are estopped (barred) from filing suit on the basis of *res judicata*. SC ¶435, pp. 488–90.

[38] SC ¶12, p. 11. The background to this event is spelt out in compelling, Godfather-esque detail in Krishna Jha and Dhirendra Jha, *Ayodhya: The Dark Night* (New Delhi: HarperCollins, 2012). Page xiv describes the *Shreeramjanmabhoomi Ka Ratka Ranjit Itihaas* (The Blood-soaked History of the Birthplace of Lord Ram), a local publication which asserted that 'on that day… Lord Rama himself redeemed his place of birth'.

[39] SC ¶12, p. 11: Section 145 enables a district magistrate, or an executive magistrate, who is satisfied from a police report or other information that a dispute likely to cause a breach of the peace exists concerning any land or water within his jurisdiction to order the parties concerned to attend court in person or by pleader.

[40] AHC (Khan, J.), p. 34. Since the night of 22–23 December, 1949, the idols have never been removed from their position under the dome of the erstwhile mosque, and have received continuous worship from court-appointed pujaris. See SC ¶30, p. 27: 'On 10 August 2015… this Court allowed the Commissioner… to replace the… tarpaulin sheets over the makeshift structure under which the idols were placed'.

[41] SC ¶12, p. 11.

[42] Ibid.

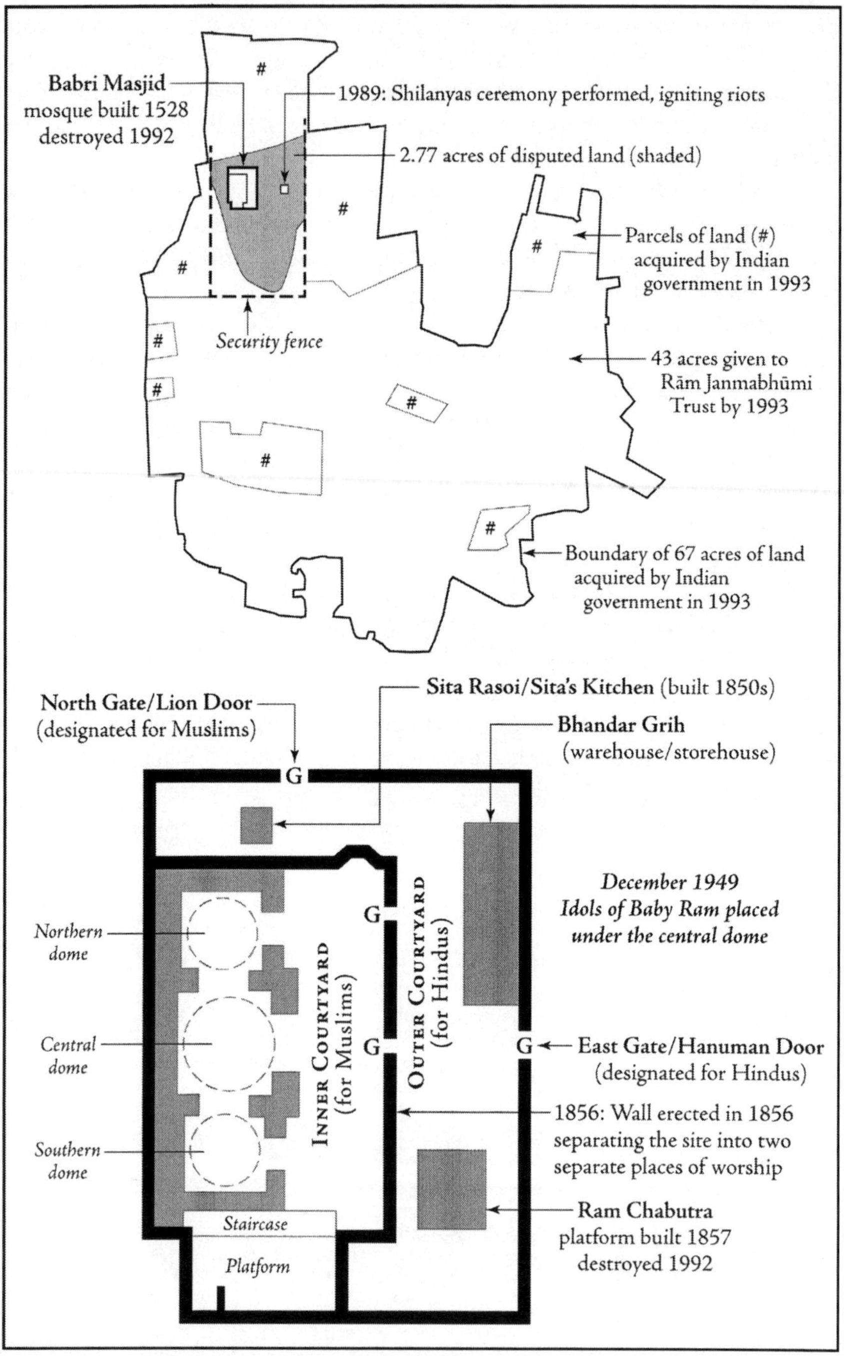

Figure 5.1 The Bābrī Masjid/Rām Janmabhūmi site: before and after 6 December 1992

mosque was destroyed by a mob, riots rocked Gujarat, and Islamic insurgents attempted to suicide-bomb his makeshift temple.[43]

Figure 5.1 shows the contested site along with various relevant historical data from the evolution of the resulting case.

5.1.4.ii The five suits of the Ayodhyā dispute

Between 1950 and 1989, five suits were filed. On 16 January 1950, Gopal Visharad (since deceased and replaced by his son in 1986) filed a suit, ***Gopal Singh Visharad since deceased and survived by Rajendra Singh v Zahoor Ahmad and others***, before the Civil Judge at Faizabad, seeking, 'a declaration… to allow the plaintiff to offer prayers in accordance with the rites and tenets of his religion ("Sanatan Dharm") at the "main Janmabhumi" near the idols within the inner courtyard without hindrance [from the state government, the local Muslim community, or the receiver]'.[44] On 19 January, 1950, 'the injunction was modified to prevent the idols from being removed from the… site and from causing interference in the performance of puja'.[45]

A second suit, filed by Paramhans Ramchandra Das on 5 December 1950, and identical to Visharad's, was withdrawn in 1990.[46] While these suits concerned the *right to worship* at the site and not a *proprietary title* to the site, the Supreme Court would frame this *right* of Hindus to worship Lord Rām at the Janmabhūmi *as* the juridical person, Rām Lalla Virajman – capable of holding title to the property.[47] In connection with Visharad's suit, the court appointed a commissioner, Shiva Shankar Lal, to prepare maps and an inventory of the disputed site. He noted

[43] For the emergence of Ayodhyā as a political fulcrum in the 1980s, see van der Veer, 'God must be Liberated!'; and Sarvepalli Gopal (ed.), *Anatomy of a Confrontation: Ayodhya and the Rise of Communal Politics in India* (London: Zed, 1992). For analysis in the wake of demolition of the Babri Masjid in December 1992, see Sheldon Pollock, 'Rāmāyaṇa and Political Imagination in India', *The Journal of Asian Studies* 52.2 (1993): 261–97; Roger Friedland, and Richard Hecht, 'The Bodies of Nations: A Comparative Study of Religious Violence in Jerusalem and Ayodhya', *History of Religions* 38.2 1998: 101–49; and David Ludden, *Making India Hindu: Religion, Community, and the Politics of Democracy in India* (Delhi: Oxford University Press, 1996). For the Godhra train burning and the 2002 Gujarat communal riots, see Jyoti Punwani, 'The Carnage of Gadhra', in Siddharth Varadarajan (ed.), *Gujarat: The Making of a Tragedy* (New Delhi: Penguin Books, 2002): 45–74; and Saifuddin Ahmed, 'The Role of the Media during Communal Riots in India: A Study of the 1984 Sikh Riots and the 2002 Gujarat Riots' *Media Asia* 37.2 (2010): 103–11. For the lesser-known (and failed) 2005 Islamist attack on Ram Virajman's makeshift temple at Ayodhya, see Richard H. Davis, 'The Rise and Fall of a Sacred Place: Ayodhya Over Three Decades', in Marc Ross (ed.), *Culture and Belonging in Divided Societies: Contestation and Symbolic Landscapes* (University of Pennsylvania Press, 2009): 25–44, 25–7.

[44] SC ¶13, p.12. Regular Suit No. 2 of 1950. Subsequently renumbered as Other Original Suit (OOS) No. 1 of 1989.

[45] Ibid., ¶13, p.12.

[46] Ibid., ¶14, p. 12, Regular Suit No 2 of 1950. This was included in the consolidated suits of 1989, and for this reason, there are five, rather than four, suits in the 2010 and 2019 verdicts.

[47] Ibid., ¶206, p. 224: 'Suit 1… is essentially a suit by a worshipper for enforcement of his right to worship Lord Ram at the Janmabhumi.'

that, 'in the central portion of the [mosque] building at the north-western corner, there is a pucca platform with two stairs, on which is installed the idol of Bal Ram (infant Ram)'.[48]

The third suit, ***Nirmohi Akhara and others v Baboo Priya Datt Ram and others***, was filed on 17 December 1959, by the Nirmohi Akhara – a monastic community of Rāmānandi Vairāgya Sadhus, through their Mahant, Jagat Das.[49] The Akhara (whose Mahant had filed suit in 1885) made a series of improbable claims. They averred that there was *never* a mosque at the disputed site, that the 'mosque' was a Hindu temple, that this temple 'belongs and has always belonged' to it, and it had been 'managing it and receiving offerings through the reigning Mahant'.[50] The suit argued that the attachment of the disputed site under Section 145 had wrongfully deprived them of 'their management and charge of the said temple' and they sought 'a decree to hand over the management and charge of the temple'.[51]

Not only did the Nirmohi Akhara display a level of strategic duplicity – in their witness statements and averments – but they also attempted to undermine the legal case of Rām Virajman in order to assert their own proprietary claims. Ironically, the Nirmohi Akhara's pursuit of its personal interests, 'without protecting the independent needs and concerns of the deity of Lord Ram', aided Rām's legal victory by providing a cause of action for a next friend to file suit on Rām's behalf.[52]

The fourth suit, ***The Sunni Central Board of Waqfs, UP and others v Gopal Singh Visharad (since deceased) and others***, was filed by the Sunni Central Board of Waqfs, Uttar Pradesh, on the 18 December 1961.[53] The suit claimed that:

> Assuming, though not admitting, that... there existed a Hindu temple... on the site of which emperor Babar built the mosque, some 433 years ago, the Muslims, by virtue of their long exclusive and continuous possession beginning from the time the mosque was built and continuing right up to the time some mischievous persons... desecrated the mosque... the Muslims perfected their title by adverse possession and the right, title or interest of... the Hindu public if any [is] extinguished.[54]

[48] Ibid., ¶15, pp. 13–15.

[49] Ibid., ¶16, p. 13. Regular Suit No 26 of 1959 (subsequently renumbered as OOS No. 3 of 1989) For a history of the Nirmohi Akhara, see Jha and Jha, *Ayodhya*; Krishna Pokharel and T. Lahiri, 'Who Are the Nirmohi Akhara?', *The Wall Street Journal India* 30 (2010); and, for the Rāmānandī's generally, Richard Burghart, 'Wandering Ascetics of the Rāmānandī Sect', *History of Religions* 22.4 (1983): 361–80

[50] SC ¶217, p. 243.

[51] Ibid., ¶217 & 16 pp. 243–4 & 13.

[52] Ibid., ¶428. p. 479. For 'next friends' in relation to Hindu deities, see Chapter 4, §4.2.3.ii, 'Filing suit in the name of the deity'. In the Common Law, a 'next friend' (*prochein ami/proximus amicus*) is a person who represents another person who is under disability or otherwise unable to maintain a suit on his or her own behalf, and who does not have a legal guardian.

[53] Regular Suit No. 12 of 1961 (subsequently renumbered as OOS No. 4 of 1989).

[54] AHC (Khan, J), pp. 55–6.

The Sunni Central Board of Waqfs sought 'a declaration that the entire disputed site of the Bābrī Masjid was a public mosque and for the delivery of possession upon removal of the idols'.[55] Furthermore, the Supreme Court notes that,

> The plaint was amended following the demolition of Babri Masjid to place subsequent facts and events on the record. According to the plaintiffs, a mosque does not require any particular structure and even after the demolition of the mosque, the land on which it stood continues to remain a mosque in which Muslims are entitled to offer prayers.[56]

On 1 July 1989, the fifth suit, ***Bhagwan Sri Ram Lala Virajman and others v Rajendra Singh and others***, was filed on behalf of two deities, 'Bhagwan Sri Ram Lala Virajman' and 'Asthan Sri Rām Janam Bhumi, Ayodhya', by a 'next friend', Deoki Nandan Agarwal, a senior advocate and retired judge of the Allahabad High Court.[57] According to the plaint, 'the first and second plaintiffs are juridical persons with Bhagwan Sri Rama as a presiding deity of the place', that the earlier suits have 'a dim prospect of their immediate hearing' and that the deities are, 'Extremely unhappy with the delay in the disposal of the suits, the deterioration in the management of the affairs of the temple and with the alleged misappropriation of the offerings of worshippers by pujaris and other temple staff.'[58] The suit claimed that 'some of the parties to the earlier suits are… involved in seeking to gratify their personal interest by obtaining control over [the] worship of the plaintiff deities' and argued that the Nirmohi Akhara, 'has put forward a personal interest in the management of the worship of the plaintiff-deities'. Due to this malfeasance, and because there was 'no other fit person' to represent the deities, Agarwal 'instituted the suit as next friend'.[59] The deities sought two forms of legal relief:

> (a) A declaration that the entire premises of Sri Ram Janmabhumi described in Annexures I, II and III belong to the plaintiff-deities; and
> (b) A permanent injunction prohibiting the defendants from interfering with or obstructing the construction of a new temple at Sri Ram Janmabhumi after the demolition and removal of the existing buildings and structures.[60]

[55] SC ¶17, p. 18.
[56] Ibid., ¶601, p. 709.
[57] Regular Suit No. 236 of 1989 (subsequently renumbered as OOS No. 5 of 1989). For Agarwal's journey to being Rāma's next friend, see 'The Man who was Ram Lalla's "next friend"', *The Times of India*, 2 October 2010.
[58] SC ¶312, pp. 358–9.
[59] SC ¶312 & 315, pp. 360–1.
[60] SC ¶315, pp. 361–2.

5.1.4.iii 1992 and its aftermath

In 1989, the suits were transferred to the Allahabad High Court. On 6 December, 1992, the mosque was destroyed by a large crowd of Kar Sevaks (religious activists) and a small, makeshift temple was erected at the location of the erstwhile mosque's central dome (wherein Rāma's idols were deposited). When the Indian army secured the site, the regular worship of Rāma's idols by court-appointed pujaris continued. The destruction of the mosque and the riots that accompanied it gained international infamy.[61] Sheldon Pollock connects the Hindu nationalist politics of the Bharatiya Janata Party (BJP) and the destruction of the Bābrī Masjid:

> From December 1992 through January 1993, more than 3,000 people were killed in 'communal' rioting across India… however complex the causal nexus of these events may be… the symbolic nexus is simple. This nexus was… the 'Chariot Procession' ('*rathyātra*') undertaken by the then-president of the Bharatiya Janata Party… L. K. Advani, in October 1990. In a Toyota truck turned into an epic chariot, Advani traveled from Somnath in Gujarat to Ayodhya… It was this *yātra* that led… to the event that inaugurated, the most recent riots, the actual demolition of the mosque on December 6, 1992, not by a mob but by what appears to have been a trained group of Hindu militants… the primary impetus for political mobilization- in the name of a Hindu theocratic politics and against the Muslim population-derived in large part from the invocation of… the figure of the warrior-god Rama, his birthplace temple in Ayodhya, and the liberation of this sacred site.[62]

While the Euro-American Academy and the Indian political sphere debated the profound implications of 1992 in terms of India's cultural identity and commitments to secularism (itself a contested term), the Indian Central Government attempted to resolve the Ayodhyā dispute through an Act of Parliament, the Acquisition of Certain Areas at Ayodhya Act, 1993.[63] The Act vested the ownership of the disputed site in the Central Government (annulling any pre-existing proprietary interests) and directed the Government to manage the property so as to 'ensure that the position existing before the commencement of this Act in the area on which the structure… stood in Ayodhya… is maintained'.[64]

Furthermore, the Act abated 'any suit, appeal or other proceeding in respect of the right, title and interest relating to any property which has vested in the Central Government under section 3… pending before any court, tribunal or other

[61] Take, for example, Rajeev Dhavan's characterization of the Kar Sevaks as 'Hindu Taliban' in front of the Supreme Court in 2018: https://timesofindia.indiatimes.com/india/babri-masjid-destroyed-by-hindu-taliban-supreme-court-told/articleshow/64979474.cms

[62] Pollock, 'Rāmāyaṇa', 261.

[63] For the Act, see www.indiacode.nic.in/bitstream/123456789/1915/3/A1993-33.pdf. For discussions of Indian secularism, see Rajeev Bhargava (ed.), *Secularism and its Critics* (Oxford: Oxford University Press, 1999).

[64] Acquisition of Certain Areas at Ayodhya Act, 1993, 3.7(2).

authority'.[65] Along with the Act, the president of India, S.D. Sharma, made a Special Reference (No. 1 of 1993) under Article 143(1) of the Constitution, requesting the Supreme Court to determine, 'whether a Hindu temple or any Hindu religious structure existed prior to the construction of the Ram Janma Bhumi-Babri Masjid in the area on which the structure stood'.[66]

Numerous legal challenges to the Act resulted in a landmark verdict from the Supreme Court in 1994, ***Dr M Ismail Faruqui v Union of India***.[67] The Court argued that, as the Special Reference, 'cannot be construed as an effective alternate dispute resolution mechanism to permit substitution of the pending suits and legal proceedings', Section 2.4(3) of the Act (which abated legal suits) was unconstitutional, and the Allahabad High Court would have to hear the cases.[68] However, the Court upheld the remainder of the Act, and ruled that the Government of India was merely the statutory receiver of the land and had a fiduciary duty to manage the land – retaining the *status quo* – until the lawsuits were heard.[69]

The Supreme Court of India issued its verdict in ***M. Siddiq v Suresh Das*** in 2019. The justices' 1,000-page opinion cites every significant case in the history of Anglo-Hindu and post-independence law on the subject in a comprehensive review of the jurisprudence of Hindu deities as juridical persons. Before turning to the details of the Ayodhyā case, it is imperative, therefore, to garner an appreciation for the core principles of the post-independence case-law concerning Hindu deities before delving into the technical application of their principles in the Bābrī Masjid dispute.

While examining the evolution of Supreme Court case law in the 1950s, 1960s, 1970s, and 1980s, it is prudent to remember that while all of these cases were being decided, the Ayodhyā dispute was brewing. While the Supreme Court was shaping the post-colonial Hindu law of religious and charitable trusts, Rām Virajman's image was safely ensconced under the dome of the mosque, receiving regular court-monitored worship. During all of these events, Deoki Nandan

[65] Ibid., 2.4(3)

[66] AIR 1995 SC 605 ¶15: Article 143 in the Constitution of India 1949: 'Power of President to consult Supreme Court (1) If at any time it appears to the President that a question of law or fact has arisen, or is likely to arise, which is of such a nature and of such public importance that it is expedient to obtain the opinion of the Supreme Court upon it, he may refer the question to that Court for consideration and the Court may, after such hearing as it thinks fit, report to the President its opinion thereon.'

[67] AIR SC 605 ¶15.

[68] Ibid., ¶149: 'The Act having been struck down, the suits as to the title… in the Allahabad High Court revive…'

[69] Ibid. Did the Court's order for the maintenance of the *status quo* ¶98(4) infringe the Muslim community's rights to religious freedom under Articles 25 and 26 of the Constitution? See ibid., ¶31: 'It is… contended that… by directing maintenance of the status quo… which enables the Hindus to exercise the right of worship of some kind in the disputed site keeping the Muslims totally excluded from that area…' CF ¶55: 'Section 7(2) of the Act freezes the situation… which was a lesser right of worship for the Hindu devotees than that in existence earlier… and it does not create a new situation more favourable to the Hindu community…'

Agarwal was reading the case reports that we are about to examine – with an eye, on his part, to crafting an argument, based on the Sanskrit jurisprudential principles of Equity and Trusts, that would secure the disputed premises for Rām Virjaman himself.

5.2 The Supreme Court of India's jurisprudential toolbox and Hindu religious endowments

During the decades since its inception in 1950, the Supreme Court of India developed a sophisticated 'toolbox' of jurisprudential principles and techniques while carving out a capacious role for judicial review within the federal republic.[70] In this section, I examine four areas of jurisprudence relating to Hindu deities and religious trusts where the Supreme Court has made great strides in developing rights-based tests in its judgments since 1950: 1) the jurisdiction of the Court in exercising a supervisory role of religious endowments and over state regulation of religious endowments; 2) the balancing of a respect for the distinctive customs and beliefs of religious communities against constitutional provisions and statutes prohibiting caste and gender-based discrimination; 3) recognising collective belief as the primary criterion for the attribution of legal personality of Hindu deities, while setting reasonable limits on the objects and rights of divine legal persons; and 4) distinguishing between the quasi-proprietary rights of *shebaits* and the nominal ownership of deities in matters of taxation, limitation, and adverse possession.

These principles emerged in case law from the 1950s onwards that used a constitutional, rights-based jurisprudence which was very much in conversation with post-independence statutes (the Hindu Codes Bills of 1955–56 in particular). Nevertheless, these cases entailed a re-examination of earlier, colonial-era case law from this new vantage point. The end result, in the aggregate, was the creation of a new body of law that enjoyed deep, and occasionally unexpected, links to Anglo-Hindu law – just as Anglo-Hindu law enjoyed deep, often unexpected links to pre-colonial jurisprudence and legal practice.

[70] For positive appraisals of the Court's performance, see Jamie Cassels, 'Judicial Activism and Public Interest Litigation in India: Attempting the Impossible?', *The American Journal of Comparative Law* 37.3 (1989): 495–519; and Manoj Mate, 'The Rise of Judicial Governance in India', *Boston University International Law Journal* 33.169 (2015). For a less effusive analysis, see Wilfried Swenden and Rekha Saxena, 'Policing the Federation: The Supreme Court Judicial Federalism in India', *Territory, Politics, Governance* 10.1 (2022): 12–31.

5.2.1 The State, the Crown, and Hindu religious endowments

Perhaps *the* core feature of the Anglo-Hindu law of religious and charitable trusts was the *parens patriae* jurisdiction, with its links to English and Sanskrit jurisprudence, of the Company, Crown, and their courts. This principle justified State intervention and supervision over, *inter alia*, temples, monasteries, charities, and the estates of women, minors, and the mentally infirm.[71] Sovereignty and jurisdiction were intimately connected in the old Anglo-Hindu law, and this often catalysed difficult questions about the relationship between the Crown, the Company, indigenous Indian princes, and public temples, which had always been subject to some measure of state interference. The Supreme Court, however, took a different view concerning the states' and courts' rights to supervise religious institutions. The protection of fundamental rights, rather than the exercise of feudal prerogative, provided the justification for governmental supervision. This jurisprudential shift in justification, however, did not entail a significant shift in the practical operation of law. The state remained *parens patriae* in practice, if not in name.[72]

Debates abound about the precise nature of sovereignty in the Republic of India.[73] While it was clear during British rule that sovereignty vested in the Crown (with the Company acting as a trustee before 1858), the situation after independence was less obvious.[74] Certainly, in the leadup to independence, the Indian Congress insisted that sovereignty vested in the people, and the pre-amble to the Constitution notes that the Indian people resolved 'to constitute India into a sovereign, democratic republic'.[75] Furthermore, early Supreme Court decisions, such as ***A.K. Gopalan v State of Madras*** (1950), and ***Virendra Singh v State of***

[71] See Chapter 4, §4.2.1, 'The Company and the Crowns: sovereignty, jurisdiction, and trusteeship (1772–1863)'.

[72] See Bhat, 'Parens Patriae', 205–6, where the author argues for an 'expansion of the provision' (§92 of the CPC 1908) which would enable 'the Judiciary to perform its inherent protectionist role' as *parens patriae*. Of course, despite the courts' reluctance in the matter of public trusts to stand forth as *parens patriae*, this feudal language appears much more commonly in guardianship proceedings. See, for example, Rakshith Shetty, 'An Analytical Study on the Appointment of Guardians to Vegetative People in Reference to the Doctrine of "Parens Patriae"', *Indian Journal of Law and Legal Research* 5.1 (2023): 1–12. Also see ***Suchita Srivastava & Anr. v Chandigarh Administration*** (2009) 9 SCC 1.

[73] A useful summary can be found in Das Acevedo, 'Temples, Courts', where the author argues for a 'dynamic equilibrium' between popular sovereignty and '"divided sovereignty" in which the state, as the agent of reform, has sovereign authority independent of citizens'.

[74] For these questions, see S. N. Dwivedi, 'Location of Sovereignty in India', *Journal of the Indian Law Institute* 9.1 (1967): 71–84. See page 71 for four options: '(1) The legislature is sovereign; (2) The legislature is sovereign within its sphere; (3) The Constitution is sovereign; and (4) The people of India are sovereign.'

[75] Ibid., 81 fn 51.

Uttar Pradesh (1954), repeatedly emphasise that sovereignty vests exclusively in the Indian people.[76]

In ***Virendra Singh v State of Uttar Pradesh***, the State of Uttar Pradesh revoked a pair of land grants that had been made by the rulers of two small princely states before their accession to the Union of India. When the grantees filed suit, the State argued that, by virtue of being the legal heir to these erstwhile princely states, it enjoyed the sovereign right to adjust or revoke grants made under the earlier regime without being subject to judicial review. Justice Bose's eloquent opinion provides a concise overview of the early Supreme Court's understanding of Indian sovereignty:

> The problem which confronts us… [is] the impact of the Constitution on the peoples and territories which joined the Indian Union and brought the Constitution into being… In our opinion, the Constitution, by reason of the authority derived from, and conferred by, the peoples of this land, blotted out in one magnificent sweep all vestiges of arbitrary and despotic power in the territories of India and over its citizens and lands and prohibited just such acts of arbitrary power as the State now seeks to uphold… At one stroke all other territorial allegiances were wiped out and the past was obliterated except where expressly preserved; at one moment of time the new order was born with its new allegiance springing from the same source for all, grounded on the same basis: the sovereign will of the peoples of India with no class, no caste, no race, no creed, no distinction, no reservation… We are no longer concerned with principalities, and powers.[77]

5.2.1.i State legislation and the Supreme Court

While this view of popular sovereignty, beautifully stated by Justice Ghose, effectively estopped the State Government (or the State acting on behalf of the Central Government) from *exercising* the despotic, feudal prerogatives of previous governments through executive *fiat*, the Government and states enjoyed significant legislative powers and semi-feudal responsibilities under the Constitution.[78] In the

[76] AIR 1950 SC 27; 1954 AIR 447; and 1955 SCR 415. See Justice Sastri's comments in ***Gopalan***, 198, 'There can be no doubt that the people of India have, in exercise of their sovereign will as expressed in the Preamble, adopted the democratic ideal… and in delegating to the legislature, the executive and the judiciary their respective powers in the Constitution, reserved to themselves certain fundamental rights, so called, I apprehend, because they have been retained by the people and made paramount to the delegated powers, as in the American model.'

[77] Ibid., ¶280–1 [Ghose, J]. Ghose effectively argues against the despotic, unmitigatedly feudal theory of Indian sovereignty accepted by the Privy Council in colonial cases such as ***Vajesingji Joravarsingji Nayak v The Secretary of State For India*** (1924) 7 MIA 476; and ***Secretary of State for India v Sardar Rustam Khan*** (1941) 68 IA 109.

[78] Articles 245–54 of the Constitution demarcate the concurrent legislative powers of the States and Centre. Article 296 affords the State the right to escheat to any properties or prerogatives which 'would have accrued to His Majesty or, as the case may be, to the Ruler of an Indian State'.

early 1950s, several state legislatures enacted statutes that significantly expanded state control over and intervention into Hindu religious endowments, and this, in turn, resulted in a flurry of Supreme Court cases that challenged those enactments on the grounds of Articles 25 and 26 of the Constitution.[79]

The Supreme Court responded by justifying the states' and Central Government's right to manage religious endowments like previous governments of India. It also justified this power of supervision as much on the Constitution as on historical fact. Furthermore, in setting itself up as the arbiter of what constitutes 'religious' and 'secular' practices within religious institutional structures, the Supreme Court implicitly slipped into the position of earlier sovereigns, who had also tasked themselves within enquiring into and subsequently regulating the conventional rules of semi-*sui-iuris* communities.

Hindu Religious Endowments, Madras v Sri Lakshmindra Thirtha Swamiar of Shri Shirur Mutt (1954) is probably the most famous early Supreme Court case that concerns the government's ability to regulate temples – subject to review from the courts.[80] The case concerned whether the Madras Hindu Religious and Charitable Endowments Act (1951), which, *inter alia*, asserted considerable control over the Shirur Mutt's financial and ritual independence (the latter including restricting temple entry) violated Articles 25 and 26 of the new Indian Constitution. The Supreme Court ruled that, 'restrictions by the State upon free exercise of religion are permitted both under articles 25 and 26 on grounds of public order, morality and health'; that, under Article 25(2.a), the State may 'regulate or restrict any economic, financial, political and other secular activities which may be associated with religious practice'; and that Article 25(2.b) empowers the State to 'legislate for social welfare and reform even though by so doing it might interfere with religious practices'.[81]

While the court noted that, 'a religious denomination or organization enjoys complete autonomy in the matter of deciding as to what rites and

[79] As Mukherjea notes in *Hindu Law*, 403, 'from the constitutional [point] of view, there is an obstacle to the formulation of one uniform code for religious and charitable trusts and endowments. Entry 28 of List III of the 7th Schedule of the Indian Constitution grants concurrent powers of legislation… in the fields of *charities and charitable institutions, charitable and religious endowments and religious institutions*.' A partial list of state acts (which appear in the appendix to Mukerjea's 3rd edition of *Hindu Law*, fn. 24) includes: the Bihar Hindu Religious Trusts Act (1950); the Travancore Cochin Hindu Religious Institution Act (1950); the Rajasthan Public Trusts Act (1950); the Bombay Public Trusts Act (1950); the Madhya Pradesh Public Trusts Act (1951); the Orissa Hindu Religious Endowments Act (1951); the Puri Jagannath Temple (Administration.) Act (1952); the Madras Hindu Religious and Charitable Endowments Act (1959); the Uttar Pradesh Public Institutions (Prevention of Dissipation of Temple Properties) Act (1962); and the Andhra Pradesh Charitable and Hindu Religious Institutions and Endowments Act (1966).

[80] 1954 AIR 282; 1954 SCR 1005.

[81] Ibid. [Mukherjea, J].

ceremonies are essential according to the tenets of the religion they hold', the court also noted that:

> The scale of expenses to be incurred in connection with these religious observances would be a matter of administration of property belonging to the religious denomination and can be controlled by secular authorities in accordance with any law laid down by a competent legislature; for it could not be the injunction, of any religion to destroy the institution and its endowments by incurring wasteful expenditure on rites and ceremonies.[82]

While the court added that, 'a law which takes away the right of administration from the hands of a religious denomination altogether and vests it in any other authority would amount to a violation of the right guaranteed under clause (d) of article 26', it also added that the Madras Act's efforts, 'to ensure that the... endowments attached to the religious institutions are properly administered and their income is duly appropriated for the purposes for which they were founded or exist' was perfectly constitutional.[83]

Even as ***Shirur Mutt*** *limits* the government's powers over religious institutions' essential practices, it *defines* and justifies 'the right of the State to employ the sovereign power to ensure peace, security and orderly living without which constitutional guarantee of civil liberty would be a mockery'.[84] In 1954, the Supreme Court ruled in two similar cases that challenged the validity of state-level regulations on religious endowments: ***Sri Jagannath v State of Orissa*** and ***Ratilal v State of Bombay***.[85] Both judgments, citing ***Shirur Mutt***, articulated the same argument, that 'it is the secular administration of the religious institutions that the Legislature seeks to control and the object, as enunciated in the Act, is to ensure that the endowments attached to the religious institutions are properly administered and their income is duly appropriated for purposes for which they were founded or exist'.[86] This closely follows the language of East India Company's Bengal, Madras, and Bombay Regulations of 1810, 1817, and 1827, respectively.[87] Rather than a foreign power articulating its authority over a subject population through enacting

[82] Ibid. One essential practice accepted by the Supreme Court was the 'traditional custom universally observed not to allow access to any outsider to the particularly sacred parts of a temple as for example, the place where the deity is located'.

[83] Ibid.

[84] The case was followed by a 1954 amendment to the Act that was also challenged in ***Sudhindra Tirtha Swamiar v Comissioner of Hindu Religious and Charitable Endowments, Madras*** ILR 1956 Mad 229.

[85] (1954) SCR 1046 and (1954) AIR SC 388, challenging the Orissa Hindu Religious Endowments Act 1952 and Bombay Public Trusts Act, 1950. Mukherjea, *Hindu Law*, 398 discusses two similar cases involving the state of Travancore–Cochin's *devaswam* board.

[86] 1954 SCR 1046. Quoted with approval in ***Mahant Moti Das v S. P. Sahi, the Special Officer*** (1959) AIR 942, 1959 SCR Supl. (2) 503.

[87] See Chapter 4, §4.2.1.i, 'The sovereign company as *parens patriae*'.

sovereignty through temple supervision, this was a native government expressing its independent sovereignty through regulating religious endowments.

A more sophisticated question concerning post-independence sovereignty and the administration of Hindu religious and charitable endowments arose in ***Tilkayat Shri Gobinda Lalji Maharaj v State of Rajasthan***, a case that involved the famous Nathdwar temple in the erstwhile princely state of Mewar.[88] The *Tilkayat* (head priest) of the Sri Nathdwar temple sued the Government of Rajasthan over the constitutionality of Nathdwar Temple Act (1959), a piece of legislation which formally vested the temple assets in Śrīnāthjī Deva. The *Tilkayat* claimed, *inter alia*, that, the temple was a private temple and, therefore, beyond the remit of the state to supervise directly.

In rejecting this contention and in asserting the public nature of the temple (and concomitant right of the State to supervise it), the Supreme Court pointed to a '*Firman* issued by the Udaipur Darbar in 1934… [which] really… shows that the Shrinathji Temple at Nathdwara is undoubtedly a public temple'.[89] The *farmān*, explicitly describes the temple as being public and allocated to the Udaipur Darbar (chancery) the 'absolute right to supervise that the property dedicated to the shrine is used for legitimate purpose of the shrine'. In 1934, however: 'The Maharana of Udaipur was an absolute monarch… [and] an absolute monarch was the fountain-head of all legislative, executive and judicial powers and it is of the very essence of sovereignty which vested in him that he could supervise and control the administration of the public charity.'[90]

This, of course, is classic *parens patriae* jurisprudence, or at least a feudal justification for the royal supervision of religious endowments, and the Supreme Court argued that as a consequence of this *farmān* being in effect when Mewar acceded to the Indian Union:

> He [the *shebait*] can claim no better and no higher rights after the Firman was issued. The said clause also declares that the Darbar has absolute right to see to it that the property is used for legitimate purpose of the shrine. This again is an assertion which is validly made to assert the sovereign's rights to supervise the administration of public charity.[91]

The Supreme Court does not take on a *parens patriae* argument of its own, but rather it acknowledges the enduring legal consequences of the erstwhile Mahārāja's jurisdiction in support of the ability of the State of Rajasthan's power to exercise *similar* legal controls under different, constitutional premises.

[88] (1963) AIR 1638; 1964 SCR (1) 561. See Chapter 3, §3.3.2.ii, 'The deity as sovereign in Vijayanagara'.
[89] Ibid.
[90] (1963) AIR 1638; 1964 SCR (1) 561 [Gajendragadkar, J].
[91] 1964 SCR (1) 561 [Gajendragadkar, J].

While the Supreme Court accepted the *parens patriae* rights of previous sovereigns in ***Tilkayat Sri Gobinda Lalji***, it remained wary of the states or the courts assuming this role in the context of private religious trusts. In ***Mahant Ram Saroop Dasji v S. P. Sahi, Special Officer-in-Charge of the Hindu Religious Endowments Board***, decided in 1959, the Mahant of the Salouna Asthal challenged the application of the State of Bihar's Hindu Religious Trusts Act (1951) to his *maṭha* on the grounds that it was a private religious trust. Private religious trusts, while immune to direct state control, are nevertheless justiciable in cases of breach of trust when an interested party files suit.[92] The advocates for the State of Bihar argued, however, that the Act applied to private and public religious trusts equally. The Supreme Court, for its part, noted that:

> So far as private religious trusts are concerned, there are no specific statutory enactments and such trusts are regulated by the general law of the land. The British Government, when it was first established in India, following the tradition of the former rulers, asserted by virtue of its sovereign authority the right to visit public religious and charitable endowments and to prevent and redress abuses in their management.[93]

The Patna High Court drew on English trusts jurisprudence and *parens patriae* jurisdiction (citing Justice Mukherjea in the process), and argued that, in English law, 'the Crown as *parens patriae* is the constitutional protector of all property subject to charitable trusts, such trusts being essentially matters of public concern'.[94] Furthermore, the High Court reasoned that, since, 'in the case of a charitable corporation where the founder is a private person, he and his heirs become visitors in law and where such heirs are extinct or incompetent, their powers devolve on the Crown or the State [in English law]', it would be 'in the interests of the general public that the State should exercise superintendence and control over the administration of private trusts as in the case of public trusts'.[95]

The Patna High Court wanted to expand the remit of the states' rights of supervision of religious trusts by invoking English theories of *parens patriae*, which, it must be said, align more closely with Dharmaśāstric theories than with the position taken by the Supreme Court. The Supreme Court dismissed the importation of English jurisprudence, noted the existence of legal remedies to

[92] (1959) AIR 942, 1959 SCR SUPL. (2) 503. Mukherjea, *Hindu Law*, 362: 'In a private or family debutter the beneficiaries are a limited and defined class of persons, as for example, the members of a family. If the trustee or shebait is guilty of mismanagement, waste, wrongful alienation of debutter property or other neglect of duties, a suit can certainly be instituted for remedying these abuses of trust. Under the general law of the land the founder of the endowment, or any of his heirs is competent to institute a suit for proper administration of the debutter, for removal of the old trustee and for appointment of a new one.' See Chapter 4, Note 56 for the public/private distinction in Anglo-Hindu law.
[93] Ibid. [Das, J].
[94] Ibid.
[95] Ibid.

the maladministration of private religious trusts, and directed the Government of Bihar to cease interfering with the *Maṭha* 'unless and until the[y]... have obtained the necessary determination that the Salouna asthal is a public trust'.[96] In the Supreme Court's estimation, the right to property in Article 19(1) of the Constitution shielded the Mahant from the statutes of the State of Bihar.

5.2.1.ii Escheated to the public good? The shebaiti rights of the 'Ruler of Travancore' in the Padmanābhasvāmi verdict (2020)

No Supreme Court case better illustrates the complicated, overlapping threads of sovereignty, public/private distinctions, and property rights with regard to Hindu religious endowments than ***Sri Marthanda Varma (D) Th. Lrs. & Anr. Petitioners v State of Kerala & Ors*** (2020).[97] The case pitted Śrī Padmanābhadāsa Śrī Uthradom Thirunal Marthanda Varma (1922–2013), the titular Mahārāja of Travancore, against the State of Kerala over the control of the fabulously endowed Padmanābhasvāmi temple in Thiruvananthapuram.[98] On the one hand, the shape of the case was simple: an erstwhile sovereign was resisting state efforts to administer a public temple, the administration of which had vested in the mahārājas for centuries. On the other hand, the case involved complex, largely unanswered questions about sovereignty, property, and the guardianship of Hindu deities. Unsurprisingly, the same Sanskrit jurisprudential themes of Equity and Trusts that were discussed in Chapters 1, 2, 3, and 4 appear in the verdicts.

Much of the complexity of ***Sri Marthanda Varma*** stems from the unusual constitutional history of the quondam Kingdom of Travancore – as a sovereign state that resisted colonial expansion rather successfully. At the Battle of Colachel in 1741, the forces of Anizham Thirunal Marthanda Varma of Travancore (r. 1729–58 CE) defeated the forces of the Dutch East India Company under Eustachius De Lannoy (1715–77 CE).[99] Captured, De Lannoy joined the Mahārāja and assisted in the creation of a modern, powerful, European-style military for Travancore that enabled the Mahārājas to retain independence and control over the lucrative Malabar spice trade.[100] In 1750, Anizham Thirunal Marthanda Varma established a new constitutional arrangement, through the *Thripaddi Dānam*, when he donated the entire

[96] Ibid.

[97] SC 639 (Civil Appeal No. 2732 of 2020). An excellent summary is, Vinod Rai, 'The Sree Padmanabhaswamy Temple Case: Landmark Ruling by the Indian Supreme Court', *ISAS Insights* 635 (2020): 1–5.

[98] The best scholarship on the case – published before the Supreme Court's verdict – is Das Acevedo, 'Divine Sovereignty'.

[99] Mark de Lannoy, *The Kulasekhara Perumals of Travancore: History and State Formation in Travancore from 1671 to 1758* (Leiden: Leiden University Press, 1997).

[100] For the Travancore spice trade in the age of the British, see K. Kusuman, *A History of Trade and Commerce in Travancore* (Delhi: Mittal, 1987), 127–58.

kingdom to Padmanābhasvāmi, the tutelary deity of the royal house. The endowment states that:

> We, Thrippappoor Keezhperur Veera Bala Marthanda Varma… have this day… transfer[red] by absolute gift and dedication, to endure as long as the Sun and Moon shall last, all the lands and functions appertaining thereto together with all rights and dignities, positions of honour and all other possessions that we have been hitherto enjoying as of right…. in favour of Perumal Sree Padmanabha Perumal. we have this day executed this deed of absolute gift and dedication.[101]

For the next two-hundred years, Śrī Padnamābhasvāmi, like Virūpākṣa at Vijayanagara in the 16th and 17th centuries, ruled as a sovereign deity with the 'mahārāja' acting as his servant (*Padmanābhadāsa*) and legal representative.[102]

Resisting Tipu Sulṭān's expansionism in southern India required acquiring military power; in 1788, Anizham's successor, Dharma Raja Karthika Thirunal Rama Varma (r. 1758–98 CE), 'entered into an agreement with the Governor of Madras to lease two British battalions'.[103] As part of the agreement, the East India Company sent an agent – later a resident – to Travancore, and in the early 19th century, John Munro (1778 –1858 CE) served as *Dīwān*.[104] Munro centralised the management of temples in Travancore in 1811, in step with the East India Company's policies in the Calcutta, Madras, and Bombay presidencies. Furthermore, during this time, the Padmanābhasvāmi temple 'had such surplus that… for the needs of the State, Travancore Kings used to steadily borrow funds from the Sree Padmanabhaswamy Temple on repayment basis and the loans were repaid with interest'.[105] Śrī Padmanābhasvāmi was possibly the wealthiest deity in India (or the world).

In the 20th century, the last independent Mahārāja, Sree Padmanābhadāsa Sree Chithira Thirunal Balarama Varma, created a centralised *Devasvom* (deities' property) Board that centralised temple regulation and issued the much-lauded Temple Entry Proclamation in 1936. This opened the doors of the kingdom's temples to Hindus of all castes.[106] In 1949, he signed a twenty-two article covenant with the Government of India.[107] Much of the covenant was much of a sameness with other accessionary agreements between princely states and the Indian Union, but Article VIII (b) was unique:

[101] Civil Appeal No. 2732 of 2020, ¶5. The Court cites Princess Aswathi Thirunal Gouri Lakshmi Bayi, *Sree Padmanabha Swamy Temple*, 3rd edn. (Mumbai: Bharatiya Vidya Bhavan, 2013) at length. Also see Uma Maheswari, *Thrip Padi Danam* (Malayalam) (Kozhikode: Mathrubhumi Books, 2020).

[102] Civil Appeal No. 2732 of 2020, ¶5.

[103] Das Acevedo, 'Divine Sovereignty', 845.

[104] Ibid., 845.

[105] Civil Appeal No. 2732 of 2020, ¶6.

[106] For temple entry, see Marc Galanter, 'Temple-entry and the Untouchability (Offences)' *Journal of the Indian Law Institute* 6.263 (1964): 185–95.

[107] Civil Appeal No. 2732 of 2020), ¶11.

> The administration of Sri Padmanabhaswamy Temple, the Sri Pandaravaga properties and all other properties and funds of the said temple now vested in trust in the Ruler of the covenanting State of Travancore… shall, with effect from the first day of August 1949, be conducted, subject to the control and supervision of the Ruler of Travancore, by an Executive Officer appointed by him. There shall be a Committee known by the name of the Sree Padmanbhaswamy Temple Committee composed of three Hindu Members, to be nominated by the Ruler of Travancore to advise him in the discharge of his functions.[108]

After Padmanābhadāsa Chithira acceded to the Union of India, the newly founded State of Travancore-Cochin explicitly recognised his right of supervision over the Padmanābhasvāmi temple in Chapter 18(2) of the Travancore-Cochin Hindu Religious Institutions Act, 1950:

> The administration of the Sree Padmanabhaswamy temple, the Sree Pandaravaga properties and all other properties and funds of the said temple vested in trust in the Ruler of Travancore and the sum of six lakhs of rupees mentioned in sub-section (1) shall be conducted, subject to the control and supervision of the Ruler of Travancore, by an executive officer appointed by him.[109]

Even after Padmanābhadāsa Chithira's death in 1991 and the ascension of Sree Padmanābhadāsa Sree Uthradom Thirunal Marthanda Varma (r. 1991–2013 CE) as the titular Mahārāja of Travancore, this remained a satisfactory agreement. In 2007, however, 'the popular Malayalam daily *Kaumudi* published an article documenting the efforts of the head of family to inventory the contents of the Padmanabhaswamy vaults, or *kallaras*' including a secret (*rahasya*) vault said to contain 'the wealth accumulated by Travancore royals since 700 AD'.[110] The *Kaumudi* articles prompted 'several readers to file writ public interest litigation suits challenging the royals' authority over the temple and its wealth' and T.P. Sundara Rajan, a retired police officer, lawyer, and Padmanābhasvāmi devotee, filed a *quo warranto* petition with the Kerala High Court.[111] These petitions, and the royal family's challenges to them were bundled as ***T.P. Sundara Rajan v The State of Kerala***.[112] Figure 5.2 displays the layout of the Padmanābhasvāmi temple along with its central shrines and sundry treasure vaults.

The argument before the Kerala High Court in 2011 was a classic question of sovereignty in post-independence India. On the one hand, Padmanābhadāsa Marthanda Varma argued that Chapter 3(2) of the Travancore-Cochin Hindu Religious Institutions Act (1950), vested control of the Padmanābhasvāmi temple

[108] Ibid., ¶11.
[109] Ibid., ¶13.3
[110] Das Acevedo, 'Divine Sovereignty', 850.
[111] Ibid., 852. For public interest litigation in India, see P. Craig and L. Deshpande, 'Rights, Autonomy and Process: Public Interest Litigation in India', *Oxford Journal of Legal Studies* 9.3 (1989): 356–73.
[112] 23 WP. 36487 of 2009.

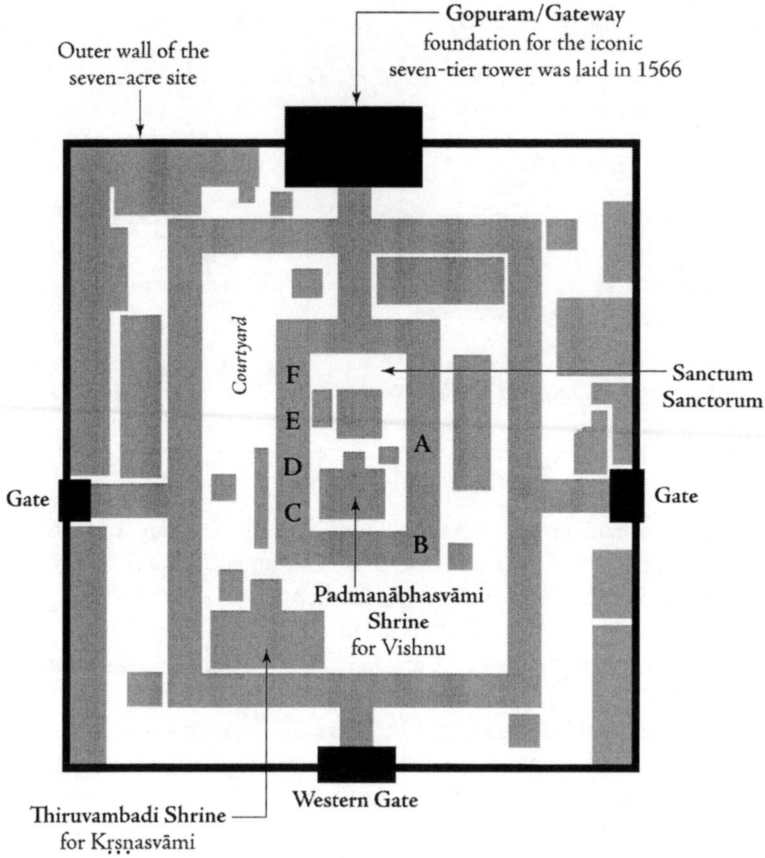

Vaults Containing Vast Riches

- **A** Possibly opened in the 1930s, but not since
- **B** Unopened since the 1880s
- **C** Opened periodically by the two priests of the temple
- **D** Opened periodically by the two priests of the temple
- **E** Opened periodically by the two priests of the temple
- **F** Opened periodically by the two priests of the temple
- **[G]** Possible subterranean vault (location unknown)
- **[H]** Possible subterranean vault (location unknown)

Figure 5.2 The Padmanābhasvāmi temple and its treasure vaults (*kallaras*)

in him, as the *titular* Ruler of Travancore. Therefore, the terms of the covenant signed by Chithira in 1949 – vesting control in the same terms – was non-justiciable on account of Article 363(1) of the Indian Constitution, and that the *shebaitship* of the temple (a public temple) was a private, heritable right that could not be expropriated by the state.[113] Sundara Rajan, for his part, averred that, with the passage of the 26th Amendment to the Indian Constitution in 1971 – which ceased state recognition of 'rulers' of former princely states and abolished privy purses – there was no recognised 'ruler' of Travancore under the terms of the Travancore-Cochin Hindu Religious Institutions Act and, so the state needed to intervene to protect the interests of Padmanābhasvāmi.[114]

In 2011, the Kerala High Court ruled against Marthanda Varma on the basis that he was not the 'ruler' of Travancore under the Travancore-Cochin Hindu Religious Institutions Act (1950) or under Article 363(1) of the Constitution.[115] In the Court's estimation, 'after the death of the last Ruler… [Chithira in 1991], there is no Ruler in the erstwhile State of Travancore'.[116] The Kerala High Court ruled that: 'Since the deity is a perpetual minor in the eye of the law, the court has jurisdiction to protect it… as parens patriae…. [and] on the death of the last Ruler [management of the temple] reverts back to the State for administration.'[117] In essence, the High Court put itself into the legal position of current Ruler of Travancore (for the purposes of the Travancore-Cochin Act) and argued that, 'in the literal sense and by virtue of the operation of Articles 295 and 296 of the Constitution, the Temple vests in [the] State Government through succession or *escheat*'.[118]

Invoking further *parens patriae* language, the Kerala High Court ruled that, to avoid 'any orphanage for the temple', and in order 'to save the Temple and to protect the interests of the devotees and the public at large', the government must 'make arrangement [for the administration of the temple] in the same way once

[113] Article 363(1): 'Notwithstanding anything in this Constitution but subject to the provisions of article 143, neither the Supreme Court nor any other court shall have jurisdiction in any dispute arising out of any provision of a treaty, agreement, covenant, engagement, sanad or other similar instrument which was entered into or executed by any Ruler of an Indian State and to which the Government of the Dominion of India or any of its predecessor Governments was a party.' Cited in Das Acevedo, 'Divine Sovereignty', 853–4.

[114] Das Acevedo, 'Divine Sovereignty', 853–4.

[115] WP (C) 36487 of 2009 ¶10.

[116] Ibid., ¶10.

[117] Ibid., ¶12–13. The Court quoted ***A.A. Gopalakrishnan v Cochin Devaswom Board & Ors*** (2007) (7) SCC 482 ¶10: 'The properties of deities… require to be protected and safeguarded by their Trustees/ Archaks/ Sebaits/employees. Instances are many where persons entrusted with the duty of managing and safeguarding the properties… deities… have usurped… by setting up false claims of ownership or tenancy, or adverse possession. This is possible only with the passive or active collusion of the concerned authorities. Such acts of "fences eating the crops" should be dealt with sternly… It is also the duty of courts to protect and safeguard the properties of religious and charitable institutions from wrongful claims or misappropriation.'

[118] Ibid., ¶13.

State-run temples were handed over to Devaswom Boards (after accession to the Union)'.[119] Unusually, the Court also ordered the Government to 'open all kallaras' and 'create a museum' to 'exhibit all the treasures of the Temple for the public, devotees and the tourists'.[120] In short, the Kerala High Court embraced its *parens patriae* jurisdiction of the otherwise guardian-less deity, Padmanābhasvāmi, on the basis of escheating to the prerogative of the erstwhile Mahārājas. The State of Kerala had become, in effect, the Padmanābhadāsa.

On appeal to the Supreme Court, Marthanda Varma was joined by the chief *tantri* of the temple as an intervenor, whose written submissions (by his advocate, J. Sai Deepak) inveighed against the High Court's invocation of *parens patriae* and escheat.[121] The written submissions included the argument that, while, 'the erstwhile Rulers of the Princely States were Hindu sovereigns as recognized by the High Court... since the India State is a secular State, it cannot arrogate to itself powers and rights enjoyed by Hindu sovereigns'.[122] The Supreme Court, for its part, took the view that the *shebaitship* of the Padmanābhasvāmi 'had vested in the Ruler of Travancore, not in his official capacity', but, rather in his personal capacity, as a private individual.[123] Consequently, 'the normal incident of heritability must get attached to the office of such *Shebaitship* in accordance with governing principles of succession and custom'.[124] In the Supreme Court's estimation, 'unless and until the line of succession of the *Shebaitship* and in-charge of the administration, is completely extinct, there can be no question of escheat'.[125]

The Supreme Court granted Marthanda Varma's appeal and ordered the settlement of a scheme – suggested by Marthanda – featuring an Administrative Committee and the Advisory Committee comprising various notables (with Marthanda occupying pride of place as *shebait*).[126] As in ***Mahant Ram Saroop Dasji***, in ***Marthanda Varma***, the Supreme Court restricted the High Court's exercise of a *parens patriae* jurisdiction that was based on the sovereign claims of prior, feudal governments. Ironically, in both cases the Supreme Court recognised the legal effects of prior rulers' sovereign powers, but rejected the *contemporary* use of those powers. Rather, the Supreme Court repeatedly eschewed sovereign prerogative in favour of the protection of constitutional rights – in

[119] Ibid., ¶13–14.
[120] Ibid., ¶16.iii. For the elaborate legal wrangling between the Court, the temple, the deity, and the mahārāja over accessing these vaults, see Das Acevedo, 'Divine Sovereignty', 854–9.
[121] Special Leave Petition (Civil) No. 11295 of 2011.
[122] Ibid., ¶22.
[123] Civil Appeal No. 2732 of 2020, ¶105.
[124] Ibid.
[125] Ibid., ¶106, citing ***Kutchi Lal Rameshwar Ashram 60 Trust Evam Anna Kshetra Trust v Collector, Haridwar*** (2017) 16 SCC 418.
[126] Civil Appeal No. 2732 of 2020, ¶114.

this case, the private proprietary rights of the Mahārājas' *shebaitship*. The Court would not permit the State to step into the shoes of the Mahārāja or the Padmanābhasvāmidāsa, but it would protect the deity – in the name of the public's right to worship.

In conclusion, Indian independence enabled vastly greater state control over Hindu religious and charitable trusts, and various Indian states passed a flurry of legislation to that effect almost as soon as the Constitution of India took effect. Given the capacious legislative powers afforded to the states under the Constitution of India and the untested limits of Article 25 and 26 (protecting freedom of religion), it was inevitable that the Supreme Court would hear many cases that challenged the states' ability to regulate religious institutions. Ironically, it was the High Courts, often favouring the states' interventions, that asserted *parens patriae* and other Anglo-Hindu, English-Sanskrit jurisprudential theories that were grounded in a feudal, property-oriented perspective.

For its part, the Supreme Court did not reject state supervision over religious endowments outright. Rather, it rejected the assertion of the despotic sovereignty of previous regimes. Instead, the Supreme Court favoured a rights-based approach that weighed the public good verses various constitutionally protected freedoms of property and religion. While this clearly constitutes a departure from Dharmaśāstric theories of the kingship in relation to religious endowments – and, indeed, to centuries of Hindu, Muslim, and English paradigms of rule – it nevertheless established an effective system of judicial and state supervision of *shebaiti* and other functionary rights in temples. Thus, we can thus say that, while the state and the courts fulfilled a similar function to their colonial predecessors in acting as the protector of temples, deities, and those who are non-*sui-iuris*, they performed that function under a constitutional, rather than a royal aegis.

5.2.2 Essential practices, custom, and equity

Many of the early Supreme Court cases that articulated the states' and courts' right to regulate Hindu religious and charitable endowments also delineated the aspects over which and the conditions under which these endowments could be regulated. Generally, the Supreme Court took the view that, while the essential belief and practices of a religious sect are protected by Articles 25 and 26 of the Constitution, the secular, financial aspects of a religious institution are nevertheless very much open to state and judicial regulation.

Even essential practices, are subject to considerations of public order, health and morality, as well as constitutional *provisions* that enshrine rights to non-discrimination and equality.[127] The passage of the Hindu Code Bills (1955–56) and the Untouchability (Offences) Act (1955), along with a raft of state-level reform legislation, set the stage for the Supreme Court's balancing of a recognition of the customs and beliefs of religious communities with the push for equality and the necessity of supervising trust finances.[128] As with the sovereignty-oriented cases that I discussed earlier in this chapter, the Supreme Court reconfigured a core feature of Anglo-Hindu law along a rights-based constitutional pattern. Anglo-Hindu jurists took the view that the courts should respect and protect the customs and practices of Hindu temples and it was on this basis that the Bombay High Court, in ***Sankaralinga Nadan v Raja Rajeswara Dorai***, prevented the Nadars from entering the Kamudhi temple.[129]

In a similar vein, the Supreme Court followed this pattern from the standpoint of Articles 25 and 26 of the Constitution. The Court would, like a Dharmaśāstric sovereign, investigate the conventions of religious communities – the *sāmayikadharmas* of Hindu Sanskrit theories of Equity – acting as the arbiter of those beliefs and their acceptability within paradigms of the Constitution.[130]

5.2.2.i The early history of the Essential Practices Test

The Essential Practices Test was born in 1954, in Justice Mukherjea's opinion in ***Commissioner, Hindu Religious Endowments, Madras v Sri Lakshmindra Thirtha Swamiar of Sri Shirur Mutt***.[131] As noted earlier, the case turned on the constitutionality of the 1951 Madras Hindu Religious and Charitable Trusts

[127] See, for example, Marc Galanter, 'Untouchability and the Law', *Economic and Political Weekly* 4.1–2 (1969): 131–70; and Marc Galanter, 'Caste Disabilities and Indian Federalism', *Journal of the Indian Law Institute* 3.2 (1961): 205–34. Galanter notes, on p. 205, that 'most of the fundamental rights conferred by the Constitution are restrictions solely on the activity of the state'. Also see Rajeev Dhawan & Fali S. Nariman, 'The Supreme Court and Group Life: Religious, Freedom, Minority Groups and Disadvantaged Communities', in B.N. Kirpal *et al.* (eds), *Supreme But Not Infallible: Essays in Honour of the Supreme Court of India* (Oxford: Oxford University Press, 2004). For the Supreme Court and women's rights, see Soumalya Ghosh, 'Supreme Court on Women's Right to Religious Freedom in India: from Shirur Mutt to Sabarimala', *Indian Journal of Law and Justice* 10.1 (2019): 162–8.

[128] For the Hindu Code Bills, see Fleming, *Ownership and Inheritance*, 215–18: 'The Indian parliament passed a series of landmark reforms of Hindu law between 1955 and 1956. The "Hindu Code Bill" was a composite body of laws, made up of distinct sets of legal enactment – the Hindu Marriage Act passed in 1955, and the Hindu Succession Act, the Hindu Minority and Guardianship Act and the Hindu Adoption and Maintenance Act, all of which were passed in 1956… The effects of the Hindu Code Bill were legion: women were granted greater property rights in their paternal estates, the rules regarding divorce, adoption and marriage were liberalized, and the legal cohesiveness of the joint family estate – the coparcenary – was greatly diminished.'

[129] (1908) 10 BOM LR 781. Also see Chapter 4, §4.2.2.ii, 'Customary usage and Dharmaśāstric Equity in Anglo-Hindu Trusts law'.

[130] For the Court's role in interpreting scripture in this context, see C.J. Fuller, 'Hinduism and Scriptural Authority in Modern Indian Law', *Comparative Studies in Society & History* 32.2 (1988): 225–48. Also see Das Acevedo, 'Gods' Homes', 553–8.

[131] (1954) AIR 282, 1954 SCR 1005.

Act. Discussing Article 26 (the right to manage religious institutions), Justice Mukherjea notes that 'the language undoubtedly suggests that there could be other affairs of a religious denomination or a section thereof which are not matters of religion and to which the guarantee [to protection] given by this clause would not apply'.[132] If, as Mukherjea, observes, 'the administration of its property by a religious denomination has... been placed on a different footing from the right to manage its own affairs in matters of religion', then 'the question is, where... [is] the line to be drawn between what are matters of religion and what are not[?]'[133]

The answer, according to the Court, is that 'what constitutes the essential part of a religion is primarily to be ascertained with reference to the doctrines of that religion itself'.[134] Although the Supreme Court ruled that much of the 1951 Act was constitutional, they objected to Section 21, which granted the Commissioner, 'and his subordinate officers and also persons authorised by them to enter the premises of any religious institution or place of worship for the purpose of exercising any power conferred, or any duty imposed by or under the Act'.[135] In what would prove to be an obstacle for claimants in cases involving temple-entry for low-caste individuals and women in subsequent times, Justice Mukherjea reasoned that:

> It is well known that there could be no... unrestricted right of entry in a public temple or other religious institution, for persons who are not connected with the spiritual functions thereof. It is a traditional custom universally observed not to allow access to any outsider to the particularly sacred parts of a temple as for example, the place where the deity is located. There are also fixed hours of worship and rest for the idol when no disturbance by any member of the public is allowed.[136]

Justice Mukherjea took up the question of temple-entry in greater depth in ***Nar Hari Sastri And Others v Shri Badrinath Temple Committee*** (also decided in 1952).[137] In this case, Justice Mukherjea distinguished between the general right of *all* Hindus to worship at public temples, from special rights that are over and beyond those 'enjoyed ordinarily by members of the Hindu public'.[138] The former category of right required only the ascertainment of the temple's public status for the court to recognise this right. The second category of right, however, 'would undoubtedly have to establish such rights on the basis of custom, usage or otherwise'.[139] Nevertheless, public temple entry is not an 'unrestricted right... [and] it is open to the trustees of a public temple to regulate the time of public visits and

[132] Ibid.
[133] Ibid.
[134] Ibid.
[135] Ibid.
[136] Ibid.
[137] (1952) AIR 245 SC, 1952 SCR 849.
[138] Ibid.
[139] Ibid.

fix certain hours of the day during which alone members of the public would be allowed access to the shrine'.[140]

This all seems reasonable and logical. What happens, however, when an essential practice of a public temple conflicts with the right of all Hindus to access a temple? This was precisely the point of contention in ***Sri Venkataramana Devaruand v The State Of Mysore***.[141] The trustees of a temple of Śrīveṅkaṭarāma in the village of Mannampady, Mysore, challenged a scheme set up under the Madras Temple Entry Authorisation Act (1947), which permitted Harijans to enter the temple. The trustees claimed that the temple was founded by and for the local Maithila Brāhmaṇa community, and as such, their use of the temple to the exclusion of all others formed an essential part of their religious denomination. The Supreme Court recognised that, because, 'during certain religious ceremonies, persons other than Gowda Saraswath Brahmins have been wholly excluded... this evidence leads irresistibly to the conclusion that the temple is a denominational one, as contended for by the appellants [the Brāhmaṇas]'.[142]

If the temple were a public denominational temple with a clear, Brāhmaṇical class of beneficiaries, then, as the Court noted, 'the question arises whether the appellants are entitled to exclude other communities from entering into it for worship on the ground that it is a matter of religion within the protection of Art. 26 (b)'.[143] The heart of the decision was 'a fundamental distinction between excluding persons from temples open for purposes of worship to the Hindu public in general on the ground that they belong to the excluded communities and excluding persons from denominational temples on the ground that they are not objects within the benefit of the foundation.'[144] The Supreme Court's conclusion was that, while the public – including Harijans – had a constitutionally protected (Article 25) right to worship at the public temple, the temple's status as a denominational temple, also, meant that the Court recognised the Brāhmaṇas' exclusion of *all* non-Brāhmaṇa Hindus during the performance of certain *essential* ceremonies as protected by Article 26, provided that this did not substantially harm the public worship.[145]

[140] Ibid.
[141] (1958) AIR 255, 1958 SCR 895. For the classification of Jains as 'Hindus' for legal purposes and its impact on temple entry, see Manisha Sethi, 'Jainism in Danger? Temple Entry and the Rhetoric of Religion and Reform in Post-colonial India', *Modern Asian Studies* 55.5 (2021): 1718–54.
[142] (1958) AIR 255, 1958 SCR 895.
[143] Ibid.
[144] Ibid.
[145] Ibid.: 'We have held that the right of a denomination to wholly exclude members of the public from worshipping in the temple, though comprised in Art. 26(b), must yield to the overriding right declared by Art. 25(2)(b) in favour of the public to enter into a temple for worship. But where the right claimed is not one of general and total exclusion of the public from worship in the temple at all times but of exclusion from certain religious services, they being limited by the rules of the foundation to the members of the denomination, then the question is not whether Art. 25(2)(b) over-rides that right so as to extinguish it, but whether it is possible-so to regulate the rights of the persons protected by Art. 25(2)(b) as to give effect to both the rights.'

In short, the goal of the court in its application of the Essential Practices Test had been to balance the need to recognise religious diversity and autonomy (within the parameters of Article 26), with the need for fundamental rights to equality.[146] This put the Court in the unusual position of delving into the scriptures, histories, and customs of diverse religious organisations in order to determine what, *according to the adherents of a religion*, the core principles and practices are. As Das Acevedo notes, '1960s cases demonstrated that the Supreme Court was willing not only to act as gatekeeper between the religious and non-religious (or the non-essentially religious), but also between "real" and "fake" religion'.[147]

During the following decades, the Court increasingly fine-tuned the finer points of the Essential Practices Test, but the core jurisprudence remained the same: the Supreme Court (and High Courts) had the twin duty, just like a Dharmaśāstric sovereign, of enquiring into the conventional by-laws and practices of religious groups, and of protecting those aspects that do not conflict with statutory law. Certainly, the statutory law of the Republic of India differs substantially from the Brāhmaṇa-centric laws envisioned in Dharmaśāstric literature, but the *role* played by the state and its justice system bears a significant similarity. In short, the Supreme Court followed a notion of Equity (in the Dharmaśāstric sense), even if the fundamental principles of equality were different.

5.2.2.ii Essential practices, Equity, and equality at the Sabarimala temple

The Śrī Ayyappan temple on Sabarimala Hill, nestled inside the Periyar National Park and Wildlife Sanctuary, attracts more than 20 lakhs of pilgrims annually during the pilgrimage season (December to January). The Sabarimala pilgrimage entails a forty-one-day vow of purification, during which the devotee abstains from alcohol, sex, meat, and other impurifying activities. The long duration of the pilgrimage creates a problem, however: women of menstruating age will cycle during any forty-one-day period. According to longstanding Hindu religious tradition, menstruation would violate the vow of purification required to access the temple during the pilgrimage season. Consequently, the Sabarimala temple has the longstanding custom – with sometimes uneven enforcement – of barring women aged ten to fifty years from entering the temple.

[146] Less equitable was the Court's ruling in ***Sardar Syedna Taher Saifuddin v The State Of Bombay*** (1962) AIR 853, 1962 SCR Supl. (2) 496, that excommunication was an 'essential' component of Tayyibi Isma'ilism which 'kept the denomination together and maintained the purity of its fellowship'. The Court took a dim view of the Swaminarayan's claim to be a distinct sect in a bid to avoid temple-entry by Harijans in ***Sastri Yagnapurushadji v Muldas Brudardas Vaishya*** (1966) AIR 1119, 1966 SCR (3) 242.

[147] Das Acevedo, 'Gods' Homes', 556.

The accepted antiquity of the custom, its application only to a subcategory of women, and its probable violation of Article 25.2(b) of the Constitution, made it an ideal subject for litigation. This litigation would stimulate the Courts' interpretation of the limits of the Essential Practices Test.[148] On the one hand, the temple had a clear, well-established custom that the High Courts viewed as an 'essential' facet of the religious practice at Sabarimala. On the other hand, banning women, either during the pilgrimage season or throughout the entire year, seems to violent the spirit of 'throwing open of Hindu religious institutions of a public character to all classes and sections of Hindus' flagrantly.[149] In overturning the High Court of Kerala's endorsement of the ban on women's participation in worship, the Supreme Court emphasised the importance of equality over custom.[150] As in many of the cases examined in this chapter, the Supreme Court reined in the High Court's Anglo-Hindu-inspired jurisprudence (emphasising feudalism, custom, and private property) in favour of a rights-based jurisprudence.

In 1991, S. Mahendran, a devotee of Śrī Ayyappan, filed a suit, ***S. Mahendran v The Secretary, Travancore Devaswom Board***, with the Kerala High Court – a suit converted into Public Interest Litigation – alleging that, 'contrary to the customs and usages followed in the temple', young women were 'trekking Sabari hills (Sabarimala) and offering prayers at the Sabarimala Shrine'.[151] This was partially true, and the Court noted in its verdict that: 'For the last 20 years women irrespective of their age were allowed to visit the temple when it opens for monthly poojas. They were not permitted to enter the temple during [the] *Mandalam*, *Makaravilakku*, and *Vishu* seasons.'[152] The respondents averred that: 1) 'under Articles 15, 25 and 26 of the Constitution of India… The Board [regulating the temple] cannot conceive of any religious practice under the Hindu religion which deprives a worshipper of his rights to enter the temple and worship therein according to his belief'; and 2) that 'the entry of young ladies in the temple during monthly poojas is not against the customs and practices followed in the temple'.[153]

The questions, then, before the Kerala High Court were whether the *partial* ban on women was an *essential* custom of the Sabarimala temple and, if so,

[148] For a superlative analysis of the litigation surrounding Sabarimala, see Deepa Das Acevedo, *The Battle for Sabarimala: Religion, Law, and Gender in Contemporary India* (New York: Oxford University Press, 2024).

[149] Indian Constitution, Article 25.2(b): '(b) providing for social welfare and reform or the throwing open of Hindu religious institutions of a public character to all classes and sections of Hindus'.

[150] The standard work of reference on Sabarimala will be Das Acevedo, *The Battle for Sabarimala*. Also see, Deepa Das Acevedo, 'Pause for Thought: Supreme Court's Verdict on Sabarimala', *Economic and Political Weekly* 53.43 (2018): 12–15.

[151] IR 1993 Ker 42, ¶2 (Balanarayana Marar, J).

[152] Ibid., ¶8.

[153] Ibid., ¶9.

whether this custom violated Articles 15, 25, and 26 of the Indian Constitution.[154] This is a classic example of Essential Practices jurisprudence – balancing customary practice against constitutional freedoms. Petitioners argued that, 'the restriction imposed on woman of a particular age group from entering the temple is a matter of religion and a matter of religious faith' and that, the temple, as a 'religious denomination' had 'every right' to bar 'a section of the people from entering the temple if it is a matter of religion'.[155] This is essentially the same argument that the Brāhmaṇas put forth in ***Sri Venkataramana Devaru***, with the caveat that, unlike in ***Venkataramana***, where the Brāhmaṇas excluded *all* non-Brāhmaṇas, the temple functionaries in ***Mahendran*** desired only to exclude *some* members of one segment of the Hindu public.

The Kerala High Court relied on ***Venkataramana Davaru***'s ruling, 'that the right of a denomination to wholly exclude members of the public from worshipping in a temple though comprised in Article 26(b), must yield to the overriding right declared by Article 25(2)(b) in favour of the public to enter into the temple for worship' when assessing the essentiality of the ban on women's worship.[156] The Court consulted the chief *Thanthri* (priest) of the temple – who had consecrated the current deity-image in 1950. He advised that 'only persons who had taken penance and followed the customs are eligible to enter the temple and it is not proper for young women to enter the temple since that is contrary to customs and usages'.[157] Furthermore, when the Ayyappan *himself* was consulted on the matter by astrologers in a series of *devapraśnas* ('divine queries'), the response was that, 'the deity does not like young ladies entering the precincts of the temple'.[158]

While Ayyappan might desire the absence of some, or all women from his temple, the Court's task was to determine if that wish violated the Indian Constitution. The Court noted that, the issue of pubescent women notwithstanding, the Sabarimala temple was notable in that, 'there is no distinction of caste, creed or colour in Sabarimala temple and there had not been any even in olden times… [when] a section of Hindus were forbidden to enter other temples in the State'.[159] The 'vital reason for imposing this restriction on young women', according to the Thanthri, was not a social prejudice against women, but a Dharmaśāstric

[154] Ibid., ¶12. There was also the matter of the Kerala Public Worship (Authorisation of Entry) Act 1965, Act 7/1965. Section 3 of the Act provides that 'every place of public worship which is open to Hindus generally or to any section or class thereof shall be open to all sections and classes of Hindus and no Hindu of whatsoever section or class'.

[155] IR 1993 Ker 42, ¶14.

[156] Ibid., ¶20.

[157] Ibid., ¶31. For discussions concerning the Court's emphasis on the authoritative dicta of the *Thanthri* over and above observed custom, see Das Acevedo, 'Gods' Homes', 563–5, esp. fn 79.

[158] IR 1993 Ker 42, ¶36. For divine queries in India, see Giles Tarabout, 'Religious Uncertainty, Astrology and the Courts in South India', in Daniela Berti, Anthony Good, and Gilles Tarabout (eds), *Of Doubt and Proof: Ritual and Legal Practices of Judgment* (Farnham: Ashgate, 2015): 59–76.

[159] IR 1993 Ker 42, ¶38.

restriction on Ayyappan as a '*brahmācārin*' (a celibate student).[160] On the basis of the essential fact of Ayyappan's celibacy, the court ruled that women, 'after menarche up to menopause are not entitled to enter the temple and offer prayers there at any time of the year'.[161]

The Kerala High Court dismissed the possibility that a ban on women of menstruating age violated the Kerala Public Worship (Authorisation of Entry) Act of 1965 (or, indeed Article 25(2b)), 'since there is no restriction between one section and another section or between one class and another class among the Hindus in the matter of entry to a temple whereas the prohibition is only in respect of women of a particular age group and not women as a class'.[162] Essentially, the Court prioritised the essential practices of the temple – and the will of the deity – over the limited, but not complete, prevention of pubescent women from worshipping at the temple.

The ban remained in place from 1991 until 2018. In 2006, the Indian Young Lawyers Association filed a writ petition under Article 32 of the Constitution, seeking 'to ensure entry of female devotees between the age group of 10 to 50 years to the Lord Ayyappa Temple at Sabarimala'.[163] In 2018, the Supreme Court issued a ruling that struck down the ban on women's entry to Sabarimala, ***Indian Young Lawyers Association v The State of Kerala***. Two key questions before the apex court were: 1) 'whether the exclusionary practice which is based upon a biological factor exclusive to the female gender... violates the very core of Articles 14, 15 and 17... of the Constitution'; and 2) 'whether the practice of excluding such women constitutes an "essential religious practice" under Article 25'.[164] With reference to the second question, the Supreme Court quoted ***Seshammal v State of Tamilnadu*** when describing an essential practice as:

> Those practices that are fundamental to follow a religious belief. It is upon the cornerstone of essential parts or practices the superstructure of religion is built. Without which, a religion will be no religion. Test to determine whether a part or practice is essential to the religion is – to find out whether the nature of religion will be changed without that part or practice. If the taking away of that part or practice could result in a fundamental change in the character of that religion or in its belief, then such part could be treated as an essential or integral part.[165]

[160] Ibid., ¶39.
[161] Ibid., ¶43.
[162] Ibid., ¶44.3.
[163] SC Writ Petition (Civil) No. 373 of 2006 ¶5 (Misra, CJI). For Article 32, see Nirmalendu Bikash Rakshit, 'Right to Constitutional Remedy: Significance of Article 32', *Economic and Political Weekly* 34.34–5 (1999): 2379–81.
[164] SC Writ Petition (Civil) No. 373 of 2006 ¶7.2.
[165] ¶121 (1972) 3 SCR 815.

On the basis of this definition of an 'Essential Practice', Justice Misra concluded that, in

> allowing women to enter into the Sabarimala temple, it cannot be imagined that the nature of Hindu religion would be fundamentally altered or changed in any manner. Therefore, the exclusionary practice… is neither an essential nor an integral part of the Hindu religion without which Hindu religion, of which the devotees of Lord Ayyappa are followers, will not survive.[166]

Consequently, the Court struck down the custom of prohibiting women aged ten to fifty from worshipping at Sabarimala – although the enforcement of that ruling has been notoriously difficult.[167]

In short, the Supreme Court's essential practices jurisprudence involves balancing a respect for the unique customs, beliefs, and practices of India's rich and diverse array of religious communities while simultaneously promoting the progressive freedoms from discrimination enshrined in the Constitution. Most of the foundational cases discussed above involved the Supreme Court reining in the High Court's prioritisation of custom over equality. The Supreme Court did so by deeming discriminatory customs as 'non-essential' to the practice of the religion under scrutiny. In many ways, the High Courts' opinions were closer to those of the old Anglo-Hindu law than the Supreme Court's opinions. The High Courts, like the old colonial courts, took a more conservative view of temple custom: declining, generally, to overturn established conventional Dharmas and respecting the limited *sui iuris* capacity of said communities. In the Supreme Court's jurisprudence, however, the Court plays an active role in interrogating their beliefs and practices, and separating their 'superstitious' and discriminatory elements from their acceptable ones.[168]

In fact, as Justice Nariman notes in his concurring opinion in ***Indian Young Lawyers Association***, the Essential Practices Test greatly expanded from its initial application to *financial* elements, to its increasingly rigorous application to reforming religious practice:

> Prior to ***Devaru***, this Court used the word 'essential' to distinguish between religious and secular practices in order to circumscribe the extent of state intervention in religious matters. The shift in judicial approach took place when 'essentially religious' (as distinct from the secular) became conflated with 'essential to religion.' The

[166] Ibid., ¶123 (Misra, CJI).

[167] See, for example, Das Acevedo, 'Pause', 15: 'In the aftermath of the IYLA verdict, Kerala has experienced massive protests, incendiary statements by public figures, and gangs of (often female) devotees stopping pilgrims en route to Sabarimala in order to ensure that none of them are women in the prohibited age range.' For an ideological criticism of the decision based on discourse analysis, see Rashmi Kumari, 'Menstruating Women and Celibate Gods: A Discourse Analysis of Women's Entry into Sabarimala Temple in Kerala, India', in Nazia Hussein and Saba Hussain (eds), *Decolonising Gender in South Asia* (London: Routledge, 2021): 80–97.

[168] For the Supreme Court's use of the essential practices test to remove 'superstitious' beliefs and practices from constitutional protection, see ***The Durgah Committee, Ajmer v Syed Hussain Ali And Others*** (1961) AIR 1402, 1962 SCR (1) 383.

> Court's enquiry into the essentiality of the practice in question represented a shift in the test, which now enjoined upon the Court the duty to decide which religious practices would be afforded constitutional protection, based on the determination of what constitutes an essential religious practice.[169]

Justice Nariman's observations help to explain why many contemporary scholars take a critical view of the Supreme Court's jurisprudence on the freedom of religion. The Essential Practices Test, which requires the Court to inquire into a community's tenets *according the tradition in question*, has also become a mechanism for altering those beliefs. In fact, as of 2023, the Supreme Court is reviewing its decision in the 2018 ***Young Lawyers*** judgment and 'the outcome may lay down a path for the Courts to reconcile the essential religious practice test with constitutional principles'.[170]

5.2.3 The juristic personality of Hindu deities and Articles 25 and 26 of the Indian Constitution

The Supreme Court's jurisprudence on *parens patriae* jurisdiction and on the inviolability of custom and usage tended to restrict the conservative principles of Anglo-Hindu law in favour of progressive constitutional principles.[171] The Supreme Court's jurisprudence concerning the juristic personality of deities, however, trends towards a significantly more capacious view of *what phenomena* can be granted personhood and *who* has an interest in these deities' welfare. The jurisprudential development is the expansion of deities' 'figurative personhood' into being an expression of devotees' pious, constitutionally protected right to worship a particular deity. While the circularity of this view of the juristic personality of Hindu deities – as the compendious expression of devotees' desire to worship the deity – is notable, it also elegantly ties together the Anglo-Hindu jurisprudence of Hindu deities (as essentially purpose trusts) with the principles of the Constitution of India.

As the Supreme Court developed its jurisprudence of Hindu deities in a constitutional framework, it relied heavily on Raghunandana Bhaṭṭācārya's maxim that, 'it is for the sake of rites of the worshippers that the (para)brahman, which is made of consciousness, which cannot be measured, which is

[169] SC Writ Petition (Civil) No. 373 of 2006 ¶32 (Nariman, J).

[170] RP (C) 3358/2018, www.scobserver.in/cases/kantaru-rajeevaru-indian-young-lawyers-association-sabrimala-review-background/. Note that the delay in hearing the review petition can be attributed to the case being bundled with several other freedom of religion cases, including ***Goolrokh Gupta v Burjor Pardiwala*** (Parsi excommunication), ***Yasmeen Zuber Ahmad Peerzade v Union of India*** (women's entry in mosques), and ***Sunita Tiwari v Union of India*** (female circumcision among the Dawoodi Bohra community).

[171] See Chapter 5, §5.2.1, 'The State, the Crown, and Hindu religious endowments' and §5.2.2, 'Essential practices, custom, and equity'.

imperishable, and which has no body, is postulated to have form (in an image)'.[172] If, as the court interpreted this maxim, Hindu deities are ascribed personality for the benefit of their devotees, then an almost infinite array of phenomena – not just temple images – could be afforded legal personality by the courts. Many of the cases reviewed in this section test the limits of what, precisely, can and cannot be recognised as a juridical person, including, temple images, Sikh sacred texts, mosques, 'self-manifesting' (*svayambhu*) images, rocks, pillars of ice, trees, and even rivers. In ***M. Siddiq v Suresh Das***, the disputed land itself appeared as a plaintiff: Rām Asthan Janmabhūmi (the deification of the contested site).

In 1953, the Supreme Court heard ***Sree Sree Ishwar Sridhar Jew v Sushila Bala Dasi And Others,*** and reaffirmed the Privy Council's ruling in ***Surendrakrishna Ray v Shree Shree Ishwar Bhubaneshwari Thakurani*** that a *shebait* cannot claim adverse possession against the very deity that they serve.[173] This case largely restated the law regarding *shebaitship* before 1950, and the Court's 1956 decision in ***Deoki Nandan v Murlidhar*** largely restated the Anglo-Hindu view of deities' personality as the compendious expression of a religious purpose.[174] The latter case involved Sheo Ghulam, a pious Hindu who built, endowed, and managed a temple to Śrī Rādhakṛṣṇajī, and died without issue. His widow, and then a distant agnatic kinsman took over control of the temple, prohibited public entry, and claimed that it was a private temple purely for the benefit of Ghulam's family.[175] The Court quotes the *Śābarabhāṣya* and ***Bhupati Nath Smritirtha v Ram Lal Maitra*** with approval and explains that: 'The Gods... can be described as their owners only in a figurative sense (*Gaunartha*), and the true purpose of a gift of properties to the idol is to... acquire spiritual benefit by providing opportunities and facilities for those who desire to worship.'[176]

The case was mostly factual: on account of the evidence presented, the court ruled that the temple was public and that the appellant had a right to worship at it. The ***Deoki Nandan*** judgment's emphasis on benefit as a determining factor in understanding deities, however, anticipates the general direction of travel for subsequent rulings, such as ***The Poohari Fakir Sadavarthy v The Commissioner, Hindu Religious Endowments, Madras***. In this case, the Court ruled that: 'A religious institution will be a temple if two conditions are satisfied. One is that it is a place of public religious worship and the other is that it is dedicated to or is for the

[172] See Note 5.
[173] (1933) AIR Cal 295 and AIR 1933 Cal 295.
[174] (1957) AIR 133, 1956 SCR 756.
[175] Ibid.
[176] (1910) ILR 37 Cal 128. For the Sanskrit principles, see Chapter 1, §1.6.2.ii, 'Divine endowments in Mīmāṃsā and Vedānta'. For the legal personality of Hindu deities in Anglo-Hindu law, see Chapter 4, §4.2.3.i, 'The legal personality of Hindu deities'.

benefit of, or is used as of right by the Hindu Community, or any section thereof, as a place of religious worship.'[177]

The concept of the Hindu community as the beneficiary of public religious endowments played a crucial role in the Supreme Court's decision in ***Bishwanath v Sri Thakur Radha Ballabhji***, quoted at the beginning of this chapter.[178] In ***Bishwanath***, the Court justified the intervention of a 'next friend' filing suit in the name of the deity for the recovery of *debutter* properties that had been illegally alienated by the *shebait* on the basis that: 'Worshippers of an idol are its beneficiaries, though only in a spiritual sense. It has also been held that persons who go in only for the purpose of devotion have, according to Hindu law and religion, a greater and deeper interest in temples than mere servants who serve there for some pecuniary advantage.'[179]

We find very similar language, evocative of Raghunandana Bhaṭṭācārya's maxim, in ***Yogendra Nath Naskar v Commissioner of Income-Tax***, a landmark tax case from 1969, in which the Court observed a:

> distinction between the spiritual and the legal aspect of the Hindu idol which is installed and worshipped. From the spiritual standpoint the idol may be to the worshipper a symbol (*pratika*) of the Supreme Godhead intended to invoke a sense of the vast and infinite reality, and suggesting the essential truth of the Real that is beyond all name or form… [and] the Hindu worshipper purports to worship the Supreme Spirit and nothing else [emphasis added].[180]

The thrust of the Court's decision in ***Yogendra Nath***, was however, limited to ruling that:

> The deity stands as the… symbol of the particular purpose which is indicated by the donor… [and] the true legal view is that in that capacity alone the dedicated property vests in it. There is no principle why a deity as such a legal person should not be taxed if such a legal person is allowed in law to own property even though in the ideal sense.[181]

Slowly, but surely, the Supreme Court associated the conception of the deity as the worshipper's pious intention with Article 25 of the Constitution, particularly when querying the range of phenomena that could be recognised as temples or deities on the basis of being treated as such by Hindu worshippers whose rights to do so are constitutionally protected. The standard authority for this proposition

[177] (1963) AIR SC 510, 1962 Supp (2) SCR 276. Quoting, with approval in, ***T.R.K. Ramaswami Servai And Anr. v The Board of Commissioners*** AIR 1951 Mad 473, (1950) 2 MLJ 511. This authority was followed by Andhra High Court in ***Marrepu Venkata Ramana Murthi v The Deity of Sri Rama Mandiram*** (1966) AIR AP 197.

[178] (1967) AIR 1044, 1967 SCR (2) 618.

[179] Ibid., citing ***Kalyana Venkataramana Ayyangar v Kasturi Ranga Ayyangar*** (1917) AIR Mad 112, with approval.

[180] 1969 AIR 1089, 1969 SCR (3) 742 [Ramaswami, J].

[181] Ibid.

is ***Ram Jankijee Deities & Ors v State of Bihar and Ors*** (1999).[182] The case turned on whether a deity that had had not been consecrated 'according to the Shastras' would, nevertheless, be recognised as a legal person. The High Court of Patna had ruled that:

> The image of the deity is to be found in *Shastras*. `Raja Rani' [one of the plaintiff deities] is not known to *Shastras*. It is unknown in [the] Hindu Pantheon. It is a particular image which is a juristic person. Idol is again an image of the deity. There cannot be a dedication to any name or image not recognised by the *Shastras*. Here, in the present case, the petitioners assert that the dedication is to both the deities `Raja Rani' but none of these have been recognised by the *Shastras*.[183]

The Supreme Court found that this was, 'a total misappreciation of the principles of Hindu law'.[184] Drawing on Mukherjea's *Hindu Law of Religious and Charitable Trusts*, the maxims of Raghunandana, and a bevy of case law, the Court concluded that, 'if the people believe in the temples' religious efficacy no other requirement exists as regards other areas… [and] it is not a particular image which is a juridical person but it is a particular bent of mind which consecrate the image'.[185] The Court repeatedly invokes variations on a theme of Raghunandana's maxim, such as: 'God is Omnipotent and Omniscient and its presence is felt not by reason of a particular form or image but by reason of the presence of the omnipotent: It is formless, it is shapeless and it is for the benefit of the worshippers that there is manifestation in images of the Supreme Being'; or; 'as noticed above, it [divinity] is formless, shapeless but it is the human concept of a particular divine existence which gives it the shape, the size and the colour'.[186] Furthermore, Justice Banerjee noted that:

> To constitute a temple, it is enough if it is a place of public religious worship and if the people believe in its religious efficacy irrespective of the fact whether there is an idol or a structure or other paraphernalia. It is enough if the devotees or the pilgrims feel that there is some super human power which they should worship and invoke its blessings.[187]

In using these maxims to overturn the High Court's ruling and to recognise the juridical personality of an extra-śāstric deity, the court firmly decided that the

[182] (1999) 5 SCC 50.
[183] Ibid., ¶10 [Banerjee, J].
[184] Ibid. [Banerjee, J].
[185] Ibid., citing, ***Shri Lakshmi Narain and others v State of Bihar and others*** (1978) BBCJ 489; ***Pramatha Nath Mullick v Pradyumna Kumar Mullick & Anr*** (1925) LR 52 IA 245; ***Rambrahma Chatterjee v Kedar Nath Banerjee*** (1922) (36) CLJ 478/483; ***Addangi Nageswara Rao v Sri Ankamma Devatha Temple*** (1973) 1 AWR 379; ***T.R.K. Ramaswami Sarvai and another v The Board of Commissioner*** ILR (1950) Madras 799; and ***Venkataramana Murthi v Sri Rama Mandhiram*** (1964) (2) An. WR 457.
[186] (1999) 5 SCC 50.
[187] Ibid.

authority for determining *what* constitutes a deity lies with the *belief and faith* of worshippers, rather than with external textual sources.

The authority of faith and belief in matters of legal personality played a central role in the Court's reasoning in ***Shiromani Gurdwara Prabandhak Committee, Amritsar v Som Nath Dass*** (2000).[188] In this case, the Court was tasked with determining if the sacred Sikh scripture, the *Guru Granth Sahib*, which is enshrined in Sikh Gurdwaras, was a 'living Guru.' As in ***Ram Jankijee***, the Court focused on the principle that, 'faith and belief cannot be judged through any judicial scrutiny', and ruled that 'this faith necessitated the creation of a unit to be recognised as a Juristic Person.'[189] The court accepted, on the principles of faith and belief (protected under Article 25 of the Constitution), that 'a Juristic Person is not roped in any defined circle.... [and] with the changing thoughts, changing needs of the society, fresh juristic personalities were created from time to time.' Consequently, the Court recognised that the Guru Granth Sahib can be afforded legal personality, but this raises the question of how far this logic can be taken.[190]

Shortly before the Supreme Court took a clear stance on the limits of faith as the basis of legal personality in ***M. Siddiq v Suresh Das***, the Uttarakhand High Court issued two rulings that afforded legal personality to the Gaṅgā and Yamunā rivers and to several glaciers, respectively: ***Mohd. Salim v State of Uttarakhand & Others*** and ***Lalit Miglani v State of Uttarakhand and Others***.[191] In ***Mohd. Salim***, the Uttarakhand High Court cited ***Yogendra Nath***, ***Ram Jankijee*** and ***Shiromani Gurdwara*** (along with other earlier cases) in support of the contention that: 'God is Omnipotent and Omniscient and its presence is felt not by reason of a particular form or image but by reason of the presence of the omnipotent: It is formless, it is shapeless and it is for the benefit of the worshippers that there is manifestation in images of the Supreme Being.'[192] While this observation is undoubtedly true as a

[188] (2000) 4 SCC 146. For the Sikh tradition of recognizing the Guru Granth Sahib as a 'living guru' and legal person, see Kristina Myrvold, 'Making the Scripture a Person: Reinventing Death Rituals of Guru Granth Sahib in Sikhism', in Kristina Myrvold (ed.), *The Death of Sacred Texts: Ritual Disposal and Renovation of Texts in World Religions* (London: Routledge, 2010): 135–56.

[189] (2000) 4 SCC 146 [Misra, J].

[190] Ibid.

[191] WPPIL 126/2014 (High Court of Uttarakhand) 2017 [19] and WPPIL 140/2015 (High Court of Uttarakhand) 2017 64. The cases have received significant scholarly attention. See, for example, Stellina Jolly and K.S. Roshan Menon, 'Of Ebbs and Flows: Understanding the Legal Consequences of Granting Personhood to Natural Entities in India', *Transnational Environmental Law* 10.3 (2021): 467–92; Julia Talbot-Jones and Jeff Bennett, 'Toward a Property Rights Theory of Legal Rights for Rivers', *Ecological Economics* 164 (2019): 1–6; Erin O'Donnell, 'At the Intersection of the Sacred and the Legal: Rights for Nature in Uttarakhand, India', *Journal of Environmental Law* 30 (2018): 135–44; Erin O'Donnell, 'Rivers as Living Beings: Rights in Law, but no Right in Water?' *Griffith Law Review* 29.4 (2020): 643–68; Erin O'Donnell and Julia Talbot-Jones, 'Creating Legal Rights for Rivers: Lessons from Australia, New Zealand, and India', *Ecology and Society* 23.1 (2018); and Kelly Alley, 'Spiritual Ecology' *Religions* 10.9 (2019): 1–17.

[192] WPPIL 126/2014 (High Court of Uttarakhand) 2017 19, ¶13 [Sharma, J].

statement of law and belief, its application to the rivers Gaṅgā and Yamunā is on far more tenuous ground. The Court ruled that:

> All the Hindus have deep Astha [faith] in rivers Ganga and Yamuna and they collectively connect with these rivers. Rivers Ganga and Yamuna are central to the existence of half of Indian population and their health and well being. The rivers have provided both physical and spiritual sustenance to all of us from time immemorial. Rivers Ganga and Yamuna have spiritual and physical sustenance. They support and assist both the life and natural resources and health and well-being of the entire community. Rivers Ganga and Yamuna are breathing, living and sustaining the communities from mountains to sea.[193]

Justice Sharma does not seem to query whether the Hindu population, its reverence for the rivers notwithstanding, *actually* treat the rivers as juridical persons. He invokes the Court's *parens patriae* jurisdiction to declare 'the Director NAMAMI Gange [a public interest group], the Chief Secretary of the State of Uttarakhand and the Advocate General of the State of Uttarakhand' to be *persons in loco parentis* (in the legal place of a parent), who 'are bound to uphold the status of Rivers Ganges and Yamuna and also to promote the health and well-being of these rivers'.[194] While the decision is very much founded on the core principles of the jurisprudence of Hindu religious and charitable trusts, it also clearly extends them beyond any standard taken in Indian case law.

The Supreme Court used faith and belief as a criterion to determine the existence of a temple of a Hindu deity as a juridical person. In ***Ram Jankijee***, ***Shiromani Gurdwara*** and similar cases, this logic was used to justify the application of Hindu trusts law to case where clear patterns of worship did not *quite* meet Sanskrit textual standards. The Uttarakhand High Court, however (followed by a 2022 case from the Madras High Court affording juridical personality to 'Mother Nature'), uses this practical, constitutional workaround for cases involving unusual temples, and expands it dramatically to include phenomena that have never been treated as legal persons under Hindu law. At the time of publishing this monograph, appeals from these two judgments are currently awaiting hearing in the Supreme Court, which stayed them soon after their issuance in 2018. I strongly suspect that the Supreme Court will overturn the High Court's verdicts.[195] We shall see later that in the Ayodhyā dispute, the Supreme Court took a dim view of

[193] Ibid., ¶17 [Sharma, J].

[194] Ibid., ¶19 [Sharma, J].

[195] ***A. Periyakaruppan v The Principal Secretary to Government, and Others*** WP (MD) Nos. 18636 of 2013 and 3070 of 2020 and WMP (MD) No.2614 of 2020. Note that Justice Srimathy at ¶21–3 cites ***Mohd. Salim*** approvingly on the question of *parens patriae*, but makes essentially a *biological* rather than a *theological* argument for affording natural personality to 'Mother Nature': www.livelaw.in/pdf_upload/mother-nature-416320.pdf. For a critical review of the Uttarakhand High Court's judgments, see Palash Srivastav, 'Legal Personality of Ganga and Ecocentrism: Critical Review', *Cambridge Law Review* 4.1 (2019): 151–68.

using Hindu faith and belief to create novel types of legal persons that frustrate the normal operation of the law.

5.2.4 Property, tax, and adverse possession, in the modern Hindu law of religious and charitable trusts

Before turning to the 2019 Supreme Court verdict in the Ayodhyā case, I want to explore the final facet of the Supreme Court's jurisprudential toolbox: the understanding of *debutter* and *shebaitship* as property rights within the wider context of Indian civil law. While Anglo-Hindu law took the view that *shebaitship* constituted a form of *proprietary* right (if not always 'property'), post-colonial law tended to view *shebaitship* in more strongly proprietary terms.[196] In asserting the proprietary aspect of *shebaits*' interests in religious endowments – often for the purposes of facilitating tax liability – the Supreme Court also opened up religious endowments to a greater liability for civil legal issues such as limitation and adverse possession. The more *shebaitship* is treated as property for the purposes of tax, the more it can be treated as property under civil law. This aspect of the jurisprudence of Hindu religious endowments was an important point of contention in the Ayodhya dispute.

When Justice Mukherjea penned the majority opinion in ***Angurbala Mullick v Debabrata Mullick*** in 1951, he explored the proprietary aspect of *shebaitship* (and *Mahantship*) in detail.[197] The case turned, in part, on whether *shebaitship* could be classified as 'property' for the purposes of the Hindu Women's Right to Property Act of 1936. Justice Mukherjea, drawing on previous rulings of the Judicial Committee of the Privy Council, noted that:

> The exact legal position of a *shebait* may not be capable of precise definition but its implications are fairly well established... But though a *shebait* is a manager and not a trustee in the technical sense, it would not he correct to describe the *shebaitship* as a mere office. The *shebait* has not only duties to discharge in connection with the endowment, but he has a beneficial interest in the *debutter* property.[198]

Justice Mukherjea's emphasis on the *shebait's* 'beneficial interest in the *debutter* property' enabled him to conclude that, the 'hereditary *shebait* of a private *debutter*', especially when the *shebaiti* right comes with significant emoluments, 'is a recognized form of property in Hindu Law'.[199]

[196] For the taxation of deities and the construal of *shebaitship* as property, see J. Duncan Derrett, 'The Liability of Deities to Pay Taxes', *The Bombay Law Reporter* 71 (1969): 38–45; and Kartick Maheshwari and Vishnu Vardhan Shankar, 'Stone Gods and Earthly Interests: The Jural Relations and Consequence of Attributing Legal Personality to Hindu Idols', *Student Bar Review* 16 (2004): 46–67, 56–67.

[197] (1951) AIR SC 293, 1951 2 SCR 1125.

[198] Ibid., ¶13 [Mukherjea, J], citing ***Vidya Varuti v Balusami*** [48 I.A. 302].

[199] (1951) AIR SC 293, 1951 2 SCR 1125, ¶22 [Mukherjea, J], citing ***Umayal Achi v Lakshmi Achi*** (1945) FCR 1 on secular trust 'property beneficially owned by the propositus'.

The theory of *shebaitship* as property in ***Angurbala Mullick*** was applied to protect a widow's *shebaiti* rights. The principle was quickly extended to property law and taxation. In ***Kalipada Chakraborti and Another v Palani Bala Devi and Others***, Justice Mukherjea examined the implications of his judgment in ***Angurbala Mullick*** within the context of limitation.[200] The case involved the heirs to a widow. The widow had alienated her *shebaiti* rights to a third party illegally. The third party in turn, claimed that the heirs were barred by limitation. The questions before the Supreme Court were: 1) are *shebaiti* rights 'property' for the purposes of limitation; and 2) if so, what class of property are they (again for the purposes of limitation). Justice Mukherjea reasoned that, '*shebaitship*, as is now well settled, combines in it both the elements of office and property… [and] the *shebaiti* interest is heritable and follows the line of inheritance from the founder'.[201] That being the case, however, '*shebaitship* is property of a peculiar and anomalous character, and it is difficult to say that it comes under the category of immovable property [and] it is quite settled that a *shebaiti* right is a hereditary office'.[202]

Mukherjea is effectively tracing the course of Anglo-Hindu law, but with greater legal precision. Two subsequent cases, ***Rai Sahib Dr Gurdittamal Kapur v Mahant Amar Das Chela Mahant Ram Saran*** and ***Sarangadeva Periya Matam v Ramaswami Goundar(Dead) by Legal Representatives***, further established the doctrine that, as property, *mahantship*, *shebaitiship*, *debutter*, and other endowed assets can be acquired and lost according to adverse possession.[203] In ***Sarangadeva Periya Matam***, the Court observed that:

> Like an idol, the math is a juristic person having the power of acquiring, owning and possessing properties and having the capacity of suing and being sued. Being an ideal person, it must of necessity act in relation to its temporal affairs through human agency… It may acquire property by prescription and may likewise lose property by adverse possession. The running of limitation against the math under Article 144 is not suspended by the absence of a legally appointed *mathadhipathi*; clearly, limitation would run against it where it is managed by a de facto *mathadhipathi*. and we think it would run equally if there is neither a de jure nor a de facto *mathadhipathi*.

As *shebaitship* and *mahantship* came to be seen as property rights, *debutter* became increasingly subject to being acquired and lost through purchase, sale, and adverse possession. The result of this process, besides ensuring that claims of divine ownership could not be used to escape the operation of property law, was to lead deities and their *shebaits* towards tax liability. Generally, Hindu religious and charitable trusts have been tax exempt since time immemorial.[204] Under the

200 (1953) AIR 125, 1953 SCR 503.
201 Ibid. [Mukherjea, J].
202 Ibid.
203 (1965) AIR SC 1966 and (1966) AIR SC 1603.
204 Maheshwari and Shankar, 'Stone Gods', 56–7.

unamended Income Tax Act of 1922, deities were exempt from assessment, and this, of course created 'an avenue for tax avoidance'.[205] The Indian Income Tax Act of 1961, however, 'did away with this liberal attitude' and 'broadly provided that exemptions would be given only up to twenty-five percent of the trust's properties'.[206] Furthermore, the Act eliminated all tax concessions for private religious trusts and for public religious trusts that directly benefited the founder or their family.[207]

As expected, the elimination of tax-exempt status led to a flurry of cases involving the question of deities' and *shebaits*' respective tax burden. The most famous of the these cases, ***Yogendra Nath Naskar v Commissioner of Income-Tax***, established the dominant legal paradigm that is still in place today.[208] The Court noted that, in a *spiritual sense*, the deity-image represents the Almighty (certainly not liable to taxation), but, 'so far as the deity stands as the… symbol of the… purpose… indicated by the donor, it can figure as a legal person… [and] the dedicated property vests in it'.[209] Although classical Sanskrit jurisprudence unequivocally exempts religious endowments from assessment for tax, the Court ruled that:

> There is no principle why a deity as such a legal person should not be taxed if such a legal person is allowed in law to own property even though in the ideal sense and to sue for the property, to realise rent and to defend such property in a court of law again in the ideal sense. Our conclusion is that the Hindu idol is a juristic entity capable of holding property and of being taxed through its *shebaits* who are entrusted with the possession and management of its property.[210]

The straightforwardness of this position probably accounts for the relative stability of tax-jurisprudence for Hindu trusts in contemporary India. For example, the fifth edition of Mukherjea's *Hindu Law of Religious and Charitable Trusts*' chapter on taxation (Chapter 10), largely reviews the relevant statutes and case law before 1969.[211] One notable case, however, ***Commissioner of Income Tax v Jagannath Jew***, established the notable principle that, when 'a substantial amount of the income of an absolute *debutter* in favor of the family deity is spent on objects of general public utility, the amount so spent is to be exempted from taxation'.[212]

Nevertheless, generally, the post-independent State has generally been keen to tax endowments, 'even at the expense of reducing the corpus available to the

[205] Ibid., 57.
[206] Ibid., 58; S.11 & S. 12, Income Tax Act, 1961.
[207] Maheshwari and Shankar, 'Stone Gods', 58; S.13, Income Tax Act, 1961.
[208] (1969) AIR 1089, 1969 SCR (3) 742.
[209] Ibid. [Ramaswami, J].
[210] Ibid. [Ramaswami, J].
[211] Mukherjea, *Hindu Law*, 468–95. The paucity of cases may also be explained by the great success of the Indian Income Tax Appellate Tribunal, which handles tax-related appeal. See R.P. Garg and Beenu Yadav, *Income Tax Appellate Tribunal (ITAT): Practice and Procedure* (New Delhi: Taxmann Publications, 2014).
[212] Mukherjea, *Hindu Law*, 493–4; (1977) AIR SC 1523.

Idol to a nullity (thereby adversely affecting the spiritual and material interests of the worshippers)'.[213] In short, the shift towards a recognition of the *shebait*'s proprietary right in *debutter* assets also led to increased taxation for the deity and a greater liability for the operation of civil law – involving limitation and adverse possession. Divine property became property in the post-Independence legal regime – freed from its pre-Independence legal immunities.

5.2.5 Inventory of the Supreme Court's jurisprudential toolbox

The Supreme Court of India inherited a vast body of case law from colonial India. That body of case law, discussed at length in Chapter 4, articulated several core features of the jurisprudence of Hindu religious and charitable trusts: 1) the right and duty of the Crown, as *parens patriae*, to protect and oversee endowments, especially in instances of breach of trust by the deities' fiduciaries; 2) the analogous relationship between deities and minors with reference to their guardians; and 3) the view of deities' personality as the compendious expression of the pious intentions of donors. The task for the Supreme Court, however, was to interpret new cases within both this body of case law and within the principles and processes enshrined in the new Constitution of India.

By all accounts, this was a highly successful process, but one that involved significant reconfigurations of the Anglo-Hindu law of Hindu religious and charitable trusts. First, the Supreme Court reined in the High Court's efforts to assert control over religious endowments through the exercise of *parens patriae* jurisdiction. Although many states passed statutory regulations concerning Hindu endowments, and although many High Courts justified this supervision on the basis of the Republic of India's assumption of the sovereign prerogatives of the British Crown (in India) and of sundry princely states, the Supreme Court took the view that all such feudal holdovers had been abolished with the implementation of the Constitution.

Second, even as the Supreme Court negatived the feudal justification for state supervision of endowments, it provided an alternative justification for these interventions. That justification, the Essential Practices Test, was born from the Supreme Court's understanding of Articles 25 and 26 of the Constitution, granting a mixture of autonomy for religious communities on *essential* matters and a judicial jurisdiction over secular and non-essential matters. Despite its averment that the determination of essentiality lies in the tenets of the community in question, the arbiter of those tenets lies with the courts. While post-colonial courts, like their colonial and pre-colonial predecessors, claim to uphold the customs and usages of Hindu religious institutions – following the old Dharmaśāstric

[213] Maheshwari and Shankar, 'Stone Gods', 61–2.

model of Equity as the supplemental laws of *sui iuris* communities – the court has also retained a substantial right to *interpret* what those conventional laws are. In essence, the Supreme Court carved out a new, constitutional justification for the right of supervision and interference that was enjoyed by Dharmaśāstric sovereigns, the Mughals, and the British. Now, the State and its agents expresses the concept of sovereignty in Constitutional, rather than feudal terms.

Third, the Supreme Court greatly expanded the concept of Hindu deities as the juridical personification of the pious purpose of a donor's intention. While Anglo-Hindu law viewed deities as the compendious expression of the donors' intent, the Supreme Court took the view that worship and belief by Hindus is sufficient to confer legal personality on the object of worship (within limits). While this was a reasonable, well-intentioned way of ensuring that the worshippers of non-traditional temples and phenomena had their constitutional rights to worship protected by the courts, it nevertheless opened up the possibility for Hindus to claim potentially legally vexing phenomena, such as rivers and land, as legal persons (more on that in the next section). This ever-closer association of deities with constitutional rights led advocates for Appayyan in ***Indian Young Lawyers Association v State of Kerala*** to introduce the 'breathtakingly circular... spectacle of a deity claiming a constitutional right to religious freedom'.[214]

Fourth, as post-colonial law increasingly viewed *shebaiti* rights as property rights, deities' assets became increasingly tied up in the mundane constraints of tax, transaction, and legal liability to adverse possession. Claims to immunity from adverse possession, from taxation, and from other civil processes were increasingly eroded – often to the detriment of the deity. Nevertheless, the effect of making deities' property more or less the same as any other types of property has probably decreased opportunities for financial mischief.

A greater appreciation for the evolution of the Hindu law of religious and charitable trusts and its jurisprudence in the Republic of India is a valuable contribution in its own right and helps us to appreciate that the Supreme Court has retained many core features of Anglo-Hindu jurisprudence while bringing them into harmony with the provisions of the Constitution. Furthermore, we shall see in the following section of this chapter that the core principles of the constitutional jurisprudence of divine endowments discussed earlier played a central role in the Supreme Court's judgment in the Ayodhyā dispute. In many ways, the verdict in ***M. Siddiq v Suresh Das*** is *the* most comprehensive and authoritative account of the contemporary jurisprudence of divine endowments. The Court employs its

[214] Das Acevedo, 'Pause', 15: 'Specifically, People for Dharma asserted in their writ petition that "[t]he Deity as the Owner of His Abode enjoys the right to privacy under Article 21, which includes the right to preserve His celibate form ... Finally the Deity has the right to follow His Dharma, like any other person under Article 25(1)." '

entire toolbox in ***M. Siddiq v Suresh Das***, and so it is vital to have gained familiarity with those tools before delving into the judgment in depth.

5.3 The Supreme Court's toolbox in the Ayodhyā dispute

This chapter now returns to the Ayodhyā dispute, which, when we left it in 1989, involved five different pending suits. On 9 November 2019, a constitutional bench of the Supreme Court of India delivered a unanimous, 1,045-page verdict in ***M. Siddiq v Suresh Das***, a series of appeals of a 2010 judgment from the Allahabad High Court, in the case of ***Gopal Singh Visharad and Ors v Zahoor Ahmad and Ors.***[215] The case concerned:

> A dispute between two religious communities... over a piece of land admeasuring 1500 square yards in the town of Ayodhya. The disputed property is of immense significance to Hindus and Muslims. The Hindu community claims it as the birthplace of Lord Ram, an incarnation of Lord Vishnu. The Muslim community claim it as the site of the historic Babri Masjid built by the first Mughal Emperor, Babur... [which] existed at the site until 6 December 1992.... the Hindus refer to the disputed site as Ram Janmabhumi or Ram. The Hindus assert that there existed at the disputed site an ancient temple dedicated to Lord Ram, which was demolished... by Mughal Emperor Babur... Though the significance of the site for the Hindus is not denied, it is the case of the Muslims that there exists no proprietary claim of the Hindus over the disputed property.[216]

The Supreme Court overturned the 2010 Allahabad High Court's verdict and awarded the ownership of the site to a divine litigant: Rām Virajman, the infant form of Rāma, the tutelary deity of the Rām Janmabhūmi. The Court ordered the Central Government to establish a trust to take possession of Rām's property (from government receivership), and to construct a temple dedicated to (and owned by) the juridical person, Rām Virajman.[217]

The Supreme Court recognised that 'the Muslims were dispossessed upon the desecration of the mosque on 22/23 December 1949 which was ultimately destroyed on 6 December 1992... through means which should not have been employed in a secular nation committed to the rule of law'.[218] Consequently, the Court employed its equitable jurisdiction under Article 142 of the Indian Constitution 'to provide

[215] ***Visharad v Ahmad***, OOS, No. 1 of 1989, All. HC, 4 (2010) – hereafter 'AHC'. ***M. Siddiq v Suresh Das***, 1 SCC 1 (2020) – hereafter 'SC'.

[216] SC ¶1–3, pp. 6–7.

[217] Ibid., ¶805, pp. 925–6. The Shri Ram Janmabhoomi Teerth Kshetra, was formed on 5 February 2020, and controls approximately seventy acres in Ayodhya. Kesava Parasaran, the lead advocate for Rām Virajman was appointed as the first chairman. On 5 August 2020, Narendra Modi laid the cornerstone of the Rām Janmabhumi Mandir.

[218] Ibid., ¶800, pp. 922–3.

restitution to the Muslim community for the unlawful destruction of their place of worship…' namely, that '5 acres be allotted to the Sunni Central Waqf Board either by the Central Government out of the acquired land or by the Government of Uttar Pradesh within the city of Ayodhya'.[219] The Supreme Court's verdict brought closure to an inter-communal dispute that, directly or indirectly, led to thousands of deaths, but it also attracted significant controversy.[220] The 2011 judgment of the Allahabad High Court and the 2019 judgment of the Supreme Court have received significant scholarly attention, particularly in relation to the suit of Rām Virajman.[221]

This section unpacks the Supreme Court of India's reasoning in the Ayodhyā verdict and situates this logic within the wider history of equity and trusts in Sanskrit jurisprudence that I have charted in this monograph. Specifically, I examine how the Supreme Court reined in some of the jurisprudential extensions of the Allahabad High Court – particularly in relation to Hindu jurisprudence – by appealing to the constitutional jurisprudence of the Hindu law of religious and charitable trusts that I outlined in the previous section of this chapter. The Allahabad and Supreme Courts' verdicts share a deep interest in four specific topics of contention: 1) the juristic personality of the two plaintiff deities, Rām Virajman and Asthan Rām Janmabhūmi; 2) the right of suit by either the worshippers of Ram, the Nirmohi Akhara, or Deoki Nandan Agarwal as 'next friend'; 3) the applicability of limitation or adverse possession to the plaintiff deities or their legal representatives; and 4) the role of the State as the guardian of the deities, custodian of the contested site, and legal heir to the British Raj.

Much of the debate between the Allahabad High Court and the Supreme Court involves the question of if and how certain Dharmaśāstric passages can or ought to trump established judicial precedent or civil procedure concerning Hindu endowments. Article 25 protects the freedom to worship, and Article

[219] Ibid., ¶801, p. 923. Also see ¶653–76, pp. 771–90, where the Court recounts 'Justice Equity and Good Conscience' as a juridical paradigm in India (from Regulation 60 of Warren Hastings' 1781 *Regulations for the Administration of Justice* to Article 142(1) of Constitution). The Court relies on Derrett, 'Justice, Equity'.

[220] See, for example, Friedland and Hecht, 'The Bodies of Nations'; and Sheetal Parikh, 'Enshrining a Secular Idol: A Judicial Response to the Violent Aftermath of Ayodhya', *Case Western Reserve Journal of International Law* 37.85 (2005): 85–109.

[221] For a comprehensive summary of the Allahabad verdict, see Aparna Chandra, 'Gopal Singh Visharad and Ors v. Zahoor Ahmad and Ors., O.S.Nos. 1/1989, 3/1989, 4/1989, 5/1989: A Summary of the Babri Masjid-Ram Janm Bhoomi Decision', 11 October 2010, https://ssrn.com/abstract=1690803 or http://dx.doi.org/10.2139/ssrn.1690803. For criticisms of the Allahabad verdict, see Kalyani Ramnath, 'Of Limited Suits and Limitless Legalities: Interpreting Legal Procedure in the Ayodhya Judgment', *NUALS Law Journal* 5.1 (2011): 1–18; and Ratna Kapur, 'The Ayodhya Case: Hindu Majoritarianism and the Right to Religious Liberty' *Maryland Journal of International Law* 29.305 (2014): 305–65. For the 2019 Supreme Court judgment, see Amit Bindal, 'Complete Justice? Silences and Erasures in the Ayodhya Judgment', *Journal of Indian Law & Society* 11.1 (2020): 48–71; and Rahul Govind, 'On the Deity of Juristic Personality: The Religious, the Secular and the Nation in the Ayodhya Dispute and the Ayodhya Judgments (2010 & 2019)', *National Law School of India Review* 33.1 (2021): 150–180.

26 protects communities' right to endow and to maintain religious institutions (temples, mosques, etc). A primary source of juridical knowledge about Hindus' Article 26 rights is Dharmaśāstra. The Ayodhyā case featured a series of novel Dharmaśāstric arguments that were introduced on the basis of Article 25 and 26 claims.

The Allahabad High Court gave these Dharmaśāstric/Article 25–6 arguments great credence; on the basis of certain Dharmaśāstric verses, the Court concluded, against the grain of judicial precedent, that Hindu deities (such as Rām Lal Virajman) are almost wholly immune from the constraints of civil law. The Allahabad High Court's three-judge panel took a split view on the jurisprudence involved in the case. The majority of the court, Justices Sharma and Agarwala gave significant credence to Dharmaśāstric jurisprudence and ruled that both plaintiff deities were legal persons, the right of suit vested in the deities, the deities were wholly immune to adverse possession and limitation, and the State had a constitutional duty to defend the interests of the deities.[222] The protection of the Article 25 and 26 rights of Hindus, these justices reasoned, required bringing case law into alignment with Dharmaśāstra.

The Supreme Court, in contrast, reined in the Dharmaśāstric extravagance of the Allahabad High Court and upheld the principles of the constitutional jurisprudence that it had developed in the seventy years since the enactment of the Constitution. In the Supreme Court's estimation, appeals to Articles 25 and 26 of the Constitution could not serve as valid warrants for the argument that Dharmaśāstric jurisprudential principles should trump the operation of civil law. In the Court's view, constitutional protections for the freedom of religion have to be balanced against the sometimes competing interests of civil procedure, secularism, and equality. These ideas all lie at the core of the Supreme Court's constitutional jurisprudence of Hindu religious and charitable trusts.

On the shared points of the contention, the Supreme Court recognised the personality of Rām Virajman on the basis of the 'longstanding belief and faith' of the Hindu worshippers, but rejected the personality of Rām Asthan Janmabhūmi on the basis that, 'the purpose for which juristic personality is conferred cannot be "evolved" into a trojan horse that permits, on the basis of religious faith and belief, the extinguishing of all competing proprietary claims over property as well stripping the property itself of the essential characteristic of immoveable property'.[223]

Both deities' legal personality hinged on the recognition that faith and belief serve as necessary and sufficient conditions for the conferral of legal personality – a development of Supreme Court jurisprudence. Furthermore, the Supreme Court

[222] Justice Sharma and Agarwal endorsed this view, while Justice Khan's judgment varied considerably from those of his colleagues on the question of Hindu trusts.
[223] 1 SCC 1 (2020) ¶201.

ruled that because the Nirmohi Akhara, the self-described servants of Rām Virajman, had acted against the interests of the Rām Virajman, 'the institution of the Suit 5 was necessitated as a result of the deity not being a party to the earlier suits and based on the apprehension that in the existing suits, the personal interests of the leading parties were being pursued without protecting the independent needs and concerns of the deity'.[224]

Additionally, the Supreme Court negatived the majority of the Allahabad High Court's ruling that deities, by virtue of Hindu law, are perpetual minors for the purposes of limitation (i.e., protected from the bar of limitation). The Supreme Court, quoted the 'prescient words of a visionary judge' from B.K. Mukherjea's *Hindu Law*, which argued that 'to build up a law of procedure upon the fiction that the idol is an infant would lead to manifestly undesirable and anomalous consequences'.[225] Invoking these dicta of Justice Mukherjea, the Supreme Court ruled that 'it is an established position that a deity cannot on the ground of being a perpetual minor stand exempted from the application of the Limitation Act'.[226] In short, the Supreme Court ensured that deities and their assets are still subject to the standard laws of procedure and property.

Considering that Rām Virajman is a legal person, without a *shebait* (but with a next friend), whose assets can be lost through adverse possession, then it would seem, at first blush, that, as the Muslim community had held the site adversely to the deity for five-hundred years, Rām Virajman's suit would be barred by limitation. However, while the Allahabad High Court took the view that Rām Virajman and/or Rām Asthan Janmabhūmi was immune to adverse possession, the Supreme Court ruled that Rām had *never* been disposed within the operative (rather than historical) property regime of the British Raj and the Republic of India. The Supreme Court notes that, in '1858, by the proclamation of Lord Canning, all property, excluding a select few estates, were confiscated by the British sovereign and the disputed property was designated as *Nazul* land (i.e. land confiscated and vesting in the government)'.[227] Referring to Articles 372(1) and 296 of the Constitution, the Supreme Court noted the 'legal continuity between the British Sovereign and the Republic of India' and established that the title to the contested site was, and remained, vested in the Government of India up to the decision in 2019.[228]

If Rām had never been dispossessed under the current property and constitutional regime (since 1858, at least), and since, 'even after the attachment of the disputed property on 29 December 1949 the *sewa-puja* of the plaintiff deities continued… it cannot be contended that the cause of action in Suit 5 arose on

[224] Ibid., ¶428.
[225] Ibid.
[226] Ibid., ¶425.
[227] Ibid., ¶650.
[228] Ibid., ¶651.

29 December 1949 and pertains to the obstruction of worship and prayer or the attachment of the disputed property'.[229] In essence, the view of the Supreme Court was that Rām Virajman had never been dispossessed, and that the Government, after attaching the disputed site, had served effectively as a guardian of the deity.

We might say that the State had operated as *parens patrie*, protecting Rām Virajman, arranging for his worship, and ensuring that his case was heard in court. The problem with this view, however, is that Rām Virajman might not have a cause for legal action. Ironically, Rām's suit claimed that one cause of action was the malfeasant actions of the Nirmohi Akhara, which, in the opinion of the Supreme Court, 'is well and truly borne out by the proceedings as they unfolded in the proceedings before this Court'.[230] In acting adversely to the deity they claimed to serve and in breaking their claimed relationship of trust, the Akhara actually created the cause for Rām to file suit – and win.

In short, while the Supreme Court rejected many of the assertive, bullish Dharmaśāstric claims of the majority of the Allahabad High Court, reigning in Anglo-Hindu jurisprudence in favour of the principles of the Constitution, it nevertheless drew deeply on the colonial and post-colonial jurisprudence of Hindu religious and charitable trusts. The Supreme Court reasoned, implicitly, that Dharmaśāstric maxims concerning Hindu religious endowments (and the legal personality of Hindu deities) would have to be interpreted in such a way as to ensure the proper application of civil law to Hindu deities.

Effectively, the Supreme Court's verdict in the Ayodhyā dispute was the culmination of the process of the Indian judiciary's project of bringing the colonial-era, Anglo-Hindu case law and jurisprudence concerning Hindu religious endowments into alignment with the Indian Constitution. In doing so, the Supreme Court not only brought the Ayodhyā dispute to a definite end, but it also provided a sophisticated, comprehensive account of the current law of Hindu trusts that may serve to explicate the Court's reasoning in future cases.

5.3.1 The juridical personality of Hindu deities in the Ayodhyā verdicts (2010 and 2019)

Visharad v Ahmad and ***M. Siddiq v Suresh Das*** are probably the two most important court decisions concerning the legal personality of Hindu deities since India's independence. This is because they examine previous precedents on the issue in great detail and either set forth, or answer several hitherto unresolved legal

[229] Ibid., 428.

[230] Ibid. For a portion of an earlier version of this section that appeared in a special issue of *Contemporary South Asia*, see Fleming, 'Dharmaśāstra'.

questions. We saw that in earlier cases, including ***Sree Sree Ishwar Sridhar Jew***, ***Surendrakrishna Ray***, ***Deoki Nandan***, ***Poohari Fakir Sadavarthy***, ***Bishwanath***, ***Yogendra Nath***, ***Ram Jankijee Deities***, and ***Shiromani Gurdwara*** that the Supreme Court had taken the position that deities represent the pious, constitutionally protected desire of Hindus to worship the deity in question.

The existence of a deity or a temple, therefore, should not be determined on the basis of architecture, religious texts, or other external tests, but rather through the faith and beliefs of the worshippers. While the Allahabad High Court took an extremely capacious view of the capacity of faith and belief to create legal persons out of land itself, the Supreme Court restricted this to the creation of conventional deities. Both courts gave credence to the view that the beliefs of the community in question determine the existence of a legal person, but in the Supreme Court's estimation such persons cannot be used as a device for defeating the operation of civil law. Both courts' rulings interact with Raghunandana's maxim, discussed previously, accepting the maxim's core premise, but arguing over its level of practical extension.

5.3.1.i Raghunandana run rampant: Asthan Rām Janmabhūmi (plaintiff 2)

One difference of opinion between the courts lay in a question concerning the extent to which Raghunandana's maxim – on its own or as enshrined in judicial precedent – could validate, on constitutional grounds, judicial recognition of a near-limitless array of phenomena as Hindu deities (and legal persons).[231] Does mere belief on the part of the Hindu community require the courts to infer the existence of a deity even in the absence of a formal deed of endowment or temple? Can a mere belief deify land – and thereby immunise it from civil legal claims?

The plaint in Suit 5 (cited verbatim in Sharma's 2010 judgment) cites Raghunandana implicitly:

> 20. The place itself... the ASTHAN SRI RAMA JANMA BHUMI... has been an object of worship... as it personifies the spirit of the Divine worshipped in the form of SRI RAMA LALA or Lord RAMA the child. The Asthan was thus Deified and has had a juridical personality of its own even before the construction of a Temple building or the installation of the idol of Bhagwan Sri Rama...

[231] Some of the authorities on the matter are, ***Yogendra Nath Naskar v CIT*** (1969) AIR 1089, 1969 SCR (3) 742, AIR 1969 SUPREME COURT 1089, ***Ram Janki Deity v State of Bihar*** 1999 (5) SCC, ***Sri Sabhanayagar Temple, Chidambaram v State of Tamil Nadu*** (2009) 4 CTC 801, ***Sri Adi Visheshwara of Kashi Vishwanath Temple v State of UP*** (1997) 4 SCC 606, and ***Shiromani Gurdwara Prabandhak Committee, Amritsar v Som Nath Dass*** (2000) 4 SCC 146 (in ***Shiromani***, the court considered the juristic personality of the Guru Granth Sahib).

> 21. ...The Hindus... worship the Divine, which has no quality or shape or form, but can be known only when it manifests ITSELF in the form of an incarnation... It is the SPIRIT of the DIVINE which is worshipped by most Hindus, and not its material form or shape in an idol.... The SPIRIT of the DIVINE is indestructible and ever remains present everywhere at all times for anyone to invoke it in any shape or form...[232]

In the Supreme Court's estimation, the essence of this argument is that, 'the faith of the devotees regards the land as a deity and prayer is offered to it... Hence... the plaintiffs in Suit 5 submit that this court must confer juristic personality on the land represented as Ram Janmasthan.'[233] Rāma's counsel's assertion that 'God is shapeless and formless and there is no requirement that the object of worship be an idol' is a representative example of the almost-ubiquitous invocation (implicit or explicit) of Raghunandana's maxim when discussing *what* sorts of Hindu religious entities can be afforded legal personality by the courts.[234] Taken to its logical conclusion, Raghunandana's proposition (as read juridically) could potentially force the courts to recognise a vast array of phenomena (rivers, land, etc.) as Hindu deities (and legal persons).

In front of the Supreme Court, the counsel for Rām relied on Raghunandana, as quoted in ***Ram Jankijee Deities v State of Bihar***, that: 'The image simply gives a name and form to the formless God and the orthodox Hindu idea is that conception of form is only for the benefit of the worshipper and nothing else' to aver that 'any method of consecration chosen by the devotees is adequate for the conferral of legal personality on the deity'.[235] In their verdicts, Agarwal and Sharma also used ***Ram Jankijee*** as an authority for their decision to recognise the juridical personality (and concomitant indestructability) of Asthan Rām Janmabhūmi. Sharma asserts that:

> The place [Asthan Janmabhūmi] according to the *Smirit* [sic] have to be considered as a deity like *Agni* and *Vayu* being worshipped. They are shapeless and formless but they attain the divinity. If the public go for worship and consider that there is divine presence then it is [a] temple which has already been held by Hon'ble apex court in... ***Ram Jankijee***.[236]

Sharma's 'Smirit' source is Raghunandana's verse from the *Devapratiṣṭhātattva* (as interpreted in ***Bhupati*** and ***Ram Jankijee***).[237] For Sharma, ***Ram Jankijee*** ensures that Hindu belief and practice (protected under Articles 25 and 26 of the Constitution) enables a deity to take on an endless array of forms – with the legal

232 AHC (Sharma, Suit 5), p. 61
233 SC ¶130, p. 167.
234 Ibid.
235 SC ¶165 p. 195; (1999) 5 SCC 50 ¶17 (citing Mukherjea's *Hindu Law*).
236 AHC (Sharma, Suit 5) 173.
237 Ibid., 49–54, 73–75, 86–87 (Sharma cites G.C. Sarkar Sastri's, *Hindu Law* 8th ed.).

consequence, in the case of the Asthan Rām Janmabhūmi, that 'the plaintiff no. 2 is the deity and public is going for worship from times immemorial with a feeling of presence of deity divine… [and] if the temple is destroyed… the place will remain a juridical person'.[238] Consequently, Sharma decrees that Asthan Rām Janmabhūmi, is, and always was, the owner of 'the entire premises of Sri Ram Janm Bhumi at Ayodhya as described and delineated in annexure nos. 1 and 2 of the plaint'.[239]

Justice Agarwal provides more juridical nuance than Justice Sharma, but he nevertheless endorses a capacious view of the juridical personality of Hindu deities. Agarwal notes that the advocates for the deities in Suit 5, 'submit that in Hindu religious scriptures the concept of "Deity" vary extremely … [including] a place or object, i.e. natural things like river, tree, stone, mountain, mound or even a part of earth connected with divine activities'.[240] In assessing 'whether a place by itself can be a Deity and be conferred status of legal person in the light of principles of Hindu Law', Agarwal quotes a vast array of Dharmaśāstric sources – and Mukherjea's *Hindu Law of Religious and Charitable Trusts* – at length.[241] In answering this question in the affirmative, Agarwal focuses on Raghunandana's verse, and invokes a series of cases wherein Raghunandana's logic was used by the courts to advance the juridical view that 'a place which creates a sense of reverence in the belief that God resides there or an edifice devoted to divine worship is a [Hindu] temple'.[242]

While Ratna Kapur indicts Agarwal's endorsement of the communitarian Hindus' 'robust and substantive claim to freedom of religion in their own interests', and Gopinath Arunima (as well as Kalyani Ramnatha) questions the Dharmaśāstric coherence of treating *land* as a *deity*, I want to foreground how the Allahabad High Court's willingness to recognise a unique, legally indestructible instantiation of a Hindu deity – and Hindu majoritarian arguments for the existence of such a deity – involve appeals to Dharmaśāstric sources as interpreted by the courts.[243] Kapur and I share, I think, Saumya Saxena's broader argument

[238] Ibid., 173.

[239] Ibid., 174.

[240] AHC (Agarwal) ¶1693 p.1807

[241] Ibid., ¶1710, p. 1843 and ¶1721, p. 1852.

[242] Ibid., ¶1736–48, pp. 1860–4. Agarwal cites ***T.R.K. Ramaswami Servai v H.R.E. Madras*** ILR 1950 Mad 799; ***Venkataramana Moorthy v Sri Rama Mandhiram*** (1964) 2 An.WR 457; ***T. V. Durairajulu Naidu v The Commissioner, the Hindu Religious and Charitable Endowments (Administration) Department*** (1986) (99) LW 630; and Mukherjea's *Hindu Law*.

[243] Kapur, 'The Ayodhya Case', 362. Despite her excellent analysis of the constitutional issues involved in the 2010 judgment, Kapur's analysis of the plaintiff deities is limited to footnotes 3 and 141–2 (pp. 306–7 and 338). Kapur notes that Agarwal accepts the contention that faith is sufficient to deify a location (pp. 343–6), but she does not trace the logic that led Justices Agarwal and Sharma to arrive at this conclusion. Also see Gopinath Arunima, 'Ayodhya Verdict: Bad Theology, Without Justice', *Economic and Political Weekly* 35.41 (2010). Arunima's argument, that the 2010 judgment involves an 'elision' of *devasthanam* (a holy place) with a *janmasthanam* (a birthplace) is cited in Ramnath, 'Of Limited Suits', 11, fn 26. Ramnath offers this following gloss: 'The former [*devasthanam*] is a holy place which may be treated as a deity, but the latter [*janmasthanam*] being treated as a deity is unprecedented in Hindu law jurisprudence.' Neither of these are legible categories in the jurisprudence of the Ayodhyā dispute, where the issue is between treating land as a deity, or treating the right to worship at a particular location as a deity.

that Hindu majoritarianism is enabled by, and transforms secularism, rather than being an expression against it.[244]

Agarwal and Sharma of the Allahabad High Court accept the notion that a 'formless' Hindu deity might take virtually any form 'for the benefit of the worshippers' – on the authority of the Supreme Court in ***Ram Jankijee***.[245] This notion enables Justices Sharma and Agarwal to endorse the argument that, because the disputed site at Ayodhyā 'is believed to be the birthplace of Lord Rama by Hindus for time immemorial and they visit it to worship and Darshan' then the site itself 'satisfies the requirement of a "deity" '.[246]

Agarwal's conclusion, that 'plaintiffs 1 and 2 are juridical person [sic]' by virtue of 'the fact that they are being visited as a matter of right by Hindus for Darshan and worship believing the Place as [the] birthplace of Lord Rama, and the idols being the image of Supreme Being having divine powers', asserts that 'this faith and belief cannot be negatived on the challenge made by those who have no such belief or faith'.[247] Consequently, this ruling expands the scope of a Hindu deity dramatically. For Agarwal, Raghunandana's maxim, as supported in a secular judicial record, enables the recognition of a unique Hindu deity – a piece of land – whose worship forms an *essential* part of the Hindu faith. On this basis, Agarwal argues that, as the contested site at Ayodhyā 'is a place of peculiar and unique significance for [Hindus]', if it 'is allowed to extinguish/[become] extinct by application of a provision of statutes', then, 'the fundamental right of practicing religion' will be 'denied to the Hindus permanently'.[248] To protect this essential practice, then, Agarwal rules that Rām's claim to ownership must succeed. Secular provisions supporting religious freedom become, in this view, a tactical tool for judicial recognition of majoritarian land claims.

[244] See Saumya Saxena, '"Courting" Hindu Nationalism: Law and the Rise of Modern Hindutva', *Contemporary South Asia* 26.4 (2018): 378–99. Also see Ratna Kapur, 'The Ayodhya Case, Freedom of Religion, and the Making of Modernist "Hinduism" ', *Contemporary South Asia* 32.1 (2023): 10–25.

[245] AHC (Agarwal) ¶1758, p. 1870 & ¶1802, p. 1904. See SC ¶165, p. 195 & (1999) 5 SCC 50 ¶16: 'The observations of the Division Bench has been in our view true to the Shastras… If the people believe in the temples' religious efficacy no other requirement exists as regards other areas… Hindus have in Shastras "Agni" Devta; "Vayu" Devta these deities are shapeless and formless but for every ritual Hindus offer their oblations before the deity. The Ahuti to the deity is the ultimate… It is not a particular image which is a juridical person but it is a particular bent of mind which consecrate the image.'

[246] AHC (Agarwal) ¶1889, p. 1975. The specific 'belief' in question was framed as: 'that the fort of King Dashrath situated at Ayodhya included the part of the building wherein Lord Rama was born according to Hindu belief and the disputed area covered that house'.

[247] Ibid., ¶1918, p. 2006.

[248] Ibid., ¶2722, p. 2615. Agarwal makes the constitutional issue clear at ¶2714, pp. 2616–17: 'the Government will have the effect of depriving the worshippers their right of worship under Article 25 of the Constitution and such an acquisition even under the statutory provision cannot be permitted… This will be infringing the fundamental right under Article 25 of the Constitution.'

5.3.1.ii Raghunandana reined in: the juridical personality of Rām Lalla Virajman (plaintiff 1)

In 2019, the Supreme Court rejected the legal personality of Asthan Rām Janmabhūmi (and the Allahabad High Court's endorsement of a juridical theory in which Hindu belief could create a near-limitless array of juridical persons) on three grounds: 1) that the legal deification of land on the basis of mere belief is not countenanced by judicial precedent; 2) that the legal deification of land would create a class of property that would frustrate the operation of civil law; and 3) that affording the Hindu community a unique method of acquiring property on the basis of belief would violate the secular principles of the Indian Constitution.

The Supreme Court did recognise Rām Virajman as a juridical person on the basis of longstanding Hindu belief, and despite the absence of a deed of dedication, a legal guardian (*shebait*), or a temple structure, defined this deity as a particular pious purpose: the right of Hindus to worship Rām at Ayodhyā.[249] The result is a tautological deity: Rām Virajman is the pious, constitutionally protected right of Hindus to worship Rām Virajman at the Janmabhūmi. In the Supreme Court's analysis, the relief sought by Gopal Visharad in Suit No. 1 of 1989: 'a declaration… to allow the plaintiff to offer prayers in accordance with the rites and tenets of his religion ("*Sanatan Dharm*") at the "main Janmabhumi" near the idols, within the inner courtyard', is subsumed, ontologically and legally, into Rām Virajman.[250]

The Supreme Court notes that the counsel for the deities, 'submitted that in Hindu Law the concept of a juridical person is not limited to idols… [and that because the land itself] is an object of worship… and prayer is offered to it… this court must confer juristic personality on the land represented as Ram Janmasthan'.[251] This contention is once again supported by an appeal to Raghunandana, as enshrined in previous judicial precedent, that 'God is shapeless and formless and there is no requirement that the object of worship be an idol'.[252] The deities' counsel asserted that 'there is a distinction between: (i) the land being a deity; (ii) the land being the abode of a deity; and (iii) the land being the property of a deity', and that, as the land 'is itself the deity', consequently, 'questions of possession, joint-possession or adverse possession' would be rendered 'infructuous'.[253]

[249] SC ¶129, p. 166. For a critique of this apparent contradiction in the Supreme Court's decision to recognize the legal personality of Rām Lalla Virajman, see Govind, 'On the Deity'.
[250] SC ¶13, p. 12.
[251] Ibid., ¶130, p. 167.
[252] Ibid., ¶130, p. 167.
[253] Ibid. This finding would render the destruction of an earlier temple irrelevant: 'Mr Vaidyanathan submitted that the disputed property, being a legal person, is *res nullius*. Since the disputed property is a juristic person, it is not alienable. It was contended that land which is *res nullius* or *res extra commercium* cannot be acquired by adverse possession. It was urged that even if the image of the idol is broken, a deity is immortal and thus, the construction of the mosque on the land did not take away from its character as a deity.'

The Court notes that by 'invoking the argument of a "juristic person" the plaintiffs have urged this Court to create an additional ground for the conferral of legal personality – the faith and belief of the devotees' and that 'amongst the ensemble of arguments advanced before this Court, this innovative legal claim is at the heart of the present dispute'.[254] In the Court's estimation, the 'recognition of the religious significance of a place as a place of public worship is conceptually distinct from recognising the place as a juristic person'.[255] Essentially, many locations are recognised religiously, culturally, and legally, as being important to the Hindu community, but very few, if any, of these locations are recognised *legally* as juristic persons. Indeed, the Supreme Court examines the 'wealth of precedent' – involving variations on a theme of Raghunandana's verse – that was cited by the Allahabad High Court in support of the legal personhood of Asthan Rām Janmabhūmi. The Supreme Court, unlike the Allahabad High Court, concludes that these decisions are authorities for the proposition that Asthan Rām Janmabhūmi, the land itself, cannot be recognised as a legal person.[256]

After working through these precedents, the Court concludes that, 'the counsel have selectively relied on extracts to support the contention that the disputed site is a juridical person'.[257] In this view, judicial precedent's Raghunanda-based recognition on the divinity of 'natural formations, animals and can even... everyday objects which have significance in a worshipper's life' must be seen from a *spiritual*, rather than a *legal* perspective.[258] In the absence of a express deed of dedication – which delineates the *pious purpose* of a testator, the Court argues, that: 'Each conferment of legal personality... must be judged on the facts of the case and [not] every manifestation of the Supreme Being results in the creation of a legal person.'[259]

The second reason that the Supreme Court rejected the legal personality of Asthan Rām Janmabhūmi is more practical: the 'conferral of "absolute title" (resulting from the conferral of legal personality on land) would... render the very concept of title meaningless'.[260] Rām's counsel's desired legal outcome for the deification of the land in question was to ensure that, as *res nullius*, it would be immunised from any historical dispossession (through, for example, the construction of the mosque) or legal process (such as sale or gift), but this move would also run contrary to the practical legal purpose of affording legal personhood to Hindu deities: creating a site of jural relations so that one *could* file suit in relation to land and other properties dedicated to a deity.

[254] Ibid., ¶161, p. 193.
[255] Ibid., ¶136, p. 172.
[256] Ibid.
[257] Ibid., ¶137, p. 173.
[258] Ibid., ¶185, pp. 210–11.
[259] Ibid.
[260] Ibid., ¶174, p. 201.

The Supreme Court concludes that, with regard to Asthan Rām Janmabhūmi, due to the absence of an 'act of dedication… the question of whom the property was dedicated to does not arise and… the need to recognise the pious purpose behind the dedication… as a legal person also does not arise'.[261] If a deity's legal personhood is the personification of the pious intentions of an endowment's founder, then, without evidence (presumed or assumed) of a foundation, then the Court cannot infer the existence of a deity. Surprisingly, however, the Supreme Court *does* recognise Rām Virajman as a pious purpose *despite the absence of a deed of dedication*.[262] Rahul Govind argues that this reflects the Court's 'inconsistency between the… exposition of the concept of juristic personality and its application of the same in this particular case'.[263] The Supreme Court's justification of this inconsistency, however, shares a common theme with the Allahabad High Court's conferral of juristic personality on Astham Ram Janmabhūmi: an expansion of the spirit of Raghunandana's maxim on the basis of Hindus' constitutionally protected right to worship. Before the Ayodhya verdict, the courts invoked Raghunandana in their conferral of legal personhood on natural phenomena, religious texts, and other non-śāstric religious phenomena. Afterward, the Ayodhya verdict added constitutional rights to Raghunandana's remit.

These first two reasons for rejecting the legal personality of Asthan Rām Janmabhūmi are very technical and the third reason – the preservation of secularism – appears to be more policy-oriented. While Justice Sharma and Agarwal of the Allahabad High Court framed the recognition of Asthan Rām Janmabhūmi as the *defence* of constitutional freedoms of religion, the Supreme Court takes the view that the rejection of this novel juridical person 'touches upon the heart of our constitutional commitment to secularism'.[264]

A major issue with this 'novel extension of the law applicable to Hindu religious endowments' is that this 'method of worship on the basis of which a proprietary claim may be sustained' is available only to the Hindu community.[265] The crux of the constitutional conundrum is that although 'religious diversity… requires the protection of diverse methods of offering worship', nevertheless, accepting that a 'method of worship unique to one religion should result in the conferral of an absolute title… over parties from another religion in an adjudication over civil property claims' would violate the Constitution's promise of equality of all faiths and render ownership a 'question of which community's faith is stronger'.[266]

[261] Ibid., ¶174, p. 201
[262] Ibid., ¶174, p. 201.
[263] Govind, 'On the Deity', 174.
[264] SC ¶202, p. 222. For discussions of Indian secularism in a legal context, see Deepa Das Acevedo, 'Secularism in the Indian Context' *Law & Soc. Inquiry* 38.138 (2013): 138–67; and Ronojoy Sen, 'Reforming Religion: the Indian Constitution, the Courts and Hinduism' in Susanna Mancini (ed.), *Constitutions and Religion* (Northampton: Edward Elgar Publishing, 2020): 222–36.
[265] SC ¶202, p. 222.
[266] Ibid., ¶203–5, pp. 222–4.

What about Rām Virajman, the tutelary deity of the contested site, who was recognised (and whose case was granted) by all three judges of the Allahabad High Court and by the Supreme Court? If he is not the *land*, what, exactly, *is* he? Rām Virajman first entered the legal record in Deoki Agarwal's plaint of 1989: 'According to the faith of the devotees of BHAGVAN SRI RAMA LALA… the spirit of BHAGWAN SRI RAMA… resides at Asthan Sri Rama Janma Bhumi and can be experienced by those who pray there… That Spirit is the Deity.'[267] Like Asthan Rām Janmabhūmi, the legal personality of Rām Virajman must be *inferred* on the basis of *faith*, *belief*, and *worship* rather than by deed. Here, then, the Supreme Court recognises the longstanding *faith* and worship of Hindus at Ayodhyā as evidence of the existence of a pious purpose (worship at Ayodhyā). In this approach, the intentions of a now-lost founder of a temple at Ayodhyā are not necessary for the Court to confer legal personality on Rām Virajman. For the Supreme Court, as for the Allahabad High Court, Rām Virajman is the pious purpose of worshiping Rām at Ayodhya: 'Hindu devotees of Lord Ram hold a… long standing… belief in… offering prayer to Lord Ram at the site they believe to be his birthplace.'[268] For Rām Virajman, therefore, belief and worship *are* sufficient for the court to recognise his legal personality:

> In the present case, the first plaintiff has been the object of worship for several hundred years and the underlying purpose of continued worship is apparent even absent [of] any express dedication or trust… At the heart of the present dispute are questions pertaining to the rightful manager of the deity and the access of the devotees of Lord Ram to the idols.[269]

One crucial distinction between the two deities is that the existence of Rām Virajman, as a pious purpose rather than a specific parcel of land, does not extinguish competing property rights, *a priori*. Rām Virajman, unlike Asthan Rām Janmabhūmi, could be relocated without being destroyed. Nevertheless, the legal principles and precedents that support the recognition of this deity in the absence of an express trust or deed – ***Ram Jankijee***, ***Bhupati***, ***Yogendra Nath***, and Mukherjea's *Hindu Law* – are the same as those cited in support of Asthan Rām Janmabhūmi. These share a core reliance on the hugely influential verse from Raghunandana's *Devapratiṣṭhātattva*.

In fact, the Supreme Court argues that as 'the right [that was] asserted' by Gopal Singh Visharad in 1950 was 'a right in common with and for the benefit of other Hindu devotees to pray at the disputed property':

> The remaining issues in contention in Suit 1 are connected with the ones argued in Suit 5. The relief sought in Suit 5 will have a direct impact on the plaintiff's right to

[267] AHC (Sharma, Suit 5), p. 11.
[268] SC ¶126, p. 164.
[269] Ibid., ¶129, p. 166.

> pray as claimed in Suit 1. Accordingly, we will deal with the contentions raised in Suit 1 at the time of addressing the contentions in Suit 5.[270]

Gopal Visharad's (and the Hindu community's) abstract right to worship is unable to own property, but it is entitled to legal protection under Article 25 of the Indian Constitution. As the Court frames the right for Hindus to pray to Rām at Ayodhya as a juridical person, the Court's decision to award the title to the disputed site to Rām Virajman affirms 'the right of the plaintiff in Suit 1 to worship at the disputed property'.[271] Divinising a constitutional right (as Rām Virajman) enables the Court to determine what property rights that divinised right might enjoy. In fact, the counsel for the Sunni Central Board of Waqfs, Rajeev Dhavan, accepted Rām Virajman as the legal personification of the Hindu community's right to worship, but 'envisaged [this] only [as] an easementary right to worship for the Hindu devotees to pray and, for that purpose, to gain access to the courtyard'.[272] Thus, for Dhavan, the Ayodhyā dispute is *not* about whether Rām Virajman (or other Hindu deities) should be recognised as legal persons. Rather, the dispute concerns what rights – proprietary, procedural, etc. – particular divine legal persons should enjoy.

In short, the courts affirmed that Rām Virajman is the juridical representation of an abstract, constitutionally protected, right to worship. For the benefit of Rām's worshippers, the court granted legal recognition to a bodiless, attributeless being. Would Raghunandana be pleased to see his venerable defence of image worship redeployed by a modern court to justify the property rights of a Hindu deity? Or would he be horrified that Rām Virajman represents the rights of people of all castes without any regard to the norms of *varṇa* (caste)? Perhaps both, but therein lies my broader point: references to Dharmaśāstric maxims have been, and will likely be, an essential point of reference for judges adjudicating cases involving Hindu law.

5.3.2 Adverse possession, next friends, and state protection

Having examined *what* Rām Lalla Virajman is – a sort of divination of the Article 25 and 26 rights of the Hindu devotees of Lord Rāma – the next important legal question in the Ayodhya judgments concerns *who* has the right to represent the deity in court proceedings, *what* rights Rāma enjoys, and *how* the history of those property rights should be construed in formulating a lawful and just resolution to the conflict. Both the Supreme Court and the Allahabad High Court rejected the Nirmohi Akhara's claims to be the *shebait* of Rām Virajman – although the Muslim

[270] Ibid., ¶215–16, pp. 242–4.
[271] Ibid., ¶805, p. 927.
[272] Ibid., ¶222, p. 249.

litigants accepted the proposition of the Nirmohi Akhara's *shebaitship* in the hopes that this would bar Rām Virajman's suit by limitation – but took a different view on limitation. The High Court believed that, on the basis of Dharmaśāstra, deities are perpetual minors and therefore immune to adverse possession.

The Supreme Court, for its part, rejected the theory of perpetual minority and argued that Rām Virajman had never been dispossessed. Rather, Rām's interests had been looked after faithfully by the State and, in the aggregate both suits 4 and 5 should be granted.

5.3.2.i Deities and adverse possession

> As milk becomes tasty curd over time, similarly, over time, possession for three generations is the cause of gift (the acquisition of title). One should not put forth possession (as proof of title) in women, in the property of gods and kings, in the property of minors and Vedic Brāhmaṇas, and (in inheritance) from the mother and from the father.
>
> *Kātyāyanasmṛti* (300–600 CE)[273]

The 'law of limitation' refers to specific time limits for different suits within which an aggrieved person can approach the court for redress or justice. If a suit is filed beyond this period, then the suit will be barred by limitation.[274] This was the logic behind Chamier's dismissal of Raghubar Das' 1885 suit and the Sunni Central Board of Waqfs' claim that the 'Muslims perfected their title by adverse possession'.[275] However, as we saw in Chapter 4, the Anglo-Hindu jurisprudence of divine endowments evolved in tandem with the formalisation of trusts law and civil procedure (including the laws of limitation) in the late 19th century.[276]

A theory, born from a mixture of Dharmaśāstra and English trusts law, of Hindu deities as 'perpetual minors' are a represented (like children and other legally incompetent individuals) by a series of fiduciaries (*shebaits*) raised complicated questions vis-à-vis civil procedure in the Anglo-Hindu law of religious and charitable trusts. These questions included: 1) who was entitled to represent a deity; 2) how could a deity be protected when its guardian acted in a *mala fide* manner; 3) what happens when a deity has no legal guardian; and 4) does

[273] P.V. Kāṇe (ed. & trans.), *Kātyāyanasmṛtisāroddhāraḥ* (Pune: Oriental Book Agency Reprint for *Hindu Law Quarterly*, 1933), 43: yathā kṣīraṃ janayati dadhi kālād rasanvitam / dānahetus tathā kālād bhogas tripuruṣāgataḥ //328// na bhogaṃ kalpayed strīṣu devarājadhaneṣu ca / bālaśrotriyavitte ca mātṛtaḥ pitṛtaḥ kramāt //330// See Kāṇe's footnote on p. 180 for an analysis of these forms of property in relation to the Indian Limitation Act (1908).

[274] For the history of the Law of Limitation in India, see Sukumar Ray and M.R. Malick (eds), *B.B. Mitra's Limitation Act* 23rd edition (Calcutta: Eastern Law House, 2014).

[275] For limitation in Dharmaśāstra, see Chapter 1, §1.4 'Guardianship' and §1.6.2.i '*Dharmasūtras, Dharmasmṛtis*, and the *Purāṇas*'.

[276] See Chapter 4, Notes 240–52.

limitation run against a deity? By the end of the colonial period, India's variegated court system produced a vast, uneven body of legal precedent. Furthermore, Article 26 guarantees religious communities the right 'to establish and maintain institutions for religious and charitable purposes' according to the belief and practices of those communities.

In the Ayodhyā dispute, the difficult question of whether Rām Virajman's suit was maintainable in law – in accordance with civil procedure – precipitated technical discussions about the analogical status of Hindu deities as 'perpetual minors' and about who was entitled to legally represent Rām. Justices Agarwal and Sharma ruled, on the basis of Dharmaśāstric reasoning and a thin body of case law, that, as a 'perpetual minor', Ram Virajman and other deities' suits could *never* be barred by limitation.[277] Justice Khan dissented, noting that, in the opinion of Justice Mukherjea, this is 'an extravagant doctrine contrary to the decision of the Judicial committee… [and] the fiction that the idol is an infant would lead to manifestly undesirable and anomalous consequences'.[278] The Supreme Court rejected Sharma and Agarwal's reasoning, arguing that 'the applicability of the law of limitation cannot be ruled out on the basis of the theory of perpetual minority'.[279]

Nevertheless, the *analogous* relationship between a deity and a minor, wherein both are represented by legal guardians (who have a fiduciary relationship of trust) played a central role in the Allahabad and Supreme Courts' acceptance of the maintainability of Suit 5 (filed by Deoki Agarwal as a *next friend* of Rām Virajman) and rejection of Suit 3 (filed by the Nirmohi Akhara). The courts drew on the Anglo-Hindu jurisprudence of the *guardianship of deities* and argued that: 1) the Nirmohi Akhara claimed to be the legal guardian (*shebait*) of Rām Virajman; 2) if the Nirmohi Akhara were the *bona fide* shebait of Rām, only they could file suit on the deity's behalf; and 3) as the Nirmohi Akhara did *not* file suit within limitation, the Akhara's suit for title would have been barred by limitation and Agarwal's suit would be dismissed as he would have no standing.

In fact, Rajeev Dhavan (counsel for the plaintiffs in Suit 4) argued for this very position.[280] As the Nirmohi Akhara were *mala fide* towards Rām and not his *de facto shebaits*, Deoki Agarwal *could* file suit as Rām's next friend. Ironically, the Nirmohi Akhara's *mala fide* actions towards Rām assisted Rām's case by providing a legal cause for action – a *felix culpa*.[281] As in the issue of Rām Virajman's legal *personality* – where the Supreme Court poured an Article 25 right to worship into the

[277] AHC (Sharma, Suit 5), p. 167; (Agarwal) ¶1945, p. 2031.
[278] Ibid. (Khan), pp. 186–7, citing Mukherjea, *Hindu Law*, 256–7. The case referred to is ***Damodar Das v Lakhan Das*** (1910) ILR 60 Cal 54.
[279] SC ¶425, p. 473.
[280] Ibid., ¶335, pp. 388–9.
[281] Ibid., ¶428, pp. 477–9.

legal mould of a Hindu deity – the Supreme Court used the fiduciary relations of Hindu trusts as a paradigm to reshape the history of Hindu worship at Ayodhyā.

The plaintiffs in Suit 4 argued that Rām's suit, filed in 1989 would be barred by limitation if the cause for that suit arose forty-nine years earlier (when the Government attached the land at Ayodhyā), or 461 years earlier (when, ostensibly, Bābur's general raised the mosque). In the 2010 Allahabad High Court hearing, Shri M.M. Pandey, an advocate for the plaintiffs in Suit 5 (the deities), argued that 'it is [a] settled proposition of Hindu law that deities cannot be deprived of their properties and their claim cannot be barred by time and thus their title cannot become extinct by dispossession also'.[282] To support this claim, Pandey turned to Dharmaśāstra, arguing that the 'statement of law in *Katyayana Smriti* is of special significance in these suits… [and] the… King's duty relating to Temples has been strongly emphasised in the Hindu Law from ancient times'.[283]

Pandey quotes many Dharmaśāstra verses that formed the juridical core of Anglo-Hindu law's theory of the Government (the 'sovereign') as the arbiter of disputes concerning Hindu trusts.[284] To this standard canon, Pandey adds, on the basis of Kātyāyana, the claim that 'temple property is never lost even if it is enjoyed by strangers for hundreds of years'.[285] Kātyāyana's verse is unique in Dharmaśāstra in that it *explicitly* lists the property of deities as being immune to adverse possession, but it reflects a Dharmaśāstric pattern – adopted in Anglo-Hindu jurisprudence – of *analogising* deities to women, minors, and other legal dependents (against whom limitation cannot run).[286] The issue in Dharmaśāstra and Anglo-Hindu law lies in how far that analogy can be extended for legal purposes.

Kātyāyana aids Pandey in arguing – successfully in the 2010 verdict – that Hindu deities are perpetual minors for the purposes of limitation. Pandey asserts that 'Hindu Law has to be applied on the rights/property and incidental matters concerning Hindu Deity… unless such law has been modified by any statute or Custom' and, Justice Agarwal agreed that:

> The idol was… in the position of a minor not because of the recognition or declaration by British Indian Courts… but because of the then existing and continuing position of the idol in Hindu law being treated as minor… Therefore, the idol enjoyed the status of a minor… [and therefore] the maxim *contra non valentem agere*

[282] AHC (Sharma, Suit 5), p. 146.

[283] Ibid., p. 148 (Paragraph 4 of Pandey's submissions). See Chapter 1, §1.4, 'Guardianship', for Sanskrit jurisprudential theories. See Chapter 2, §2.1.1, 'Theory' for the practical instantiation of these theories.

[284] Ibid., p. 148. The key precedent cited (wherein much Dharmaśāstric justification for the state's 'sovereign's' right of visitation is quoted) is ***Raja Muttu Ramalinga Setupati v Perianayagum Pillai*** (1874) 1 IA 209.

[285] AHC (Sharma, Suit 5) p. 157.

[286] For deities as minors in Anglo-Hindu law, see Chapter 4, §4.2.3.iii, 'Deities, minors, and the law of limitation'.

> *non currit praescriptio*... comes into effect and should be made applicable in the case of idol.[287]

While Agarwal's logic is *Dharmaśāstrically* sound, it runs counter to established precedents – as Justice Khan and the Supreme Court note at length.[288] Surprisingly, on the strength of this reasoning, Justices Agarwal and Sharma turn to ***Bishwanath v Radha Ballabhji***, the pre-Ayodhyā authority from the Supreme Court on the juridical personality of Hindu deities. On the basis of an observation that, 'an idol is in the position of a minor when the person representing it leaves it in a lurch', Justices Agarwal and Sharma set conflicting case law aside and ruled that a deity cannot be subject to limitation.[289]

Khan's observation, that 'it cannot be said that the Supreme Court in Biswanath's case just by one sentence... intended to impliedly overrule scores of cases... on the question that the idol is not a minor... for the purposes of limitation' was confirmed by the Supreme Court.[290] The Supreme Court observed that:

> The analysis of the legal position on the applicability of the law on perpetual minority by... Khan commends itself... The submission which was urged by Mr C.S. Vaidyanathan [counsel for the deities] is contrary to the jurisprudence of close to a century on the issue... The applicability of the law of limitation cannot be ruled out on the basis of the theory of perpetual minority.[291]

This restriction on the legal analogy between deities and minors has the legal effect of preventing an unwanted consequence, which is that the perpetual minority of all deities for the purposes of limitation would lead to a torrent of litigation concerning contested alienations of properties from endowments stretching back centuries.

5.3.2.ii Rām Virajman's ostensible shebaits, next friends, and State-appointed guardians

A deity may not be in the position of a minor for the purposes of limitation (Dharmaśāstric arguments to that effect notwithstanding), but the essence of the

[287] AHC (Sharma, Suit 5), p. 153; (Agarwal) ¶2580–1, pp. 2653–5.

[288] Ibid. (Khan), pp. 165–89. Khan's authorities (demonstrating that limitation runs against deities) are: ***Chitarmal v Panchu Lal*** (1926) AIR All 392 (DB), ***Jagdindra v Hemantah*** 31 Indian Appeals 203, ***Damodar Das v Adhikari Lakhan Das*** 37 Indian Appeals 147, ***Parkasdas v Janki Ballabha*** (1926) AIR Oudh 444, ***Naurangi Lal v Ram Charan Das*** (1930) AIR Patna 455 (DB), ***Ram Charan Das v Naurangi Lal and Ors.*** (1933) AIR PC75, ***Radha Krishan Das v Radha Raman*** (1949) AIR Orissa 1, and ***Surendra v Sri Sri Bhubaneswari*** (1933) AIR Cal 295. Khan also cites ***Dr Guranditta Mal Kapur v Amar Das*** (1965) AIR SC 1966, and ***Sarangadeva Periya Matam v R. Goundar*** (1966) AIR SC 1603 (Supreme Court judgments that clarify that limitation runs against deities). In Justice Sharma and Agarwal's defence, in ***Rama Reddy v Ranga Dasan*** (1925) (1926) 50 MLJ 589, Justice Devadoss concluded that, 'a person who acquires title from a trustee of a temple cannot acquire any title adverse to the idol, for the idol is an infant for all time'.

[289] AHC (Sharma, Suit 5), pp. 167–8; (Agarwal) ¶1945, p. 2031.

[290] Ibid. (Khan), p. 183. Also see SC ¶425, p. 473.

[291] SC ¶425.

Anglo-Hindu jurisprudence of divine endowments is an analogical comparison between deities' legal representatives (*shebaits*) and the guardians of infants.[292] Despite *not* being recognised as Rām Virajman's *shebait* (not for want of trying), the Nirmohi Akhara's *mala fide* actions towards Rām justified Deoki Agarwal's suit on Rām's behalf. Although the absence of a *de facto shebait* would not save Rām Virajman from limitation *per se*, the Supreme Court ruled that, from the British acquisition of Oudh in 1856 (the Court's declared origin of contested rights of Hindus and Muslims over the Ayodhya site), Rām Virajman (Hindus' right to worship) had suffered no substantive harm *until* the Nirmohi Akhara filed suit in an attempt to claim the site for themselves in 1959.

The State (through its receiver) had, in the estimation of the Court, served as a responsible legal guardian for Rām Virajman (ensuring that his idols were worshipped regularly and not removed from the site). Consequently, Rām's suit was saved from limitation by a combination of the State's positive (temporary) guardianship of an orphaned Rām's interests *and* the Nirmohi Akhara's malfeasance vis-à-vis the deity they claimed to protect.

The Supreme Court relied on ***Bishwanath*** – the same case on which the Allahabad High Court had relied – as the standard account of the perpetual minority of Hindu deities. Setting limitation aside, ***Bishwanath*** delineates the circumstances in which a *next friend* can file suit on a deity's behalf: 'An idol is in the position of a minor when the person representing it leaves it in a lurch, a person interested in the worship of the idol can certainly be clothed with an *ad hoc* power of representation to protect its interest.'[293]

Among a range of dubious averments, the Nirmohi Akhara, in Suit 3, contested the maintainability of Suit 5, on the basis that, as Rām's *shebaits*, the Akhara, and only the Akhara could file suit on the deity's behalf.[294] Unfortunately, for the Nirmohi Akhara, the Allahabad and Supreme Courts concluded that, although the 'Nirmohi Akhara existed at the disputed site, the claim of Nirmohi Akhara... is that of an intermittent exercise of certain management rights [which] does not confer... the position... of a *de facto shebait*'. Fortunately for Rām Virajman, being 'left in the lurch' without a *shebait* ensured that Suit 5 was maintainable by his next friend, Deoki Agarwal.[295] *Had* the Nirmohi Akhara been recognised as the *shebait* of Rām, Suits 3 *and* 5 would have failed: Suit 5 due to the existence of a *shebait*; and Suit 3 because the Nirmohi Akhara, having filed suit in 1959, *was* barred by limitation.[296]

[292] See Chapter 4, §4.2.3.ii, 'Filing suit in the name of the deity'.

[293] SC ¶343 pp. 395–6

[294] Ibid., ¶220–2, pp. 246–8.

[295] Ibid., ¶401, p. 443. The phrase 'left in the lurch' comes from Chief Justice Subba Rao's speech in ***Bishwanath*** (¶10). It is cited with approval by the Supreme Court at ¶413.

[296] Ibid., ¶225, 246, 248, & 255, pp. 257, 295–296 & 304–5. Article 120 of the Limitation Act 1908 stipulates six years for a 'suit for which no period of limitation is provided elsewhere in this schedule', while Article 142 stipulates twelve years 'for possession of immoveable property when the plaintiff... has been dispossessed'. While the Akhara's grievance was the loss of 'management and charge of the

The deficiency of the Nirmohi Akhara's suit explains why, given that 'the maintainability of Suit 5 hinges on the question whether Nirmohi Akhara were *shebaits*', it was strategic when 'Dr Rajeev Dhavan, leading the arguments for the Sunni Central Waqf Board submitted that though Suit 3 is barred by limitation, that does not extinguish the right of Nirmohi Akhara to pursue its claim as a shebait'.[297]

Although the Nirmohi Akhara's failure to provide its status as *de facto shebait* (despite the strategic efforts of Sunni Central Waqf Board, the plaintiffs in Suit 4) ensured the validity of Deoki Agarwal's right to file suit on behalf of Rām Virajman, the absence of a *shebait*, *per se*, would not save Rām from the bar of limitation.[298] The issue of limitation, therefore, turned on the question of *when* Rām's cause for legal action arise. If the deity's cause arose in 1949, when the disputed site was attached under Section 145, then his suit, filed in 1989, would be well beyond the twelve years stipulated for suits regarding immoveable property under Article 120 of the Limitation Act (1908).

Surprisingly, the Supreme Court found that, as 'even after the attachment of the disputed property… the *sewa-puja* of the plaintiff deities continued [via a court-appointed *purjari*]… it cannot be contended that the cause of action in Suit 5 arose on 29 December 1949 and pertains to the obstruction of worship and prayer or the attachment of the disputed property'.[299] In fact, the claim the Government of India (through magistrates, court-appointed trustees and pujaris, and even the Indian army) had, in maintaining the *status quo* throughout the nearly seventy years that the case had remained pending, fulfilled its fiduciary obligation to look after Rām Virajman's interests – even when Rām was not a party in any suit.[300] As the State had served as a responsible guardian to an orphaned infant Rām, the State's actions could not be construed as a cause of action for the running of limitation.

One might be forgiven, as F.E.A. Chamier did in 1885, for assuming that Rām's cause of action arose in 1528 when a mosque was raised on the contested site (assuming that this was raised on the ruins of a pre-Mughal temple). At that time, presumably, the Hindu community's right to worship (Rām Virajman) had been extinguished by the right of conquest of the Mughal emperor. For the plaintiffs

temple as a result of the order of attachment under Section 145 [to which Article 120 applies]' the court observed that 'an ingenious effort has been made to gloss over the contents of the suit in the written submissions', as well as to establish their case as one of title over the land (to which Article 142 applies). The Court was not persuaded and as the cause of 'action arose on 5 January 1950… [and] the suit was instituted on 17 December 1959… the suit is outside the prescribed period of limitation and is barred'.

297 Ibid., ¶358, p. 405 & ¶428, p. 478.

298 The Supreme Court (¶423, pp. 469–71) accepted the finding of in ***Sarangadeva Periya Matam v Ramaswami Goundar (Dead) by Legal Representatives*** (1966) AIR SC 1603 that 'when possession of… property became[s] adverse, limitation against the Math would run even in the absence of a *de jure* or *de facto* Mathadhipathi'.

299 SC ¶428, p. 477.

300 Ibid., ¶426, pp. 474–7.

in Suit 4 (the Uttar Pradesh Sunni Central Waqf Board), however, there was no evidence of a deed of dedication or of exclusive possession during the Mughal period – a fact that seems to have eluded most critics of the 2010 and 2019 verdicts.[301] The Supreme Court concurred with Justice Agarwal's conclusion, 'that in the preceding few hundred years, the only action which may have arisen to adversely affect the interest of the plaintiffs was the raising of the disputed structure. In spite of this, the place in dispute continued to be used by the Hindus for the purposes of worship.'[302] The Supreme Court, noted that the 'disputed property has fallen within the territory of various rulers and legal regimes', but, citing precedent, concluded that 'the legal consequences of actions taken, proprietary rights perfected, or injuries suffered in previous legal regimes can only be enforced by this Court if they received implied or express recognition by subsequent sovereigns'.[303] Consequently, even *if* a 'Hindu temple which vested title to the disputed site in the plaintiff deities' had existed before the Mughal period, there is 'no evidence… that upon the change in legal regime to the Mughal sovereign' this right was respected.[304]

This logic cuts against the Muslim community's claim to have perfected their title by adverse possession. This is because the Muslim community's presumed, exclusive Mughal-era title to the land was *not* upheld during the change in legal regime to the British East India Company. As the Court notes, 'upon the annexation of Oudh by the British sovereign [1856], no actions were taken… to exclude… the Hindu devotees of Lord Ram from worship', and, in '1858… the disputed property was designated as *Nazul* land (…confiscated and vesting in the government)'.[305] As Article 372 of the Indian Constitution establishes a legal continuity between the British sovereign and the Union of India, the Court recognises only the 'rights of the parties… which occurred during the colonial regime'.[306]

Ironically, the Supreme Court's history of the disputed site – in which Rām Virajman was *never* dispossessed in the active legal regime and in which his

[301] Ibid., ¶677–8, pp. 791–2.
[302] Ibid., ¶426, pp. 474–6.
[303] Ibid., ¶633 & 646, pp. 756 & 766. The cases are: ***Secretary of State Council in India v Kamachee Boye Sahaba*** (1857–60) 7 Moo IA 476, ***Thomas and James Cook v Sir James Sprigg*** (1899) AC 572, ***Secretary of State of India in Council v Bai Rajbai*** (1915) ILR 39 Bom 625, ***Promod Chandra Deb v State of Orissa*** (1962) Supp (1) SCR 405, ***State of Gujarat v Vora Fiddali Badruddin Mithibarwala*** (1964) 6 SCR 461, ***Pema Chibar v Union of India*** (1966) 1 SCR 357, and ***Union of India v Sudhansu Mazumdar*** (1971) 3 SCC 265.
[304] SC ¶648, p. 767.
[305] Ibid., ¶650, p. 768.
[306] Ibid., ¶651, pp. 769–70. Article 372(1): 'Notwithstanding the repeal by this Constitution of the enactments referred to in article 395 but subject to the other provisions of this Constitution, all the law in force in the territory of India immediately before the commencement of this Constitution shall continue in force therein until altered or repealed or amended by a competent Legislature or other competent authority.'

interests were *always* safeguarded by the Government – leads to a conclusion whereby Rām's *only* legal cause for a suit for title to the land is the malfeasance of the Nirmohi Akhara. The Supreme Court noted that:

> Suit 5 was necessitated... [because] in the existing suits, the personal interests of the leading parties were being pursued without protecting the... concerns of the deity... borne out by the proceedings as they unfolded in the proceedings before this Court.... The Sunni Central Waqf Board made joint cause with Nirmohi Akhara by supporting the cause of Nirmohi Akhara as a *shebait*, to buttress its challenge to the entitlement of the deity to protect its interests through a next friend... In this backdrop, the cause pleaded in Suit 5 at the behest of the deity... cannot be held to be beyond limitation.[307]

Although the Supreme Court rejected the Allahabad High Court's strong Dharmaśāstric, Kātyāyaṇa-based analogy between deities and minors in terms of an absolute immunity to limitation, the Court relied on the juridical minority of deities in relation to guardianship. While the Court, on the basis of Article 25 of the Constitution, viewed Rām Virajman as the legal personification of a Hindu right to worship, the Court, on the basis of Article 26 of the Constitution delineated the relationship between that legal person and his legal guardians.

A combination of the State's responsible care of Rām, and the Nirmohi Akhara's breach of trust created a unique mixture of circumstances whereby Rām was recognised by the court as having a superior history of possession, and, consequently, title to the site. The Court was correct to note that while 'the Muslims were dispossessed upon the desecration of the mosque on 22/23 December 1949', Rām was not.[308]

5.3.3 Ayodhyā's conclusion

The Courts viewed Rām Virajman as the legal personification of a Hindu belief in the efficacy of worship at the disputed site in Ayodhyā, but the Supreme Court concluded that there are *legal limits* to this belief. Sanskrit and Anglo-Hindu jurisprudential principles about the legal personality of Hindu deities could not be used as a Trojan horse to defeat the property claims of Muslim parties. Belief cannot, in the ruling of the Supreme Court, trump the operation of civil law – of adverse possession, limitation, etc., or to create unique legal entities (Asthan Rām Janmabhūmi) that would defy the application of *any* legal procedure. In setting limits on the scope of Raghunandana's observation that a formless deity takes

[307] SC ¶428, pp. 479–80.
[308] Ibid., ¶800, pp. 922–3.

form for the benefit of the worshippers, the Court largely foreclosed the possibility of recognising the juridical personality of rivers such as the Gaṅgā and Yamunā.[309]

Once the Court recognised Hindu belief as a juridical person, Rām Virajman, they clothed that person, despite the absence of any deed of dedication or of a *shebait*, in the legal vestments of a Hindu religious endowment and re-read the history of the Ayodhyā dispute as a history of the guardianship of Rām at the disputed site. In this fiduciary history, the *State* (beginning with the Union of India's direct legal antecedent, the British East India Company) had protected Rām Virajman's interests by permitting Hindus to worship at the disputed site. Even after the attachment of the disputed premises in 1949 (and the destruction of the mosque in 1992), the State had ensured the regular worship of Rām Virajman. In Dharmaśāstric terms, the State (as sovereign) had fulfilled its duty as *parens patriae*, to safeguard the interests of 'orphaned' deities like Rām Virajman. Ironically, as the Supreme Court concludes, the only legal harm that Rām Virajman suffered was the *mala fide* suit of the Nirmohi Akhara – the entity that had managed Rām's idols on the Rām Chabutra for centuries. Effectively, the Supreme Court viewed its verdict as safeguarding Rām (whatever be the deity's characterisation in constitutional jurisprudence or in religious metaphysics).

This narrative relies on two axioms: 1) taking 1856 as the starting point for the existence of legal rights that are justiciable by contemporary courts; and 2) projecting, perhaps anachronistically, the legal principles of Hindu trusts onto the history of Hindu worship at Ayodhyā. Drawing a line under the Mughal regime (in the former Oudh, at least), the Supreme Court, so that the 'law cannot be used as a device to reach back in time and provide a legal remedy to every person who disagrees with the course which history has taken'.[310] This limited the potential efficacy of suits filed in the name of deities at Mathurā and Vārāṇasī, where, during the British regime, no right of Hindu worship was recognised.[311] Even as the Supreme Court projected the principles of Hindu trusts law on the history of Rām worship at Ayodhyā, it curtailed the Allahabad High Court's expansion of those principles (based on Kātyāyaṇa, etc.) as they apply to Hindu deities.

The Supreme Court's attempts to rein in a rights-based, Dharmaśāstric expansion of the law of Hindu trusts also sets the stage and the terms of debate for future suits over Mathurā, Vārāṇasī and other disputed sites. The Supreme Court invoked the Places of Worship (Special Provisions) Act 1991, which imposes 'a positive obligation to maintain the religious character of every place of worship as it existed on 15 August 1947, when India achieved independence from colonial

[309] See Chapter 5, §5.2.3, 'The juristic personality of Hindu deities and Articles 25 and 26 of the Indian Constitution'.
[310] SC ¶633, p. 756.
[311] Ibid.

rule' as a bar to such suits.[312] Unsurprisingly, the Act has recently become the target of public interest litigation.[313]

Nevertheless, on 9 April 2021, a senior judge of the Vārāṇasī Court ordered the ASI to perform a survey of the Kāśīviśvanātha/Jñān Vāpi mosque site in response to a suit filed on behalf of the deity Lord Vishweshvar Kashi Vishwanath.[314] That report was completed in 2023 and reporting on its contents in January of 2024 indicates that it recognised the existence of the Hindu temple that was constructed before the Jñān Vāpi Mosque.[315] In April 2024, the Supreme Court declined to interfere with a Vārāṇasī court's order that allowed a priest nominated by the Kashi Vishwanath Trust to conduct daily worship (*pūjā*) in the cellar of the mosque (where a series of Hindu images are ensconced).[316]

The fear that the Allahabad High Court's endorsement of a faith-based application of Sanskrit jurisprudence will expand the Hindu community's constitutionally-protected rights to freedom of religion into a legal weapon with which to assert control over India's contested geography is in many respects assuaged by the Supreme Court of India's ruling. Nevertheless, communal conflict over contested sites has increased and, invariably, has taken on the language of the Courts – of deities as legal persons, of broken fiduciary relations, of historical claims about worship, and about the potential legislative obstacles to a Hindutva agenda.

5.4 Conclusion: Kashi-Mathura Baaqi Hain?

The Supreme Court's observation that 'the Muslims were dispossessed… through means which should not have been employed in a secular nation committed to the rule of law', when juxtaposed with its order that '5 [alternative] acres be allotted to the Sunni Central Waqf Board… within the city of Ayodhya' gives credence to the American historian, Audrey Truschke's criticism that 'what the mob began

312 SC ¶78, p. 116. Section 5 of the Act expressly exempts the Ayodhyā dispute: 'Nothing contained in this Act shall apply to the place or place of worship commonly known as Ram Janma Bhumi-Babri Masjid situated in Ayodhya.'

313 Much of that challenge comes from litigation filed by Ashwini Kumar Upadhyay, a veteran public interest litigator at the Supreme Court of India. See, for example: www.scobserver.in/tag/ashwini-kumar-upadhyay/. Also see the coverage of the ongoing case ***Ashwini Kumar Upadhyay v Union of India*** (WP (C) 1216/2020) concerning the constitutionality of the Places of Worship Act: www.scobserver.in/cases/ashwini-kumar-upadhyay-union-of-india-constitutionality-of-the-places-of-worship-act-case-background/

314 https://theprint.in/judiciary/varanasi-court-orders-asi-probe-to-settle-kashi-vishwanath-temple-gyanvapi-mosque-dispute/636829/

315 www.reuters.com/world/india/survey-finds-mosque-indias-varanasi-was-built-over-temple-hindu-petitioners-2024-01-26/

316 https://timesofindia.indiatimes.com/india/supreme-court-declines-to-stop-puja-of-deities-in-gyanvapi-cellar/articleshow/108957653.cms

extrajudicially, the Supreme Court finished through judicial opinion'.[317] Despite this, this chapter has shown that a detailed reading of the 2010 and 2019 Ayodhyā verdicts in conjunction with the Supreme Court's wider jurisprudential toolbox reveals that the protection of Hindu *belief* was only one facet of the courts' logic.

The Ayodhyā verdict is extremely important because it clarifies numerous ambiguous points of jurisprudence in the wider law of Hindu religious and charitable trusts. These include: what types of phenomena will the court recognise as deities on the basis of Hindu belief and faith; who is fit to represent a deity in judicial proceedings, especially when claimants to the *shebaitship* of deities act fraudulently; when and how can deities gain or lose assets through adverse possession and other operations of law; and where do we draw historical limits on the criminal wrongs or legal rights of the past – Mughal, colonial, etc. – when adjudicating contemporary communal conflicts?

Although the Supreme Court argued that the 'law cannot be used as a device to reach back in time and provide a legal remedy to every person who disagrees with the course which history has taken', this is precisely what has happened subsequently.[318] Faith-based applications of Sanskrit jurisprudence have been employed to transform the Hindu community's constitutionally protected rights to freedom of religion into a legal device with which to assert control over India's contested geography. This jurisprudential shift lies at the heart of lawsuits filed in the name of deities at Mathurā and Vārāṇasī. Chapter 3 discussed the destruction of Hindu temples at these sites during the reign of Aurangzeb.[319] Although the Supreme Court invoked the Places of Worship (Special Provisions) Act 1991, as a bar to these suits (when discussing the Act in the Ayodhyā verdict), the Act has recently become the target of public interest litigation.[320] It appears to be highly likely that, in the coming years, the Supreme Court will be tasked with applying the principles of its ruling in ***M. Siddiq v Suresh Das*** to the fact patterns of the Mathurā and Vārāṇasī disputes.

On 20 May 2022, a judge of the district court in Mathura ruled that a lawsuit, filed by a 'next friend' on behalf of two deities, 'Bhagwan Shrikrishna Virajman' and 'Asthan Shrikrishna Janam Bhoomi' (note the remarkable similarity to divine litigants in the Ayodhyā case), for possession of the disputed site (occupied in part

[317] Audrey Truschke, 'Historical Right', *Caravan*, 6 December 2019 https://caravanmagazine.in/religion/ayodhya-babri-masjid-ram-mandir-supreme-court-audrey-truschke.

[318] SC ¶633.

[319] See Chapter 3, §3.4.1.iii, 'The ambiguous position of Aurangzeb'.

[320] SC ¶78, p. 116. Section 5 of the act expressly exempts the Ayodhyā dispute: 'nothing contained in this Act shall apply to the place or place of worship commonly known as Ram Janma Bhumi-Babri Masjid situated in Ayodhya': https://theprint.in/opinion/politically-correct/did-modi-give-hindus-closure-a-pil-against-the-places-of-worship-act-will-decide-the-answer/621753/https://timesofindia.indiatimes.com/india/sc-agrees-to-examine-validity-of-places-of-worship-act/articleshow/81463934.cms

by the Shahi Idgah mosque), was not barred by the Places of Worship Act.[321] On 9 April 2021, a senior judge of the Vārāṇasī Court ordered the ASI to perform a survey of the Kāśīviśvanātha/Jñān Vāpi mosque site in response to a suit filed on behalf of the deity Lord Vishweshvar Kashi Vishwanath by a next friend.[322] In this case, advocates for the plaintiff deity aver that, since it is the location of an eternal, self-revealed (*svayambhū*) Śivaliṅga, the destruction of the physical temple could not result in the termination of the deity's ownership over the disputed site.[323]

As noted earlier, the resulting ASI report (unreleased) indicated that a Hindu temple was constructed on the site before the Jñān Vāpi mosque, and in April 2024, the Supreme Court permitted a Hindu priest to conduct daily worship (*pūjā*) in the cellar of the mosque (where a series of Hindu images are ensconced).[324] Jurisprudentially, the case at Vārāṇasī will probably turn on a question of the religious character of the mosque/temple as it existed on 15 August 1947 (under the Places of Worship Act). Nevertheless, even as all of these cases engage with broad questions of constitutional jurisprudence (as articulated in depth in ***M. Siddiq v Suresh Das***) they also entail a significant amount of Sanskrit jurisprudential concepts regarding Equity and Trusts. There are questions of *parens patriae* jurisdiction, of Equity as the legally protected conventions of religious communities, and of deities' secondary, figurative ownership of endowed assets. Some of the jurisprudential terms concepts used in adjudicating practical disputes over religious and charitable endowments have changed over the centuries, but many have remained constant. In that sense, the *spirit* of Equity and Trusts in Sanskrit jurisprudence has endured.

Of course, appreciating the nuances of the 2010 and 2019 verdicts in the Ayodhyā dispute also requires us to understand the pre-constitutional history of the Hindu Law of Religious and Charitable Trusts as well as its transformation after the introduction of the Constitution and Supreme Court in 1950. Broadly, even as the Supreme Court shifted some of the norms of Anglo-Hindu jurisprudence in line with the provisions of the Constitution, its justices also carved out new legal tests for intervention and new jurisprudential justifications for that

[321] Civil Revision No. 02/2021, ***Bhagwan Shrikrishna Virajman etc. v U.P. Sunni Central Waqf Board etc.*** For an excellent discussion of the Mathurā dispute, see Nick Tackes, 'The View from Mathura: Nationalist Projects in a Local Dispute', *Contemporary South Asia* 32.1 (2024): 84–100.

[322] For an excellent discussion of the Vārāṇasī dispute, see https://theprint.in/judiciary/varanasi-court-orders-asi-probe-to-settle-kashi-vishwanath-temple-gyanvapi-mosque-dispute/636829/

[323] The case is ongoing. See, Vera Lazaretti, 'Ayodhya 2.0 in Banaras? Judicial Discourses and Rituals of Place in the Making of Hindu Majoritarianism', *Contemporary South Asia* 32.1 (2023): 66–83. Also see, www.firstpost.com/india/kashi-gyanvapi-dispute-case-next-friend-of-lord-vishweshwar-says-temple-was-destroyed-but-its-religious-character-didnt-change-10549441.html; www.livelaw.in/news-updates/vishweshwar-jyotirlinga-is-situated-below-gyanvapi-mosque-which-is-self-manifested-lords-next-friend-argues-in-allahabad-hc-199695; and www.livelaw.in/news-updates/gyanvapi-lord-vishweshwara-through-next-friend-move-varanasi-court-seeking-impleadment-in-suit-by-hindu-worshippers-200427

[324] See Conclusion, §6.1.1, 'Communitarian concerns'.

intervention. Rather than assert feudal prerogatives as the sovereign heir to the British Crown – as virtually all Indian rulers had done before – the Court took the claim that the Constitution inaugurated a new era in Indian history, law, and society (with numerous connections to the past), seriously. Often, this meant that the Supreme Court, as in the Sabarimala case, encouraged a progressive telos to Hindu religious institutional practices by emphasising only those practices which conform to gender and caste equality as being 'essential' and therefore protected.

In the context of juridical personality, the shift from the proprietary Anglo-Hindu legal regime to the constitutional jurisprudence of the present day did not involve a wholesale rejection of earlier case law. Far from it. In fact, constitutional jurisprudence allowed for the judicial recognition of a greater variety of phenomena as juridical persons on the basis of Hindu belief and faith. This is a laudable process, but as the Supreme Court's ruling in the Ayodhyā verdict demonstrates, these deities must be construed in such a way that they do not infringe on the operation of civil law.

Different rulers at different times in Indian history have drawn on the Sanskrit jurisprudence of Equity and Trusts when crafting legal regulations for the Hindu religious and charitable endowments. In the medieval ages, Dharmaśāstric sovereigns in the Sanskrit cosmopolis drew on Sanskrit jurisprudential principles such as conventional laws (*sāmayikadharmas*) when issuing edicts (*śāsanas*) that endowed Hindu deities. During the Indo-Islamic period, Hindu rulers endowed and regulated Hindu religious institutions using the bureaucratic technology of the Persian Cosmopolis in accordance with political-theological principles of Sanskrit jurisprudence (especially the *parens patriae* jurisdiction of the king in protecting deities from desecration by Muslims). During the age of European colonialism, the jurists and administrators of the British East India Company created a hybrid, Anglo-Hindu jurisprudence for temples and other related institutions that combined elements of English Chancery Law (trusts etc.) and Dharmaśāstric jurisprudence.

Finally, the Supreme Court brought the legacy of centuries' worth of legal developments in line with the principles of the Indian Constitution. At each level of history, however, the Sanskrit jurisprudence of Equity and Trusts played an important role in the practical administration of religious and charitable endowments.

Conclusion: Hindu Deities in the 21st-Century Global Order

> *There is a purpose underlying the enactment of the Places of Worship Act. The law speaks to our history and to the future of the nation. Cognizant as we are of our history and of the need for the nation to confront it, Independence was a watershed moment to heal the wounds of the past. Historical wrongs cannot be remedied by the people taking the law in their own hands. In preserving the character of places of public worship, Parliament has mandated in no uncertain terms that history and its wrongs shall not be used as instruments to oppress the present and the future.*
>
> Supreme Court of India in ***M. Siddiq v Suresh Das***[1]

In the final paragraphs of its monumental verdict (that brought the Ayodhyā dispute to a close) in 2019, the Supreme Court of India invoked the Places of Worship (Special Provisions) Act of 1991. In doing so the justices appealed as much to the higher moral principles of the Indian people as they did to the force of statute.[2] The Ayodhyā dispute, broadly representative of India's wider history of intercommunal conflict, was a divisive, bloody, and internationally provocative affair whose resolution, whatever be its perceived justice, should be an occasion for confronting the past and reflecting on what sort of future India should pursue.

In Himanchal Pradesh, the 2022 election victory of the Indian National Congress over the BJP threatens to re-ignite the long-running dispute between the State Government and the erstwhile Rajpūt rulers of the Kullu principality over control of the Raghunāthajī temple in Kullu.[3] Finally, debates over affording

[1] 1 SCC 1 (2020).

[2] The Act imposes 'a positive obligation to maintain the religious character of every place of worship as it existed on 15 August 1947, when India achieved independence from colonial rule' on the Government and courts.

[3] For an introduction to the history of the Kullu Raghunāthajī temple, see Daniela Berti, 'Divine Jurisdictions and Forms of Government in Himachal Pradesh (Northern India)', in Daniela Berti and Gilles Tarabout (eds), *Territory, Soil and Society in South Asia* (New Delhi: Manoharlal Banarsidass, 2009): 311–39.

legal rights to sacred environmental phenomena are far from limited to ***Mohd. Salim v State of Uttarakhand & Others*** and ***Lalit Miglani v State of Uttarakhand and Others.***[4] The recognition of the sacrality of local environmental phenomena by the courts has served, with mixed efficacy, as barriers to development in various regions of India.[5] The Gods have awakened as legal and political entities. How will the judiciary respond?

Having outlined the core Sanskrit jurisprudential principles of the Hindu law of religious and charitable trusts (in Chapter 1) and having sketched the history of their application to the practical administration of religious endowments in classical, Islamic, British, and independent India (in Chapters 2, 3, 4, and 5), I want to query the place of deities in contemporary India and the wider world by way of conclusion. On the one hand, Indian deities have returned, once again, to the forefront of the Indian public consciousness. Perhaps more so than at any time in history since the Islamic conquest of India in the 12th century, India's deities play a central role in the political, economic, social, religious, and legal life of the Indian nation. Whatever be the explanation – metaphysical, political, communitarian, or otherwise – the gods have awoken and now assert themselves as robust legal persons.

On the other hand, India's pivotal role in the Commonwealth and in the wider global order as a peaceful, secular, and ambitious republic with more than a billion citizens – and even more people in the South Asian diaspora – has brought Hindus and their deities, or Hindu deities and their devotees, to the United Kingdom, North America, and beyond. How those deities and their attendant financial, ritual, and cultural practices have adapted to new legal and social contexts is as much a story of acceptance as it is of transformation. The novelty of Hindu deities being recognised as juridical persons in England or America by Anglo-American courts should coincide, however, with a critical appraisal of our own legally idiosyncratic property-owning 'idols': the vast, multinational corporations whose juridical personality, arrogation of political freedoms, exacerbation of wealth inequality, and degradation of the environment are enacted corporate boards under the pretext of fulfilling their fiduciary duties to investors.[6]

[4] WPPIL 126/2014 (High Court of Uttarakhand) 2017 [19] & WPPIL 140/2015 (High Court of Uttarakhand) 2017 64.

[5] See Eliza Kent, *Sacred Groves and Local Gods: Religion and Environmentalism in South India* (Oxford: Oxford University Press, 2013). Also see Bijayashree Satpathy, 'Forest Rights Act Implementation in Odisha: Redressing Historical Injustices', *South Asia Research* 37.3 (2017): 259–76; and Leah Temper and Joan Martinez-Alier, 'The God of the Mountain and Godavarman: Net Present Value, Indigenous Territorial Rights and Sacredness in a Bauxite Mining Conflict in India', *Ecological Economics* 96 (2013): 79–87.

[6] See, for example, Adam Winkler, *We the Corporations: How American Businesses Won their Civil Rights* (New York: Norton, 2018).

When we examine the legal history and possible futures of Hindu deities within the context of the present, two key themes emerge. First, Hindu trusts, like most of the world's trust systems or foundations, are the product of a somewhat haphazard amalgamation of different jurisprudential solutions to the practical problem of alienating assets for particular purposes and placing those assets in the care of another party (or retaining them for oneself). Successions of authorities drew on various jurisprudential traditions– Dharmaśāstric, Islamic, English, or Constitutional – and devised remedies for maladministration. That these solutions sometimes bore only partial resemblance to the practices of previous administrations by no means marks them as flawed or failed. The nature of Equity has, I would contend, always entailed an element of flexibility conditioned by a genuine appeal to a set of core principles. India's contribution to the history of religious trusts certainly typifies that aspect of Equity.

Second, in order to debate effectively about what might be wrong, or what might be worth changing by statute or by judicial intervention, about the contemporary Hindu law of religious and charitable trusts, it is absolutely *vital* that we take stock of the two-millennia worth of legal developments that brought us to the present situation. It is wrong to attribute to malice that which is explained by ignorance, especially in the context of contemporary discussions of Hindu law.

Through no fault of their own, a great many popular and scholarly commentators' opinions on the Ayodhyā dispute in particular, and on the juridical personality of Hindu deities generally, have undermined their analysis of modern legal developments, through adopting distorted (or inaccurate) assumptions about the nature of Sanskritic or pre-colonial theories of practices of divine trusts. This is understandable because Sanskrit theories of trust are diffusely spread among some of the more difficult and under-studied portions of Dharmaśāstric and Mīmāṃsā literature. Nevertheless, confronting the difficulties of the present requires far more than simply rejecting two-hundred years' worth of jurisprudence as the fruit of colonial misunderstanding. Rather, it requires a longer view. That longer view, of course, is the telos of this monograph.

6.1 The gods awaken: Hindu deities in contemporary Indian society

> Gods die. And when they truly die, they are unmourned and unremembered. Ideas are more difficult to kill than people, but they can be killed, in the end.
>
> Neil Gaiman, *American Gods*[7]

[7] Neil Gaiman, *American Gods* (London: Headline Review, 2004).

Hindu deities and religion more generally, constitute an essential, ubiquitous fixture of life in contemporary India. While the Western world has generally witnessed a steady decline in religiosity – notable exceptions notwithstanding, of course – in conjunction with economic development and modernisation, India has grown more religious in the face of similar social transitions.[8] One could explain the increasingly prominent role of deities in Indian life using different sociological, economic, legal, or metaphysical terminology. Meera Nanda, for example, attributes the 'Hinduisation' of India to the cumulative effects of globalisation, the liberalisation of India's domestic economy, and the political mobilisation of Hindu middle classes as an electoral strategy, for the increasing presence of Hindu religion in contemporary Indian life.[9]

Legally, however, we might say that, as the Supreme Court of India recognises the juristic personality of Hindu deities as the compendious expression of the pious, constitutionally protected desire of Hindus to worship those same deities, it is completely logical that these deities would become more robust and assertive as their collective worship grows. Metaphysically, we would be remiss not to acknowledge that a śāstric or Purāṇic account of the re-emergence of deities as social and political agents would be expressed in different terms: the suppression of the deities' cults under foreign political regimes, the re-allocation of funds that would have traditionally been dedicated to deities to the building of Indian mosques, madrassas, and palaces, or even stately homes in Britain, along with the generally declining conditions of the *Kaliyuga*, greatly impinged on the ability of the community of the faithful to maintain and to protect their deities. The end of colonialism, and the emergence of India as a prosperous nation with strong constitutional provisions for the protection of the practice of religion has allowed deities to emerge, once again, as true agents in the unfolding of history.

Whatever the truth of any of these explanations, the undeniable reality is that deities now play a more prominent role in Indian society than during the colonial age. At the same time, and unlike other areas of Hindu law, the Parliament of India has declined to pass comprehensive legislation outlining the Hindu law of religious and charitable trusts. The law and jurisprudence governing Hindu deities, their assets, and their cults, has been almost entirely judge-made. This makes the legal regulation of deities a pressing and enduring topic for the Indian judiciary.

[8] For Indian religiosity, see Meera Nanda, *The God Market: How Globalization is Making India more Hindu* (New York: NYU Press, 2011). For declining religiosity in Europe, see Hugh McLeod and Werner Ustorf (eds), *The Decline of Christendom in Western Europe, 1750–2000* (Cambridge: Cambridge University Press, 2003); and Loek Halman and Veerle Draulans, 'How Secular is Europe?', *The British Journal of Sociology* 57.2 (2006): 263–88. For challenges to the general 'secularisation thesis', see David Voas and Mark Chaves, 'Is the United States a Counterexample to the Secularization Thesis?', *American Journal of Sociology* 121.5 (2016): 1517–56.

[9] Nanda, *The God Market*, 1–11.

Two areas of law are of particular concern: 1) communitarian relations; and 2) environmental protection. These are central issues for the wider development of India in the 21st century and it therefore comes as no surprise that they would be reflected in legal debates concerning Hindu deities. More simply, given that Hindu deities have become cyphers for the beliefs and practices of the wider Hindu community in the eyes of the law, it is implausible that these deities would not share in the same fundamental social concerns as their worshippers.

6.1.1 Communitarian concerns

The communitarian facet of Hindu deities' increasing prominence has received the most scholarly attention. Various crucial moments in the Ayodhyā dispute – the 1992 destruction of the Bābrī Masjid, the 2010 Allahabad High Court Ruling, and the 2019 Supreme Court verdict – elicited a flurry of scholarship that sought to understand the relationship between Hindu nationalist (Hindutva) politics and the secular judicial system.[10] In the wake of the 2019 verdict, the faith-based Sanskrit jurisprudence of divine personality was utilised in two new cases that assert the right of the Hindu community to worship at two similarly contested religious sites in India: the Kṛṣṇajanmastha temple/Shahi Eidgah mosque in Mathurā and the Kāśīviśvanātha temple/Jñān Vāpī mosque in Vārāṇasī.[11] Of note, the plaintiffs in both suits were clearly modelled on Deoki Agarwal's suit on behalf of Rām Virajman in 1989: the Mathurā case was filed by a next friend on behalf of 'Bhagwan Shrikrishna Virajman' and 'Asthan Shrikrishna Janam Bhoom' while the Vārāṇasī case was filed by a next friend on behalf of Lord 'Vishweshvar Kashi Vishwanath', who is claimed to be an eternal, self-revealed (*svayambhū*) Śivaliṅga.[12]

Although one might expect that the Places of Worship (Special Provisions) Act 1991 would be an insurmountable bar to the success of these deities' claims to the ownership of the contested locations, it has not, as of yet, led to these cases' dismissal. In fact, a unique facet of both disputes is the claim that the Places of Worship Act does not apply because the deities at both sites were *never*

[10] For reactions to the demolition in 1992, see van der Veer, 'God must be Liberated!'; Gopal, Anatomy of a Confrontation; Pollock, 'Rāmāyaṇa'; Friedland and Hecht, 'The Bodies of Nations'; and Ludden, Making India Hindu. For analyses of the 2010 Allahabad High Court Verdict, see Aparna Chandra, 'Gopal Singh Visharad and Ors v. Zahoor Ahmad and Ors., O.S.Nos. 1/1989, 3/1989, 4/1989, 5/1989: A Summary of the Babri Masjid-Ram Janm Bhoomi Decision', 11 October 2010, https://ssrn.com/abstract=1690803 or http://dx.doi.org/10.2139/ssrn.1690803; Ramnath, 'Of Limited Suits'; and Kapur, 'The Ayodhya Case' (2014). For the 2019 Supreme Court Judgment, see Bindal, 'Complete Justice?'; Govind, 'On the Deity'; and Sarath Mathew, 'Applying Adverse Possession Rules to the Ayodhya Case', *Journal of Indian Law and Society* 11.1 (2020): xi–xxiv.

[11] Shashank Rai, Shabarna Choudhury, and Sai Snigdha Kantamneni, 'Aftermath of Ayodhya Verdict: Impact on Kashi and Mathura', *Jus Corpus Law Journal* 1 (2020): 90–100.

[12] Civil Revision No. 02/2021 ***Bhagwan Shrikrishna Virajman etc. v UP Sunni Central Waqf Board etc.***

dispossessed and the character of both locations was never wholly Islamic. Take, for example, the following claim by Lord Visheshwar's advocate, and next friend, Vijay Shankar Rastogi:

> It is clear from the averments of the plaint that the property in question, i.e. the temple of Lord Visheshwar has been in existence from ancient time, i.e., Satyug up till now and the Swayambhu Lord Visheshwar is situated in the disputed structure. It is further argued that if the temple has been destroyed by any means, the religious character never changed, therefore, Section 4 of the Places of Worship (Special Provisions) Act, 1991 is not applicable because the structure of old temple was built prior to the 15th Century.[13]

This is an intriguing argument, especially given the fact that the Jñān Vāpī Mosque retains many architectural features (perhaps even the *liṅga*) of the erstwhile temple of Kāśīviśvanātha. The results of the Archeological Survey of India's court-appointed (but unreleased) study of the site may introduce an entirely new question for the Supreme Court to decide eventually: can deities be subject to the adverse possession of their temple when their *worshippers* rather than their images (*mūrtis*), are excluded from the temple?[14] The consequences of this ruling could be enormous: India is home to hundreds, if not thousands of disputed religious sites on which mosques or temples were built from the spoliated remnants of earlier temples. Acknowledging the enduring legal personality of deities from erstwhile temples (or the continuing nature of a site as a temple even after the construction of a new structure on top of it) could lead to a tidal wave of title suits.

6.1.2 Environmental protections

While the communitarian aspect of the legal personality of Hindu deities has received the most scholarly attention in recent years, the role of deities in environmental concerns has also been the subject of extended scholastic discussion.[15] I discussed the extension of legal personality to the rivers Gaṅgā and Yamunā in ***Mohd. Salim v State of Uttarakhand & Others*** & ***Lalit Miglani v State of Uttarakhand and Others*** in Chapter 5, but these cases are representative of a wider phenomenon in contemporary India of employing juridical personality as a mechanism for preserving the environment.

[13] www.firstpost.com/india/kashi-gyanvapi-dispute-case-next-friend-of-lord-vishweshwar-says-temple-was-destroyed-but-its-religious-character-didnt-change-10549441.html

[14] The completed report's release to the public has been the subject of much reporting and litigation. See, for example: www.thehindu.com/news/national/other-states/gyanvapi-mosque-survey-varanasi-court-allows-all-parties-to-have-access-to-asi-report/article67772164.ece

[15] Most notable in this context is the work of Daniela Berti, see 'Divine Jurisdictions'; and 'Gods' Rights vs Hydroelectric Projects: Environmental Conflicts and the Judicialization of Nature in India' *Rivista Degli Studi Orientali* 88.2 (2015): 111–29. Also see Ehud Halperin, 'Winds of Change: Religion and Climate in the Western Himalayas', *Journal of the American Academy of Religion* 85.1 (2017): 64–111.

Ram Jankijee, ***Shiromani Gurdwara***, and similar cases involve the recognition, on the basis of collective faith and belief, of the legal personality of Hindu deities that do not quite meet the normative standards of Dharmaśāstra. These cases have been applied to ecological phenomena, such as sacred groves, rivers, and mountains, that were never treated as legal persons in classical Sanskrit jurisprudence or in pre-colonial legal practice. For example, Daniela Berti discusses a case from Himanchal Pradesh in 2006, during which the heir to the Ford family (of automakers) attempted to build a 'Ski Village development project in the Kullu district of Himachal Pradesh.'[16] When the local population consulted their local pantheon on the matter, 'God after god spoke and made it clear that they did not want the ski village in the area since it would desecrate holy places. They warned the people that if the project was approved, the gods would leave and destroy the area.'[17] Additionally, Berti demonstrates that 'the environmental issue is also put forward by gods' followers regarding the recent practice attested to in various Himalayan regions of India to create "god's protected forests" '.[18]

The broader point is that in many circumstances far humbler than the Uttarakhand High Court's recognition of the entire Gaṅgā as a legal person, the juridical personality of Hindu deities has been adapted to local contexts in support of environmental preservation.

One final example from Berti's work should suffice to prove this wider point. In 2006, 'Water Miller, a private energy and water supplier, signed an agreement with the state of Himachal Pradesh to set up a 1 megawatt Hydro Electric Project in the forest near the village of Vashist, in the Kullu valley'.[19] This industrial progress ran afoul of the inhabitants of Vashist, 'the village closest to the place selected by the Water Miller Company, who said that the work would damage the forest where the goddess Joginī supposedly lived'.[20] Joginī was believed to dwell in a waterfall within the forest. As in the case of the Ford family's ski lodge, the local deities, including Joginī, were consulted (by the villagers) and they vehemently opposed Water Miller's dam proposals. The situation rapidly spun out of control, with a flurry of court cases filed by multiple parties in 2011, but in the wake of evidence being presented that, 'the goddess is the owner of the land and that villagers are tenants and they have either to serve the goddess or to pay a tax', the Company abandoned its plans for the dam.[21]

[16] Berti, 'Divine Jurisdictions', 7.

[17] Ibid., 8. Citing Vibha Varshney, 'Divine Wrath Could Put Ski Resort Deal on Ice', *Down to Earth*, 15 March 2006, www.downtoearth.org.in/node/7429

[18] Berti, 'Divine Jurisdictions'. Discussing Safia Aggarwal, 'The Role of Religion in Conservation and Degradation of Forests: Examples from the Kumaun Himalaya', in Arjun Guneratne (ed.), *Culture and the Environment in the Himalaya* (Abingdon: Routledge, 2010): 132–50.

[19] Ibid., 13–14.

[20] Ibid., 14.

[21] Ibid., 19. The Company filed suit with the Uttarakhand High Court, but according to Berti, the case has languished for years without any resolution.

Deities might serve effectively as a legal bulwark against the environmental degradation caused by the rapid industrialisation of natural spaces, but it also creates legal and political problems. On the one hand, as Berti notes:

> One area where religion has joined the environmental debate is in the Hindutva (Hindu right-wing fundamentalist) movement. One example is the longstanding campaign against the Tehri dam, in what today is Uttarakhand, where the religious arguments used by environmental activists – that the building of a dam on the headwaters of the river Ganga would disturb the Ganges (goddess) self-purification powers – has been reinterpreted according to the rhetoric used by Hindutva leaders active in the region, who are more concerned with the discourse about the Ganges as a symbol of Hindu culture and nation.[22]

Berti's observation serves as a timely reminder that expanding the remit of juridical personality on the basis of faith in an environmental context might have undesirable consequences in the communitarian context. Affording juristic personality to the Gaṅgā may prove effective in holding public and private institutions to account for pollution, but this novel use of the jurisprudence of Hindu religious and charitable trusts, like the claim in the Ayodhya dispute that the *land* in question was the legal person Rām Asthan Janmabhūmi, creates a form of ownership that is essentially immune to the operation of civil law. The Supreme Court rejected this proposition in the Ayodhya Dispute, ruling that: 'The purpose for which juristic personality is conferred cannot be "evolved" into a trojan horse that permits, on the basis of religious faith and belief, the extinguishing of all competing proprietary claims over property as well stripping the property itself of the essential characteristic of immoveable property.'[23]

It remains to be seen how the Supreme Court will rule in ***Mohd. Salim v State of Uttarakhand & Others*** & ***Lalit Miglani v State of Uttarakhand and Others***. But, if the Ayodhya verdict is any indication, it seems likely that the Court will reject the juridical personality of the Gaṅgā and Yamunā. Nevertheless, we may say with certainty that the Hindu law of religious and charitable trusts and the juridical rights of Hindu deities are very much dynamic in the environmental context, and future cases may resolve some of the tensions discussed here. Furthermore, recent examples of attributing legal personality to rivers in New Zealand and in Colombia demonstrate that the Indian example is not an outlier. For example, in 2016, a Constitutional Court in Bogotá, Colombia ruled that: 'The

[22] Ibid., 3, citing Emma Tomalin, 'Bio-Divinity and Biodiversity: Perspectives on Religion and Environmental Conservation in India' *Numen* 51.3 (2004): 265–95; Mukul Sharma, 'Passages from Nature to Nationalism: Sunderlal Bahuguna and Tehri Dam Opposition in Garhwal', *Economic and Political Weekly* 8 (2009): 35–42; and Emma Mawdsley, 'The Abuse of Religion and Ecology: the Vishva Hindu Parishad and Tehri Dam', in Arjun Guneratne (ed.), *Culture and the Environment in the Himalaya* (Abingdon: Routledge, 2010): 151–65.

[23] 1 SCC 1 (2020) ¶201.

river Atrato, including its basins and contributors, is recognized as a *public corporation* with a right to protection, conservation, and recovery by the state and the ethnic communities.'[24]

6.2 The gods go West: Indian deities in Euro-American society and law

As Indians have spread out across the world in search of opportunity and as India has grown increasingly prosperous and politically influential, questions of Hindu law have appeared in foreign courts. Take, for example, Richard Davis' introduction to ***Bumper Development Corporation v Commissioner of Police of the Metropolis and Others***: '"Suing Shiva Dismays Dealers", read the headline on the Sunday Times of London, February 21, 1988. The Hindu God Śiva, it appeared, had come to the old imperial capital to bring a suit before the Queen's Bench for the return of his stolen property… a classic man-bites-dog story.'[25]

The British Broadcasting Corporation loves a good 'exotic Indian phenomenon is amusing' story, whatever be the veracity of its sometimes hackneyed presentation of the phenomenon in question.[26] The BBC's coverage and Richard Davis' excellent analysis of Śiva's suit has probably made ***Bumper Development Corporation*** the most well-known case involving Hindu law to have been adjudicated at the Queen's Bench in London.[27]

The facts of the case are relatively simple: in 1976, a landless labourer in southern India unearthed bronze sculptures of Śiva and his divine retinue on the former site of a 'temple which had been endowed in the late thirteenth century by a Hindu notable called Avui Thiru Vishwanatha… [but] had lain in ruins and unworshipped for a matter of centuries.'[28] The labourer sold the sculptures to local criminals, and they eventually ended up in London via the extensive, illicit black market in antiquities that has vexed the Government of India for decades.[29] The

[24] No. T-622/2016, paras. ¶10.2, emphasis added. Cited in Andreas Fischer-Lescano, 'Nature as a Legal Person: Proxy Constellations in Law', *Law and Literature* 32.2 (2020): 237–62.

[25] Davis, Lives of Indian Images, 195. ***Bumper Development Corporation Ltd v Commissioner of Police of the Metropolis*** (1991) 1 WLR 1362, (1991) 4 All ER 638.

[26] Recent examples include 'PhD Student Solves 2,500-Year-Old Sanskrit Problem', 15 December 2022, www.bbc.com/news/articles/cg3gw9v7jnvo; 'Carbon Dating Reveals Earliest Origins of Zero Symbol', 15 September 2017; and 'When Gods Were Hauled into Indian Courts', 29 February 2016, www.bbc.com/news/world-asia-india-35629805

[27] Of perhaps greater legal import, however, is ***Bal Mohinder Singh v Jasminder Singh and Another*** (2014) EWHC 1060 (Ch), where the Chancery Division heard a case involving a substantial fortune ostensibly held in a family trust according to the *Mitākṣarā* school of law.

[28] [1991] 4 All ER 638, 640 [Purchass, LJ].

[29] For the art market and repatriation, see Tapati Guha-Thakurta, 'Our Gods, Their Museums: The Contrary Careers of India's Art Object', *Art History* 30.4 (2007): 628–57; and S.K. Pachauri, 'Plunder of Cultural and Art Treasures: The Indian Experience', in Neil Brodie and Kathryn Walker Tubb

Śiva statue was sold to a Canadian businessman, Robert Borden. When Borden sent the statue to the British Museum for restoration, it was impounded by Scotland Yard, in 1982 'as part of a policy of returning religious artifacts… to their owners in India'.[30] Naturally, Borden sued the police for recovery of the statue, and the proceedings were joined by the State of Tamil Nadu.

Of note, as the proceedings progressed, the ruined temple was explored by the Indian Government, and 'amongst the surviving ruins and materials… was a… Sivalingam'. The local population 'reinstated [it] as an object of religious worship at the site of the [former] temple'.[31] The case turned on two questions: 1) whether the statue impounded by Scotland Yard was the same statue that had been dug up in Tamil Nadu (the Court answered in the affirmative); and 2) whether the Government of Tamil Nadu had better claim to the ownership of the statue than Borden's Bumper Corporation. At the King's Bench, Justice Ian Kennedy held that 'the "pious" intention of the twelfth century notable who gave the land and built the Pathur temple remained in being and was personified by the Sivalingam of the temple which itself had a title superior to that of Bumper'.[32]

Ironically, Justice Kennedy endorsement of the legal personality of the temple flowed from a 'hypothetical' recognition of a church as a legal person in medieval English law:

> (Sir John) Salmond recognizes the possibilities which may not be farfetched, of (say) a foreign Roman Catholic cathedral having legal personality under the law of the country where it is situated; and, in order to make the concept more comprehensible, let it be assumed that it is given that personality by legislation specifically empowering it to sue by its proper officer for the protection and recovery of its contents. It would, we think, be a strong thing for the English court to refuse the cathedral access simply on the ground that our own law would not recognize a similarly constituted entity as a legal person. The touchstone for determining whether access should be given or refused is the comity of nations, defined by the *Shorter Oxford English Dictionary* as: 'The courteous and friendly understanding by which each nation respects the laws and usages of every other, so far as may be without prejudice to its own rights and interests.'[33]

On appeal, the appellate judges noted that the 'true status in Hindu law' of the temple and its legal representative 'is central to the issues raised'.[34] The justices noted that 'it is trite law that foreign law in our courts is treated as a question of fact [and thereby governed by evidentiary standards]', and ruled that Justice

(eds), *Illicit Antiquities: The Theft of Culture and the Extinction of Archeology* (London: Routledge, 2002): 268–79.

[30] [1991] 4 All ER 638, 641 [Purchass, LJ].

[31] Ibid., 642.

[32] Ibid., 643.

[33] (1991) 4 All ER 638, 647–8 [Purchass, LJ].

[34] Ibid., 643 [Purchass, LJ].

Kennedy's interpretation of Indian Supreme Court law concerning Hindu religious and charitable trusts was flawed.[35]

Furthermore, the Court ruled, on the same basis that Justice Kennedy was 'not entitled to rely on his own researches based on passages from Mukherjea['s] *Hindu Law of Religious and Charitable Trusts* (1951) without having the assistance of the expert witness', but nevertheless accepted Mukherjea's textbook as evidence on account of its having been referred to at trial by expert witnesses (a technical, procedural point).[36] On the basis of Mukherjea's textbook, their lordships accepted the juristic personality of the temple under Hindu (and therefore English) law, but declined to comment on the question of whether the *deity* rather than the *temple* could be recognised as a legal person under English law.[37]

The courts formulated the juridical personality of Hindu deities in the following terms: 'The pious intention of the 12th Century notable, who gave the land and built the Pathur temple, remains in being and is, personified by the temple itself, a juristic entity which has a title to the Nataraja superior to that of the defendant.'[38] This is not entirely accurate, but it comes close enough to the established Indian jurisprudence of Hindu religious and charitable trusts that it was cited by the Supreme Court of India with approval in ***M. Siddiq v Suresh Das***.[39]

While some have noted the chilling effect of ***Bumper*** on 'the prestige and credibility of London as a centre of the international art market', one could also argue, perhaps more persuasively, that the courts' efforts to ensure the return of stolen cultural heritage is a laudable example of the judiciary prioritising equity – in the general sense of fairness – and working to understand the intricacies of a jurisprudence that might have seemed remarkably exotic.[40] It is deeply ironic that an English court in the former imperial metropole would recognise the legal personality of deities as exotic foreign law, when jurists from those very courts had shaped that law using the principles of English trusts.

Bumper is representative of the wider inclusion of Hindu religious institutions and practices in the secular legal systems of the West. Focusing on Britain, my adopted home, Hindu religious institutions are almost universally registered as charities under the Charities Act of 2011. This, of course, raises interesting questions concerning the assimilation of Hindu religious practices and activities into

[35] Ibid., 644. Kennedy cited ***Reddy v Reddy*** (1967) AIR 1967 SC 436 & ***Vikrama Das v Daulat Ram*** (1956) AIR SC 382.

[36] (1991) 4 All ER 638, 646.

[37] Ibid., 648–9. Note that Davis, *Lives of Indian Images*, 251, inaccurately relates that Kennedy recognises the juristic personality of Śiva – rather than the temple.

[38] Kennedy, J. Cited in Sandy Ghandhi and Jennifer James, 'The God That Won', *International Journal of Cultural Property* 1.2 (1992): 369–382.

[39] 1 SCC 1 (2020) ¶103.

[40] For the complaint, see Robert Paterson, 'The Curse of the London Nataraj', *International Journal of Cultural Property* 5.2 (1996): 330–8.

the wider rubric of English conceptions of 'charity' and concerning the prohibition on discrimination under the Equality Act of 2010.[41]

Although the British Hindu community numbers only about 800,000 individuals (a little over 1 per cent of the total population of the UK), Hindus are widely represented in politics, law, culture, commerce, and education. While many Hindus proudly practise their religion in the UK, the discourse around British Hindus, unlike British Muslims of South Asian extraction, has been one of remarkable and positive assimilation.[42] The ever-increasing cultural and economic ties between India and Britain – now built on mutual self-interest and the comity of nations, rather than on colonial exploitation – as well as the presence of a growing, prosperous and pious Hindu diasporic community in the UK and in Europe, will likely lead to a greater interaction between the judiciary and the Hindu religious institutions.

While it is unlikely that the legal personality of Hindu deities will ever be utilised *within* Britain – the establishment of registered charities seems to be an effective mechanism at present – it is highly likely that the story of Hinduism flourishing in Britain will include the assimilation of Hindu temples and monasteries to English charity law. That, however, is a question for future academic research.

6.3 Summary of chapters

This monograph examined the theory and practice of Equity and Trusts in Sanskrit jurisprudential literature (Dharmaśāstra) and in Indian legal history over roughly two millennia. The core argument of the book was that Sanskrit jurists articulated complex theories of Equity as a form of supplemental (*pāribhāṣika*)

[41] For an account of global Hindu deities, see Joanne Waghorne, *Diaspora of the Gods: Modern Hindu Temples in an Urban Middle-Class World* (Oxford: Oxford University Press, 2004). For discussions of Hindu institutions within the rubric of British Charities law, see Frank Canmer, 'Paying the Piper? Public Funding and Supervision of Religion in a Secularized Society (United Kingdom)', in Francis Messner (ed.), *Public Funding of Religions in Europe* (London: Routledge, 2015): 171–98. An extensive discussion of two cases involving the Kṛṣṇa worshipping sect, ISKON – ***ISKON v Secretary of State for the Environment and Hertsmere Borough Council*** (1992) 16 March (unreported) and ***ISKON v United Kingdom*** (1994) 76-A Dec & Rep 90 – appears in S. Poulter, *Ethnicity, Law and Human Rights – The English Experience* (Oxford: Oxford University Press, 1998). Also see Sidharthan Maunaguru, '"Homeless" Deities and Refugee Devotees: Hindu Temples, Sri Lankan Tamil Diaspora, and Politics in the United Kingdom', *American Anthropologist* 123.3 (2021): 552–64. For issues of caste discrimination at British Hindu temples, see Prakash Shah, *Against Caste in British Law: A Critical Perspective on the Caste Discrimination Provision in the Equality* (London: Palgrave Macmillan, 2015); and Annapurna Waughray, *Capturing Caste in Law: The Legal Regulation of Caste Discrimination* (London: Taylor & Francis, 2022).

[42] See Werner Menski, 'Asians In Britain and the Question of Adaptation to a New Legal Order: Asian Laws in Britain', in Milton Israel and N. K. Wagle (eds), *Ethnicity, Identity, Migration: The South Asian Context.* (Toronto: University of Toronto Press, 1993): 238–69.

or conventional (*sāmayika*) law that the Crown, as *parens patriae*, had a duty to protect. This model of Indian Equity is remarkably similar to theories of Equity from the ancient world, including Babylon, Greece, Rome, and the early Christian Church. Those ancient, Western systems of jurisprudence influenced the development of Equity jurisprudence at the English Court of Chancery. In the introduction to this monograph, I argued that, even though these systems of Equity had notable differences from one another – the product of the unique historical circumstances of their creation and evolution – they nevertheless shared core principles such as *parens patriae* jurisdiction, guardianship, fiduciary duties, and *trust*.

As with Equity, I argued that Dharmaśāstra articulates a theory of trusts which, while not identical to the highly technical English variety, shares the core principle of a fiduciary who must employ property for stipulated purposes. It seems that every developed legal system in world history developed a theory of fiduciaries; the likely explanation for this, I would argue, is the ubiquitous phenomenon of individuals making bequests and other charitable ventures. India, however, developed a distinctive form of trust – one shared to an extent with Babylon, Greece, and Rome – in which deities were recognised as legal persons, who owned assets, and engaged in commercial activities. India's compendious epigraphic records reveal that Hindu deities were numerous and legally robust during the classical and medieval periods. In the course of time, however, ancient Roman, Greek, and Babylonian religions died out, while Hindu deities have enjoyed a longevity rivalled only by the God of the Abrahamic faiths.

While Hindu deities have been recognised as legal persons for more than two-thousand years, the precise implications of that personality have shifted over the centuries. Different rulers brought different conceptions of legal personality and its incidents to India, yet they all contributed to the modern incarnation of the Hindu law of religious and charitable trusts. Another objective of this monograph has been, therefore, to examine different epochs in the history of the Sanskrit jurisprudence of Equity and Trusts in an effort to understand where that law came from and where it will head in the coming decades (or centuries).

6.3.1 Chapter 1

This chapter argued that notwithstanding Justice Mukherjea's claim to the contrary, Sanskrit jurisprudence articulates a comprehensive, if diffusely spread, jurisprudence of Equity and Trusts. By working *synchronically* through numerous Dharmaśāstric, Arthaśāstric, and philosophical treatises, and collecting maxims concerning Equity and Trusts alongside these texts, Chapter 1 added several new passages to the material that has been collected before. In the aggregate, these *dicta* demonstrate that there is substantially more material than many scholars have assumed. Furthermore, there are, in fact, many discussions of legal phenomena that one would associate with Courts of Equity in English jurisprudence: trusts, guardianship, and the administration of the estates of legal incompetents. The Crown in Sanskrit jurisprudence, like the Crown in English or Roman jurisprudence, must, as *parens patriae*, protect the property and legal interests of its most vulnerable subjects.

The jurisprudence of divine endowments, however diffuse, is consistent: temples and other religious endowments are ancient and consistently afforded royal protection; their assets are managed by guardians who owe fiduciary duties towards those institutions; various secular and religious communities have the right to establish the conventional legal rules which govern the management of the endowment (either through writing or through the intentions of a founder); when guardians breach their fiduciary duties the Crown must hold them accountable for breach of trust; deities share an analogous relationship with women, minors, and other protected categories of individuals; and, whatever the metaphysical explanation used to explain it, deities' juridical personhood (their nominal ownership of assets) is recognised as a customary (and therefore legal) convention.

The wider scholarly intervention of the chapter was the problematisation of the common scholarly assumption of a divide between 'popular' conventions and elite jurisprudence. Günther-Dietz Sontheimer, among others, probably overemphasised the importance of some Mīmāṃsā and related Dharmaśastra arguments that ostensibly deny the legal personality of Hindu deities.[43] The *textual* data (independent of the corroborating epigraphic data) indicate that at every historical level of its development, the Dharmaśāstric tradition *accommodates* image worship within its wider jurisprudence of Equity and Trusts. Admittedly, the Brāhmaṇical tradition often expressed anxiety about image worship, but a close reading of the Mīmāṃsā treatises that purportedly reject the ownership of deities furnish some of the most detailed legal accounts concerning the practical operation of temple trusts (involving servants who enact the wishes of deities in return for compensation). The legal personality for Hindu deities forms a ubiquitous facet of Dharmaśāstra.

6.3.2 Chapter 2

Chapter 2 surveys approximately two-thousand years' worth of Indian epigraphs in an effort to follow Gerard Colas' recommendation that, 'Only an extensive enquiry into the phraseology of inscriptions would make it possible to define and organize in a[n] historical perspective the various political, social, and religious

[43] Sontheimer, 'Religious Endowments in India'.

circumstances of the rise of the concept of deity-image in epigraphy'.[44] My central argument was that Dharmaśāstric theories of Equity and Trusts served as the jurisprudential foundation for the practical creation and regulation of religious endowments in classical and medieval India.

In the aggregate, the data strongly suggest a clear linear evolution of trusts from the Mauryan Empire (321–185 BCE) to the establishment of the Delhi Sulṭānate (1206 CE). Initially, classical Indian trusts tended to be fairly simple allocations of tax-free land to particular monastic (typically Jain or Buddhist) tradition and were written in Prakrit languages. For example, Aśoka Maurya's dedication of income (to the Buddhist monks who possessed the Buddha's relics at Lumbinī) became the template for more elaborate dedications of perpetual endowments (*akṣayanīvīs*) by the Kuṣāṇas, Śakas, and Sātavāhanas during the Age Between the Empires (~100 BCE–300 CE). There were a few temple endowments made during this period, but Hindus deities rarely, if ever, appeared as robust legal persons.

The advent of the Gupta era ushered in significant advancements in the law of Equity and Trusts. The legal instruments that earlier rulers had used to endow Buddhist and Jain institutions were deployed to support the newly ascendent cults of Purāṇic deities, such as Viṣṇu, Śiva, and the goddess. At the same time, endowments to deities began to invoke Brāhmaṇical, Dharmaśāstric concepts, and use Sanskrit, rather than Prakrit. This effectively inaugurated the constitutional order of the Sanskrit Cosmopolis, in which a common linguistic and jurisprudential idiom anchored a stable, pan-Indic model of sovereign power involving a series of porous, layered political polities.[45] Even though Hindu deities were clearly recognised as legal persons in endowments (the endowments almost always mention the deity as the recipient), the deity was usually just the beneficiary of these endowments.

Later, between the 6th and 9th centuries, deities and their endowments played increasingly important political roles as the eponymous, tutelary deities of consolidated dynasties with pan-Indian imperial ambitions. At this point, temple endowments became significantly more complex and deities' property portfolios grew. As the deities' fortunes grew, however, they became more likely to be plundered by rival dynasties.[46] At the same time, the panegyric and legal language of these grants grew increasingly Sanskritic, even as the regional vernaculars such as Kannada and Tamil were used for the first time. During the 8th century, the 'Tripartite Struggle' between the Rāṣṭrakūṭas, Pālas, and Gurjara-Pratihāras, dominated Indian politics. At the same time, deities owned intricate property portfolios and their trustees held increasingly sophisticated rights over divine

[44] Colas, 'Images and Territory of Gods', 114.
[45] For the Sanskrit Cosmopolis, see Pollock, Language of the Gods. For an analysis of the relationship between the cosmopolis and law, see Davis, 'Historical Overview', 17–20.
[46] See, for example, Davis, 'Indian Art'.

endowments.[47] Deities owned fields, endowments, shops, and offered loans at interest to public and private individuals. Deities even found themselves as parties in legal disputes between deities.

The theory and practice of the law of Equity and Trusts reached its pre-Islamic zenith around the turn of the second millennium, CE. While the great Kalyāṇa Cālukya and Cōḷa empires battled for sub-continental supremacy, they, their subordinates, and their sometimes overambitious rivals, left behind elaborate records of divine and charitable trusts.[48] The charters for these endowments, although often written in Kannada and in Tamil nevertheless utilised the jurisprudential theories of Dharmaśāstra and the legal instruments of earlier eras. Furthermore, the increasing connection between imperial dynasties and the endowment and supervision of temples and monasteries as strategy of rule, led to the spoliation of many religious endowments.

6.3.3 Chapter 3

Chapter 3 examines the transformation of Sanskrit theories and practices of Equity and Trusts in Islamic India.[49] Islamic rulers came to India as early as 711 CE, when Muḥammad ibn al-Qāsim conquered Sind.[50] Over the centuries, vast swaths of the Indian subcontinent fell under the sway of Turkic conquerors from Central Asia. With the establishment of the Delhi Sulṭānate in 1206, Islamic hegemony became a key feature of life in India. The advent of Islamic rule in India precipitated profound changes to India's religious, political, linguistic, and legal landscapes: Muslim communities immigrated to India (and many Indians converted to Islam); a series of Islamic dynasties established emirates and sulṭānates over most of India; Persian largely supplanted Sanskrit as the predominant language of literature and administration; and highly centralised bureaucratic regimes replaced the decentralised, administrative polities of the Sanskrit cosmopolis.

A new constitutional paradigm, designated the 'Persian cosmopolis' by Richard Eaton, largely supplanted the Sanskrit cosmopolis of the early medieval era.[51] Contrary to what some communalists would expect, Hindu and Muslim rulers alike embraced the administrative and cultural technologies of the Persian cosmopolis. While some Muslim rulers before the Mughal emperors (1526–1857 CE) tolerated or patronised Hindu religious institutions, the most significant developments occurred in the Vijayanagara Empire (1336–1646 CE).[52] The Vijayanagara

[47] Schmiedchen, 'Imperial Rulers'.
[48] See, for example, Inden *et al.*, Querying the Medieval.
[49] I take my lead from Truschke, The Language of History.
[50] For the *Chachnāma*, see Ahmed, Book of Conquest.
[51] Eaton, 'Persian Cosmopolis'.
[52] For the history of Vijayanagara, see Stein, New Cambridge History.

emperors, styled as Hindu sulṭāns, applied the centralised administrative techniques of the sulṭānates to a jurisprudentially Dharmaśāstric realm. The emperors, like some of their contemporaries dedicated the entire kingdom to their tutelary deity, Virūpākṣa and ruled as stewards on the deity's behalf. In short, a fusion between Dharmaśāstric *theory* and Persianate *practice* fundamentally changed the system of administration of Hindu religious endowments.

In later times, the Mughal emperors (1526–1857 CE) and the Marāṭhā Confederacy (1674–1818 CE), endowed many Hindu temples within the parameters of a Sanskritised-Persianate chancery practice of revenue allocation.[53] In the Mughal context, state patronage, protection, and legal supervision of Hindu religious trusts under an Islamic, Persianate legal regime was integral to a laudable effort to build an inclusive state, in which ecumenical imperial patronage went hand-in-glove with Mughal authority. The telos of the chapter is, in short, that notwithstanding many instances of interreligious conflict and temple desecration, Islamic India served as a productive environment for the development of a more sophisticated, centralised theory and practice of Hindu Equity and Trusts.

6.3.4 Chapter 4

In 1765, the British East India Company acquired *dīwānī* (tax collection) rights over the provinces of Bengal, Bihar, and Orissa via a decree (*farmān*) from the Mughal Emperor Shāh ʿĀlam II. At this moment, the Company began its momentous transition from being a mercantile outfit towards becoming an ever-expanding territorial power. Effectively, the Company stepped into Persianate Mughal administrative vestments as a nominal agent of the emperor and used that as a springboard to slowly annex increasingly greater portions of the subcontinent. Under the Mughal constitutional order *dīwānī* rights also entailed the responsibility for the administration of law. Consequently, the Company adopted Warren Hastings' Judicial Plan in 1772, whereby British judges would dispense civil justice to the native population according to native law.[54]

The Anglo-Hindu law of religious and charitable trusts was in a large part shaped by these wider constitutional issues between 1772 and 1862, as well as by the principles of Sanskrit jurisprudence and English practices from the Court of Chancery. At first, the Government assumed the power of regulating religious endowments – especially temples – on the basis of their *parens patriae* rights as the *Dīwān* of Bengal, Bihar, and Orissa, and other native titles of sovereignty. These

[53] For an overview of Persianate chancery practices, see Green, 'Introduction'. Also see Arjomand, 'Evolution'.

[54] For an account of early Company suzerainty and its impact on the development of Anglo-Hindu law, see Fleming, Ownership and Inheritance, Chapter 2.

actions, especially as we saw in the context of the Jagannātha temple in Puri, were largely the practices of pre-colonial sovereigns and the jurisprudential theory of Dharmaśāstra, but they also relegated earlier kings to the status of mere trustee, rather than sovereign.[55]

The era of Crown rule changed India's legal landscape dramatically. The High Courts Act of 1861 led to the creation of unified High Courts within each presidency. The Religious Endowments Act of 1863 formally dissociated the Central Government from its role as administrator of religious endowments (a *de facto* dissociation had been in effect since the 1840s) and shifted responsibility for the supervision of temple trustees to the courts.[56] Between 1863 and approximately 1900, the courts focused on the fiduciary duties of trustees in public and private Hindu religious institutions. *Shebaits*, *dharmakartas*, *mahants*, and other categories of agents who managed endowed assets on behalf of deities did not assimilate *precisely* to the English concept of a trustee – in which property vested *in the trustee* rather than in the beneficiary.[57] Nevertheless, in holding fiduciaries accountable for their malfeasance, the courts also delineated *shebaits*' and *dharmakartas*' positive rights as trustees, including the use of endowed assets for the commercial benefit of the deity and its endowment.

The 20th century saw the courts shift the focus of their legal analysis to the question of deities' status under the law. The codification of civil procedure and more substantive law by the legislature meant that the courts had to resolve several ambiguities in the judicial precedents governing Hindu religious endowments within the wider remit of civil law. In essence, this meant testing earlier rulings concerning the legal personhood of Hindu deities (and the fiduciary duties of their guardians) within the context of the right to suit, the law of limitation, adverse possession, and even taxation.

Furthermore, suits were increasingly being filed *with the deity as the primary plaintiff or defendant* – a novel development for Anglo-Hindu law.[58] In delineating *who* could serve as a 'next friend' – usually on the basis of having a beneficial interest in the endowment – the courts began to frame the legal personality of Hindu deities as a 'compendious expression' of the pious purpose of the worshipper to worship the deity. This effectively reframed divine endowments as a novel form of purpose trusts.

In short, the Anglo-Hindu law of religious and charitable trusts produced a complex, sophisticated hybrid system of jurisprudence that combined features of Sanskrit legal discourse and practice with the characteristic features of the

[55] See, for example, Kulke, 'Juggernaut'.
[56] The standard work of reference is Birla, Stages of Capital.
[57] Justice Ali discusses this at length in ***Vidya Varuthi Thirtha v Balusami Ayyar*** (1922) 24 Bom LR.
[58] To my knowledge, the first case to be filed in the name of the deity is ***Sri Sri Kalimata Debi and Anr. v Nagendra Nath Chuckerbutty*** (1927) AIR Cal 244.

Common Law, including binding judicial precedent and universally applicable statutes. The jurisprudence supporting this hybrid law, however, remained largely faithful to Dharmaśāstric principles, even when it took its cue from English Equity. Ironically, in my estimation, the absence of significantly detailed formal rules governing trusts in Sanskrit jurisprudential literature – a feature discussed at length in Chapter 1 – led British jurists away from the issue which vexed them in the context of inheritance law: the misconstrual of scholastic jurisprudential *theory* as practical positive law. In effect, limiting their use of Dharmaśāstric resources to general principles led British jurists to take a more authentically indigenous approach, *jurisprudentially* and practically, to the supervision of Hindu religious endowments.

6.3.5 Chapter 5

Chapter 5 turns to the independence of the Dominion of India in 1947, the introduction of the Constitution of the Republic of India in 1950, and the Supreme Court of India's jurisprudence of Hindu religious and charitable trusts over the past seventy years. The chapter does so with an eye towards exploring how the Supreme Court of India deployed the sundry components of its jurisprudential 'toolbox' of the Hindu law of religious and charitable trusts in its verdict on the infamous 'Ayodhyā dispute', ***M. Siddiq v Suresh Das,*** delivered in 2019.[59]

I focus on four jurisprudential 'tools' in the Supreme Court's arsenal: 1) the jurisdiction of the Court in exercising a supervisory role of religious endowments and over State regulation of religious endowments; 2) the balancing of a respect for the distinctive customs and beliefs of religious communities against constitutional provisions and statues prohibiting caste and gender-based discrimination; 3) recognising collective belief as the primary criterion for the attribution of legal personality of Hindu deities, while setting reasonable limits on the objects and rights of divine legal persons; and 4) distinguishing between the quasi-proprietary rights of *shebaits* and the nominal ownership of deities in matters of taxation, limitation, and adverse possession.

The Supreme Court inherited the vast body of Anglo-Hindu case law (and colonial law more generally) under Articles 296 and 372 of the Constitution.[60]

[59] ***M. Siddiq v Suresh Das*** 1 SCC 1 (2020).

[60] **Article 296:** 'Subject as hereinafter provided, any property in the territory of India which, if this Constitution had not come into operation, would have accrued to His Majesty or, as the case may be, to the Ruler of an Indian State by escheat or lapse, or as *bona vacantia* for want of a rightful owner, shall, if it is property situate in a State, vest in such State, and shall, in any other case, vest in the Union'; **Article 372(1):** '1) Notwithstanding the repeal by this Constitution of the enactments referred to in article 395 but subject to the other provisions of this Constitution, all the law in force in the territory of India immediately before the commencement of this Constitution shall continue in force therein until altered or repealed or amended by a competent Legislature or other competent authority.'

Furthermore, Articles 25–28 (although mostly 25 and 26) of the Indian Constitution establish fundamental rights to practice one's religion freely, although these rights are not absolute. Rather, they must be balanced against other rights – such as freedom from discrimination – and the wider application of civil law.[61]

Under the old Anglo-Hindu jurisprudence, however, deities tended to be viewed primarily within the rubric of private property rights: donors, fiduciaries, and beneficiaries all being bound by contract or by trust. Under the Constitution, however, deities' juridical personality increasingly functioned as a legal cypher for the right to worship: belief and faith, became as important as contract in assessing the relationship between deities and their human co-agents. As Rajeev Dhawan notes:

> A very important section of the case law [of the Supreme Court on religious endowments] has been constitutional. Religious rights which under Anglo-Hindu law had been translated into proprietary interests had to be re-translated into constitutional terminology and adjusted into the framework of constitutional limitations. Apart from this proprietary facet, religious rights were protected by the Constitution. Thus, constitutional claims could be made by those that made worship possible and the worshipper.[62]

In the decades since 1950, the Supreme Court has worked steadily and admirably to bring Anglo-Hindu case law into alignment with the principles of the Constitution, and to develop a rights-based jurisprudence of Hindu religious and charitable trusts that respects the faith and belief of the Hindu community without protecting gender or caste-based discrimination, or without encouraging communalistic conflict.

All of these developments were tested in the Ayodhyā dispute. To say that the Ayodhyā dispute and the Supreme Court's verdict concerning it were controversial would be an understatement. Nevertheless, while many critics and scholars have criticised the Supreme Court's decision to award the contested site of the erstwhile Bābrī Masjid to the divine litigant, Rām Lalla Virajman, even controversial decisions have logic. Furthermore, the 1,000-plus-page unanimous ruling from the Supreme Court in 2019 is, without question, the most sophisticated and authoritative disquisition on the jurisprudence of the Hindu law of religious and charitable trusts in Indian history. Consequently, the Court's opinion in ***M. Siddiq v Suresh Das*** provides invaluable information about future communitarian cases – involving Mathurā and Vārāṇasī, among many other historically contested sites – as about cases involving environmental concerns or caste and gender-based discrimination.[63]

[61] See Das Acevedo, 'Gods' Homes'; and Das Acevedo, 'Temples, Courts'.

[62] Dhawan, 'The Supreme Court'.

[63] Jolly and Menon, 'Of Ebbs and Flows'. For gender discrimination, see Das Acevedo, The Battle for Sabarimala.

6.4 A final thought

In many ways, this monograph is the fruit of my efforts to offer a Sanskritist's comments on Chief Justice B.K. Mukherjea's renowned *Hindu Law of Religious and Charitable Endowments*, which has been cited often by scholars and courts since its first edition was published in 1951. The aim of *Equity and Trusts in Sanskrit Jurisprudence* was to explore how, when, and why different jurists at different moments in Indian history drew on the principles and maxims of Sanskrit Equity to develop practical systems to manage Hindu religious and charitable trusts.

The problem with such a task, as the reader must appreciate after having read the chapters of this monograph, is that, as Mukherjea notes, there is a 'paucity of materials on the subject of endowments in Hindu law'.[64] This paucity is perhaps overstated, and in carefully combing through the Dharmaśāstric and related textual sources, I was able to glean several additional, and highly relevant *dicta*. Using these, it was possible to provide a more nuanced and complete account of Equity and Trusts in Sanskrit jurisprudence and of Sanskrit jurisprudence in the practical legal history of Indian trusts.

The Indian story of trusts is much more interesting than its portrayal as an abstruse scholastic Sanskrit glass-bead-game. A familiarity with these technical facets of Equity and Trusts is vital in appreciating the law, for an appreciation for the law of trusts allows us to appreciate some of India's greatest historical moments from new perspectives. Aśoka Maurya's vast Indian realm was held together in no small part by the *parens patriae* jurisdiction that he articulated in his pan-Indian inscriptions. The rise of Temple Hinduism around the time of the Gupta Empire's ascendency witnessed the deities *themselves* becoming the direct beneficiaries of religious trusts. The great power politics of early medieval India involved imperial deities who were named after the ruling sovereign.

All of this was complicated and transformed by the advent of Islamic rule in India. While Mahṃūds Ghazni and Ghūrid destroyed many Hindu, Jain, and Buddhist institutions, they paved the way for the introduction of a more centralised, Persianate constitutional order. When the Vijayanagara emperors asserted their sovereignty and power, they did so by using a Sanskritised Persiante and sulṭānate idiom even as they endowed their tutelary deity with the entire realm. When the British stepped into the administrative vestments of the Mughal and Marāṭhā empires in the 18th century, they too continued the grand, venerable Indian tradition of sovereigns serving as custodians of Hindu deities.

The English introduced elements of English Equity and Trusts to India. Several of these English elements of Equity and Trusts share conceptual (if not historical) linkages to Dharmaśāstric accounts. As Justice Mukherjea notes: 'Religious and

[64] Mukherjea, *Hindu Law*, 1.

charitable trusts are found to exist... in almost all the civilized countries and their origin can be traced primarily to the instincts of piety and benevolence which are implanted in human nature.'[65] Ancient Sanskrit scholars created a sophisticated jurisprudence of Equity and Trusts, and:

> Whatever changes were brought about by time... the fundamental, moral and religious ideas of the Hindus which lie at the root of their religious and charitable institutions, remained substantially the same; and the system that we can see around us can be said to be an evolutionary product of the spirit and genius of the people passing through different phases of their cultural development.[66]

To Justice Mukherjea's wise utterance, I would only add that in understanding and appreciating these past phases of cultural development we will be in a better position to contribute to the future of the theory and practice of the Hindu law of religious and charitable trusts.

[65] Ibid.
[66] Ibid.

Bibliography

Primary sources

Alberuni's India: An Account of the Religion, Philosophy, Literature, Chronology, Astronomy, Customs, Laws, and Astrology of India. Edward Sachau (ed.) (London: Trübner & Co, 1887/88)

Alberuni's India: An Account of the Religion, Philosophy, Literature, Geography, Chronology, Astronomy, Customs, Laws and Astrology of India about AD 1030, Vol. 1. Edward Sachau (ed. & trans.) (Delhi: S. Chand, 1964)

Aparārka: Commentary on the Yājñavalkya-dharmaśāstra. Hari Nārāyaṇa Āpate (ed.) (Poona: Ānandāśrama Sanskrit Series, no. 46, 1903)

Bhagavantabhāskaraḥ. Veṇīmādhava Śāstrī (ed.) (Delhi: Caukhambā Saṃskṛta Pratiṣṭhāna, Vrajajīvana prācya bhāratī granthamālā, no. 9, 1985)

Brahmanical Theories of the Gift: A Critical Edition and Annotated Translation of the Dānakānda of the Krtyakalpataru. David Brick (ed. & trans.) (Cambridge, MA: Harvard University Press, 2015)

Brahmavaivarta Purāṇa. Greg Bailey (trans.) (New Delhi: Motilal Banarsidass, 2022)

Bṛhaspatismṛti. Rangaswami Aiyangar (ed.) (Calcutta: Baroda Oriental Institute, 1941)

Dānamayūkha. Ratna Gopal Bhatta (ed.) (Benares: Chowkhamba Sanskrit Series, Kāśī Saṃskr̥ta Granthamālā, no. 44, 1909)

Dānasāgara of Ballāla Sena. Bhabatosh Bhattacarya (ed.) (Calcutta: Asiatic Society, Bibliotecha Indica, Vol. 273, 1956)

Dharmasūtras: The Law Codes of Āpastamba, Gautama, Baudhāyana, and Vasiṣṭha, Patrick Olivelle (ed. & trans.) (Oxford: Oxford University Press, 1999)

Ibn Khallikan's Biographical Dictionary. Baron MacGukin de Slane (ed.) (Paris: Oriental Translation Fund, Vol. 3, 1868)

Kātyāyanasmṛtisāroddhāraḥ. P.V. Kāṇe (ed. & trans.) (Pune: Oriental Book Agency Reprint for *Hindu Law Quarterly*, 1933)

The Kauṭilīya Arthaśāstra: A Critical Edition with a Glossary, 2nd edn. R. P. Kangle (ed.) (Bombay: University of Bombay, 1969)

Kauṭalīyamarthaśāstram of Ācārya Viṣṇugupta: with Four Commentaries, Vol. 2.1. Śrī Viśvanātha Śāstrī Dātāra (ed.) (Varanasi Sarasvatībhāvana-Granthamālā, no. 130, 1991)

The Law Code of Viṣṇu: A Critical Edition and Annotated Translation of the Vaiṣṇavadharmaśāstra. Patrick Olivelle (ed.) (Cambridge MA: Harvard University Press, 2010)

Manu-Smṛti with the 'Manubhāṣya' of Medhātithi. Gaṅgānātha Jha (ed.) (Calcutta: Asiatic Society of Bengal, Vol. 1, 1932)

Muntakẖabu-t-tawārīkẖ. George Ranking (ed. & trans.) (Calcutta: Asiatic Society of Bengal, Vol. 1, 1898)

Nāradasmṛti. Richard Lariviere (ed. & trans.) (Philadelphia: University of Pennsylvania, 1989)

The New Oxford American Dictionary, 2nd edn. Erin McKean (ed.) (Oxford: Oxford University Press, 2005)

Nicomachean Ethics, 2nd edn. Terence Irwin (trans.) (Indianapolis: Hackett, 1999)

Padmapurāṇa. N.A. Deshpande (trans.) (Delhi: Motilal Banarsidass, 1988–92)

Pūrtakamalāra, Bhandarkar Oriental Research Institute Ms. No 838

Rājadharmakaustubha. Kamala Kṛṣṇa Smṛtitīrtha (ed.) (Baroda: Oriental Institute, Gaekwad Oriental Series 122, 1935)

Die Rāma-Tāpanīya-Upanishad. Albrecht Weber (ed.) (Berlin: Königl. Akademie der Wissenschaften, 1864)

Sanskrit Documents: Being Sanskrit Letters and Other Documents Preserved in the Oriental Collection at the National Archives of India. Surendranath Sen and Umesha Mishra (ed. & trans.) (Allahabad: Ganganatha Jha Research Institute, 1951)

Sarasvatīvilāsa. R. Shama Sastry (ed.) (Mysore: University of Mysore Oriental Library Publications, Sanskrit Series, no. 71, 1927)

Smṛticandrikā. Searchable Electronic Edition of the Vyavahārakāṇḍa of the Smṛticandrikā by Devaṇṇabhaṭṭa, transcribed, edited, formatted, by Patrick Olivelle, https://docs.google.com/document/d/1pm1UjraMz8O4gkP3hmFv9-ltw1Kx2TvCOtkGGAlNa9o/edit

St Thomas Aquinas Summa Theologiæ, Vol. 28. Thomas Gilby (ed.) (Cambridge: Blackfriars 1966)

Viṣṇudharmottapurāṇa (Hyderabad: Sarvodaya Sāhitya Mandira, 1929)

Vyavahāracintāmaṇi by Vācaspati Miśra: A Digest on Hindu Legal Procedure Ludo Rocher (ed. & trans.) (Gent: Gentse Orientalistiche Bijdragen 1. 1956)

Vyavahārasaukhya: The Treatise on Legal Procedure in the Ṭoḍarānanda Composed at the Instance of Ṭoḍaramalla During the Reign of Akbar. Ludo Rocher (ed. & trans.) (Florence: Società Editrice Fiorentina, 2016)

Vyavasthāchandrikā: A Digest of Hindu Law, as Current in all the Provinces of India, Except Bengal Proper. Shyāmācharan Sarkār (ed.) (Calcutta: I.C. Bose & Co., 1878)

Vyavasthādarpana: Digest of Hindu Law as Current in Bengal, 3rd edn. Shyāmācharan Sarkār (ed.) (Calcutta: I.C. Bose & Co., 1883)

The Works of Sir John Fortescue. Thomas Fortescue, Lord Clermont (ed.) (London: Privately Printed, 1869)

The Yājñavalkyasmṛti with the Commentary Bālakrīda of Visvarūpāchārya. Two Parts. Ganapati Sastri (ed.) (Trivandrum: Government Press, 1922–24)

Yājñvalkyasmṛti with the Mitākṣarā of Vijñāneśvara. R.K. Panda (ed.) (Delhi: Bharatiya Kala Prakashan, 2011)

Secondary sources

Abbasi, Muhammad, 'Colonial State and Muslim Institutions: History of Regulatory Framework for Awqāf (Religious Endowment) in British India', in Rajeswary Brown and Justin Pierce (eds), *Charities in the Non-Western World* (Abingdon: Routledge, 2013): 311–32

Acharya, Diwakar, *Early Tantric Vaiṣṇavism: Three Newly Discovered Works of the Pañcarātra: Devāmṛtapañcarātra and Aṣṭādaśavidhāna: Critically Edited from their 11th and 12th-Century Nepalese Palm Leaf Manuscripts with an Introduction and Texts* (Paris: EFEO, 2015)

Aggarwal, Safia, 'The Role of Religion in Conservation and Degradation of Forests: Examples from the Kumaun Himalaya', in Arjun Guneratne (ed.), *Culture and the Environment in the Himalaya* (Abingdon: Routledge, 2010): 132–50

Ahmad, Aziz, 'Epic and Counter-Epic in Medieval India', *Journal of the American Oriental Society* 83.4 (1963): 470–6

Ahmed, Manan, *A Book of Conquest: The Chachnama and Muslim Origins in South Asia* (Cambridge, MA: Harvard University Press, 2016)

Ahmed, Saifuddin, 'The Role of the Media during Communal Riots in India: A Study of the 1984 Sikh Riots and the 2002 Gujarat Riots', *Media Asia* 37.2 (2010): 103–11

Aitchison, C.U., *A Collection of Treaties, Engagements, and Sanads Relating to India and Neighboring Countries*, Vol 8: Madras Presidency (Calcutta: Government Press, 1892)

Aiyangar, S. Krishnaswami, *A History of Tirupati*, 2 vols (Madras: Tirumalai Tirupati Devasthanam Committee, 1940–41)

Aiyar, Swarna, '"August Anarchy": The Partition Massacres in Punjab, 1947', *South Asia: Journal of South Asian Studies* (2007): 13–36

Ali, Daud, 'Royal Eulogy as World History: Rethinking Copper-plate Inscriptions in Cōḷa History', in Ronald Inden, Jonathan Walters, and Daud Ali (eds), *Querying the Medieval: Texts and the History of Practices in South Asia* (Oxford: Oxford University Press, 2000): 165–229

Alkire, Jennifer, 'Incompetency from an Equitable Perspective: Chancery and the Guardianship Doctrine', *The Journal of Legal Medicine* 1.1 (1979): 80–109

Alley, Kelly, 'Spiritual Ecology', *Religions* 10.9 (2019): 1–17

Ames, James 'The Origin of Uses and Trusts', *Harvard Law Review* 21.4 (1908): 261–74

Anand, Adarsh, 'Accession of Jammu and Kashmir State: Historical and Legal Perspective', *Journal of the Indian Law Institute* 43.4 (2001): 455–68

Anderson, Michael, 'Islamic Law and the Colonial Encounter in British India', in David Arnold and Peter Robb (eds), *Institutions and Ideologies: A SOAS South Asia Reader* (London: Routledge, 1993): 148–64

Appadurai, Arjun, *Worship and Conflict Under Colonial Rule: A South Indian Case* (Cambridge: Cambridge University Press, 1981)

Appadurai Breckenridge, Carol, 'From Protector to Litigant: Changing Relations Between Hindu Temples and the Rājā of Ramnad', *Indian Economic and Social History Review* 14.1 (1977): 75–106

Arjomand, Said, 'Evolution of the Persianate Polity and its Transmission to India', *Journal of Persianate Studies* 2 (2009): 115–36

Armstrong, Gregory 'Church and State Relations: The Changes Wrought by Constantine', *Journal of the American Academy of Religion* 32.1 (1964): 1–7

Arnaoutoglou, Ilias, 'Roman Law and Collegia in Asia Minor', *Revue Internationale des droits de l'"Antiquité* 49 (2002): 27–44

Arunima, Gopinath, 'Ayodhya Verdict: Bad Theology, Without Justice', *Economic and Political Weekly* 35.41 (2010)

Arvind, T.T., 'Religious Endowments and Trusts Law in Colonial India', in Liew Ying Khai and Wu Ying-Chieh (eds), *Asia-Pacific Trusts Law* (London: Bloomsbury, 2022): 55–76

Ashfaque, S.M., 'The Grand Mosque of Banbhore', *Pakistan Archaeology* 6 (1969): 182–209

Ayyar, A.S. Nataraja, *Mīmāmsā Jurisprudence: The Sources of Hindu Law* (Allahabad: Gaṅgānātha Jha Research Institute, 1952)

Bagchi, Jhunu, *The History and Culture of the Pālas of Bengal and Bihar, cir. 750–1200 AD* (Delhi: Abhinav, 1993)

Bagchi, S.C., *Juristic Personality of Hindu Deities* (Calcutta: University of Calcutta, 1933)

Bahuguna, Rameshwar Prasad, 'Religion and State in Eighteenth Century Rajasthan: Sawai Jai Singh and "Reformed" Vaishnavism', *Proceedings of the Indian Historical Congress* 74 (2013): 353–62

Baker, J.H., *The Oxford History of the Laws of England VI: 1483–1558* (Oxford: Oxford University Press, 2003)

Bakker, Hans (ed.), *The Vākāṭaka Heritage: Indian Culture at the Crossroads* (Groningen: Egbert Forsten, 2004)

Bakker, Hans (ed.), *Mansar: The Discovery of Pravareśvara and Pravarapura Temple and Residence of the Vākāṭaka King Pravarasena II* (Groningen: Library of the University of Groningen, 2008)

Bakker, Hans, 'Royal Patronage and Religious Tolerance The Formative Period of Gupta-Vākāṭaka Culture', *Journal of the Royal Asiatic Society* 20.4 (2010): 461–75

Bakker, Hans, 'The Gupta-Vakataka Relationship: A New Interpretation of the Ramagiri Evidence (2)', *Religions of South Asia* 5.1–2 (2012): 293–302

Bakker, Hans, 'Throne and Temple: Political Power and Religious Prestige in Vidarbha', in Hans Bakker (ed.), *Holy Ground: Where Art and Text Meet* (Leiden: Brill, 2019): 149–66

Bakker, Hans, and Harunaga Isaacson, 'The Ramtek Inscriptions II: The Vākāṭaka Inscription at the Kevala-Narasiṃha Temple', in Hans Bakker (ed.), *Holy Ground: Where Art and Text Meet* (Leiden: Brill, 2019): 113–47

Balogh, Dániel, *Inscriptions of the Aulikaras and Their Associates* (Berlin: Walter de Gruyter, 2019)

Baltutis, Michael C., 'Recognition and Legislation of Private Religious Endowments in Indian Law', in Robert Baird (ed.), *Religion and Law in Independent India*, 2nd edn. (New Delhi: Manoharlal Banarsidass, 2005): 443–68

Banerjee, Gooroodass, *The Hindu Law of Marriage and Stridhan* (Calcutta: Thacker, Spink & Co, 1879)

Bangash, Yaqoob, 'Implementing Partition: Proceedings of the Punjab Partition Committee, July–August, 1947', *Modern Asian Studies* 55.6 (2021): 1883–925

Barry, John Vincent, 'Suicide and the Law', *Melbourne University Law Review* 5.1 (1965): 1–16

Barua, B.M., 'The Sohgaura Copper Plate Inscription', *Journal of the Bhandarkar Oriental Research Institute* 11.1 (1930): 32–48

Baums, Stefan, 'Catalog and Revised Texts and Translations of Gandharan Reliquary Inscriptions', in David Jongeward, Elizabeth Errington, Richard Salomon, and Stefan Baums (eds), *Gandharan Buddhist Reliquaries* (Seattle: Early Buddhist Manuscripts Project, 2012): 211–12

Bayi, Princess Aswathi Thirunal Gouri Lakshmi, *Sree Padmanabha Swamy Temple*, 3rd edn. (Mumbai: Bharatiya Vidya Bhavan, 2013)

Beever, Allan, 'Aristotle on Equity, Law, and Justice', *Legal Theory* 10.1 (2004): 33–50

Behrens, Georg, 'An Early Tudor Debate on the Relation between Law and Equity', *The Journal of Legal History* 19.2 (1998): 143–61

Bell, H.E., *An Introduction to the History and Records of the Court of Wards and Liveries* (Cambridge: Cambridge University Press, 1953)

Benton, Lauren, *A Search for Sovereignty: Law and Geography in European Empires, 1400–1900* (New York: Cambridge University Press, 2010)

Berti, Daniela, 'Fighting Enemies and Protecting Territory: Deities as Local Rulers in Kullu, Himachal Pradesh', *European Bulletin of Himalayan Research* 29–30 (2006): 62–81

Berti, Daniela, 'Ritual Kingship, Divine Bureaucracy and Electoral Politics in Kullu' *European Bulletin of Himalayan Research* 29–30 (2006): 39–61

Berti, Daniela, 'Divine Jurisdictions and Forms of Government in Himachal Pradesh (Northern India)', in Daniela Berti and Gilles Tarabout (eds), *Territory, Soil and Society in South Asia* (New Delhi: Manoharlal Banarsidass, 2009): 311–39

Berti, Daniela, 'Gods' Rights vs Hydroelectric Projects: Environmental Conflicts and the Judicialization of Nature in India', *Rivista Degli Studi Orientali* 88.2 (2015): 111–29

Beth, Loren, 'The Judicial Committee as Constitutional Court for the British Empire 1833–1971', *Georgia Journal of International and Comparative Law* 7.1 (1977): 47–84

Betts, Raymond, 'The Allusion to Rome in British Imperialist Thought of the Late Nineteenth and Early Twentieth Centuries', *Victorian Studies* 15.2 (1972): 149–59

Bhargava, Rajeev (ed.), *Secularism and its Critics* (Oxford: Oxford University Press, 1999)

Bhargava, Rajeev, 'An Ancient Indian Secular Age?', in Akeel Bilgrami (ed.), *Beyond the Secular West* (New York: Columbia University Press, 2016): 188–214

Bhat, P. Ishwara, 'The Parens Patriae Role of the Courts in the Matter of Public Trusts Under §92 of the Civil Procedure Code: Expectations, Contributions, Limitations', *NUJS Law Review* 7.3–4 (2014): 205–24

Bhattacharya, Neeladri, 'Remaking Custom: The Discourse and Practice of Colonial Codification', in R. Champakalakshmi and S. Gopal (eds), *Tradition, Dissent and Ideology: Essays in Honour of Romila Thapar* (New Delhi: Oxford University Press, 1996), 20–51

Bhattacharyya, Dinesh, 'A Newly Discovered Copperplate from Tippera [The Gunaighar Grant of Vainyagupta: The Year 188 Current (Gupta Era)]', *The Indian Historical Quarterly* 6:1 (1930): 45–60

Bhatia, Gautam, 'Horizontal Discrimination and Article 15(2) of the Indian Constitution: A Transformative Approach', *Asian Journal of Comparative Law* 11.1 (2016): 87–109

Bhosle, Prince Pratap Sinh Serfoji Raje, *Contributions of Thanjavur Maratha Kings*, 2nd edn. (Channai: Notion Press, 2017)

Bilfrāmī, Rafat, *Religious and Quasi-Religious Departments of the Mughal Period (1556–1707)* (New Delhi: Munshiram Manoharlal, 1984)

Bindal, Amit, 'Complete Justice? Silences and Erasures in the Ayodhya Judgment', *Journal of Indian Law & Society* 11.1 (2020): 48–71

Bingham, Thomas (Lord), *The Rule of Law* (London: Penguin, 2011)

Birla, Ritua, *Stages of Capital: Law, Culture, and Market Governance in Late Colonial India* (Durham: Duke University Press, 2009)

Bisschop, Peter, 'Śaivism in the Gupta-Vākāṭaka Age', *Journal of the Royal Asiatic Society* 20.4 (2010): 477–88

Bisschop, Peter, and Elizabeth Cecil, 'Jayati Bhagavāñ Jinendraḥ! Jainism and Royal Representation in the Kadamba Plates of Palāśikā', *Journal of the American Oriental Society* 141.3 (2021): 613–35

Bisschop, Peter, and Elizabeth Cecil, 'Primary Sources and Asian Pasts: Beyond the Boundaries of the "Gupta Period"', in Peter Bisschop and Elizabeth Cecil (eds), *Primary Sources and Asian Pasts* (Berlin: De Grunter, 2021): 1–17

Bogaert, Raymond, *Banques et Banquiers dans les Cités Grecques* (Leiden: Sijthoff, 1968)

Borgolte, Michael, *World History as the History of Foundation, 3000 BCE to 1500 CE*, translated by Zachary Chitwood (Leiden: Brill, 2020)

Branfoot, Crispin, 'Remaking the Past: Tamil Sacred Landscape and Temple Renovations', *Bulletin of SAOS* 76.1 (2013): 21–47

Brimnes, Niels, 'Beyond Colonial Law: Indigenous Litigation and the Contestation of Property in the Mayor's Court in Late Eighteenth-Century Madras', *Modern Asian Studies* 37.3 (2003): 513–50

Bromberg, Benjamin, 'Temple Banking in Ancient Rome', *The Economic History Review* 10.2 (1940): 128–31

Bryk, Franciszek, *What Role Do Religious Institutions Play in Aristotle's Ideal Polis?* (Unpublished MSt Thesis: University of Oxford, 2023)

Buckland, William, *A Text-Book of Roman Law: From Augustus to Justinian* (Cambridge: Cambridge University Press, 1921)

Burghart, Richard, 'Wandering Ascetics of the Rāmānandī Sect', *History of Religions* 22.4 (1983): 361–80

Busch, Allison, 'Literary Responses to the Mughal Imperium: The Historical Poems of Keśavdās', *South Asia Research* 25: 1 (2005): 34–7

Busch, Allison, '"Unhitching the Oxcart of Delhi": A Mughal-Period Hindi Account of Political Insurgency', *JRAS* 28.3 (2018): 415–39

Calabria, Michael, 'The Unorthodox "Orthodoxy" of Shah Jahan: A Reassessment of His Religiosity', *South Asia: Journal of South Asian Studies* 41.3 (2018): 579–600

Calhoun, George, 'The Jurisprudence of the Greek City', *Columbia Law Review* 24.2 (1924): 154–71

Canmer, Frank, 'Paying the Piper? Public Funding and Supervision of Religion in a Secularized Society (United Kingdom)' , in Francis Messner (ed.), *Public Funding of Religions in Europe* (London: Routledge, 2015): 171–98

Cappalletti, Sara, 'The Avatāra in Medieval South Asian Contexts: Dynamic Translation Across Hindu, Buddhist and Islamic Traditions in the Ghaznavid Period', in Blain Auer and Ingo Strauch (eds), *Encountering Buddhism and Islam in Premodern Central and South Asia* (Berlin: De Grunter, 2019): 161–76

Carey, Christopher, 'Legal Space in Classical Athens', *Greece & Rome*, 41.2 (2009): 172–86

Carey, Christopher, Ifigeneia Giannadaki, and Brenda Griffith-Williams (eds), *Use and Abuse of Law in the Athenian Courts* (Leiden: Brill, 2018)

Carne, William Lindsay, 'A Sketch of the History of the High Court of Chancery from its Origin to the Chancellorship of Wolsey', *Virginia Law Register* 13.7 (1927): 391–421

Cassels, Jamie, 'Judicial Activism and Public Interest Litigation in India: Attempting the Impossible?', *The American Journal of Comparative Law* 37.3 (1989): 495–519

Catlin, Amy, '"Vātāpi Gaṇapatim": Sculptural, Poetic, and Musical Text in a Hymn to Gaṇeśa', in Robert Brown (ed.), *Ganesh: Studies of an Asian God* (Albany: SUNY, 1991): 141–70

Cecil, Elizabeth, *Mapping the Pāśupāta Landscape: Narrative, Place, and the Śaiva Imaginary in Early Medieval North India* (Leiden: Brill, 2020)

Cecil, Elizabeth, and Mekhola Gomes, 'Kāma at the Kadamba Court: The Guḍnāpur Pillar Inscription of Ravivarman as a Text-Monument', *Indo-Iranian Journal* 64 (2021): 10–50

Chakrabarty, Bidyut, 'B.R. Ambedkar and the History of Constitutionalizing India', *Contemporary South Asia* 24 (2016): 133–48

Chambers, John, *A Practical Treatise on the Jurisdiction of the High Court of Chancery Over the Persons and Property of Infants* (London: Saunders and Bennin, 1842)

Chandra, Aparna, *Gopal Singh Visharad and Ors v. Zahoor Ahmad and Ors., O.S.Nos. 1/1989, 3/1989, 4/1989, 5/1989: A Summary of the Babri Masjid-Ram Janm Bhoomi Decision* (11 October 2010), https://ssrn.com/abstract=1690803 or http://dx.doi.org/10.2139/ssrn.1690803

Chandra, Jnan, 'Aurangzib and Hindu Temples', *Journal of the Pakistan Historical Society* 5.4 (1957): 247–54

Chandra, Jnan, 'Alamgir's Tolerance in Light of Contemporary Jain Literature', *Journal of Pakistan Historical Society* 6.4 (1958): 269–72

Chandra, Satish, 'Some Religious Grants of Aurangzeb to "Maths" in the State of Marwar', *Proceedings of the Indian History Congress* 32.1 (1970): 405–7

Chandrachud, Abhinav, *An Independent, Colonial Judiciary: A History of the Bombay High Court during the British Raj, 1862–1947* (New York: Oxford University Press, 2015)

Chankowski, Véronique, *Athenes et Delos a l'epoque Classique: Recherches sur l'administration du Sanctuaire d'apollon Delien* (Unpublished PhD Dissertation: EPHE, 1999)

Chankowski, Véronique, 'Techniques Financières, Influences, Performances dans les Activités Bancaires des Sanctuaires Grecs', *Topoi Orient-Occident* 12.1 (2005): 69–93

Chankowski, Véronique, 'Les Places Financières dans le monde Grec Classique et hellénistique des Cités', *Pallas* (2007): 93–112

Chankowski, Véronique, 'Divine Financiers: Cults as Consumers and Generators of Value', in Zosia Archibald, John Davies, and Vincent Gabrielsen (eds), *The Economies of Hellenistic Societies, Third to First Centuries BC* (Oxford: Oxford University Press, 2011): 142–65

Chankowski, Véronique, *Parasites du Dieu: Comptables, Financiers et Commerçants dans la Délos Hellénistique* (Athens: École Française d"Athènes, 2020)

Chatterjee, Nandini, *The Making of Indian Secularism: Empire, Law and Christianity, 1830–1960* (Cambridge: Cambridge University Press, 2011)

Chatterjee, Partha, *A Princely Impostor? The Kumar of Bhawal and the Secret History of Indian Nationalism* (New Delhi: Orient Blackswan, 2004)

Chatterjee, Tarender, and Bhujendro Bhushan Chatterjee, *G.M. Tagore, versus Woopendermohun Tagore, and Others: Being a Full Report of the Proceedings in the Above Containing the Will of the Late Honorable Prosonocoomar Tagore, C.S.I., the Judgment of the High Court both of Original and Appellate, Sides, Grounds of Appeal of Parties in the Privy Council, Brief Extract of Argument in the Privy Council During Hearing, and Judgment of the Lords Justices of the Privy Council* (Calcutta: Indian Mirror Press, 1872)

Chattopadhyaya, D. *et al.* (eds), *Inscriptions and Agrarian Issues in Indian History: Essays in Memory of D.C. Sircar* (Kolkata: The Asiatic Society, 2017)

Chetty, A. Subbarraya, 'Tipu's Endowments to Hindus and Hindu Institutions', *Proceedings of the Indian History Congress* 7 (1944): 416–19

Chiera, Edward, *They Wrote on Clay: The Babylonian Tablets Speak Today* (Cambridge: Cambridge University Press, 1939)

Chiriyankandath, James, '"Creating a Secular State in a Religious Country": The Debate in the Indian Constituent Assembly', *Commonwealth & Comparative Politics* 38.2 (2000): 1–28

Choudhry, Sujit, Madhav Khosla, and Pratap Bhanu Mehta (eds), *The Oxford Handbook of the Indian Constitution* (Oxford: Oxford University Press, 2016)

Clooney, Francis X., 'Why the Veda Has No Author: Language as Ritual in Early Mīmāṃsā and Post-Modern Theology', *Journal of the American Academy of Religion* 55.4 (1987): 659–84

Clooney, Francis X., *Thinking Ritually: Rediscovering the Pūrva Mīmāṃsā of Jaimini* (Vienna: Nobili Research Library, 1990)

Clooney, Francis X., 'What's a God? The Quest for the Right Understanding of Devatā in Brāhmaṇical Ritual Theory (Mīmāṃsā)', *International Journal of Hindu Studies* 1.2 (1997): 337–85

Clooney, Francis X., 'Śaṅkara's Theological Realism: The Meaning and Usefulness of Gods (*Devatā*) in the Uttara Mīmāṃsā Sūtra Bhāṣya', in Bradley J. Malkovsky (ed.), *New Perspectives on Advaita Vedanta: Essays in Commemoration of Professor Richard De Smet, S.J.* (Leiden: Brill, 2000): 30–50

Cobban, Alan, *The Medieval English Universities: Oxford and Cambridge to C. 1500* (London: Routledge, 1988)

Cohen, Benjamin, 'The Court of Wards in a Princely State: Bank Robber or Babysitter?', *Modern Asian Studies* 41.2 (2007): 395–420

Cohen, Benjamin, *Kingship and Colonialism in India's Deccan 1850–1948* (New York: Palgrave Macmillan, 2007)

Cohn, Bernard, *Colonialism and Its Forms of Knowledge: The British in India* (Princeton, NJ: Princeton University Press, 1996)

Cohn, Bernard, *The Bernard Cohn Omnibus* (New Delhi: Oxford University Press, 2004)

Coing, Helmut, 'English Equity and the Denunciatio Evangelica of the Canon Law', *Law Quarterly Review* 71 (1955): 223–41

Colas, Gérard, *Viṣṇù, ses Images et ses Feux* (Paris: EFEO, 1996)

Colas, Gerard, 'The Competing Hermeneutics of Image Worship in Hinduism (Fifth to Eleventh Century AD)', in Phyllis Granoff *et al.* (eds), *Images in Asian* Religions (Vancouver: UBC Press, 2004): 149–79

Colas, Gerard, 'Images and Territory of Gods: From Precepts to Epigraphs', in Daniela Berti and Gilles Tarabout (eds), *Territory, Soil and Society in South Asia* (New Delhi: Manohar, 2009): 99–142

Copland, Ian, 'The Princely States, the Muslim League, and the Partition of India in 1947', *The International History Review* 13.1 (1991): 38–69

Craig, P. and L. Deshpande, 'Rights, Autonomy and Process: Public Interest Litigation in India', *Oxford Journal of Legal Studies* 9.3 (1989): 356–73

Custer, Lawrence, 'The Origins of the Doctrine of *Parens Patriae*', *Emory Law Journal* 27.2 (1978): 195–208

Das Acevedo, Deepa, 'Secularism in the Indian Context', *Law & Social Inquiry* 38.138 (2013): 138–67

Das Acevedo, Deepa, 'Celibate Gods and "Essential Practices" Jurisprudence at Sabarimala, 1991–2011', in Daniela Berti *et al.* (eds), *Filing Religion: State, Hinduism, and Courts of Law* (Oxford: Oxford University Press, 2016): 101–23

Das Acevedo, Deepa, 'Divine Sovereignty, Indian Property Law, and the Dispute Over the Padmanabhaswamy Temple', *Modern Asian Studies* 50.3 (2016): 841–65

Das Acevedo, Deepa, 'Temples, Courts, and Dynamic Equilibrium in the Indian Constitution', *The American Journal of Comparative Law* 64.3 (2016): 555–82

Das Acevedo, Deepa, 'Gods' Homes, Men's Courts, Women's Rights', *International Journal of Constitutional Law* 16.2 (2018): 552–73

Das Acevedo, Deepa, 'Pause for Thought: Supreme Court's Verdict on Sabarimala', *Economic and Political Weekly* 53.43 (2018): 12–15

Das Acevedo, Deepa, *The Battle for Sabarimala: Religion Law, and Gender in Contemporary India* (New York: Oxford University Press, 2024)

Davis, Donald, 'Intermediate Realms of Law: Corporate Groups and Rulers in Medieval India', *Journal of the Economic and Social History of the Orient* 48.1 (2005): 92–117

Davis, Donald, 'Hinduism as a Legal Tradition', *Journal of the American Academy of Religion* 75.2 (2007): 241–67

Davis, Donald, 'The Non-Observance of Conventions: A Title of Hindu Law in the Smṛticandrikā', *Zeitschrift der Deutschen Morganländischen Gesellschaft* 157.1 (2007): 103–24

Davis, Donald, 'Law', in S. Mittal and G. Thursby (eds), *Studying Hinduism* (New York: Routledge, 2008)

Davis, Donald, 'A Historical Overview of Hindu Law', in Timothy Lubin, Donald Davis, and Jayanth Krishnan (eds), *Hinduism and Law: An Introduction* (Cambridge: Cambridge University Press, 2010): 17–27

Davis, Donald, *The Spirit of Hindu Law* (Cambridge: Cambridge University Press, 2010)

Davis, Donald, 'Centres of Law: Duties, Rights, and Jurisdictional Pluralism in Medieval India', in Paul Dresch and Hannah Skoda (eds), *Legalism: Anthropology and History* (Oxford: Oxford University Press, 2012): 85–113

Davis, Donald, 'Toward a History of Documents in Medieval India: The Encounter of Scholasticism and Regional Law in the *Smṛticandrikā*', *The Medieval Globe* 2.2 (2016): 167–97

Davis, Donald, '*Ownership and Inheritance in Sanskrit Jurisprudence* by Christopher T. Fleming (Review)', *Philosophy East and West* 72.3 (2022): 1–6

Davis, Richard, *Ritual in an Oscillating Universe* (Princeton: Princeton University Press, 1991)

Davis, Richard, 'Indian Art Objects as Loot', *The Journal of Asian Studies* 52.1 (1993): 22–48

Davis, Richard, 'The Rebuilding of a Hindu Temple', in Donald Lopez (ed.), *Religions of India in Practice* (Princeton: Princeton University Press, 1995): 627–48

Davis, Richard, *Lives of Indian Images* (Princeton: Princeton University Press, 1997)

Davis, Richard, 'Indian Image-Worship and its Discontents', in Jan Assmann and Albert I. Baumgartner (eds), *Representation in Religion* (Leiden: Brill, 2001): 107–32

Davis, Richard, 'The Rise and Fall of a Sacred Place: Ayodhya Over Three Decades', in Marc Ross (ed.), *Culture and Belonging in Divided Societies: Contestation and Symbolic Landscapes* (Philadelphia: University of Pennsylvania Press, 2009): 25–44

Davis, Richard, 'Temples, Deities, and the Law', in Timothy Lubin, Donald Davis, and Jayanth Krishnan (eds), *Hinduism and Law: An Introduction* (Cambridge: Cambridge University Press, 2010): 195–206

Davis, Richard, 'Images and Temples', in Patrick Olivelle and Donald R. Davis (eds), *The Oxford History of Hinduism: Hindu Law* (Oxford: Oxford University Press, 2018): 347–67

Davis, Seth, 'Empire in Equity', *Notre Dame Law Review* 97.5 (2022): 1985–2017

De, Rohit, '"A Peripatetic World Court": Cosmopolitan Courts, Nationalist Judges and the Indian Appeal to the Privy Council', *Law and History Review* 32.4 (2014): 821–51

De, Rohit, 'The Federal Court and Civil Liberties in Late Colonial India', in T. Halliday, L. Karpik, and M. Feeley (eds), *Fates of Political Liberalism in the British Post-Colony: The Politics of the Legal Complex* (Cambridge: Cambridge University Press, 2012): 59–90

Derrett, J. Duncan, 'An Example of Tax-evasion in Medieval India', *Bulletin of the School of Oriental and African Studies* 19.1 (1957): 162–6

Derrett, J. Duncan, 'Justice, Equity, and Good Conscience', in J.D. Anderson (ed.), *Changing Law In Developing Countries* (New York Frederick Praeger, 1963): 114–54

Derrett, J. Duncan, 'The Reform of Hindu Religious Endowments', in D.E. Smith (ed.), *South Asian Politics and Religion* (Princeton: Princeton University Press, 1966): 311–36

Derrett, J. Duncan, 'The British as Patrons of the Śāstra', in J. Duncan Derrett (ed.), *Religion, Law and the State in India* (London: Faber & Faber, 1968): 225–73

Derrett, J. Duncan, 'The Liability of Deities to Pay Taxes', *The Bombay Law Reporter* 71 (1969): 38–45

Derrett, J. Duncan, 'The Development of the Concept of Property in India, c. AD 800–1800', in J. Duncan Derrett (ed.), *Essays in Classical and Modern Indian Law*, Vol. 2 (Leiden: E. J. Brill, 1977): 8–130

Derrett, J. Duncan, 'A Juridical Fabrication of Early British India: The *Mahānirvāṇa Tantra*', in J. Duncan Derrett (ed.), *Essays in Classical and Modern Hindu Law*, V.II (Leiden: Brill, 1977)

Derrett, J. Duncan, 'Religious Endowments, Public and Private', in J. Duncan Derrett (ed.), *Religion, Law and the State in India* (Delhi: Oxford University Press, 1999): 482–512

Derrett, J. Duncan, 'Nīvī', *Vishveshvaranand Indological Journal* 12.1–2 (1974): 89–5

Deshpande, Prachi, 'The Marathi *Kaulnāmā:* Property, Sovereignty and Documentation in a Persianate Form', *Journal of the Economic and Social History of the Orient* 64 (2021): 583–614

Dewey, John, 'The Historic Background of Corporate Legal Personality', *Yale Law Journal* 35.6 (1926): 655–73

Dhawan, Rajeev, 'The Supreme Court and Hindu Religious Endowments 1950–1975', *Journal of the Indian Law Institute* 20.1 (1978): 52–102

Dhawan, Rajeev, and Fali S. Nariman, 'The Supreme Court and Group Life: Religious, Freedom, Minority Groups and Disadvantaged Communities', in B.N. Kirpal *et al.* (eds), *Supreme But Not Infallible: Essays in Honour of the Supreme Court of India* (Oxford: Oxford University Press, 2004)

Dignas, Beate, *Economy of the Sacred in Hellenistic and Roman Asia Minor* (Oxford: Oxford University Press, 2002)

Dikshit, D.P., *Political History of the Calukyas of Badami* (New Delhi: Abhinav, 1980)

Dirks, Nicholas, 'From Little King to Landlord: Property, Law, and the Gift Under the Madras Permanent Settlement', *Comparative Studies in Society and History* 28.2 (1986): 307–33

Dirks, Nicolas, *The Hollow Crown: Ethnohistory of an Indian Kingdom*, 2nd edn. (Cambridge: Cambridge University Press, 1993)

Dobie, Alisdair, 'The Development of Financial Management and Control in Monastic Houses and Estates in England c. 1200–1540', *Accounting, Business & Financial History* 18.2 (1980): 141–59

Doe, N., *Fundamental Authority in Late Medieval English Law* (Cambridge: Cambridge University Press, 1990)

Dossal, Mariam, 'The Bombay Revenue Survey (1865–1872) and the Need for State Empowerment', *Proceedings of the Indian History Congress* 56 (1995): 594–60

Duff, Patrick, *Personality in Roman Private Law* (Cambridge: Cambridge University Press, 1938)

Dwight, Theodore, 'The Jurisdiction of the Court of Chancery to Enforce Charitable Uses', *University of Pennsylvania Law Review* 10.3 (1862): 129–47

Dwivedi, S.N., 'Location of Sovereignty in India', *Journal of the Indian Law Institute* 9.1 (1967): 71–84

Eaton, Richard, *The Sufis of Bijapur, 1300–1700: Social Roles of Sufis in Medieval India* (Princeton: Princeton University Press, 1972)

Eaton, Richard, *The Rise of Islam and the Bengal Frontier, 1204–1760* (Berkeley: University of California Press, 1993)

Eaton, Richard, 'Temple Desecration and Indo-Muslim States', *Journal of Islamic Studies* 11.3 (2000): 283–319

Eaton, Richard, 'The Persian Cosmopolis (900–1900) and the Sanskrit Cosmopolis (400–1400)', in Abbas Amanat and Assef Ashraf (eds), *The Persianate World: Rethinking a Shared Sphere* (Leiden: Brill, 2018): 63–83

Eaton, Richard, *India in the Persianate Age* (Berkeley: University of California Press, 2019)

Eaton, Richard, and Phillip Wagoner, *Power, Memory, Architecture: Contested Sites on India's Deccan Plateau, 1300–1600* (Oxford: Oxford University Press, 2017)

Ekelund, Robert, *et al.*, *Sacred Trust: The Medieval Church as an Economic Firm* (Oxford: Oxford University Press, 1996)

Endicott, Timothy, 'The Conscience of the King: Christopher St. German and Thomas More and the Development of English Equity', *University of Toronto Faculty of Law Review* 47.2 (1989): 549–70

Falk, Harry, 'A Copper Plate Donation Record and Some Seals from the Kashmir Smast', in *Beiträge Zur Allgemeinen und Vergleichenden Archäologie 23* (Mainz am Rhein: Verlag Phillip von Zabern, 2003): 1–19

Falk, Harry, 'The Tidal Waves of Indian History: Between the Empires and Beyond', in Patrick Olivelle (ed.), *Between the Empires: Society in India 300 BCE to 400 CE* (Oxford: Oxford University Press, 2006): 145–66

Falk, Harry, 'Ten Thoughts on the Mathura Lion Capital Reliquary', in Shailendra Bhandare and Sanjay Garg (eds), *Felicitas: Essays in Numismatic, Epigraphy and History in Honour of Joe Cribb* (Mumbai: Reesha Books, 2011): 121–42

Falk, Harry, 'The Fate of Aśoka's Donations at Lumbinī', in Patrick Olivelle, Janice Leoshko, and Himanshu Prabha Ray (eds), *Reimagining Aśoka* (Oxford: Oxford University Press, 2012): 204–16

Finn, Jennifer, *Much Ado About Marduk: Questioning Discourses of Royalty in First Millennium Mesopotamian Literature* (Berlin: De Gruyter, 2017)

Fischer-Lescano, Andreas, 'Nature as a Legal Person: Proxy Constellations in Law', *Law and Literature* 32.2 (2020): 237–62

Fisher, Elaine, 'A Microhistory of a South Indian Monastery: The Hooli Bṛhanmaṭha and the History of Sanskritic Vīraśaivism', *Journal of Indian Intellectual History* 1 (2018): 13–47

Fleming, Christopher T., *Ownership and Inheritance in Sanskrit Jurisprudence* (Oxford: Oxford University Press, 2020)

Fleming, Christopher T., 'Dharmaśāstra and the Legal Personality of Deities in the Ayodhya Verdicts (2010 & 2019)', *Contemporary South Asia* 32.1 (2023): 26–39

Fleming, Christopher T., 'Introduction', in Christopher T. Fleming *et al.* (eds), *Science and Society in the Sanskrit World* (Leiden: Brill, 2023): 1–46

Flood, Finbarr, 'Pillars, Palimpsests, and Princely Practices: Translating the Past in Sultanate India', *Res: Anthropology and Aesthetics* 43 (2003): 95–116

Flood, Finbarr, 'Conflict and Cosmopolitanism in Arab Sind', in Deborah Hutton and Rebecca Brown (eds), *A Companion to Asian Art and Architecture* (Oxford: Blackwell, 2011): 365–97

Flood, Finnbar, 'Refiguring Iconoclasm in the Early Indian Mosque', in Anne McClanan and Jeff Johnson (eds), *Negating the Image: Case Studies in Iconoclasm* (London: Routledge, 2016): 15–40

Flood, Gavin, 'The Śaiva Traditions', in Gavin Flood (ed.), *The Blackwell Companion to Hinduism* (Oxford: Blackwell, 2003): 200–28

Francis, Emmanuel, *Le Discours Royal dans l'Inde du Sud Ancienne: Inscriptions et Monuments Pallava, IVème-IXème Siècles* (Louvain-la-Neuve: Université Catholique de Louvain, 2013)

Frankel, Tamar, 'Fiduciary Law', *California Law Review* 71.3 (1983): 795–836

Fredungberg, Mirza, *The Chachnamah: An Ancient History of Sind* (Karachi: Commissioner's Press, 1900)

Friedland, Roger, and Richard Hecht, 'The Bodies of Nations: A Comparative Study of Religious Violence in Jerusalem and Ayodhya', *History of Religions* 38.2 1998: 101–49

Friedmann, Yohanan, 'The Temple of Multān: A Note on Early Muslim Attitudes to Idolatry', *Israel Oriental Studies* 2 (1972): 176–82

Friedmann, Yohanan, 'Medieval Muslim Views of Indian Religions', *Journal of the American Oriental Society* 95.2 (1975): 214–21

Fuller, C.J., 'Hinduism and Scriptural Authority in Modern Indian Law', *Comparative Studies in Society & History* 32.2 (1988): 225–48

Fuller, C.J., *Servants of the Goddess: The Priests of a South Indian Temple* (Cambridge: Cambridge University Press, 2008)

Furui, Ryosuke, 'Rangpur Copper Plate Inscription of Mahīpāla I, Year 5', *Journal of Ancient Indian History* 27 (2011): 232–45

Furui, Ryosuke, 'Ājīvikas, Maṇibhadra and Early History of Eastern Bengal: A New Copperplate Inscription of Vainyagupta and its Implications', *Journal of the Royal Asiatic Society* 26.4 (2016): 657–81

Furui, Ryosuke, 'Bharat Kala Bhavan Copper Plate Inscription of Rājyapāla, Year 2: Re-edition and Reinterpretation', *Puravritta: Journal of the Directorate of Archaeology & Museums* 1 (2016): 41–56

Furui, Ryosuke, *Land and Society in Early South Asia: Eastern India 400–1250 AD* (New Delhi: Routledge, 2019)

Furui, Ryosuke, 'Sujanagar Stone Inscription of the Time of Bhojavarman, Year 7', *Pratna Samiksha: A Journal of Archeology* 10 (2019): 115–22

Gadbois, George, 'The Federal Court of India: 1937–1950'. *Journal of the Indian Law Institute* 6.2/3 (1964): 253–315

Gadbois, George, *Supreme Court of India: The Beginnings*, edited and introduced by Vikram Raghavan and Vasujith Ram (New Delhi: Oxford University Press, 2017)

Gai, G.S., *Inscriptions of the Early Kadambas* (New Delhi: Pratibha Prakashan, 1996)

Galanter, Marc, 'Hinduism, Secularism, and the Indian Judiciary', *Philosophy East and West* 21.4 (1971): 467–87

Galanter, Marc, 'Caste Disabilities and Indian Federalism', *Journal of the Indian Law Institute* 3.2 (1961): 205–34

Galanter, Marc, 'Temple-entry and the Untouchability (Offences)', *Journal of the Indian Law Institute* 6.263 (1964): 185–95

Galanter, Marc, 'Untouchability and the Law', *Economic and Political Weekly* 4.1–2 (1969): 131–70

Ghandhi, Sandy, and Jennifer James, 'The God That Won', *International Journal of Cultural Property* 1.2 (1992): 369–382

Gandhi, Supriya, '*Dharmaśāstra* in Aurangzeb's India: A Persian Translation of the *Yājñavalkya Smṛti* and *Mitākṣarā*', *Journal of Hindu Studies* 16 (2023): 33–56

Garg, R.P., and Beenu Yadav, *Income Tax Appellate Tribunal (ITAT): Practice and Procedure* (New Delhi: Taxmann Publications, 2014)

Gaudiosi, Monica, 'The Influence of the Islamic Law of *Waqf* on the Development of the Trust in England: The Case of Merton College', *University of Pennsylvania Law Review* 136 (1987): 1231–61

Gauthier, Albert, *Roman Law and its Contribution to the Development of Canon Law* (Ottawa: Faculty of Canon Law, Saint Paul University, 1996)

Ghosal, H.R., 'Resumption of Rent-Free Tenures for Assessment by the Company's Government (1819–1850)', *Proceedings of the Indian History Congress* 13(1950): 316–19

Ghose, J.C., *The Hindu Law of Impartible Property* (Calcutta: S.C. Auddy, 1908)

Ghose, Rashberhary, *The Law of Mortgage in India* (Calcutta: Thacker Spink & Co., 1877)

Ghosh, Soumalya, 'Supreme Court on Women's Right to Religious Freedom in India: from Shirur Mutt to Sabarimala', *Indian Journal of Law and Justice* 10.1 (2019): 162–8

Ghosh, Suchandra, 'A Hoard of Copper Plates: Patronage and the Early Valkhā State', *Studies in History* 31.1 (2015): 1–29

Goldberg, John, Henry E. Smith, and P.G. Turner (eds), *Equity and Law: Fusion and Fission* (Cambridge: Cambridge University Press, 2019)

Gopal, Sarvepalli (ed.), *Anatomy of a Confrontation: Ayodhya and the Rise of Communal Politics in India* (London: Zed, 1992)

Gornall, Alastair, *Rewriting Buddhism: Pali Literature and Monastic Reform in Sri Lanka, 1157–1270* (London: UCL Press, 2020)

Govind, Rahul, 'On the Deity of Juristic Personality: The Religious, the Secular and the Nation in the Ayodhya Dispute and the Ayodhya Judgments (2010 & 2019)', *National Law School of India Review* 33.1 (2021): 150–80

Grande, Francesco, 'Definiteness Marking in Earlier Stages of Arabic Areal Evidence from Classical Arabic Idols' Names', *Annali di Ca' Foscari Serie Orientale* 57 (2021): 19–52

Granoff, Phyllis, 'Reading Between the Lines: Colliding Attitudes Towards Image Worship in Indian Religious Texts', in Gerard Colas and Giles Tarabout (eds), *Hindu Rites, Transfer, and Transformations* (Paris: Ecole de Des Hautes Etudes, 2006): 389–422

Granoff, Phyllis, 'Images and Their Ritual Use in Medieval India: Hesitations and Contradictions', in Phyllis Granoff *et al.* (eds), *Images in Asian Religions* (Vancouver: UBC Press, 2004): 19–55

Granoff, Phyllis, 'Tales of Broken Limbs and Bleeding Wounds: Responses to Muslim Iconoclasm in Medieval India', *East and West* 41.1 (1991): 189–203

Green, Nile, 'Introduction: The Frontiers of the Persianate World (800–1900)', in Nile Green (ed.), *The Persianate World: Frontiers of a Eurasian Lingua Franca* (Oakland: University of California Press, 2019): 1–74

Guenther, A.M., 'Ḥanafī fiqh in Mughal India: The *Fatawa-i 'Alamgiri*', in Richard Eaton (ed.), *India's Islamic Traditions, 711–1750* (New Delhi: Oxford University Press, 2003): 209–33

Guha, Ranajit, *A Rule of Property for Bengal: An Essay on the Idea of Permanent Settlement* (Paris: Mouton, 1964)

Guha, Sumit, 'An Indian Penal Regime: Maharasthra in the Eighteenth Century', *Past and Present* 147.1 (1995): 101–26

Guha-Thakurta, Tapati, 'Our Gods, Their Museums: The Contrary Careers of India's Art Object', *Art History* 30.4 (2007): 628–57

Gune, V.T., *The Judicial System of the Marathas* (Poona: Deccan College, 1953)

Gupta, Nirmala, 'Land Grants of Mughal Emperors to Jangamavadi Matha of Benares, A Centre of Veershaivism', Quarterly *Journal of the Pakistan Historical Society* 57.1 (2009): 29–40

Gupta, S. Sen, 'A Note on Resumption of Lekheraj Lands in Bengal and the Landholders Society', *Proceedings of the Indian Historical Society* 43 (1982): 487–93

Halman, Loek, and Veerle Draulans, 'How Secular is Europe?', *The British Journal of Sociology* 57.2 (2006): 263–88

Halperin, Ehud, 'Winds of Change: Religion and Climate in the Western Himalayas', *Journal of the American Academy of Religion*, 85.1 (2017): 64–111

Harrington, Thomas, 'Stewardship and Ownership of Material Goods: Discipline and Order in the Pre-Constantinian Church', *Catholic Lawyer* 33.2 (1990): 109–30

Haskett, Timothy, 'The Medieval English Court of Chancery', *Law and History Review* 14.2 (1996): 245–314

Hawkes, Lisa, '*Parens Patriae* and the Union Carbide Case: The Disaster at Bhopal Continues', *Cornell International Law Journal* 21 (1988): 181–200

Hazra, R.C., *Studies in the Purāṇic Records on Hindu Rites and Customs* (Dacca: University of Dacca, 1940)

Helmholz, R.H., 'Canon Law and Roman Law', in David Johnston (ed.), *The Cambridge Companion to Roman Law* (Cambridge: Cambridge University Press, 2015): 396–422

Helmholz, Richard, 'Roman Law of Guardianship in England, 1300–1600', *Tulane Law Review* 52 (1978): 223–47

Heitzman, James, *Gifts of Power: Lordship in an Early Indian State* (New Delhi: Oxford University Press, 1997)

Hemmingham, Stephen, 'The Raj Darbhanga and the Court of Wards, 1860–1879: Managerial Reorganization and Elite Education', *Indian Economic and Social History Review* 19.3–4 (1982): 347–63

Hodges, Leonard, 'Between Litigation and Arbitration: Administering Legal Pluralism in Eighteenth-Century Bombay', *Itinerario* 42.3 (2018): 490–515

Hogben, Murray, 'An Imperial Dilemma: The Reluctant Indianization of the Indian Political Service', *Modern Asian Studies* 15.4 (1981): 751–69

Hölkeskamp, Karl, 'Written Law in Archaic Greece', *Proceedings of the Cambridge Philological Society (Second Series)* 38 (1993): 87–117

Holland, Bernard, *Imperium Et Libertas: A Study in History and Politics* (London: Edward Arnold, 1901)

Holmes, Oliver Wendell, 'Early English Equity', *Law Quarterly Review* 1.2 (1885): 162–74

Hooker, M.B., 'The East India Company and the Crown: 1773–1858', *Malaya Law Review* 11.1 (1969): 1–37

Horstmann, Monika, 'Govindadevjī of Vrindaban and Jaipur and its Kachvāhā Patrons from the Mid-Seventeenth to the Mid-Eighteenth Century', in Alan W. Entwistle and Françoise Mallinson (eds), *Studies in South Asian Devotional Literature: Research Papers, 1988–1991 Presented at the Fifth Conference on Devotional Literature in New Indo-Aryan Languages* (New Delhi & Paris: Manohar & École Française d'Extrême-Orient, 1994): 82–93

Horstmann, Monika, 'Govindadeva and His Custodians from 1643 through the Time of Jaya Siṃha II (1700–1743)', in Margaret Case (ed.), *Govindadeva: A Dialogue in Stone* (New Delhi: Indira Gandhi National Centre for the Arts, 1996): 185–93

Horstmann, Monika, *In Favour of Govindadevjī: Historical Documents Relating to a Deity of Vrindaban and Eastern Rajasthan* (New Delhi: Indira Gandhi National Centre for the Arts & Manohar Publishers & Distributors, 1999)

Horstmann, Monika, 'The Mālik in Rāmānandī Documents of the 18th and 19th Centuries', in Simon Cubelic, Axel Michaels, and Astrid Zotter (eds), *Studies in Historical Documents from Nepal and India* (Heidelberg: Heidelberg University Publishing, 2018): 401–44

Howell, P.A., *The Judicial Committee of the Privy Council: 1833–1876* (Cambridge: Cambridge University Press, 1979)

Hudson, Alastair, *Equity and Trusts*, 10th edn. (London: Routledge, 2021)

Hultzsch, E., *Corpus Inscriptionum Indicarum Vol 1: Inscriptions of Asoka* (Oxford: Clarendon Press, 1925)

Huttenback, Robert, 'The Emasculation of a Princely State: The Case of Kashmir', *Journal of Asian History* 7.1 (1973): 1–29

Inden, Ronald 'Changes in the Vedic Priesthood', in A.W. Van den Hoek *et al.* (eds), *Ritual, State and History in South Asia: Essays in Honour of J.C. Heesterman* (Leiden: Brill, 1992): 556–78

Inden, Ronald, 'Imperial Purāṇas: Kashmir as the Center of the World', in Ronald Inden, Jonathan Walters, and Daud Ali (eds), *Querying the Medieval: Texts and the History of Practices in South Asia* (Oxford: Oxford University Press, 2000): 29–98

Inden, Ronald, Jonathan Walters, and Daud Ali (eds), *Querying the Medieval: Texts and the History of Practices in South Asia* (Oxford: Oxford University Press, 2000)

Iyer, Pudukota, *The Law Relating to Hindu and Mahomedan Endowments*, 2nd edn. (Madras: Modern Printing Works, 1918)

Jain, M.P., *Outlines of Indian Legal History* (New Delhi: University of Delhi Press, 1952)

Jain, M.P., 'Law Reporting in India', *Journal of the Indian Law Institute* 24.2/3 (1982): 560–74

Jalal, Ayesha, 'Inheriting the Raj: Jinnah and the Governor-Generalship Issue', *Modern Asian Studies* 19.1 (2008): 29–53

Jha, Gaṅgānātha, *The Prābhākara School of Pūrva Mīmāṃsā* (Allahabad: University of Allahabad, 1911)

Jha, Krishna, and Dhirendra Jha, *Ayodhya: The Dark Night* (New Delhi: HarperCollins, 2012)

Johnston, David, *The Roman Law of Trusts* (Oxford: Oxford University Press, 1988)

Johns, Claude, *Assyrian Deeds and Documents Recording the Transfer of Property, Volume 3* (Cambridge: Cambridge University Press, 1901)

Jolly, Julius, *Outlines of an History of the Hindu Law of Partition, Inheritance, and Adoption, as Contained in the Original Sanskrit Treatises* (Calcutta: Thacker, Spink, & Co., 1885)

Jolly, Stellina, and K.S. Roshan Menon, 'Of Ebbs and Flows: Understanding the Legal Consequences of Granting Personhood to Natural Entities in India', *Transnational Environmental Law* 10.3 (2021): 467–92

Jones, Gareth, *History of the Law of Charity, 1532–1827* (Cambridge: Cambridge University Press 1969)

Jones, Gareth, *History of the Law of Charity, 1532–1827*, 2nd edn. (Cambridge: Cambridge University Press, 2011)

Jones, W.J., *The Elizabethan Court of Chancery* (Oxford: Oxford University Press, 1967)

Juncu, Meera, *India in the Italian Renaissance: Visions of a Contemporary Pagan World 1300* (London: Routledge, 2015)

Kāṇe, P.V., *History of Dharmaśāstra*, Vol. 1 (Pune: Bhandarkar Oriental Research Institute, 1930)

Kāṇe, P.V., *History of Dharmaśāstra*, Vol. 2.2 (Pune: Bhandarkar Oriental Research Institute, 1941)

Kāṇe, P.V., *A History of Dharmaśāstra*, Vol. 5.2 (Pune: Bhandarkar Oriental Research Institute, 1962)

Kāṇe, P.V., *History of Dharmaśāstra*, Vol. 3, 2nd edn. (Pune: Bhandarkar Oriental Research Institute, 1973)

Kannabiran, Kalpana, *Tools of Justice: Non-discrimination and the Indian Constitution* (Abingdon: Routledge, 2012)

Kapur, Ratna, 'The Ayodhya Case: Hindu Majoritarianism and the Right to Religious Liberty', *Maryland Journal of International Law* 29.305 (2014): 305–65

Kapur, Ratna, 'The Ayodhya Case, Freedom of Religion, and the Making of Modernist "Hinduism"' *Contemporary South Asia* 32.1 (2023): 10–25

Kent, Eliza, *Sacred Groves and Local Gods: Religion and Environmentalism in South India* (Oxford: Oxford University Press, 2013)

Kenyon, Frederic, *Aristotle on the Athenian Constitution* (London: George Bell and Sons, 1901)

Keul, Istvan (ed.), *Consecration Rituals in South Asia* (Leiden: Brill, 2017)

Khan, Fazal Ahmad, 'Excavations at Banbhore', *Pakistan Archaeology* 1 (1964): 48–55

Khan, Hussain, 'The Institution of Iqṭā' and it Impact on Muslim Rule in India', *Islamic Studies* 22.1 (1983): 1–9

Khan, M.S., 'al-Bīrūnī and the Political History of India', *Oriens* 25/26 (1976): 86–115

Khanna, H.R., *Making of India's Constitution*, 2nd edn. (Lucknow: Eastern Book Company, 2008)

Kozah, Mario, *The Birth of Indology as an Islamic Science: Al-Bīrūnī's Treatise on Yoga Psychology* (Leiden: Brill, 2015)

Kozlowski, Gregory, *Muslim Endowments and Society in British India* (Cambridge: Cambridge University Press, 1985)

Kozlowski, Gregory, 'The Changing Political and Social Contexts of Muslim Endowments (*waqfs*)', in R. Deguilhem (ed.), *Le waqfdans l'espace islamique, Outil depouvoir socio-économique* (Damascus: Institut Français d'Etudes Arabes de Damas 1995): 355–70

Krishnaswami, A., *The Tamil Country Under Vijayanagara* (Annamalainagar: Annamalai University, 1964)

Kroppenberg, Inge, 'Law, Religion, and Constitution of the Vestal Virgins', *Law & Literature* 22.3 (2010): 418–39

Kroll, Ethan, *A Logical Approach to Law* (PhD Dissertation, University of Chicago, 2010)

Kulke, Hermann, 'Kings without a Kingdom: The Rajas of Khurda and the Jagannatha Cult', *South Asia: Journal of South Asian Studies* 4.1 (1974): 60–77

Kulke, Herman, '"Juggernaut" Under British Supremacy and the Resurgence of the Kurda Rājās as "Rājās of Puri"', in Anncharlott Eschmann, Hermann Kulke, and G.C. Tripathi (eds), *The Cult of Jagannatha and the Regional Tradition of Orissa* (New Delhi: Manorharlal, 1978): 345–57

Kulke, Hermann, 'Fragmentation and Segmentation versus Integration? Reflections on the Concepts of Indian Feudalism and the Segmentary State in Indian History', *Studies in Indian History* 4 (1982): 237–63

Kulke, Herman, 'King Anaṅgabhīma III, the Veritable Founder of the Gajapati Kingship and of the Jagannātha Trinity at Puri', *Journal of the Royal Asiatic Society of Great Britain and Ireland* 1 (1989): 26–39

Kulke, Hermann, 'The Early and Imperial Kingdom: A Processural Model of Integrative State Formation in Early Medieval India', in Hermann Kulke (ed.), *The State in India, 1000–1700* (New Delhi: Oxford University Press, 1995)

Kulke, Hermann, 'Ritual Sovereignty and Ritual Policy: Some Historiographic Reflections', in Margo Kitts *et al.* (eds), *State, Power, and Violence* (Wiesbaden: Harrassowitz Verlag, 2010): 603–26

Kumarasingham, Harshan, '"The Tropical Dominions": The Appeal of Dominion Status in the Decolonization of India, Pakistan, and Ceylon', *Transactions of the Royal Historical Society* 23 (2013): 223–45

Kumari, Koutha, *History of Religious Endowments in Andhra Pradesh* (New Delhi: Northern Book Centre, 1998)

Kumari, Rashmi, 'Menstruating Women and Celibate Gods: A Discourse Analysis of Women's Entry into Sabarimala Temple in Kerala, India', in Nazia Hussein and Saba Hussain (eds), *Decolonising Gender in South Asia* (London: Routledge: 2021): 80–97

Kunal, Kishore, *Ayodhyā Revisited* (New Delhi: Ocean Books, 2016)

Kusuman, K., *A History of Trade and Commerce in Travancore* (Delhi: Mittal, 1987)

Laine, James, 'The *Dharma* of Islam and the *Dīn* of Hinduism: Hindus and Muslims in the Age of Śivājī', *International Journal of Hindu Studies* 3.3 (1999): 299–318

Lakshminath, A., *Precedent in the Indian Legal System*, 2nd edn. (Lucknow: Eastern Book House, 2005)

Lal, Kishori Saran, *History of the Khaljis (1290–1320)* (Allahabad: The Indian Press, 1950)

Lane-Pool, Stanley, *Aurangzīb and the Decay of the Mughal Empire* (Oxford: Oxford University Press, 1908)

Lannoy, Mark de, *The Kulasekhara Perumals of Travancore: History and State Formation in Travancore from 1671 to 1758* (Leiden: Leiden University Press, 1997)

Lazaretti, Vera, 'Ayodhya 2.0 in Banaras? Judicial Discourses and Rituals of Place in the Making of Hindu Majoritarianism', *Contemporary South Asia* 32.1 (2023): 66–83

Lewin, Thomas, *A Practical Treatise on the Law of Trusts and Trustees*, 10th edn. (London: Maxell, 1837)

Ligt, Luuk de, 'D. 47,22, 1, pr.-1 and the Formation of Semi-Public "Collegia"', *Latomus* 60.2 (2001): 345–58

Lingat, Robert, *The Classical Law of India*, trans. J. Duncan Derrett (Berkeley: University of California Press, 1973)

Lobban, Michael, 'Preparing for Fusion: Reforming the Nineteenth-Century Court of Chancery (Parts 1 and 2)', *Law and History Review* 22.2–3 (2004)

Long, Joseph, 'The Definition of a Trust', *Virginia Law Review* 8.6 (1922): 426–33

Lott, J. Bert, 'The Earliest Augustan Gods Outside of Rome', *The Classical Journal* 110.2 (2014–15): 129–58

Loughlin, Martin, 'Constitutional Theory: A 25th Anniversary Essay', *Oxford Journal of Legal Studies* 25 (2005): 183–202

Lubin, Timothy, 'The Theory and Practice of Property in Premodern South Asia: Disparities and Convergences', *Journal of the Economic and Social History of the Orient* 61.5/6 (2018): 803–50

Lubin, Timothy, 'Towards a South Asian Diplomatics: Cosmopolitan Norms and Regional Idioms in the Use of Documents', in Simon Cubelic, Axel Michaels, and Astrid Zotter (eds), *Studies in Historical Documents from Nepal and India* (Heidelberg: Heidelberg University Publishing, 2018): 37–84

Lubin, Timothy, 'Religious Endowments in Ancient India and the Institutionalization of Brahmin Caste Status', *American Journal of Legal History* 63.2 (2023): 97–114

Ludden, David, *Making India Hindu: Religion, Community, and the Politics of Democracy in India* (Delhi: Oxford University Press, 1996)

Lüders, Heinrich, *Mathurā Inscriptions* (Göttingen: Vandenhoeck & Ruprecht, 1961)

Lutjeharms, Rembert, 'A Temple of Stone and a Temple of Love: Govindadeva in the Religious Imagination of Early Gauḍīya Vaiṣṇavas', in Kiyokazu Okita and Rembert Lutjeharms (eds), *The Building of Vṛndāvana: Architecture, Theology, and Practice in an Early Modern Pilgrimage Town* (Leiden: Brill, 2024): 149–96

MacKinnon, Catharine, 'Sex Equality Under the Constitution of India: Problems, Prospects, and "Personal Laws"', *International Journal of Constitutional Law* 4.2 (2006): 181–202

Maclean, Derryl, *Religion and Society in Arab Sind* (Leiden: Brill, 1989)

MacNair, Mike, 'Equity and Conscience', *Oxford Journal of Legal Studies* 27.4 (2007): 659–81

MacNair, Mike, 'Arbitrary Chancellors and the Problem of Predictability', in W.J. Zwalve and E. Koops (eds.), *Law & Equity Approaches in Roman Law and Common Law* (Leiden: Brill, 2013): 80–104

MacRae, Duncan, 'The Laws of the Rites of the Priests: Varro and Late Republican Roman Sacral Jurisprudence', *Bulletin of the Institute of Classical Studies* 60.2 (2017): 34–48

Maheshwari, Kartick, and Vishnu Vardhan Shankar, 'Stone Gods and Earthly Interests: The Jural Relations and Consequence of Attributing Legal Personality to Hindu Idols', *Student Bar Review* 16 (2004): 46–67

Maheswari, Uma, *Thrip Padi Danam* (Malayalam) (Kozhikode: Mathrubhumi Books, 2020)

Maita, Keya, 'Ambedkar and the Constitution of India: A Deweyan Experiment', *Contemporary Pragmatism* 9.2 (2012): 301–20

Maitland, F.W., *Equity: Also the Forms of Action at Common Law* (Cambridge: Cambridge University Press, 1910)

Maitland, F.W., *State, Trust and Corporation*, eds. David Runciman and Magnus Ryan (Cambridge: Cambridge University Press, 2003)

Makdisi, George, 'The Guilds of Law in Medieval Legal History: An Inquiry into the Origins of the Inns of Court', *Cleveland State Law Review* 34.1 (1985–86): 3–18

Malik, Jamal, 'From Universal Dominion to Principalities (approx. 1650–1800)', in Jamal Malik (ed.), *Islam In South Asia* (Leiden: Brill, 2020): 255–92

Mann, Michael, 'A Permanent Settlement for the Ceded and Conquered Provinces: Revenue Administration in North India 1801–33', *Indian Economic and Social History Review* 32.2 (1995): 245–69

Marchant, Ronald, *The Church under the Law: Justice, Administration and Discipline in the Diocese of York, 1560–1640* (Cambridge: Cambridge University Press, 1969)

Marsh, Alfred, *History of the Court of Chancery and of the Rise and Development of the Doctrines of Equity* (Toronto: Carswell & Co, 1890)

Martini, Kelsey, 'The Origin of Akṣayanīvī and the Historical Context of the Arthaśāstra', *Indo-Iranian Journal* 65 (2022): 144–69

Mate, Manoj, 'The Rise of Judicial Governance in India', *Boston University International Law Journal* 33.169 (2015)

Mathew, Sarath, 'Applying Adverse Possession Rules to the Ayodhya Case', *Journal of Indian Law and Society* 11.1 (2020): xi–xxiv

Maunaguru, Sidharthan, '"Homeless" Deities and Refugee Devotees: Hindu Temples, Sri Lankan Tamil Diaspora, and Politics in the United Kingdom', *American Anthropologist* 123.3 (2021): 552–64

Mawdsley, Emma, 'The Abuse of Religion and Ecology: The Vishva Hindu Parishad and Tehri Dam', in Arjun Guneratne (ed.), *Culture and the Environment in the Himalaya* (Abingdon: Routledge, 2010): 151–65

McClish, Mark, 'Is the Arthaśāstra a Mauryan Document?', in Patrick Olivelle *et al.* (eds), *Reimagining Asoka* (Oxford: Oxford University Press, 2012): 280–309

McClish, Mark, 'Titles of Law: *Vyavahārapada*', in Patrick Olivelle and Donald Davis (eds), *Hindu Law: A New History of Dharmaśāstra* (New York: Oxford University Press, 2018), 299–312

McClish, Mark, *The History of the Arthaśāstra: Sovereignty and Sacred Law in Ancient India* (Cambridge: Cambridge University Press, 2019)

McCrea, Lawrence, 'Hindu Jurisprudence and Scriptural Hermeneutics', in Timothy Lubin *et al.* (eds), *Hinduism and Law: An Introduction* (Cambridge: Cambridge University Press, 2010): 123–36

McLeod, Hugh, and Werner Ustorf (eds), *The Decline of Christendom in Western Europe, 1750–2000* (Cambridge: Cambridge University Press, 2003)

Menon, Parvathi, 'The Carnatic Debts and the Agrarian Crisis of the Eighteenth Century', *Review of Agrarian Studies* 9.1 (2019): 10–32

Menski, Werner, 'Asians In Britain and the Question of Adaptation to a New Legal Order: Asian Laws in Britain', in Milton Israel and N. K. Wagle (eds), *Ethnicity, Identity, Migration: The South Asian Context* (Toronto: University of Toronto Press, 1993): 238–69

Merrill, Christi, 'The Afterlives of Panditry: Rethinking Fidelity in Sacred Texts with Multiple Origins', in Judy Wakabayashi and Rita Kothari (eds), *Decentering Translation Studies* (Amsterdam: John Benjamin, 2009): 75–94

Michaels, Axel, *Homo Ritualis: Hindu Ritual and Its Significance to Ritual Theory* (New York: Oxford University Press, 2016)

Migeottee, Léopold, 'La Gestion des Biens Sacrés dans les Cités Grecques', in H. Rupprecht (ed.), *Symposion 2003, Vorträge zur griechischen und Hellenistischen Rechtsgeschichte* (Vienna: Austrian Academy of Sciences 2006): 233–46

Mirashi, Vasudev Vishnu, 'Three Ancient and Famous Temples of the Sun', *Purāṇa* 8 (1966): 38–51

Mirashi, Vasudev Vishnu, *Bhavabhūti: His Life Date and Works* (Delhi: Motilal Banarsidass, 1974): 102–9

Mirashi, Vasudev Vishnu, *The History and Inscriptions of the Sātavāhanas and the Western Kshatrapas* (Bombay: Government Press, 1981)

Mishra, Aman, 'Sīyaḍoṇī: An Unplanned Town of the Gurjara-Pratīhāra Times', *Urban History* 50.4 (2022): 1–18

Mishra, S.C., *Evolution of Kauṭilya's Arthaśāstra: An Inscriptional Approach* (Delhi: Anamaka Prakashan, 1993)

Misra, B.B., *The Judicial Administration of the East India Company in Bengal, 1765–1782* (London: SOAS, 1947)

Mitchell, Lynette, and Charles Melville (eds), *Every Inch a King: Comparative Studies on Kings and Kingship in the Ancient and Medieval Worlds* (Leiden: Brill, 2013)

Mookerjee, Prasad, *A Diary of Sir Asutosh Mookerjee, with his Life Sketch* (Calcutta: Asutosh Mookerjee Memorial Institute, 1998)

Mookerji, Radhakumud, *Candragupta and His Times* (New Delhi: Motilal Banarsidass, 1966)

Moran, Arik, 'Rajpūt Kingship', in *Oxford Research Encyclopedia of Asian History* (Oxford: Oxford University Press, 2023)

Morcillo, Marta García, 'Sacred Gifts, Profane Uses? Transfers and the Roman Religious Sphere', in Andrew Wilson, Nick Ray, and Angela Trentacoste (eds), *The Economy of Roman Religion* (Oxford: Oxford University Press, 2023): 245–66

Morton, T.C., *Decisions of the Supreme Court of Judicature at Fort William in Bengal. On the Plea, Equity, Ecclesiastical, Admiralty and Crown Sides, from the Date of the Charter of 1774 to 1841* (Calcutta: Samuel Smith & Co., 1841)

Mudaliar, Chandra, *The Secular State and Religious Institutions in India: A Study of the Administration of Hindu Public Religious Trusts in Madras* (Wiesbaden: Franz Steiner Verlag, 1974)

Mukherjea, B.K., *The Hindu Law of Religious and Charitable Trusts*, 5th edn. (Calcutta: Eastern Law House, 2016)

Mukherjee, Asutosh, *The Law of Perpetuities in British India* (Calcutta: Thacker, Spink, & Co, 1902)

Mukherjee, Prabhat and Nancy Gardner Cassels (eds), *Pilgrim Tax and Temple Scandals: A Critical Study of the Important Jagannath Temple Records During British Rule* (Bangkok: Orchid Press, 2000)

Mukherjee Tarapada, and Irfan Habib, 'Akbar and the Temples of Mathura and its Environs', *Proceedings of the Indian History Congress* 48 (1987): 234–50

Mukherjee, Tarapada, and Irfan Habib, 'The Mughal Administration and the Vrindaban During the Reigns of Jahangir and Shah Jahan', *Proceedings of the Indian History Congress* 49 (1988): 287–300

Mukherjee, Tarapada, and Irfan Habib, 'Land Rights in the Reign of Akbar (the Evidence of the Sale-Deeds of Vrindaban and Ariṭha', *Proceedings of the Indian History Congress* 50 (1989): 236–55

Mukherjee Tarapada, and J.C. Wright, 'An Early Testamentary Document in Sanskrit', *Bulletin of the School of Oriental and African Studies* 42.2 (1979): 297–320

Mukherji, Saugata, 'A Note on Lekhiraj Lands', *Proceedings of the Indian Historical Congress* 21 (1958): 426–30

Mustafa, Faizan, and Jagteshwar Sohi, 'Freedom of Religion in India: Current Issues and Supreme Court Acting as Clergy', *BYU Law Review* (2017): 915–56

Mustafa, Mohammed, 'The Shaping of Land Revenue Policy in Madras Presidency: Revenue Experiments – the Case of Chittoor District', *Indian Economic and Social History Review* 42.2 (2007): 111–267

Myrvold, Kristina, 'Making the Scripture a Person: Reinventing Death Rituals of Guru Granth Sahib in Sikhism', in Kristina Myrvold (ed.), *The Death of Sacred Texts: Ritual Disposal and Renovation of Texts in World Religions* (London: Routledge, 2010): 135–56

Nanda, Meera, *The God Market: How Globalization is Making India More Hindu* (New York: NYU Press, 2011)

Narain, Jagat, 'Equal Protection Guarantee and the Right of Property Under the Indian Constitution', *International and Comparative Law Quarterly* 15.1 (1966): 199–230

Nardi, Isabella, 'Mobility and Festivity: Krishna Icons and the Reunion of the Seven Svarūps of 1739–1740', *South Asian Studies* 39.1 (2023): 21–34

Natarajan, Prema, 'High Courts in India as Palladium of People's Rights Against Administrative Discretion (1861–1900)', *Proceedings of the Indian History Congress* 39.2 (1978): 691–9

Neuberger, Lord, 'Equity: the Soul and Spirit of all Law or a Roguish Thing? Lehane Lecture 2014', *Australian Law Journal* 88.11 (2014): 802–11

Neuborne, Burt, 'The Supreme Court of India', *International Journal of Constitutional Law* 1.3 (2003): 476–510

Neumann, Hans, 'Mesopotamien', in Albrecht Jockenhovel (ed.), *Grundlagen der Globalen Welt vom Beginn bis 1200 v. Chr* (Darmstadt: Wissenschaftliches Buchgesellschaft, 2009): 184–215

Newbigin, Eleanor, 'The Codification of Personal Law and Secular Citizenship: Revisiting the History of Law Reform in Late Colonial India', *Indian Economic and Social History Review* 46.1 (2009): 83–104

Newbigin, Eleanor, *The Hindu Family and the Emergence of Modern India: Law, Citizenship and Community* (Cambridge: Cambridge University Press, 2013)

Newman, John, 'Islam in the *Kālacakratantra*', *Journal of the International Association of Buddhist Studies* 21.2 (1998): 311–72

Norman, K.R., 'The Languages of the Composition and Transmission of the Aśokan Edicts', in Patrick Olivelle, Janice Leoshko, and Himanshu Prabha Ray (eds), *Reimagining Aśoka* (Oxford: Oxford University Press, 2012): 38–64

Nottingham, Lord, 'Prolegomena of Chancery and Equity', in D.E.C. Yale (ed.), *Lord Nottingham's 'Manual of Chancery Practice' and 'Prolegomena of Chancery and Equity'* (Cambridge: Cambridge University Press, 1965)

O'Donnell, Erin, 'At the Intersection of the Sacred and the Legal: Rights for Nature in Uttarakhand, India', *Journal of Environmental Law* 30 (2018): 135–44

O'Donnell, Erin, 'Rivers as Living Beings: Rights in Law, but no Right in Water?', *Griffith Law Review* 29.4 (2020): 643–68

O'Donnell, Erin, and Julia Talbot-Jones, 'Creating Legal Rights for Rivers: Lessons from Australia, New Zealand, and India', *Ecology and Society* 23.1 (2018)

O'Hanlon, Rosalind, 'The Social Worth of Scribes: Brahmins, Kāyasthas, and the Social Order in Early Modern India', *Indian Economic and Social History Review* 47.4 (2010): 563–95

Oleck, Howard, 'Historical Nature of Equity Jurisprudence' *Fordham Law Review* 20.23 (1951): 23–44

Olivelle, Patrick, 'Introduction', *Journal of Indian Philosophy* 32.5–6 (2004): 421–2

Olivelle, Patrick (ed.), *Between the Empires: Society in India 300 BCE–400 CE* (New York: Oxford University Press, 2006)

Olivelle, Patrick, 'The Temple in Sanskrit Legal Literature', in H. P. Ray (ed.), *Archaeology and Text: Temple in South Asia* (Delhi: Oxford University Press, 2010): 191–204

Olivelle, Patrick, 'Aśoka's Inscriptions as Text and Ideology', in Patrick Olivelle, Janice Leoshko, and Himanshu Prabha Ray (eds), *Reimagining Aśoka* (Oxford: Oxford University Press, 2012): 157–83

Olivelle, Patrick, 'Introduction', in Patrick Olivelle, Janice Leoshko, and Himanshu Prabha Ray (eds), *Reimagining Aśoka* (Oxford: Oxford University Press, 2012): 1–16

Olivelle, Patrick, *King, Governance, and Law in Ancient India: Kauṭilya's Arthaśāstra* (Oxford: Oxford University Press, 2013)

Olivelle, Patrick, *Ashoka: Portrait of a Philosopher King* (New Haven: Yale University Press, 2024)

Olivelle, Patrick, David Brick, and Mark McClish (eds), *A Sanskrit Dictionary of Law and Stutecraft* (New Delhi: Primus, 2015)

Olivelle, Patrick, and Mark McClish, 'The Four Feet of Legal Procedure and the Origins of Jurisprudence in Ancient India', *Journal of the American Oriental Society* 135.1 (2015): 33–47

Ollett, Andrew, *The Language of the Snakes: Prakrit, Sanskrit, and the Language Order of Premodern India* (Berkeley: University of California Press, 2017)

Ollett, Andrew, 'Attempted Iconoclasm: Mahmud of Ghazna, King Yoga, and the Poet Dhanapāla', *Comparative Studies of South Asia, Africa and the Middle East* 42.2 (2022): 309–24

Orr, Leslie, 'Women in the Temple, the Palace, and the Family: The Construction of Women's Identities in Pre-Colonial Tamilnāḍu', in Kenneth Hall (ed.), *Structure and Society in Early South India: Essays in Honour of Noboru Karashima* (New Delhi: Oxford University Press, 2001): 198–234

Orr, Leslie, 'Michael Willis, *The Archaeology of Hindu Ritual: Temples and the Establishment of the Gods*', *South Asian Studies* 26.2 (2010): 238–42

Pacciolla, Paolo, *The Indian Drum of the King-God and the Pakhāvaj of Nathdwara* (London: Routledge, 2020)

Pachauri, S.K., 'Plunder of Cultural and Art Treasures: The Indian Experience', in Neil Brodie and Kathryn Walker Tubb (eds), *Illicit Antiquities: The Theft of Culture and the Extinction of Archeology* (London: Routledge, 2002): 268–79

Parikh, Sheetal, 'Enshrining a Secular Idol: A Judicial Response to the Violent Aftermath of Ayodhya', *Case Western Reserve Journal of International Law* 37.85 (2005): 85–109

Paterson, Robert, 'The Curse of the London Nataraj', *International Journal of Cultural Property* 5.2 (1996): 330–8

Patra, K.M., 'The Temple of Jagannath and Pilgrim Tax (1803–1840)', *Proceedings of the Indian History Congress* 30 (1968): 92–301

Patton, David, 'The Queen, the Attorney General, and the Modern Charitable Fiduciary: A Historical Perspective on Charitable Enforcement Reform', *University of Florida Journal of Law and Public Policy* 11.2 (2000): 131–78

Pauwels, Heidi, 'The Saint, the Warlord, and the Emperor: Discourses of Braj Bhakti and Bundelā Loyalty', *Journal of the Economic and Social History of the Orient* 52: 2 (2009): 187–228

Pauwels, Heidi, 'A Tale of Two Temples: Mathurā's Keśavadeva and Orcchā's Caturbhujadeva', in Rosalind O'Hanlon and David Washbroom (eds), *Religious Cultures in Early Modern India* (London: Routledge, 2012): 278–99

Pauwels, Heidi, and Emilia Bachrach, 'Aurangzeb as Iconoclast? Vaishnava Accounts of the Krishna Images' Exodus from Braj', *Journal of the Royal Asiatic Society* 28.3 (2018): 485–508

Peabody, Norbert, 'In Whose Turban Does the Lord Reside? The Objectification of Charisma and the Fetishization of Objects in the Hindu Kingdom of Kota', *Comparative Studies in Society and History* 33.4 (1991): 726–54

Peabody, Norbert, *Hindu Kingship and Polity in Pre-Colonial India* (Cambridge: Cambridge University Press, 2003)

Peralta, Padilla, *Divine Institutions: Religions and Community in the Middle Roman Republic* (Princeton: Princeton University Press, 2020)

Phillips, Jim, 'A Successor to the Moguls: The Nawab of the Garnatic and the East India Company, 1763–1785', *International History Review* 7.3 (1985): 364–89

Poitras, Geoffrey, 'The *Societas Publicanorum* and Corporate Personality in Roman Private Law', *Business History* 63.7 (2021): 1055–78

Pokharel, Krishna, and T. Lahiri, 'Who Are the Nirmohi Akhara?', *The Wall Street Journal India* 30 (2010)

Pollock, Frederick, and Frederic William Maitland, *The History of English Law Before the Time of Edward I*, 2nd edn., Vol. 1 (Cambridge: Cambridge University Press, 1898)

Pollock, Sheldon, 'Rāmāyaṇa and Political Imagination in India', *The Journal of Asian Studies* 52.2 (1993): 261–97

Pollock, Sheldon, *The Language of the Gods in the World of Men* (Berkeley: University of California Press, 2006)

Pongratz-Leisten, Beate, *Religion and Ideology in Assyria* (Berlin: De Gruyte, 2015)

Poulter, S., *Ethnicity, Law and Human Rights: The English Experience* (Oxford: Oxford University Press, 1998)

Prasad, Pushpa, *Inscriptions of the Delhi Sultanate 1191–1526* (Delhi: Oxford University Press, 1990)

Punwani, Jyoti, 'The Carnage of Gadhra', in Siddharth Varadarajan (eds), *Gujarat: The Making of a Tragedy* (New Delhi: Penguin Books, 2002): 45–74

Puri, B.N., *The History of the Gurjara-Pratiharas* (Delhi: Munshiram Manoharlal, 1957)

Purushotham, Sunil, 'Federating the Raj: Hyderabad, Sovereign Kingship, and Partition', *Modern Asian Studies* 54.1 (2020): 157–98

Pylee, M.V., *An Introduction to the Constitution of India*, 5th edn. (Noida: Vikas, 2007)

Quintanilla, Sonya, *History of Early Stone Sculpture at Mathura: Ca. 150 BCE–100 CE* (Leiden: Brill, 2007)

Rabe, Michael D., 'Royal Temple Dedications', in Donald Lopez (ed.), *Religions of India in Practice* (Princeton: Princeton University Press, 1995): 235–43

Raddock, Elisabeth, *Listen How the Wise One Begins Construction of a House for Visnu: Chapters 1–14 of the Hayasirsa Pancaratra* (Unpublished PhD Dissertation: UC Berkeley, 2011)

Rai, Shashank, Shabarna Choudhury, and Sai Snigdha Kantamneni, 'Aftermath of Ayodhya Verdict: Impact on Kashi and Mathura', *Jus Corpus Law Journal* 1 (2020): 90–100

Rai, Vinod, 'The Sree Padmanabhaswamy Temple Case: Landmark Ruling by the Indian Supreme Court', *ISAS Insights* 635 (2020): 1–5

Raju, K.H. Cheluva, 'Dr. B.R. Ambedkar and Making of the Constitution', *Indian Journal of Political Science* 52.2 (1991): 153–64

Rakshit, Nirmalendu Bikash, 'Right to Constitutional Remedy: Significance of Article 32', *Economic and Political Weekly* 34.34–5 (1999): 2379–81

Ramesh, K.V., *The Cālukyas of Vātāpi* (Delhi: Kala Prakashan, 1984)

Ramesh, K.V., and S.P. Tewari (eds), *A Copper-Plate Hoard of the Gupta Period from Bagh, Madhya Pradesh* (New Delhi: Archeological Survey of India, 1990)

Ramjohn, Mohamed, *Unlocking Equity and Trusts*, 7th edn. (London: Routledge, 2019)

Ramnath, Kalyani, 'ADM Jabalpur's Antecedents: Political Emergencies, Civil Liberties, and Arguments from Colonial Continuities in India', *American University International Law Review* 31.2 (2016): 209–52

Ramnath, Kalyani, 'Of Limited Suits and Limitless Legalities: Interpreting Legal Procedure in the Ayodhya Judgment', *NUALS Law Journal* 5.1 (2011): 1–18

Rani, J. Jemi Merlin, 'The Religious Legacy of Tipu Sultan', *IOSR Journal Of Humanities and Social Science* 23.4 (2018): 84–8

Rankin, George, *Background to Indian Law* (Cambridge: Cambridge University Press, 1946)

Rao, C. Hayavadano, 'Stephen, Sir Harry Lushington', in *The Indian Biographical Dictionary* (Madras: Pillar & Co., 1915)

Rastelli, Marion, 'The 'Pāñcarātra Passages in *Agnipurāṇa* 21–70', in *Melanges tantriques a la memoir d'Helene Brunner* (Pondicherry: EFEO, 2007): 187–229

Rauh, Nicholas, *The Sacred Bonds of Commerce: Religion, Economy, and Trade Society at Hellenistic Roman Delos, 166–87 BC* (Leiden: Brill, 1993)

Rawlinson, H.C., 'Notes on a Newly-Discovered Clay Cylinder of Cyrus the Great', *Journal of the Royal Asiatic Society of Great Britain and Ireland* New Series 12.1 (1880): 70–97

Ray, Himanshu, 'The Mauryan Empire', in Peter Bang, C.A. Bayly, and Walter Scheidel (eds), *The Oxford History of Empire: Volume 2: The History of Empires* (Oxford: Oxford University Press, 2021): 198–217

Ray, Sukumar, and M.R. Malick (eds), *B.B. Mitra's Limitation Act*, 23rd edn. (Calcutta: Eastern Law House, 2014)

Renger, Johannes, 'Interaction of Temple, Palace, and "Private Enterprise" in the Old Babylonian Economy', in Edward Lipinski (ed.), *State and Temple Economy*, Vol. 1 (Leuven: Departement Oriëntalistiek 1979): 249–56

Renger, Johannes, 'Institutional, Communal, and Individual Ownership or Possession of Arable Land in Ancient Mesopotamia from the end of the Fourth to the end of the First Millennium BC', *Chicago-Kent Law Review* 71.1 (1995): 269–319

Renger, Johannes, 'Economy of Ancient Mesopotamia: A General Outline', in Gwendolyn Leick (ed.), *The Babylonian World* (London: Routledge, 2007): 187–97

Rezavi, Syed Ali Nadeem, 'Antiquarian Interests in Medeival India: The Relocation of Ashokan Pillars by Firuzshah Tughluq', *Proceedings of the Indian History Congress* 70 (2009–10): 994–1010

Ribaravić, Luka, 'Leviathan and Medieval "Universitas": Hobbes' Debt to Canon Law', *History of Political Thought*, 38.1 (2017): 92–109

Rice, Lewis, 'Nagamangala Copper Plate Inscription', *Indian Antiquary* 2 (1873): 155–61

Richter, Susan, '*Pater Patriae Sinensis*: The Discovery of Patriarchal Rule in China and Its Significance for German Theories of State in the Eighteenth Century', in A. Flüchter and S. Richter (eds), *Structures on the Move: Technologies of Governance in Transcultural Encounter* (Berlin: Springer, 2012)

Robertson, J.F., *Redistributive Economies in Ancient Mesopotamian Society: A Case Study from Isin-Larsa Period Nippur* (Unpublished PhD Dissertation: University of Michigan, 1981)

Robertson, J.F., 'The Internal Political and Economic Structure of Old Babylonian Nippur: The *Guennakkum* and His "House"', *Journal of Cuneiform Studies* 36 (1984): 145–90

Robertson, J.F., 'The Temple Economy of Old Babylonian Nippur: The Evidence for Centralized Management', in J. Ellis (ed.), *Nippur at the Centennial: Papers Read at the 35 Rencontre Assyriologique Internationale, Philadelphia* (Philadelphia: University Museum Press, 1988): 177–88

Rocher, Ludo, *The Purāṇas* (Wiesbaden: Otto Harrassowitz, 1986)

Rocher, Ludo, 'Jīmūtavāhana's Dāyabhāga and the Maxim Factum Valet', in Donald Davis (ed.), *Studies in Hindu Law and Dharmaśāstra* (New York: Anthem Press, 2014): 305–13

Rocher, Ludo, 'Schools of Hindu Law', in Donald Davis (ed.), *Studies in Hindu Law and Dharmaśāstra* (London: Anthem, 2014): 119–28

Rocher, Ludo, *Vyavahārasaukhya: The Treatise on Legal Procedure in the Ṭodarānanda Composed at the Instance of Ṭoḍaramalla During the Reign of Akbar* (Florence: Società Editrice Fiorentina, 2016)

Rocher, Rosane, 'The Career of Rādhākānta Tarkavāgīśa, an Eighteenth-Century Pandit in British Employ', *Journal of the American Oriental Society* 109.4 (1989): 627–33

Rocher, Rosane, 'Weaving Knowledge: Sir William Jones and Indian Pandits', in Garland Cannon and Kevin Brine (eds), *Objects of Enquiry: The Life, Contributions, and Influences of Sir William Jones, 1746–1794* (New York: New York University Press, 1995): 51–79

Rocher, Rosane, 'The Creation of Anglo-Hindu Law', in Timothy Lubin, Donald Davis, and Jayanth Krishnan (eds), *Hinduism and Law: An Introduction* (Cambridge: Cambridge University Press, 2010): 78–104

Rocher, Rosane, and Ludo Rocher, *The Making of Western Indology: Henry Thomas Colebrooke and the East India Company* (London: Routledge, 2012)

Rorabacher, J. Albert, *Property, Land, Revenue, and Policy: The East India Company, c. 1757–1825* (London: Routledge, 2016)

Roth, Martha, 'Mesopotamian Legal Traditions and the Laws of Hammurabi', *Chicago-Kent Law Review* 71.1 (1995): 13–40

Rotman, Leonard, 'Fiduciary Law's Holy Grail: Reconciling Theory and Practice in Fiduciary Jurisprudence', *Boston University Law Review* 91.3 (2011): 921–72

Saletore, B.A., 'Tipu Sultan as Defender of the Hindu *Dharma*', in Irfan Habib (ed.), *Confronting Colonialism: Resistance and Modernization Under Haider Ali and Tipu Sultan* (London: Anthem Press, 2002): 115–30

Salomon, Richard, *Indian Epigraphy: A Guide to the Study of Inscriptions in Sanskrit, Prakrit, and the other Indo-Aryan languages* (New York: Oxford University Press, 1998)

Salomon, Richard, 'Aśoka and the "Epigraphic Habit" in India', in Patrick Olivelle (ed.), *Aśoka in History and Historical Memory* (Delhi: Motilal Banarsidass, 2009): 45–52

Salomon, Richard, 'The Fine Art of Forgery in India', in Gérard Colas and Gerdi Gerschheimer (eds), *Écrire et transmettre en Inde Classique* (Paris: École Française d'Extrême-Orient, 2009): 107–134

Salomon, Richard, 'Aṣṭabhujasvāmin: A Reinterpretation of the Ābhīra Inscription from Nagarjunakonda', *Indo-Iranian Journal* 56 (2013): 397–417

Samons, Loren, *Empire of the Owl: Athenian Imperial Finance* (Stuttgart: Franz Steiner, 2000)

Sanderson, Alexis, 'The Śaiva Religion Among the Khmers (Part 1)', *Bulletin de l'Ecole française d'Extrême-Orient* 90–91 (2003): 349–462

Sanderson, Alexis, 'The Śaiva Age: The Rise and Dominance of Śaivism During the Early Medieval Period', in Shingo Einoo (ed.), *Genesis and Development of Tantrism* (Tokyo: University of Tokyo, 2009): 41–350

Sanderson, Alexis, 'How Public was Śaivism?', in Nina Mirnig, Marion Rastelli, and Vincent Eltschinger (eds), *Tantric Communities in Context* (Vienna: Austrian Academy of Sciences Press, 2019): 1–48

Sankaranarayana, S., *The Viṣṇukuṇḍis and their Times: An Epigraphic Study* (Delhi: Agam Prakashan, 1977)

Sarasvati, Prannath, *The Hindu Law of Endowments* (Calcutta: Thacker, Spink, & Co., 1897)

Sarkar, Bihani, *Heroic Shāktism: The Cult of Durgā in Ancient Indian Kingship* (Oxford: Oxford University Press, 2017)

Sarkar, Golapchandra, *The Hindu Law of Adoption* (Calcutta: Thacker, Spink, & Co., 1891)

Sato, Tsugitaka, *State and Rural Society in Medieval Islam Sultans, Muqta's and Fallahun* (Ledien: Brill, 1997)

Satpathy, Bijayashree, 'Forest Rights Act Implementation in Odisha: Redressing Historical Injustices', *South Asia Research* 37.3 (2017): 259–76

Saxena, Saumya, '"Courting" Hindu Nationalism: Law and the Rise of Modern Hindutva', *Contemporary South Asia* 26.4 (2018): 378–99

Scheppler, Bill, *Al-Biruni: Master Astronomer and Muslim Scholar of the Eleventh Century* (New York: Rosen Publishing, 2006)

Schlosser, Andrea, and Pankaj Tandon, 'The Channapatna Plates: A New Set of Copperplates of the Western Gaṅgas', *Studien zur Indologie und Iranistik* 29 (2009): 219–49

Schopen, Gregory, 'The Buddha as an Owner of Property and Permanent Resident in Medieval Indian Monasteries', *Journal of Indian Philosophy* 18.3 (1990): 181–217

Schopen, Gregory, 'Doing Business for the Lord: Lending on Interest and Written Loan Contracts in the Mūlasarvāstivāda-vinaya', *Journal of the American Oriental Society* 114.4 (1994): 527–54

Schmiedchen, Annette, *Herrschergenealogie und religiöses Patronat: Die Inschriftenkultur der Rāṣṭrakūṭas, Śilāhāras und Yādavas (8. bis 13. Jahrhundert)* (Leiden: Brill, 2014)

Schmiedchen, Annette, 'Imperial Rulers and Regional Elites in Early Medieval Central India (8th to 13th Centuries)', in Herman Kulke and Bhairabi Sahu (eds), *The Routledge Handbook of the State in Pre-Modern India* (London: Routledge, 2022): 291–308

Schwartz, Jason, 'The King Must Protect the Difference: The Juridical Foundations of Tantric Knowledge', *Religions* 9.4 (2018): 1–25

Scott, Austin, 'The Nature and Rights of *Cestui Que Trust*', *Columbia Law Review* 17.4 (1917): 269–90

Sealy, Len, 'Fiduciary Relationships', *Cambridge Law Journal* 20.1 (1962): 119–40

Sen, Priyanath, *The General Principles of Hindu Jurisprudence* (Calcutta: University of Calcutta, 1989)

Sen, Ranjit, 'The Emergence of a Service Elite in Bengal in the Second Half of the Eighteenth Century: A New Dimension of Collaboration', *Proceeding of the Indian History Congress* 36 (1975): 511–22

Sen, Ronojoy, *Legalizing Religion: The Indian Supreme Court and Secularism* (Washington, DC: East West Center, 2007)

Sen, Ronojoy, *Articles of Faith: Religion, Secularism, and the Indian Supreme Court*, updated and revised edition (New Delhi: Oxford University Press, 2019)

Sen, Ronojoy, 'Reforming Religion: the Indian Constitution, the Courts and Hinduism', in Susanna Mancini (ed.), *Constitutions and Religion* (Northampton: Edward Elgar Publishing, 2020): 222–36.

Sen, Sarbani, *The Constitution of India: Popular Sovereignty and Democratic Transformations* (Oxford: Oxford University Press, 2011)

Seth, Sudev, 'Revenue Farming Reconsidered: Tenurial Rights and Tenurial Duties in Early Modern India, ca. 1556–1818', *Journal of the Economic and Social History of the Orient* 61 (2018): 878–918

Sethi, Manisha, 'Jainism in Danger? Temple Entry and the Rhetoric of Religion and Reform in Post-colonial India' *Modern Asian Studies* 55.5 (2021): 1718–54

Seymour, John, 'Parens Patriae and Wardship Powers: Their Nature and Origins', *Oxford Journal of Legal Studies* 14.2 (1994): 159–88

Seipp, David, 'The Reception of Canon Law and Civil Law in the Common Law Courts before 1600', *Oxford Journal of Legal Studies* 13.3 (1993): 388–420

Seipp, David, 'Trust and Fiduciary Duty in the Early Common Law', *Boston University Law Review* 91.3 (2011): 1011–38

Shah, Prakash, *Against Caste in British Law: A Critical Perspective on the Caste Discrimination Provision in the Equality* (London: Palgrave Macmillan, 2015)

Sharma, Mukul, 'Passages from Nature to Nationalism: Sunderlal Bahuguna and Tehri Dam Opposition in Garhwal', *Economic and Political Weekly* 8 (2009): 35–42

Sherman, Charles, 'Debt of the Modern Law of Guardianship to Roman Law', *Michigan Law Review* 12.2 (1913–14): 124–31

Shetty, Rakshith, 'An Analytical Study on the Appointment of Guardians to Vegetative People in Reference to the Doctrine of "Parens Patriae"', *Indian Journal of Law and Legal Research* 5.1 (2023): 1–12

Shobhi, Prithvi Datta Chandra, 'Kalyāṇa Is Wrecked: The Remaking of a Medieval Capital in Popular Imagination', *South Asian Studies* 32.1 (2006): 90–8

Siddiq, Mohammad, *Epigraphy and Islamic Culture: Inscriptions of the Early Muslim Rulers of Bengal (1205–1494)* (London: Routledge, 2015)

Siddique, Asheesh, 'William Jones, Esq.', *Global Intellectual History* (2023): 1–7

Singh, Surinder, 'Dynamics of Statecraft in the Delhi Sultanate: A Reconstruction from the Letters of Ainul Mulk Mahru', *Proceedings of the Indian History Congress* 61.1 (2000–01): 285–93

Singh, Upinder, 'Cults and Shrines in Early Historical Mathura (c. 200 BC–AD 200)', *World Archeology* 36.3 (2004): 378–98

Sinha, Chittaranjan, 'A Judiciary at Odds with the Executive: The Calcutta Supreme Court and the Bengal Administration 1781–1833', *Journal of the Indian Law Institute* 10.3 (1968): 499–519

Sircar, Dineschandra, *Successor of the Sātavāhanas in Lower Deccan* (Calutta: University of Calcutta, 1939)

Sircar, Dineschandra, *Epochs in Indian Legal History* (Hoshiarpur: Vishveshvaranand Vedic Research Institute, 1958)

Sircar, Dineschandra, *Indian Epigraphy* (Delhi: Motilal Banarsidass, 1965)

Sircar, Dineschandra, *Select Inscriptions Bearing on Indian History and Civilization*, 2 vols., 2nd edn. (Calcutta: University of Calcutta: 1965)

Sircar, Dineschandra, *Aśokan Studies* (Calcutta: Indian Museum, 1979)

Sircar, Dineschandra, *The Kānyakubja-Gauḍa Struggle: From the Sixth to the Twelfth Century AD* (Calcutta: Asiatic Society, 1985)

Skinner, Michael, *Urbanization and Interactions in the Early Historic Deccan: The Sātavāhana, Western Ksatrapa, and Iksvāku Dynasties* (Unpublished MA Dissertation, University of Washington, 2012)

Skinner, Michael, *Marks of Empire: Extracting a Narrative from the Corpus of Kuṣāṇa Inscriptions* (Unpublished PhD Dissertation: University of Washington, 2017)

Smith, Henry E., 'Equity as Second-Order Law: The Problem of Opportunism', *Harvard Public Law Working Paper No. 15-13* (2015)

Smith, Henry E., 'Equity as Meta-Law', *Yale Law Journal* 130 (2021): 1050–134

Sohm, Rudolph, *Institutes of Roman Law* (Oxford: Oxford University Press, 1892)

Sontheimer, Günther-Dietz, 'Religious Endowments in India: The Juristic Personality of Hindu Deities', in Heidrun Brückner *et al.* (eds), *Essays on Religion, Literature and Law* (New Delhi: Manohar, 2004): 15–68

Spencer, George W., 'Crisis of Authority in a Hindu Temple under the Impact of Islam: Śrīraṅgam in the Fourteenth Century', in B.L. Smith (ed.), *Religion and the Legitimation of Power South Asia* (Leiden: Brill, 1978)

Srinivasn, Doris (ed.), *Mathurā: The Cultural Heritage* (New Delhi: American Institute of Indian Studies, 1989)

Srivastav, Palash, 'Legal Personality of Ganga and Ecocentrism: Critical Review', *Cambridge Law Review* 4.1 (2019): 151–68

Srivastava, Ramesh, *Development of Judicial System in India Under the East India Company, 1833–1858* (Lucknow: Lucknow Publishing House, 1971)

Starling, M.H., *The Indian Limitation Act, 1877*, 4th edn. (Bombay: Education Society Press, 1900)

Starza, O.M., *The Jagannatha Temple at Puri: Its Architecture, Art, and Cult* (Leiden: Brill, 1993)

Stein, Burton, *The New Cambridge History of India: Vijayanagara* (Cambridge: Cambridge University Press, 2008)

Stein, Deborah, *The Hegemony of Heritage: Ritual and Record in Stone* (Oakland: University of California Press, 2018)

Stern, Phillip, *The Company-State: Corporate Sovereignty and the Early Modern Foundations of the British Empire in India* (Oxford: Oxford University Press, 2011)

Stevenson, Tom, 'Acceptance of the Title *Pater Patriae* in 2 BC', *Antichthon* 43 (2009): 97–108

Stietencron, Heinrich von, 'Orthodox Attitudes Towards Temple Service and Image Worship in Ancient India', *Central Asiatic Journal* 21.2 (1977): 126–38

Stoker, Valerie, 'Polemics and Patronage in Sixteenth-Century Vijayanagara: Vyāsatīrtha and the Dynamics of Hindu Sectarian Relations', *Journal of the American Academy of Religion* 51.2 (2011): 129–55

Stoker, Valerie, *Polemics and Patronage in the City of Victory: Vyasatirtha, Hindu Sectarianism and the Sixteenth Century Vijayanagara Court* (Oakland: University of California Press, 2016)

Story, Joseph, *Equity Jurisprudence*, 2nd edn. (England: Stevens and Haynes, 1892)

Strange, Thomas, *Notes of Cases in the Court of the Recorder and in the Supreme Court of Judicature at Madras: 1798–1816*, Vol. 1 (Madras: Asylum Press, 1816)

Strange, Thomas, *Hindu Law*, Vol. 1 (London: Parbury Allen & Co., 1830)

Strauch, Ingo, 'Money for Rituals: Akṣayanīvī and Related Inscriptions form Āndhradeśa', in Henry Albery, Jens-Uwe Hartmann, and Himanshu Prabha Ray (eds), *Power, Presence and Space South Asian Rituals in Archaeological Context* (London: Routledge, 2020): 193–214

Strong, John, *The Legend of King Aśoka: A Study and Translation of the Aśokavadana* (Princeton: Princeton University Press, 1984)

Sturman, Rachel, 'Property and Attachments: Defining Autonomy and the Claims of Family in Nineteenth-Century Western India', *Comparative Studies in Society and History* 47.3 (2005-07): 611–37

Subbarayalu, Y., *South India Under the Cholas* (New Delhi: Oxford University Press, 2012)

Sundaram, Chandar, *Indianization, the Officer Corps, and the Indian Army: The Forgotten Debate, 1817–1917* (Lanham: Lexington Books, 2019)

Swenden, Wilfried, and Rekha Saxena, 'Policing the Federation: The Supreme Court Judicial Federalism in India', *Territory, Politics, Governance* 10.1 (2022): 12–31

Tackes, Nick, 'The View from Mathura: Nationalist Projects in a Local Dispute', *Contemporary South Asia* 32.1 (2024): 84–100

Tagore, Rajah, *Hindu Loyalty* (Calcutta: I.C. Bose & Co., 1883)

Talbot, Cynthia, *The Last Hindu Emperor: Prithviraj and the Indian Past 1200–2000* (Cambridge: Cambridge University Press, 2016)

Talbot, Cynthia, 'A Poetic Record of the Rajpūt Rebellion, c. 1680', *JRAS* 3.28 (2018): 461–83

Talbot, Ian, 'Mountbatten and the Partition of India: A Rejoinder', *History* 69.225 (1984): 29–35

Talbot, Ian, 'Partition of India: The Human Dimension', *Journal of the Social History Society* 6.4 (2009): 403–10

Talbot, Ian, and Gurharpal Singh (eds), *Partition and Region: Bengal, Punjab and the Partition of the Subcontinent* (Karachi: Oxford University Press, 1999)

Talbot-Jones, Julia, and Jeff Bennett, 'Toward a Property Rights Theory of Legal Rights for Rivers', *Ecological Economics* 164 (2019): 1–6

Tambiah, Stanley, *World Conqueror, World Renouncer* (Cambridge: Cambridge University Press, 2010)

Tarabout, Giles, 'Religious Uncertainty, Astrology and the Courts in South India', in Daniela Berti, Anthony Good, and Gilles Tarabout (eds), *Of Doubt and Proof: Ritual and Legal Practices of Judgment* (Farnham: Ashgate, 2015): 59–76

Tejani, Shabnum, 'Untouchable Demands for Justice or the Problem of Religious "Non-Interference": The Case of Temple Entry Movements in Late-Colonial India', *Journal of Colonialism and Colonial History* 14.3 (2013)

Tellegen-Couperu, Olga, 'Sacred Law and Civil Law', in Olga Tellegen-Couperu (ed.), *Law and Religion in the Roman Republic* (Leiden: Brill, 2012): 145–64

Temper, Leah, and Joan Martinez-Alier, 'The God of the Mountain and Godavarman: Net Present Value, Indigenous Territorial Rights and Sacredness in a Bauxite Mining Conflict in India', *Ecological Economics* 96 (2013): 79–87

Thapar, Romila, *Aśoka and the Decline of the Mauryas*, revised edition (New Delhi: Oxford University Press, 1997)

Thapar, Romila, *Somnath, the Many Voices of a History* (New Delhi: Penguin, 2004)

Thapar, Romila, 'Aśoka: A Retrospective', in Patrick Olivelle, Janice Leoshko, and Himanshu Prabha Ray (eds), *Reimagining Aśoka* (Oxford: Oxford University Press, 2012): 18–37

Thelen, Elizabeth, 'Disputed Transactions: Documents, Language, and Authority in Eighteenth Century Marwar', *Journal of the Economic and Social History of the Orient* 64 (2021): 792–825

Thomas, Yan, '*Res Religiosae*: On the Categories of Religion and Commerce Under Roman Law', in Alain Pottage and Martha Mundy (eds), *Law, Anthropology, and the Constitution of the Social: Making Persons and Things* (Cambridge: Cambridge University Press, 2009): 40–72

Tillin, Louise, 'United in Diversity? Asymmetry in Indian Federalism', *Publius: The Journal of Federalism* 37.1 (2007): 45–67

Tomalin, Emma, 'Bio-Divinity and Biodiversity: Perspectives on Religion and Environmental Conservation in India', *Numen* 51.3 (2004): 265–95

Tran, N., *Les membres des associations Romaines: Le rang social des collegiati en Italie et en Gaules sous le haut-empire* (Rome: Collection de l'École française de Rome 367, 2006)

Trevelyan, Ernest, *The Law Relating to Minors: As Administered in the Provinces Subject to the High Courts of British India. Together with the Practice of the Courts of Wards in Bengal, Madras, Bombay, and the United Provinces of Agra and Oudh*, 4th edn. (London: W. Thacker & Company, 1912)

Trevelyan, Ernest, *The Law Relating to Minors: As Administered in the Provinces Subject to the High Courts of British India: Together with the Practice of the Courts of Wards in Bengal, Bihar and Orissa, Madras, Bombay, and the United Provinces of Agra and Oudh*, 5th edn. (Calcutta: W. Thacker & Company, 1916)

Truschke, Audrey, *Aurangzeb: The Life and Legacy of India's Most Controversial King* (Stanford: Stanford University Press, 2017)

Truschke, Audrey, *The Language of History: Sanskrit Narratives of Indo-Muslim Rule* (New York: Columbia University Press, 2021)

Truschke, Audrey, 'Hindu: A History', *Comparative Studies in Society and History* 65.2 (2023): 246–71

Tushnet, Mark, 'Constitution', in Michel Rosenfeld and Andras Sajo (eds), *The Oxford Handbook of Comparative Constitutional Law* (Oxford: Oxford University Press, 2012)

Vajpeyi, Ananya, *Righteous Republic* (Cambridge, MA: Harvard University Press, 2012)

van der Veer, Peter, '"God Must be Liberated!" A Hindu Liberation Movement in Ayodhya', *Modern Asian Studies* 21.2 (1987): 283–301

Varshney, Ashutosh, 'How has Indian Federalism Done?', *Studies in Indian Politics* 1.1 (2013): 43–63

Vattanky, John, 'Aspects of Early Nyāya Theism', *Journal of Indian Philosophy* 6.4 (1978): 393–404

Venkatkrishnan, Anand, 'Ritual, Reflection, and Religion: The Devas of Banaras', *South Asian History and Culture* 6.1 (2015): 147–71

Venkatkrishnan, Anand, 'Are There Atheists in Potholes? Mīmāṃsakas Debate the Path of Bhakti', in Gil Ben-Herut *et al.* (eds), *Regional Communities of Devotion in South Asia: Insiders, Outsiders, and Interlopers* (London: Routledge, 2020): 177–91

Verboven, Koenraad, 'Guilds and Gods Religious Profiles of Occupational *Collegia* and the Problem of the *Dendrophori*', in Andrew Wilson, Nick Ray, and Angela Trentacoste (eds), *The Economy of Roman Religion* (Oxford: Oxford University Press, 2023): 267–309

Verpoorten, Jean-Marie, *Mīmāṃsā Literature* (Wiesbaden: O. Harrassowitz, 1987)

Vinogradoff, Paul, *Outlines of Historical Jurisprudence, Volume 2: The Jurisprudence of the Greek City* (Oxford: Oxford University Press, 1922)

Viraraghavacharya, T.K.T., *History of Tirupati*, Vol 2. (Tirupati: Tirumala Tirupati Devasthanam Committee, 2003)

Virgo, Graham, *The Principles of Equity and Trusts*, 4th edn. (Oxford: Oxford University Press, 2020)

Voas, David, and Mark Chaves, 'Is the United States a Counterexample to the Secularization Thesis?', *American Journal of Sociology* 121.5 (2016): 1517–56

Waghorne, Joanne, *Diaspora of the Gods: Modern Hindu Temples in an Urban Middle-Class World* (Oxford: Oxford University Press, 2004)

Wagoner, Phillip, *Tidings of the King: A Translation and Ethnohistorical Analysis of the Rāyavācakamu* (Honolulu: University of Hawai'i Press, 1993)

Wagoner, Phillip, 'From "Pampa's Crossing" to "The Place of Lord Virupaksa": Architecture, Cult, and Patronage at Hampi before the Founding of Vijayanagara', in D. Devaraj and C.S. Patil (eds), *Vijayanagara: Progress of Research, 1988–1991* (Mysore: Directorate of Archaeology and Museums, 1996): 141–74

Wagoner, Phillip, '"Sultan among Hindu Kings": Dress, Titles, and the Islamicization of Hindu culture at Vijayanagara', *The Journal of Asian Studies* 55.4 (1996): 851–80

Wagoner, Phillip, 'Fortuitous Convergences and Essential Ambiguities: Transcultural Political Elites in the Medieval Deccan', *International Journal of Hindu Studies* 3.3 (1998): 241–64

Wagoner, Phillip, 'Harihara, Bukka, and the Sultan: The Delhi Sultanate in the Political Imagination of Vijayanagara', in David Gilmartin and Bruce Lawrence (eds), *Beyond Turk and Hindu: Rethinking Religious Identities in Islamicate South Asia* (Gainesville: University of Florida Press, 2000): 300–26

Wagoner, Philip, *Objects of Translation: Material Culture and Medieval 'Hindu-Muslim' Encounter* (Princeton: Princeton University Press, 2009)

Wagoner, Philip, 'India c. 1200–c. 1500', in Anne Curry and David Graff (eds), *The Cambridge History of War*, Vol. 2 (Cambridge: Cambridge University Press, 2020)

Waheeduzzaman, Abu Mohammad, *Land Resumption in Bengal: 1819–1846* (Unpublished PhD Dissertation, SOAS, 1969)

Walters, Jonathan S., 'Multireligion on the Bus: Beyond "Influence" and "Syncretism" in the Study of Religious Meetings', in Pradeep Jeganathan and Qadri Ismail (eds), *Unmaking the Nation: The Politics of Identity and History in Modern Sri Lanka* (Colombo: Social Scientists' Association, 1995): 25–54

Walters, Jonathan S., 'Buddhist History: The Sri Lankan Pāli Vaṃsas and Their Commentary', in Ronald Inden, Jonathan Walters, and Daud Ali (eds), *Querying the Medieval: Texts and the History of Practices in South Asia* (Oxford: Oxford University Press, 2000): 99–164

Warren, Nancy, *Spiritual Economies: Female Monasticism in Later Medieval England* (Philadelphia: University of Pennsylvania Press, 2001)

Washbrook, David, 'Law, State, and Agrarian Society in Colonial India', *Modern Asian Studies*, 15:3 (1981): 649–741

Watt, Gary, *Trusts and Equity*, 9th edn. (Oxford: Oxford University Press, 2020)

Waughray, Annapurna, *Capturing Caste in Law: The Legal Regulation of Caste Discrimination* (London: Taylor & Francis, 2022)

Wheeler, Brannon, *Mecca and Eden: Ritual, Relics, and Territory in Islam* (Chicago: University of Chicago Press, 2006)

Wigg-Wolf, David, 'Moneychangers in the Temple? Coins and Religion in the Roman World', in Andrew Wilson, Nick Ray, and Angela Trentacoste (eds), *The Economy of Roman Religion* (Oxford: Oxford University Press, 2023): 130–54

Williams, Donovan, 'The Council of India and the Relationship between the Home and Supreme Governments, 1858–1870', *The English Historical* 81.318 (1966): 56–73

Willis, Michael, 'Religious and Royal Patronage in North India', in Vishakha Desai and Darielle Mason (eds), *Gods, Guardians, and Lovers: Temple Sculptures from North India A.D. 700–1200* (London: Asia Society Galleries, 1993): 48–65

Willis, Michael, *The Archaeology of Hindu Ritual: Temples and the Establishment of the Gods* (Cambridge: Cambridge University Press, 2009)

Williston, Samuel, 'History of the Law of Business Corporations before 1800. I', *Harvard Law Review* 2.3 (1888): 105–24

Wilson, Andrew, 'Introduction', in Andrew Wilson, Nick Ray, and Angela Trentacoste (eds), *The Economy of Roman Religion* (Oxford: Oxford University Press, 2023): 1–29

Wilson, Deborah, *Women and Legal Guardianship* (Manchester: Manchester University Press, 2013)

Wink, Andre, *Land and Sovereignty in India: Agrarian Society and Politics Under the Eighteenth-century Maratha Svarājya* (Cambridge: Cambridge University Press, 1986)

Wink, Andre, *Al-Hind: The Making of the Indo-Islamic World, Vol 1: Early Medieval India and the Expansion of Islam*, 3rd edn. (Leiden: Brill, 2002)

Wink, Andre, *Al-Hind: The Making of the Islamic World, Vol 2: The Slave Kings and the Islamic Conquest 11th–13th Centuries* (Leiden: Brill, 2002)

Winkler, Adam, *We the Corporations: How American Businesses Won their Civil Rights* (New York: Norton, 2018)

Witte, John, 'Introduction', in John Witte and Frank Alexander (eds), *Christianity and Law: An Introduction* (Cambridge: Cambridge University Press, 2008): 1–32

Wohl, Victoria, *Law's Cosmos: Juridical Discourse in Athenian Forensic Oratory* (Cambridge: Cambridge University Press, 2010)

Wood, Cyrus, 'The New Friend-Extent of Authority to Compromise Suit' *Central Law Journal* 41 (1895): 342–4

Wood, Susan, *The Proprietary Church in the Medieval West* (Oxford: Oxford University Press, 2006)

Yang, Anand, 'An Institutional Shelter: The Court of Wards in Late Nineteenth-Century Bihar', *Modern Asian Studies* 13.2 (1979): 247–64

Zaweed, Salim, 'The Waqf Estates of Pāṇḍūa: Historical Analysis (from Fifteenth to Twentieth Centuries)', *Indian Historical Review* 48.2 (2021)

Ziad, Waleed, '"Islamic Coins" from a Hindu Temple', *Journal of the Economic and Social History of the Orient* 59 (2016): 618–59

Zwalve, W.J., and E. Koops, 'Introduction: The Equity Phenomenon', in W.J. Zwalve and E. Koops (eds), *Law & Equity Approaches in Roman Law and Common Law* (Leiden: Brill, 2013): 1–13

Index

Note: for Sanskrit, Arabic, and Persian texts, see authors' names; for court cases, see the Table of Cases on pp. *x–xvi*.